PREFACE

The *Research Guide to American Historical Biography* contains bibliographical and other reference aids that allow the reader to explore more fully the lives of 278 prominent men and women who have helped to shape the contours of United States history. The *Research Guide* is designed to facilitate the research process for college and secondary school term papers, to assist graduate students and professors in areas outside their fields of expertise, and to provide librarians with an acquisitions tool, information to expedite interlibrary loans, and a ready reference. Our contributors, most of whom are historians affiliated with universities or state historical societies, have sifted through an abundance of sources to direct the reader to those which are most useful.

Each entry is divided into several sections for quick reference: the Chronology provides a synopsis of major events in the subject's life; the Activities of Historical Significance interprets the subject's accomplishments and places them in context; the Overview of Biographical Sources notes any difficulties that the subject's biographers have encountered and comments on changes in scholarly opinion that have occurred over the years; the Evaluation of Principal Biographical Sources is an annotated bibliography that evaluates the most important secondary sources for content, readability, and accuracy; the Evaluation of Biographies for Young People is a separate listing of biographies written for a young audience, which appears in articles whose subjects have inspired at least three works in this genre; the Overview and Evaluation of Primary Sources cites autobiographical works by the subject, memoirs by the subject's family and acquaintances, pertinent government documents, and manuscript collections that contain an abundance of unpublished material; Fiction and Adaptations describes novels, films, plays, or other creative interpretations of the subject's activities; Museums, Historical Landmarks, Societies provides the name, location, and a brief description of relevant organizations or points of interest; and Other Sources is a bibliography of journal and encyclopedia articles, monographs, and works on the subject's era that put his or her role in historical context. The works cited in the Evaluation of Principal Biographical Sources and in the Overview and Evaluation of Primary Sources have A, G, or Y designations appended to the bibliographical information to indicate whether the work is most appropriate for an academic, general, or young audience. A work's audience designation is based on a combination of readability, subject matter, and availability. Finally, selected U.S. Postal Service commemorative stamps illustrate some of the articles. The events that the stamps commemorate relate to the historical achievements of the figures. Each stamp's caption contains the USPS official name of the stamp and the date of its release.

As a further aid to students not well-versed in all areas of American history, we have designed an appendix that groups the contents by the era in which each subject made his or her greatest contributions. Also included in each volume is an appendix that groups by state the most popular sites described in the Museums, Historical Landmarks, Societies section of the articles. If the figure to whom the site relates is not self-evident, his or her name follows in parentheses, except in cases, such as battlefields, where the site is pertinent to several figures. Volume 3 contains a third appendix that lists addresses and telephone numbers for the research libraries most often cited in the articles, as well as for a representative historical society for each state.

Because this reference work is a basic research tool, the contents are largely a reflection of the availability of biographical and primary sources that are appropriate for our intended audience. We have endeavored to take into account those individuals most often studied in the areas of politics and statecraft, business and labor, education, journalism, religion, and the military. Also included are noted feminists, minority figures, jurists, explorers, scientists, and inventors. Literary figures are generally excluded because they are covered in Beacham Publishing's *Research Guide to Biography and Criticism*. Only writers such as Harriet Beecher Stowe and Edward Bellamy, whose works had a very direct impact on American social thought, are included. In a few cases, individuals for whom extensive biographical information does not exist are briefly treated because of the roles they have played in significant movements or events (e.g., Betty Friedan is included for her role in the women's movement).

The *Research Guide to American Historical Biography* owes its existence to the labor of many individuals who have given generously of their time and talent, and I wish to acknowledge my gratitude to all our contributors.

Beacham Publishing is continually interested in producing books devoted to improving the research capabilities of students and welcomes any suggestions for revising this title or ideas for other types of books. Write to: Beacham Publishing, 2100 "S" Street NW, Washington, D.C. 20008.

Robert Muccigrosso
Brooklyn College of the City
University of New York

CONTRIBUTORS

Charles H. Adams
University of Arkansas-Fayetteville

A. Owen Aldridge
University of Illinois

Thomas G. Alexander
Brigham Young University

Leonard J. Arrington
Brigham Young University

Barbara Bair
University of California-Los
    Angeles

Jean V. Berlin
Correspondence of William T.
    Sherman
Wofford College

Frederick J. Blue
Youngstown State University

Ruth Bordin
Bentley Historical Library
University of Michigan

Larry G. Bowman
University of North Texas

Jo Ann Boydston
Center for Dewey Studies
Southern Illinois University,
    Carbondale

James C. Bradford
Texas A&M University

John Braeman
University of Nebraska-Lincoln

Mary Jo Bratton
East Carolina University

Douglas G. Brinkley
Hofstra University

Alan S. Brown
Western Michigan University

Mary Lynn McCree Bryan
Jane Addams Papers

Edwin G. Burrows
Brooklyn College, CUNY

David H. Burton
St. Joseph's University

Allan C. Carlson
The Rockford Institute

Betty Boyd Caroli
Kingsborough Community College,
    CUNY

Albert Castel
Western Michigan University

Robert J. Chaffin
University of Wisconsin-Oshkosh

Ellen Chesler

Patricia P. Clark
Andrew Johnson Project
University of Tennessee-Knoxville

Paolo E. Coletta
U.S. Naval Academy (Ret.)

Gary L. Collison
Pennsylvania State University-York

David R. Contosta
Chestnut Hill College

Michael Cook
The Strong Museum

Lynda Lasswell Crist
The Papers of Jefferson Davis
Rice University

Robert Rhodes Crout
Oregon State University

Thomas J. Curran
St. John's University, New York

Nelson S. Dearmont
Papers of Robert Morris
Queens College, CUNY

Julian J. DelGaudio
California State University-Long
  Beach

David C. Dennard
East Carolina University

Justus D. Doenecke
New College of the University of
  South Florida

Jacob H. Dorn
Wright State University

Diane Eidelman

J. Christopher Eisele
Illinois State University

Candace Falk
Emma Goldman Papers
University of California-Berkeley

Henry C. Ferrell, Jr.
East Carolina University

Linda Firestone

Thomas Fleming
The Rockford Institute

Morris D. Forkosch
Emeritus, Brooklyn Law School

Robert J. Forman
St. John's University, New York

Maurice G. Fortin
University of North Texas Libraries

George W. Franz
Pennsylvania State University-
  Delaware County

Steven H. Gale
Kentucky State University

William M. Gargan
Brooklyn College, CUNY

Donald F. M. Gerardi
Brooklyn College, CUNY

H. Roger Grant
University of Akron

Lloyd J. Graybar
Eastern Kentucky University

Ivan Greenberg
Graduate and University Center,
  CUNY

Lionel W. Greer
The Papers of Albert Gallatin
Baruch College, CUNY

Lenore Gussin

Jack L. Hammersmith
West Virginia University

Ralph W. Haskins
University of Tennessee-Knoxville

Charles C. Hay III
Eastern Kentucky University

Melba Porter Hay
The Papers of Henry Clay
University of Kentucky

Richard Allen Heckman
California State Polytechnic
  University-Pomona

Joseph P. Hobbs
North Carolina State University

Diane Long Hoeveler
Marquette University

J. David Hoeveler, Jr.
University of Wisconsin-Milwaukee

Melvin G. Holli
University of Illinois-Chicago

Ari Hoogenboom
Brooklyn College and Graduate
  Center, CUNY

Charles F. Howlett

William D. Jenkins
Youngstown State University

Veda Jones

Jacob Judd
Lehman College and Graduate
  Center, CUNY

John L. King, Jr.

Robert S. La Forte
University of North Texas

Roger D. Launius
Department of the Air Force

Arlene Lazarowitz
California State University-Long
  Beach

William M. Leary
University of Georgia

J. Perry Leavell, Jr.
Drew University

David W. Levy
University of Oklahoma

Kirsten E. Lewis

Kenneth Lipartito
Baker & Botts

Gloria Ricci Lothrop
California State Polytechnic
  University-Pomona

David S. Lux
Virginia Polytechnic Institute and
  State University

Arnold Markoe
Brooklyn College, CUNY

Joan Marshall
Brooklyn College, CUNY (Ret.)

David B. Mattern
Papers of James Madison
University of Virginia

Joseph M. McCarthy
Suffolk University

Thomas C. McClintock
Oregon State University

John F. McClymer
Assumption College

Linda O. McMurry
North Carolina State University

Tamara Moser Melia
Naval Historical Center

Christopher C. Meyers

Randall M. Miller
St. Joseph's University

H. Wayne Morgan
University of Oklahoma

Robert Muccigrosso
Brooklyn College, CUNY

Michael Musuraca
Graduate Center, CUNY

Pellegrino Nazzaro
Rochester Institute of Technology

Elizabeth M. Nuxoll
Papers of Robert Morris
Queens College, CUNY

Thomas Ofcansky
Department of Defense

William L. O'Neill
Rutgers University

Beverly Wilson Palmer
Charles Sumner Correspondence
Pomona College

Jacqueline K. Parker
Cleveland State University

Jack Patrick
Youngstown State University

Donald K. Pickens
University of North Texas

Harold T. Pinkett

Keith Ian Polakoff
California State University-Long
    Beach

Nicholas C. Polos
University of La Verne

J. Tracy Power
South Carolina Department of
    Archives and History

Howard L. Preston

Paul M. Pruitt, Jr.
University of Alabama School of
    Law Library

Fred D. Ragan
East Carolina University

Honora Raphael
Brooklyn College, CUNY

Joanne R. Reitano
LaGuardia Community College

Donald J. Richards
Lehman College, CUNY

Tommy W. Rogers

Marc Rothenberg
Joseph Henry Papers
Smithsonian Institution

Udo Sautter
University of Windsor

Edward L. Schapsmeier
Illinois State University

Frederick H. Schapsmeier
University of Wisconsin-Oshkosh

John R. Schmidt

Kenneth E. Shewmaker
Dartmouth College

E. Thomson Shields, Jr.
University of Tennessee-Knoxville

Richard K. Showman
The Nathanael Greene Papers
Rhode Island Historical Society

Jack Shreve
Allegany Community College

John Y. Simon
The Papers of Ulysses S. Grant
Southern Illinois University-
    Carbondale

Brooks D. Simpson
Wofford College

Mary Lee Spence
University of Illinois-
    Urbana/Champaign

John C. Super
West Virginia University

Jacob L. Susskind
Pennsylvania State University

Gretchen R. Sutherland
Cornell College

Eugene M. Tobin
Hamilton College

C. David Tompkins
Northeastern Illinois University

Hans L. Trefousse
Brooklyn College and Graduate
   Center, CUNY

John C. Van Horne
Library Company of Philadelphia

William T. Walker
Philadelphia College of Pharmacy
   and Science

Peter Wallenstein
Virginia Polytechnic Institute and
   State University

Melvin R. Williams
Brooklyn College, CUNY

Clyde N. Wilson
Papers of John C. Calhoun
University of South Carolina

John Scott Wilson
University of South Carolina

W. Kirk Wood
Alabama State University

CONTENTS

Richard T. Ely
Ralph Waldo Emerson
David Farragut
Millard Fillmore
Gerald R. Ford
Henry Ford
Nathan Bedford Forrest
Felix Frankfurter
Benjamin Franklin
John C. Frémont
Betty Friedan
J. William Fulbright
Margaret Fuller
Robert Fulton
Albert Gallatin
James A. Garfield
William Lloyd Garrison
Marcus M. Garvey
Charlotte Perkins Gilman
Washington Gladden
Emma Goldman
Samuel Gompers
Billy Graham
Ulysses S. Grant
Horace Greeley
Nathanael Greene
D. W. Griffith
Angelina & Sarah Grimké
Alexander Hamilton
Marcus Alonzo Hanna
Warren G. Harding
Benjamin Harrison
William Henry Harrison
John Hay
Rutherford B. Hayes
William D. Haywood
William Randolph Hearst
Joseph Henry
Patrick Henry
Alger Hiss
Oliver Wendell Holmes, Jr.
Herbert Hoover
J. Edgar Hoover

Sam Houston
Charles Evans Hughes
Cordell Hull
Hubert H. Humphrey
Anne Hutchinson
Thomas Hutchinson
Andrew Jackson
Stonewall Jackson
Jesse James
William James
John Jay
Thomas Jefferson
Andrew Johnson
Lyndon B. Johnson
John Paul Jones
Chief Joseph
Florence Kelley
John F. Kennedy
Robert F. Kennedy
Martin Luther King, Jr.
Henry A. Kissinger
Marquis de Lafayette
Robert M. La Follette
Fiorello La Guardia
Benjamin Henry Latrobe
Robert E. Lee
John L. Lewis
Meriwether Lewis & William Clark
Abraham Lincoln
Charles A. Lindbergh, Jr.
Walter Lippmann
Henry Cabot Lodge
Huey Long
Clare Boothe Luce
Henry R. Luce
Douglas MacArthur
Dolley Madison
James Madison
Alfred Thayer Mahan
Malcolm X
Horace Mann
Francis Marion
George C. Marshall

John Marshall
Cotton Mather
Joseph R. McCarthy
George B. McClellan
William McKinley
Aimee Semple McPherson
Margaret Mead
H. L. Mencken
Thomas Merton
Billy Mitchell
James Monroe
J. Pierpont Morgan
Gouverneur Morris
Robert Morris
Samuel F. B. Morse
John Muir
Ralph Nader
Thomas Nast
Carry Nation
Richard M. Nixon
Albert Jay Nock
George W. Norris
J. Robert Oppenheimer
Thomas Paine
Theodore Parker
Francis Parkman
George S. Patton, Jr.
William Penn
Frances Perkins
Matthew Calbraith Perry
Oliver Hazard Perry
John J. Pershing
Ulrich B. Phillips
Wendell Phillips
Franklin Pierce
Gifford Pinchot
Pocahontas
James K. Polk
Chief Pontiac
Terence V. Powderly
William Hickling Prescott
Sir Walter Raleigh
A. Philip Randolph

Ronald Reagan
John Reed
Jacob Riis
Jackie Robinson
John D. Rockefeller
Nelson A. Rockefeller
Eleanor Roosevelt
Franklin D. Roosevelt
Theodore Roosevelt
Elihu Root
Julius & Ethel Rosenberg
Benjamin Rush
Nicola Sacco & Bartolomeo Vanzetti
Margaret Sanger
Carl Schurz
Winfield Scott
Junípero Serra
William Seward
William T. Sherman
William Gilmore Simms
Alfred E. Smith
John Smith
Joseph Smith
Hernando de Soto
Edwin M. Stanton
Elizabeth Cady Stanton
Lincoln Steffens
Alexander H. Stephens
Thaddeus Stevens
Adlai E. Stevenson
Henry L. Stimson
Harriet Beecher Stowe
Charles Sumner
William Graham Sumner
Robert A. Taft
William H. Taft
Roger Brooke Taney
Frederick W. Taylor
Zachary Taylor
Tecumseh
Norman Thomas
Henry David Thoreau
Harry S Truman

Harriet Tubman
Frederick Jackson Turner
Nat Turner
William M. Tweed
John Tyler
Martin Van Buren
Thorstein Veblen
George C. Wallace
Henry A. Wallace
Lester Frank Ward
Earl Warren
Booker T. Washington
George Washington

Thomas Watson
Daniel Webster
Gideon Welles
William Allen White
Walt Whitman
Eli Whitney
Frances Willard
Roger Williams
Wendell L. Willkie
Woodrow Wilson
John Winthrop
Wilbur & Orville Wright
Brigham Young

RESEARCH GUIDE
TO AMERICAN
HISTORICAL BIOGRAPHY

DEAN ACHESON
1893–1971

Chronology

Born Dean Gooderham Acheson on April 11, 1893, in Middletown, Connecticut, the son of Edward Campion Acheson, an Episcopal bishop, and Eleanor Gertrude Gooderham Acheson; *1915* graduates from Yale University with "gentleman C's," having first attended the Groton School; *1917* marries Alice Stanley, with whom he will have three children; *1918–1920* graduates from Harvard Law School; serves as law clerk to Supreme Court Justice Louis D. Brandeis; *1921* joins law firm of Covington and Burling, with which he will be affiliated for the rest of his life; *1933* President Franklin D. Roosevelt appoints him undersecretary of the treasury at the recommendation of Felix Frankfurter; resigns six months later in protest against the reduction of the gold content of the dollar; *1936* joins the Yale Corporation, on which he serves until 1961; *1941* appointed assistant secretary of state, and serves under Cordell Hull and Edward Stettinius; *1941–1944* helps coordinate the lend-lease program during World War II; *1941–1953* at State Department, he is responsible for the Bretton Woods agreement leading to the establishment of the World Bank, assistance to Greece and Turkey under the Truman Doctrine, groundwork for the Marshall Plan, development of American atomic policy, formation of NATO, peace treaty with Japan, diplomacy over the Korean conflict, U.S. policy toward the People's Republic of China, creation and rearmament of West Germany, and the era of bipartisanship in foreign policy; *1945–1947* appointed undersecretary of state serving under James F. Byrnes and George C. Marshall; retires temporarily from State Department in July 1947; *1949* returns to State Department as President Truman's secretary of state; *1953* leaves office under a hail of criticism and McCarthyite accusations of being "soft on communism"; *1953–1960* returns to law and becomes outspoken critic of the Eisenhower-Dulles foreign policy; *1957–1960* serves as chairman of the Foreign Policy Committee of the Democratic Advisory Council; *1960–1963* becomes important unofficial foreign policy advisor to President Kennedy on the Berlin and Cuban crises; *1964–1968* advises President Johnson on the Vietnam War; *March 1968* tells President Johnson he should pull the U.S. out of Vietnam; *1968–1971* serves as important unofficial advisor to President Nixon; *1970* wins the Pulitzer Prize for his sixth book, the autobiographical *Present at the Creation*; *1971* dies on October 12 of a stroke, at his country home in Sandy Spring, Maryland.

Activities of Historical Significance

Dean Acheson was the U.S. secretary of state under President Harry S Truman and a major architect of the nation's foreign policy after World War II. The son of

1

an Episcopal bishop of Connecticut, Acheson grew up in that state, attended Groton School and graduated from Yale in 1915. After serving in the Navy during World War I, he received a law degree from Harvard in 1918 and became private secretary to Supreme Court Justice Louis Brandeis. He then entered law practice in Washington with the new firm of Covington & Burling. In 1933, he was appointed undersecretary of the treasury, but resigned after a few months in protest of what he considered the reckless and unconstitutional action by the president in reducing the gold content of the dollar. Acheson returned to public service in 1941 as assistant secretary of state and from 1945 to 1947 he served as undersecretary of state, the department's second-ranking post, where he was instrumental in planning the United Nations and developing a policy of containment toward Soviet expansionism, and secured aid for Greece and Turkey against Communist-backed insurgents in what is commonly referred to as the Truman Doctrine. He was appointed secretary of state by President Truman and served in this post through 1952.

While at the State Department, Acheson helped formulate the early American response to Soviet expansionism, recommending that the U.S. give economic, political, and military aid to countries on the rim of the Communist bloc to prevent or "contain" future Soviet expansion. In his view Germany played the key role in the redevelopment of Europe, and Acheson's ideas were influential in the formulation of the Marshall Plan of massive aid to war-torn Europe.

As secretary of state, Acheson was instrumental in the creation of the North Atlantic Treaty Organization (NATO), the rebuilding and rearming of Germany, and the development of atomic energy policy. Although he believed that the North Atlantic community represented the peak of man's cultural and political growth (and therefore made it the focus of his diplomacy), Acheson perforce spent a large portion of his time on Asian affairs. Following the fall of Chiang Kai-Shek, Acheson pursued a nonrecognition policy toward Communist China. In 1950, he used the Soviet boycott of the United Nations Security Council to secure U.N. support for U.S. intervention in the Korean War.

He retired from government service in the summer of 1947, resuming his legal practice; but he could not entirely avoid public affairs. In November 1948, President Truman asked Acheson to replace the ailing George Marshall as secretary of state and Acheson accepted.

During his years as secretary, Dean Acheson was sorely tested to keep up with the rapid developments of the fall of Chiang Kai-Shek and the Korean War. The virulently anti-Communist Acheson was soon attacked by Senator Joseph McCarthy and other Republicans for "losing" China, pursuing a "no win" policy in the Korean War, and "coddling" Communists in government. He survived these accusations, remained in office until the end of Truman's presidency, and continued implementing the containment policy in East Asia by signing a peace treaty with Japan and supporting the French in Indochina. Acheson's European policy was largely successful, hinging upon a vigorous NATO and the early European Community movement. A hallmark of the Truman-Acheson period is the successful implementation of a bipartisan U.S. foreign policy. Acheson left office at the end of the Truman administration to return to his private law practice. He continued speaking out on foreign policy issues and served as an unofficial advisor to the Kennedy, Johnson, and Nixon administrations. The author of eight books, Acheson's autobiographical *Present at the Creation* (1969) won a Pulitzer Price.

Acheson viewed U.S.-Soviet relations both in terms of power politics and as a contest between democratic and totalitarian values. He opposed a Wilsonian emphasis on internationalism and appeals to abstract principles of right and wrong in the formation of policy, believing such appeals were attempts to avoid the practical responsibility of exercising power. He accepted the inevitability of a bipolar world, at least within the forseeable future. His major goals, therefore, were to contain Communist expansion and to develop a strong military presence and alliances so that the West could negotiate with the Soviet Union "from positions of strength."

Overview of Biographical Sources

There is no comprehensive biography of Dean Acheson, partly because Acheson himself wrote with such authoritative ability and literary flare, most notably demonstrated in his Pulitzer Prize-winning memoir of his years in the State Department, *Present at the Creation* (1969). To date, three published biographical profiles exist, and one of these, Walter Isaacson and Evan Thomas's *The Wise Men: Six Friends and the World They Made* (1986), portrays Acheson along with five others (Chip Bohlen, Averell Harriman, George Kennan, Robert Lovett, and John J. McCloy) as a premier architect of U.S. postwar foreign policy. Gaddis Smith's *Dean Acheson* (1972) is a volume in the American Secretaries of State and Their Diplomacy series, and therefore focuses primarily on his foreign policy achievements and blunders while he held that office from 1949 to 1953.

David S. McLellan's *Dean Acheson: The State Department Years* (1976) is the nearest thing to a full-scale biography, although the book gives short shrift to the last seventeen years of Acheson's life. McLellan concentrates mainly on the political as contrasted with the economic and elitist interpretations of Acheson's foreign policy. Forrest Pogue's masterful *George C. Marshall: Statesman 1945–1959* (1987) and Robert Donavan's *Tumultuous Years: The Presidency of Harry S Truman, 1949–1953* (1982) both offer important historical and biographical portraits of Acheson in government.

Evaluation of Principal Biographical Sources

Isaacson, Walter and Evan Thomas. *The Wise Men: Six Friends and The World They Made*. New York: Simon and Schuster, 1986. (**A, G**) An intimate biography of Dean Acheson, Chip Bohlen, Averell Harriman, George Kennan, Robert Lovett, and John McCloy, this work emphasizes the roles these men played in bringing order to the postwar chaos, and their attempts to contain Soviet expansionism. Acheson is given credit for being the creative force behind the Marshall Plan and Truman Doctrine. Although an enjoyable read, the book relies too heavily on anecdotes at the expense of scholarship.

McLellan, David S. *Dean Acheson: The State Department Years*. New York: Dodd, Mead, 1976. (**A, G**) A thoroughly researched and balanced biography. The author concludes that Dean Acheson, as much as any single individual, can justify being called the architect of post-World War II American foreign policy. He argues that Acheson's policies in regard to Europe were, for the most part, about the best that the country could do at the time; Acheson's major errors, he argues, were in dealing with Asia.

Smith, Gaddis. *American Secretaries of State and Their Diplomacy: Dean Acheson*. New York: Cooper Square Publishers, 1972. (**A, G**) The author, a distinguished diplomatic historian, has written a splendid, eminently readable profile of Dean Acheson in government. It is particularly strong on the role of NATO, the formation of the West German government and its integration into a system of European defense, and the Korean conflict, and also offers the best explanation of Acheson's perception of the Soviet menace.

Stupak, Ronald. *The Shaping of Foreign Policy: The Role of the Secretary of State as Seen by Dean Acheson*. Cleveland: The Odyssey Press, 1969. (**A**) Analyzes Acheson's perspectives on the proper role of the secretary of state in American government.

Overview and Evaluation of Primary Sources

Dean Acheson was the author of six books, plus three volumes of collected articles and speeches edited posthumously. The first of these, *A Democrat Looks at His Party* (New York: Harper and Brothers, 1955; **A, G**), is a polemic presenting the virtues of the party from 1933 to 1953, in which he also touches briskly upon such topics as pollsters, intellectuals in government, demagogues, the New Deal, war, and life itself. There soon followed an updated reassessment of Woodrow Wilson's famous book, *Congressional Government* (1885), entitled *A Citizen Looks at Congress* (New York: Harper and Brothers, 1956; **A, G**), a penetrating analysis of Congress, its relation to the Chief Executive, and the role of the committee system in the House and Senate. The William L. Clayton Lectures that Acheson delivered at the Fletcher School of Law and Diplomacy, later published under the title of *Power and Diplomacy* (Cambridge: Harvard University Press, 1958; **A, G**), deal with NATO's military requirements and political precepts for coalitions of free states. *Sketches from Life of Men I Have Known* (New York: Harper and Brothers, 1961; **A, G**), contains wonderful personal vignettes of Acheson's close association with world leaders including Churchill, Adenauer, and Marshall. Acheson's next book, *Morning and Noon* (Boston: Houghton Mifflin, 1965; **A, G**), is a charming and nostalgic autobiographical account of his childhood in Middletown, Connecticut, his time spent at Yale and Harvard, his years as law clerk to Justice Brandeis, and his service in the Roosevelt administration. *Present at the Creation* (New York: W. W. Norton, 1969; **A, G**) is the brilliant Pulitzer Prize-winning account of his years in the State Department (1945-1953), when he was a key architect and manager of American foreign policy during the presidency of Harry S Truman. *Fragments of My Fleece* (New York: W. W. Norton, 1971; **A, G**), *Grapes from Thorns* (New York: W. W. Norton, 1972; **A, G**), and *This Vast External Realm* (New York: W. W. Norton, 1973; **A, G**) are collections of posthumously published essays covering a wide range of topics related to law, government, politics, and foreign-policy decision making. The central public papers of Dean Acheson as secretary of state can be found in *The Pattern of Responsibility: From the Record of Dean Acheson*, edited by McGeorge Bundy (Boston: Houghton Mifflin, 1952; **A, G**). *Among Friends: Personal Letters of Dean Acheson*, edited by David S. McLellan and David C. Acheson (New York: Dodd, Mead, 1980; **A, G**), is a wonderful selection of witty and informal personal letters written to friends, associates, and family.

In addition to his own published writings, the collected primary material is rich. The Sterling Memorial Library at Yale University is the repository of his personal papers including all his post-secretarial papers from 1953-1971. Acheson's own records and correspondence from his tours of public service are located at the Harry S Truman Library in Independence, Missouri. His oral history pertaining to his role as foreign policy advisor to President Kennedy can be found at the John F. Kennedy Library in Boston. The Dean Acheson oral history seminars on his State Department years, including accounts given by his aides Averell Harriman and Paul Nitze at Princeton University, 1952-1953, are available on microfilm at the Truman Library. The *Department of State Bulletin* (1941-1953) and the *Foreign Relations of the United States* (1945-1953) are helpful government sources.

Museums, Historical Landmarks, Societies

Harewood (near Sandy Spring, MD). After his retirement in 1953, Acheson moved to this farmhouse, which had been his summer home since 1925; while living here, he wrote *Present at the Creation*. The house is now privately owned and closed to the public.

Other Sources

Brinkley, Douglas G. "Intimidating Seniority: Dean Acheson as Elder Statesman 1953-1971." Ph.D. dissertation, Georgetown University, 1988. One of the few accounts of his later years.

Donavan, Robert. *Tumultuous Years: The Presidency of Harry S Truman, 1949–1953*. New York: W. W. Norton, 1982. The second volume of Donavan's Truman biography offers important biographical and historical insights into Acheson as secretary of state.

Ferrell, Robert H., and David McLellan. "Dean Acheson: Architect of a Manageable World Order." In *Makers of American Diplomacy: From Theodore Roosevelt to Henry Kissinger*, edited by F. J. Merli and T. A. Wilson. New York: Scribners, 1974. A well-rounded, straightforward assessment of Acheson's career in government.

Gardner, Lloyd. *Architects of Illusion*. Chicago: Quadrangle, 1970. A revisionist perspective of Acheson's diplomacy.

Pogue, Forrest. *George C. Marshall: Statesman, 1945–1959*. New York: Viking Press, 1987. The fourth and final volume of Pogue's authorized biography of Marshall includes valuable information on Acheson's years in the State Department.

Rosenau, James. "The Senate and Dean Acheson: A Case Study in Legislative Attitudes." Ph.D. dissertation, Princeton University, 1957. One of the earliest studies.

Douglas G. Brinkley
Hofstra University

Atoms for Peace, 1955

ABIGAIL ADAMS
1744-1818

Chronology

Born Abigail Smith on November 11, 1744, in Weymouth, Massachusetts, the second of four children of the Reverend William Smith, a Harvard graduate with connections to successful merchants, and Elizabeth Quincy Smith, whose family included the colony's leading religious figures; *1744-1764* is educated at home by other family members, including her Grandmother Quincy and later her elder sister's husband, Richard Cranch, who also introduces her to her future husband; *1764-1774* marries lawyer, John Adams, nine years her senior, and gives birth to five children, four of whom survive to adulthood; *1774-1783* raises the children almost as a single parent while her husband is absent, engaged in the independence movement and then in representing his new country abroad; takes prime responsibility for managing the family farm and keeping the household solvent; corresponds extensively with her husband and others regarding the independence movement and her own feelings about many subjects, including revolution, equality, and education; *1783-1788* joins her husband in Paris and then in London where he serves as first minister to England; *1789-1801* continues during her husband's vice presidency (1789-1797) and presidency (1797-1801) to add to her reputation as a woman of sharp intellect and strong opinion; is increasingly ill in the 1790s and spends more time in Massachusetts; presides over the relocation from Philadelphia to Washington, D.C., of the official residence of the President and then, when the results of the 1800 election become clear, returns to Massachusetts; *1801-1818* spends the remainder of her life in the Quincy house which she and John had purchased on their return from Europe; sees her son, John Quincy, become Secretary of State in the cabinet of James Monroe; *1818* dies on October 28 in Quincy, Massachusetts.

Activities of Historical Significance

As wife of the second President of the United States and mother of the sixth, Abigail Adams gained considerable attention, but it is in her own right, as reporter and thinker, that she merits most consideration. Because she lived at the center of American political life for most of her adult years and wrote such lively commentary on events and her own reactions to them, she has achieved prominence as chronicler of late eighteenth-century American life. Her views have been taken as evidence that the war for independence fostered a new respect for women, especially in their roles as mothers in a new republic. As First Lady she spoke out on her husband's political foes and on policies, differing from Martha Washington, who had kept her own counsel on significant matters. Although her opinions were voiced in private, through family letters, they remained no secret, and one political opponent sarcastically referred to her as "Mrs. President, not of the country but of a faction." She was particularly upset by what she considered to be unfair criticism of her husband and her son. Her grandson singled out her greatest contribution as keeping the family solvent. Charles Francis Adams wrote that had it not been for her prudent operation of the farm and her firm control over family finances, the Adams men might not have had the freedom to devote their lives to politics.

Overview of Biographical Sources

The Adams family, eminent in the country's history for four generations, has been the subject of many treatments, both on page and screen, and Abigail Adams always figures prominently in these accounts. Paul C. Nagel assigns her an important role in *Descent From Glory: Four Generations of the John Adams Family* (1983) and an even more central place in *The Adams Women* (1987). Dutiful and strong, Abigail Adams emerges in the Nagel books as intelligent and concerned with matters ranging from her country's future to the education of her children. At the same time, Nagel spends considerable energy describing the small details of her day.

Nearly every book on John Adams gives considerable attention to his wife's strong influence and to his respect for her opinions. In a two-volume work, *John Adams* (1962–1963), presidential biographer Page Smith describes her as acting as "minister without portfolio."

In her own right, Abigail Adams gained new, more focused attention in the 1970s as the United States celebrated the bicentennial of its independence and singled out figures of the revolutionary period. Renewed interest in women's history added to her fame. Vera Laska pointed to Adams, along with Mercy Otis Warren and Deborah Sampson Gannett, as a Massachusetts leader in *Remember the Ladies: Outstanding Women of the American Revolution* (1976).

Her penchant for letter writing supplied material for many biographies and most of them (whether aimed at juvenile or adult audiences) quote from her letters. The most complete, Phyllis Lee Levin, *Abigail Adams: A Biography* (1987), is richly documented and reveals a strong, independent subject but pays relatively little attention to the setting in which she operated or to the scholarship surrounding her and her peers. Older biographies, such as Charles W. Akers, *Abigail Adams: An American Woman* (1980), and Janet Whitney, *Abigail Adams* (1947), also fail to give sufficient attention to scholarship on women's roles. For that kind of context, readers will want to look at Mary Beth Norton, *Liberty's Daughters* (1980).

Evaluation of Principal Biographical Sources

Akers, Charles W. *Abigail Adams: An American Woman*. Boston: Little, Brown,

1980. **(A, G)** The author has attempted a traditional, well-researched biography (without footnotes) and quotes from the Adams letters. The valuable bibliographic essay summarizes much of the scholarship on the topic and is particularly useful in citing relevant journal articles.

Laska, Vera O. *Remember the Ladies: Outstanding Women of the American Revolution*. Boston: Commonwealth of Massachusetts Bicentennial Commission, 1976. **(G)** In separate sections, Laska treats admiringly the contributions of three Massachusetts women who played important parts in the Revolution: Adams, Mercy Otis Warren, the historian, and Deborah Sampson Gannett, the soldier.

Levin, Phyllis Lee. *Abigail Adams: A Biography*. New York: St. Martin's Press, 1987. **(A, G)** Based on extensive examination of the Adams Papers, this large, richly documented book is a very readable account of the subject's life. Unlike so many of the biographies, which concentrate on the revolutionary period, this one gives considerable attention to her youth and old age.

Whitney, Janet Payne. *Abigail Adams*. Boston: Little, Brown, 1947. **(G)** Although it includes imagined conversations, this biography also contains quotations from the Adams papers.

Withey, Lynne. *Dearest Friend: A Life of Abigail Adams*. New York: Free Press, 1981. **(G)** Author sees her subject as ambivalent about the proper role for women. Although she admired strength, she also praised demureness.

Evaluation of Biographies for Young People
Lee, Susan, and John Lee. *Abigail Adams*. Chicago: Children's Press, 1977. Intended for very young children, this book includes some quotations from Adams's letters in which vocabulary (such as "uncouth") may need explanation.

Witter, Evelyn. *Abigail Adams: First Lady of Faith and Courage*. Milford, MI: Mott Media, 1976. Aimed at grades 3–6, this work portrays Adams as a "born-again Christian, her whole life guided by His Word."

Overview and Evaluation of Primary Sources
The full text of Abigail Adams's letters can be found in the 608 microfilm reels of *Adams Papers* owned by the Massachusetts Historical Society. Several published versions of parts of the collection exist as well. Among the most reliable are L. H. Butterfield, *The Adams Family Correspondence* (4 vols.; Cambridge, MA: Harvard University Press, 1963–1973; **A, G**), and Stewart Mitchell, *New Letters of Abigail Adams, 1788–1801* (Boston: Houghton, Mifflin, 1947; **A, G**). Charles Francis Adams edited two volumes of his grandmother's letters and added his own memoir

in *Letters of Mrs. Adams* (Boston: Little, Brown, 1840; **A, G**) and *Familiar Letters of John Adams and His Wife During the Revolution* (Freeport, NY: Library Press, 1970; **A, G**). Whether in the full text or in abbreviated form, Abigail Adams's letters show a woman of learning and wit. Grammar, punctuation, and spelling are often wrong, but her wry comments on the state of the country and her household, interspersed with her judgments of people and places, are never dull. Her correspondence with Thomas Jefferson, with whom she had a warm friendship, then a political battle, and finally a wary accommodation, is included with that of her husband in John Adams, *The Adams-Jefferson Letters: The Complete Correspondence Between Thomas Jefferson and Abigail and John Adams*, edited by Lester J. Cappon (Chapel Hill: University of North Carolina, 1959; **A, G**).

Several portraits of Abigail Adams appear in Andrew Oliver, *Portraits of John and Abigail Adams* (Cambridge, MA: Harvard University Press, 1967; **A, G**). In addition to the much reproduced pastel by Benjamin Blyth, completed soon after Abigail married John Adams, Oliver includes the 1785 oil painting by Mather Brown and two oil paintings by Gilbert Stuart.

Fiction and Adaptations

The relationship between Abigail and John Adams became the subject of Irving Stone's *Those Who Love: A Biographical Novel of Abigail and John Adams* (1965). Although the author researched the Adams record for several years and quotes from the Adams Papers, this is fiction.

The Broadway musical "1776" opened in New York on March 16, 1969, to extremely positive reviews. In the cast consisting primarily of male signers of the Declaration of Independence, only two female characters appear: one is Abigail Adams, who delivers her famous "Remember the Ladies" line to husband John.

A script for theater, based on the Adams letters, was written by William Gibson and presented first as "Abigail and John." Later the title was changed to "American Primitive: The Words of John and Abigail Adams Put into a Sequence for the Theater, with Addenda in Rhyme" (1972). The cast of three men, three women, one boy and one girl perform in front of a large map. Dialogue comes from letters written between 1774 and 1777; comments include those on family matters as well as on the independence movement.

The popular television series on the Adams family was accompanied by a book of the same title: Jack Shepherd, *The Adams Chronicles: Four Generations of Greatness* (1975).

Museums, Historical Landmarks, Societies

Adams Historic Site (135 Adams Street, Quincy, MA). This is the house which John and Abigail bought after their return from Europe and used as their residence until their deaths. Four generations of Adamses called this house their home, and the furnishings, along with a library of 14,000 volumes, reflect their tastes. Nearby, at 141 Franklin Street, is the smaller house where John and Abigail lived after their marriage and where their son, John Quincy, was born. Reproductions of the original furnishings help visitors understand what it looked like in the eighteenth century. Only part of the original structure of Abigail Adams's birthplace remains at North and Norton Streets in East Weymouth, Massachusetts, but that building is also open to the public.

Other Sources

Butterfield, L. H. "Abigail Adams." In *Notable American Women*, edited by Edward James. Cambridge MA: Harvard University Press, 1971. An excellent, concise summary of Abigail Adams's life and the scholarship in the field, written by the major editor of the Adams Papers.

Betty Boyd Caroli
Kingsborough Community College, City University of New York

Abigail Adams, 1985

CHARLES FRANCIS ADAMS
1807–1886

Chronology

Born Charles Francis Adams on August 18, 1807, in Boston, Massachusetts, the son of President John Quincy Adams and Louisa Johnson Adams, and grandson of President John Adams; *1809–1815* moves to St. Petersburg with family, where his father is U.S. Minister to Russia; learns to speak fluent French while there; *1815–1817* moves to Great Britain when father is made U.S. Minister to London; attends English boarding school; *1817–1829* returns to United States and studies at Boston Latin School; graduates from Harvard College at age 18; reads law in Boston office of Daniel Webster; is admitted to bar; 1829 marries Abigail Brooks, daughter of the immensely wealthy Peter Chardon Brooks; *1829–1848* writes articles for the prestigious and influential *North American Review*; becomes outspoken opponent of slavery and leads the Conscience Whigs; receives nomination for vice president of the U.S. from the unsuccessful Free Soil party in 1848; *1848–1861* edits 10-volume *Works of John Adams* (1850–1856); joins new Republican party and is elected to the U.S. House of Representatives in 1858 and 1860; *1861–1868* serves as U.S. Minister to Great Britain where he is much responsible for keeping that country from recognizing the American Confederacy, as well as for handling numerous crises between the two nations during the Civil War; *1868–1886* is one of U.S. arbiters in the Alabama cases; is seriously considered as a presidential candidate by the Liberal Republicans in 1872; edits John Quincy Adams's *Diary* (1874–1877); *1886* dies on November 21 in Boston.

Activities of Historical Significance

A member of the nation's premier political family, Charles Francis Adams was undoubtedly one of the U.S.'s most accomplished diplomats. His diplomatic "apprenticeships" under his father in St. Petersburg and then in London were unparalleled. His thorough mastery of French was also a valuable asset at a time when French was still the diplomatic language of Europe.

Through his firm but skillful negotiations while Minister to Great Britain, he was influential in persuading the British, and by extension the French, not to recognize the Civil War Confederacy. He was also able to soothe British anger during the Trent affair, so called because an American warship, the *San Jacinto*, seized two Confederate agents (Mason and Slidell) from the British mail packet *Trent*. Later he convinced British authorities to confiscate two iron-clad warships from the Laird shipyard that were destined for the Confederates. He had been unsuccessful, however, in stopping sale of the *Alabama* to the rebel government, and after the war he played a central role in obtaining compensation from Great Britain.

Adams was probably unsuited temperamentally for high elective office and was sincerely relieved when the Liberal Republicans nominated Horace Greeley rather than himself for president in 1872.

Overview of Biographical Sources

Despite his prominence and undoubted ability, there are only two book-length biographies of Charles Francis Adams. The first, *Charles Francis Adams* (1900), is by his son, Charles Francis Adams, Jr. The second is Martin Duberman, *Charles Francis Adams, 1807–1886* (1961). Francis Russell, *Adams An American Dynasty* (1976), contains several chapters of useful information on Charles Francis Adams.

Evaluation of Principal Biographical Sources

Adams, Charles Francis, Jr. *Charles Francis Adams*. Cambridge: Harvard University Press, 1900. **(A)** Written by Adams's son, it contains personal information that cannot be found elsewhere. Understandably, the work suffers from the biases of an author so intimately related to his subject.

Duberman, Martin. *Charles Francis Adams, 1807–1886*. Boston: Houghton Mifflin, 1961. **(A)** Extraordinarily well-researched and well-written, this large volume is destined to remain the definitive biography of Charles Francis Adams for years to come.

Overview and Evaluation of Primary Sources

Charles Francis Adams and his sons Charles Francis Jr. and Henry were all accomplished writers and left valuable autobiographical accounts. Charles Francis Adams's *Diary*, 6 vols. (Cambridge: Harvard University Press, 1964–1974; **A,G**), supplies a great deal of primary material and gives important insights into the politics and diplomacy of his times. Adams also wrote prolifically for the *North American Review*. Charles Francis Adams, Jr., *Autobiography* (Boston: Houghton Mifflin, 1916; **A, G**), contains very telling descriptions of the father's character and of his qualities as a father and a family man. Henry Adams, *The Education of Henry Adams* (1907; Boston: Houghton Mifflin, 1973; **A, G**), contains a lengthy and important account of the elder Adams's years as Minister to Great Britain.

Also, the Massachusetts Historical Society houses the largest collection of Adams's papers, as well as those of his illustrious family.

Fiction and Adaptations

Charles Francis Adams is treated extensively in several episodes of a PBS series, *The Adams Chronicles*, first televised in 1975. The presentation gives an especially accurate and vivid picture of his difficult yet highly successful tenure as Minister to Great Britain.

Museums, Historical Landmarks, Societies

Adams National Historic Site (Quincy, MA). Includes the Adams family mansion where Charles Francis Adams's parents lived in their later years and where he and his family spent many summers.

Other Sources

Adams, James Truslow. *The Adams Family*. Westport, CT: Greenwood Press, 1974. A well-written overview of four generations of the Adams family which endeavors to show how succeeding generations were influenced by those that went before.

Bemis, Samuel Flagg. "Charles Francis Adams." In *Encyclopedia Americana*. Vol. 1. Danbury, CT: Grolier, 1986. A brief outline of Adams's life by an accomplished historian.

Ford, Worthington Chauncy. "Charles Francis Adams." In *Dictionary of American Biography*. Vol. 1. New York: Charles Scribner's Sons, 1928. A thorough sketch by a capable student of the Adams family.

Russell, Francis. *Adams: An American Dynasty*. New York: American Heritage, 1976. Like James Truslow Adams, Russell explores the theme of intergenerational influence. He also carries the family's history up to the mid-1970s.

David R. Contosta
Chestnut Hill College

HENRY ADAMS
1838–1918

Chronology

Born Henry Brooks Adams on February 16, 1838, in Boston, fourth of six children of Charles Francis Adams, American Congressman and diplomat, and Abigail Brooks Adams, and great-grandson of President John Adams, and grandson of President John Quincy Adams; *1838–1858* grows up in Boston, Massachusetts, summers at family homestead in nearby Quincy; attends series of private schools; *1858* graduates from Harvard College; *1858–1860* studies briefly in Germany and takes extensive grand tour of Europe; *1860–1861* is private secretary to father who is now a U.S. Congressman in Washington; while there observes disintegration of Union and beginning of Civil War; *1861–1868* lives in London as private secretary to his father, who has been appointed Minister to Great Britain; while there meets leading figures from British literary, political, and academic life and publishes first serious articles on history and politics; *1868–1870* works as free-lance journalist in Washington, exposing political corruption during the early Grant administration; *1870–1877* teaches history at Harvard, edits the prestigious *North American Review*; continues to write articles on reform politics, history, and other subjects; begins his *Life of Albert Gallatin*; *1872* marries Marian Hooper; *1877–1885* lives in Washington, D.C., where he commences his massive *History of the United States During the Administrations of Thomas Jefferson and James Madison* and, with wife, presides over a celebrated Washington salon; *1885* Marian Adams commits suicide following depression in wake of her father's death; *1885–1891* finishes history of Jefferson and Madison administrations, and travels widely with friends, including a round-the-world trip with painter John LaFarge in 1890–1891; *1891–1912* spends seven to eight months each year in Paris and rest of time in Washington; becomes fascinated by Middle Ages; writes *Mont-Saint-Michel and Chartres* and *The Education of Henry Adams*; *1912* suffers first stroke; *1912–1918* is looked after by nieces, and passes days trying to reconstruct medieval songs; *1918* dies peacefully in sleep on March 27 at home in Washington, D.C.

Activities of Historical Significance

Unlike his famous ancestors, Henry Adams was never in the forefront of American politics and diplomacy. But his trenchant criticisms of American life and thought have made him one of the nation's most important writers and critics. He was especially critical of incompetent or corrupt politicians during the post-Civil War period and of the country's conquest of an island empire during the Spanish-American War of 1898. He was similarly critical of American faith in technology and devotion to unbridled capitalism.

Adams was also a pioneer in historical scholarship, teaching the country's first graduate seminar in history while a professor at Harvard. Some of his own historical works became a model for exhaustive research and careful writing.

Finally, as the fourth generation of Adamses to achieve great success, he provides a rare example of continuing distinction within one family.

Overview of Biographical/Critical Sources

Few American writers or historians have inspired more biographical studies than Henry Adams. The most substantial biography is a three-volume work by Ernest Samuels: *The Young Henry Adams* (1948); *Henry Adams: The Middle Years* (1958); and *Henry Adams: The Major Phase* (1964). Samuels's work is exceedingly well written and painstakingly researched.

An excellent, one-volume biography is Elizabeth Stevenson's *Henry Adams* (1955). Focusing on Adams's earliest years is Edward Chalfant's *A Biography of Henry Adams: His First Life, 1838–1862* (1982). The best literary criticism per se is Richard P. Blackmur's *Henry Adams* (1980). Works concentrating on Adams's thought are Max I. Baym, *The French Education of Henry Adams* (1951); J. C. Levenson, *The Mind and Art of Henry Adams* (1957); and William H. Jordy, *Henry Adams: Scientific Historian* (1952).

The many important and creative people in Adams's life are discussed in Ernst Scheyer, *Circle of Henry Adams* (1970). Also revealing in this regard is Harold Dean Cater's lengthy introduction to a selection of letters called *Henry Adams and His Friends* (1947). For Adams's controversial relationship with Elizabeth Cameron, see Arlene B. Tehan, *Henry Adams in Love: The Pursuit of Elizabeth Sherman Cameron* (1983). On Adams's wife Marian there are Otto Friedrich's *Clover* (1979) and Eugenia Kaledin's *The Education of Mrs. Henry Adams* (1981). Continuing family influences on Adams are treated in Earl N. Harbert, *The Force So Much Closer Home: Henry Adams and His Family* (1977), and Francis Russell, *Adams, An American Dynasty* (1976). Useful insights into Adams as an historian may be found in Timothy Paul Donovan, *Henry Adams and Brooks Adams* (1961). Books on various themes in Adams's life and thought are David R. Contosta, *Henry Adams and the American Experiment* (1980), and William Dusinberre, *Henry Adams and the Myth of Failure* (1980).

Evaluation of Principal Biographical Sources

Blackmur, Richard P. *Henry Adams*. New York: Harcourt Brace Jovanovich, 1980. **(A)** Although informed by brilliant insights into Adams's works, Blackmur's posthumously published book is a collection of essays that he wrote over a period of nearly 50 years. It is often difficult to read and is in no sense a biography of Adams.

Chalfant, Edward. *A Biography of Henry Adams: His First Life, 1838–1862*. Hamden, CT: Archon Books, 1982. **(A, G)** The initial installment of a projected three-volume project on Adams, this work covers its subject up to age 24. With considerable exaggeration, Chalfant claims that Adams had become a successful politician by early adulthood.

Contosta, David R. *Henry Adams and the American Experiment*. Boston: Little, Brown, 1980. **(A, G)** This brief biography focuses on Adams's life-long fascination with what he and his family called the American experiment and pays particular attention to Adams's own ambivalent role as a critic of that experiment.

Donovan, Timothy Paul. *Henry Adams and Brooks Adams*. Norman, OK: Oklahoma University Press, 1961. **(A)** This study examines Henry Adams's and his brother Brooks Adams's attempts to create a science of history, in addition to treating the intellectual influences that the brothers exerted on each other.

Dusinberre, William. *Henry Adams: The Myth of Failure*. Charlottesville, VA: University Press of Virginia, 1980. **(A)** Dwelling on Adams's self-proclaimed image of failure, the author attempts to explain both the reasons and realities behind this studied pose.

Friedrich, Otto. *Clover*. New York: Simon and Schuster, 1979. **(A, G)** Although the author has not come much closer than others in lifting the veil on Marian "Clover" Adams's psyche and ultimate suicide, his study has much to reveal about the Adamses' famous salon in Washington from 1877 to 1885.

Harbert, Earl N. *The Force So Much Closer Home: Henry Adams and His Family*. New York: New York University Press, 1977. **(A)** Here the author traces the influence of three generations of family habit and thought on Henry Adams.

Homans, Abigail Adams. *Education by Uncles*. Boston: Houghton Mifflin, 1966. **(A, G)** Written by one of Adams's nieces, this charming book offers much insight into the closeness and importance of his family.

Kalendin, Eugenia. *The Education of Mrs. Henry Adams*. Philadelphia: Temple University Press, 1981. **(A)** This work examines the ideas and currents that shaped Marian Adams's thinking, and the intellectual and social relationship between Adams and his wife.

Levenson, J. C. *The Mind and Art of Henry Adams*. Stanford, CA: Stanford University Press, 1957. **(A)** Essentially an intellectual and cultural biography of Adams, Levenson's study of Adams is one of the best by a literary critic.

Russell, Francis. *Adams, An American Dynasty*. New York: American Heritage Publications, 1976. **(A, G)** An excellent overview of four generations of America's most famous family.

Samuels, Ernest. *The Young Henry Adams*; *Henry Adams: The Middle Years*; and *Henry Adams: The Major Phase*. Cambridge, MA: Harvard University Press, 1948, 1958, 1964. **(A)** This most definitive life of Adams to date is more a narrative than an interpretive biography, in which the author tries to get beneath the irony and self-deprecation of Adams's *Education of Henry Adams*.

Scheyer, Ernst. *Circle of Henry Adams*. Detroit: Wayne State University Press, 1970. **(A)** Concentrates on the wide circle of Adams's friends, many of them the leading artists, intellectuals, and statesmen of the day, who gathered around Henry Adams during his adult life and especially at the Adams salon in Washington.

Stevenson, Elizabeth. *Henry Adams*. New York: Macmillan, 1955. **(A, G)** Although a full, one-volume biography of Adams, Stevenson has taken special pains to contradict Adams's constant protestations of personal failure.

Overview and Evaluation of Primary Sources

Adams wrote nearly every day of his adult life, as letters, articles, reviews, novels, and essays poured forth from his pen. When finished, the most complete and authoritative collection of Adams's correspondence will be that edited by J. C. Levenson *et al*. Three of six volumes, covering the years 1858–1892, have now been published as *Letters of Henry Adams* (Cambridge, MA: Harvard University Press, 1982; **A)**. Other collections of Adams's correspondence are Harold Dean Cater, ed., *Henry Adams and His Friends* (Boston: Houghton Mifflin, 1947; **A)**, and the three titles edited by Worthington Chauncey Ford: *A Cycle of Adams Letters, 1861–1865*, 2 vols.; (Boston: Houghton Mifflin, 1920; **A)**; *Letters of Henry Adams, 1858–1891* (Boston: Houghton Mifflin, 1930; **A)**; and *Letters of Henry Adams, 1892–1918* (Boston: Houghton Mifflin, 1938; **A)**. A selection of the letters of Adams's wife Marian were edited by Ward Thoron as *The Letters of Mrs. Henry Adams* (Boston: Little, Brown, 1936; **A)**.

Also shedding light on Adams's life is his autobiographical *The Education of Henry Adams* (Boston: Houghton Mifflin, 1918; **A, G)**. It should be read with much circumspection, however, since it is filled with omissions, distortions, and constant self-deprecations.

Adams's major historical writings are *The Life of Albert Gallatin* (Philadelphia: J. B. Lippincott, 1879; **A)**; *The History of the United States During the Administrations of Thomas Jefferson and James Madison* (New York: Charles Scribner's Sons, 1889–1891; **A)**; and *John Randolph* (Boston: Houghton Mifflin, 1890; **A)**. In addition to these, there are two semi-historical works that defy standard categories: *Mont-Saint-Michel and Chartres* (privately printed in 1905 and since reprinted in several editions; **A, G)** and *Tahiti* (privately printed in 1901 and also reprinted in several editions; **A, G)**.

Finally, there are Adams's two novels, *Democracy* (New York: Henry Holt, 1880; **A, G)** and *Esther* (New York: Henry Holt, 1884; **A, G)**. Although mediocre novels at best, they reveal a great deal about Adams's thought on contemporary issues—*Democracy*, on Gilded Age American politics, and *Esther*, on American women.

Anyone who is interested in studying Adams thoroughly should also consult his many articles, essays, and reviews. The most complete listing of these may be found in each of Ernest Samuels's three volumes on Adams. Some of these periodical writings have been collected: *Historical Essays* (New York: Charles Scribner's Sons, 1891; **A**) and *Henry Adams: The Great Secession Winter and Other Essays*, edited by George E. Hochfield (New York: A. E. Barnes, 1963; **A**).

The Massachusetts Historical Society houses the largest body of Adams's letters and manuscripts as part of its collection of Adams Family Papers.

Fiction and Adaptations

Henry Adams figures prominently in the final episodes of a vivid and accurate PBS series entitled *The Adams Chronicles*, which was first broadcast in 1975.

Museums, Historical Landmarks, Societies

Adams National Historic Site (Quincy, MA). Contains the Adams family mansion where Henry Adams spent his childhood summers and where the entire family often gathered for reunions.

Houghton Library, Harvard University (Cambridge, MA). Contains correspondence of Henry and Brooks Adams, as well as other Henry Adams manuscripts.

Rock Creek Cemetery (Washington, DC). Location of Henry and Marian Adams's graves, with the figure of a mysterious, seated woman sculpted by the famous Augustus Saint-Gaudens.

Other Sources

Johnson, Allen. "Henry Brooks Adams." In *Dictionary of American Biography*. New York: Charles Scribner's Sons, 1928. Offers a brief sketch of Adams's life and work.

David R. Contosta
Chestnut Hill College

JOHN ADAMS
1735–1826

Chronology

Born John Adams on October 30, 1735, in Braintree (now Quincy), Massachusetts, to John Adams, a farmer and local office holder, and Susanna Boylston Adams; *1735–1755* grows up and attends school in Braintree; *1755* graduates from Harvard college; *1755–1764* teaches school for a year in Worcester, Massachusetts, while deciding upon a career; reads law with James Putnam of Worcester and is presented to Boston bar by Jeremiah Gridley in 1758; law practice grows slowly but steadily; *1764* marries Abigail Smith; *1765–1770* writes a series of essays for the *Boston Gazette*, later collected and published as *A Dissertation on the Canon and Feudal Law*; joins James Otis in writing protests against the Stamp Act; defends John Hancock, who is accused of smuggling, as well as British Captain Thomas Preston, charged with murder in the Boston Massacre of March 1770; *1771–1775* applauds Boston Tea Party of 1773; is elected a delegate to First Continental Congress in 1774 and there helps to draft a petition to George III; returns to Boston where he is elected to provincial congress and then chosen to provincial council; writes "Novanglus," a series of essays in the press on the origins of the dispute with Great Britain; *1776–1777* writes *Thoughts on Government* in answer to Thomas Paine's *Common Sense*; is elected to Second Continental Congress; proposes George Washington as commander-in-chief of Continental army; is early and most vocal advocate of independence in Congress and serves on committee to draft the Declaration of Independence; is subsequently a member of many important committees in Congress and is largely responsible for creation of first United States navy; *1778* Congress sends him as one of three commissioners to France, but he is recalled after a year; *1779–1783* is sent back to France to negotiate, with John Jay, a treaty of peace with Great Britain; arranges for a loan from the Dutch; achieves success in peace talks with Britain, over opposition of French Foreign Minister Vergennes, where he negotiates for enlarged western boundaries and the rights of Americans to fish off Newfoundland Coast; begins writing his *Defense of the Constitutions of the United States of America*, the first volume of which is published while delegates are assembling for the Constitutional Convention of 1787; *1789–1796* supports ratification of the new Constitution; is elected first vice president of the United States, and is reelected in 1792; *1796–1801* is elected second president of the United States; saves the country from war with France in 1798–1799; is denied a second term, in large part by his political enemy Alexander Hamilton; *1801–1826* returns to home in Quincy, Massachusetts, where he carries on extensive correspondence with numerous persons, the most important being with Thomas Jefferson; assists son John Quincy Adams with his rising political career and sees him elected sixth president of the United States in 1824; *1826* dies on July 4 in Quincy, exactly 50 years after the Declaration of Independence was proclaimed; Thomas Jefferson dies the same day.

Activities of Historical Significance

Although John Adams was one of the most important of the American founding fathers, he was neglected for decades by historians and nearly forgotten by the general public. There are several reasons for this: Adams was known for being blunt, quarrelsome, and sometimes aloof, traits that did not endear him to his contemporaries and which, for a long time thereafter, obscured his very real capacity for warmth and humor. His conservative philosophy and concerns about the excesses of democracy also alienated many historians, who have tended to accept the more liberal "Whig" interpretation of their country's past. And despite his intimate involvement in national affairs on the highest level, Adams has not been strongly associated with any one great event, as, for example, were George Washington and Thomas Jefferson. Conditions since the end of World War II, however, have led to much greater appreciation of Adams. Among these are a growing interest in political conservatism, renewed recognition of the dangers of unchecked power, the decision to open Adams's papers to the public, and the bicentennial of American independence in 1976.

Adams's most important achievements were his leadership of the independence movement in the Second Continental Congress, his preservation of American fishing rights and insistence on generous western boundaries during peace negotiations with Great Britain in 1783, and his successful efforts to preserve the peace with France in 1798–1799, despite popular demands for war.

Adams's political thought also provides a good example of early conservatism in the United States. Sharing his Puritan ancestors' strong doubts about human perfectibility, Adams believed that human nature was a mixture of good and evil, and that life was a struggle to realize one's better self. An essential approach to winning this struggle, according to Adams, was a constant application of reason, coupled with a refusal to give into purely emotional demands. It followed that citizens should select the most intelligent and moral men to govern—what Adams saw as a natural aristocracy of wisdom and virtue. Such a philosophy has been understandably unpopular among those who would extoll the virtues of common men.

Overview of Biographical Sources

Because of the general neglect of Adams's life and thought, there were few biographies until the second half of the twentieth century. The definitive biography to date is Page Smith's two-volume *John Adams* (1962). Another fine work is the two-volume *John Adams* (1871) by his son, John Quincy Adams, and his grandson, Charles Francis Adams. An excellent one-volume life is Gilbert Chinard's *Honest*

John Adams (1933). A more recent but less useful biography is Anne Husten Burleigh's *John Adams* (1970).

Concentrating on Adams's thought and personality is Peter Shaw's *The Character of John Adams* (1976). Other intellectual studies are Haraszti Zoltán, *John Adams and the Prophets of Progress* (1952); John R. Howe, Jr., *The Changing Political Thought of John Adams* (1966); and Edward Handler, *America and Europe in the Political Thought of John Adams* (1964). An informative comparison between John Adams and his sometime political foe, Thomas Jefferson, is Merrill D. Peterson, *Adams and Jefferson: A Revolutionary Dialogue* (1976).

On various aspects of Adams's political and diplomatic career, there are Catherine Drinker Bowen's, *John Adams and The American Revolution* (1950); James H. Hutson, *John Adams and the Diplomacy of the American Revolution* (1980); Manning J. Dauer, *The Adams Federalists* (1953); and Ralph Adams Brown, *The Presidency of John Adams* (1975).

Accounts of Adams's intelligent and resourceful wife, Abigail, are Charles W. Akers, *Abigail Adams: An American Woman* (1980); Janet Whitney, *Abigail Adams* (1948); and Paul C. Nagel, *The Adams Women: Abigail Adams and Louisa Adams, Their Sisters and Daughters* (1987).

On the Adams family as a whole, see James Truslow Adams, *The Adams Family* (1930), and Francis Russell, *Adams: An American Dynasty* (1976).

Evaluation of Principal Biographical Sources

Adams, John Quincy, and Charles Francis Adams. *John Adams*. 1871. Reprint. New York: Chelsea House, 1980. **(A)** This generally well-written and well-researched biography by Adams's son and grandson emphasizes what the authors considered the four crises in his public life: his legal defense of Captain Preston, his premature call for independence in 1775, his resistance to French Foreign Minister Vergennes during the peace negotiations with Great Britain in 1783, and his decision to avoid war with France in 1798. Unfortunately, in their efforts to be objective, the authors neglect to use their extensive personal knowledge of John Adams that might have made him appear much more likeable and human.

Bowen, Catherine Drinker. *John Adams and the American Revolution*. Boston: Little, Brown, 1950. **(A, G)** This volume by a skilled and well-known biographer focuses on the first half of Adams's life and career. It gives Adams the full credit that he deserves as a leader of the American Revolution.

Brown, Ralph Adams. *The Presidency of John Adams*. Lawrence: The University of Kansas Press, 1975. **(A)** This volume concentrates on the problems John Adams confronted during his presidency, the solutions that he offered, and an assessment of his actions. Adams generally receives high marks from Brown for his performance.

Chinard, Gilbert. *Honest John Adams*. Boston: Little, Brown, 1933. (**A, G**) Often called the most readable one-volume biography of Adams, Chinard's work did much to shed sympathetic light on a hitherto neglected man. Chinard examines his subject's political ideas and the reasons behind them. He also portrays the more colorful and human side of Adams's personality.

Shaw, Peter. *The Character of John Adams*. Chapel Hill: University of North Carolina Press, 1976. (**A**) Like Chinard, Shaw tries to depict Adams in all his complexity. Shaw goes further, however, in attempting to explain Adams's seemingly contradictory character by placing his thoughts and actions within the wider social and cultural environment that helped to shape them.

Smith, Page. *John Adams*. Garden City, NY: Doubleday, 1962. (**A, G**) A superbly written, definitive biography made possible, in part, by a family decision to make Adams's papers available to scholars for the first time. Smith labors to treat all sides of Adams's complex character, explaining his life and thought as an integral part of his eighteenth century world.

Overview and Evaluation of Primary Sources

Like all the other famous Adamses, John Adams was a prolific writer. His extensive writings, first made public in the mid-1950s, are housed in the Massachusetts Historical Society in Boston; they are also available on microfilm at many libraries. A large selection of Adams's papers were edited and published by his grandson, Charles Francis Adams, in the ten-volume *Works of John Adams, Second President of the United States, With a Life of the Author* (Boston: Little, Brown, 1850–1856; **A**). Much more exhaustive, when completed, will be the *Papers of John Adams*, edited by Lyman Butterfield et al. (Cambridge: Harvard University Press; **A**). Briefer collections of Adams letters include *The Spur of Fame: Dialogues of John Adams and Benjamin Rush, 1805–1813*, edited by John A. Schultz and Douglas Adair (San Marino, CA: The Huntington Library, 1966; **A**) and *The Book of Abigail and John: Selected Letters of the Adams Family, 1762–1784*, edited by Lyman Butterfield et al. (Cambridge: Harvard University Press, 1975; **A, G**).

Fiction and Adaptations

John Adams figures prominently in the early episodes of a PBS series entitled *The Adams Chronicles*, which was first broadcast in 1975. It gives a generally accurate and entertaining view of the multi-faceted Adams.

The broadway musical, *1776*, by Peter Stone and Sherman Edwards, first staged in 1969, depicts a serious but human John Adams as he leads the debate for American independence.

John Adams's relationship with his wife is the subject of Irving Stone's novel *Those Who Love: A Biographical Novel of Abigail and John Adams* (1965). Although Stone undertook extensive research and includes quotations from the Adams Papers, the work is fictional.

Museums, Historical Landmarks, Societies

Adams National Historical Site (Quincy, MA). The Adams family mansion, with furnishings, where John and Abigail Adams spent the latter years of their lives.

John Adams and John Quincy Adams Birthplaces (Quincy, MA). These early eighteenth-century "saltbox" houses are furnished to represent the way they may have looked during the lives of their most famous occupants.

Other Sources

Claude Moore Fuess. "John Adams." In the *Dictionary of American Biography*. New York: Charles Scribner's Sons, 1928. A brief sketch of Adams's life and work.

David R. Contosta
Chestnut Hill College

JOHN QUINCY ADAMS
1767–1848

Chronology

Born John Quincy Adams on July 11, 1767, in Braintree (now Quincy), Massachusetts, the eldest son and second of five children of John Adams, who will become the second president of the U.S., and Abigail Smith Adams; *1778–1779* joins father on diplomatic mission to Paris; *1779–1785* undertakes second overseas sojourn with father, attending school in Paris, Amsterdam, Leyden, and The Hague; *1781–1782* serves as private secretary to Francis Dana on a mission to Russia; *1785–1787* returns home to study at Harvard College, graduating with honors; *1787–1790* studies law at Newburyport, winning admission to the bar in 1790; *1791* publishes an attack on Thomas Paine's *The Rights of Man*, using the pseudonym "Publicola"; *1793* defends Washington's Proclamation of Neutrality in a series of essays under the name "Marcellus"; *1794* is appointed minister to The Hague by President George Washington; *July 26, 1797* marries Louisa Catherine Johnson, daughter of the American consul in London, with whom he will have four children; *November 1797* arrives in Berlin as minister to Prussia, having been appointed by his father; *1801* returns to the United States; *April 5, 1802* elected as a Federalist to the Massachusetts State Senate; *February 3, 1803* elected to the United States Senate; *1805* appointed professor of oratory and rhetoric at Harvard, a position he holds until 1810; *June 8, 1808* resigns his Senate seat; *March 6, 1809* appointed minister to Russia by President James Madison; *1811* declines offer of a seat on the Supreme Court; *1813–1814* serves on United States commission appointed to negotiate a peace settlement with the British; *December 24, 1814* signs Treaty of Ghent, ending the War of 1812; *1815* appointed minister to Great Britain; *1817* named secretary of state by President James Monroe; *1818* concludes a treaty with Great Britain covering disputed boundaries, fishing rights, slavery, and commerce; *February 22, 1819* signs Adams-Onis Treaty with the Spanish minister, transferring Florida to the United States and fixing the American-Spanish boundary west along the 42nd parallel to the Pacific Ocean; *1823* plays major role in the framing of the Monroe Doctrine, which is announced in the president's annual message on December 2; *1824* is nominated for the presidency; in the ensuing four-way race, no candidate secures a majority of the electoral vote, with Adams finishing behind Andrew Jackson and ahead of William H. Crawford and Henry Clay; the election is turned over to the House of Representatives; *February 9, 1825* Adams is chosen president by the House of Representatives by a slim margin over Jackson and Crawford amid charges that he made a "corrupt bargain" with Clay; *March 4, 1825* is sworn in as the sixth president; appoints Clay secretary of state, causing an uproar among Jackson's partisans; *1828* after a tumultuous administration in which his policy proposals are obstructed by Congress, Adams loses his bid for reelection to Jackson; *March 4, 1829* slips out of Washington, D.C., on the morning of Jackson's inauguration; *1830* wins election to the House of Representatives; *1836–1844* engages in "Gag Rule Controversy" over the reception of anti-slavery petitions by the House of Representatives; *1841* goes before the Supreme Court to successfully defend black passengers of the slave ship *Amistad* against attempts to re-enslave them; *1843* makes successful tour of the Old Northwest; *1848* suffers a stroke on the floor of the House of Representatives on February 21; dies two days later in Washington, D.C., and is buried in Quincy.

Activities of Historical Significance

John Quincy Adams led a long, varied, and useful life dedicated to public service. His lackluster presidency, a personality that combined candor with conceit and intelligence with injured pride, and his all-too-obvious sense of self-importance have hindered his quest for fame among Americans both in his time and today. Yet his contributions as a diplomat were crucial to the development of the young nation, and his defense of the right of petition and his attacks on slavery provided a beacon for freedom.

Adams's experiences in diplomacy stretched all the way back to his youth, when, as a ten-year-old boy, he accompanied his father to Europe. His wide training and deep learning earned him diplomatic posts during Washington's and his father's administrations, and his nominal federalism proved an easily surmountable obstacle when he resumed diplomatic service during the Madison administration. He played a key role in bringing the War of 1812 to a close at the peace table in Ghent, Belgium, in 1814, for which he was rewarded with the mission to Great Britain, a post once held by his father (and one which would be held in turn by his son Charles during and after the American Civil War).

In 1817 Adams returned to the United States to serve as secretary of state under James Monroe. During the next eight years he established the foundations for a powerful transcontinental empire through skillful negotiation. After settling several outstanding issues with England in 1818, he worked to obtain not only the Floridas but also a recognition from Spain that the borders of the United States extended all the way to the Pacific Ocean, a goal achieved with the signing of the Adams-Onis Treaty in 1819. One way to enhance the power of the United States was to prevent encroachments in the Americas by European powers, a likely prospect in reaction to a series of independence movements in Latin America. In 1823, Adams played a key role in the framing and promulgation of the Monroe Doctrine, a declaration of principle closing off the Americas from European colonization, interference, or intrigue. The Monroe Doctrine remains to this day a cornerstone of America foreign policy.

Such accomplishments seemed to merit Adams's elevation to the highest office in the land, yet his bid for the White House in 1824 and his subsequent administration were perhaps the low points of his public life, as well as the cause of increasing tensions and tragedies within his family. With no candidate receiving a majority of the electoral vote, the choice of the next president fell to the House of Representatives, where Adams triumphed over the more popular war hero Andrew Jackson. Ironically, it was Adams's defense of Jackson's behavior in Florida during the first Seminole War which had rescued the hero of New Orleans from a possible court-martial. Henry Clay's support proved vital to Adams's victory; when Adams tendered the Kentuckian the position of secretary of state, the murmurs of a "corrupt bargain" swelled into a loud chorus of denunciation. For the next four years Adams's legislative and diplomatic initiatives were usually thwarted by an unruly Congress more intent on the election of 1828 than on current policy concerns. Thrashed by Jackson in the ensuing presidential contest, Adams slipped out of Washington on the morning of Jackson's inauguration, much as his father had in 1801 when Thomas Jefferson succeeded him as president.

Unlike most ex-presidents, retirement from the White House did not mean an end to public service for John Quincy Adams. In 1830 his fellow-citizens elected him to the first of nine terms in the House of Representatives. In Congress, Adams battled proslavery advocates seeking to suppress discussion of the possible abolition of the "peculiar institution" in what became known as the Gag Rule Controversy. At the same time, his defense proved instrumental in the release of the black slaves who had seized control of the Spanish ship *Amistad* in a revolt. Abolitionist and antislavery forces sang his praises, and Adams enjoyed more popularity than he had ever known. His opposition to slavery led him to oppose the annexation of Texas and the Mexican War, an ironic stance in light of his earlier lust for transcontinental expansion.

Overview of Biographical Sources

Although history may not have always been kind to John Quincy Adams, he has been fortunate in the biographers who have selected him as their subject of study. Foremost among these studies is Samuel Flagg Bemis's magisterial two-volume work, *John Quincy Adams and the Foundations of American Foreign Policy* (1949) and *John Quincy Adams and the Union* (1956), both models of biography. Mary Hargreaves's study, *The Presidency of John Quincy Adams* (1985), remedies the only significant weak spot in Bemis's work. More recent studies have contributed much to an understanding of John Quincy Adams the man. Most important among these are Jack Shepherd's *Cannibals of the Heart* (1980), a touching account of Adams's marriage and family, and Paul C. Nagel's two studies of the Adams family, *Descent From Glory* (1983) and *The Adams Women* (1987). Finally, Leonard Richards's *The Life and Times of Congressman John Quincy Adams* (1986) is a gem of a biography on Adams's post-presidential career.

Evaluation of Principal Biographical Sources

Adams, Henry. *The Degradation of the Democratic Dogma*. Introduction by Brooks Adams. New York: Macmillan, 1920. (**A**) Although ostensibly about the grandson of John Quincy Adams, one section, "The Heritage of Henry Adams," by Brooks Adams, contains much biographical information about the sixth president.

Bemis, Samuel Flagg. *John Quincy Adams and the Foundations of American Foreign Policy*. New York: Alfred A. Knopf, 1949. (**A, G**) The first volume of a two-volume biography, containing a masterly discussion of Adams's diplomatic career.

————. *John Quincy Adams and the Union*. New York: Alfred A. Knopf, 1956. (**A, G**) The second volume of Bemis's study covers Adams's ill-starred presidency and congressional career. An absorbing and thoroughly researched account.

East, Robert A. *John Quincy Adams: The Critical Years, 1785–1794*. New York: Bookman Associates, 1962. (**A, G**) A rather straightforward account of Adams's early career, culminating in his appointment by President Washington to The Hague.

Hargreaves, Mary W. M. *The Presidency of John Quincy Adams*. Lawrence: University Press of Kansas, 1985. (**A**) The best examination of the Adams administration, covering all aspects of the troubled White House tenure of the sixth president.

Hecht, Marie B. *John Quincy Adams: A Personal History of an Independent Man*. New York: Macmillan, 1972. (**G**) A well-written account, relying heavily and uncritically on the Adams Papers, which tends to magnify its subject's accomplishments while minimizing his flaws and mistakes.

Lipsky, George A. *John Quincy Adams: His Theory and Ideas*. New York: Thomas Y. Crowell, 1950. (**A**) The best examination of Adams's thoughts on federal power, slavery, and foreign policy available.

Morse, John T. *John Quincy Adams*. Boston: Houghton Mifflin, 1882. (**A, G**) Issued as a volume in the American Statesman Series, Morse's biography offers a short and concise overview.

Nagel, Paul C. *Descent From Glory: Four Generations of the John Adams Family*. New York: Oxford University Press, 1983. (**A, G**) Contains a great deal of information about John Quincy Adams as son, husband, father, and grandfather in the Adams clan.

Richards, Leonard L. *The Life and Times of Congressman John Quincy Adams*. New York: Oxford University Press, 1986. (**A, G**) A clear and concise exploration of the former president's congressional career, illuminating the roots of the political antislavery struggle and the debate over territorial expansion in the 1840s.

Seward, William Henry. *Life and Public Services of John Quincy Adams*. 1849. Reprint. Port Washington, NY: Kennikat Press, 1971. (**A**) Seward, an antislavery Whig and follower of Adams, commemorates his leader in a biography originally issued a year after Adams's death.

Shepherd, Jack. *Cannibals of the Heart: A Personal Biography of Louisa Catherine and John Quincy Adams*. New York: McGraw-Hill, 1980. (**A, G**) An engrossing look at the private tragedies and torments of John Quincy Adams's marriage and family life, emphasizing the emotional toll on Louisa Catherine Adams as she struggled to establish an independent identity.

Overview and Evaluation of Primary Sources

The vast bulk of the papers of John Quincy Adams are located at the Massachusetts Historical Society; this collection is part of the 608-reel microfilm edition of the Adams Family Papers. Other official documents, pertaining mostly to Adams's diplomatic career, are at the National Archives. There have also been several attempts to provide letterpress editions of Adams's writings. Worthington C. Ford edited seven volumes of *The Writings of John Quincy Adams* (New York: Macmillan, 1913–1917; **A**), but this effort only reached Adams's writings to 1823.

Adams's voluminous diary has been printed in edited form several times. Charles Francis Adams issued an edition of his father's diary in the 1870s, but the awkwardly-titled *Memoirs of John Quincy Adams, Comprising Portions of His Diary from 1795 to 1848*, 12 vols. (Philadelphia: J. B. Lippincott, 1874–1877; **A**) is uneven in quality and excludes much sensitive material. Allan Nevins's condensed single volume version of this work, *Diary of John Quincy Adams, 1794–1845* (New York: Scribner's, 1951; **A, G**), makes for more enjoyable reading. In 1982 the Adams Family Papers Project and Harvard University Press began publishing the complete diary under the direction of David Grayson Allen, but the snail's pace at which this work has proceeded makes it unlikely that it will be of much use for decades to come. The first two volumes take the reader to 1788. There is little sign that the various other series of letterpress publications by the Adams Papers Project will be completed with any greater dispatch. For those readers who can not afford to wait decades, Adrienne Koch and William Peden, eds., *The Selected Writings of John and John Quincy Adams* (New York: Alfred A. Knopf, 1946; **A, G**), is a good place to start, while Walter LaFeber's *John Quincy Adams and American Continental Empire* (Chicago: Quadrangle, 1965; **G**) contains a concise selection of excerpts from letters, speeches, and papers. The researcher wishing for more is directed to the microfilm edition of the Adams Family Papers.

Fiction and Adaptations

The most notable and widely acclaimed adaptation of the Adams legacy is *The*

Adams Chronicles, which originally aired on PBS stations in 1976. The twelve episodes were produced by the Educational Broadcasting Corporation, and drew critical raves despite minor inaccuracies. David Birney portrayed the young John Quincy Adams, while William Daniels played the mature statesman and diplomat.

Museums, Historical Landmarks, Societies

Adams National Historic Site (Quincy, MA). The main structure on this property, built in 1731, housed four generations of the Adams family.

First Parish (Unitarian) Church (Quincy, MA). Louisa Catherine Adams and John Quincy Adams are buried here in a crypt, as are John and Abigail Adams.

John Quincy Adams Birthplace (Quincy, MA). Adjacent to John Adams's birthplace, this saltbox structure dates from 1663.

Statuary Hall, United States Capitol (Washington, DC). This area once served as the chamber for the House of Representatives; the spot where John Quincy Adams collapsed on February 21, 1848, is marked.

Other Sources

Butterfield, L. H. "Tending a Dragon-killer: Notes for the Biographer of Mrs. John Quincy Adams." *Proceedings of the American Philosophical Society* 118 (April 1974): 165–78. A suggestive list of ideas about the wife of John Quincy Adams.

Dangerfield, George. *The Era of Good Feelings*. New York: Harcourt, Brace, and World, 1952. A very readable and enjoyable account of the time during John Quincy Adams's stint on the Ghent Commission and as secretary of state.

————. *The Awakening of American Nationalism, 1815–1828*. New York: Harper and Row, 1965. A survey of the most significant years of Adams's public life.

Graebner, Norman. "John Quincy Adams: Empiricism and Empire." In *Makers of American Diplomacy*, edited by Frank J. Merli and Theodore A. Wilson. New York: Scribner's, 1974. A good overview of Adams's accomplishments as a diplomat from a realist perspective.

Jones, Howard. *Mutiny on the "Amistad": The Saga of a Slave Revolt and Its Impact on American Abolition, Law, and Diplomacy*. New York: Oxford University Press, 1987. A fascinating study of this incident and the legal defense in which Adams played a key role.

Musto, David F. "The Youth of John Quincy Adams." *Proceedings of the American Philosophical Society* 113 (August 1969): 269–82. A discussion of the pressures of parental expectation upon young John Quincy Adams, focusing on the role of Abigail Adams.

Nagel, Paul C. *The Adams Women: Abigail and Louisa Adams, Their Sisters and Daughters*. New York: Oxford University Press, 1987. A very able exploration of the lives of John Quincy Adams's mother and wife.

Oliver, Andrew. *Portraits of John Quincy Adams and His Wife*. Cambridge: Harvard University Press, 1970. A complete pictorial collection with commentary.

Perkins, Bradford. *Castlereagh and Adams*. Berkeley: University of California Press, 1964. The concluding volume of Perkins's trilogy on Anglo-American relations between the Jay Treaty and the Monroe Doctrine, this study covers Adams's tenure as secretary of state.

Shepherd, Jack. *The Adams Chronicles: Four Generations of Greatness*. Boston: Little, Brown, 1975. A profusely illustrated volume prepared to accompany the Educational Broadcasting Corporation's television series of the same name.

Brooks D. Simpson
Wofford College

SAMUEL ADAMS
1722–1803

Chronology

Born Samuel Adams on September 17, 1722, in Boston, son of Samuel Adams, a successful brewer, deacon of Old South Church, sometime justice of the peace, selectman, member of the Massachusetts House of Representatives, and Mary Fifield Adams; *1736–1740* attends Harvard College with a social rank of fifth in a class of twenty-two; *1740* receives B.A.; *1740–1748* briefly studies law; receives M.A.; works a few months in the counting house of Thomas Cushing; borrows £1000 from his father to start a business that soon fails; joins his father's brewing business; *1748* after his father's death, inherits one-third of a comfortable estate; *1749–1756* depletes his inheritance and faces creditors; *1749* marries Elizabeth Checkley; *1754* his wife dies; *1756–1764* works ineffectively as a tax collector, falling about £8000 in arrears, but becomes active in Boston politics, eventually joining the Caucus Club, a base for opposing the power of Lieutenant Governor Thomas Hutchinson and his circle; *1764* marries Elizabeth Wells; joins critics of the Sugar Act as the Empire begins a more rigorous colonial policy; *1765* leads protests against the Stamp Act, encourages formation of the Sons of Liberty, and becomes a member of the Massachusetts House of Representatives; *1766* is re-elected to the House where the new radical majority makes him clerk, a position he retains until 1774; emerges as a leader of "patriots" alarmed by alleged abuses of government power; *1767* protests the Townshend Acts; *1768* cultivates Boston merchants by enlisting the help of John Hancock and develops the Non-Importation Association; drafts a "Circular Letter" to other colonies to broaden support for resistance to imperial measures and another to Massachusetts towns for a "patriot" convention in Boston; *1770–1772* works to maintain public awareness of the dangers of imperial power in a period of relative calm after the repeal of the Townshend Acts; *1772* sets up the rudiments of a revolutionary network by starting the Massachusetts Committee of Correspondence and encouraging similar intercolonial committees; *1773* embarrasses Thomas Hutchinson by releasing letters in which the governor recommended a firmer colonial policy to London; his release of the Hutchinson letters also embarrasses Benjamin Franklin, who had supplied the letters from London on the understanding they would not be made public; is an organizer of the Boston Tea Party; *1774* leads opposition to the Intolerable Acts and proposes a Continental Congress; *1774–1781* as a delegate to the Continental Congress, he opposes compromise with the British and helps draft the Articles of Confederation; *1776* signs the Declaration of Independence; *1779–1781* participates in the Massachusetts convention to draft a state constitution; *1781* returns to Massachusetts political life as a state senator; *1786–1787* opposes Shays's Rebellion; *1788* after some hesitation, supports the Federal Constitution at the state ratifying convention; *1789–1793* serves as lieutenant governor of Massachusetts; *1793* succeeds to the governorship after Hancock's death; *1794* elected governor and serves until 1797; *1803* dies on October 2 in Boston.

Activities of Historical Significance

Adams's role in leading Boston's opposition to imperial policies after 1764 made him one of the most important members of the American revolutionary generation. His contemporaries regarded him as vital to the cause of American independence because he was in large part responsible for the public perception that American rights were in danger. His skills as a political organizer created a strong base of support in Massachusetts and created mechanisms, such as the committees of correspondences and the non-importation associations, which served as the foundations for revolutionary government after 1775. His ability to shape opinion kept the royal authorities on the defensive. With his second cousin, John Adams, Adams worked effectively at the Continental Congress to oppose suggestions for compromise. After the adoption of the Declaration of Independence in 1776, Adams's significant role in national life ended.

Overview of Biographical Sources

For a figure of such importance to the American Revolution, Adams has remained elusive and controversial. He had to wait longer than most of the founders for a biographer. The favorable biography by a descendant, William Wells, *The Life and Public Services of Samuel Adams*, was not published until 1865. A largely reverent biography by James Hosmer, *Samuel Adams* (1885), suggests that Adams had sometimes used less than fair means to shape opinion. Later biographers have stressed themes of demagogy and political manipulation, portraying him as an intolerant and suspicious troublemaker. Among such portrayals are Ralph Volney Harlow's *Samuel Adams: Promoter of the American Revolution* (1923), John C. Miller's *Sam Adams: Pioneer in Propaganda* (1936), and Clifford Shipton's "Samuel Adams" (1958). More recent studies, most notably Pauline Maier in *The Old Revolutionaries* (1980), argue that these negative portrayals fail to do justice to Adams as a historical figure.

Evaluation of Principal Biographical Sources

Beach, Stewart. *Samuel Adams: The Fateful Years, 1764–1776*. New York: Dodd, Mead, 1965. (**A, G**) In this study of Adams's most significant years, Beach opposes the view that Adams was a manipulative demagogue. He argues that Adams did not start out believing that the colonies should break with England and that he was a fascinating and complex figure who has been largely misunderstood.

Harlow, Ralph Volney. *Samuel Adams: Promoter of the American Revolution*. New York: H. Holt, 1923. (**G**) This biography suggests that Adams was motivated by a hatred for the mother country fueled by an inferiority complex that made his political actions partly irrational. The book is an example of the misuse of a superficial understanding of Freudian theory.

Hosmer, James Kendall. *Samuel Adams*. 1885. Reprint. Cambridge, MA: Riverside Press, 1896. (**A, G**) Intended to be a laudatory portrayal of a founding father, this book suggests that Adams was, regrettably, something less than a gentleman in his methods. Hosmer has a higher opinion of Hutchinson's character in a later biography of the Loyalist governor.

Miller, John C. *Sam Adams: Pioneer in Propaganda*. 1936. Reprint. Stanford, CA: Stanford University Press, 1960. (**A, G**) Miller sees Adams as a talented political manipulator who orchestrated opinion with the fixed aim of separating the colonies from Britain. This book remains the most scholarly and comprehensive twentieth-century biography.

Wells, William V. *The Life and Public Services of Samuel Adams*. 1865. Reprint. Freeport, NY: Books for Libraries Press, 1969. (**A, G**) A descendant of Adams, Wells sees his subject as a hero who held to his dream of American independence from the earliest days of the struggle. This carefully researched work contains useful materials on Adams's private life.

Overview and Evaluation of Primary Sources
One reason for the paucity of Adams biographies is that he left few papers. His second cousin John Adams said that Samuel destroyed much of his correspondence during the years of the Continental Congress. Historians have been suspicious of the authenticity of some papers that survive a man who generally believed in covering his tracks. Some of the material, including letters written by Adams, can be read in *The Writings of Samuel Adams*, 3 vols., edited by Harry Alonza Cushing (1904–1908. Reprint. New York: Octagon Books, 1968; **A, G**). Surviving manuscripts are collected in the Samuel Adams Papers in the New York Public Library. The calendar to the papers contains summaries of missing letters.

Museums, Historical Landmarks, Societies
Park Street Church (Boston, MA). Contains Adams's grave along with those of John Hancock, Robert Treat Paine, Paul Revere, and James Otis.

Other Sources

Ackers, Charles W. "Sam Adams—and Much More." *New England Quarterly* 47 (1974): 120–131. Charges that the view of Adams as a political manipulator who pushed Americans into rebellion is a myth that should be discarded.

Becker, Carl L. "Samuel Adams." In *The Dictionary of American Biography*, edited by Allen Johnson. Vol. 1. New York: Charles Scribner's Sons, 1928. This full sketch by a respected historian of the revolutionary period gives a generally balanced account but sees Adams as essentially a revolutionary agitator.

Maier, Pauline. "A New Englander As Revolutionary: Samuel Adams." In *The Old Revolutionaries: Political Lives in the Age of Samuel Adams*. New York: Alfred A. Knopf, 1980. Provides an excellent review of the literature and places Adams in historical context.

Shipton, Clifford. "Samuel Adams." In *Sibley's Harvard Graduates*. Vol. 10, 1736–1740. Boston: Massachusetts Historical Society, 1958. This highly critical sketch portrays Adams as a demagogue.

Williams, William Appleman. "Samuel Adams: Calvinist, Mercantilist, Revolutionary." *Studies on the Left* 1 (1960): 47–57. This essay is an important step in the modern reconsideration of Adams as a significant and complex revolutionary figure.

Donald F. M. Gerardi
Brooklyn College,
City University of New York

JANE ADDAMS
1860–1935

Chronology

Born Laura Jane Addams on September 6, 1860, in Cedarville, Illinois, the eighth of nine children to John Huy Addams, eight-term Republican member of the Illinois Senate, farmer, miller, bank president, Sunday school teacher, self-described Quaker, and influential community leader, and Sarah Weber Addams, who dies in childbirth in 1862; *1860–1877* grows up in Cedarville, in rural, northern Illinois; reared until she is eight primarily by father and oldest sister, Mary Addams, and then by stepmother, Anna Hostetter Haldeman; *1877–1882* studies a curriculum with strong religious emphasis at Rockford Female Seminary, Rockford, Illinois; graduates valedictorian, June 1881, and receives one of first A.B. degrees awarded by Rockford College in 1882; attends Woman's Medical College, Philadelphia, for approximately six months; *1882* undergoes medical treatment to correct spinal curvature; *1883–1889* lives with stepmother in Cedarville and Baltimore; travels through Europe twice, 1883–1885 and 1887–1888; *June 1888* visits and is inspired by Toynbee Hall, the prototypical settlement house founded in the East End of London in 1884; *September 1889* with Rockford Female Seminary classmate Ellen Gates Starr, opens Hull-House on Halsted Street, the third settlement in America and the first in Chicago; *1889–1935* serves as Head Resident of Hull-House, attracting a creative group of reform-minded associates who come into residence at the peace settlement; develops Hull-House programs and lectures nationwide on social settlements and reform issues, establishing a national reputation as a social reformer; *1892* speaks on Hull-House and the settlement idea at Plymouth School of Ethics Conference, Plymouth, Massachusetts, and is identified as the leader in the emerging American settlement movement; *1895* is appointed garbage inspector, 19th ward, Chicago; *1895–1935* authors eleven books and hundreds of articles on national reform issues and peace; *1904* receives an honorary LL.D. from University of Wisconsin, Madison, the first of fourteen honorary degrees during her lifetime from various institutions; *1905–1909* serves as a member of the Chicago School Board; *1908* named America's foremost living woman by the *Ladies' Home Journal*; *1909–1910* selected as the first woman president of the National Conference of Charities and Corrections; *1911–1914* serves as vice president of the National American Woman Suffrage Association; *1912* seconds nomination of Theodore Roosevelt for president on the Progressive party ticket and becomes a member of the Progressive National Committee as well as serving on the Illinois and Cook County Progressive committees; *1914–1918* opposes U.S. entrance into World War I; *January 1915* helps found the Woman's Peace party, Washington, D.C., and is elected its chairman; *April-June 1915* presides at the International Congress of Women held at The Hague, Netherlands, elected president of the International Committee of Women for Permanent Peace, and travels in Europe with Aletta Jacobs and Rosa Genoni, presenting mediation plans at the capitals of belligerent countries; *1915–1920* castigated as a peace advocate; *1917– 1918* lectures nationwide for U.S. Food Administration, and opposes federal and local sedition and espionage legislation, as well as government policy regarding conscientious objectors and political prisoners; *May 1919* presides at the second International Congress of Women in Zurich, Switzerland, and is elected president of the Women's International League for Peace and Freedom (WILPF), which is founded at the meeting; *1919–1929* serves as president of WILPF, becoming honorary president for life in 1929; *1923* travels around the world, and has emergency mastectomy in Tokyo; *1927* joins efforts to prevent execution of Sacco and Vanzetti; *1928* presides at Pan-Pacific Woman's Conference, Honolulu; *1931* identified in a poll conducted by *Good Housekeeping Magazine* as America's most famous woman; undergoes surgery for removal of ovarian cyst; shares Nobel Peace Prize with Nicholas Murray Butler; *1935* dies on May 21 at Passavant Hospital in Chicago, after surgery for abdominal obstruction caused by cancer, and is buried on May 24, in the family plot in Cedarville, Illinois.

Activities of Historical Significance

Jane Addams chose the epitaph, "Jane Addams of Hull-House and the Women's International League for Peace and Freedom." Indeed, when Addams is identified today, it is most often as the founder of those two organizations and as the recipient of the 1931 Nobel Peace Prize. Yet her contemporary and historical significance extends beyond these accomplishments.

Late nineteenth and early twentieth century America was characterized by a rapid industrial development fired by technological advances and a flood of immigrants providing cheap labor. It was also a period of social inequality and urban squalor in which living and working conditions demanded reform. The American settlement movement, started in 1886, evolved to reform poor living and working conditions. By 1892, settlements were at the forefront of reform in America and Jane Addams was the acknowledged leader of the settlement movement.

Addams's involvement in the settlement movement began in September 1889, when she and Ellen Gates Starr founded Hull-House, a social settlement in Chicago. It was the third settlement in America and, like most of the several hundred founded in urban America during the next twenty years, it was modeled after London's Toynbee Hall, begun in 1884 by Canon and Mrs. Samuel A. Barnett. At Hull-House, well-educated, financially independent young women and men settled in a dilapidated but gracious house on Halsted Street in the middle of a crowded, dowdy immigrant neighborhood. The new residents sought to better themselves and society by learning firsthand about the problems their slum-dwelling neighbors faced, and using their education to help the neighbors solve these problems. Addams's idea was not to dispense charity, but rather to create opportunities for self-help. The settlement provided a social and educational center for the neighborhood. Jane Addams and her followers soon found themselves involved in most of the reform movements of their day: they led the fight for compulsory education and the end of child labor, for improved working conditions and fair wages, and for a better environment; they promoted playgrounds, clean, well-lighted streets, and improved housing; and fought for health care, education and opportunity for immigrants, and woman suffrage.

Addams's supportive and open leadership attracted an assortment of creative, intelligent men and women. They formed a network of leaders, promoting the reform tradition they brought from their Hull-House experience. Among Addams's associates were Robert Weaver and Frances Perkins, respectively the first black and first woman in a U.S. Cabinet; Jeanette Rankin, first woman in Congress; Gerard Swope, president of General Electric; Ramsey McDonald, Prime Minister of Great Britain; MacKenzie King, Prime Minister of Canada; Alice Hamilton, pioneer in industrial medicine and the first woman on the Harvard medical faculty; and Florence Kelley, the founder of the National Consumers League.

Addams's commitment to peace stemmed naturally from her reform perspective. The dynamics of the Hull-House neighborhood convinced her that different ethnic groups could learn to respect and appreciate one another, despite centuries-old antagonisms. With the onset of World War I, she became a leader in the women's peace movement in America, helping to found, and serving as the president and spokesperson of the Woman's Peace party in America. In this role, Addams testified before Congress and urged President Wilson through private meetings and correspondence to keep America out of war. She was also chosen president of an International Congress of Women, held at The Hague in April-May 1915, to promote a mediated settlement to the hostilities. Though unsuccessful, these European and American women continued to promote peace throughout the war, and reconvened in Zurich after the armistice. At that meeting, they founded the Women's International League for Peace and Freedom, of which the Woman's Peace party became the U.S. section. Jane Addams was elected to serve as the League's first president, holding office until 1929, when she became honorary president until her death in 1935. On behalf of the major peace organizations she headed, Addams opposed military preparedness and compulsory military training in schools, and supported civil liberties, the fair treatment of conscientious objectors, disarmament, and mediation of international disputes.

Continuing her peace efforts after America entered the conflict in 1917, Addams disappointed thousands of patriotic Americans who considered her to be the epitome of American womanhood. Addams chose to make her contribution to the war effort by speaking for the U.S. Food Administration to encourage the preservation and conservation of food. Unfortunately, that activity provided insufficient evidence of her patriotism, and the rift between Addams and the American people continued. The stature she had achieved as a reformer, as a leader in the Progressive party, and in the fight for woman suffrage seemed forgotten.

By the late 1920s, as America put World War I behind it, the infamous Jane Addams regained public esteem. Aside from the several honorary degrees added to her collection, she was given the M. Carey Thomas Award, the *Pictorial Review Magazine* Award, and the recognition of *Good Housekeeping Magazine* as the most famous woman in America. The capstone of her life and career came in 1931, when she became the first American woman to receive the Nobel Peace Prize, which she shared with Nicholas Murry Butler.

Addams's fame, based on her reform activities, was revealed to a national and international audience through her writings and speeches. She produced eleven books which were widely reviewed and read, together with hundreds of articles in popular magazines and scholarly journals; these, combined with her lecture tours, and, toward the end of her life, radio addresses, made her a household name. As an articulate publicist, she popularized the reform ideas she espoused and helped create a demand for change. Her activities as a writer, speaker, organizer, and leader resulted in her becoming a powerful role model for young women, which is particularly significant because of the untraditional lifestyle she chose, living unmarried and outside the confines of the family, and in a community with other women and men. She also helped open an array of employment opportunities for women, and led the way to a new profession for women: that of social work.

Overview of Biographical Sources

During her lifetime, thousands of articles about Jane Addams and her activities appeared in newspapers, journals, and popular magazines throughout Europe and America. Addams's papers in the Swarthmore College Peace Collection, Swarthmore, Pennsylvania, include over 130,000 clippings relating to her activities from 1892–1935. These can be found in the microfilm edition of *The Jane Addams Papers* (1984–1985).

In contrast to this wide journalistic coverage, only two book-length biographies of Addams appeared during her lifetime. Winfred Wise, *Jane Addams of Hull House* (1935), a biography for young people, and James Weber Linn (Addams's nephew), *Jane Addams: A Biography* (1935), were both highly laudatory works authorized by Addams, who provided selected primary sources. Biographical sketches of Addams began to appear in anthologies during her lifetime, and modern anthologies continue to cover aspects of her life.

At the time of her death, numerous biographical memorials appeared, many of which were provided by groups with which Addams was associated: the National Association of Social Workers, the Women's International League for Peace and Freedom, and National Federation of Settlements. The July 15, 1935, issue of *Unity*, published by the Unitarians in Chicago, was devoted to Addams. In England, S. K. Ratcliffe wrote, "Jane Addams of Chicago," *Contemporary Review* (July 1935), which was reprinted with additions. Elisabeth Rotten offered a fifty-page study, *Jane Addams, 1860–1935* (1936).

Until 1959, scholarly biographers neglected Addams, though several lives were written for young audiences. However, with the centennial celebration of Addams's birth, her life and contributions attracted renewed interest. The Women's International League for Peace and Freedom issued several smaller publications about their founder and sponsored Margaret Tims, *Jane Addams of Hull-House, 1860–1935: A Centennial Study* (1961), summarizing previously published works. Rockford College, Hull-House, and the Illinois State Historical Society also offered centennial works, and historians and scholars began to rediscover Addams. Largely through the works of Jill Conway, Merle Curti, Allen Davis, Christopher Lasch, Daniel Levine, Staughton Lynd, and Anne Scott, Addams began to emerge as a leading figure in the American reform movement of the late nineteenth and early twentieth centuries.

The growth of women's studies resulting from the rebirth of the women's movement in the 1960s and 1970s gave rise to feminist interpretations of Addams's contributions. Jill Conway's published dissertation, *The First Generation of American Women Graduates* (1987), offers a book-length example of the first wave of scholarly feminist treatments.

Finally, much can be learned about Addams from studies of the organizations she founded. Noteworthy works include Allen F. Davis, *Spearheads for Reform* (1967); Clark Chambers, *Seedtime of Reform* (1963); Davis and Mary Lynn McCree, eds., *Eighty Years at Hull-House* (1969); Mary Louise Degan, *The Woman's Peace Party* (1974); Gertrude Bussey and Margaret Tims, *The Women's International League for Peace and Freedom, 1915–1965; A Record of Fifty Years Work* (1965); and Mitchell F. Ducey, *The Women's International League for Peace and Freedom Papers, 1915–1978. A Guide to the Microfilm Edition* (1983).

Evaluation of Principal Biographical Sources

Conway, Jill K. *The First Generation of American Women Graduates*. Edited by Barbara M. Solomon. New York: Garland, 1987. **(A)** Originally a dissertation, this book compares significant life experiences of the first generation of college women. It follows seven women—Jane Addams, Ellen Gates Starr, Lillian Wald, Florence Kelley, Julia Lathrop, Alice Hamilton, and Ida Cannon—but focuses primarily on Addams. This feminist critique examines Addams's life in terms of her feminist philosophy and her needs as a woman of her day.

Davis, Allen F. *American Heroine: The Life and Legend of Jane Addams*. New York: Oxford University Press, 1973. **(A, G)** Written over a period of more than ten years, this most recent biography of Addams is also the most thoroughly researched, the author having access to most of the Addams materials presently available. Davis focuses on the woman behind the facade of myths and public image. His portrayal reveals an Addams who sought every opportunity to promote not only her own causes but her own popularity, and he does not hesitate to debunk, whenever possible, her perfect "Saint Jane" image. Davis has done a masterful job of selecting and condensing an enormous number of facts into a manageable, readable, chronological study.

Farrell, John C. *Beloved Lady: A History of Jane Addams' Ideas on Reform and Peace*. Baltimore: Johns Hopkins Press, 1967. (A) This first intellectual history of the philosophy of Jane Addams, based on an extensive examination of available primary sources, attempts to identify her ideas in order to explain her actions. Farrell presents her as a creative thinker and an activist. Contains an extensive bibliographic essay on sources by and about Jane Addams, her activities and her time, and an annotated bibliography of her writings.

Levine, Daniel. *Jane Addams and the Liberal Tradition*. Madison, WI: State Historical Society of Wisconsin, 1971. (A) In this intellectual biography, the author argues that Jane Addams is part of the American radical tradition. Based on her writings, speeches, and activities, Levine identifies Addams as a leader in the reform movements that swept American society in the late nineteenth and early twentieth centuries. He argues that she even prepared the way for the reforms that came after her death, especially during the New Deal.

Linn, James Weber. *Jane Addams: A Biography*. New York: Appleton-Century, 1935. (A, G) This authorized biography written by Jane Addams's nephew, an English professor at the University of Chicago, is still the most revealing about her personal life and activities. Easy to read, it is full of anecdotes, together with quoted letters and diary entries for which the originals may have been lost. Jane Addams selected the material from which the biography was written; indeed, she read, corrected, and approved of the first eight chapters. Linn finished the work in the wake of her death in May 1935, so that it could be published that year. This chronological biography emphasizes her early life, her activities, and her accomplishments, rather than her philosophy.

Scott, Anne F. "Introduction." In the reprint of Jane Addams, *Democracy and Social Ethics*. Cambridge, MA: The Belknap Press of Harvard University Press, 1964. (A, G) Focusing on her childhood and preparation for Hull-House, Scott reflects on Jane Addams's life as an example of the changing role of women in America.

Tims, Margaret. *Jane Addams of Hull-House, 1860–1935: A Centennial Study*. New York: Macmillan, 1961. (G) Written by a leader of the British section of the Women's International League for Peace and Freedom, this work is primarily a summary of already published sources, particularly of Jane Addams's autobiographies and Linn's biography.

Evaluation of Biographies for Young People

Fishwick, Marshall W. *Jane Addams*. Edited by Sam Wells. Morristown, NJ: Silver Burdett, 1968. Heavily illustrated with a letter-sized format, this pleasant and easily read work is based primarily on published sources.

Gilbert, Miriam. *Jane Addams, World Neighbor*. New York: Abingdon Press, 1960. One of the Makers of America Series for third and fourth grade readers, this biography stresses Addams's childhood, and her Hull-House activities. It includes topical chapters on working children, immigrants, working women, and a cooperative living arrangement called the Jane Club.

Johnson, Ann Donegan. *The Value of Friendship, The Story of Jane Addams*. La Jolla, CA: Value Communications, 1979. For third or fourth grade readers, this description of Addams's social conscience shows the changes she effected.

Judson, Clara Ingram. *City Neighbor: The Story of Jane Addams*. New York: Charles Scribner's Sons, 1951. Written primarily about Addams's childhood and Hull-House experiences, this children's book for third to fifth graders is anecdotal and captures the flavor of social settlements. It is based largely on *Twenty Years at Hull-House*.

Keller, Gail Faithful. *Jane Addams*. New York: Thomas Y. Crowell, 1971. An excellent, accurate children's biography of Addams for grades five to eight. Keller mentions Addams's peace work, but concentrates more on her contributions through Hull-House, and her efforts for reform.

Meigs, Cornelia. *Jane Addams: Pioneer for Social Justice*. Boston: Little, Brown, 1970. This well-written Junior Literary Guild selection for sixth grade through junior high school focuses on Addams's childhood, the development of Hull-House, and Addams's related national reform activities.

Peterson, Helen Stone. *Jane Addams, Pioneer of Hull-House*. Champaign, IL: Garrard, 1965. For third grade level readers, this work concentrates on her childhood and Hull-House adventures.

Wagoner, Jean Brown. *Jane Addams, Little Lame Girl*. New York and Indianapolis, IN: Bobbs-Merrill, 1944. The author provides childhood vignettes for third or fourth grade readers. All but the last two chapters of the book take place before Jane Addams was eight years old. Based on research conducted under the direction of the author, the work relies on first hand accounts by some of the people who knew Addams during her childhood in Cedarville, Illinois.

Wise, Winifred E. *Jane Addams of Hull-House*. New York: Harcourt, Brace, 1935. Written with Jane Addams's approval, this biographical effort is based largely on *Twenty Years at Hull-House*, on Addams's college and travel letters and papers, and on early diaries provided by Addams. Focuses primarily on her youth and Hull-House activities, portraying Addams as a heroine.

Overview of Primary Sources

The papers and writings of Jane Addams are voluminous. Addams began to deposit her peace papers in the Swarthmore College Peace Collection in the early 1930s. After her death, her archive there was augmented with materials sent from Hull-House, the U.S. section of the WILPF, family, and friends. Another collection of Addams papers was developed in the 1960s and 1970s at the restored Jane Addams' Hull-House, University of Illinois, Chicago. Addams's documents and writings may be found in many other collections and repositories throughout America and in other countries. The Jane Addams Papers Project, undertaken in 1975 to gather and organize all of the Addams papers that could be found, has resulted in the microfilm edition of *The Jane Addams Papers* (1984–1985).

Addams spread information about her reform and peace philosophy and activities through her speeches and writings, and the Addams Project has identified approximately one thousand manuscripts or printed versions of her articles that appeared in popular and scholarly periodicals. In addition, she authored eleven books, wrote chapters for others, and made significant contributions to the writing and editing of two other books that are often identified as hers: *Hull-House Maps and Papers* (1895) and *Women at The Hague* (1915). Her books, often rewritten from a series of speeches or articles, were widely reviewed and went through several printings. New editions and reprints of many of them have been issued since 1960; most are still in print.

Evaluation of Primary Sources

Addams, Jane. *Democracy and Social Ethics*. New York: Macmillan, 1902. **(A, G)** Addams's first book, a treatise on morals, consists of a series of related essays in which she confirms her faith in democracy and examines human relationships, observing the need for a set of social rules to improve conditions when society is rapidly changing.

————. *The Excellent Becomes the Permanent*. New York: Macmillan, 1932. **(A, G)** Addams tries to define her beliefs about life after death in this series of memorial addresses she had given for friends.

————. *Forty Years at Hull-House*. New York: Macmillan, 1935. **(A, G)** Issued shortly after her death, this work combines into one volume the two volumes of Addams's famous autobiography: *Twenty Years at Hull-House* (1910) and *Second Twenty Years at Hull-House* (1929). The first part of the book begins with her childhood and progresses through her preparation for founding Hull-House and its first twenty years. Addams takes some liberties with the facts in order to moralize and to portray herself as a heroine. The second part of the book, covering the years 1910–1929, is topically arranged. Written by an older Addams who had suffered through public disapproval during and after World War I, this somewhat nostalgic second part lacks the message and hopefulness of the first, but is still revealing of settlement activities and national reform efforts. An afterword by Addams's friend Lillian D. Wald covers Addams's life from 1929 until her death.

————. *The Long Road of Woman's Memory*. New York: Macmillan, 1916. **(A, G)** This work, which Addams considered to be her best, contains her views on the social value of women who choose to live unconventionally; women who oppose war are, for Addams, the best examples of female wisdom. In discussing the female psyche, Addams claims memory as well as intuition are special female powers.

————. *My Friend, Julia Lathrop*. Edited by Alice Hamilton. New York: Macmillan, 1935. **(A, G)** Addams's last book is a biography of one of her best friends.

————. *A New Conscience and an Ancient Evil*. New York: Macmillan, 1912. **(A, G)** Addams tried her hand at writing about prostitution, something she knew little about, and added little to contemporary views. Reinforcing the prevailing belief that women succumbed to prostitution only when trapped into evil ways by male exploiters or when in economic hardship, this sentimental appeal is not one of her better works.

————. *Newer Ideals of Peace*. New York: Macmillan, 1907. **(A, G)** In these essays on ethics, Addams examines the lives of urban working men and women of different nationalities and believes she sees a new internationalism emerging as old nationalist alignments become obsolete. She considers how to replace the spirit of militarism with the ideal of peace.

————. *Peace and Bread in Time of War*. New York: Macmillan, 1929. **(A, G)** The reworked speeches that Addams gave on behalf of the Food and Drug Administration during World War I form the basis of this work. Addams's pacifist philosophy comes through as she insists that women have a duty to preserve life even in the face of war.

————. *The Spirit of Youth and the City Streets*. New York: Macmillan, 1909. **(A, G)** Composed of essays and speeches developed over a two-year period, this eloquent work shows Addams's concern with the problem of youth in the industrial city, where children joined the labor force by the age of fourteen. Six chapters offer descriptions of what it was like to be young in the Chicago slums.

Addams, Jane, Emily G. Balch, and Alice Hamilton. *Women at The Hague*. New York: Macmillan, 1915. **(A, G)** This is a journalistic account of the International Congress of Women at The Hague in April 1915 and of the two delegations from the Congress that visited European capitals to promote a mediation plan. Three essays by Addams, three by Balch, and one by Hamilton report on the wartime conditions in Europe from a pacifist perspective.

Addams, Jane, and Florence Kelley, eds. *Hull-House Maps and Papers: A Presentation of Nationalities and Wages in a Congested District of Chicago, together with Comments and Essays on Problems Growing Out of the Social Conditions. By Residents of Hull-House.* New York: Thomas Y. Crowell, 1895. **(A)** This first attempt to study an urban working-class neighborhood in America is composed of a series of essays by the people who carried out the investigation. The results of the 1893 block-by-block survey of the Hull-House neighborhood are presented in color on two large folding maps, one indicating nationality, the other income. The text provides an excellent discussion of neighborhood problems and of Hull-House programs. Aside from co-editing the work, Addams contributed an essay and a description of the settlement program.

Bryan, Mary Lynn McCree, et al., eds. *The Jane Addams Papers.* Sanford, NC: Microfilming Corporation of America, 1984; Ann Arbor: University Microfilms International, 1985. **(A)** These eighty-two reels of microfilm comprise the most complete edition of Addams's papers and are indispensable to any scholar studying Addams and her times. The papers are presented in five series: Correspondence, 1867–1935; Documents, 1870–1935; Writings, 1877–1936; Hull-House Association Records, 1889–1935; and Clippings File, 1892–1936. A printed *Guide* to the content and organization of the microfilm edition is available with the microfilm or separately.

Haldeman-Julius, Marcet. "Jane Addams as I Knew Her." In *Reviewers Library.* Vol. 7. Girard, KS: Haldeman-Julius Publications, 1936. **(G)** Revealing of Addams's personality, this short critical work is written from her niece's socialist perspective.

Johnson, Emily Cooper. *Jane Addams: A Centennial Reader.* New York: Macmillan, 1960. **(A, G)** The most comprehensive anthology of Addams's writings. Created under the direction of the WILPF in commemoration of her birth, it was developed to show the breadth of Addams's interests, offering sections on social work, women, child welfare, the arts, trade unions, civil liberties, and international peace.

Lagemann, Ellen C., ed. *Jane Addams on Education.* Classics in Education series. New York: Teachers College Press, 1985. **(A, G)** An anthology focusing on Addams's writings as an educator.

Lasch, Christopher, ed. *The Social Thought of Jane Addams.* Indianapolis: Bobbs-Merrill, 1965. **(A, G)** An anthology of Addams's writings on social reform.

Philanthropy and Social Progress: Seven Essays by Miss Jane Addams, Robert A. Woods, Father J. O. S. Huntington, Professor Franklin H. Giddings, and Bernard Bosanquet. Delivered before the School of Applied Ethics at Plymouth, Mass., during the Session of 1892. New York: Thomas Y. Crowell, 1893. **(A)** Contains two significant essays by Addams on the philosophy and programs of Hull-House. These essays had a great deal of influence on Addams's ascension to the leadership of the settlement movement.

Fiction and Adaptations

Hundreds of poems were dedicated to or written about Jane Addams. Some were composed by ordinary people who were impressed by her efforts, while others were written by well-known poets such as Witter Bynner, who produced "Jane Addams—1915," which can be found in his collection entitled *A Canticle of Pan and Other Poems* (1920).

Addams's life has been the subject of numerous radio play adaptations throughout the years. One of the best known dramatic works began as a studio reading created and given by Violet Oakley in 1942. The limited, printed edition of *Cathedral of Compassion, Dramatic Outline of the Life of Jane Addams, 1860–1935* (1955), was also handsomely illustrated by Oakley, who knew Addams and was committed to her peace ideas. Highly laudatory and symbolic, it embraces the "Saint Jane" image of Addams.

Among other dramatizations of Addams's life and work are Dorothy Elderdice, *Jane Addams Speaks: A Dramatized Biography for the Centennial Celebration of Jane Addams' Birth, 1960* (1960) and *A Memory Book of Jane Addams: Excerpts from the Story of Her Life in Her Own Words and Accompanied by Living Pictures* (1955); Jane Clements and Winifred Bealy, *Cathedral of Humanity* (1946), presented by the Chase Park Radio Workshop in Cooperation with WGNB; William Schueman, *Jane Addams*, a half-hour radio play performed over WNYC on June 1, 1941; Meridith Page and Virginia Lee Tracy, *The Red Cloak*, in the series "Men Who Made History," presented by Ohio School of the Air; and Mary Lynn Mc-Cree, *The Unique Contribution . . . Hull-House*, twenty, five-minute broadcasts on Jane Addams and Hull-House, performed by Kay Canady and Mary Lynn Mc-Cree on the Chicago Circle Campus Information Network, 1968–1969.

A musical comedy entitled *Jane* is an adaptation of the life of Jane Addams from 1877 to 1898, with music by Oscar Haugland, lyrics by Willard Welsh, and book by Nelson James and Willard Welsh. It was produced at the Northern Illinois Theatre with the Northern Illinois University Department of Music, April 1974. It has since been given at least once in concert. A revised and shortened version will be presented in 1989.

A thirty-three-minute documentary film, *Crossing Borders: The Story of the Women's International League for Peace and Freedom*, produced by Barbara Laing, Jeanne Kracher and Linda Balek, contains film footage as well as still photographs of Jane Addams. Filmstrips of varying length, together with biographical scripts on her life, have been produced by the Encyclopedia Britannica, American Baptist Board of Education and Publication, and the Society for Visual Education.

Among novels that mention Addams, feature characters who seem to be based upon her, or that relate in some way to the settlement are Charles King, *A Tame Surrender, A Story of the Chicago Strike* (1896), and Elia M. Peattie, *The Precipice* (1914). Herman Brandau dedicated his anti-war novel, *The Great Destroyer* (1932), to Addams, and she appears in the story as well.

Museums, Historical Landmarks, Societies

Cedarville Area Museum (Cedarville, IL). Contains memorabilia including clothing and personal possessions, books, and papers relating to the period in which Addams was a member of the community and to Addams herself.

Cedarville Town Cemetery (Cedarville, IL). The family plot where Jane Addams is buried, along with her mother, stepmother, father, brothers, and sisters, is located on a hill to the northwest of the village.

Hall of Fame for Great Americans (New York, NY). Addams was inducted into the Hall of Fame on May 19, 1968, and her likeness, sculpted by Granville W. Carter, may be seen in the Hall of Fame Building on the campus of New York University.

Jane Addams' Hull-House (Chicago, IL). Located at the University of Illinois, this building is one of the most interesting of the Addams sites. In 1963, the university acquired the thirteen-building Hull-House settlement complex for a site on which to build its new Chicago campus. Between 1963 and 1965, all but two of the Hull-House buildings were destroyed to make way for the school, but the two remaining structures were restored by the university as a memorial and include exhibits.

National Women's Hall of Fame (Seneca Falls, NY). Also has a likeness of Addams.

Rockford College (Rockford, IL). Has a collection which includes Addams's class ring and the academic hoods associated with her honorary degrees.

Stephenson County Historical Society (Freeport, IL). Features a collection of Addams's personal and family mementos.

Swarthmore College Peace Collection (Swarthmore, PA). In addition to holding the core of the Jane Addams peace papers, this collection also contains a great number of candid and posed photographs of Addams, and some artifacts. There is often a small exhibit on Jane Addams in the Peace Collection reading room.

Other Sources

Clark, Chambers. "Jane Addams." In *American Writers: A Collection of Literary Biographies*, edited by Leonard Ungar. Supp. 1. New York: Charles Scribner's Sons, 1979. An extended analysis of Addams the writer.

Davis, Allen F. "Jane Addams." In *Notable American Women*, edited by Ed James, J. W. James, and P. S. Boyer. Vol. 1. Cambridge: Belknap Press of Harvard University Press, 1971. The best short biographical sketch.

Deegan, Mary Jo. *Jane Addams and the Men of the Chicago School.* New Brunswick, NJ: Transaction Books, 1988. The author, a sociologist, provides evidence that Addams was a pioneer sociologist and identifies her contributions to sociology. Relying heavily on archival sources, she explores the existence of a sexual division of labor during the founding years of the discipline and the role Addams played with her women's network in influencing the development of sociology through her working relationship with men of the Chicago school.

Elson, Alex. "First Principles of Jane Addams." *Social Service Review* 28 (March 1954): 3–11. Addams's contributions to social work are examined by a Hull-House associate.

Peattie, Elia W. "Women of the Hour." *Harpers Bazaar* 38 (October 1904): 1003–1008. Emphasizes Addams's personality.

Slote, Nancy. "Jane Addams." In *Biographical Dictionary of Modern Peace Leaders*, edited by Harold Josephson, et al. Westport, CT: Greenwood Press, 1984. A succint and readable biographical sketch emphasizing Addams's pacifist activities.

Mary Lynn McCree Bryan
Editor, Jane Addams Papers

LOUIS AGASSIZ
1807–1873

Chronology

Born Jean Louis Rodolphe Agassiz on May 28, 1807, in Motier-en-Vuly, Switzerland, the son of Rodolphe Agassiz, a minister, and Rose Mayor Agassiz; *1807–1824* grows up in the Swiss cantons of Fribourg, Vaud, and Neuchâtel; *1824–1829* studies at the universities of Zurich, Heidelberg, and Munich; *1829* earns his doctorate in philosophy at the universities of Munich and Erlanger and publishes a monograph on the fish of Brazil; *1830* receives a doctor of medicine degree from Munich; *1830–1832* studies under Georges Cuvier in Paris; *1832* marries Cecil Braun, sister of a Heidelberg classmate; *1832–1846* serves as Professor of Natural History at the College of Neuchâtel; publishes his multi-volume study of fossil fish; develops concept of an "Ice Age" to explain glaciation of Europe; *1846* comes to the United States to lecture at the Lowell Institute in Boston and to examine the natural history of North America; *1847* suffers the death of his wife; decides to stay in the United States; *1847–1873* teaches at the Lawrence Scientific School of Harvard University; *1850* marries Elizabeth Cabot Cary, the daughter of Thomas G. Cary, one of Boston's leading citizens; *1859* establishes the Museum of Comparative Zoology at Harvard University; *1859–1873* becomes a leading American scientist in opposition to Darwin's theory of evolution; *1863* helps found the National Academy of Sciences; *1873* establishes the Anderson School of Natural History, a combined summer school and marine biological station; *1873* dies on December 14 in Cambridge, Massachusetts, of a cerebral hemorrhage.

Activities of Historical Significance

While in Europe, Agassiz published very significant monographs in the fields of geology, ichthyology, and paleontology. Typically, he gathered and synthesized large quantities of data. His study of European glacial formations led him to argue that in the recent geological past there was a period when most of northern Europe was covered by ice. When the earth warmed, the ice receded northward, leaving its mark on the earth's surface in the form of geological configurations. His decision to stay in the United States proved important in raising the status and visibility of natural history research in this country. Agassiz's significance, subsequent to his arrival in the United States, was not due to any additional major scientific discoveries, but to his role as the founder of a great research and training institution and his encouragement of research. The Museum of Comparative Zoology, established through a combination of private and public contributions, including support from the state of Massachusetts, became a center of biological research. Agassiz was an inspiring teacher and popularizer. Not only did he train a generation of American naturalists, but his public lectures generated enthusiasm and funds wherever he spoke.

Despite his reputation and status, his opposition to Darwin's theory of evolution had little impact on the scientific community, who generally preferred the arguments of Asa Gray, Agassiz's colleague on the Harvard faculty and one of Darwin's earliest supporters.

Overview of Biographical Sources

Most chronicles of Agassiz written prior to 1960 depended upon the Agassiz correspondence published in two early biographical studies, one compiled by his wife, and the other by his colleague Jules Marcou. Characteristically, such chronicles have displayed a pro-Agassiz bias and downplayed or ignored Agassiz's opposition to evolution.

In contrast to these uncritical accounts, a wide range of scholarly, contextual studies have appeared during the last thirty years. The cornerstone of these later studies has been Edward Lurie's biography of Agassiz (1960). Lurie used a wide range of published and manuscript sources in order to analyze Agassiz in the context of the developing mid-century American scientific community. Lurie's study has been complemented by other analytical studies of Agassiz resulting from the rise in scholarly interest in nineteenth-century American science. Also valuable for understanding Agassiz are the studies of his second wife by Paton and Tharp, because through his marriage Agassiz became integrated into the power structure of Boston.

Evaluation of Principal Biographical Sources

Agassiz, Elizabeth Cary, ed. *Louis Agassiz: His Life and Correspondence.* 2 vols. Boston: Houghton Mifflin, 1885. **(A, G)** Agassiz's wife intersperses narrative with excerpts from his correspondence. Although an unobjective study, it is still useful for the insight it provides.

Lurie, Edward. *Louis Agassiz: A Life in Science.* Chicago: University of Chicago Press, 1960. **(A, G)** The standard, scholarly biography of Agassiz, it is balanced and insightful. Lurie is neither apologetic nor defensive about Agassiz's opposition to Darwin, but explains it in terms of his philosophical and scientific thought.

Marcou, Jules. *Life, Letters, and Works of Louis Agassiz.* 2 vols. New York: Macmillan, 1896. **(A, G)** This perspective of Agassiz's scientific work is unbalanced. Marcou also decided not to translate any of Agassiz's French correspondence.

Robinson, Mabel L. *Runner of the Mountain Top: The Life of Louis Agassiz.* New York: Random House, 1939. **(G)** This is an uncritical account, based on little or no original research, and lacking footnotes.

Evaluation of Biographies for Young People

Peare, Catherine Owens. *A Scientist of Two Worlds: Louis Agassiz.* Philadelphia: J. B. Lippincott, 1958. An accurate, balanced account for grades 6 through 12.

Tharp, Louise Hall. *Louis Agassiz: Adventurous Scientist.* Boston: Little, Brown, 1961. Aimed at grades 4 through 8, this book provides a good introduction to Agassiz's life and science.

Overview and Evaluation of Primary Sources

There is no complete list of Agassiz's scientific publications. Perhaps the best bibliography for older works, despite some inaccuracies, appears at the end of Marcou's 1896 biography. For Agassiz's early American publications, see Max Meisel, *A Bibliography of American Natural History: The Pioneer Century, 1796–1865,* 3 vols. (1924–1929; Reprint. New York: Hafner Publishing, 1967; **A**).

The vast number and range of Agassiz's publications can be daunting. He published hundreds of articles and monographs in scientific and general journals. Two of his most significant monographs have been reprinted with historical introductions which place them in context. Originally published in 1859, the same year as Darwin's *Origin of Species,* Agassiz, *Essay on Classification,* edited by Edward Lurie (Cambridge: Harvard University Press, 1962; **A**), lays out his vision of the structure of the natural world. *Studies of Glaciers, Preceded by the Discourse of Neuchâtel,* translated and edited by Albert V. Carozzi (New York: Hafner Publishing, 1967; **A**), is an excellent translation of Agassiz's discussion of the Ice Age and shows the scientist at his best.

Manuscript material is concentrated at Harvard University, with collections of Agassiz papers at the Houghton Library, the Museum of Comparative Zoology, and in the Harvard University Archives. Useful material can also be found in the Asa Gray Papers at the Gray Herbarium. In addition, the manuscript collections of almost any American naturalist of the mid-nineteenth century will probably contain correspondence pertaining to Agassiz. Of particular interest because of his role as Assistant Secretary of the Smithsonian are the papers of S. F. Baird in the Smithsonian Institution Archives.

Museums, Historical Landmarks, Societies

Museum of Comparative Zoology (Cambridge, MA). Agassiz's specimens are preserved in this natural history museum on the Harvard campus.

Other Sources

Cooper, Lane. *Louis Agassiz as a Teacher: Illustrative Extracts on his Method of Instruction*. Rev. ed. Ithaca: Comstock Publishing, 1945. An English teacher utilizes the testimony of Agassiz's students to demonstrate the effectiveness of his teaching.

Dupree, A. Hunter. *Asa Gray, 1810–1888*. Cambridge: Harvard University Press, 1959. A detailed, scholarly, yet highly readable study of Agassiz's Harvard colleague and scientific rival.

Lowenberg, Bert James. "The Reaction of American Scientists to Darwinism." *American Historical Review* 38 (1933): 687–701. The classic discussion of three representative scientists: Gray, the leader of the evolutionists; Agassiz, the spokesman of the opponents; and James Dwight Dana, who initially rejected evolution but eventually changed his mind.

Mayr, Ernst. "Agassiz, Darwin, and Evolution." *Harvard Library Bulletin* 13 (1959): 165–194. An important attempt to identify the characteristics of Agassiz's thought which made him unsympathetic to evolution.

Paton, Lucy Allen. *Elizabeth Cary Agassiz: A Biography*. Boston: Houghton, Mifflin, 1919. Paton provides extensive extracts from Mrs. Agassiz's correspondence.

Tharp, Louis Hall. *Adventurous Alliance: The Story of the Agassiz Family of Boston*. Boston: Little, Brown, 1959. A study of Agassiz's second wife and her family. It provides a well-researched description of the Boston community which Agassiz joined.

Winsor, Mary Pickard. "Louis Agassiz and the Species Question." *Studies in History of Biology* 3 (1979): 89–117. Criticizes Mayr's conclusion and argues that Agassiz's opposition to evolution was caused by his unwillingness to admit error.

Marc Rothenberg
Joseph Henry Papers, Smithsonian Institution

Bighorn Sheep, 1972

HORATIO ALGER, JR.
1832–1899

Chronology

Born Horatio Alger on January 13, 1832, in Revere, Massachusetts, to the Reverend Horatio Alger, a Unitarian clergyman who wants his son to follow in his footsteps, and Olive Fenno Alger; grows up in a strict, pious atmosphere; *1845–1848* attends Gates Academy, where his education focuses on religion; his self-righteousness earns him the nickname "Holy Horatio"; *1848–1852* attends and graduates from Harvard University, where he studies French and the classics; *1852* expresses a desire to marry Patience Stires, but his father disapproves and he never does wed; *1853–1856* works as a journalist and teacher; *1856* writes his first known fiction, *Bertha's Christmas Vision*, which is never published; *1857–1860* attends and graduates from Harvard Divinity School; *1860* lives in Paris; *1864* although not enthused about the ministry, is ordained as a Unitarian minister and serves at a church in Brewster, Massachusetts; *1866* moves to New York City and begins writing novels, but receives no recognition; *1867* befriends Charles O'Connor, superintendent of the Newsboys' Lodging House, and soon becomes involved with the orphanage; the street boys' lives become the basis for his juvenile stories; publishes his first serial story, "Ragged Dick," in *Student and Schoolmate* magazine, and it is an immediate best seller, launching his phenomenally successful publishing career; *1868* signs a contract with A. K. Loring for six stories to appear in the *New York Weekly*; *1873* makes a second trip to Paris; *1880* his contract with the *New York Weekly* expires; begins publishing stories with smaller, less influential periodicals and writing stories designed specifically for popularity; *1896* moves to Natick, Massachusetts, where he lives with his sister; *1899* dies on July 18 in Natick.

Activities of Historical Significance

Alger's legacy can be found in his many stories which, although not critically acclaimed, reflect the social trends of nineteenth-century America as well as Alger's own gospel for success. His 135 novels sold over 20,000,000 copies, providing "Holy Horatio" ample opportunity to preach his ideals.

Many critics, however, characterize Alger's morality as a secondary concern, accusing him of writing substanceless books for profit. One critic described his books as "greenback pastoral . . . Like the U.S. Mint, Alger and his boys trusted in God."

Despite the just accusations that he wrote "moral journalism," Alger's works expressed the Protestant work ethic, which remains a subtle part of the American Dream. The boys' adventure stories preached the gospel of success through hard work, and Alger served as America's social philosopher, a latter-day Ben Franklin. Though Alger achieved mass popularity, he failed to write the "Great American Novel" that he longed to author.

Overview of Biographical Sources

Few reliable biographical sources exist for Horatio Alger. The obituary notices in the *New York World*, the *New York Post*, and the *New York Tribune*, all dated July 19, 1899, contain biographical outlines. The first book-length biography, Herbert R. Mayes, *A Biography Without a Hero: Horatio Alger* (1928), has been proven unreliable by subsequent research. Roy Russell, *Holy Horatio* (1976), offers an interesting vignette on Alger, complemented by sharp insights into the darker corners of his life. John Tebbell wrote one of the best works on Alger, entitled *From Rags to Riches, Horatio Alger, Jr., and the American Dream* (1963). Also valuable are Edwin P. Hoyt, *Horatio's Boys: The Life and Works of Horatio Alger, Jr.* (1974), and Gary Scharnhorst and Jack Bales, *The Lost Life of Horatio Alger, Jr.* (1985).

Useful journal articles include H. F. Pringle, "Rebellious Parson," *Saturday Evening Post* (February 10, 1951); Marshall Fishwick, "The Rise and Fall of Horatio Alger," *The Saturday Review of Literature* (November 17, 1956); and B. Blackbird, "Novels that Boys of a Century Ago Couldn't Put Down," *Smithsonian* (November 1977). Very little critical attention has been paid to Alger's works.

Evaluation of Principal Biographical Sources

Hoyt, Edwin P. *Horatio's Boys: The Life and Works of Horatio Alger, Jr.* 1974. Reprint. Briarcliff Manor, NY: Stein & Day, 1983. (**A**) Provides a sound description of Alger's works and impact on American literature.

Mayes, Herbert R. *A Biography Without a Hero: Horatio Alger.* New York: Macy-Masiuss, 1928. (**A, G**) Though this was once considered the standard reference work and a fair biographical treatment, later research proved much of the information unreliable. Mayes has been accused of "absurd fabrications," and he may have invented an Alger diary, given him a stammer he never had, and erroneously described him frolicking with a prostitute in Paris at a time when he was actually attending divinity school in Massachusetts. Though fascinating reading, the book abounds in contradictions and should not be trusted.

Russell, Roy. *Holy Horatio.* Santa Barbara, CA: Capra Press, 1976. (**A, G**) A valuable work, offering rare insight into Alger's psychological problems and unflattering secrets.

Scharnhorst, Gary, and Jack Bales. *The Lost Life of Horatio Alger, Jr.* Bloomington: Indiana University Press, 1985. **(A, G)** A sympathetic, thoroughly documented biography. Perhaps the most readily available work on Alger.

Tebbell, John. *From Rags to Riches, Horatio Alger, Jr., and the American Dream.* New York: Macmillan, 1963. **(A, G)** A reliable, comprehensive, and thoroughly researched study drawn from a diversity of sources.

Overview and Evaluation of Primary Sources

Alger never wrote an autobiography, and no volumes of his letters have been published. Bibliographies of the Alger primary materials are offered in Bob Bennet, *Horatio Alger, Jr.: A Comprehensive Bibliography* (Mt. Pleasant, MI: Flying Eagle, 1980; **A**); Gary Scharnhorst and Jack Bales, *Horatio Alger, Jr.: An Annotated Bibliography of Comment and Criticism* (Metuchen, NJ: Scarecrow, 1981; **A**); and in Scharnhorst and Bale's aforementioned biography.

The best collection of primary sources is in the Houghton Library, Harvard University, including letters, papers, and correspondence. There are also some materials at the New York Public Library and in the Library of Congress.

Museums, Historical Landmarks, Societies

Honnold Library (Claremont, CA). Houses a collection of over 150 early editions of Alger works.

Horatio Alger Society (Lansing, MI). This organization possesses some interesting primary materials.

Other Sources

Bates, Ernest Sutherland. "Horatio Alger." *Dictionary of American Biography*, edited by Dumas Malone. Vol. 1. New York: Charles Scribner's Sons, 1928. A well-written, clear analysis of Alger and his work.

Edes, Grace W. *The Annals of the Harvard Class of 1852.* Cambridge, MA: Harvard University Press, 1922. Discusses Alger's life and creative writing.

Seelye, John, ed. *The Young Miner; or Tom Nelson in California by Horatio Alger, Jr.* 1879. Reprint. San Francisco: San Francisco Book Club of California, 1965. A unique piece on Alger's writings on the West, especially California.

Nicholas C. Polos
University of La Verne

SUSAN B. ANTHONY
1820-1906

Chronology

Born Susan Brownell Anthony on February 15, 1820, near Adams, Massachusetts, the second of eight children of Daniel Anthony, a descendant of Rhode Island settlers, and Lucy Read Anthony; *1826–1837* moves to Battenville, New York, where her father manages a cotton mill; educated at public school and at home; *1837–1838* attends Quaker boarding school near Philadelphia; returns home when family loses its fortune during the Panic of 1837; moves with family to Hardscrabble, New York; *1839–1849* teaches at, then heads, the Female Department at Canajoharie Academy in Rochester, New York; lives with her mother's relatives; begins temperance activities; *1848* attends Unitarian church because of anti-slavery position; *1849* quits teaching and returns to farm near Rochester, purchased in 1845 with mother's inheritance; *1850–1851* meets Elizabeth Cady Stanton and begins life-long collaboration; *1852* after being denied permission to speak at Sons of Temperance meeting in Albany, establishes first Woman's State Temperance Society of New York, installing Stanton as president and herself as organizing agent; attends her first woman's rights convention in Syracuse; adopts Bloomer costume to support dress reform; *1853* speaks out for equal pay at New York State Teachers Convention; *1854–1855* petitions to expand married women's property rights; *1856–1861* replaces Lucy Stone as paid agent of American Anti-Slavery Society, organizing speakers' programs throughout the state; *1863–1864* organizes the Women's Loyal League to support expansion of black emancipation after Lincoln's Proclamation; *1864* supports Frémont for president; *1866–1869* combines black and woman's suffrage goals in new American Equal Rights Association; *1866–1867* campaigns with Stanton in New York and Kansas for woman's suffrage; *1868–1870* publishes the *Revolution* with backing of George Francis Train; *1868* helps organize Working Women's Association in New York City; is delegate to National Labor Union, but is expelled the following year; *1869–1890* creates National Woman's Suffrage Association; *1870–1876* lectures on Lyceum circuit to pay off debts of defunct *Revolution*; *1872* illegally registers and votes for President Grant, for which she is tried and convicted, but never pays fine; *1876* disrupts Philadelphia Centennial Celebration with Woman's Declaration; begins work with Stanton and Matilda Joslyn Gage on *History of Woman Suffrage*; *1878* Anthony Amendment is introduced into Congress for the first time; *1883* organizes International Committee for Women's Rights in London; *1888* plans Washington, D.C., convention that results in permanent International Council of Women; *1892–1900* elected president of National American Woman Association; *1893* lauded at Chicago World's Fair; *1898* publishes authorized biography; *1904* joins Carrie Chapman Catt in Berlin to establish International Woman's Suffrage Association; *1905* discusses woman suffrage with President Theodore Roosevelt; *1906* dies on March 13, from pneumonia, at home in Rochester.

Activities of Historical Significance

Susan B. Anthony transformed the abstract idea of unequal treatment of women, as expressed in the 1848 Seneca Falls Declaration of Sentiments, into a mass mobilization of women and elite second-generation suffrage leaders to win the vote for women. Using her executive and organizational skills, she created support and funding for the suffrage struggle.

Specific outcomes of Anthony's activism include the 1860 Married Women's Property Act (New York State), the 1872 test cases of the franchise as a right of citizenship (brought to the U.S. Supreme Court by a St. Louis couple in *Minor v. Happerset*), the 1890 amalgamation of the two wings of the suffrage movement, and the introduction and passage of the Nineteenth Amendment to the Constitution (1878–1920), which guaranteed women the right to vote.

In addition, Anthony provided the data for an unsystematic but radical critique of institutions that she and Stanton believed oppressed women—marriage, the church, the workplace, and the polity. Under Anthony's compelling direction, her followers produced both a radical journal and a multi-volume archival history that reflected the ideas and activities of the Anthony-Stanton wing of the movement.

While Anthony is best known for her organizational skills, she has also emerged as a cultural heroine. For some, she is embodied as a cross-eyed, man-hating spinster; for others, she is the great sweet-spirited soul of the suffrage movement. First inspired by Elizabeth Cady Stanton, she eventually developed a persuasive forensic style of her own, gaining a loyal following and training a generation of "Aunt Susan's girls" to carry on the movement.

Overview of Biographical Sources

Five biographies of Anthony have appeared. The first, Ida Husted Harper's *Life and Works of Susan B. Anthony* (1898–1908), was authorized by Anthony and published during her lifetime. Journalist Rheta Dorr's *Susan B. Anthony: The Woman Who Changed the Mind of a Nation* (1928) was published two decades after Anthony's death. Anthony's niece, Lucy Anthony, asked Alma Lutz to write *Susan B. Anthony: Rebel, Crusader, Humanitarian* (1959). Katharine Anthony produced a psychological biography, *Susan B. Anthony: Her Personal History and Her Era* (1954). The latest work is scholar Kathleen Barry's *Susan B. Anthony: A Life for the Love of Woman* (1987).

Among the early, adulatory pieces on Anthony are chapters in *Eminent Women of the Age* (1868), by Elizabeth Cady Stanton and Theodore Tilton; *Makers of Freedom* (1926), by George Sherwood Eddy and Kirby Page; and *The Great Woman*

Statesman (1925), a book written by Nanette B. Paul for the Susan B. Anthony Foundation.

The Anthony/Stanton partnership is illuminated in the autobiography of Elizabeth Cady Stanton, *Eighty Years and More* (1898); the autobiography of Stanton's daughter, Harriot Stanton Blatch, *Challenging Years* (1940); and the work of contemporary Stanton scholars such as Lois Banner and Elizabeth Griffin. Other important insights are provided by "Aunt Susan's girls," especially Carrie Chapman Catt, the master strategist in the final phases of the suffrage movement, whose *Woman Suffrage Politics: The Inner Story of the Suffrage Movement* (1923), was written with Nettie Rogers Shuler.

The broad contours of the suffrage movement, and Anthony's place within it, are interpreted by Eleanor Flexner, *Century of Struggle* (1959; rev. ed., 1975), who sees Anthony as an incomparable organizer, the fixed star giving direction and force to the suffrage movement for half a century. Robert Edgar Riegel's *American Feminists* (1963) addresses Anthony's honesty, sense of duty, and ability to attract younger women to the movement.

Revisionist historians of the 1970s, including Ellen Carol DuBois, dispute structuring the development of the suffragist's ideas, from social justice abstractions to the politics of expediency, into mutually exclusive decades, pointing to Anthony's use of women's actual grievances to trigger anger and commitment in others, as well as her early tactical militancy. DuBois addresses this theory in a number of her works, including the introductory sections in the *Stanton/Anthony Correspondence* (1981). In "Contemporary Rhetorical Criticism: Genres, Analogs, and Susan B. Anthony," in *Jensen Lectures: Contemporary Communication Studies* (1982), Karlyn Kohrs Campbell analyzes Anthony's speeches in defense of her illegal vote in the 1872 presidential election.

Evaluation of Principal Biographical Sources

Anthony, Katharine. *Susan B. Anthony: Her Personal History and Her Era.* Garden City, NY: Doubleday, 1954. (A, G) The author (no relation to her subject) uses Anthony's diaries, scrapbooks, and other primary sources to create a psychological biography.

Barry, Kathleen. *Susan B. Anthony: A Life for the Love of Woman.* New York: Free Press, 1987. (A, G) Written by a scholar, this is a sophisticated and authoritative biography.

Dorr, Rheta Childe. *Susan B. Anthony: The Woman Who Changed the Mind of a Nation.* 1928. Reprint. New York: AMS Press, 1978. (A, G) A newspaper reporter who covered NAWSA conventions, Dorr mines the Harper biography and reminiscences of Anthony associates to humanize her subject while glorifying her accomplishments.

Harper, Ida Husted. *Life and Work of Susan B. Anthony*. Indianapolis: Bobbs-Merrill, 1898–1908. **(A, G)** Entrusted by Anthony as guardian of the record, Harper narrates a meticulous chronological summary of activities, speeches, letters, party planks, hearings, diary entries, travels, and other events and episodes that made up the historical landscape of Anthony's life and career. The chronology, uncritical detail, and transcriptions have influenced all subsequent accounts. The absolute accuracy of this account may never be proven, for legend has it that Harper burned original documents from Anthony's collection after citing them in the biography.

Lutz, Alma. *Susan B. Anthony: Rebel, Crusader, Humanitarian*. 1959. Reprint. Washington, DC: Zenger, 1975. **(A, G)** Lutz places Anthony's contributions in the larger context of the nineteenth-century women's reform movements.

Evaluation of Biographies for Young People

Clinton, Susan. *The Story of Susan B. Anthony*. Chicago: Children's Press, 1986. Highlights the test of the vote in 1872, and Anthony's efforts to pay off the *Revolution* debt. Illustrations caricature U.S. marshals (pot-bellied) and women temperance marchers (with drunken men slouched in the foreground).

Cooper, Ilene. *Susan B. Anthony*. New York: F. Watts, 1984. Describes Anthony's disabilities, including her surgery for turned-out eyes, which her doctor blamed on her trying to read while recovering from whooping cough.

Monsell, Helen Albee. *Susan B. Anthony*. 1960. Reprint. Indianapolis: Bobbs-Merrill, 1984. A lighthearted portrait of Anthony's family and professional life. Temperance and anti-slavery activities are omitted.

Overview and Evaluation of Primary Sources

The six-volume *History of Woman Suffrage* (1881–1922. Reprint. New York: Arno Press and the New York Times, 1969; **A**) is an enormous collection of documents, the compiling of which was undertaken and directed by Anthony during her lifetime, and completed by Ida Husted Harper, who was also Anthony's authorized biographer, and Matilda Joslyn Gage. The volumes give a vivid sense of the campaigns and activities of the movement's leaders and followers through transcripts of speeches, convention reports, legal documents, letters, and reminiscences, as well as articles and correspondence from the *Revolution*. Anthony distributed copies of the first four volumes to many libraries and schools during her lifetime.

A one-volume collection of excerpts from the *History*, edited by Mari Jo and Paul Buhl, was published as *The Concise History of Woman Suffrage* (Urbana: University of Illinois Press, 1978; **A, G**).

For Anthony's version of the illegal voting scandal, see *An Account of the Proceedings on the Trial of Susan B. Anthony on the Charge of Illegal Voting* (New York: Arno Press, 1974; **A, G**).

Elizabeth Cady Stanton/Susan B. Anthony: Correspondence, Writings, Speeches, edited by Ellen C. DuBois (New York: Schocken, 1981; **A**), focuses on the leadership qualities of both women, and the historical context of their partnership. For this collection, DuBois attempted to restore the original texts of many letters that were severely edited by Stanton's children, Theodore Stanton and Harriot Stanton Blatch, in their biography of their mother, *Elizabeth Cady Stanton as Revealed in Her Letters, Diary, and Reminiscences* (New York: Harper and Brothers, 1929; **A, G**). Despite the expurgation of so much material, the Stanton children's work does offer insight into the relationship between their mother and Susan B. Anthony.

The creation of a comprehensive microfilm and book edition of the papers of Stanton and Anthony has been underway since 1979 at the University of Massachusetts, in Amherst, with publication scheduled for 1989. The editors describe their project in Ann D. Gordon and Patricia G. Holland, "The Papers of Elizabeth Cady Stanton and Susan B. Anthony," in the *OAH Newsletter* 14 (November 1986; **A, G**). Because of the editors' view of the intellectual unity of the Stanton/Anthony partnership, the papers will be chronologically interfiled.

The papers of Susan B. Anthony are concentrated in the Library of Congress; the University of Rochester Library; the Schlesinger Library on the History of Women at Radcliffe College; and the Huntington Library in San Marino, California. While these are the major collections, some 36 smaller collections, 29 libraries, and 13 states also hold materials related to Anthony. With the publication of the Gordon/Holland microfilm edition of the Stanton/Anthony papers, access to these many and scattered primary sources will be significantly enhanced.

Fiction and Adaptations

Anthony has been the subject of opera, plays, television vignettes, filmstrips, and recordings. Virgil Thomson's opera, "The Mother of Us All" (1946–1947), has a sophisticated simplicity that combines his dissociated scales and triads with the fragments of words and phrases from Gertrude Stein's text. On a more popular level, Anthony's adopted hometown was the scene of the Rochester Opera Theater production of "The Woman Who Dared" (1984), composed by Zelman Bokser, with a libretto by Cynthia File.

One-act plays portraying Anthony as a cultural heroine include Tim Kelly's "The Remarkable Susan" (1973), which centers on the 1873 illegal voting trial; and Claribel Speiner's sketch of the Anthony sisters at home, in *Easy Sketches of Famous Women* (1960).

Television productions that include representations of Anthony include the eleventh and twelfth segments of the second season of Steve Allen's "Meeting of the

Minds" series (1979), which places Anthony in the conversational company of Socrates, Francis Bacon, and Emil Zapata, discussing philosophy and reform. Other television productions featuring Anthony include "The Years Between" (1977), part of the ABC News *Directions* series, hosted by Harry Chapin, in which Anthony finds herself in the company of such other human rights proponents as Jane Addams, Henry David Thoreau, Eugene V. Debs, and Franklin Roosevelt; and the CBS News production "The Trial of Susan B. Anthony" (1972). CBS also produced an earlier adaptation of the trial for the *You Are There* series (1955). Anthony's public partnership with Elizabeth Cady Stanton was dramatized in "Susan and Mrs. Stanton," for the *Truly American* series aired by WVIZ-TV (1979). Another television film, "How We Got the Vote" (1976), was produced as part of the *American Document* series by Post-Newsweek Stations.

The Childhood of Susan B. Anthony, a film produced and directed by Joanne Parrent in 1988, is an educational production, geared toward grades 5 through 8, that uses vintage artworks and dramatizations of Anthony's younger years to portray her early development and schooling. The film is available from FilmFair Communications.

Museums, Historical Landmarks, Societies
National Women's Hall of Fame (Seneca Falls, NY). Features a tribute to Anthony.

Susan B. Anthony Birthplace (Adams, MA). Built in the early nineteenth century by Anthony's father, her birthplace and home until the age of six still stands at East Rd. and East St., but is closed to the public.

Susan B. Anthony House (Rochester, NY). The house where Anthony lived out her last years contains her furniture and other period pieces, memorabilia, and the Carrie Chapman Catt photograph collection of suffrage leaders and activities.

Susan B. Anthony Memorial Building (Rochester, NY). A social center for women on the University of Rochester campus (where Anthony helped introduce coeducation) built as a memorial in 1914, contained a gymnasium, parlors, and a lunch room. It is now in private hands.

U.S. Capitol (Washington, DC). Displays a famous group composition sculpted by Adelaide Johnson, depicting several suffrage leaders, including Anthony, Stanton, and Lucretia Mott.

Other Sources
DuBois, Ellen C. "The Radicalism of the Woman Suffrage Movement." *Feminist Studies* 3 (Fall 1975): 63–71. Addresses Anthony's radical activities.

————. "Outgrowing the Compact of the Fathers: Equal Rights, Woman Suffrage, and the United States Constitution, 1820–1878." *Journal of American History* 74 (December 1987): 836–862. Shows how the suffrage movement, with Anthony's leadership, evolved into an undeniable social and political force.

Holland, Patricia G. "Anthony, Susan Brownell." In *American Reformers*, edited by Alden Whitman. New York: H. W. Wilson, 1985. Biographical sketch, emphasizing Anthony's social activism and accomplishments. Written by one of the editors of the microfilm project.

Lutz, Alma. "Anthony, Susan Brownell." In *Notable American Women*, edited by Edward T. James. Vol. 1. Cambridge, MA: Belknap Press, 1971. Sketch written by one of Anthony's more notable biographers.

Papachristou, Judith. "Woman's Suffrage Movement: New Research and New Perspectives." *OAH Newsletter* 14 (August 1986): 6–8. Draws out the complexity of the movement, offering a positive interpretation of the twentieth-century phase.

Scott, Anne Firor. "Anthony, Susan Brownell." In *Encyclopedia of American Biography*, edited by John A. Garraty. New York: Harper and Row, 1974. Thumbnail sketch of Anthony's life and works.

Starr, Harris Elwood. "Anthony, Susan Brownell." In *Dictionary of American Biography*, edited by Dumas Malone. Vol. 1. New York: Charles Scribner's Sons, 1927. An early, brief biographical description.

Jacqueline K. Parker
Cleveland State University

Susan B. Anthony, 1936

BENEDICT ARNOLD
1741–1801

Chronology

Born Benedict Arnold on January 14, 1741, in Norwich, Connecticut, one of two surviving children of Benedict Arnold, a cooper and merchant, and Hannah Waterman King Arnold; *1741–1752* is raised in strict New England Congregational household; *1752–1755* attends boarding school in Canterbury, Connecticut; *1755* begins apprenticeship in an apothecary's shop; *1758–1762* runs away from home to join a militia unit in the French and Indian War, deserts and returns home, then rejoins his unit but leaves soon after; travels to West Indies; *1762* moves to New Haven; opens a drug and book shop; *1767* marries Margaret Mansfield, daughter of socially prominent Sheriff Samuel Mansfield; *1775* is appointed captain of a Connecticut militia company that takes part in the siege of Boston, and is promoted to colonel; helps Ethan Allen capture Fort Ticonderoga; wife dies on June 19; proposes attack on Canada; leads expedition overland to Quebec, which he and Richard Montgomery fail to capture in December; *1776* is promoted by Congress to Brigadier General in Continental Army; leads makeshift fleet that fights two naval battles on Lake Champlain, preventing the British from taking Fort Ticonderoga; *1777* opposes the British raid on Danbury, Connecticut, and is promoted to Major General; joins Horatio Gates at the battle of Saratoga and is wounded; *1778* rejoins the army and is made commander of Philadelphia; *1779* marries Margaret Shippen of a wealthy merchant family; is court-martialed for profiting from his public position and receives reprimand from George Washington; begins treasonable correspondence with Sir Henry Clinton; *1780* takes command of West Point, which he attempts to betray to the British, fails and deserts; is made a British Brigadier General of provincial troops; leads an expedition into Virginia; *1781* leads an expedition in Connecticut and burns New London; sails for England; *1787* moves to St. John, New Brunswick, and establishes himself in trade; *1792* moves back to England; *1793* begins frequent commercial voyages to the West Indies; *1797–1799* makes several unsuccessful attempts to get active service in British army; *1801* dies on June 14 of dropsy in London.

Activities of Historical Significance

For Americans, the name of Benedict Arnold is synonymous with treason. Arnold's attempt in 1780 to surrender the garrison at West Point shocked and horrified his contemporaries and has ranked him ever since as one of America's great villains. Linked forever with the tragic fate of Major John André, who was hanged as a spy when the traitorous plot was exposed, Arnold remains in the eyes of the world a monster of greed and dishonor.

Before his treason, however, Arnold ranked as one of America's heroes, a status confirmed by his energy and passion for the revolutionary cause and his brilliant military exploits. His leadership of the Canadian expedition and brave but unsuccessful attack on Quebec in 1775–1776 showed spirit and enterprise that were sadly lacking elsewhere in the ranks of the Continental Army. The construction of a fleet on Lake Champlain and his defense of the approaches to Fort Ticonderoga earned him deserved commendation, as did his response to the British raid at Danbury, Connecticut. But it was at Saratoga that he reinforced his reputation for bravery and military prowess. While recovering from the leg wound he received at Saratoga, Arnold served as commander of Philadelphia, where, as in his field commands, he was again involved in controversy. He was soon court-martialed for profiting from his public position.

After Arnold deserted to the British in 1780, he participated in two expeditions against the United States. The campaign in Virginia in December 1780 was short but effective; the New London attack in 1781 ended in a massacre of militia at Fort Griswold and the burning of the town.

Overview of Biographical Sources

The dramatic story of Benedict Arnold has kept a strong hold on American consciousness, with each passing generation demanding its own version. From the beginning, Arnold played a large role in the theology of the Revolution as the fallen angel, a Satan so full of evil that his name could not be invoked without shame. Jared Spark's *Life and Treason of Benedict Arnold* (1847) reflected what was the dominant view until Isaac Arnold's *The Life of Benedict Arnold: His Patriotism and His Treason* (1880), which attempted to "give the devil his due" by evaluating Arnold's military contributions to the patriot cause without condoning his later betrayal. Even this apologetic effort to correct the record was ill-received, as the review by John Stevens, "Benedict Arnold and his Apologist," in the *Magazine of American History* (1880), attests. Yet Isaac Arnold's book remained the standard biography into the 1950s, and still reads well today. More importantly, it set the tone and pattern for most subsequent efforts to retell the story.

Evaluation of Principal Biographical Sources

Arnold, Isaac N. *The Life of Benedict Arnold; his Patriotism and his Treason.* Chicago: Jansen, McClurg, 1880. **(A, G)** This first attempt to resuscitate Arnold's reputation set the tone for subsequent biographies. While not excusing Arnold's treason, the author feels a great injustice was done by ignoring the general's patriotic service. The work includes the subject's "Thoughts on the American War," written after he arrived in England in 1782, and is valuable mostly for its genealogy, anecdotes not found elsewhere and many letters.

Boylan, Brian Richard. *Benedict Arnold: The Dark Eagle*. New York: W. W. Norton, 1973. **(G)** Written with dramatic flair (and poetic license), the author emphasizes Arnold's best qualities, especially his military abilities. Boylan also accepts at face value Arnold's reason for betraying his country—that he attempted to hasten the end of an unwinnable war. With illustrations and maps.

Decker, Malcolm. *Benedict Arnold: Son of the Havens*. Tarrytown, NY: W. Abbatt, 1932. **(G)** An unflattering portrait of a man whose chief motivation was money. Overly dramatized and overwritten, it includes, nonetheless, a wealth of letters.

―――――. *Ten Days of Infamy: An Illustrated Memoir of the Arnold-André Conspiracy*. New York: Arno, 1969. **(G)** More useful than the author's biography of Arnold, this book contains many rare illustrations and photos of historical sites.

Flexner, James T. *The Traitor and the Spy: Benedict Arnold and John André*. New York: Harcourt, Brace, 1953. **(A, G)** A combination of careful research and vivid writing makes this a good introductory read. While its main focus is the treason, it covers Arnold's wartime career adequately and includes a great deal of material on André. Unfortunately, source references were published separately.

Fritz, Jean. *Traitor: The Case of Benedict Arnold*. New York: Putman's, 1981. **(Y)** A carefully drawn and convincing portrait engagingly written for teenagers.

Lengyel, Cornel. *I, Benedict Arnold: The Anatomy of Treason*. New York: Doubleday, 1960. **(G)** A short, imaginative reconstruction of the treason story.

Murdoch, Richard K. "Benedict Arnold and the Owners of the *Charming Nancy*." *Pennsylvania Magazine of History and Biography* 84 (January 1960): 22–55. **(A)** This is a detailed look at Arnold's activities while in Philadelphia which, according to the author, were those of a hard-headed businessman and not a traitor.

Paine, Lauran. *Benedict Arnold: Hero and Traitor*. London: Robert Hale, 1965. **(G)** A short, readable biography that examines the paradox of Arnold's life: the same intensity of spirit that made him successful also led to his infamous act.

Sellers, Charles C. *Benedict Arnold: The Proud Warrior*. New York: Minton, Balch, 1930. **(G)** The author focuses on Arnold's wartime career in a highly colored fashion, offering Arnold's materialism as an explanation for the treason.

Sherwin, Oscar. *Benedict Arnold: Patriot and Traitor*. New York: Century, 1931. **(G)** In a book dedicated to Arnold's second wife, Peggy Shippen Arnold, the author makes liberal use of traditional accounts (most without substantiation) to explain the general's anger, resentment and need for money.

Stevens, John A. "Benedict Arnold and His Apologist." *Magazine of American History* 4 (March 1880): 181–191. **(A, G)** This review of Isaac Arnold's biography is a good example of the hatred that Benedict Arnold continued to inspire even one hundred years after the event.

Sullivan, Edward D. *Benedict Arnold: Military Racketeer*. New York: Vanguard, 1932. **(G)** A one-sided and superficial view of Arnold as an unmitigated scoundrel whose only loyalty was to himself.

Todd, Charles B. *The Real Benedict Arnold*. New York: A. S. Barnes, 1903. **(G)** Another one-dimensional picture of Arnold which blames his second wife for leading him to betray his country through her extravagance, blandishments and ambition.

Van Doren, Carl. *Secret History of the American Revolution*. New York: Viking, 1941. **(A, G)** This book, the bulk of which focusses on the Arnold conspiracy, was the first to make use of the papers of Sir Henry Clinton, British commander in North America in 1780. The valuable appendix contains Arnold-André correspondence and Clinton's narrative account of Arnold's plot.

Wallace, Willard M. *Traitorous Hero: The Life and Fortunes of Benedict Arnold*. New York: Harper, 1954. **(A, G)** This careful and balanced character study is the best treatment of Arnold's life so far. The author explains Arnold's betrayal in terms of his lifetime pursuit of respectability, social acceptance, and confirmation of his military abilities. Engagingly written, thoroughly researched, and with an extensive bibliography, it is marred only by a lack of good maps and the author's tendency to generalize on the nature of treason.

Overview and Evaluation of Primary Sources

Materials for research into the life of Benedict Arnold are scattered in a number of archives and published collections. Arnold published little of what he wrote, and left little to posterity other than his correspondence and the letterbooks he kept while on duty in the Continental Army. Some of this material is printed in the *Pennsylvania Magazine of History and Biography* 8 (1884; **A**), *Historical Magazine* 1 (January 1857; **A**) and the *Magazine of History* 3 (1906; **A**). A number of Arnold's early business papers are found in the New Haven (Connecticut) Colony Historical Society.

The published documents of military leaders and statesmen of the Revolution are also valuable sources for materials on Arnold. Among the best of these are John C. Fitzpatrick's *Writings of George Washington* (Washington, DC: U.S. Government Printing Office, 1931–1944; **A**), which is gradually being replaced by William Abbott's *Papers of George Washington* (Charlottesville: University Press of Virginia, ongoing; **A**); Fitzpatrick's *Journals of the Continental Congress* (Washington, DC: U.S. Government Printing Office, 1904–1937; **A**); Edmund C. Burnett's

Letters of Members of the Continental Congress (Reprint. Gloucester, MA: Peter Smith, 1963; **A**); and Peter Force's multi-volume *American Archives* (1837–1846. Reprint. New York: Johnson Reprint, 1972; **A**). The Massachusetts Historical Society's *Collections*, as well as the publications of the historical societies of Connecticut and New York, are also sources of extensive material relating to Arnold. Kenneth Roberts collected the journals of soldiers who followed Arnold to Canada in 1775, and published them as *March to Quebec* (New York: Doubleday, 1938; **A**).

For sources dealing directly with the treason plot, one should consult the Arnold-André correspondence, found in the appendix of Van Doren's aforementioned *Secret History of the Revolution*. An investigation of one of Arnold's aides was published as *The Varick Court of Inquiry* (Boston: Bibliophile Society, 1907; **A**). André's trial testimony was published as *Proceedings of a Board of Officers . . . Respecting Major John André* (New York: Rivington, 1780; **A**).

An interesting source on Arnold's life in England are the letters written to Peggy Shippen Arnold from her father, edited by Lewis B. Walker as the "Life of Margaret Shippen," in the *Pennsylvania Magazine of History and Biography* 24–26 (1900–1902; **A**), which also includes Arnold's last will and testament.

Arnold material is also found in many manuscript collections, some of which are available on microfilm. A treasure trove is the Papers of the Continental Congress, which are accompanied by a thorough index. The papers of Horatio Gates, Phillip Schuyler and Silas Deane are at the New-York Historical Society. The Emmett Collection at the New York Public Library contains important correspondence between revolutionary leaders, as do the Dreer and Gratz Collections at the Historical Society of Pennsylvania. The Clinton Papers are at the Clements Library of the University of Michigan. For information about Arnold's post-war business career, the Arnold-Hayt correspondence at the Library Archives of the University of New Brunswick should be consulted.

Fiction and Adaptations

There have been many novels based on the life and treason of Benedict Arnold. Robert Gessner's 1944 novel, *Treason*, tells the Arnold story by focusing on one of his young aides, Matthew Clarkson, and Haym Salomon, a Jewish patriot. The novel is heavily influenced by ongoing events in Europe in World War II. Frank O. Hough's fictionalized biography, *Renown* (1938), seeks to explain Arnold's motives in betraying his country. The sympathetic author concludes that Arnold's overarching ambition led him to try and save his country through noble treason.

Bart Spicer's *Brother to the Enemy* (1958) is a well-written, exciting fictional treatment of a little known episode involving John Champe, sergeant-major of

Lee's Legion. After Arnold's flight to New York, George Washington induced Champe to desert, follow Arnold, kidnap him and bring him back. Champe failed, of course, but his adventures make absorbing reading.

Francis Lynde's *Mr. Arnold: A Romance of the Revolution* (1923) is a blander retelling of the John Champe story, with an added fictional sidekick who narrates the story. *Arundel* (1930), by Kenneth Roberts, is a solid, satisfying full-length novel of the famous march to Canada and the attack on Quebec. *Rabble in Arms* (1933), Roberts's sequel to *Arundel*, continues the story through the battle of Saratoga.

An older work, Henry Peterson's *Pemberton: Or One Hundred Years Ago* (1899) is an historical romance focusing on the Pembertons, a Quaker family torn between loyalism and the Revolution. The portrait of Arnold is generally accurate, but many of the writer's attitudes would be offensive today.

Museums, Historical Landmarks, Societies

New Haven Colony Historical Society (New Haven, CT). Has a collection of artifacts from Arnold's pharmacy and magnificent home, both of which were mainstays of the community until Arnold's reputation turned sour.

Saratoga National Battlefield Park (Saratoga Springs, NY). There is an unnamed monument in the shape of a boot "in the memory of the most brilliant soldier in the Continental Army."

United States Military Academy (West Point, NY). In the chapel, among a series of plaques dedicated to the American generals of the Revolution, there is one with no name, just the dates 1741–1801, in memory of Arnold.

Other Sources

Gocek, Matilda A. *Benedict Arnold: A Reader's Guide and Bibliography*. Monroe, NY: Library Research, 1973. A reference guide providing resource information on works relating to the life of Benedict Arnold.

David B. Mattern
Papers of James Madison
University of Virginia

CHESTER A. ARTHUR
1829-1886

Chronology

Born Chester Alan Arthur on October 5, 1829, in Fairfield, Vermont, the son of William Arthur, a Baptist minister, and Malvena Stone Arthur; *1829-1845* grows up in various parishes in Vermont and New York State; *1845-1848* attends and graduates from Union College, Schenectady, where he is elected to Phi Beta Kappa; *1848-1851* holds secondary school teaching posts at Schaghticoke, New York; North Pownal, Vermont; Cohoes, New York; *1851-1861* practices law in New York City; *1859* marries Ellen Lewis Herndon; *1861-1863* works as engineer-in-chief, inspector general, quartermaster general of the New York State Militia; holds rank of brigadier general; *1863-1871* rises steadily in New York State Republican ranks, becoming the leading lieutenant of Senator Roscoe Conkling; *1871-1878* appointed Collector of the New York Customhouse by President Grant; serves until suspended by President Hayes on the grounds that operations were corrupt and inefficient; *1878-1880* returns to practice of law while remaining active in New York State politics; *1880* wife dies; is nominated as Republican candidate for vice president; *1881-1885* accedes to the presidency upon the assassination of Garfield; *1885-1886* is inactive counsel for his former law firm; *1886* dies on November 18 of Bright's disease in New York City.

Activities of Historical Significance

This son of an itinerant minister spent his first three decades as a model of youthful idealism, first as a beloved school teacher, then as a young lawyer directly involved in the anti-slavery movement, then as a conscientious and honest quartermaster general for New York State during the Civil War. However, he has gone down in history as an embarrassment—political conniver, spoilsman par excellence, and "gentleman boss." His closeness to Roscoe Conkling and the New York Customs House always tainted his reputation, and his inertness while in the White House has added little to public esteem. Perhaps the least known of U.S. presidents, Arthur has usually been described in terms of twenty-one-course dinners and elegant waistcoats, so inert and bland that it seems doubtful that he himself could remember having done anything in particular.

However, in reality, Arthur was one of the nation's great political surprises, particularly as few expected a man of his background to perform capably. He provided calm and reassurance to a nation shocked by Garfield's murder. As president he supported passage of the Pendleton Civil Service Reform bill of 1883 and approved laws modernizing the navy. Not lacking courage, he vetoed a Chinese exclusion bill and a "pork-barrel" rivers and harbors proposal, endorsed the findings of a tariff commission, conscientiously tried to administer the new civil-service program, and prosecuted the Star Route cases. His reputation for laziness was a bit undeserved, for he was suffering from fatal Bright's disease during much of his presidency.

Overview of Biographical Sources

Until 1935, when George Frederick Howe's *Chester A. Arthur: A Quarter-Century of Machine Politics* was published, virtually nothing was written about Chester Alan Arthur. Even the campaign biographies of 1880, a frequent if dubious source of "instant" history, focussed on Garfield, the Republican standard-bearer, and touched on his running-mate only in passing. Howe's book was once the major—indeed the only—serious work but has been discovered incorrect or misleading on a series of points, ranging from the year of Arthur's birth to failure to note his knowledge that he had Bright's disease. In *Gentleman Boss: The Life of Chester Alan Arthur* (1975), Thomas C. Reeves draws upon thousands of Arthur documents that he personally discovered to write an appreciative, thorough account. Here Arthur is portrayed as quite a good president, one who overcame his shady past. Reeves's sentiments are echoed in Justus D. Doenecke, *The Presidencies of James A. Garfield and Chester A. Arthur* (1981), as Doenecke finds Arthur successful to a degree not acknowledged by his fellow politicians, the press, the great mass of his countrymen—and, most of all, historians.

Evaluation of Principal Biographical Sources

Doenecke, Justus D. *The Presidencies of James A. Garfield and Chester A. Arthur.* Lawrence: University Press of Kansas, 1981. **(A, G)** In the first general study of Arthur's presidency, Doenecke concedes that he initiated little new legislation and was not an active president. However, Doenecke claims that Arthur conducted himself in office with dignity and restraint. The author notes that Arthur's administration pioneered in the development of the navy, sought foreign markets for American surpluses, and pressed for a scientific tariff. He goes into much detail on the condition of blacks and Indians, Arthur's strategy to secure power for the Republican party in the South, a wide assortment of diplomatic crises, and the nature of the spoils system.

Howe, George Frederick. *Chester A. Arthur: A Quarter-Century of Machine Politics.* New York: Dodd, Mead, 1935. Reprint. New York: Frederick A. Ungar, 1957. **(A, G)** Though Reeves's research has shown it to be inaccurate on numerous matters, this book is a pioneering work, both in offering a scholarly life of Arthur and in presenting some view of machine politics in the Empire State during the Gilded Age.

Pletcher, David A. *The Awkward Years: American Foreign Relations under Garfield and Arthur.* Columbia: University of Missouri Press, 1961. **(A)** A leading diplomatic historian shows why the expansionist policies of Arthur and Secretary of State Frederick Theodore Frelinghuysen collapsed. Particularly good is his treatment of the Arthur administration's policies concerning the tariff, the navy, an imbroglio in Korea, the War of the Pacific between Chile and Peru, and the "pork war" with Germany.

Reeves, Thomas C. *Gentleman Boss: The Life of Chester Alan Arthur.* New York: Alfred A. Knopf, 1975. **(A, G)** Reeves breaks down one stereotype after another concerning both Arthur the man and his era. He portrays his subject as a deeply emotional, even romantic person, who never had a moment of real happiness after the death of his wife. While by no means glossing over Arthur's role as a skilled spoilsman who placed politics above efficiency, he stresses the man's accomplishments as president. According to Reeves, Arthur usually made sound appointments, worked sincerely for civil service reform, and contributed significantly to the birth of the modern navy. If his terminal illness, a Reeves discovery that made national headlines in 1972, often made him lethargic and depressed, he still can appear more decisive and straightforward than his vacillating predecessor, James A. Garfield.

Overview and Evaluation of Primary Sources

On the day before his death, Arthur ordered all his papers burned. Large garbage cans were repeatedly filled with documents, and their contents burned while his son watched. As late as 1918, the Library of Congress possessed only two documents written by Arthur. Fortunately, however, in 1970 Professor Thomas C. Reeves found some 2,143 documents relating to Arthur's role in the 1880 campaign and subsequently found others all over the country. One collection had been lying in the cluttered flat of a ninety-nine-year-old Arthur descendant who was an astrologer and guru. All Arthur documents are now in the Library of Congress and the National Archives except for a special collection in the New-York Historical Society. The only published collection of Arthur papers is found in Volume 7 of James D. Richardson, ed., *A Compilation of the Messages and Papers of the Presidents*, 10 vols. (Washington, DC: Government Printing Office, 1896–1907; **A**). His state papers were often far-sighted, showing a grasp of such issues as consular reform, commercial agreements, currency policy, and presidential liability.

Museums, Historical Landmarks, Societies

President Chester A. Arthur Birthplace (Fairfield, VT). Arthur's birthplace houses period furnishings and artifacts.

Other Sources

"Chester Alan Arthur." In *Dictionary of American Biography,* vol. 1, edited by Allen Johnson. New York: Scribners, 1927. Three-page summary concentrating on Arthur's political career and the difficulties he encountered therein.

Justus D. Doenecke
New College of the University of South Florida

JOHN JACOB ASTOR
1763–1848

Chronology

Born John Jacob Astor on July 17, 1763, in the village of Walldorf, near Heidelberg, now West Germany, to Jacob Astor, a butcher; *1763–1779* attends school until fourteen, learns butcher's trade from his father; *1779–1783* joins brother George in London and works as musical instrument maker; *1783* migrates to New York, learns fur trading business and establishes trading firm; *1785* marries Sarah Todd whose widowed mother is related to prominent Brevoort family; *1789* imitating brother Henry, a butcher, begins practice of reinvesting profits in New York real estate; *1795* expands fur trading operations and imports firearms; *1800* participates in profitable China trade; increases Manhattan real estate investments; *1808* arranges corporate charter as sole stockholder of American Fur Company to develop trade in area acquired by Louisiana Purchase; *1810–1813* his Pacific Fur Co. establishes trading post at Astoria, in Oregon Territory; *1813* suffers major financial loss when Astoria is surrendered to British; *1813–1814* invests heavily in United States bonds, sold to finance the War of 1812; *1815–1827* establishes American Fur Company's Western Department and absorbs Columbia Fur Company, dominates but fails to achieve complete monopoly in fur trade throughout the West; *after 1827* withdraws from China and India trade; invests in securities of railroads, canal and insurance companies, 2nd Bank of the U.S. and other banks, as well as real estate; *1830s* withdraws from fur trading and other commerce; *1837* takes advantage of financial panic by buying property at low prices; turns management of business over to son, William Backhouse Astor; *1848* dies on March 29 in New York.

Activities of Historical Significance

The sheer size of the Astor fortune and his fame among contemporaries as "the richest man in America" are less important than the role he played as a prototypical nineteenth-century entrepreneur who achieved financial success by combining keen business skills with intelligence, imagination, cunning and ruthlessness. In none of these attributes was he very different from many businessmen of his time, but he was able to employ them with a purposefulness that carried him far beyond the accomplishments of others.

Diversification was the hallmark of Astor's business activities. He functioned as a wholesaler and a retailer of imported and domestic products. He exported American goods and acted as a commission agent for other trading concerns. Astor operated his ships, which were often built to his own specifications, as a common carrier for other foreign traders. He helped plan and create the 2nd Bank of the

U.S. Much of his wealth was acquired through shrewd investments. Besides major investments in securities of governments and private companies, he invested in real estate in Manhattan, upstate New York, Ontario and Wisconsin. In New York City, he enhanced the value of his property with the construction of a luxury hotel, theater and other buildings. He conducted his affairs with ability and a fine sense of timing. His abandoning of the Far East trade after 1827 and the fur trade in the 1830s followed his recognition that the profitability of these ventures had peaked and that his capital could better be employed elsewhere.

Astor's historical reputation has hinged on questions concerning his business methods and practices. If viewed in the world of his contemporaries, he appears to have differed little from them, except in the degree of canniness and opportunism that he demonstrated. Probably the most damaging accusation against him has been made by a twentieth-century writer, Gustavus Myers, who accused him of bribing Lewis Cass, then governor of Michigan. The evidence, found in 1909, was inconclusive and has since disappeared. The disbursement to Cass recorded in an American Fur Company account book could have a legitimate business explanation. There is no doubt that Astor's employees supplied whiskey to the Indians from whom they were buying furs, a common practice that violated federal laws. The universal extent of the custom and Astor's attention to detail mean he cannot be excused because of ignorance. To his credit, he had earlier sought stricter enforcement of those laws. The best example of his trickery, just narrowly within the law, was his obtaining a license to send a ship to China despite the trade prohibitions of the Embargo Act of 1808. Employing a supposed Chinese dignitary to petition for a ship to return him to his homeland, Astor won the unsuspecting approval of the voyage from President Thomas Jefferson. Before the masquerade could be revealed, Astor's ship sailed with the one passenger and a cargo of merchandise. Astor was skilled at cultivating the powerful figures of the day, such as James Madison (while serving as Secretary of State), Albert Gallatin (while Secretary of the Treasury), and Daniel Tompkins, Governor of New York. Like other New York property owners, he insisted on payment when streets running through his land were levelled and earth was removed but he did not pay to have city landfill dumped in low and swampy parts of his land. National and local governments were to be used and not respected. In these characteristics Astor stands out, not for uniqueness, but because he epitomized the behavior and attitudes of his day.

At the time of his death, his estate was estimated at over $20,000,000—the largest fortune ever amassed at that time by an American. His will bequeathed $400,000 for the Astor Library (later subsumed by the New York Public Library) and $100,000 for other public causes. The remainder of his estate was passed on to his son, William Backhouse Astor, and other heirs.

Overview of Biographical Sources

Although more than thirty biographers have written about Astor, beginning with

Washington Irving's *Astoria* (1836), very few have relied on primary sources for their information. Of those writing about the full range of Astor's commercial activities, only Kenneth Wiggins Porter's *John Jacob Astor, Business Man* (1931), made extensive use of the Astor papers in the Baker Library at Harvard, but even this work fails to take advantage of valuable material located elsewhere. Hiram Martin Chittenden's *American Fur Trade of the Far West* (1902) is the classic work on the subject. Subsequent writers have drawn heavily on the books by Porter and Chittenden as well as the four earliest biographies: Irving's *Astoria*; Wilhelm Oertel *Johann Jacob Astor* (1860); Joseph Alfred Scoville, *The Old Merchants of New York City* (1863); and James Parton, *Life of John Jacob Astor* (1865). Most Astor biographies have leaned sharply toward being either laudatory or critical. Few, other than Porter and Chittenden, maintain a balanced and objective approach. Anecdotes told by the early writers have been repeated uncritically throughout the literature on Astor. A new level of strident criticism was introduced by the muckraker generation of writers early in the twentieth century. Gustavus Myers, in his *History of Great American Fortunes* (1909), gleaned the works of his predecessors for every derogatory fact or inference, sometimes distorting the context to suit his purpose of showing that wealth such as Astor's could be gained only by dishonest and antisocial means. Two later works demonstrate Myers's strong influence: Matthew Josephson, *The Robber Barons* (1934), and Ferdinand Lundberg, *The Rich and the Super-Rich* (1968). Lundberg states his view succinctly, "Business is crime." William J. Ghent, author of the article on Astor in *Dictionary of American Biography*, acknowledged his debt to Parton and Myers. Astor biographers have also been misled by works that have later been proven to be hoaxes. Several widely repeated anecdotes picturing Astor as an ill-mannered boor are traced to *A Great Peace Maker, the Diary of James Gallatin, Secretary to Albert Gallatin*, Count Gallatin, editor (1914). Raymond Walters, Jr., has exposed the diary as a fraud (*American Historical Review* 62). Similarly, Franklin Harvey Head's *A Notable Law Suit* (1896), gives an imaginative account of a fictitious lawsuit brought by the famed landscape architect Frederick Law Olmstead against the Astor family. According to Head's account, the Astor fortune was derived from Captain Kidd's buried treasure which had been improperly removed by an Astor employee from Olmstead family property in Maine. At least one later biographer, Virginia Cowles, was so impressed with the yarn that she reprinted it in full. There is a clear need for a comprehensive work updating Porter's landmark effort and embracing the material not used by him. There is also need for more specialized study of the Astor real estate activities.

Evaluation of Principal Biographical Sources

Chittenden, Hiram Martin. *The American Fur Trade of the Far West*. New York: F. P. Harper, 1902. **(A, G)** Chittenden's classic work combines reliability with an enjoyable narrative style. The analysis of controversial issues is thoughtfully done.

Gates, John D. *The Astor Family*. Garden City, NY: Doubleday, 1981. **(G)** The book covers the many generations from the founder of the family fortune down to the present. The fifty pages devoted to John Jacob Astor are a concise and well-balanced account of his career.

Greenbie, Sydney, and Marjorie Greenbie. *Gold of Ophir: The China Trade in the Making of America*. New York: Wilson-Erickson, 1937. **(G)** A useful source for the history of the China trade and Astor's role in it. It suffers from the authors' attempt to popularize their work.

Hone, Philip. *The Diary of Philip Hone: 1828–1851*. Edited by Allan Nevins. New York: Dodd, Mead, 1936. **(A, G, Y)** Though Astor plays a minor role in Hone's diary, it is fascinating reading with vivid descriptions of the people and events observed by this wealthy auctioneer and former mayor of New York. It is a valuable book for anyone interested in the period.

Irving, Washington. *Astoria; or Anecdotes of an Enterprise Beyond the Rocky Mountains*. Philadelphia: Carey, Lea and Blanchard, 1836. **(A, G, Y)** Irving, a friend of Astor, is generally judged to have told the story of the Astoria misadventure accurately and objectively.

Myers, Gustavus. *History of the Great American Fortunes*. Chicago: Charles H. Kerr, 1909. **(A, G)** While interesting as an example of the social criticism stirring in the early twentieth century, Myers's work is an unreliable study of Astor because of the biased and selective use of sources.

O'Connor, Harvey. *The Astors*. New York: Alfred A. Knopf, 1941. **(G)** The first part of the book concerns the original John Jacob Astor and is a popularized retelling of the old, critical anecdotes.

Oertel, Wilhelm (W. E. Van Horn). *Johann Jacob Astor* (in German). Wiesbaden: Kreidel and Niedner, 1860. **(A)** Oertel visited Astor's home village of Walldorf and collected the reminiscences of Astor's boyhood neighbors.

Parton, James. *Life of John Jacob Astor*. New York: American News, 1865 **(A, G, Y)** Parton, though a respected historian, relied on unsubstantiated anecdotes, mostly uncomplimentary. He borrowed freely from Irving, Scoville and Oertel.

Phillips, Paul Chrisler. *The Fur Trade*. Norman: University of Oklahoma Press, 1961. **(A, G)** A thorough, well-documented study covering the sixteenth through the nineteenth centuries. The discussion of Astor, in volume two, is authoritative and even-handed.

Porter, Kenneth Higgins. *John Jacob Astor, Business Man*. Cambridge, MA: Harvard University Press, 1931. **(A, G)** The best Astor biography yet written. Porter used many primary sources, though not all that are now available. He carefully identifies the old unverified myths and analyzes them.

Scoville, Joseph Alfred (William Barrett). *The Old Merchants of New York City*. 5 vols. New York: Carleton, 1863. **(G)** This highly unreliable collection of gossip and anecdotes is, unfortunately, the source for subsequent popular biographers.

Sinclair, David. *Dynasty: The Astors and Their Times*. New York: Beaufort Books, 1984. **(G, Y)** A popular narrative of seven generations of Astors with emphasis on the British descendants. It is a competent and balanced treatment of the first Astor's accomplishments and character.

Smith, Arthur D. Howden. *John Jacob Astor, Landlord of New York*. New York: Blue Ribbon Books, 1931. **(G, Y)** Smith employs an imaginative and fictionalized style and uses ethnic stereotypes that are now considered offensive.

Terrell, John Upton. *Furs by Astor*. New York: William Morrow, 1963. **(G)** This work shows a strong anti-Astor bias. It appears to be derived from Chittenden and influenced by Myers.

Overview and Evaluation of Primary Sources
A great deal of Astor material was destroyed in the 1870s and 1880s when the offices of his estate were moved. A few remaining account books and some correspondence were later given to the Baker Library at Harvard Business School. Over the years, however, considerably more Astor correspondence and records, (including the records of the American Fur Company) have come to light in the holdings of various repositories. The New-York Historical Society has a large quantity of documentary material concerning the Astor real estate holdings, and the Gallatin Papers at that institution include over 150 letters written between 1812 and 1836 by Astor to Albert Gallatin. The Missouri Historical Society (St. Louis), the Minnesota Historical Society (St. Paul), the Clarke Historical Library (Central Michigan University) and the Burton Library (Detroit, MI) have records and papers of the American Fur Company. The New York Public Library's Astor Papers collection has correspondence and records of land holdings, legal affairs and loans, dating from 1792 to 1849. That library also has the papers of Ramsay Crooks, Astor's general manager at the American Fur Company. Lesser quantities of Astor material are found in more than a dozen other locations indexed in the *National Union Catalog of Manuscript Collections* (NUCMC).

Washington Irving's *Astoria* is the only book-length biography that was written while Astor was alive, and it is believed that Irving included information and anecdotes that he heard directly from Astor. However, it is not possible now to determine what was derived from Astor and what came from other sources.

Fiction and Adaptations
River to the West: A Novel of the Astor Adventure, by John Edward Jennings

(1948), is the story of the voyage to Astoria of Astor's ship *Tonquin* in 1810–1811, the massacre of the crew by Indians and a survivor's return east as described by a fictional participant. Though based on historical events, the author takes liberties with the facts. It is an entertaining adventure story but should not be relied on for accuracy.

Hollywood has not found Astor to be a worthy subject for a movie, but he does appear as a supporting character in *Little Old New York,* starring Marion Davies and released in 1923. The role of Astor was played by Andrew Dillon.

The fur trade and adventures of fur trappers were popular subjects for films in silent-movie days but less so in more recent years. The plots usually featured Mounties chasing evil-doers through the wilderness, sometimes helped by the faithful dog Rin Tin Tin, but the setting was usually Canada and so Astor and his fur company were not part of the story.

Museums, Historical Landmarks, Societies

Astor House (Mackinac Island, MI). Once the headquarters for the American Fur Company.

The Astor Library (425 Lafayette Street, New York, NY). Astor's will provided funds, added to by his son William Backhouse Astor, to build the library building and purchase its collection of books. It opened in 1854 and merged in 1911 with the Lenox Library to form the New York Public Library. The original building has been designated a landmark and is the home of the New York Shakespeare Festival.

Fort Astoria (Astoria, OR). This outpost, built on the site abandoned during the War of 1812 and regained in 1815, is now open to the public.

Fort Union Trading Post National Historical Site (near Williston, ND). Headquarters of American Fur Company's operation on the Upper Missouri River from 1829 to 1867, archeological excavations are being conducted and will be followed by a partial restoration of the fort.

John Jacob Astor Memorial (Bellevue, NE). A monument honors Astor as the founder of Bellevue in 1810, though he was never this far west. The first settlers were American Fur Company employees.

Other Sources

Ghent, William J. "John Jacob Astor." In *Dictionary of American Biography*, edited by Allen Johnson, vol. 1, pp. 397–400. New York: Charles Scribner's Sons,

1928. Falls short of the usual high quality of this reference work. The author relies principally on Parton and Myers and reflects their biases.

Lionel W. Greer
The Papers of Albert Gallatin
Baruch College, City University of New York

IRVING BABBITT
1865–1933

Chronology

Born Irving Babbitt on August 2, 1865, in Dayton, Ohio, the third son and fourth child of Edwin Dwight, a physician and author of books on spiritualism, and Augusta Darling Babbitt; *1865–1876* moves frequently with family, going as far east as New York City, where he attends the public schools and derives a small income by selling newspapers on the city streets; *c.1876* his mother dies and Irving moves with the other children to his grandparents' farm outside of Cincinnati; *1881* spends a summer at his uncle's ranch in Wyoming, becoming an enthusiastic horseman and relishing the robust life of the outdoors; *1885* with the financial help of his uncle, enrolls in Harvard University, concentrating his studies in foreign languages and literature; *1887* travels to Europe with classmate and after five days in Paris they embark on a series of long hikes over the continent, with numerous visits to places outside the familiar itinerary of tourists; later finds several attractive qualities about Spain at a time when that nation was an object of vilification in the American public mind, and will later express his views in "Lights and Shades of Spanish Character," published in the *Atlantic Monthly*; *1889* graduates with honors from Harvard with a major in classics; in September departs for a teaching job in Deer Lodge, Montana; *1891* takes an important new departure by going to Paris to study Sanskrit and Pali and to immerse himself in Indian philosophy, a major interest hereafter; *1892* returns to Harvard for graduate work and forms friendship with Paul Elmer More; *1893* earns M.A. degree from Harvard and takes one-year appointment at Williams College, where he teaches romance languages; *1894* returns to Harvard as an instructor in the Classics Department, but relocates to Romance Languages and teaches French; *1895* publishes "The Rational Study of the Classics," in *Atlantic Monthly*, his first appearance in print; *1900* in London, marries Dora May Drew, the twenty-three year old daughter of a Protestant missionary to China; returns to Cambridge with wife; Josiah Royce and William James are their neighbors; *1901* his daughter Esther is born on October 2; *1903* his son Edwin Sturges is born on June 12; *1908* publishes first book, *Literature and the American College*; *1910* publishes *The New Laokoon: An Essay on the Confusion of the Arts*; has become an established and popular teacher at Harvard and his students include Walter Lippmann, Stuart Sherman, Norman Foerster, Van Wyck Brooks, and T. S. Eliot; is openly dissatisfied with the Harvard educational philosophy and with the lack of recognition given him by the university; *1912* wins an offer from the University of Illinois and only then does Harvard promote him to full professor; publishes *The Masters of Modern French Criticism*; *1919* publishes *Rousseau and Romanticism*; *1923* is exchange professor at the Sorbonne; *1924* publishes *Democracy and Leadership*; *1930* is elected to the American Academy of Arts and Letters; debates the New Humanism with Carl Van Doren and Henry

Seidel Canby in Carnegie Hall; contributes the lead essay, "Humanism: An Essay at Definition," in *Humanism and America,* edited by Norman Foerster; *1932* is afflicted by declining health; delivers his last public lecture before the American Academy of Arts and Letters; publishes his book of essays, *On Being Creative*; *1933* dies on July 15 at his home in Cambridge.

Activities of Historical Significance

Babbitt's prominence in American intellectual history lies in his leadership of a movement that came to be called "The New Humanism." It had influential and controversial affiliates: Paul Elmer More, editor of the *Nation*, noted literary critic, author of *The Shelburne Essays*, and professor of the classics at Princeton University; Stuart Sherman, professor of English at the University of Illinois and author of *On Contemporary Literature, The Genius of America*, and *Points of View*; and Norman Foerster, professor of English at the University of North Carolina and the University of Iowa, an editor of the *Cambridge History of American Literature*, and author of *American Criticism, The American Scholar*, and *The American State University*. The New Humanism also had dozens of enthusiasts in American colleges and universities and included among qualified sympathizers Babbitt's former student T. S. Eliot. The movement acquired a surprising, popular interest in 1930, and in that year Foerster organized essays by supporters in the collection *Humanism in America*. At the same time, G. Hartley Grattan edited a rival volume of critical essays, *The Critique of Humanism*.

Babbitt's humanism defended a dualistic view of human nature, emphasizing a principle of discipline and control that is in constant conflict with an expansive impulse seeking liberation from all restraints. In his writings Babbitt judged the French romantic Jean-Jacques Rousseau the major corrupting influence of modern culture. Babbitt associated romanticism with a celebration of individual instinct and the uniqueness of personality which denied the universal aspects of human nature depicted in classical and neo-classical literature. On the other hand, Babbitt also criticized a more recent tendency of intellectual culture, naturalism. Depicting man as the reflex agent of natural forces, naturalism dissolved the principle of control and rationalized all human behavior by stressing the dominance of environment over individual will and responsibility. For Babbitt, naturalism simply reinforced the dreadful legacy of romanticism, and indeed he often referred to naturalism as "romanticism on all fours." Babbitt found the negative effects of romanticism and naturalism to be especially acute in the United States. America, he said, had produced a culture that was mechanistic, worshipping power and force in all aspects of its society, and at the same time sentimental and emotionally indulgent, as witnessed by the popularity of Hollywood and frivolous, romantic novels.

However simple in outline, Babbitt's basic philosophy was presented with much subtlety, sophistication, and, above all, great erudition. Babbitt's writings suggest an intellectual with the world's wisdom at his fingertips; they draw quotations and references from a variety of writers that spans the centuries and includes the seminal voices of both Western and Eastern civilizations. Babbitt's versatility was impressive: he applied his humanistic dualism to literature and literary criticism, education, politics, and religion. A conservative in the traditionalist, Burkean mode, Babbitt remains a dominant influence, his works cited by conservative thinkers from Peter Viereck to Russell Kirk to George Will.

Overview of Biographical Sources

Despite his influence in American thought, Babbitt has not received considerable scholarly attention. A good starting point in the available literature is the collection of personal reminiscences edited by Frederick Manchester and Odell Shepard, *Irving Babbitt: Man and Teacher* (1941). Its thirty-nine contributors range from Babbitt's wife to former students, and they offer collectively a lively personal portrait of the energetic professor.

An early study of the New Humanism is Louis J. A. Mercier, *The Challenge of Humanism: An Essay in Comparative Criticism* (1936), which includes several sections on Babbitt. A chapter on Babbitt appears in Keith F. McKean, *The Moral Measure of Literature* (1961). J. David Hoeveler, Jr., *The New Humanism: A Critique of Modern America, 1900–1940* (1977), deals with the New Humanism as an intellectual movement and analyzes the positions taken by its various exponents. Two books that examine Babbitt as an intellectual are Thomas R. Nevin's *Irving Babbitt: An Intellectual Study* (1984), and Claes G. Ryn's *Will, Imagination, and Reason: Irving Babbitt and the Problem of Reality* (1986). A collection of essays that assesses Babbitt's legacy and influence is *Irving Babbitt in Our Time* (1986), edited by George A. Panichas and Claes G. Ryn.

Evaluation of Principal Biographical/Critical Sources

Hoeveler, J. David, Jr. *The New Humanism: A Critique of Modern America, 1900–1940.* Charlottesville: University Press of Virginia, 1977. **(A)** A generally sympathetic account of the intellectual movement led by Babbitt, this work illustrates the diversity within the New Humanism, showing in particular how Babbitt differed from liberal humanists like Sherman and more religious thinkers like More.

Manchester, Frederick, and Odell Shepard, eds. *Irving Babbitt: Man and Teacher.* New York: G. P. Putnam's Sons, 1941. **(A, G)** Students and friends remember Babbitt as personality as much as thinker, and this series of reminiscences is a wonderful account of the many facets of Babbitt, inside the classroom and out.

Nevin, Thomas R. *Irving Babbitt: An Intellectual Study.* Chapel Hill: University of North Carolina Press, 1984. **(A)** This is the most comprehensive portrait of Babbitt's thought. Contains a useful bibliographical essay.

Panichas, George A., and Claes G. Ryn, eds. *Irving Babbitt in Our Time.* Washington, DC: Catholic University of America Press, 1986. **(A)** Nine contributors consider Babbitt's views in relation to other major thinkers and intellectual traditions. The book also contains a helpful chronology of Babbitt's life and major works, by Mary E. Slayton.

Ryn, Claes G. *Will, Imagination and Reason: Irving Babbitt and the Problem of Reality.* Chicago: Regnery Books, 1986. **(A)** A very technical work that concentrates on Babbitt's esthetic views, particularly in comparison with those of the Italian philosopher Benedetto Croce; recommended for the philosophical specialist.

Overview and Evaluation of Primary Sources

Paul Elmer More once said that Babbitt's central ideas did not change at all over a thirty-five year period of writing and teaching. More was correct, but Babbitt's philosophy was reinforced as he increased the depth and breadth of his learning. An excellent introduction to his writings is George A. Panichas, ed., *Irving Babbitt: Representative Writings* (Lincoln: University of Nebraska Press, 1981; **A**), which contains some of Babbitt's most famous essays and key selections from his books.

The lasting relevance of three of Babbitt's major works is attested to by their release in new editions in the past few years: *Literature and the American College: Essays in Defense of the Humanities* (1908; Washington, D.C.: National Humanities Institute, 1986; **A**), *Rousseau and Romanticism* (1919; Austin: University of Texas Press, 1977; **A**), and *Democracy and Leadership* (1924; Indianapolis: Liberty Classics, 1981; **A**). *The Masters of Modern French Criticism* (Boston: Houghton Mifflin, 1912; **A**) is the best source for Babbitt's philosophy of art and literary criticism. Less useful is *The New Laokoon: An Essay on the Confusion of the Arts* (Boston: Houghton Mifflin, 1910; **A**). *Spanish Character and Other Essays* (Boston: Houghton Mifflin, 1940; **A**) includes his important early essay on Spain. Babbitt's great interest in Eastern religion and the importance of the East for his humanism is best summarized in his essay "Buddha and the Occident," which appears in his translation, *The Dhammapada: Translated from the Pali with an Essay on Buddha and the Occident* (New York: Oxford University Press, 1936; **A, G**). *On Being Creative and Other Essays* (Boston: Houghton Mifflin, 1932; **A**) supplements these works but is not essential.

Valuable collections of Babbitt's papers include his extensive correspondence with Paul Elmer More, privately held by Babbitt's daughter, Mrs. Esther Babbitt Howe, in Washington, D.C. Other letters, as well as lecture and reading notes, may be found in the Harvard University Archives. The Stuart Sherman Papers in the University of Illinois Archives also contain Babbitt letters, but most of these are reproduced, in whole or in part, in Jacob Zeitlin and Homer Woodbridge, eds., *The Life and Letters of Stuart Sherman* (1929; Freeport, NY: Books for Libraries Press, 1971; **A**). Additional materials may be found in the Papers of the American Academy of Arts and Letters in New York City and at the Houghton Library, Harvard University, which contain Babbitt's extensive correspondence with his publisher, the Houghton Mifflin Company. The Harry Hayden Clark Papers at the University of Wisconsin contain the extensive lecture notes of Babbitt's student assistant in comparative literature.

Other Sources
Blackmur, R. P. "Humanism and Symbolic Imagination." *Southern Review* 7 (1941): 309–325. Blackmur attacks Babbitt's writings on the role of the imagination.

Eliot, T. S. "Second Thoughts About Humanism." *Bookman* 7 (1929–1930): 225–233. Eliot greatly admired his former teacher, but they disagreed sharply on the dependency of humanism on religion, as this essay indicates.

Kazin, Alfred. "Liberals and New Humanists." In *On Native Grounds*. New York: Alfred A. Knopf, 1942. An engaging chapter in a book that bristles with the author's rapid-fire judgments.

Kirk, Russell. "Introduction" to Babbitt's *Literature and the American College*. 1908. Washington, DC: American Humanities Institute, 1986. A valuable essay that indicates the influence of Babbitt on the conservative intellectual movement of the later twentieth century.

Lippmann, Walter. "Humanism as Dogma." *Saturday Review of Literature* 6 (1930): 817–819. This is a critical essay from a former Babbitt student. And yet Lippmann's book of 1955, *The Public Philosophy*, reflects Babbitt's influence on every page.

Lora, Ronald. "The New Humanism of Irving Babbitt and Paul Elmer More." In *Conservative Minds in America*. Chicago: Rand-McNally, 1972. One of the best brief summaries of the New Humanism available.

Mercier, Louis. *The Challenge of Humanism*. New York: Oxford University Press, 1936. A staunch defender of Babbitt, Mercier locates him in a European intellectual tradition but overstates the case for Babbitt as a religious thinker.

More, Paul Elmer. "Irving Babbitt." In *On Being Human*. Princeton: Princeton University Press, 1936. An important, memorable essay by Babbitt's co-leader in the New Humanism movement.

Panichas, George A. "The Critical Mission of Irving Babbitt." *Modern Age* 20 (1976): 242–253. One of Babbitt's most trenchant disciples and interpreters, Panichas reviews Babbitt's critical principles; reprinted with slight changes as the "Introduction" to *Irving Babbitt: Representative Writings*.

Ryn, Claes. "The Humanism of Irving Babbitt." *Modern Age* 21 (1977): 251–262. Ryn is another Babbitt disciple and writes this essay in a journal that is itself a testimonial to Babbitt's influence.

Wilson, Edmund. "Notes on Babbitt and More." In *The Shores of Light*. New York: Farrar, Straus, and Young, 1952. Wilson was a vigorous opponent of Babbitt and in this essay he faults Babbitt's use of Greek.

J. David Hoeveler, Jr.
University of Wisconsin-Milwaukee

GEORGE BANCROFT
1800-1891

Chronology

Born George Bancroft on October 3, 1800, in Worcester, Massachusetts, one of thirteen children of Aaron Bancroft, an author and liberal Congregational minister with Arminian theological views, and Lucretia Candler Bancroft, who has a long and illustrious New England ancestry; *1800–1811* grows up in Worcester, where he receives early schooling; *1811–1813* attends Phillips Exeter Academy in Exeter, New Hampshire, to prepare for Harvard; *1813–1818* attends Harvard, graduates and remains there an additional year as a divinity student; *1818* enters Gottingen University in Germany to study theology and philology; *1820* receives the M.A. and Ph.D. degrees; *1821* meets the German poet Goethe; continues studies in Berlin under leading German Romantic scholars; travels extensively on the Continent, visiting Paris, Geneva, Milan, Venice, Florence, Rome, and Naples; *1822* returns to America; becomes a less than enthusiastic tutor of Greek at Harvard and part-time minister in Worcester; *1823* publishes a collection of poems; seeking new directions in his life, he and his partner, J. C. Cogswell, establish Round Hill Academy in Northampton, Massachusetts, which remains his chief occupation until 1827; *1826* delivers a memorable Fourth of July oration at Northampton; begins writing articles on German literature and book reviews for the *North American Review*; translates Arnold H. L. Hereen's historical works and Phillipp Karl Buttmann's *Greek Grammar*; *March 1, 1827* marries Sarah H. Dwight, and becomes involved in her family's extensive banking operation; *1831* pens a famous article for the *North American Review* attacking the Second Bank of the United States, attracting the attention of Democratic party leaders; *1834* begins political career by being defeated as a candidate for the Massachusetts General Court; becomes editor of the *Baystate Democrat*; publishes the first volume of *A History of the United States from the Discovery of the Continent*; publishes article on "Slavery in Rome" for the *North American Review*; *1837* his first wife dies; is appointed by President Martin Van Buren as collector of the Port of Boston, a reward for his loyalty and service to the party; publishes second volume of *A History of the United States from the Discovery of the Continent*; *1838* marries his second wife, Elizabeth Davis Bliss; *1840* publishes volume 3 of the *History*; *1844* is defeated as gubernatorial candidate; *1845* after eight years in Boston is appointed secretary of the navy by President James K. Polk; during his eighteen-month tenure, the United States Naval Academy is founded; *1846* appointed by Polk as U.S. minister to Great Britain, a position that also provides access to archives in London and Paris for research essential to his *History of the United States*; *1849* returns to the United States after a successful tenure in Britain; *1849–1867* devotes time to historical research and writing and publishes volumes 4 through 9 of his *History*; publishes *Literary and*

Historical Miscellanies in 1855; a staunch nationalist, unionist, and anti-slavery advocate, he strongly supports the Northern war effort, viewing the conflict of 1861–1865 as "the instrument of Divine Providence to root out social slavery" and make the United States not only free, but unified as a nation as well; although a Democrat, he ultimately supports Abraham Lincoln and writes an article for the *Atlantic Magazine* on Lincoln's place in history following the president's assassination; defends policies of President Andrew Johnson, whose first annual message he authors; *1867–1874* serves as U.S. minister to Berlin; meets Bismarck (whom he praises for "renovating Europe") and historians Ranke and Mommsen; *1874* returns to the United States and settles in Washington, D.C.; publishes volume 10 of *A History of the United States*; *1876* publishes six-volume revised *History*; *1882* publishes a *History of the Formation of the Constitution of the United States of America*; *1883–1885* undertakes last revision of his *History*; *1889* authors a biography of Martin Van Buren; *1891* dies on January 17, in Washington, D.C., and is buried in Worcester, Massachusetts.

Activities of Historical Significance

Bancroft's fame is based primarily on his multi-volume *History of the United States from the Discovery of the Continent*, a great work of literature and history that earned him the appellation of "Father of American History." More than any other nineteenth-century historian, Bancroft popularized the study of the American past. Indeed, his highly nationalistic and optimistic tone, together with his belief in unlimited progress through Divine Providence, captured and encapsulated the dominant American mood. As sales of his *History* increased (18,000 copies were sold in 1876) so too did his wealth and fame. Equally important, the research materials he collected now form an important historical collection at the New York Public Library, and his own letters provide valuable insights into significant political and literary developments of the nineteenth century.

Bancroft's active political career was also significant. As a leading spokesman of the Democratic party, cabinet member, presidential advisor, and diplomat, Bancroft influenced the course of American history during the fateful years between 1830 and 1890 that saw the defeat of the South in the Civil War and the emergence of modern industrial and imperial America.

Bancroft remains a controversial figure; nearly a century after his death, historians continue to tackle the complex questions surrounding his life: was he a radical or a conservative in his political, social, religious, and economic beliefs? did he really believe in the will or sovereignty of the people or did he stand for public order and stability? was he a loyal Democrat who championed that party's states' rights dogma, or was he a national Whig turned Republican who espoused a consolidated and perpetual view of the constitution and union? does his remarkable career and personal life resemble a Horatio Alger success story or was it the result

of cold and cunning calculation on his part? Bancroft's disinheritance and disown-
ing of his stepson George following his first wife's death also raises questions about
his personality and his larger relationship with his family.

Overview of Biographical Sources

No single biography deals satisfactorily with all of the issues raised about Bancroft, which is to be expected given his complex personality, his longevity, the
multifaceted nature of his family and personal relations, and the various public
roles he assumed.

Mark A. DeWolfe Howe's authorized biography, *The Life and Letters of George
Bancroft*, 2 vols. (1908), is less concerned with minute details and psychoanalysis
than with providing the major outlines of a remarkable literary and political career,
offering just enough narrative to serve as essential background for the letters presented. Although admitting Bancroft's democratic bias ("Bancroft the politician
and Bancroft the historian were consistent exponents of the same democratic principle"), Howe is content to let Bancroft speak for himself through his letters and
thus avoids making judgments about Bancroft's *History*, his character, and his
public services.

More successful in tracing the elements that shaped Bancroft's life is Russel B.
Nye's *George Bancroft: Brahmin Rebel* (1944), which focuses on the mainspring of
Bancroft's thought and actions. Seeking to understand Bancroft not only as an
individual but also as a political figure and historian, Nye identifies Romanticism
as the common thread that unites Bancroft's personal, philosophical, and historical
views. Nye finds that, as a reflection of his own background and training, Bancroft
emphasized man's inherent goodness and perfectibility, and believed in the inevitability of progress and the sovereignty of the people. Nye also analyzes the shortcomings of Bancroft's *History* as Romantic literature: "With his powerful urge to
write not merely original but transcendental history, he could never be content
with . . . slavish adherence to particular documents . . . ."

Although not strictly a biography, David Levin's *History as Romantic Art* (1959)
provides important insights into Bancroft's literary style and methods by comparing
him with such eminent literati as William H. Prescott, John Lothrop Motley, and
Francis Parkman. Levin concludes that all of these writers belong in the mainstream of American Romantic thought, as evidenced by their concern that writing
should be artistic in nature, aesthetically pleasing, dramatic, and thematic—hence
the grand style and broad sweep of their histories. Bancroft's romanticism and
nationalism is also underscored by Richard C. Vitzthum, *The American Compromise: Theme and Method in the Histories of Bancroft, Parkman, and Adams*
(1974).

Taking exception to most previous analyses of Bancroft's life is Lillian Handlin's
biography, *George Bancroft: The Intellectual as Democrat* (1984), which attempts

to provide a new perspective on Bancroft the man and a greater appreciation of his *History*. Handlin denies the central influence of Romanticism upon Bancroft's thought and development as a historian, emphasizes his essential conservatism (he was a Democrat but not democratic), and defends his *History* as being less politically motivated than is generally presumed. In effect, Handlin seeks to reverse the accepted image of Bancroft as an advocate of democracy and nationalism.

Although many scholars have recognized Bancroft's democratic nationalistic bias, they have not appreciated his role in creating a "myth of democracy" that has helped to obscure the original republican beliefs of the founding fathers. This is the viewpoint presented in W. Kirk Wood, "George Bancroft," in volume 30 of the *Dictionary of Literary Biography* (1984). Drawing upon the work of Nye, Vitzthum, and other scholars, this interpretative piece, while admitting Bancroft's Romanticism, nevertheless carries that insight to its logical conclusion: Romanticism, as a nineteenth-century phenomenon, gave rise to another system of beliefs and values—individualism, materialism, nationalism, majoritarianism, and capitalism—that ultimately triumphed over the older republicanism and, in the process, transformed the Republic itself.

The years after 1830 also witnessed the rise of a highly nationalist historiography that was opposed and criticized in the South and the North. As the nation itself was democratized and nationalized, its history was also transformed by historians like Bancroft who had to legitimatize their revolutionary beliefs by reinterpreting the American past to make it more liberal and egalitarian than it really was. In this sense, Bancroft truly is the "Father of American History" at least in its modern, consensus form.

Evaluation of Principal Biographical Sources

Handlin, Lillian. *George Bancroft: The Intellectual as Democrat*. New York: Harper & Row, 1984. (**A, G**) This biography offers a new interpretation that takes exception to Nye's emphasis upon Romanticism as the key to Bancroft's life and mind. In Handlin's view, Bancroft was neither a radical nor a democrat; rather, he was basically conservative and anti-individualist, characteristics she attributes to native American (not European) influences, most notably the Congregational religious tradition to which he was exposed in his youth. In turn, this insight is used to explain his *History*, which was written "to reassure himself and his audience" that America was providentially destined to improve and progress despite threats to its existence, and to explore his less than satisfactory personal relations. In addition to revealing Bancroft's "inner life," the author also provides the most detailed analysis yet of the *History* itself.

Howe, Mark A. DeWolfe. *The Life and Letters of George Bancroft*. 2 vols. New York: Scribners, 1908. (**A, G**) Written and edited by a leading man of letters, this key study covers the salient points of a long life and career. Although the author approaches his subject in a sympathetic and non-controversial fashion, the study is still valuable, particularly with respect to the letters it contains.

Levin, David. *History as Romantic Art: Bancroft, Prescott, Motley, and Parkman.* Stanford, CT: Stanford University Press, 1959. (**A, G**) This comparative analysis from a literary perspective firmly establishes Bancroft as a leading practitioner of Romantic history. An essential book for understanding the content and style of Romantic history.

Nye, Russel Blaine. *George Bancroft: Brahmin Rebel.* New York: Alfred A. Knopf, 1944. (**A, G**) Begun as a dissertation, this well-researched, highly readable, and balanced account by a respected historian provides a welcome synthesis of fact and interpretation. The author emphasizes the influence of Romanticism upon Bancroft's personal beliefs, political activities, and historical method.

————. *George Bancroft.* New York: Washington Square Press, 1964. (**A, G**) The author's revised version of his earlier biography.

Vitzthum, Richard C. *The American Compromise: Theme and Method in the Histories of Bancroft, Parkman, and Adams.* Norman: University of Oklahoma Press, 1974. (**A, G**) A comparative analysis that characterizes the work of all three historians as presenting American history in terms of a basic "conflict between separatist, decentralizing, anarchic forces on the one hand and unifying forces of central authority and sovereignty on the other."

Overview and Evaluation of Primary Sources

Bancroft's *History of the United States from the Discovery of the Continent,* 10 vols. (Boston: L. C. Little and J. Brown, 1842–1854; **A, G**), including the two-volume *History of the Formation of the Constitution of the United States* (1882. Reprint. Littleton, CO: Rothman, 1983; **A**), provides the best introduction to his historical method, style, and interpretation. They also provide valuable clues to his political beliefs.

Repositories that contain significant collections of Bancroft's letters and papers include the Library of Congress (Bancroft-Bliss Papers), Massachusetts Historical Society, and the New York Public Library. Additional manuscript sources may be found in the Boston Public Library, Cornell University Library, and the Phillips Exeter Academy Library. In addition to Mark DeWolfe Howe's two volumes (see Biographical Sources), published letters are available in Martin Van Buren-George Bancroft Correspondence, 1830–1845, in the *Proceedings of the Massachusetts Historical Society* 42 (October 1908–June 1909; **A, G**), and in John Spencer Bassett, ed., "The Correspondence of George Bancroft and Jared Sparks," *Smith College Studies in History* 2 (January 1917; **A, G**).

Other Sources

Bassett, John Spencer. "George Bancroft." In *The Middle Group of American Historians*. New York: Macmillan, 1917. Written by an early Jacksonian scholar, this lengthy sketch presents Bancroft as a political opportunist with a "lack of continuous ideals" and a highly partisan historian whose extreme Americanism ultimately lessened the future value of his *History*. In light of Handlin's recent study, the author's references to Bancroft's Unitarian background, his states' rights views, his driving ambition, and his highly emotional nature are perceptive indeed.

Kraus, Michael. *The Writing of American History*. Norman: University of Oklahoma Press, 1953. A useful, brief account that focuses on Bancroft the historian and his larger role in American historiography.

Wish, Harvey. "George Bancroft and German Idealism." In *The American Historian: A Social-Intellectual History of the Writing of the American Past*. New York: Oxford University Press, 1960. A philosophical treatment of Bancroft's life that places him and his *History* in the larger context of Romantic philosophy and German historiography. Agreeing with Kraus, the author believes that despite its shortcomings, Bancroft's *History* is still praiseworthy in many respects.

Walter Kirk Wood
Alabama State University

U.S. Naval Cadets, 1937

CLARA BARTON
1821–1912

Chronology

Born on December 25, 1821, in North Oxford, Massachusetts, the youngest of five children born to Stephen and Sarah Stone Barton, substantial farmers who were descended from early New England families; *1821–1850* grows up, attends school, and teaches in the vicinity of North Oxford; *1850* enrolls for a year in the Liberal Institute of Clinton, New York; *1852–1854* teaches in New Jersey, establishing the state's first "free" public school; *1854–1857* works as a clerk in the U.S. Patent Office in Washington, D.C.; *1857–1860* deprived of her position because of a Democratic victory, she passes three years in North Oxford; *1860* is recalled to her Patent Office position; *1861* aids and befriends Civil War troops; *1864* is appointed head nurse in Benjamin Butler's Army of the James; *1865–1868* receives appointment from Lincoln to gather information on missing military; lectures about her battlefield experiences; *1869–1871* becomes familiar with the International Committee of the Red Cross during a European lecture tour and joins their efforts during the Franco-Prussian War; *1877–1881* works to organize an American Red Cross Society and secure U.S. adherence to the Geneva Conventions; *1881–1904* as head of the American Red Cross, she personally oversees the distribution of more than $2 million of relief in twenty-one disasters; *1906* organizes the National First Aid Association of America; *1912* dies on April 12 of pneumonia at Glen Echo, Maryland.

Activities of Historical Significance

Clara Barton was one of the most famous women of nineteenth-century America. During the Civil War she became known as the Angel of the Battlefield. In later years she was honored internationally for championing American participation in the International Red Cross. During the four decades she headed the organization in the U.S., she personally supervised and distributed aid to victims of flood, fire, and political violence in the United States, Armenia, and Cuba.

While her disinclination to delegate responsibility or to use acceptable accounting procedures resulted in organizational factions and little articulation between local and national offices, Barton successfully organized an aid program noted for its economy, comprehensiveness, and efficiency. Barton, a public supporter of various social reforms, was particularly committed to women's suffrage and equal pay for equal work.

Overview of Biographical Sources

Numerous biographical accounts of Clara Barton's life have drawn from her extensive and vividly written correspondence and personal papers. Considerable insight is provided by the candid entries in her 35-volume diary that she maintained throughout her adult life. These papers, amounting to more than 100,000 items, were used by Elizabeth Brown Pryor in *Clara Barton: Professional Angel* (1987), which goes beyond the triumphs and the public image to examine the paradox of an heroic figure who often feared confronting the realities of her own life. Accounts placing Barton in a broader context include Foster Rhea Dulles, *The American Red Cross: A History* (1950), and L. P. Brochett and Mary C. Vaughan, *Women's Work in the Civil War* (1867).

Evaluation of Principal Biographical Sources

Barton, William E. *The Life of Clara Barton*, 2 vols. Boston: Houghton Mifflin, 1922. (A, G) One of Clara Barton's favorite cousins wrote this richly detailed authorized biography. Using the personal materials available at that time, the author produced a readable and accurate biography that is somewhat generous in dealing with Barton's shortcomings.

Boardman, Mabel T. *Under the Red Cross Flag at Home and Abroad*. Philadelphia: Lippincott, 1915. (A, G) The author, Clara Barton's leading adversary in the American Red Cross, develops the opposition viewpoint. This volume does not, however, minimize Barton's achievements in the Spanish-American War and at the turn of the century.

Boylston, Helen Dove. *Clara Barton: Founder of the American Red Cross*. New York: Random House, 1955. (G, Y) This balanced study of Clara Barton, designed for juvenile readers, focuses on the organization she headed and is most informative in its final chapters.

Dulles, Foster Rhea. *The American Red Cross: A History*. New York: Harper, 1950. (A, G) This carefully documented study provides a history of the American Red Cross movement. It demonstrates the rapid growth of the Red Cross and places an honestly portrayed Clara Barton in the context of her work.

Epler, Percy H. *The Life of Clara Barton*. New York: Macmillan, 1941. (A, G, Y) Although this early volume does not benefit from more recently available materials, it is a candid portrayal which captures Clara Barton's dynamism. Relying on conversations with Barton, eyewitness accounts and extensive research, Epler has produced an honest and persuasive portrait.

Fishwick, Marshall W. *Illustrious Americans: Clara Barton*. Morristown: Silver Bardette, 1966. (G, Y) Although designed as a biography for juveniles, this richly illustrated volume, half of which is devoted to Barton's own writings, is an accurate, readable volume that is also of interest to the general reader. An additional strength is the use of timeliness and illustrations to place Barton in a broader historical context.

Kite, Elizabeth S. *Antoinette Margot and Clara Barton*. Philadelphia: Catholic Historical Society of Philadelphia Records, 1944. **(A, G, Y)** This volume, which emphasizes religious themes, highlights the very important friendship of two women who were dedicated to the International Red Cross.

Memorial to Clara Barton. Washington: Government Printing Office, 1917. **(G)** A compilation of memorials designed largely to invoke a zealous patriotism as the U.S. entered World War I.

Pryor, Elizabeth Brown. *Clara Barton: Professional Angel*. Philadelphia: University of Pennsylvania Press, 1987. **(A, G)** If a definitive volume is possible, this is it. The product of ten years of research into the recently released Barton diaries, as well as the more well-known depositories, the account is well-written, richly detailed and effective in portraying Barton as both a legend and a human being. After careful study of Barton's archival legacy, Pryor judiciously and gracefully reconciles the public image and private sphere of Clara Barton.

Ross, Ishbel. *Angel of the Battlefield*. New York: Harper & Row, 1956. **(A, G)** This well-written book is both enjoyable and accurate. Written long after the period of public controversy surrounding Barton had subsided, it is objective, persuasive, and evocative of the era.

Williams, Blanche Colton. *Clara Barton: Daughter of Destiny*. New York: Lippincott, 1941. **(A, G, Y)** Although this biography is sympathetic, it is not overburdened by clichés. Its particular strength lies in portraying Barton's search for a life purpose and in exploring her motivations.

Young, Charles Sumner. *Clara Barton: A Centenary Tribute*. Boston: Gorham Press, 1922. **(G)** The glowing accolades in this volume provide little new information, but the compilation underscores the stature Barton was accorded even in the cynical 1920s.

Overview and Evaluation of Primary Sources

Clara Barton's attempts to modify reality to fit an heroic vision of herself led to slight exaggerations in her accounts and alterations of events to create a more dramatic effect. This led to controversies even during her lifetime. Examples of this somewhat weaken Barton's autobiographical accounts, *The Story of My Childhood* (Meriden, CT: Journal Publishing, 1907; **A, G, Y**), *The Red Cross* (Washington, DC: The American Red Cross, 1898; republished as *The Red Cross in Peace and War;* **A, G, Y**), and *A Story of the Red Cross* (New York: D. Appleton, 1904; **A, G, Y**). The numerous manuscripts, including a sequel to her biography, are available in the Library of Congress. A more candid insight into both her aspirations and motives is provided by Barton's 35-volume diary in the Manuscript Division of the Library of Congress. Her range of interests, financial and family concerns, and personal relationships is revealed in her extensive correspondence, portions of which can be found in the Sophia Smith Collection, Smith College; the Henry E. Huntington Library, San Marino, California; the Library of Congress; the American Antiquarian Society, Worcester, Massachusetts; and the National Archives and Records Service.

Speeches, scrapbooks of clippings and photographs, letter-books, and account books are in the Library of Congress. The national headquarters of the American Red Cross has personal materials. Also useful are the official transcripts of her Congressional Testimony supporting Senate Resolution No. 73, subsequently published in the *Woman's Journal* (April 1, 1882).

Reminiscences include "Reminiscences of Miss Clara Barton," n.d., Austin Craig and Family Papers, Minnesota Historical Society, St. Paul, MN **(A, G)**; Cora Bacon Foster, *Clara Barton: Humanitarian* (Washington: Columbia Historical Society, 1918; **A, G**); Interview with Clara Barton in the *National Repository* 5, no. 2 (February 1879): 15 **(A, G)**.

Fiction and Adaptations

Barton's contributions have been the subject of several visual presentations including: "Angel of Mercy" (1940), a ten-minute black and white film, available from the Media Center of Syracuse University, and "Heroism of Clara Barton" (1956), a thirty-minute black and white television presentation produced as part of the "You Are There" series and available from the AV Library Services of the University of Minnesota.

Museums, Historical Landmarks, Societies

American Red Cross (Washington, DC). Some of Clara Barton's personal effects are on display in the national headquarters of the organization that she founded.

Clara Barton Birthplace (North Oxford, MA). Maintains a collection of artifacts from the lives of Barton and her family.

Clara Barton National Historic Site (Glen Echo, MD). Site of Barton's home from 1891 until 1912, and site of national headquarters of the American Red Cross from 1891 to 1904, contains archival material as well as personal records and artifacts.

Free Public School (Bordentown, NJ). Organized by Barton, this one-room schoolhouse was one of the country's first free public schools, and is operated as a historic site by the Bordentown Historical Society. Open by appointment.

Other Sources

Curti, Merle. "Clara Barton." In *Notable American Women,* edited by Edward T. James, et al. Cambridge: Belknap Press of Harvard University Press, 1971. Provides a comprehensive biographical profile.

Gloria Ricci Lothrop
California State Polytechnic University

Clara Barton, 1948

BERNARD M. BARUCH
1870–1965

Chronology

Born Bernard Mannes Baruch on August 19, 1870, in Camden, South Carolina, the second of four sons of Simon Baruch, a Jewish immigrant from East Prussia and former Confederate surgeon, and Isabelle (Belle) Wolfe Baruch, daughter of an established plantation family; *1870–1881* spends childhood in post-Reconstruction South; attends Wallace, a private school in Camden; identifies with the Democratic party and is influenced considerably by his mother; *1881* moves with family to New York City; *1884* enrolls at City College of New York; receives indifferent grades but succeeds in social and athletic activities; elected senior class president; *1889* declines a medical career and is employed as office boy for wholesale glass dealer Whitall, Tatum and Company; *1890* meets father's patient, Daniel Guggenheim, but refuses his offer to be an ore buyer in Mexico in deference to mother's objections; *1891* becomes a bond salesman for the brokerage firm of A. A. Housman and Company; *1895* becomes partner in the firm and earns $48,000 for the year; buys seat on the New York stock exchange; *October 20, 1897* marries Episcopalian Annie Griffen, and their three children, Belle (1899), Bernard, Jr. (1903), and Renee (1905), are reared as Christians; *1897–1900* becomes a millionaire owing to plunges in sugar, tobacco, and railroad stocks and bonds; *1903* opens his own investment office specializing in raw materials and individual development; allies himself with the Guggenheims in copper, sulfur, rubber, tungsten, zinc, and gold speculation; *1904–1917* invests in Texas Gulf Sulphur, Utah Copper, Intercontinental Rubber, and Alaska Juneau Gold Mining companies; *1905* acquires the Hobcaw Barony, a 13,900 acre tract on the Waccamaw River in South Carolina, which becomes a retreat for business associates and politicians; *1912* meets Woodrow Wilson and, with other Wall Street associates, bankrolls his presidential campaign; *1913–1915* supports enactment of New Freedom legislation; *1915* joins military preparedness movement and advocates war planning; *1916* contributes heavily to the Wilson reelection campaign; becomes chairperson of the raw materials and minerals committee of the Advisory Commission of the Council of National Defense; *1918* gains chairmanship of War Industries Board; develops a cadre of associates including Herbert B. Swope, Albert C. Ritchie, Hugh S. Johnson, and George Peek, who become known as "Baruch Men"; declines a Treasury appointment in December, resigns from the War Industries Board, and joins the United States delegation to the Paris peace conference; *1919* while serving as Wilson's economic advisor, advocates commercial credits to Europe; advances Wilson's new diplomacy at Paris; *1920* publishes *Making of the Reparation and Economic Sections of the Treaty* as a rebuttal to John Maynard Keynes's *Economic Consequences of the Peace*; *1920–1924* supports William G. McAdoo's presidential aspirations;

1920–1932 builds friendships with most of the Democratic senatorial leadership through association and campaign contributions while confirming key journalistic ties such as Arthur C. Krock; *1928* contributes to Alfred E. Smith's presidential campaign; *1929–1933* amid the Great Depression urges courage and confidence in the United States economic system and argues for deflation; *1932* joins Franklin D. Roosevelt's presidential campaign following his nomination; *1933–1939* becomes occasional Roosevelt consultant and indirect participant in the New Deal; emerges as critic of isolationism; *1941* advocates price controls; *1942* heads Rubber Survey Committee that recommends gas rationing; *1943* perfects "Park Bench Statesman" image but declines chairmanship of the War Production Board; *1944* endorses the draconian Morgenthau plan for postwar Germany; *1945* depends upon public opinion to maintain his great prestige; *1946* becomes U.S. Representative to United Nations Atomic Energy Commission and unfolds his plan for international control of atomic energy; *1948* breaks with President Harry Truman; *1952* endorses Dwight Eisenhower's presidential candidacy; *1953–1965* performs role as public commentator opposing inflation and survives to be last Wilsonian; *1965* dies on June 20 in New York from a heart attack.

Activities of Historical Significance

Baruch's two great moments occurred as director of the War Industries Board (WIB) and as United States Representative to the United Nations Atomic Energy Commission. As director of the WIB, he discovered the potential influence of the commission as opposed to the traditional legislative, judicial, and executive components of government. Thereafter, the implementation of many of his recommendations required some form of special committee. He also cleaved to the presidential policies of Woodrow Wilson and introduced himself into the core of Democratic leadership in the Senate. These relationships along with those he cemented among publicists, journalists, and younger bureaucrats on the rise gave him entry into federal councils for the next fifty years.

As a proponent of the creation of an international body for the development and control of atomic energy, he offered one of the alternatives to the ensuing cold war. Altering suggestions of a State Department committee composed in part of David E. Lilienthal and Dean Acheson, Baruch proposed an enforcement body containing elements of the Wilson League of Nations. These conditions encouraged a movement toward confrontation with the Soviets and helped engender the postwar armaments race.

From 1920–1940, Baruch may have influenced key leaders of the Senate by his initiation of dialogues on the issue of war planning. Roosevelt used Baruch to salve the frayed political nerves of conservatives inside and outside of the New Deal administration. Truman was less drawn to the South Carolinian, but his secretary of state, James F. Byrnes, continued, for a while, associations made during World War II and earlier.

More importantly, Baruch's public career illustrates vividly what great wealth and a wily intelligence may accomplish in modern America when aided and abetted by willing journalists and public relations adjuncts.

Overview of Biographical Sources

Very little has been written dealing with Baruch's life in its entirety. Carter Field, *Bernard Baruch: Park Bench Statesman* (1944), provides a full life of Baruch but is uncritical in his laudatory interpretation. Pulitzer Prize-winning author Margaret Coit planned to write an authorized and definitive biography that would portray his career as a reflection of American history since the Civil War. Baruch originally agreed to help Coit with the project, but later rescinded his offer. Consequently, *Mr. Baruch* (1957) does not live up to the original expectations. The most recently attempted comprehensive evaluation of Baruch, Jordan A. Schwarz, *The Speculator: Bernard M. Baruch in Washington, 1917–1965* (1981), is thoroughly researched and well written.

There is no shortage of material assessing the various phases of Baruch's career. Grosvenor Clarkson, *Industrial America in the World War: The Strategy Behind the Line, 1917–1918* (1923), and Robert Cuff, *The War Industries Board: Business-Government Relations During World War I* (1973), provide different perspectives on the nature and effectiveness of the War Industries Board and Baruch's performance as the director. James Grant, *Bernard M. Baruch: The Adventures of a Wall Street Legend* (1983), provides a detailed description of Baruch's skill in speculation and investment.

Evaluation of Principal Biographical Sources

Clarkson, Grosvenor B. *Industrial America in the World War: The Strategy Behind the Line, 1917–1918*. Boston: Houghton Mifflin, 1923. Reprint. Englewood, NJ: Jerome Ozer, 1974. (**A**) Clarkson served as secretary and then director of the Committee on National Defense and presents an account of the War Industries Board that treats Baruch's role favorably. The narrative reveals that the board spent much of the war grasping for ill-defined economic goals through frequently conflicting means.

Coit, Margaret. *Mr. Baruch*. Boston: Houghton Mifflin, 1957. (**A, G**) The Pulitzer Prize-winning author sought to use Baruch's career as a portrait of the United States since the Civil War. Initially Baruch sponsored the biography, but later deprived Coit of materials he had invited her to use.

Cuff, Robert D. *The War Industries Board: Business-Government Relations Dur-*

ing World War I. Baltimore: Johns Hopkins University Press, 1973. **(A)** The Board, according to Cuff, stressed voluntary cooperation over political coercion, and Baruch, among others, unsuccessfully attempted to reconcile individualism to scientific control. Given the fragmented and informal nature of the nation's business establishment, sufficient organization from the WIB was never forthcoming.

Field, Carter. *Bernard Baruch: Park Bench Statesman.* New York: McGraw-Hill, 1944. **(G)** A writer on the staff of *Business Week*, Field produces a flattering biography of his former creditor.

Grant, James. *Bernard M. Baruch: The Adventures of a Wall Street Legend.* New York: Simon and Schuster, 1983. **(A, G)** Emphasizes Baruch's speculation and corrects tales of his investment prowess. It also relates many personal episodes with such persons as Hugh Johnson and Arthur Krock.

Kahn, E. J., Jr. *The World of Swope.* New York: Simon and Schuster, 1965. **(A, G)** The most celebrated journalist of the 1920s and former WIB member, Herbert Bayard Swope's association with Baruch is detailed with considerable insight into the nature of Baruch's cronyism with the editor of the *New York World.*

Rosenbloom, Morris V. *Peace and Strength: Bernard Baruch and a Blueprint for Security.* New York: Farrar, Straus and Young, 1952. **(A, G)** Includes Baruch's testimony before the Senate in May 1952, calling for armed preparedness. Rosenbloom also excerpts statements from the Wilson years onward that relate to the economy and foreign policy. A useful selected list of Baruch's published writings is appended.

Schwarz, Jordan A. *The Speculator: Bernard M. Baruch in Washington, 1917–1965.* Chapel Hill: University of North Carolina Press, 1981. **(A, G)** In a finely written and well-researched manner, the author provides the most recent comprehensive evaluation. Guilty of intellectual arrogance, Baruch remained a Wilsonian in spirit by advocating economic planning and a strong central government; progress would be obtained by bureaucratic elites rather than by representative political processes.

White, William L. *Bernard M. Baruch: Portrait of a Citizen.* New York: Harcourt Brace, 1950. **(A, G)** Particularly useful for its reprint of Baruch's two statements before the United Nations Atomic Energy Commission in June and December 1946 that outline the United States atomic proposals and his plan for international control of atomic energy. White also lists contemporary magazine articles on Baruch.

Overview and Evaluation of Primary Sources
Baruch expended considerable effort to chronicle his public activities and his many policy recommendations. *American Industry in the War: A Report of the War*

Industries Board, edited by Richard H. Hippelheuser (Washington, DC: Government Printing Office, 1921; **A**), reports the board's activities during World War I. Baruch reissued the work in 1941 to impress authorities and influence policies at the onset of another great war. *Taking the Profit Out of War*, edited by Richard H. Hippelheuser (New York: Prentice-Hall, 1941; **A**), served similar purposes and contained Baruch's original report of WIB activities, his 1931 statement before the War Policies Commission relating to total mobilization, and 1941 commentaries treating price fixing. Baruch published *The Making of the Reparation and Economic Sections of the Treaty* (New York: Harper and Brothers, 1920; **A**) in response to John M. Keynes's highly critical *The Economic Consequences of Peace* (New York: Harcourt, Brace and Howe, 1920; **A**). Baruch advanced his earlier arguments opposing inflation and favoring careful planning for future wars in *A Philosophy for Our Time* (New York: Simon and Schuster, 1954; **A**). Finally, Baruch oversaw the production of a two-volume autobiography, providing primary materials and offering oral interviews to the writers he carefully selected for the task. *Baruch: My Own Story*, edited by Samuel Lubell (New York: Holt, Rinehart and Winston, 1957; **A, G**), and *Baruch: The Public Years*, edited by Lubell and Harold Epstein (New York: Holt, Rinehart and Winston, 1960; **A, G**), furnish invaluable career commentaries and a record of Baruch's world views. However, the works of Jordan A. Schwarz and James Grant should be consulted for a balanced study.

Prominent participants in and commentators on governmental affairs from World War I through John F. Kennedy's presidency mention Baruch and his activities in their memoirs, diaries, and published manuscripts. David E. Cronon, ed., *The Cabinet Diaries of Josephus Daniels, 1913–1921* (Lincoln: University of Nebraska, 1963; **A**), despite its fragmented nature, reveals much about Baruch's daily role in the Navy's war materiel procurement process. Arthur Krock, a writer for the *New York Times*, reveals the reasoning behind his own support for Baruch's policies in his *Memoirs: Sixty Years on the Firing Line* (New York: Funk and Wagnalls, 1968; **A, G**). Helen Lawrenceson, *Stranger at the Party: A Memoir* (New York: Random House, 1972; **A, G**), recounts her 1930s experiences as managing editor of *Vanity Fair*, replete with stories of Baruch and his cronies. David E. Lilienthal, *The Journals of David E. Lilienthal: The Atomic Energy Years, 1946–1950* (New York: Harper and Row, 1964; **A**) and *The Journals of David E. Lilienthal: The Harvest Years, 1959–1963* (New York: Harper and Row, 1971; **A**), recount the evolution of the elder statesman's thought. Dean Acheson, *Present at the Creation: My Years in the State Department* (New York: Norton, 1969; **A**), contains evidence of a continuing antagonism toward Baruch's ideas.

Baruch's carefully organized and indexed career papers, including those of the WIB and the United Nations Atomic Energy Commission, are housed at the Seeley J. Mudd Manuscript Library at Princeton University, along with the papers of Arthur Krock and other associates. The Manuscripts of Carter Glass and Harry Flood Byrd, Sr., in the Manuscripts Department, University of Virginia, and of

James F. Byrnes, Robert Muldrow Cooper Library, Clemson University, give insight into Baruch's southern political friends. Other rich resources on Baruch are the presidential papers of Woodrow Wilson, in the Library of Congress and Firestone Library, Princeton University; Franklin Roosevelt, at Hyde Park, New York; and Harry S Truman, at Independence, Missouri. Manuscript diaries such as those of Henry L. Stimson, in the Yale University Library, also contain invaluable commentaries.

Museums, Historical Landmarks, Societies

Seeley G. Mudd Manuscript Library, Princeton University (Princeton, NJ). Contains the largest collection of memorabilia relating to Baruch's career. Photographs, artifacts and manuscripts, as Baruch and his attendants arranged them, recreate much of his world view, his vocations, and his avocations.

Other Sources

Cuff, Bernard D. "Bernard Mannes Baruch." In *Dictionary of American Biography, Supplement Seven, 1961–1965*, edited by John A. Garraty. New York: Charles Scribner's Sons, 1981. A factual and concise overview of Baruch's life.

Cuff, Robert D. "Bernard Baruch: Symbol and Myth in Industrial Mobilization." *Business History Review* 43 (Summer 1969): 115–133. The primary evaluator of the War Industries Board interprets, in a short and succinct manner, Baruch and the WIB.

Fite, Gilbert C. *George N. Peek and the Fight for Farm Parity*. Norman: University of Oklahoma, 1954. One of the outstanding contemporary agricultural historians analyzes Moline tractor dealer Peek, the War Industry Board days, and Baruch.

Koistinen, Paul A. C. "The Industrial-Military Complex in Historical Perspective: The Inter War Years." *Journal of American History* 56 (March 1970): 819–839. Provides an insightful interpretation of the movement toward stabilization of the industrial war-making potential of the United States.

Pusey, Merlo. *Eugene Meyer*. New York: Knopf, 1974. Both Baruch and Meyer, later owner of the *Washington Post*, were involved and occasional associates in the speculative market of the early twentieth century. This work provides an excellent introduction into the era and an evaluation of the relationship between Meyer and Baruch.

Henry C. Ferrell, Jr.
East Carolina University

CHARLES A. BEARD
1874–1948

Chronology

Born Charles Austin Beard on November 27, 1874, on a farm near Knightstown, Indiana, the younger of two sons of William Henry Harrison Beard, a successful farmer, building contractor, and land speculator, and Mary J. Payne Beard; *1874–1898* grows up in Indiana; attends a local Quaker-run school and Knightstown High School; receives bachelor's degree from DePauw University; *1898–1902* pursues further study in history at Oxford University in England; marries college sweetheart Mary Ritter; plays leading role in founding the pioneer workingmen's college, Ruskin Hall; *1902–1904* returns to the U.S. and receives Ph.D. from Columbia University; *1904–1917* teaches at Columbia until his resignation in protest over the firing of antiwar faculty; *1913* publishes his landmark *An Economic Interpretation of the Constitution of the United States;* named supervisor of the Training School for Public Service of the New York Bureau of Municipal Research; *1918–1924* serves as director of the Bureau of Municipal Research; helps found the New School for Social Research; visits Japan twice, to advise first on Tokyo municipal administration and then on rebuilding the city after the 1923 earthquake; *1924–1927* completes with his wife *The Rise of American Civilization; 1927–1936* sees his hopes for a future of "unlimited progress" through the advance of technology dashed by the Great Depression; advocates national planning and welcomes the New Deal; calls for a redefinition of the concept of national interest to avoid the danger of American involvement in international conflicts; is the dominant figure on the American Historical Association's Commission on the Social Studies; champions historical relativism; *1936–1941* grows disillusioned with the New Deal; becomes a leading opponent of intervention in World War II; *1941–1946* devotes himself to elucidating the essential elements of the United States as a distinctive and unique civilization; is the moving spirit behind the report by the Committee on Historiography of the Social Science Research Council on *Theory and Practice in Historical Study; 1946–1948* publishes two volumes on Franklin D. Roosevelt's foreign policy that accuse Roosevelt of duplicity in secretly plotting war; *1948* dies on September 1 from aplastic anemia at Yale University Hospital in New Haven, Connecticut.

Activities of Historical Significance

Few, if any, of his contemporaries matched Beard's impact upon American intellectual life. He was a major contributor to the transformation of political science from the description of formal institutions to the realistic analysis of how things actually work. An apostle of the gospel of efficiency, he was one of the progressive era's foremost experts on municipal government, and a pioneer in public administration as a field of study. At the same time, he was the leading exponent-practitioner of what became known as the "New History," with its twin goals of broadening the scope of historical study beyond politics to encompass the full range of human experience, and using knowledge of the past as an instrument for understanding the present and improving the future. His championship of historical relativism did much to sensitize the profession to how the historian's personal values and attitudes influence his interpretation of the past.

He was probably best known for his pathbreaking application of the economic interpretation to American history. After Beard, no one could ignore the role of economic forces in shaping ideas and events. A 1938 survey of intellectuals showed him second only to economist and social theorist Thorstein Veblen in his influence upon their thinking. And a poll of educators, editors, and public figures shortly after Beard's death gave first place to *The Rise of American Civilization* as the work that best explained American democracy.

Nor was Beard a library-bound scholar. A longtime supporter of workingmen's and adult education, he was a founder of England's Ruskin College, the New School for Social Research, and the Workers' Education Bureau of the United States. Through his labors on the American Historical Association's Commission on the Social Studies, he had a major impact upon revision of the secondary school curriculum to make education more relevant to contemporary needs and problems. His resignation from Columbia was a signal event in the history of academic freedom in the U.S. that did much to advance its acceptance. Through his books and articles, he reached a larger popular audience than probably any other American scholar of the twentieth century.

His career was marked by controversy. Conservatives were outraged by his depiction of the Constitution as an "economic document" aimed at protecting the propertied few from popular majorities, even more by his intimation that the framers had been animated by motives of personal financial gain. His isolationism placed him at the center of the political storm in the years before Pearl Harbor, and his bitter attacks upon Franklin Roosevelt alienated many former admirers. After his death, historians increasingly challenged what was seen as his oversimplistic treatment of the role of economic conflict in American history. But even his critics acknowledge that Beard has been the single most influential figure of his time in shaping his fellow Americans' view of the nation's past.

Overview of Biographical Sources

No single, comprehensive biography covers the full range of Beard's multifacted activities. John Braeman examines in depth his boyhood and undergraduate years in "Charles A. Beard: The Formative Years in Indiana" (*Indiana Magazine of History* 78 [June 1982]: 93–127), and his four years in England in "Charles A. Beard: The English Experience" (*Journal of American Studies* 18 [August 1981]:

165–189). Howard K. Beale, ed., *Charles A. Beard: A Reappraisal* (1954), contains reminiscences and evaluations by friends and admirers. There are two attempts at tracing his intellectual development over the full span of his life: Richard Hofstadter, *The Progressive Historians* (1968), and Ellen Nore, *Charles A. Beard: An Intellectual Biography* (1983). The rest of the voluminous body of writing upon Beard is topical in approach, focusing upon particular aspects of his thought, activities, and influence.

Evaluation of Principal Biographical Sources

Benson, Lee. *Turner and Beard: American Historical Writing Reconsidered.* Glencoe, IL: Free Press, 1960. **(A)** A sympathetic evaluation of Beard's application of the economic interpretation that defends his methodology and approach against later critics.

Berg, Elias. *The Historical Thinking of Charles A. Beard.* Stockholm: Almqvist & Wicksell, 1957. **(A)** An abstruse excursion into the realm of the philosophy of history that will lose all but the most dogged readers.

Blinkoff, Maurice. *The Influence of Charles A. Beard upon American Historiography.* Buffalo: Committee on Publication on the Roswell Park Publication Fund, 1936. **(A)** A pedestrian and unimaginative—but still helpful—survey of the impact of Beard's work upon later scholars up to the time of publication.

Borning, Bernard C. *The Political and Social Thought of Charles A. Beard.* Seattle: University of Washington Press, 1962. **(A)** A detailed examination of Beard's social and political thought that suffers from overly rigid periodization, and exclusive reliance upon the published writings.

Brown, Robert E. *Charles A. Beard and the Constitution: A Critical Analysis of "An Economic Interpretation of the Constitution."* **(A)** A polemical, and at times unfair and exaggerated, attack upon the evidentiary bases and ideological underpinnings of Beard's most famous work.

Hofstadter, Richard. *The Progressive Historians: Turner, Beard, Parrington.* New York: Alfred A. Knopf, 1968. **(A, G)** An extraordinarily perceptive and lucidly written analysis that combines a sympathetic appreciation of Beard's stature with an awareness of his intellectual shortcomings. The most important single treatment for any student.

Kennedy, Thomas G. *Charles A. Beard and American Foreign Policy.* Gainesville: University Presses of Florida, 1975. **(A)** A workmanlike job that traces Beard's transformation from internationalism to isolationism.

Marcell, David W. *Progress and Pragmatism: James, Dewey, Beard, and the American Idea of Progress.* Westport, CT: Greenwood Press, 1974. **(A)** A provocative analysis that shows the affinities between Beard and the pragmatic philosophers William James and John Dewey.

Nore, Ellen. *Charles A. Beard: An Intellectual Biography.* Carbondale: Southern Illinois University Press, 1983. **(A)** The closest approximation to a full-scale biography. The author is generally sound in tracing the broad contours of Beard's intellectual growth; but despite her extensive research in manuscript sources, the man never fully emerges as a human being.

Strout, Cushing. *The Pragmatic Revolt in American History: Carl Becker and Charles Beard.* New Haven: Yale University Press, 1958. **(A)** Focuses upon Beard's reaction against the positivism of late-nineteenth-century scientific history and his resulting advocacy of historical relativism.

Overview and Evaluation of Primary Sources

Beard took the position that he should be evaluated exclusively on the basis of his published writings. More broadly, he distrusted biography. In part, he thought the individual was more the instrument than the shaper of larger historical forces. Even more important, he derived from his Quaker background a deep respect for the sanctity of individual privacy. He accordingly rebuffed urgings that he write his autobiography. Beard undertook a rare exercise in introspection during a speech at the Social Science Research Council's 1926 Hanover Conference. This attempt to trace the influences that shaped his own thinking is reprinted in John Braeman, "Charles A. Beard at Mid-Career: 'Reflections' " (*International Journal of Social Education* 2 [Spring 1987]: 60–98; **A**).

Before their deaths, Beard and his wife destroyed the bulk of their private papers. The surviving materials have been deposited in the DePauw University Archives, Greencastle, Indiana. The central files of Columbia University in New York City have extensive materials on Beard's years as a faculty member; a sizable body of Beard correspondence is to be found in different collections in Special Collections, Butler Library, Columbia University. Additional manuscript collections containing significant Beard correspondence include Harry Elmer Barnes Papers, American Heritage Center, University of Wyoming; George S. Counts Papers, Souther Illinois University Library; Merle Curti Papers, State Historical Society of Wisconsin; A. C. Krey Papers, University of Minnesota Archives; Macmillan Company Records, New York Public Library; Arthur M. Schlesinger, Sr., Papers, Harvard University Archives; and Oswald Garrison Villard Papers, Houghton Library, Harvard University. The fullest bibliographies of Beard's published writings are in Beale, ed., *Charles A. Beard: A Reappraisal* (1954), and Borning, *The Political and Social Thought of Charles A. Beard* (1962).

Other Sources

Braeman, John. "The Historian as Activist: Charles A. Beard and the New Deal." *South Atlantic Quarterly* 79 (Autumn 1980): 364–374. Traces Beard's changing response to Franklin D. Roosevelt from enthusiastic support to bitter hostility.

Cohen, Warren I. *The American Revisionists: The Lessons of Intervention in World War I.* Chicago: University of Chicago Press, 1967. Shows Beard as a pioneer in revising the accepted view about Germany's responsibility for World War I, and how his disillusionment over American involvement in that conflict shaped his attitude toward intervention in World War II.

Dahlberg, Jane S. *The New York Bureau of Municipal Research: Pioneer in Government Administration.* New York: New York University Press, 1966. Includes details about Beard's role in the movement for more efficient city government.

Higham, John, et al. *History.* Englewood Cliffs: Prentice-Hall, 1965. A perceptive account of the development of American historical scholarship that is indispensable for evaluating Beard's influence upon the profession.

Kenyon, Cecilia M. " 'An Economic Interpretation of the Constitution' after Fifty Years." *Centennial Review* 7 (Summer 1963): 327–352. A valuable analysis of post-Beardian scholarship on the framing and adoption of the Constitution.

Lane, Ann J. *Mary Ritter Beard: American Historical Writings Reconsidered.* New York: Schocken, 1977. Mary Ritter Beard not only collaborated with her husband on works such as *The Rise of American Civilization*, but was herself a pioneer in the study of women's history. This is the fullest biographical account.

Mosher, Frederick C., ed. *American Public Administration: Past, Present, Future.* University: University of Alabama Press, 1975. A collection of essays that illuminates Beard's contribution to the establishment of public administration as a field of study.

Pole, J. R. "The New History and the Sense of Social Purpose in American Historical Writing." *Transactions of the Royal Historical Society*, Fifth Series, 23 (1973): 220–242. An important elucidation and assessment of Beard's view of history as a tool for understanding the present and improving the future.

Pressly, Thomas J. *Americans Interpret Their Civil War.* Princeton: Princeton University Press, 1959. How Beard's conception in *The Rise of American Civilization* of the Civil War as a second American Revolution resulting in the triumph of industrial capitalism over agrarianism influenced later scholarship on the topic.

Radosh, Ronald. *Prophets on the Right: Profiles of Conservative Critics of American Globalism*. New York: Simon & Schuster, 1975. Documents how Beard's isolationism colored his response to the post-World War II Cold War.

Skotheim, Robert A. *American Intellectual Histories and Historians*. Princeton: Princeton University Press, 1966. Includes an illuminating analysis of Beard's changing conception of the role of ideas in history.

White, Morton G. *Social Thought in America: The Revolt against Formalism*. New York: Viking Press, 1949. A seminal work that places Beard in the context of the larger shift in American social thought after the turn of the century from formalistic description to realistic analysis.

John Braeman
University of Nebraska-Lincoln

Columbia University 200th Anniversary, 1954

P. G. T. BEAUREGARD
1818–1893

Chronology

Born Pierre Gustave Toutant-Beauregard on May 28, 1818, in St. Bernard Parish, Louisiana, to Jacques Toutant-Beauregard and Hélène Judith Di Reggio Toutant-Beauregard, descended from Italian aristocracy (the family eventually dropped the hyphen and became simply Beauregard); *1818–1834* grows up in Louisiana, educated in New Orleans and in New York; *1834* enters the United States Military Academy at West Point; *1838* graduates second in his class; on graduation is commissioned 2nd lieutenant in the Corps of Engineers; *1838–1846* serves as an engineer and rises to the rank of 1st lieutenant; *September 1841* marries Marie Laure Villere, of a distinguished Creole family of Louisiana; *1846– 1847* serves in the Mexican War as an engineer under General Winfield Scott, distinguishing himself and gaining the honorary brevet rank of major; *1847–1860* serves as an engineer; *March 1850* his wife dies in childbirth; *1853* is promoted to regular rank of captain; marries Caroline Deslonde, also of a distinguished Creole family; *January 1861* is appointed Superintendent of the United States Military Academy at West Point, but is relieved after a few days because of his pro-Southern views on secession; *February–March 1861* resigns his commission in the United States Army and accepts a commission as brigadier general in the Confederate States Army; *April 12–14, 1861* commands the Confederate forces bombarding Fort Sumter, in Charleston Harbor, and compels the surrender of the Union garrison there, beginning the Civil War; *June-July 1861* is appointed to command one of the two major Southern armies in Virginia, the other army being commanded by Brigadier General Joseph E. Johnston; the two armies merge and Beauregard is nominally second in command; *July 21, 1861* the first major battle of the war is a narrow Southern victory at Bull Run (also called Manassas); *August 1861* is promoted to full general; *January 1862* is ordered to the western theater, second in command under General Albert Sidney Johnston in the Army of Tennessee; *April 6–7, 1862* when Johnston is killed late on the first day of the battle at Shiloh, Beauregard takes command of the army and is forced to retreat on the second day; *May–June 1862* retreats to Corinth, Mississippi, then evacuates the city; turns over command of the army to a subordinate due to illness; *June–August 1862* recuperates and is ordered to take command of the coastal defenses of South Carolina and Georgia; *June 1862–April 1864* is in command at Charleston; *April 1864* ordered to Virginia to help defend Richmond and Petersburg from the southeast; *May 16, 1864* defeats a Union army at Drewry's Bluff and traps it on the peninsula at Bermuda Hundred; *June 1864* begins the siege of Petersburg, saving the Richmond-Petersburg line; *October 1864* is ordered to serve as military advisor in the West, an administrative position; *February 1865* is assigned to duty with the remnants of the Army of Tennessee; *April 26, 1865* surrenders with Johnston's army near Durham, North Carolina; *1865–1870* serves as officer in two Louisiana railroads; *1866–1870* declines several offers to command the armies of Egypt and Romania; *1877–1893* serves as a supervisor of the Louisiana State Lottery; *1879–1888* serves as adjutant general of Louisiana; *1893* dies on February 20 at his home in New Orleans.

Activities of Historical Significance

Few Civil War military leaders saw such a wide variety of service as Beauregard during the war. He was one of eight full generals in the Confederacy and was second in command at the first two great battles of the war: First Bull Run and Shiloh. He served in both major theaters, in Virginia, Tennessee, Mississippi, North Carolina, and South Carolina.

After the fall of Fort Sumter, and even more so after the victory at First Bull Run, Beauregard was idolized throughout the South. A major factor in his popularity was undoubtedly his French ancestry, with its aristocratic bearing and romantic air, something new and intriguing to most Southerners. Although his bitter disputes with others often hampered military operations, they did not seriously affect his public image.

Beauregard, for all his pomposity and bluster, and his grandiose Napoleonic battle plans, was a good soldier. His strategy was generally sound, and his performance at Charleston from 1862 to 1864 and at Petersburg in 1864 was particularly valuable to the Confederate war effort.

After the war, Beauregard, though still a hero in Louisiana, endured a measure of criticism. Much of the censure was for prospering financially during Reconstruction, particularly by his association with a lottery, and for entering into acrimonious and futile quarrels among ex-Confederates over the blame for Southern defeat.

Overview of Biographical Sources

Despite his significant role in the Civil War, there are only two biographies of Beauregard. T. Harry Williams, *P. G. T. Beauregard: Napoleon in Gray* (1955), is by far the best work; few biographical sources exist other than primary sources.

Evaluation of Principal Biographical Sources

Basso, Hamilton. *Beauregard: The Great Creole.* New York: Charles Scribner's Sons, 1933. **(A, G)** This admiring and uncritical biography argues that Beauregard has been ignored by Civil War historians because he does not fit the traditional Anglo-Saxon view of the Confederate hero. Basso, a Southern novelist, emphasizes the drama of Beauregard's life; the book is at times interesting but ultimately unsuccessful.

Williams, T. Harry. *P. G. T. Beauregard: Napoleon in Gray*. Baton Rouge: Louisiana State University Press, 1955. **(A, G)** Only the second true biography of Beauregard, and the first scholarly study, Williams's work is easily the best book on the controversial general. The writing is clear, particularly in its description of such confusing battles as Bull Run and Shiloh; Williams's skillful use of the primary sources ensures that his appraisal is realistic but fair.

Overview and Evaluation of Primary Sources

Alfred Roman, *Military Operations of General Beauregard in the War Between the States 1861–1865*, 2 vols. (New York: Harper and Brothers, 1884; **A, G**), is actually Beauregard's own effort, disguised so as to deflect criticism of its attacks on Jefferson Davis, Joseph E. Johnston, Albert S. Johnston, and others. Beauregard devotes much of his memoir to major arguments over minor disputes and includes long appendices filled with documents intended to support his contentions; this is a defense of his strategy, tactics, and leadership.

A useful account of Beauregard's Mexican War experiences is T. Harry Williams, ed., *With Beauregard in Mexico: The Mexican Reminiscences of P. G. T. Beauregard* (Baton Rouge: Louisiana State University Press, 1956; **A, G**). Predictably self-serving, the work is largely an exaggeration of Beauregard's exploits.

The standard reference work for any student of the Civil War is *War of the Rebellion: Official Records of the Union and Confederate Armies*, 128 vols. (Washington: U.S. Government Printing Office, 1880–1901; **A, G**). Care must be exercised in using official reports, however, as commanders tended to exaggerate both their own deeds and the odds against them in any particular engagement. The collection contains most of the important correspondence and battle reports of major and minor Union and Confederate officers; essential for any detailed examination of Beauregard's career.

Just as Roman's two-volume "biography" is actually the subject's own memoirs, most of Beauregard's articles on his Confederate service were actually ghostwritten by Roman. Of the five postwar articles published under his name, only one, "The First Battle of Bull Run," was actually his work. All of them are justifications of Beauregard's strategy and tactics, and are sharply critical of his real or supposed enemies, particularly Davis. They are "The First Battle of Bull Run," "The Campaign of Shiloh," "The Defense of Drewry's Bluff," and "The Defense of Charleston Harbor," all reprinted in Robert U. Johnson and Clarence C. Buel, eds., *Battles and Leaders of the Civil War*, 4 vols. (New York: Century, 1888; **A, G**); and "Torpedo Service in Charleston Harbor," reprinted in *The Annals of the War Written by Leading Participants North and South* (Philadelphia: The Times, 1879; **A**). Beauregard's book *A Commentary on the Campaign and Battle of Manassas . . . With a Summary of the Art of War* (New York: Putnam's Sons, 1891; **A**) is a justification of his elaborate battle plans for the war's first major battle and his claim to being in actual command of the army on the field; it also reprints a wartime pamphlet of Beauregard's views on strategy and tactics.

Many Beauregard manuscripts cover both his Confederate career and his postwar life. Significant collections are at the Library of Congress; the National Archives; Louisiana State University; Tulane University; Duke University; Columbia University; and the Museum of the Confederacy.

Fiction and Adaptations

Frances Parkinson Keyes's *Madame Castel's Lodger* (1962) is an entertaining fictionalized biography, written after substantial research in primary and secondary sources.

Museums, Historical Landmarks, Societies

Beauregard House (New Orleans, LA). This house, where Beauregard lived for a short time while writing his memoirs, is operated as a museum.

Confederate Museum (New Orleans, LA). This museum contains several important Beauregard items, including one of his wartime uniforms and an unusual straw military cap.

Fort Sumter National Monument (Charleston Harbor, Charleston, SC). This park includes the site of the opening of the Civil War in April 1861 and, like the other battlesites listed below, is maintained by the National Park Service.

Manassas National Battlefield Park (Manassas, VA). This park includes the site of the battle of July 1861, often called Bull Run.

Petersburg National Battlefield (Petersburg, VA). This park includes the sites of the fighting around Petersburg in May-August 1864.

Shiloh National Military Park (Shiloh, TN). This park includes the site of the battle of April 1862.

Other Sources

Connelly, Thomas L. *Army of the Heartland: The Army of Tennessee, 1861–1862.* Baton Rouge: Louisiana State University Press, 1967. The first volume of a two-volume study that is the only modern and scholarly analysis of the army's commanders and campaigns. Connelly's work, quite critical of Beauregard, is particularly useful for its view of him at and immediately after Shiloh.

Freeman, Douglas Southall. *Lee's Lieutenants: A Study in Command.* Vols. 1 and 3. New York: Charles Scribner's Sons, 1942–1944. Freeman, a Richmond journalist, wrote this command study of the Army of Northern Virginia after his Pulitzer Prize-winning *R. E. Lee*. The first and third volumes contain his detailed criticism of Beauregard's generalship at Bull Run and Petersburg.

J. Tracy Power
South Carolina Department of
Archives and History

Shiloh, 1962

HENRY WARD BEECHER
1813–1887

Chronology

Born Henry Ward Beecher on June 24, 1813, in Litchfield, Connecticut, the eighth of nine children born to evangelist Lyman Beecher and his first wife, Roxana Foote Beecher, and the brother of Harriet Beecher (Stowe), who is two years older; *1826* enrolls in the Mount Pleasant Classical Institute in Amherst, Massachusetts; *1830* enters Amherst College; *1834* graduates and enters Lane Theological Seminary in Cincinnati, which his father runs; *1836* edits the *Cincinnati Journal & Western Luminary*; *1837* is licensed to preach by the Cincinnati Presbytery, and goes to Lawrenceburg, Indiana; *August 3, 1837* marries Eunice Bullard; *1838* the Old School Miami Presbytery rejects his application for ordination, and his Lawrenceburg congregation withdraws from the presbytery; is ordained by the New School Presbytery of Cincinnati; *1839* becomes pastor of the Second Presbyterian Church of Indianapolis; *1844* publishes his enormously popular series of addresses on vices as *Seven Lectures to Young Men*; *1846* gives his first sermons denouncing slavery; *1847* takes the pulpit of the Congregational Plymouth Church of Brooklyn, New York; *1849* the Plymouth Church building burns, and a larger one, with a semicircular auditorium designed to display Beecher's oratorical talents, is erected in its place; *1850* gives the "Shall We Compromise?" sermon, denouncing slavery and the Compromise of 1850; spends the summer in Europe; *1854* reads his "Defence of Kansas" sermon, upholding the settlers' right to forcible opposition and asks his congregation to give money for rifles (known as "Beecher Bibles" because they were shipped in boxes marked "Bibles") to arm the Kansans; *1855* publishes his controversial *Conflict of Northern and Southern Theories of Men and Society*, which predicts that the "irreconcilable differences" between the sections would end in bloodshed; *1856* affiliates himself with the Republican party; *1860* campaigns for Lincoln; *1861–1864* edits the New York *Independent*; *1863* visits England and delivers series of lectures supporting the North; *1865* is chosen by Lincoln to speak at the raising of the United States flag over Fort Sumter on April 14; *1866* makes the major address at the Woman's Rights Convention; is criticized for his "Cleveland Letter" expressing sympathy with the Cleveland convention of soldiers and sailors who supported Andrew Johnson; *1867* publishes *Norwood, or Village Life in New England*; *1868* supports Grant's presidential bid; *1869* is elected president of the less radical, New England-based American Woman Suffrage Association, offending the more militant, New York-based National Woman Suffrage Association, one of whose leaders is Victoria Woodhull; *1870–1881* edits the *Christian Union*; *1870* Theodore Tilton accuses him of having an affair with his wife, Elizabeth Tilton; *1871* publishes the first volume of *The Life of Jesus Christ*; *1872–1875* is the first Lyman Beecher Lecturer in Preaching at Yale; *1872* Victoria

Woodhull publishes the story of the Beecher-Tilton affair in *Woodhull and Claflin's Weekly*; *1874–1875* Tilton files a complaint in court against Beecher, accusing him of adultery and alienation of affection, and demands $100,000 in damages—the trial lasts six months and the jury splits 6–3 in favor of Beecher; *1876* Council of Congregational Churches convenes at Plymouth Church and, after an examination of the facts, declares Beecher innocent of wrongdoing in the Tilton affair; *1877* discards the theological notion of hell; *1882* withdraws from the Association of Congregational Ministers because of his disbelief in a literal hell and advocacy of evolution; *1885* publishes *Evolution and Religion*; *1886* preaches and lectures in England for four months; *1887* dies on March 8 of a severe cerebral hemorrhage in Brooklyn, New York; is interred in the Greenwood Cemetery in Brooklyn.

Activities of Historical Significance

Henry Ward Beecher's interpretation of Christian doctrine marked America's transition to the Victorian Age and her final rejection of Puritan theology. For nearly forty years, his electrifying, popular presence at the pulpit of the Brooklyn church reassured Americans that God was kind, forgiving, and full of love; that material prosperity was not a sign of wickedness; and that they were capable of infinite progress. And the country responded with an outpouring of love, respect, and admiration for the man who helped them to make sense of the Industrial Revolution, the Civil War, and even evolution.

As a youngster, Beecher felt unloved and unwanted by his father and his step-mother. He was a shy, awkward child who spoke with a stutter and lived in fear of his father's unbending Calvinism and vengeful God. It was not until he went away to school that Beecher began to find an identity for himself and became an accomplished public speaker. After an undistinguished academic career at Amherst, Henry entered the seminary his father headed in Cincinnati, despite his reluctance to be so near the stifling patriarchal presence. But it was during these years, on a beautiful May afternoon in the woods, that he experienced an epiphanic moment: the beauty, regularity, and order of nature convinced him that God must be good and loving, and that he must share this message through his preaching. In time he would come to represent a complete reaction against everything his father symbolized.

From the start, he inspired devotion in his congregations, as witnessed by the Lawrenceburg church's withdrawal from the Old School Presbytery when it refused to ordain Beecher. This loyalty grew out of his formulation of a theology and philosophy that appealed to middle-class Americans of the time in an entirely new way. He preached a comforting religion, with a friendly lord and savior instead of hellfire and brimstone, held a moderate position on public issues, and relied on persuasion rather than threats in moral matters. His popularity grew on a national scale with his move to the prosperous Plymouth Church in Brooklyn, and he became arguably the most widely known (as well as the richest) religious figure of the day.

No foe to material wealth, Beecher nonetheless advocated reform issues, such as abolition and women's rights, but always in a moderate, gradual way with which many Americans could agree without feeling that they were espousing radical revolution. While his moderation and caution earned him the scorn of more devoted and rigorous reformers, his approach successfully popularized their causes with the average citizen.

Beecher's popularity made Theodore Tilton's 1870 accusation that he had committed adultery with his wife Elizabeth all the more shocking and disturbing. Although the evidence was never conclusive, the widespread and public nature of the scandal convinced many that some sort of impropriety had taken place. But once the scandal was laid to rest, Beecher regained his popularity and influence, although his renunciation of the concept of a literal hell and his embrace of evolution put him increasingly at odds with fellow churchmen. But the populace still loved him; after he died, over 40,000 mourners paid their respects at the viewing of his body.

Overview of Biographical Sources

The first biographies of Beecher, notably *A Biography of Henry Ward Beecher* (1888) by his son William and son-in-law Samuel Scoville and *Henry Ward Beecher* (1903) by Lyman Abbott, his assistant and successor at Plymouth Church, were excessively laudatory and insufficiently critical or objective. Paxton Hibben's *Henry Ward Beecher, An American Portrait* (1927) presented a new interpretation of the man as a heartless hypocrite, indicative of the way Beecher biographers were becoming obsessed with his moral character.

William G. McLoughlin's interpretive work, *The Meaning of Henry Ward Beecher* (1970), was a refreshing change. It redirected inquiry toward the importance of Beecher's thought in American history and the important role he played in the social transformation of the country during the nineteenth century. Clifford E. Clark's *Henry Ward Beecher: Spokesman for a Middle-Class America* (1978), was an excellent biography in this new tradition and remains the definitive work. Meanwhile, Milton Rugoff's *The Beechers* (1981) provided an excellent interpretation of Beecher within the context of his family.

Evaluation of Principal Biographical Sources

Abbott, Lyman. *Henry Ward Beecher*. 1903. Reprint. New York: Chelsea House, 1980. **(G)** Although his work has a reverential tone, Abbott, trusted friend and associate of Beecher, does make some interesting insights and comments.

Beecher, William C., and Samuel Scoville. *A Biography of Henry Ward Beecher.* New York: Charles L. Webster, 1888. **(A, G)** The "authorized" biography, which acknowledges the aid of Mrs. Henry Ward Beecher under the authors' names, this work is highly subjective, but does offer useful and accurate microscopic details.

Clark, Clifford E. *Henry Ward Beecher: Spokesman for a Middle-Class America.* Urbana: University of Illinois Press, 1978. **(A, G)** A sophisticated and clear interpretive biography of Beecher.

Elsmere, Jane Shaffer. *Henry Ward Beecher: The Indiana Years, 1837-1847.* Indianapolis: Indiana Historical Society, 1973. **(A, G)** Although Elsmere's account is descriptive rather than interpretive and sheds no new light on the roots of Beecher's thought, it nonetheless provides a thorough and accurate record of his first two pastorates.

Hibben, Paxton. *Henry Ward Beecher: An American Portrait.* New York: George H. Doran, 1927. **(G)** Hibben's debunking biography is certainly a change from its predecessors, but its unrelenting malice and spite weaken its credibility.

McLoughlin, William G. *The Meaning of Henry Ward Beecher.* New York: Alfred Knopf, 1970. **(A, G)** McLoughlin's groundbreaking work shows that Beecher's significance for American history extends beyond the scandal involving Elizabeth Tilton.

Rugoff, Milton. *The Beechers: An American Family in the Nineteenth Century.* New York: Harper & Row, 1981. **(A, G)** A highly readable and enjoyable family biography that adds to the scholarship on Beecher by analyzing him in the context of his redoubtable kin.

Stowe, Lyman Beecher. *Saints, Sinners, and Beechers.* Indianapolis: Bobbs-Merrill, 1934. **(A, G)** The first biography of the clan as a whole, written by a member, benefits from inside knowledge and anecdotes, but does not offer any startling insights or information.

Overview and Evaluation of Primary Sources
Beecher's sermons and addresses are important sources of his thought. The sermons are reprinted in *Plymouth Pulpit*, 18 vols. in 2 series (New York: J. B. Ford, 1868-1884; **A**). *Patriotic Addresses*, edited by John R. Howard (New York: Fords, Howard, & G. Hulbert, 1888; **A, G**), and *Lectures and Orations by Henry Ward Beecher*, edited by N. D. Hillis (New York: Fleming H. Revell, 1913; **A, G**), remain the best sources for the addresses. Also important among Beecher's works are the addresses, pamphlets, and books mentioned in the chronology, notably his "Defence of Kansas" (Washington, DC: Buell & Blanchard, 1854; **A, G**), and *Evolution and Religion* (New York: Fords, Howard, & G. Hulbert, 1885; **A, G**).

There is a large collection of Beecher Family Papers at Yale University, including much of Henry's informative correspondence. The largest body of Henry's papers is at the Library of Congress; the Houghton Library of Harvard University, the New York Public Library, and the Rutherford B. Hayes Presidential Library have small but interesting collections. An important collection of Harriet Beecher Stowe and Beecher Family Papers is at the Schlesinger Library on the History of Women in America at Radcliffe College (Harvard University).

Museums, Historical Landmarks, Societies

Beecher Birthplace (Litchfield, CT). The original house in which Beecher and his sister, Harriet Beecher Stowe, were born has been moved to the Forman School, where it is closed to the public; but the original site of the house is designated by an historic marker on State Highway 63.

Beecher Bible and Rifle Church (Wabaunsee, KS). This 1862 structure was built by settlers who were provided with rifles and funded by Beecher's congregation.

Plymouth Church of the Pilgrims (Brooklyn, NY). The building, designed in 1849–1850 with Beecher's crowd-drawing capacity in mind, has changed little since he preached there.

Stowe House Community Center (Cincinnati, OH). Located in the Walnut Hills section, this was once the home of the Beecher family. Henry Ward Beecher lived here until 1837. Most of the center is devoted to collections on black history, but one room has been set aside for artifacts of the Beecher family.

Other Sources

Filler, Louis. "Liberalism, Anti-Slavery, and the Founders of the *Independent*." In *New England Quarterly* 27 (1954): 291–306. Filler has written an interesting history of this influential paper and a good account of Beecher's role in it.

Sklar, Kathryn Kish. *Catharine Beecher: A Study in Domesticity.* New Haven, CT: Yale University Press, 1973. Sklar's excellent biography of Henry's older sister has some profound insights on the nature of Lyman Beecher's influence on his children.

Starr, Harris Elwood. "Henry Ward Beecher." In *Dictionary of American Biography*. New York: Charles Scribner's Sons, 1929. This is a useful, short sketch of Beecher and his significance in America, presaging McLoughlin and Clark.

Waller, Altina L. *Reverend Beecher and Mrs. Tilton: Sex and Class in Victorian America*. Amherst: University of Massachusetts Press, 1982. This succinct and eloquent book provides a surprising and compelling political and social explanation for the eruption of the Beecher scandal.

Jean V. Berlin
Wofford College

ALEXANDER GRAHAM BELL
1847–1921

Chronology

Born Alexander Graham Bell on March 3, 1847, in Edinburgh, Scotland, the second of three sons of Alexander Melville Bell, an elocutionist, and Eliza Grace Symonds Bell, a miniature-painter; *1847–1870* grows up in Edinburgh and is educated at the Royal High School; at age 16, works as a pupil-teacher of music and elocution at Weston House Academy in Elgin and helps his father and brother complete Visible Speech; spends brief time at University of Edinburgh but leaves before completing his degree; teaches at Somerset College in Bath and then moves with father to London, where he takes courses at University College; *1870–1875* departs with family for Canada; takes a position in Boston at Sarah Fuller's school for the deaf; later teaches at Clarke Institute for the Deaf in Northhampton, Massachusetts; meets Gardiner Greene Hubbard and Thomas Sanders, both of whose deaf children he tutors; receives financial backing from Hubbard and Sanders to continue experiments with a multiple telegraph he has been working on for several years; moves from telegraph to ideas that form the basis of the telephone; *1875* completes a crude, partially successful version of telephone; *1876* files for patent based on previous experiments and achieves success in transmitting voice over wires on March 10; demonstrates the new device at the Centennial Exhibition in Philadelphia; *1877–1882* marries Hubbard's daughter Mabel, his former student; the Bell Telephone Company begins to license agents to rent telephones throughout the nation; after a settlement with chief competitor Western Union, use of the Bell device begins to grow steadily, making Bell an increasingly wealthy man; *1882* his company is taken over by financiers from Boston, and Bell becomes a minority stockholder, ending his direct involvement in the enterprise; *1883–1921* enjoys a long and fruitful life financed by his telephone stock; makes no further original contributions to science or industry but stays very active in scientific circles and continues to work on a number of projects; *1921* dies on August 2 at Beinn Bhreagh, his Canadian home.

Activities of Historical Significance

Bell's invention of the telephone is an intriguing scientific and commercial story. With his training in elocution and music, his work on the physiology of speech, his fine ear, and his acquired knowledge of electricity, Bell was almost ideally suited to produce the invention. But he did not start with this goal in mind. Beginning first with work on a multiple telegraph, a device which would allow the transmission of more than one message over a single telegraph line, Bell gradually moved toward the principles of the telephone in 1875. Receiving strong resistance from his backers, particularly Gardiner Greene Hubbard, Bell and his assistant Thomas Watson nonetheless continued their experiments in voice transmission. Their first success, an abortive one, came in 1875 with Bell's construction of the "gallows" telephone, so named for its shape. Based on the magneto-induction principle, the device failed to consistently transmit distinct words, although it now seems that the failure was due not to its design or principle but to improper use.

Though disappointed, Bell continued his experiments and in 1876 filed for a patent on his work. The diagrams he brought to the United States patent office did not even use the word telephone, but were labeled an improvement on the telegraph. In the margin of this application, however, Bell added a description of variable resistance transmission—electrically transmitting the human voice by varying the resistance of a circuit—though he had produced no device capable of such a feat. The variable resistance principle became the basis for his successful telephone of 1876 and has remained the foundation of telephony. Working in an attic laboratory in Boston, Bell and Watson built a telephone consisting of a diaphragm attached to a wire in a cup of acid water. The speaker's voice hitting the diaphragm changed the level of immersion of the wire, thereby varying its resistance and generating an undulatory current that mirrored the air vibrations of speech. It was through this telephone that Bell successfully communicated with Thomas Watson on March 10, 1876.

Bell's success was the result of hard work and the practical application of scientific principles, but Bell was clearly not an inventive genius in the category of a Thomas Edison. He never repeated his achievement in telephony with any other invention or discovery, though he actively pursued a number of scientific and technological projects in the following forty-five years of his life. Bell's historical reputation is in good part a matter of luck and timing. One of several men working in isolation from each other on voice transmission, his fame rests chiefly on the patent application of 1876, filed just hours before another inventor, Elisha Gray, reached the patent office. The basis for Bell's claim to priority, and hence the entire Bell Telephone Company (AT&T), came from the marginal addition describing the principle of variable resistance made at the last minute in the 1876 patent application. So close were Gray's and Bell's applications in time and description, that for years the Bell patent was subjected to numerous suits by competitors, beginning with those filed by Western Union, the telegraph corporation that bought Gray's telephone. The issue was put to rest in the *Dowd* suit, settled in an 1881 consent decree declaring the Bell patents wholly valid.

Bell also differs from many other inventors of the late nineteenth century in his lack of interest in the commercial side of technology, something he readily admitted. Bell participated little in the exploitation of telephony's commercial possibilities, though his early patents provided the basis of the Bell Telephone Company's monopoly of the field between 1880 and 1894. He received a substantial share of stock in the company that bears his name, but the only position he officially held was electrician. His formal connection to the Bell company ended quickly, as aggressive Boston financiers took charge of telephone promotion after 1879. In his subsequent experimenting, he paid little attention to commercial applications, preferring to see himself as a scientist rather than an inventor.

The other area in which Bell is widely remembered is his work with the deaf. Here his reputation is also controversial. The system of Visible Speech, a vocabulary of symbols indicating the position of the vocal organs in speech devised by Bell's father and taught by Alexander, still exists, but it has had little application in the teaching of speech to the deaf. The practice of teaching the deaf to speak itself has come under attack, moreover, as an inferior form of education to sign language. In his time, Bell stood squarely in the camp of those who believed that sign language isolated the deaf. He maintained that deaf people would be better off learning to read the speech of others and speak themselves. In this position, he opposed Edward Gallaudet, the other important leader in deaf education in the nineteenth century.

Overview of Biographical Sources

Bell has not been the subject of many biographies, perhaps due to the limited nature of his historical achievements. No serious biographer rejects Bell as the inventor of the telephone, despite the long controversy surrounding this issue in his own time. Other aspects of the man's life are of too little historical significance to generate any controversy, with the possible exception of his work with the deaf. No historian has tackled this subject in depth, however. The best available biography of Bell is Robert Bruce's *Alexander Graham Bell and the Conquest of Solitude* (1973). Bruce believes that Bell's later scientific experiments still showed the trace of genius that went into his telephone work and rates Bell close to Edison in stature. Joseph Goulden's *Monopoly* (1968) offers the most sympathetic hearing to those who challenged Bell's patents, though he stops short of awarding credit to anyone else. Thomas B. Costain's *The Chord of Steel* (1960) focuses narrowly on the events leading up to and immediately following Bell's invention of the telephone. Costain also addresses the one continual controversy surrounding the telephone— the question of where it was invented. Canadians have claimed that Bell conceived of the device in Brantford, Ontario, where Bell's father and mother settled and where Bell spent much of his time. Americans generally claim Boston as the site of invention, where Bell's and Watson's laboratory was located. Costain takes a pluralist view, giving credit to both places.

Evaluation of Principal Biographical Sources

Brooks, John. *Telephone: The First Hundred Years.* New York: Harper and Row, 1975. (G) Commissioned by AT&T on the one-hundredth anniversary of the telephone, this even-handed treatment of AT&T's history provides a good, brief sketch of the invention of the telephone. It is light on detail, however, and relies heavily on previously published work.

Bruce, Robert. *Alexander Graham Bell and the Conquest of Solitude.* Boston: Little, Brown, 1973. **(A)** This detailed scholarly study is the official Bell biography, written with access to Bell's personal papers. Covering all aspects of Bell's professional, family, and scientific life, Bruce places the man firmly in the context of his time. His detailed account of Bell's invention of the telephone is superb. Though generally fair and objective in his treatment of his subject, Bruce at times gives more weight to Bell's later achievements than seems warranted. Overall, however, it is by far the best source available on Alexander Graham Bell.

Costain, Thomas B. *The Chord of Steel: The Story of the Invention of the Telephone.* New York: Doubleday, 1960. **(G)** A popular history of the invention of the telephone, emphasizing Bell's life in Brantford, Canada, where he resided part of the time.

Deland, Fred. *Dumb No Longer: Romance of the Telephone.* Washington, DC: Volta Bureau, 1906. **(G)** Primarily the history of deaf education in the nineteenth century, Deland's book places Bell's work with the deaf in historical context. He emphasizes Bell's and Bell's father's work on Visible Speech, and not Alexander's later, more important efforts on behalf of the deaf. The later chapters provide a brief recounting of the invention of the telephone and laudatory stories from Bell's life.

Goulden, Joseph C. *Monopoly.* New York: Putnam, 1968. **(G)** Goulden's main concern is AT&T, but he gives a somewhat sympathetic hearing to those who claimed priority to Bell in the invention of the telephone.

Mackenzie, Catherine D. *Alexander Graham Bell: The Man who Contracted Space.* Boston: Houghton Mifflin, 1928. **(G)** Mackenzie was Bell's personal secretary in the years before his death and helped him collect biographical material and prepare his memoirs. While her work is more a series of sketches than a full-scale biography or a scholarly study, she did have the firsthand contact with Bell unavailable to any other biographer. Her work covers in some detail the invention and development of the telephone and the controversial patent disputes following.

Rhodes, Frederick L. *Beginnings of Telephony.* New York: Harper, 1929. **(A, G)** This book is primarily a history of telephone technology, but the opening chapters provide a solid sketch of Bell's invention, strong on technical detail. Rhodes, an AT&T employee, gives a strong defense of Bell's patent claims.

Overview and Evaluation of Primary Sources

Bell's extensive personal papers are deposited with the National Geographic Society in Washington, D.C. The AT&T Company Historical Archives in New York City (soon to be moved to Warren, New Jersey) also has much useful material on Bell, the invention of the telephone, and the device's early technological and commercial development. According to Robert Bruce, the following are also useful sources of manuscript material on Bell: the Volta Bureau Library of the Alexander Graham Bell Association for the Deaf, Washington, DC; the Charles Sumner Tainter Manuscripts, Division of Mechanical and Civil Engineering, Smithsonian Institution, Washington, DC; the Special Collections of the Boston University Library; and the Thomas Borthwick Manuscripts in the Scottish National Library, Edinburgh. The best sources on the patent disputes are James J. Storrow's "Proofs by and About Alexander G. Bell" (A), and AT&T's *The Bell Telephone* (A). The former is a compilation of court testimony by Bell or bearing on Bell's work; the latter contains Bell's testimony from court cases in 1892. Both are available in the AT&T Historical Archives and the Bell Collection in Washington. Bell's own published writings were extensive, though none stands out as particularly important or insightful. Harold S. Osborne, "Biographical Memoir of Alexander Graham Bell, 1847–1922," *Biographical Memoirs* 23 (Washington, DC: National Academy of Sciences, 1943; A), contains a complete list of Bell's writings, as well as his patents.

Museums, Historical Landmarks, Societies

AT&T (New York, NY). AT&T and the regional Bell Telephone companies frequently offer displays of early telephone technology. AT&T has in the past reconstructed Bell's Boston laboratory for public display, though it has no permanent collection of these materials.

Bell Memorial (Brantford, Ontario). Recounts Bell's work on the telephone done in Canada. His family home in Tutelo Heights has been dedicated as a public park.

Smithsonian Institution (Washington, DC). Holds a collection of early Bell telephones and equipment.

Other Sources

Finn, Bernard S. "Alexander Graham Bell's Experiments with the Variable Resistance Transmitter." *Smithsonian Journal of History* 1 (1966). Finn provides a detailed recounting of Bell's various experiments leading up to and immediately following his March 10 success.

Garnet, Robert W. *The Telephone Enterprise: The Evolution of the Bell System's Horizontal Structure.* Baltimore: Johns Hopkins University Press, 1985. This scholarly study is concerned more with the commercial development of the telephone. It has interesting information on Bell's early efforts at commercial exploitation of his invention and the formation of the Bell Telephone Company.

Kenneth Lipartito
Baker & Botts

EDWARD BELLAMY
1850–1898

Chronology

Born Edward Bellamy on March 26, 1850, in Chicopee Falls, Massachusetts, the third son of Rufus King Bellamy, a prominent Baptist minister, and Maria Louisa Putnam Bellamy; *1850–1867* grows up in Chicopee Falls; *1867* studies literature briefly at Union College in Schenectady, New York; *1868* travels abroad, spending considerable time in the Germanies where he becomes interested in social problems and the efficiency of the Prussian army; *1869–1880* reads law and gains admission to the Massachusetts bar, but subsequently joins the editorial staff of the *Springfield Union*; *1880* co-founds with his brother Charles, the *Springfield Daily News*; *1882* marries Emma Sanderson of Chicopee Falls; soon his enthusiasm for journalism wanes and he begins his literary career; *1888* writes the popular *Looking Backward: 2000–1887*; *1891* launches a short-lived weekly publication, the *New Nation*; *1897* writes his final novel, *Equality*; moves to Colorado in an unsuccessful attempt to overcome tuberculosis; *1898* dies on May 22 in Chicopee Falls.

Activities of Historical Significance

Edward Bellamy's book *Looking Backward: 2000–1887* (1888) ranks him as one of history's great writers of utopian literature. This romantic novel, which by the end of the nineteenth century had outsold every book published in the United States except the *Bible* and *Uncle Tom's Cabin*, immediately made this young social critic one of the country's spokesmen for reform. Arthur Morgan, the first biographer of Bellamy, may have exaggerated when he said, "He probably started more men on the road of pioneer social thought and action than has any other American"; but Arthur Lipow, the most recent student of Bellamy and "Bellamyism," is correct in suggesting that Bellamy inspired many of his readers to think about alternatives to the capitalistic structure of Gilded Age America. Soon after *Looking Backward* appeared, scores of "Bellamy Clubs" or "Nationalist Clubs" sprang up throughout the country, and some enthusiasts even created intentional communities where they sought to prove that cooperation and Nationalism offered practical ways to save society. As the People's Party movement gained strength after 1891, Bellamy and his followers adopted its principles.

Although contemporary and latter-day supporters of Bellamy Nationalism saw *Loking Backward* as a statement for popular rule, when scrutinized, this novel instead reveals a strong anti-democratic flavor. Bellamy wished to create a new bureaucratic order that would resemble the collectivist European states of the post-World War I era and not be controlled by the working classes. Indeed, his utopia glorified a government run by a talented and all-powerful elite which abolished universal suffrage and imposed a military-like discipline upon the masses. But Bellamy's thinking changed. It was probably the impact of the populist revolt that moved him and many of his backers toward democracy. For in 1897, shortly before his death, Bellamy wrote *Equality*. In this dense tract, he advocated a much less authoritarian vision of the perfect society, one that embraced the concept of direct democracy, most notably the initiative and referendum.

Even after his death in 1898 and the rapid demise of the Nationalist phenomenon, Bellamy's *Looking Backward* affected others, including social scientists, labor leaders, and politicians. The 1888 work also served as a model for numerous literary utopias.

Overview of Biographical/Critical Sources

Bellamy did not attract serious scholarly attention until Arthur E. Morgan, former head of the Tennessee Valley Authority, wrote *Edward Bellamy* (1944). This is not a traditional biography, for Morgan condenses the chronological story of Bellamy's life into only two chapters. Sylvia E. Bowman penned *The Year 2000: A Critical Biography of Edward Bellamy* (1958) and co-authored *Edward Bellamy Abroad: An American Prophet's Influence* (1962). During this same period, Everett McNair examined the Nationalist phenomenon in his work, *Edward Bellamy and the Nationalist Movement* (1957). The most interpretative book to appear on Bellamy and his overall impact on American life is Arthur Lipow, *Authoritarian Socialism in America: Edward Bellamy & the Nationalist Movement* (1982).

Evaluation of Principal Biographical/Critical Sources

Bowman, Sylvia E., et al. *Edward Bellamy Abroad: An American Prophet's Influence.* New York: Twayne, 1962. **(A, G)** The authors trace the impact of Bellamy's social thought in major areas of the world, including Australia, Canada, France, Great Britain, Russia, and Scandinavia. They conclude that "there were no frantic enthusiasts who preached that Bellamy was the new messiah [and] . . .no violent opposition to his ideas."

Bowman, Sylvia E. *The Year 2000: A Critical Biography of Edward Bellamy.* New York: Bookman Associates, 1958. **(A, G)** This is a biography of Bellamy that fails to add much information to what Arthur Morgan wrote in 1944, although it provides a useful account of the antecedents of many of Bellamy's ideas. Bowman's literary style is often verbose and turgid.

Lipow, Arthur. *Authoritarian Socialism in America: Edward Bellamy & the Nationalist Movement.* Berkeley: University of California Press, 1982. **(A, G)** This thoughtful work offers a careful analysis of Bellamy's worldview in which Lipow contends that Bellamy embraced anti-democratic beliefs before mellowing, somewhat, in the late 1890s. Bellamy's core Nationalist vision was so conceptually authoritarian that it lacked any truly democratic qualities.

McNair, Everett. *Edward Bellamy and the Nationalist Movement*. Milwaukee: Fitzgerald, 1957. **(G)** This is an obscure and rather pedestrian review of Bellamy's labors as a social reformer between 1889 and 1894.

Morgan, Arthur E. *Edward Bellamy*. New York: Columbia University Press, 1944. **(A, G)** Written by a sympathetic scholar, this is an able account of Bellamy and the Nationalist crusade. Morgan, most of all, argues that Bellamy fortified the American mind against Marxism. He also shows that Bellamy enjoyed enormous appeal with the reading public and that he emerged as a type of folk hero.

Overview and Evaluation of Primary Sources

Fortunately, much of Bellamy's writings, correspondence, and the like are available in the Houghton Library of Harvard University in Cambridge, Massachusetts. Arthur E. Morgan gathered much of this collection, and he frequently translated Bellamy's nearly indecipherable handwriting into typescript. In the early 1960s Joseph Schiffman edited Bellamy's unpublished historical novel about Shays' Rebellion of the 1780s, *Duke of Stockbridge: A Romance of Shays' Rebellion* (Cambridge: Harvard University Press, 1962; **G**).

Other Sources

Filler, Louis. "Edward Bellamy and the Spiritual Unrest." *American Journal of Economics and Sociology* 8 (April 1949): 239–249. An interpretative biographical overview of Bellamy in the context of nineteenth-century reform.

Forbes, Allyn B. "The Literary Quest for Utopia, 1880–1890." *Social Forces* 6 (December 1927): 179–189. Places Bellamy's *Looking Backward* into the larger context of late-nineteenth-century utopian novels.

Sadler, Elizabeth. "One Book's Influence: Edward Bellamy's *Looking Backward*." *New England Quarterly* 17 (December 1944): 530–555. Reveals the enormous impact of *Looking Backward* upon contemporary and latter-day authors and social critics.

Shurter, Robert L. "The Writing of *Looking Backward*." *South Atlantic Quarterly* 38 (July 1939): 255–261. Explains the thought and motivations of Bellamy in creating *Looking Backward*.

Wilson, R. Jackson. "Experience and Utopia: The Making of Edward Bellamy's *Looking Backward*." *Journal of American Studies* 11 (1977): 45–60. Points out the powerful notions of pre-industrial thought in Bellamy's writings.

Zornow, William F. "Bellamy Nationalism in Ohio, 1891 to 1896." *Ohio State Archaeological and Historical Quarterly* 58 (April 1949): 152–170. Provides a useful review of the impact of nationalism at the grass-roots level.

H. Roger Grant
The University of Akron

JUDAH P. BENJAMIN
1811-1884

Chronology

Born Judah Philip Benjamin on August 6, 1811, on the island of St. Croix, British West Indies, the third child of Philip Benjamin, an English businessman of Jewish heritage, and Rebecca de Mendes Benjamin, descended from a family of Portugese Jews; *1813-1825* grows up in the American southeast, particularly Wilmington, North Carolina; is educated broadly in public schools and at Fayetteville Academy, Fayetteville, North Carolina; *1825-1827* attends Yale University, but leaves in 1827 without taking a degree; *1828-1832* settles in New Orleans, Louisiana, and earns living as an English tutor among the French Creoles of the city while studying for admittance to the bar; as a tutor, meets Natalie St. Martin, daughter of a wealthy Creole businessman, whom he marries in 1833; *1832-1842* practices law in New Orleans and becomes one of the most prosperous attorneys in the region; his influence is considerably enhanced with the publication of his *Digest of the Reported Decisions of the Superior Court of the Late Territory of Orleans and the Supreme Court of the State of Louisiana* (1834), prepared with Thomas Slidell; *1842-1852* as a member of the Whig Party, serves in the state legislature, as a delegate to the state constitutional convention (1844-1845), and as a presidential elector on the Whig ticket (1848); his eyesight temporarily fails and he retires to sugar plantation south of New Orleans, Bellechasse, and engages in scientific farming; *1853-1861* with eyesight fully restored, serves in U.S. Senate, forceful champion of Southern rights; after election of Abraham Lincoln to presidency, advocates separate secession of Louisiana from Union; *February 1861* is appointed Attorney General of the Confederacy by Jefferson Davis, a post in which his legal background and organizational abilities are clearly demonstrated; *September 1861-March 1862* serves as Confederate Secretary of War; *March 1862-1865* serves ably as Confederate Secretary of State; *1865-1883* with the collapse of the Confederacy, escapes to England and is admitted to the bar; conducts a legal career nothing less than spectacular until his retirement; *1883-1884* retires in Paris, France, the home of his wife since before the American Civil War; *1884* dies on May 6 at his Paris home and is buried at the cemetery of Père Lachaise.

Activities of Historical Significance

Judah P. Benjamin led three successful careers in two separate nations. The first was the practice of his legal profession in New Orleans before the Civil War. He became one of the most successful lawyers in the nation and certainly the best known in the American South. His forte was commercial law, a speciality that was particularly useful in the bustling seaport of New Orleans, and undoubtedly his

129

success can be attributed to several strengths that would be demonstrated throughout his life: his profound acquaintance with the principles of law and precedent, his capacity for logical analysis, and the extraordinary facility with which he expressed his arguments. Those who knew him said that he could overwhelm adversaries with the logic, presentation, sequence, and form of his position.

Benjamin's second career was in antebellum and Civil War politics. Again, the hardheaded approach he took toward legal matters and the manner in which he argued issues served him well in politics. Both as a participant in local politics and as Senator from Louisiana between 1853 and 1861, Benjamin distinguished himself as a formidable defender of what he considered, probably correctly, the wishes of the citizens of his state. Accordingly, Benjamin was a strong voice in the Senate for Southern rights and, hesitantly, for secession. He culminated his career in politics with a series of increasingly responsible positions within the Confederate Cabinet. As Attorney General, Secretary of War, and Secretary of State, Benjamin again used his skills as an organizer and master of logic to manage his organizations. He also became the confidant of Jefferson Davis, the harried and nervous President of the Confederacy, a development that caused considerable tension and mistrust within the government as others of lesser talent and envious nature accused Benjamin of manipulating Davis for his own ends. Benjamin weathered this controversy in silence, but it was one of the factors that led to his permanent estrangement from the Southern people. In spite of his able management of his responsibilities and his sacrifices as a member of the Confederacy's Cabinet, Benjamin has not received many of the accolades that have gone to other leaders of the "Lost Cause."

Unlike some of the other Confederate officials, Benjamin recognized the end of the rebellion in 1865 and successfully escaped to Great Britain, where he began his third career. This time, he returned to the legal profession and attained a stature even more revered than he had enjoyed as an attorney in New Orleans. As before, Benjamin specialized in commercial law and in appeals cases. He was particularly effective before the Judicial Committee and the House of Lords, where the gravity of the issues and the exceptional intellectual strength of the tribunal appeared to call forth all of his mental endowment and argumentative power.

All three of these careers were historically significant, and each would have been sufficient in itself to warrant close examination. Because he led all these careers, Judah P. Benjamin merits careful historical consideration.

Overview of Biographical Sources

In spite of the importance of the careers of Judah P. Benjamin, very little in the way of biographical research has appeared. Only five full-length biographies have appeared, and the second (Osterweis, *Judah P. Benjamin* [1934]) and the fourth (Neiman, *Judah Benjamin* [1963]) are essentially rehashes of earlier scholarship. The earliest biography, Pierce Butler's *Judah P. Benjamin* (1906), is a belated attempt to place Benjamin in the proper context in American history. It is belated in the sense that most of the other leaders of the "Lost Cause" had enjoyed laudatory biographical treatment from Southern writers. By far the most detailed, judicious, and interesting biography is Robert D. Meade's *Judah P. Benjamin: Confederate Statesman* (1943), although it is now some forty-five years old. Meade's portrait acknowledges Benjamin's obvious brilliance and persistence, but never falls into sentimentality. He perceives Benjamin as a capable man who worked hard, used his talents well, and made enormous mistakes when he tried to venture outside his tried skills. Nonetheless, Meade interprets Benjamin as a statesman in the best sense of the word. Eli Evans's new biography, *Judah P. Benjamin: The Jewish Confederate* (1987), is a welcome addition to the literature. Most of the remaining scholarship considers Benjamin as a member of a larger group, as a member of the legal profession, as a member of the Confederate Cabinet, or as one of the several defenders of Southern rights.

Evaluation of Principal Biographical Sources

Butler, Pierce. *Judah P. Benjamin*. Philadelphia: Macrae-Smith, 1906. Reprint. New York: Chelsea House, 1981. **(A, G)** The first biography of Judah P. Benjamin and still a good one, though it is highly partisan in tone.

Evans, Eli. *Judah P. Benjamin: The Jewish Confederate*. New York: The Free Press, 1987. **(A, G)** This is the most significant study of Benjamin since Meade's 1943 work. It covers his life in detail.

Meade, Robert D. *Judah P. Benjamin: Confederate Statesman*. New York: Oxford University Press, 1943. Reprint. New York: Ayer, 1975. **(A, G)** This is a solid scholarly work that covers Benjamin's life in detail. It is the best biography available.

Neiman, Simon I. *Judah Benjamin*. Indianapolis: Bobbs-Merrill, 1963. **(G)** A chatty rehash of the work of earlier scholars which tries to read some questionable insights into his emotional life.

Osterweis, Rollin C. *Judah P. Benjamin: Statesman of the Lost Cause*. New York: Harper and Brothers, 1934. **(A, G)** This biography was published between the early work of Pierce Butler and the more recent and authoritative work of Robert Meade. It has very little distinction otherwise.

Patrick, Rembert W. *Jefferson Davis and His Cabinet*. Baton Rouge: Louisiana State University Press, 1944. **(A, G)** This book is the best summary of the activities of the executive branch of the Confederacy, paying careful attention to the close relationship between Benjamin and Jefferson Davis.

Pollock, Charles. "Reminiscenses of Judah Philip Benjamin." *Fortnightly Review*

69 (March 1898): 354–361. **(A, G)** A positive remembrance of Benjamin by a close associate in England.

Strode, Hudson. "Judah P. Benjamin's Loyalty to Jefferson Davis." *Georgia Review* 20 (Spring 1966): 251–260. **(A, G)** This short article is a useful study of the relationship between Benjamin and Davis in the Confederate Cabinet.

Overview and Evaluation of Primary Sources

Biographer Robert D. Meade called Judah P. Benjamin "one of the most secretive men who ever lived." He left no autobiographical accounts and no large corpus of personal papers. Some of his speeches, most from his Senatorial career, have been included in Volume 1 of *The Library of Southern Literature* (Atlanta: n.p., 1907). A compilation of important papers from the Confederacy, including most of the diplomatic correspondence with which Benjamin was associated, can be found in James D. Richardson's two-volume *The Messages and Papers of Jefferson Davis and the Confederacy, Including Diplomatic Correspondence, 1861–1865* (Washington, DC: Government Printing Office, 1907. Reprint. New York: Chelsea House, 1966). Benjamin's War Department activities for the Confederacy can be traced using the U.S. War Department, *War of the Rebellion: A Compilation of the Official Records of the Union and Confederate Armies*, 128 vols. (Washington, DC: Government Printing Office, 1880–1901). Benjamin published two legal works during his lifetime: *Digest of the Reported Decisions of the Superior Court of the Late Territory of Orleans and the Supreme Court of the State of Louisiana* (New Orleans: n.p., 1834), with Thomas Slidell, and *A Treatise on the Law of Sale of Personal Property, with Reference to the American Decisions, to the French Code and Civil Law* (London: n.p., 1868).

Benjamin's unpublished primary documents are even less plentiful. Perhaps the most extensive collection is located at the American Jewish Archives, Cincinnati, Ohio, but it is still less than one hundred items and, in part, is made up of transcripts and photocopies of papers in other repositories. Other, albeit much smaller, collections can be found at the American Jewish Historical Society, Waltham, Massachusetts; the Library of Congress, Washington, D.C., which has a Benjamin diary; the Louisiana State Museum, New Orleans; and the Alderman Library of the University of Virginia, Charlottesville.

Two of Benjamin's associates left first-hand accounts that are useful sources. For Benjamin's political life, Jefferson Davis's *The Rise and the Fall of the Confederate Government*, 2 vols. (New York: Appleton, 1881; **A, G**) is an able defense of the attempted revolution that led to the Civil War. Benjamin played a major role in the government of the Confederacy, and his ideas and policies are discussed here from the perspective of a close associate. For Benjamin's personal life, Virginia Clay-Clopton's *A Belle of the Fifties* (New York: Doubleday, Doran, 1905; **A, G**) is a lively presentation of society in the nation's capital when Benjamin resided there as

Senator from Louisiana. The author, wife of Clement Clay, Senator from Alabama, relates several stories concerning Benjamin, including that of an extended visit from his wife, Natalie, who did not live with him and had been rumored to have been involved in affairs with other men.

Fiction and Adaptations

Only one fictional work of note has appeared. Vina Delmar's *Beloved* (1956) is a syrupy romance story. Using the distressed marriage of Judah P. Benjamin and Natalie St. Martin as a starting point, the author presents a story of true love juxtaposed against divergent ideals, goals, and capabilities. From the 1840s, Natalie lived in Paris, ostensibly to allow for the proper education of their daughter, while her husband continued his career in Louisiana. They never divorced and apparently maintained an amiable relationship from afar, although rumors of infidelity on both sides surfaced periodically. Near the end of his life Benjamin returned to his wife's home and eventually died there. All this is grist for Delmar's historical romance. While the basic facts of the life of Benjamin are correct, the author takes considerable literary license with the weaving of the plot around the historical framework

Museums, Historical Landmarks, Societies

American Jewish Archives (Cincinnati, OH). Holds photograph collection on Judah Benjamin, his career, and his period.

American Jewish Historical Society (Waltham, MA). In addition to some Benjamin personal papers, houses memorabilia about Jewish Americans.

Judah P. Benjamin Confederate Memorial At Gamble Plantation State Historic Site (Ellenton, FL). This antebellum plantation with period furnishings and artifacts serves as a memorial to Benjamin.

Louisiana State Museum (New Orleans, LA). Houses a portrait and other memorabilia of Judah P. Benjamin.

Museum of the Confederacy (Richmond, VA). Contains displays of Richmond during the Confederacy and memorabilia from period.

Other Sources

Curron, C. "The Three Lives of Judah P. Benjamin." *History Today* 17 (September 1967): 583–592. A reasonable interpretation of the three stages of Benjamin's career.

Owsley, Frank L. *King Cotton Diplomacy: Foreign Relations of the Confederate States of America.* Chicago: University of Chicago Press, 1931; rev. ed. 1959. A classic account of the execution of foreign relations by the Confederate States during the Civil War. Benjamin, as Secretary of State throughout much of the period, plays a central role in this analysis.

Thomas, Emory M. *The Confederate Nation.* New York: Harper and Row, 1979. An excellent general account of the rise and fall of the Confederacy, emphasizing the nationalism of the region. Benjamin plays a role in the work because of his high position in the government.

Roger D. Launius
Military Airlift Command

Fort Sumter, 1961

THOMAS HART BENTON
1782–1858

Chronology

Born Thomas Hart Benton on March 14, 1782, in Hillsboro, North Carolina, the son of Jesse Benton, a former secretary of the royal governor of Virginia, and Ann Gooch Benton, also of Virginia stock; *1782–1798* grows up on a plantation near Hillsboro, reared mainly by his mother who is widowed when Thomas is eight; *1799* briefly attends the University of North Carolina, where he is expelled for stealing from fellow students; *1801* moves with his mother and seven other siblings to a plantation south of Nashville, Tennessee; *1809* is elected a state senator; *1811* is admitted to the bar; *1812–1815* serves as colonel of Tennessee volunteer regiment but sees no combat other than a brawl in Nashville on September 4, 1813, in which he and his brother Jesse nearly kill Andrew Jackson; *1815–1820* moves to St. Louis, Missouri, practices law, edits a newspaper, and is elected to United States Senate when Missouri becomes a state; *1821* marries Elizabeth McDowell of Virginia, a union that produces seven children; *1821–1851* serves in Senate, during which period he becomes acknowledged representative of western interests, promotes exploration and settlement of West, acts as Senate spokesman of President Jackson (with whom he is reconciled), champions gold and silver currency with result that he acquires sobriquet of "Old Bullion," favors moderate policy regarding acquisition of Texas and Oregon, and opposes the extreme proslavery and secessionist tendencies of the South; *1853–1855* serves in House of Representatives where he opposes the Kansas-Nebraska bill's repeal of the Missouri Compromise; *1854–1856* publishes *Thirty Years View*; *1856* runs unsuccessfully for governor of Missouri; *1857* publishes first volumes of *Abridgement of the Debates of Congress from 1789 to 1856* and *Historical and Legal Examination . . . of the Dred Scott Case*; *1858* dies on April 10 in Washington, D.C., of cancer.

Activities of Historical Significance

Benton was one of the giants of the Senate in its Golden Age. Just as Daniel Webster spoke for New England and John C. Calhoun for the Old South, Benton advocated the interests of the emerging West. Thus he was one of the first to propose what eventually became the Homestead Act, was an eloquent and effective champion of "Manifest Destiny," and in particular provided both backing and inspiration for the western explorations of his son-in-law, the "Pathfinder" John C. Frémont, whose conquest of California at the outbreak of the Mexican War in 1846 was probably executed at the request of Benton.

The most dramatic period in Benton's long Senate career occurred when President Andrew Jackson campaigned to abolish the Bank of the United States. Siding with Jackson, Benton helped to initiate the "Bank War," held his own in fierce debates with such defenders of the Bank as Daniel Webster and Henry Clay, and successfully led the fight to expunge a Senate resolution condemning Jackson for removing the government's deposits from the Bank. Although historians continue to debate the consequences of Jackson's triumph over the Bank, there is no doubt that Benton played a key role in achieving it.

Largely because of his western outlook Benton, although a southerner and slave-holder, broke with his native section over the issue of slavery expansion. In his opinion, which seems justified both in logic and fact, slavery was incompatible with the geography, climate, social and economic needs, and the very spirit of the West; hence, it was both wrong and futile for the South to insist upon maintaining the right to hold slaves there. Because of his stand on slavery, he sacrificed his hitherto invincible political domination of Missouri and lost his seat in the Senate. Nonetheless, by championing the cause of the Union, he helped keep Missouri from seceding when the Civil War came three years after his death.

Overview of Biographical Sources

Many of his contemporaries considered Benton equal, even superior, to Daniel Webster, Henry Clay, and John C. Calhoun in ability and influence. Nonetheless, because he never ran for president, served in the cabinet, or developed a distinctive ideology, he has not achieved their historical status. The first biography did not appear until 1886, a short and superficial work written by the young Theodore Roosevelt. Next came William M. Meig, *The Life of Thomas Hart Benton* (1904), and Joseph M. Rogers, *Thomas H. Benton* (1905), both of which are superior to Roosevelt's effort but still deficient in research and interpretation. Not until the appearance of William Nisbet Chambers, *Old Bullion Benton: Senator from the New West* (1956), and Elbert R. Smith, *Magnificent Missourian: The Life of Thomas Hart Benton* (1958), did his private life and public career receive full, scholarly, and perhaps definitive treatment. Finally, various issues of the *Missouri Historical Review* contain scholarly articles dealing with aspects of Benton's career.

Evaluation of Principal Biographical Sources

Chambers, William Nisbet. *Old Bullion Benton: Senator From the New West.* Boston: Little, Brown, 1956. Reprint. New York: Russell & Russell, 1970. **(A, G)** This is the most detailed and scholarly biography, based on exhaustive research of both primary and secondary sources. Although sympathetic to Benton, it criticizes him regarding particular matters and generally is balanced in its analyses.

James, Marquis. *Andrew Jackson: The Border Captain* and *Andrew Jackson: Portrait of a President.* Indianapolis and New York: Bobbs-Merrill, 1933–1937. **(A, G)** These works, which can be found in a one-volume edition, provide much information about Benton's careers in Tennessee and Washington, D.C., particularly as they related to Jackson.

Nevins, Allan. *Frémont: Pathmarker of the West*. 1939. Rev. ed. New York: Longmans, Green, 1955. **(A, G)** This provides the most detailed, best documented, and most objective account of the relationship between Benton and Frémont, particularly as regards Frémont's controversial activities in California during the Mexican War.

Remini, Robert V. *Andrew Jackson and the Course of American Empire, 1767–1821; Andrew Jackson and the Course of American Freedom, 1822–1832; Andrew Jackson and the Course of American Democracy, 1833–1845*. New York: Harper & Row, 1977–1984. **(A, G)** Supplements and on some matters corrects James's biography of Jackson with reference to relationships between Jackson and Benton. The best general history of the period covered by the balance of Benton's career.

Schlesinger, Arthur M., Jr. *The Age of Jackson*. Boston: Little, Brown, 1945. **(A, G)** Written with a strong pro-Jackson, pro-Democratic bias, this gives a dramatic, multi-faceted account of the Jacksonian era and contains much about Benton's part in it.

Smith, Elbert A. *Magnificent Missourian: The Life of Thomas Hart Benton*. Philadelphia and New York: J. B. Lippincott, 1958. **(A, G)** Although scholarly, this work is not as thoroughly researched and documented as Chambers's biography. On the other hand, it is more readable and, apart from a tendency to speculate beyond what the factual record supports, sometimes more perceptive in its analyses.

Overview and Evaluation of Primary Sources
The main published primary source on Benton's life is his *Thirty Years View*, 2 vols. (New York: D. Appleton, 1854–1856; **A**), particularly those editions containing his "Auto-Biographical Sketch," which was dictated from his death bed. (Not all editions contain this sketch.) Most of this work consists of summaries of Congressional debates and long quotations from Benton's own speeches, but it also contains much valuable information on leading men and events of his time and his views on both. Benton's daughter, Jessie Benton Frémont, provides some firsthand information about him in "Biographical Sketch of Senator Benton in Connection with Western Expansion" contained in John Charles Frémont, *Memoirs of My Life* (Chicago: Belford, Clarke, 1886; **A, G**); in "Senator Thomas Hart Benton," *Independent* (January 1903); and in *Souvenirs of My Time* (Boston: D. Lothrop, 1887; **A, G**).

Also of great value is the diary of President James K. Polk, which is available in two editions: Milo M. Quaife, ed., *The Diary of James K. Polk during his Presi-*

dency, 1845 to 1849 (Chicago: Chicago Historical Society, 1910; **A**), and Allan Nevins, ed., *The Diary of a President, 1845–1849* (London and New York: Longmans, Green, 1952; **A**). Until he had a falling out with Polk over Frémont's activities in California, Benton was highly influential in his administration and this diary reveals the nature and extent of that influence.

The largest collection of Benton's personal papers is at the Missouri Historical Society, St. Louis. Many letters to and from Benton are found in the papers of Andrew Jackson, Martin Van Buren, and James K. Polk, all in the Library of Congress, Washington, D.C.

Museums, Historical Landmarks, Societies

Bellefontaine Cemetery (St. Louis, MO). Benton's tomb.

Capitol (Washington, DC). Statue of Benton.

Lafayette Park (St. Louis, MO). Monument to Benton erected in 1869. Consists of a statue of him standing on a base inscribed with a quotation from one of his speeches urging expansion to the Pacific: "There is the East, there is India."

Other Sources

Castel, Albert. "Thomas Hart Benton—Champion of the West." *American History Illustrated* 2 (July 1967): 12–20. A "personality profile" of Benton emphasizing his role in promoting western exploration and expansion.

Chambers, William N. "Thomas Hart Benton." In *The Encyclopedia of American Biography*, edited by John A. Garraty and Jerome L. Sternstein. New York: Harper & Row, 1974. Concise account and interpretation of Benton's career by his leading biographer.

Albert Castel
Western Michigan University

Missouri 1821·1971 United States 8c

Missouri 150th Anniversary, 1971

MARY McLEOD BETHUNE
1875–1955

Chronology

Born Mary McLeod on July 10, 1875, one of seventeen children on a plantation in Mayesville, South Carolina, where her parents, Samuel and Patsy McLeod, have worked since the Civil War; *1880–1884* works as a field hand on a neighboring farm, picking cotton on the McLeod and McIntosh plantations; *1884* sent to a mission school supported by a northern Presbyterian church five miles from her home; *1890* graduates from the Mayesville School after six years of study; ambitions to continue her education are thwarted by the death of the family mule, a financial disaster for the large family; takes turns shouldering the yoke and planting cotton for the family's survival; receives a scholarship funded by a woman in Denver, Colorado, and leaves to study at the Scotia Seminary for Girls in Concord, North Carolina, where she distinguishes herself in public speaking and debate; *1893* receives a scholarship to the Moody Bible Institute in Chicago, where she spends the next two years; *1895–1900* joins Lucy Laney and teaches at the Haines Institute in Augusta, Georgia; moves to Sumter, South Carolina, to teach for two years; meets and marries Albertus Bethune; they move to Savannah, Georgia, where she gives birth to her only child, a son; the family moves to Palatka, Florida, where her husband dies; *1904* establishes a small school in Daytona, Florida, with six children in attendance; *1905* a charter is granted to the school and it officially becomes the Dayton Normal and Industrial Institute for Negro Scholars; *1907* the school moves into a new building and continues to expand; *1922* the school comes under the Methodist Episcopal Church, which suggests that it merge with Cookman College for Boys in Jacksonville; the new institution is renamed Bethune-Cookman College; *1924–1928* is founder and president of the National Association of Colored Women's Clubs; *1934* appointed by President Roosevelt to direct the Division of Negro Affairs of the National Youth Administration; further serves Roosevelt as a special advisor on minority affairs; *1935–1936* receives the Spingarn Medal and the Francis A. Drexel Award for services to the black race; *1942–1955* retires as president of the college; serves as special assistant to the secretary of war for selection of the first schools for WAC officer candidates; receives many honorary degrees, awards, and citations for her work; serves as vice president of both the National Urban League and the National Association for the Advancement of Colored People; *1955* dies on May 18 in Daytona Beach, Florida.

Activities of Historical Significance

Bethune's reputation rests on her achievements as an educator of black people in the South. At the time she founded her college, she was a product and exponent of the educational theories of Booker T. Washington, who advocated the manual arts as the proper curriculum for black people. Bethune's college stressed instruction in cooking, sewing, farming, foods, health, child care, animal husbandry, agriculture, and the mechanical trades. She has been criticized for not advocating professional training for blacks, and thereby contributing to their continued lower socio-economic status. However, her contemporaries viewed her approach to education as pragmatic and necessary. Bethune was praised in her own lifetime by Ida M. Tarbell as "one of the most potent factors in the growth of interracial good will in America."

Bethune was also one of the earliest archivists and historians of black women in America. She worked with Mary Beard at the World Center for Women's Archives to preserve documents relating to black women's history. She also established the National Archives for Black Women's History in Washington, D.C., in order, as she herself stated, "to tell in concrete form the story of the contribution of Negro Women to American life."

Overview of Biographical Sources

A satisfactory life of Bethune has yet to be written. Ralph Bullock, *In Spite of Handicaps* (1927), the only full length biography written for adults, presents Bethune as a role model for black women. Predictably, this laudatory account bears a closer resemblance to a hagiography than to a scholarly biography. Ella Kaiser Carruth, *She Wanted to Read: The Story of Mary McLeod Bethune* (1966), offers eighty pages of praise about Bethune in a biography written for young readers.

The lack of biographical data on Bethune is balanced by a plentitude of critical evaluation of her work. Though recent critics have disapproved of Bethune's advocacy of manual labor at the expense of professional training for blacks, her contemporaries praised her pragmatism. These early supporters extolled Bethune's oratorical skills, woman's rights activities, and educational contributions.

Bethune's life and work have been summarized in a number of general surveys appearing in anthologies and reference works.

Evaluation of Principal Biographical Sources

Brawley, Benjamin. *Negro Builders and Heroes*. Chapel Hill: University of North Carolina Press, 1937. **(A, G)** Contains a brief sketch of Bethune's life and work.

————. *Women of Achievement*. Chicago: Baptist Society, 1919. **(A)** A period piece of black history containing a sketch of Bethune's early work.

Bullock, Ralph. *In Spite of Handicaps*. New York: Association Press, 1927. **(A, G)** Like other early black histories, this work verges on hagiography in presenting

Bethune as a role model for black women, but is valuable as the only comprehensive biography for adults.

Carruth, Ella Kaiser. *She Wanted to Read: The Story of Mary McLeod Bethune*. Nashville: Abingdon, 1966. (**Y**) This eighty-page biography is written especially for young people.

Lerner, Gerda. *Black Women in White America: A Documentary History*. New York: Pantheon, 1972. (**A**) Lerner collects documentation on aspects of black women's experiences in America, including the typical education provided for black women as well as the National Club Movement, of which Bethune was a leader.

Massie, Dorothy C. *The Legacy of Mary McLeod Bethune*. Washington, DC: National Education Association, 1974. (**A, G**) This thirty-five-page pamphlet attempts to restore Bethune's reputation as a prominent black educator and role model for contemporary black teachers and administrators.

Overview and Evaluation of Primary Sources

Bethune's primary sources are limited to just three brief magazine articles. She discusses the need for black youths to learn about their history and culture in an article entitled "Clarifying Our Vision with the Facts," *Journal of Negro History* 23 (1938; **A, G**). Bethune contends that this knowledge would give youths confidence, self-reliance, and courage. In "I Work with Youth," *Brown American* 1 (1939; **A, G**), she writes about the joy she found in preparing young blacks for the work world. *Ebony* (September 1963; **A, G**) published Bethune's "My Last Will and Testament" in a special issue dedicated to her legacy.

Museums, Historical Landmarks, Societies

Amistad Research Center (New Orleans, LA). The repository of all of Bethune's private papers, this center also holds one of the largest collections of documents related to black history, including 8,000,000 manuscripts, 10,000 pictures, 3,500 microforms, and 500 audiotapes.

Bethune Historical Development Project (Washington, DC). The headquarters of the National Council for Negro Women, founded by Bethune.

Mary McLeod Bethune Home (Daytona Beach, FL). Called the "Retreat," this house was built in 1920 by Bethune's friends for her retirement. Located on the campus of Bethune-Cookman College, the two-story frame house was proclaimed a National Historic Landmark in 1974.

Mary McLeod Bethune Landmark (Washington, DC). Located in Lincoln Park, this statue of Bethune was erected in 1947.

Other Sources

Bartlett, R. M. *They Did Something About It*. New York: Association Press, 1939. A discussion of Bethune's efforts to transform the black community through education.

Boulware, Marcus. *The Oratory of Negro Leaders: 1900–1968*. Westport, CT: Negro University Press, 1969. Contains a brief overview of Bethune as an effective orator, particularly in regard to fund raising efforts for her college.

Brewer, William M. "Mary McLeod Bethune." *Negro History Bulletin* 19 (1955): 36. A short piece stressing Bethune's activities as a woman's rights leader.

Daniels, Sadie I. *Women Builders*. Washington, DC: Association Press, 1931. Contains a section on Bethune's educational contributions.

Dannett, Sylvia. *Profiles of Negro Womanhood*. Vol. 1. Chicago: Educational Heritage, 1964. Contains an analysis of Bethune's life and work.

Fleming, Alice. *Great Women Teachers*. Philadelphia: J. B. Lippincott, 1965. Bethune is the only black woman in this collection of life stories of ten great educators.

Low, W. Augustus, and Virgil A. Clift, eds. *Encyclopedia of Black America*. New York: McGraw-Hill, 1981. Contains entries on Bethune and the history of Bethune-Cookman College.

Peters, Margaret. *The Ebony Book of Black Achievement*. Chicago: Johnson Publishing, 1970. Contains an overview of Bethune's educational accomplishments.

Ploski, Harry, and James Williams, eds. *The Negro Almanac: A Reference Work on the Afro-American*. 4th ed. New York: Wiley, 1983. Contains a sketch of Bethune.

Richardson, Ben. *Great American Negroes*. New York: Crowell, 1956. Contains a sketch of Bethune's life and achievements.

Diane Long Hoeveler
Marquette University

BILLY THE KID
c.1859–1881

Chronology

Born Henry McCarty, probably on November 23, 1859, and probably in New York City, to Michael and Catherine McCarty; *1861–1865* father is killed in the Civil War, and the family moves to Indianapolis; *1870* with a friend, William Antrim, mother and sons move to Wichita, Kansas, where she operates a laundry; *1871* the group leaves Wichita and moves either to Colorado or New Mexico; *1873* Catherine McCarty marries William Antrim in Santa Fe, New Mexico, and they move to Silver City, where Henry attends school; *1874* his mother dies; *1875* Henry is arrested for stealing clothing, a crime he did not commit; imprisoned, he escapes, fleeing to Globe, Arizona; *1875–1876* works as a ranch hand, teamster, or sheepherder and is sometimes a "saddle tramp"; *1877* kills his first victim, Frank P. "Windy" Cahill, near Camp Grant, Arizona, is arrested and escapes; *Fall 1877* assumes the name of William H. Bonney and appears in Lincoln County, New Mexico, to work for John H. Tunstall; variously known as William Antrim, "Kid" Antrim, Billy Bonney, Billy Kid, or Billy the Kid for the remainder of his life; *1878–1879* becomes involved in the "Lincoln County War," a political, financial, and land struggle between contending groups of politicians, bankers, and speculators; shoots one man and perhaps several more, but the leaders of his group, Tunstall and Alexander McSween, are killed, and another erstwhile friend, John Chisum, withdraws from the struggle; *1880* accused of murder and cattle theft; is pursued by newly appointed Lincoln County sheriff, Pat Garrett, who captures and jails him; *1881* convicted of murder and sentenced to be hanged, escapes, killing two guards; dies on July 14 when Garrett corners him at the home of Pete Maxwell in Fort Sumner, New Mexico, shoots and kills him.

Activities of Historical Significance

The historical Billy the Kid is relatively unimportant. He lived just 21 years and attracted attention for two or three years. His fame was as a western "gunslinger," but his life, as it is reconstructed, does not entirely bear this out. He was caught up in the Lincoln County War in the New Mexico Territory as a hired man who became involved in the fighting; he was generally mistreated by all sides. At the end of the "war" he turned to cattle rustling and still faced a murder charge. He was subsequently captured, tried, and convicted of the murder of Sheriff William Brady, who may have been shot by Billy but was surely shot by others as well. The sheriff, a henchman of the group opposing the Kid's friends, suffered eight bullet wounds in a general gunfight that involved at least 11 men. Billy the Kid later

143

escaped, killing his two guards. He was subsequently shot to death by Sheriff Pat Garrett.

History has produced far more ghastly killers than Billy the Kid, and far more spectacular bad men. He claimed that he killed 21 men, but the true figure is much less. In fact, the Lincoln County War involved abler gunfighters and more competent desperadoes.

Billy the Kid became significant not for what he did, but for what others said he did. As one of his best biographers puts it, the Kid was "invented." He was a media figure almost from the beginning, one of the nation's earliest. The New Mexico press covered his exploits intently, while correspondents from eastern newspapers and magazines elaborated and glorified the minute details of his few years as an outlaw. Moreover, dime novels, especially western tales, were in vogue during the late nineteenth century, and stories of Billy the Kid proved to be particularly popular. From these rather humble beginnings more serious mythologizers took over.

Although no one can say for certain why Billy became the premier western bad man, he did. More so than Jesse James, the Daltons, or John Wesley Hardin, he was the prototype of what a true western villain should be, angelic and at times devilishly bad. Perhaps his youth was a reason for his immense legendary fame. He coupled the tenderness of years with the incongruity of a passion for homicide. It may be that his larger-than-legend stature is the result of confusion about the Lincoln County War. Some saw his side as the underdog in that brief bloody moment when the economically and culturally oppressed struggled mightily and unsuccessfully against their oppressors.

It has been suggested that Billy the Kid became legendary as an expression of opposition to the industrial-urban dislocation underway in America. It is generally believed that western cowboys enjoyed a freedom that urban dwellers no longer possess, and that a yearning to return to simpler times explains Billy the Kid's popularity. Interestingly, the industrial progress of the 1880s and 1890s that created America's cities helped the legend of Billy the Kid grow. Progress provided improved communications and publishing methods that allowed tales of his exploits to be spread around the country.

Overview of Biographical Sources

Pat Garrett and Ash Upson, a pioneer New Mexico newpaperman, wrote *The Authentic Life of Billy the Kid* (1882) and provided the impetus for some of the more believable aspects of the legend. At least they claimed they were correcting the exaggerations of dime novelists. During the late nineteenth century many writers began to weave the character of Billy the Kid into their more general books about the West. Emerson Hough's *The Story of the Cowboy* (1897) was especially influential. Biographies of the legendary figure have continued since. The Billy the Kid who emerges from these works is a dichotomized character. To some he is a dashing, romantic, kind-hearted, carefree "Robin Hood of the West," to others, a heartless, evil, mean-spirited, fiendish shootist.

Serious biographies of him have been rare indeed. Some of the best scholarship is found in regional historical journals and in papers presented by individuals at popular history associations. Since the 1950s several outstanding critical bibliographies of studies have been produced. The organization of each is such that they present the essentials of his life and ought to be considered as representatives of a relatively new historical genre, the bio-bibliography. Several of these are listed as biographies since they represent the best work done thus far. Of special note is J. C. Dykes, *Billy the Kid: The Bibliography of a Legend* (1952).

Obviously, publications about the Kid have been troubled by the legend-making process, requiring caution on the part of readers who want more than entertainment. Of the Kid's twenty-one years, only those from 1877 to 1881 receive much attention. These four years were the most exciting and the only ones for which there is much documentation.

Evaluation of Principal Biographical Sources

Adams, Ramon F. *A Fitting Death for Billy the Kid*. Norman: University of Oklahoma Press, 1960. **(A, G)** Adams was the West's most famous critical bibliographer, intent on removing the hokum, errors, and straight-out lies from "Western Studies." In this "bio-bibliography" he attempts to correct "accounts that have already been written about [Billy the Kid] under the guise of fact." Adams is concerned with the printed word in newspapers, magazines, novels, biographies, general histories, etc. Unlike J. C. Dykes, Adams gives a narrative presentation. Although both men were excellent bibliographers, Adams appears to have had the more critical eye.

Burns, Walter Noble. *The Saga of Billy the Kid*. Garden City: Doubleday Page, 1926. **(A, G)** Burns, a journalist, interviewed several women involved in Billy the Kid's life, including his sweetheart, Paulita Maxwell, the daughter of the man who owned the ranch where he was killed. Burns is credited with creating the "Janus image," the notion that Billy the Kid was a "good guy" and at times a "bad hombre." He used the Garrett-Upson biography and invented some legends of his own. These include such errors as the assertion that the Kid's dad was named William H. Bonney, Sr., and that he died in Coffeyville, Kansas, in 1862, long before there was such a town. He claimed that Billy was a big-time cattle rustler, and that the song Mrs. McSween supposedly played on her piano while her house burnt during a gunfight was the "Star Spangled Banner." Burns also invented dialogue. There is some doubt about whether this book should be considered biography.

Cline, Donald. *Alias Billy the Kid: The Man Behind the Legend*. Santa Fe: Sunstone Press, 1986. **(A, G)** As the most recent biography of the Kid, this volume incorporates a great deal of modern scholarship and concludes that Billy the Kid was a poor excuse for a hero and does not deserve the image of a noble outlaw. Some will decry this conclusion as being misleading and as unnecessarily perpetuating the negative side of the myth.

Dykes, J. C. *Billy the Kid: The Bibliography of a Legend*. Albuquerque: University of New Mexico Press, 1952. **(A, G)** Dykes includes 437 annotated entries and asks his readers to inform him of any he missed.

Garrett, Pat F. *The Authentic Life of Billy the Kid, The Noted Desperado of the Southwest*. Santa Fe: New Mexico Printing and Publishing, 1882. **(A, G)** The biography credited with starting the legend. Most believe it to have been written by Ash Upson, a pioneer New Mexico newspaperman, who was told the story by Garrett. Although it has influenced almost all subsequent writings on the Kid, it is replete with errors. Tuska in his bio-bibliography lists 75 major mistakes and says there are many more minor ones. The greatest error is the statement that Billy the Kid was born William H. Bonney. Others concern the number of people he supposedly killed, that he was a heavy drinker, a superb marksman, a keen horseman, and that he was a major cattle thief. Perhaps the most incriminating assertion is that Billy the Kid was armed when Garrett shot him. This bit of dissembling is said to be the main reason that Garrett helped write the book.

Hunt, Frazier. *The Tragic Days of Billy the Kid*. New York: Hastings House, 1956. **(A, G)** Ramon Adams calls this a "splendid and accurate" account, but not all other bibliographers and biographers agree. They note various errors of fact and emphasize that Hunt depended heavily on the Garrett-Upson and Walter Burns books for his information. Hunt presents the Kid as a quixotic romantic destined to meet a tragic death at the hands of the law. Hunt is more sympathetically inclined than Garrett-Upson.

Otero, Miguel Antonio. *The Real Billy The Kid with New Light on the Lincoln County War*. New York: Rufus Rockwell Wison, 1936. **(A)** A former governor of New Mexico, Otero wrote this book to correct errors in Garrett-Upson's biography. He made mistakes of his own but was the first writer to prove conclusively that Billy the Kid was not armed with a pistol when Garrett shot him. Otero, who favored the Tunstall-McSween faction, called Garrett "a horse thief and a coward." Despite his avowed purpose, he used a great deal of the Garrett-Upson account in this volume.

Tatum, Stephen. *Inventing Billy the Kid, Visions of the Outlaw in America, 1881–1891*. Albuquerque: The University of New Mexico Press, 1982. **(A)** Examines how the legend was invented and discusses the "cultural preoccupation" of his interpreters. In the process, Tatum reveals how modern America has created and dealt with its legends. His brief biographical account is less skeptical of earlier works than some students of this era, and it incorporates information that earlier writers doubted or considered wrong. Thus, he has Billy the Kid armed with a butcher knife and having a Colt .41 in his waistband when Garrett shot him. It is not as biography that this book should be judged, but rather as the study of a legend. As such, it is an interesting, provoking account based on various types of coverage of its subject: movies, novels, and books.

Tuska, Jon. *Billy the Kid, A Bio-bibliography*. Westport, CT: Greenwood Press, 1983. **(A, G)** This volume advances the study of Billy the Kid about as far as it can go. If one reads only one book, it should be this. The first 100 pages are a deftly crafted biography based on the latest scholarship and textual criticism. Other sections consider the character of Billy the Kid in history, fiction, film, and legend. Of course, concern with the legend overlaps all parts of the book. Tuska carries forward, supplements, and expands the work of J. C. Dykes and Ramon Adams. This volume complements Stephen Tatum's study, a work Tuska criticizes severely. Tuska reissued the book as *Billy the Kid: A Handbook* (Lincoln: University of Nebraska Press, 1986).

Overview and Evaluation of Primary Sources

Several of the secondary works listed above include original source materials on the life of Billy the Kid, but the main printed resources are a few autobiographies of individuals involved in his life and death. Pat Garrett's unreliable *The Authentic Life of Billy the Kid* is a primary source, as is that of Garrett's deputy, John W. Poe, *The Death of Billy the Kid* (Boston and New York: Houghton Mifflin Company, 1933; **A, G**). As the title page notes, Poe was "present at the killing" in 1881.

An account considered more accurate than either of the above is Eve Ball's *Ma'am Jones of the Pecos* (Tucson: University of Arizona Press, 1969; **A, G**). This is an oral history presentation of a woman who knew Billy the Kid and is deemed reliable.

Accounts that are suspect and should be used with caution include George W. Coe, *Frontier Fighter: The Autobiography of George W. Coe Who Fought and Rode with Billy the Kid as Related to Nan Hillary Harrison* (Boston: Houghton Mifflin, 1934; **A, G**); Lily Klassner, *My Girlhood Among Outlaws*, edited with introduction by Eve Ball (Tucson: University of Arizona Press, 1972; **A, G**); and two by Charles A. Siringo, *A History of "Billy the Kid,"* (Santa Fe: n.p., 1920; **A, G**) and *A Texas Cowboy; Or Fifteen Years on the Hurricane Deck of a Spanish Pony— Taken From Real Life*, edited with an introduction by J. Frank Dobie (Lincoln: University of Nebraska Press, 1966; **A, G**). This latter is a reprint of an 1885 edition and is considered to be the first ever autobiography of a cowboy.

In addition to contemporary government documents, newspapers, and magazine accounts, several manuscript collections can be consulted: Thomas B. Catron Papers, University of New Mexico Library, Albuquerque; Colonel Maurice Garland Fulton Papers, University of Arizona Library, Tucson; Robert N. Mullin Papers,

Evetts Haley Library, Midland, Texas; and various oral history interviews at the Panhandle-Plains Historical Museum, Canyon, Texas.

Like other notorious people, Billy the Kid has at least one book that claims he was not shot in 1881, but lived to a ripe old age in the twentieth century. The fact that a well-known western historian, C. L. Sonnichsen, helped prepare the book entitles it to more than passing notice. The narrative, which is brief, is supplied by Brushy Bill Roberts, alias Billy the Kid, and included are public documents bearing on the Kid's trial and affidavits from individuals who claim to have met him after his supposed death. See C. L. Sonnichsen and William V. Morrison, *Alias Billy The Kid, ". . . I want to die a free man . . ."* (Albuquerque: University of New Mexico Press, 1955; **A, G**).

Fiction and Adaptations

Billy the Kid has appeared often in American fiction, too often to be more than briefly commented on here. J. C. Dykes lists 25 novels, 13 short stories, 33 compilations of ballads, songs, records and poetry, and 16 plays in 1952. He also includes comic books, folklore, and juvenile publications.

The fictionalized story began with the novels of the 1880s, which expanded upon a *National Police Gazette* article about a Colorado bandit named Billy LeRoy. The first was Thomas Daggett's *The Life and Deeds of Billy LeRoy, alias the Kid, King of American Highwaymen* (1881). Although there may be disagreement about which genre Daggett's book represents, most consider it to be a historical novelization of episodes in the life of Billy the Kid.

Emerson Hough, who published non-fictional accounts of Billy the Kid, also wrote the first important modern novel about him, which is similar in style and format to present day novels. The volume, *Heart's Desire* (1905), is supposedly based on stories Hough heard as a young attorney in New Mexico in the early 1880s. It concerns a chase and capture of Billy the Kid and his gang of outlaws.

Just prior to *Heart's Desire*, one of the Southwest's most famous literary sons, William Sydney Porter (O. Henry), included a short story about Billy in the anthology, *Heart of the West* (1904). The story, "The Caballero's Way," ends with the lover of a Mexican girl mistakenly shooting her while gunning for Billy the Kid.

The famed western writer, Zane Grey, in his novel, *Nevada* (1927), uses Billy the Kid as a minor character and creates circumstances and characters that are taken from the general view that existed in the 1920s.

Two moderately successful novels published prior to World War II were E. B. Mann, *Gamblin' Man* (1934) and Nelson Nye, *Pistols for Hire* (1941). In each, Billy the Kid is a major figure but is portrayed as an ambivalent character, fluctuating between the good and the bad desperado.

Three postwar novels are worth mentioning: Charles Neider, *The Authentic Death of Hendry Jones* (1956); Amelia Bean, *Time For Outrage* (1967); and Matt Braun, *Jury of Six* (1980). The Neider book became the basis for the 1961 Paramount movie "One-Eyed Jacks." In it Billy the Kid is presented as a pensive, betrayed, yet heroic figure. Jon Tuska believes Amelia Bean's novel is "the finest" ever inspired by the Lincoln County War. *Jury of Six* is the first of a series of novels by Matt Braun featuring Luke Starbuck, manhunter; Starbuck becomes involved with Billy the Kid's affairs.

Billy the Kid continues to capture the imagination of novelists. In 1988, Pulitzer Prize-winning author Larry McMurtry published his version of the Kid's adventures as *Anything for Billy*.

Other interesting fictional portrayals of the Kid include Aaron Copland's 1938 ballet, "Billy the Kid," which has been performed and recorded on numerous occasions; Walter Wood's 1903 drama, *Billy the Kid*, which more than 10 million Americans saw during a twelve-year run that closed in 1918; and Michael Ondaatje's avant-garde, epic poetry, *The Collected Works of Billy the Kid* (1970).

Billy the Kid has been featured in at least 41 movies, in most as the main character. He has been portrayed by some of Hollywood's most famous Saturday afternoon cowboys, including Johnny Mack Brown, Roy Rogers, Bob Steele, Buster Crabbe, Don Barry, and Audie Murphy. In one of these low budget oaters, Lash LaRue plays the son Billy the Kid never had.

More recently, some of the nation's most prominent movie stars have played Billy the Kid in higher quality productions. Robert Taylor was the first (1941), then Joel McCrae, Marlon Brando, Paul Newman, Michael Pollard, Scott Brady, Nick Adams, and Kris Kristofferson. Equally impressive is the list of men who have directed films about him: King Vidor, Howard Hughes, Mervyn LeRoy, Arthur Penn, Marlon Brando, Andrew V. McLaglen, and Sam Peckinpah. There have also been notable writers at work on these movies, Gene Fowler and Gore Vidal, to name the best known.

Most of the movies bear little relationship to reality, although a few do concern real moments in the Kid's life. Even these instances are handled in ways that would bring little comfort to those seeking realism. Perhaps the most outlandish, and this is saying quite a bit, is the 1972 release by Embassy Pictures entitled, *Billy the Kid vs. Dracula*. Seventeen movies were part of a low cost series of Billy the Kid films made by Producers Releasing Corporation between July 1940 and August 1943. In these vintage B-movie horse operas, Billy the Kid is an outlaw who helps the weak and promotes law and order.

The four best or best known films about the Kid are King Vidor's *Billy the Kid*, MGM, 1930; *The Outlaws*, Hughes Productions, 1943, which established Jane Russell as a Hollywood star; *The Left Handed Gun*, Warner's, 1958, which was adapted from Vidal's teleplay, *The Death of Billy the Kid*, NBC-TV, 1955; and *Pat Garrett and Billy the Kid*, MGM, 1973, for which Bob Dylan did the soundtrack and played a bit part.

Billy the Kid has also been presented in radio programs such as "Death Valley Days" episodes, and on television, including the NBC-TV series, "The Tall Man"

(1961), but the crowning glory of his stature as a mass culture legend was achieved when Walt Disney animated him in a 1950s cartoon. Obviously, Billy the Kid has been vastly more important in death than he ever was in life.

Museums, Historical Landmarks, Societies

Billy the Kid Days (Lincoln, NM) A three-day pageant celebrated annually during the first week of August. An outdoor drama, "The Last Escape of Billy the Kid," is re-enacted during the pageant.

Billy the Kid Museum (Ft. Sumner, NM). Maintains an eclectic collection of Wild West memorabilia and other regional artifacts.

Other Sources

Adams, Ramon F. *Burs Under the Saddle: A Second Look at Books and Histories of the West*. Norman: University of Oklahoma Press, 1964; *Six-Guns and Saddle Leather: A Bibliography of Books and Pamphlets on Western Outlaws and Gunmen*. Norman: University of Oklahoma Press, 1969; *More Burs Under the Saddle*. Norman: University of Oklahoma Press, 1979. This group of western bibliographies contains a considerable number of entries on Billy the Kid and related subjects.

Adler, Alfred. "Billy the Kid, A Case Study in Epic Origins." *Western Folklore* 10 (April 1951): 143–152. This small essay by the founder of Individual Psychology concludes that late nineteenth-century America needed a legend and that the public created one in Billy the Kid.

Fulton, Maurice Garland. *History of the Lincoln County War*. Edited by Robert N. Mullin. Tucson: University of Arizona Press, 1968. This is the most accurate and factual account ever published on the Lincoln County War. Fulton, who died in 1955, spent much of his life pursuing documents, maps, photographs, interviews, and other source materials to use in the writing of this history. He had not completed the story at the time of his death, and it befell his literary executor, Robert Mullin, to do that.

Keleher, W. A. "In 'Re' Billy the Kid." *New Mexico Folklore Record* 4 (1949/1950): 11–13. In this brief article, Keleher, an Albuquerque attorney, raised questions that dominated the critical historiography of Billy the Kid for the next two decades. He helped to answer some of these questions in *Violence in Lincoln County, 1869–1881* (Albuquerque: University of New Mexico Press, 1957).

Metz, Leon C. *Pat Garrett: The Story of a Western Lawman*. Norman: University of Oklahoma Press, 1974. The best biography of the man who shot Billy the Kid.

Rasch, Philip J. "A Man Named Antrim." *Los Angeles Westerners' Brand Book*

6 (1950): 48–54+. The first article to discuss Billy the Kid's stepfather, William Henry Harrison Antrim, in a factual way.

————. "The Twenty-One Men He Put Bullets Through." *New Mexico Folklore Record* 9 (1954/1955): 8–14. Provides more information about Billy the Kid's "gunslinging" in New Mexico.

Rasch, Philip J., and Robert N. Mullin. "Dim Trails: The Pursuit of the Mc-Carty Family." *New Mexico Folklore Record* 8 (1953/1954): 6–11. Two of the main authorities on Billy the Kid convincingly demonstrate that historians will probably never know much about Billy the Kid before his Lincoln County days. They do supply much of what is probable and provable.

Utley, Robert M. *Four Fighters of Lincoln County*. Albuquerque: University of New Mexico Press, 1986. These are well-written vignettes about four major participants in the Lincoln County War: Alexander McSween; Colonel Nathan A. M. Dudley, commander at Fort Stanton; Governor Lew Wallace; and Billy the Kid. Utley, a well known western historian, uses the fruits of modern scholarship to present these judicious, exciting mini-biographies.

Robert S. La Forte
University of North Texas

Overland Mail, 1958

JAMES G. BLAINE
1830–1893

Chronology

Born James Gillespie Blaine on January 31, 1830, in West Brownsville, Pennsylvania, the fifth of seven children of Ephraim Lyon Blaine, a businessman-lawyer of Scotch-Irish Presbyterian descent, and Maria Louise Gillespie Blaine, daughter of a prosperous farmer-merchant of Irish Catholic background; *1830–1847* is educated at home by his mother, at public school, and at Lancaster Academy in Ohio while staying with the family of Whig politician Thomas Ewing, his mother's cousin; obtains baccalaureate from Washington and Jefferson College at age 17 after studying rhetoric, classical languages, moral philosophy, and mathematics; *1847–1854* teaches for four years at Western Military Institute in Georgetown, Kentucky; studies law while teaching for two years at Pennsylvania Institute for the Education of the Blind in Philadelphia; *March 29, 1850* marries Harriet Stanwood of Maine, who teaches in Kentucky; *1854–1856* settles in Augusta, Maine; with financial help from his wife's family, purchases interest in *Kennebec Journal*, and begins working as journalist; political career in the new Republican party advances rapidly; *1856* serves as delegate to party's first national convention; *1858–1861* is elected to Maine House of Representatives; is twice chosen Speaker; becomes chairman of Republican State Committee in 1859 and will serve in that post for 22 years; *1862* is elected to first of six terms as member of U.S. House of Representatives; *1863–1881* is Speaker of the House for three terms; is elected to U.S. Senate in 1875; narrowly misses winning Republican nomination for president in 1876 and 1880; *1881* serves as secretary of state in ill-fated administration of James A. Garfield, instituting aggressive new approach toward Latin America and calling first inter-American conference, later canceled; *1884* receives Republican nomination for the presidency but is defeated by Democrat Grover Cleveland in one of the century's closest elections; *1889–1892* serves as secretary of state under Benjamin Harrison; presides over first Pan-American Conference in 1889–1890; in declining health, becomes increasingly cautious as Harrison dictates vigorous stand in controversy with Canada and Great Britain over pelagic sealing in Bering Sea, and with Germany over bases in Samoa and exclusion of American pork from European markets; *1893* dies on January 27 of Bright's disease in Washington, D.C.

Activities of Historical Significance

During the 20-year political stalemate that followed the collapse of Reconstruction in the South, Blaine was the most popular public figure in the United States. He was blessed with an extraordinary memory for facts and figures, names and faces. He overcame the handicap of representing a small state by building a personal network of contacts across the country, concentrating on midwestern and western states. He mastered the minutest details of parliamentary procedure and most of the leading issues of his time, particularly the tariff. Invariably, he staked out a position near the center of Republican opinion. In an age when political speechmaking was an important form of public entertainment, Blaine consciously polished his skills, striving for logical clarity sustained by a compelling array of factual data. However, he was at his best in the extemporaneous role of a debater. His verbal clashes on the floor of the House of Representatives with fellow Republican Roscoe Conkling, with Benjamin H. Hill of Georgia over amnesty for Jefferson Davis, and with various Democrats over his investments in railroad securities, are legendary.

Blaine advanced rapidly up the political ladder, yet the presidency eluded him. He was chosen Speaker of the House of Representatives after only six years in Washington. His independence on Reconstruction put him at odds with President Ulysses S. Grant and the Stalwarts in the Republican party—Conkling in New York, Simon Cameron in Pennsylvania, Oliver P. Morton in Indiana—whose power in their own states was based in large part on their influence over federal patronage. At the other extreme, civil service reformers rejected Blaine because of alleged conflicts-of-interest in some of his railroad investments. In fact, Blaine's ethics were typical of his generation, and his popular strength was never dependent on machine politics.

In 1876 Blaine was the leading candidate at the Republican convention, but he was unable to gain a majority of the delegates when all of his opponents united in favor of Rutherford B. Hayes. Four years later the Republican delegates deadlocked among Blaine and Ohio's John Sherman as the leaders of the moderate Half-Breeds, and former President Grant, the candidate of the Stalwarts. Blaine and Sherman then threw their support to James A. Garfield, who was nominated.

Blaine finally received his long-coveted presidential nomination in 1884, only to lose the election to Democrat Grover Cleveland. The bolt to Cleveland of Republican civil service reformers—the Mugwumps—hurt. So, too, did the characterization of the Democrats as the party of "Rum, Romanism, and Rebellion" by an otherwise obscure clergyman introducing Blaine at a New York rally. The tired candidate, whose own family was partly Catholic and who had been assiduously courting Irish voters for years, may or may not have heard the alliterative remark. At any rate, he failed to respond to it. Blaine had many potential supporters in 1888 and even 1892, but by then his time had passed.

As the senior statesman in the Republican party, Blaine was twice made secretary of state, enthusiastically by Garfield in 1881, and grudgingly by Benjamin Harrison in 1889. Blaine had little preparation for the office, other than a desire to promote American exports and a deep-seated distrust of England. During his first term he devoted most of his attention to Latin America, where he had to contend with the War of the Pacific between Chile and Peru and several potentially violent boundary disputes. His impulsive handling of these matters did not bring the countries involved closer to agreement. He then devised the ingenious notion of an inter-American conference to promote and foster peace. But when Garfield was assassinated, his successor, the Stalwart Chester A. Arthur, accepted Blaine's resignation and withdrew the conference invitations.

When Blaine began his second term, his health was already failing. He had the satisfaction of presiding over the first Pan-American Conference in 1889–1890, but the gathering produced few positive results. He devoted his remaining energy to the controversy with Canada and England over pelagic sealing in the Bering Sea, tests of will with Germany over the independence of Samoa and the exclusion of American pork from European markets, and the negotiation of reciprocal trade agreements with Latin America. President Harrison carried progressively more of the burden of conducting foreign relations during his secretary of state's long periods of confinement. Blaine finally resigned in June 1892, bringing his public career to an end.

Overview of Biographical Sources

The published materials about Blaine are more notable for quantity than quality. His nomination for the presidency in 1884 spawned a large number of hastily written biographies, and his death in 1893 was the occasion of several more. Most of these volumes are of little value except as reflections of the esteem felt by Blaine's admirers. Edward Stanwood, a cousin by marriage, was the first professional historian to assess Blaine's career. His brief *James Gillespie Blaine* (1908) is predictably sympathetic and without footnotes or even a bibliography, but it is thoughtful and well written. The only full-length scholarly biography is David Saville Muzzey's *James G. Blaine* (1934). Muzzey's understanding of the events and issues of Blaine's time is dated, but his handling of Blaine the man is balanced and thorough. Although a modern biography drawing on the more sophisticated research of the last fifty years is needed, Muzzey's work will adequately meet most people's needs until something better comes along.

If interest in Blaine's political career has diminished, his diplomatic career has been the subject of growing attention. Alice Felt Tyler's *The Foreign Policy of James G. Blaine* (1927) and Joseph B. Lockey's two extended essays in Samuel Flagg Bemis's *The American Secretaries of State and Their Diplomacy* (1928) emphasize Blaine's pivotal role in developing a more active foreign policy, especially for Latin America. Russell H. Bastert, "A New Approach to the Origins of Blaine's Pan American Policy" (1959), and David M. Pletcher, *The Awkward Years* (1962), agree with these earlier scholars that Blaine's first term as secretary of state represented an important step in the evolution of what would eventually become "dollar diplomacy." They do not agree that his diplomatic ideas were worked out in advance; the Pan-American Conference, in particular, was a response to the pressure of events. More recently, Justus D. Doenecke, *The Presidencies of James A.*

Garfield & Chester A. Arthur (1981), and Homer E. Socolofsky and Allan B. Spetter, *The Presidency of Benjamin Harrison* (1987), have harshly criticized Blaine's performance as inexperienced and inept. Their extreme views will present a challenge to any future biographer.

Evaluation of Principal Biographical Sources

Crawford, Theron Clark. *James G. Blaine: A Study of His Life and Career.* Philadelphia: Edgewood Publishing, 1893. (**A, G**) As a Democratic correspondent in Washington, Crawford personally covered some of the major events in Blaine's career, beginning with his tenure as Speaker of the House. Written as a eulogy, his account is uncritical but rich in personal detail.

Doenecke, Justus D. "Mr. Secretary Blaine." In *The Presidencies of James A. Garfield & Chester A. Arthur.* Lawrence: Regents Press of Kansas, 1981. (**A, G**) Drawing upon the insights of modern diplomatic scholarship, Doenecke is more impressed by the problems Blaine caused by his impulsiveness and lack of experience than by the advantages he gained by breaking with traditional isolationism. The result is a far different portrait from the one painted by Blaine's biographers.

Hamilton, Gail [Mary Abigail Dodge]. *Biography of James G. Blaine.* Norwich, CT: Henry Bill Publishing, 1895. (**A**) The author, a popular essayist and cousin of Blaine's wife, often stayed in the Blaine home in Washington. Her firsthand knowledge of her subject and access to family correspondence give her account lasting value despite the tedious style and eulogistic tone. Every chapter is supplemented by scores of letters to and from Blaine, most not otherwise available in print. The period after 1876 is oddly compressed.

Harrison, Robert. "Blaine and the Camerons: A Study in the Limits of Machine Power." *Pennsylvania History* 49 (1982): 157–175. (**A, G**) Harrison argues that the power of nineteenth-century political "bosses" has been exaggerated. He notes that Senator Donald Cameron was able to impose the unit rule on the Pennsylvania delegates attending the 1876 and 1880 Republican National Conventions, thereby disregarding rank-and-file support for Blaine, only at the cost of a serious revolt against his leadership. Neither Cameron nor his successor, Matthew S. Quay, repeated the mistake. This article can also be read as a measure of Blaine's immense grass-roots popularity.

Langley, Lester D. "James Gillespie Blaine: The Ideologue as Diplomatist." In *Makers of American Diplomacy: From Benjamin Franklin to Henry Kissinger,* edited by Frank J. Merli and Theodore A. Wilson. New York: Charles Scribner's Sons, 1974. (**A, G**) Latin American policy constitutes the principal focus of this sympathetic but balanced account. Langley stresses Blaine's superior intellect and argues that among American diplomats of the post-Civil War generation he ranked in importance behind only William H. Seward. Langley depicts Blaine as a nationalist who foresaw and sought to assure a dominant role for the U.S. in Western Hemisphere affairs.

Lockey, Joseph B. "James G. Blaine, Secretary of State, March 7, 1881, to December 18, 1881 (First Term)" and "James G. Blaine, Secretary of State, March 5, 1889, to June 4, 1892 (Second Term)." In *The American Secretaries of State and Their Diplomacy*, edited by Samuel Flagg Bemis. Vols. 7 and 8. New York: Alfred A. Knopf, 1928. **(A, G)** Lockey gives an uncritically sympathetic portrait of Blaine and his handling of the Latin American disputes, the inter-American conference, the Samoan and Hawaiian policies, the Bering Sea controversy, and other problems he faced during his tenure as secretary of state.

Muzzey, David Saville. *James G. Blaine: A Political Idol of Other Days*. New York: Dodd, Mead, 1934. **(A, G)** Despite Muzzey's occasionally dated explanations of events, his is by far the best available full-length biography. Unlike Hamilton and Russell, he emphasizes Blaine's political accomplishments after 1876.

Russell, Charles Edward. *Blaine of Maine: His Life and Times*. New York: Cosmopolitan Book Corporation, 1931. **(G)** Russell was a young Washington correspondent when Blaine served as Harrison's secretary of state. He vividly depicts his subject's magnetic personality and what he considered a flawed personality. Russell was belatedly refuting Gail Hamilton; his book closely follows hers in skimming over the years after 1876.

Socolofsky, Homer E., and Allan B. Spetter. "Blaine and the State Department" and "Harrison's Foreign Policy." In *The Presidency of Benjamin Harrison*. Lawrence: University Press of Kansas, 1987. **(A, G)** Drawing on their own primary research as well as on secondary sources, the authors show that Blaine's deteriorating health and the coolness that existed between Harrison and his secretary of state led the president increasingly to develop and conduct his own foreign policy. They argue that it was Harrison who assumed an aggressive stance toward Germany over Samoa, toward Britain over pelagic sealing in the Bering Sea, toward several European nations over their exclusion of American pork, and toward Congress over the need for reciprocal trade agreements with Latin America, while Blaine invariably urged caution.

Stanwood, Edward. *James Gillespie Blaine*. Boston: Houghton Mifflin, 1908. **(A, G)** Written for the American Statesmen series, this highly favorable biography emphasizes Blaine's extraordinary political skills, quickness and finesse in debate, mastery of detail, and essential moderation. It also portrays his foreign policy initiatives as a conscious break with the past.

Tyler, Alice Felt. *The Foreign Policy of James G. Blaine*. Minneapolis: University of Minnesota Press, 1927. **(A, G)** In the most comprehensive account of Blaine's work as a diplomatist, Tyler argues that, inspired by the ideas of Henry Clay, Blaine intended from the first to establish a new approach toward the Western

Hemisphere. She concludes that his thinking paralleled and may even have been influenced by Europe's emerging economic imperialism, yet he did not foresee the end results of his political changes. Anticipating later scholars, she agrees that his handling of the seal controversy was clumsy and that his performance in his second term was less vigorous and less impetuous than in his first.

Overview and Evaluation of Primary Sources

The absence of recent biographies of Blaine is undoubtedly related to the scarcity of primary sources. He maintained a substantial correspondence but did not keep copies of his own letters. The James G. Blaine Papers in the Library of Congress consist mostly of incoming letters; few are really important. Scattered letters from Blaine can be found in the papers of other Republican leaders, in the Library of Congress and elsewhere.

Gail Hamilton's aforementioned biography includes excerpts from several hundred letters to and from Blaine. Albert T. Volwiler painstakingly assembled *The Correspondence between Benjamin Harrison and James G. Blaine, 1882–1893* (Philadelphia: American Philosophical Society, 1940; **A**); the most important materials relate to foreign policy in the years 1889–1892. The two-volume *Letters of Mrs. James G. Blaine*, edited by Harriet S. Blaine Beale (New York: Duffield, 1908; **A**), is a useful source because Blaine's wife reliably reported her husband's thoughts to family and friends. Thomas H. Sherman, *Twenty Years with James G. Blaine* (New York: Grafton Press, 1928; **A, G**), contains the anecdotal recollections of Blaine's private secretary.

Blaine devoted the years of his involuntary retirement during Arthur's presidency to the composition of *Twenty Years of Congress: From Lincoln to Garfield* (Norwich, CT: Henry Bill Publishing, 1884–1886; **A**). But these two huge volumes are not memoirs; they are Blaine's interpretation of U.S. political history from the struggle over slavery in the territories to the election of 1880. Congressional personalities and debates loom large, yet Blaine himself hardly appears. Blaine also collected what he regarded as his most important speeches and diplomatic correspondence from his first term as secretary of state in *Political Discussions, Legislative, Diplomatic, and Popular, 1856–1886* (Norwich, CT: Henry Bill Publishing, 1887; **A**).

Museums, Historical Landmarks, Societies

Blaine House (Augusta, ME). Built about 1830 and purchased in 1862, this house was Blaine's principal residence for 31 years. It has served as Maine's Executive Mansion since the 1920s, but public tours are available. Blaine's study has been preserved unchanged.

Other Sources

Bastert, Russell H. "A New Approach to the Origins of Blaine's Pan American Policy." *Hispanic American Historical Review* 39 (August 1959): 375–412. Bastert demonstrates that Blaine conceived of an inter-American conference to find collective solutions to actual and potential hemispheric wars only after his unilateral approaches to dealing with territorial disputes had been rebuffed. Not until President Arthur and Secretary of State Frederick T. Frelinghuysen withdrew his invitations did Blaine first offer the rationale that the conference would also promote trade with Latin America.

————. "Diplomatic Reversal: Frelinghuysen's Opposition to Blaine's Pan-American Policy in 1882." *Mississippi Valley Historical Review* 42 (March 1956): 653–671. In this companion article Bastert examines the considerations that led Arthur and Frelinghuysen to withdraw Blaine's invitation to attend an inter-American peace conference.

Campbell, Charles S., Jr. "The Anglo-American Crisis in the Bering Sea, 1890–1891." *Mississippi Valley Historical Review* 58 (December 1961): 393–414. Campbell reconstructs the tortuous road to settlement of the controversy over pelagic sealing. The author shows that Blaine's handling of the situation he inherited from the Cleveland administration was less than straightforward, partly because of his own hostility to England and partly because he had unwittingly awarded a new 20-year sealing lease on Alaska's Pribilof Islands to a company in which close political associates were the major investors.

Coulter, E. Merton. "Amnesty for All Except Jefferson Davis: The Hill-Blaine Debate of 1876." *Georgia Historical Quarterly* 56 (Winter 1972): 453–494. Writing from a distinctly unfriendly point of view, Coulter retells the story of one of Blaine's most famous congressional speeches. He tries to show that the Northern press was largely unsympathetic to such waving of the bloody shirt more than a decade after the Civil War had ended, yet the speech helped bolster Blaine's popularity with Republican voters.

Farrelly, David G. " 'Rum, Romanism and Rebellion' Resurrected." *Western Political Quarterly* 8 (June 1955): 262–270. Farrelly discusses a memorandum Supreme Court Justice John M. Harlan wrote in 1893, recounting a conversation in the winter of 1884–1885 in which Blaine admitted hearing Burchard's disastrous alliteration. The candidate did not immediately respond because he did not think many others had heard the remark. Only too late did he recognize his error. Even before this conversation, Blaine had remarked to a journalist, "The Lord sent upon us an ass in the shape of a preacher."

Peskin, Allan. "Blaine, Garfield and Latin America: A New Look." *Americas* 36 (July 1979): 79–89. Peskin argues that the main outlines of American foreign policy in 1881 were established as much by President Garfield as by Secretary Blaine. He presents only circumstantial evidence to support his point of view.

Pletcher, David M. *The Awkward Years: American Foreign Relations under Garfield and Arthur.* Columbia: University of Missouri Press, 1962. Pletcher argues that Blaine's principal goal in his first term as secretary of state was to augment American prestige abroad, foreshadowing later expansionist policies. Pletcher also notes that Blaine moved slowly in implementing his more active approach until Garfield died. Then, knowing his days in office were numbered, he rushed to complete an agenda he would be remembered for in 1884.

―――――. "Reciprocity and Latin America in the Early 1890s: A Foretaste of Dollar Diplomacy." *Pacific Historical Review* 47 (February 1978): 53–89. Pletcher details Blaine's efforts, following the inter-American conference of 1889–1890, to negotiate reciprocal trade agreements with several Western Hemisphere countries.

Rosenberg, Marvin, and Dorothy Rosenberg. "The District Election." *American Heritage* 13 (August 1962): 4–9, 97–101. This illustrated article presents a highly readable, detailed, but undocumented and conventional account of the presidential campaign of 1884.

Keith Ian Polakoff
California State University, Long Beach

Pan American Union, 1940

DANIEL BOONE
1734–1820

Chronology

Born Daniel Boone on November 2, 1734, in Oley (later Exter) Township, Berks County, Pennsylvania, the sixth child of Squire Boone, a weaver, blacksmith, and farmer, and Sara Morgan; *1734–1755* is reared as a Quaker; has little formal schooling, instead spends time hunting and trapping; *1751* moves with family to Yadkin River Valley, on the North Carolina frontier; *1755* serves as a wagoner in General William Braddock's disastrous expedition against Fort Duquesne; hears first stories of Kentucky from long hunter John Findley; *1756* returns to North Carolina and marries neighbor Rebecca Bryan; *1758* Cherokee Indian wars begin; becomes member of Forbes expedition against Fort Duquesne; *1759* moves to Culpeper County, Virginia; *1760* crosses Blue Ridge Mountains for first time and explores Tennessee; *1763* meets Judge Richard Henderson, who defends him in suit for debt and later engages him as a land scout; *1765* leads party to West Florida; Rebecca rejects moving there; *1769* with John Findley and four others, finds Cumberland Gap and crosses into Kentucky bluegrass country; *1773* leads settlement party toward Kentucky; is attacked by Indians, loses son James, and returns party to North Carolina; *1774* commands three Clinch Valley forts in Lord Dunmore's War; *1775* is present at Sycamore Shoals when Henderson buys Kentucky from the Cherokee Indians; leads party blazing Wilderness Trail to establish Fort Boonesborough, and quickly becomes leader of Transylvania Colony; *1776* rescues daughter Jemima and Callaway sisters from Indian kidnapping; *1778* is captured by Shawnees, taken to Detroit, and escapes; defends Boonesborough during great siege; is court-martialed for treason but is acquitted and promoted to major; *1779–1781* leaves Boonesborough, and establishes own station in Fayette County; is robbed of $50,000, mostly money entrusted to him by friends to buy land warrants; is captured by British raiders in Charlottesville, Va.; *1782* participates at siege of Bryan's Station and crucial battle of Blue Licks; *1783–1799* moves around Kentucky and western Virginia, serving as deputy land surveyor, tavernkeeper, and farmer; loses most of his land due to improper filing of claims and legal action; *1799* follows son Daniel Morgan to Missouri and receives large grant from Spanish governor; *1804* loses all claims to Missouri land; *1813* wife Rebecca dies; *1814* U.S. Congress awards him 1,000 acres of land; Kentucky creditors besiege him and he surrenders all of it; *1820* dies on September 26 at son Nathan's house in St. Charles County, Missouri.

Activities of Historical Significance

Daniel Boone achieved fame as an explorer and advanced agent of civilization in the Trans-Allegheny west during the last quarter of the eighteenth century. He was a restless spirit who preferred the rough and raw adventures which the nascent American frontier offered. Numerous legends have developed around Boone's pioneering exploits, especially in Kentucky, during the formative period of westward expansion.

Boone's quest for the exciting life of a lone hunter began in 1755 when he met the explorer John Findley. Findley attracted Boone's attention with stories of incredible, lush forests teeming with animal life in lands beyond the Appalachian Mountains. By 1769 Boone traveled through the Cumberland Gap at the Virginia and North Carolina border and saw for the first time the "beautiful level" of Central Kentucky. Later, his familiarity with Indian culture, and knowledge of the "dark and bloody ground," which the Cherokee Indians called Kentucky, impressed North Carolina judge Richard Henderson who had plans to colonize the area.

In 1775 Boone helped negotiate a treaty with the Cherokees which secured one million acres of land south of the Kentucky River for Henderson's Transylvania Company. Henderson employed Boone to blaze a trail for settlers coming from North Carolina to Kentucky. This fateful 1775 expedition along the Wilderness Trail led to the establishment of Fort Boonesborough—a permanent Western fortification on the banks of the Kentucky River. Boone quickly assumed control of Boonesborough, which was named in his honor, and helped Henderson establish a government. When Virginia refused to accept Henderson's claim and assumed control over the proprietary colony in 1776, Boone was deprived of many acres of land which he had been promised.

Boone's heroic reputation was acquired largely through his amazing exploits in 1778. While attempting to bring salt back to Boonesborough, he and twenty-seven other men were captured by Shawnee Indians. Boone, who was popular with the Indians, was taken to Detroit where British Governor Henry Hamilton offered a hundred pounds sterling for his release. The Indians refused and took him back to their camp in Ohio where he was adopted by Chief Blackfish. Several months later he escaped and returned to Boonesborough to warn the settlers of an impending Indian raid. The great siege of Boonesborough lasted eleven days, and Boone's leadership ultimately saved the fort. This event, combined with George Rogers Clark's capture of several British outposts in Indian territory, helped secure American independence from Britain by dooming their domination of the western frontier. Unfortunately, one of Boone's relatives by marriage, Richard Callaway, accused him of treason in dealing with the Indians. He was court-martialed but was fully acquitted.

The remainder of Boone's Kentucky years were filled with pain and frustration. In what historians refer to as the last battle of the American Revolution—the Battle of Blue Licks in 1782—Kentucky militia commander Colonel Levi Todd refused to heed Boone's warnings of an Indian ambush for soldiers pursuing the Indians who had just attacked Bryan's Station. Sixty settlers, including Boone's son Israel, died within five minutes in this bloody massacre.

Ironically, Boone dealt effectively with Indians and the untamed frontier but was unable to function as well within the confines of a rapidly growing Kentucky society. Many new settlers, including farmers, lawyers, and speculators, traveled the Wilderness Trail to seek new land, only to encounter disappointment because of improper land surveys. Boone, continually in financial difficulty, lost thousands of acres due to his ineptitude in obtaining clear titles, and he, too, fell victim to the vagaries of a chaotic legal system. Finally, in 1799 he sought more "elbow room" by migrating westward to Missouri where he received a large land grant from Spanish authorities who hoped that his popularity would attract more settlers. Unfortunately, he lost most of this land, as well, and died virtually penniless.

The enduring legend of Daniel Boone, whose life typifies many frontiersmen, actually began long before his death. In 1784 John Filson published *The Discovery, Settlement, and Present State of Kentucke . . .* which contained Boone's alleged autobiography. From this book and a series of early adaptations, the exploits of his life have been used to personify the pioneer who paves the way for civilization, and to typify the natural man who prefers the simplicity and rugged vitality of the wilderness. From this image much of Boone's historical significance is derived.

Overview of Biographical Sources

Biographies about Daniel Boone and his frontier exploits abound. Many present a highly romanticized version of the pioneer's life, but several well-researched and competent, scholarly studies have also been produced. Reputed autobiographies by Boone were printed long before his death in 1820. John Filson published Kentucky's first history, *The Discovery, Settlement, and Present State of Kentucke . . . To which is added . . . I. The Adventures of Col. Daniel Boon* (1784), which allegedly contained Boone's autobiography. Since Boone was barely literate, he could not have written it; actually Filson penned the words. This work concentrated on Boone's exploits from 1769–1782 and presented the frontiersman as a rugged spirit who was in harmony with nature. For several generations, biographies continued to echo these themes of Boone as the natural man who helped to spread civilization.

John Trumbull's popular condensed edition of Filson's work, *The Adventures of Colonel Daniel Boon* (1786), and Gilbert Imlay's *A Topographical Description of the Western Territory of North America . . . to which is added I. The Adventures of Daniel Boon* (1793), along with Filson's book, were translated into French and German and spread Boone's fame through the continent. Timothy Flint's *Biographical Memoir of Daniel Boone, the First Settler of Kentucky* (1833) became a runaway best seller of its day (reprinted fourteen times), partly because of a number of romantic fabrications; but it is a work that should not be dismissed out of hand, because it contains interviews with Boone. John Mason Peck's *Life of Daniel*

Boone, the Pioneer of Kentucky (1847) in the library of American Biography, edited by historian Jared Sparks, is a minister's idealized view of the frontiersman, but again was based upon personal interviews and use of the Draper manuscript collection. William H. Bogart's *Daniel Boone and the Hunters of Kentucky* (1845), and Cecil B. Hartley's *Life and Times of Colonel Daniel Boone . . .* (1859) rely heavily on Filson's and Peck's works.

By the beginning of the twentieth century, the Boone legend was undergoing a critical reassessment. Use of the Lyman Draper manuscripts at the State Historical Society of Wisconsin threw new light on Boone and the Trans-Allegheny frontier experience. Draper's long-time Wisconsin associate, Reuben Gold Thwaites, *Daniel Boone* (1902), provides a readable and competent account using the Draper manuscripts extensively. Eminent middle west frontier historian Clarence Walworth Alvord's "The Boone Myth," in *Journal of the Illinois State Historical Society* (1926), successfully refutes many of the legends that surrounded Boone's pioneer exploits and opened the door for a more realistic evaluation of the frontiersman. In John Bakeless, *Daniel Boone: Master of the Wilderness* (1939), a clear and balanced picture of Boone's life and accomplishments is presented. Most historians and literary critics still consider the Bakeless study to be the most comprehensive and thorough biography of Boone ever written. The latest work is Michael Lofaro's *The Life and Adventures of Daniel Boone* (1978), an outgrowth of his doctoral dissertation. The biography is a clear, concise, objective, and scholarly account that carefully examines many of the myths that developed about Boone.

Evaluation of Principal Biographical Sources

Abbott, John S. C. *Daniel Boone: The Pioneer of Kentucky.* New York: Dodd, Mead, 1874. **(G)** This work, part of the American Pioneers and Patriots series, presents Boone as the true American hero who is "mild mannered; feminine as a woman in his tastes and deportment, never uttering a coarse word." The frontier is portrayed as a struggle between the forces of civilization and barbarism. Inaccurate information mars the biography.

Bakeless, John. *Daniel Boone: Master of the Wilderness.* New York: William Morrow, 1939. **(A, G)** Probably the best biography ever produced on Boone, making extensive use of primary source materials, especially the Draper manuscripts. It corrects many previously held views and presents much new data, mainly about the Kentucky years. Written in a readable style, the work at times is more a social history of the Trans-Allegheny frontier experience than a biography.

Bogart, William H. *Daniel Boone and the Hunters of Kentucky.* Philadelphia: J. B. Lippincott, 1854. **(G)** One of the earlier and very popular lives of Boone which relies heavily on Filson's autobiography and John Mason Peck's 1847 biography. It is greatly biased in favor of Boone against the "barbaric" Indians.

Bruce, H. Addington. *Daniel Boone and the Wilderness Road*. New York: Macmillan, 1910. **(A, G)** This work serves as a biography of Boone, and as a study of the first phase of American territorial growth. Boone's contributions are adequately chronicled with use of mainly secondary sources.

Bryan, William S. and Rose, Robert. *A History of the Pioneer Families of Missouri*. St. Louis: Bryan and Brand, 1876. **(A, G)** Fifty-four pages are devoted to Boone. Rose, an itinerant peddler, interviewed many early Missouri pioneers who knew Boone. This work is occasionally punctuated with Boone documents. The authors rely on John Mason Peck's 1847 biography.

Elliott, Lawrence. *The Long Hunter: A New Life of Daniel Boone*. New York: Reader's Digest Press, 1976. **(A, G)** A well-written study of Boone the man, stripped of many of the legends. The author focuses on the frontiersman's private life and attempts to analyze the "complex dimension of Daniel Boone." A useful chronology of Boone's life, a good bibliography, and numerous references in the footnotes to the Draper manuscripts make the work worthwhile.

Filson, John. *The Discovery, Settlement, and Present State of Kentucke . . . To which is added I. The Adventures of Col. Daniel Boon*. Wilmington, DE: n.p., 1784. **(A, G)** This reputed autobiography of Boone, actually written by Filson from a series of interviews with the pioneer, covers the years 1769 to 1782 and established the frontiersman's legend. It strongly emphasizes Boone as a child of nature, advanced agent of civilization and progress, and hunter-Indian fighter.

Flint, Timothy. *Biographical Memoir of Daniel Boone, the First Settler of Kentucky*. Cincinnati: N. & G. Gilford, 1833. **(G)** There are fourteen different editions of this early work on Boone. The titles vary but each was published in Cincinnati from 1833 to 1868. The author presents a highly romanticized view of the pioneer and has altered several facts, especially Boone's relation with his wife, Rebecca, in order to sell the book. It has strongly contributed to the Boone legend.

Lofaro, Michael A. *The Life and Adventures of Daniel Boone*. Lexington, KY: University Press of Kentucky, 1978. **(A, G)** A highly readable, scholarly account which uses primary source material extensively to dispel many misconceptions. It is probably the best interpretative analysis of Boone within the context of the frontier experience.

Lossing, Benson J. "Daniel Boone." *Harper's New Monthly Magazine* 19 (October 1859): 577–601. **(G)** A brief account of Boone as an agent of civilization, this study relies on Flint's and Filson's works. The author was a research associate of Lyman Draper.

Peck, John Mason. *Life of Daniel Boone, the Pioneer of Kentucky*. New York: The University Society, 1847. **(A, G)** Although marred by obvious idolatry, the author does use primary source material to correct some previous biographies (he is the first biographer to date correctly the Great Siege of Boonesborough). It comprises part of the Library of American Biography series, edited by historian Jared Sparks.

Skinner, Constance L. *Pioneers of the Old Southwest*. New Haven: Yale University Press, 1921. **(A, G)** This work presents a Turnerian view of the frontier and sees Boone as agent of civilization and natural man.

Spraker, Hazel Atterbury. *The Boone Family: A Genealogical History of the Descendants of George and Mary Boone*. Rutland, VT: Tuttle, 1922. **(G)** Presents the best genealogical account of the Boone family. It contains a biographical essay on Daniel written by Jesse Procter Crump, and an occasional Boone letter or document.

Thwaites, Reuben Gold. *Daniel Boone*. New York: D. Appleton, 1902. **(A, G)** A short and accurate account of Boone's life and adventures, this study is based on the Draper manuscripts and earlier printed sources with no bibliography or footnotes. It is dedicated to Lyman Draper, Thwaites's close friend who planned to write a biography of Boone but never completed it.

Trumbull, John. *The Adventures of Colonel Daniel Boon*. Norwich, CT, 1786. **(G)** This popular condensed edition of Filson's autobiography modifies Filson's emphasis on Boone as a hunter-Indian fighter.

Van Noppen, John J. and Ima W. *Daniel Boone: Backwoodsman*. Boone, NC: The Appalachian Press, 1966. **(A, G)** Focuses on the early Boone family in Britain and analyzes the social forces, especially Quakerism, which helped shape Boone's life. It has an index and bibliography, but no footnotes.

Evaluation of Biographies for Young People

Brown, John Mason. *Daniel Boone and the Opening of the Wilderness*. New York: Random House, 1952. This work by a noted author of children's books and associate editor of *The Saturday Review of Literature* relies heavily on John Bakeless's authoritative biography of Boone. It devotes considerable space to vivid descriptions of Indian warfare and the dangers of the frontier environment. It is written for the junior high school level.

Daughtery, James H. *Daniel Boone*. New York: The Viking Press, 1939. A biography for young readers, this book also serves as a study of the dynamic forces on the American frontier. It is lavishly illustrated and is written for the elementary school level.

Ellis, Edward S. *The Life and Times of Col. Daniel Boone, Soldier, Pioneer with Sketches of Simon Kenton, Lewis Wetzel and other Leaders in the Settlement of the West*. Philadelphia: Porter and Coates, 1884. One of the common lives of Boone, this work appeared earlier with the same title as one of the series of Beadle's Dime Biographies. It presents a glorified view of Boone as the simple and honest woodsman who has an unaltering faith in country and God, and is written for the high school level.

Gulliver, Lucille. *Daniel Boone*. New York: Macmillan, 1916. A selection for the True Stories of Great Americans Series, this work (written during World War I) uses Boone as the classic example of patriotism.

Hawks, Francis Lister. *The Adventures of Daniel Boone*. New York: Appleton, 1846. Written for the Library for My Young Countrymen Series, this biography uses Filson's narrative as a source, but incorrectly gives Boone's year of death as 1818.

Hill, George Canning. *Life and Adventures of Daniel Boone*. New York: Hurst, 1859. One of the commonplace lives of the frontier hunter and explorer, this book, written for the high school level, exaggerates Boone's morality by stating "though he never made any profession of religion before the public, it can't be denied that he was the most thoroughly religious man that ever lived."

McGuire, Edna. *Daniel Boone*. Chicago: Wheeler, 1945. Part of the American Adventures Series, the work, written for the elementary school level, emphasizes Boone's life within the context of the family and the difficulties faced on the frontier.

Perry, Francis M. *Four American Pioneers—Daniel Boone, George Rogers Clark, David Crockett, and Kit Carson—Book for Young Persons*. New York: American Book, 1900. A juvenile story in Baldwin Biographical Booklets.

White, Stewart Edward. *Daniel Boone: Wilderness Scout*. New York: Allyn & Bacon, 1926. Part of the Academic Classes series, this book emphasizes Boone's qualities—unfaltering courage, good sportsmanship, initiative, love of adventure, loyalty, and perseverance—that Boy Scouts and Camp Fire Girls should emulate. The work also includes topics for discussion and composition, practical suggestions for dramatizing scenes, and a list of difficult words.

Overview and Evaluation of Primary Sources

Although Daniel Boone was barely literate and did not write much, a surprisingly large quantity of his personal manuscripts and public documents have been preserved. His early recollections were recorded in his alleged autobiography in the appendix of John Filson's *The Discovery, Settlement, and Present State of Kentucke . . .* (1784). Later biographers Timothy Flint, *Biographical Memoir of Daniel Boone* (1833), and John Mason Peck, *Life of Daniel Boone, The Pioneer of Kentucky* (1847), went to Missouri and interviewed the frontiersman. Unfortunately, while fleeing down the Missouri River in 1814 from British inspired Indian raids, Boone's son-in-law, Flanders Callaway, capsized his canoe and lost an auto-biography which Boone had dictated to his grandson.

Unquestionably the best source for Boone manuscripts is the unique collection of 500 volumes of Trans-Allegheny pioneer historical documents assiduously assembled over a fifty year period by Dr. Lyman Draper and housed in the State Historical Society of Wisconsin. Draper traveled throughout the South and old Mid-West acquiring numerous original documents from pioneer families, including the Boone family. He also conducted interviews and gathered recollections of Boone's relatives and friends in preparation for a biography of the frontiersman. In addition to the five-volume unpublished biography (Series B—Draper's Life of Boone) that chronicles Boone's life until 1778, Draper left approximately forty other volumes of manuscripts and notes about the pioneer. They are contained in Series C—Boone Papers; Series J—George Rogers Clark Papers; Series S—Draper's Notes; and Series CC—Kentucky Papers. All of the Draper papers have been microfilmed. An excellent reference source for using the collection is Josephine L. Harper, *Guide to the Draper Manuscripts* (Madison: State Historical Society of Wisconsin, 1983; **A**).

Like Draper, Colonel Reuben T. Durrett of Louisville, Kentucky, amassed a large collection of pioneer Kentucky manuscript material. He sold the collection to the University of Chicago in 1913. The Durrett Collection, preserved at the Joseph Regenstein Library, has some Boone manuscripts. In addition, there are scattered Boone documents at the office of the Yearly Meeting of the Religious Society of Friends, Philadelphia; the Friends Historical Library of Swarthmore College; the State Historical Society of Pennsylvania; the Huntington Library, San Marino, California; the courthouses of Bucks and Berks Counties in Pennsylvania; and the St. Charles County courthouse in Missouri. William P. Palmer and Sherwin McRae's *Calendar of Virginia State Papers and Other Manuscripts* (Richmond: Walker, Goode, and Derr, 1875–1885; **A**) has additional Boone material.

The best source of information about the location of individual Boone documents appears in John Bakeless's comprehensive biography, *Daniel Boone: Master of the Wilderness* (New York: William Morrow, 1939; **A, G**). In the bibliography and notes section he provides a chronological list of every extant Boone manuscript or document. Roy T. King, "Portraits of Daniel Boone," *Missouri Historical Review* 33 (1939; **A, G**), reproduces eight photographs of the many portraits of Boone, including the only painting of Boone from life by Chester Harding in 1819, and discusses the historical details of each as given by their owners.

Fiction and Adaptations

Historical novels and fictionalized accounts about the life and times of Daniel Boone abound. Several of the Leatherstocking Tales, written by James Fenimore

Cooper, portray many of Boone's frontier exploits. In Cooper's popular novels, *The Pioneers, or The Sources of the Susquehanna, a Descriptive Tale* (1823); *The Pathfinder, or the Inland Sea* (1840); and *The Deerslayer, or The First Warpath* (1841), the protagonist resembles Boone, with strong emphasis on the "natural man" theme.

Emerson Bennett's *The Renegade* (1848) depicts life with Daniel Boone on the Kentucky border in 1781. John B. Jones's novel, *Wild Western Scenes: a Narrative of Adventures in the Western Wilderness, Wherein the Exploits of Daniel Boone . . .are Particularly Described* (1853), emphasizes the romantic nature of the Boone story in a wilderness environment. Frank H. Norton's novel, *The Days of Daniel Boone: A Romance of the Dark and Bloody Ground* (1882), is a highly romanticized picture of Boone, focusing on his North Carolina years from 1768 to 1775.

In the 1880s several popular dime novels about Boone appeared: Joseph F. Badger, Jr., *The King of the Woods or Daniel Boone's Last Trail* (1884); Henry J. Wehman, *Books on the Adventures of Daniel Boone* (1885); and John H. Robinson, *Daniel Boone or the Pioneer of Kentucky* (1886). Charles H. Forbes-Lindsay's *Daniel Boone: Backwoodsman* (1908) is a historical novel which views the rugged Trans-Appalachian frontier through the eyes of Hardy Goodfellow. There are also chapters on Simon Kenton and the Girty brothers. Daniel Henderson's *Boone of the Wilderness: A Tale of Pioneer Adventures and Achievement in the Dark and Bloody Ground* (1921) begins in 1752 and focuses on Boone's relationship with his Kentucky antagonist, Anthony Arnold. Kentuckian Elizabeth Madox Robert's *The Great Meadow* (1930) is a novel of the adventures of the Jervis family being led over the Wilderness Trail by Evan Muir. It captures the rich regional dialect and folkways of the mountain people.

Popular author of frontier novels Allan W. Eckert's *The Court-Martial of Daniel Boone* (1973) presents a dramatic account of Captain Boone's controversial court-martial in which Boone is unquestionably the hero, and Colonel Richard Callaway, his accuser, is condemned. Eckert uses existing letters and diaries to reconstruct the court-martial scene. Neal Barrett, Jr.'s *Daniel Boone; Westwood Trail* (1982) provides a highly fictionalized account of Boone's conflict between family honor and the lure of the boundless frontier. The language is sometimes crude, with several references to Boone's sexual relations with Indian women.

There have been a number of children's novels written about Boone. Some of the significant accounts are: Garrett M. Davis's *In the Footsteps of Boone: An Historical Romance of Pioneer Days in Kentucky* (1903); Everett T. Tomilson's *Scouting with Daniel Boone* (1914), lavishly illustrated by Norman Rockwell; and Katherine Clugston's *Wilderness Road* (1937), an adaptation from a CBS radio story by Richard Stevenson. Alexander Key's *With Daniel Boone on the Caroliny Trail* (1941) presents an account of Boone and George Washington meeting on the Pennsylvania border. Augusta Stevenson's *Daniel Boone, Boy Hunter* (1943) is poorly written and extremely inaccurate. Two novels by Enid L. Meadowcraft, *On Indian*

Trails with Daniel Boone (1947) and *Holding the Fort with Daniel Boone* (1958), concentrate on the crucial year of 1778. All of these novels are suitable for elementary through junior high school students. *Daniel Boone* (1955), a three act play by Leona Baptist, focuses on Boone's capture by the Shawnees and the siege at Boonesborough in 1778.

Several poems have been composed about the frontiersman. Boone's nephew, Daniel Bryan, wrote *The Mountain Muse: Comprising the Adventures of Daniel Boone and the Powers of Virtuous and Refined Beauty* (1813), an epic poem that offers a highly romanticized account emphasizing the natural man theme, but marred by many historical inaccuracies. Several years later the famous English romanticist, Lord George Byron, composed a poem entitled *Don Juan* (1821) which devotes eight cantos to Boone as an apostle of republicanism and an example of the natural man who tamed the rugged frontier. A long poem, Ruby Dell Baugher's *Listening Hills* (1947), studies Boone's Kentucky life within the context of a man ordained by God to open up the Western wilderness to civilization.

Portions of Boone's life have provided the subject for two Hollywood movies and one television series. Released in 1936, *Daniel Boone*, starring George O'Brien, directed by David Howard, and written by Daniel Jarrett (based on a story by Edgecumb Pinchon), is a romantic version of Boone's Kentucky years, focussing on the founding and later siege of Boonesborough, relations with Indians and the renegade Simon Girty (played by John Carradine), and the treacherous Virginia aristocrats who usurp all the pioneers' land. In 1957 *Daniel Boone, Trailblazer* was released, starring Bruce Bennett, directed by Ismael Rodriguez and Albert C. Gannaway, and written by Tom Hubbard and John Patrick. Filmed in Mexico, the movie focuses on Boone leading a group of settlers from the Yadkin Valley to Boonesborough, and their trouble with the Indians who are incited by a French renegade and British redcoats. Both films were box office disappointments. From 1964 to 1970, NBC television produced 165 episodes of *Daniel Boone*, starring Fess Parker and produced by George Sherman, which presents Boone as a literate, heroic figure.

The National Information Center for Educational Media has produced several videotapes dealing with Boone's life. "Daniel Boone," a fifteen-minute tape, examines how Boone's first experiences as a hunter prepared him for later wilderness adventures; and "Daniel Boone in America's Story," a sixteen-minute tape, traces Boone's life, placing it in the context of the French and Indian War, the Revolutionary War, and the Louisiana Purchase. Both tapes are suitable for junior and senior high school students. Boone's life has also been adapted into an outdoor drama, *The Legend of Daniel Boone*, written by Jan Hartman, which has played every summer since 1970 at Harrodsburg, Kentucky. Even a song about Daniel Boone exists: "Air: The Girl I Left Behind Me" appears in the Boy Scout Song Book, with words by F. H. Martens.

Museums, Historical Landmarks, Societies

The Boone Family Association. Composed of descendants of Daniel and Rebecca Boone, there are several active chapters throughout the United States. The California Chapter (Columbia, CA) has an official publication, *Sierra Echoes*, dedicated to assisting persons interested in Boone family genealogy.

Boone's Lick State Historical Site (Booneville, MO). The location of a salt lick discovered by Boone in 1805.

Boone Memorial Gardens (Boone, NC). This location has a replica of a cabin used by Daniel Boone or one of his family. Adjacent to the gardens is an outdoor drama, "Horn in the West," featuring Boone.

The Daniel Boone Home (Defiance, MO). This first stone dwelling in Missouri was built by Boone's son, Nathan. It contains documents, furniture, and artifacts of the Boone family, and is open for tours.

Daniel Boone Homestead (Birdsboro, PA). The birthsite and homestead of Daniel Boone, built about 1730, where Boone lived from 1734 to 1750. It has a smokehouse, blacksmith shop, barn, log house, and water powered sawmill. The house and grounds are open for tours.

Daniel Boone State Park (Mocksville, NC). This location has a replica of a log cabin built by Daniel's father, Squire Boone, shortly after the Boone family arrived in North Carolina.

Fort Boonesborough State Park (Madison County, KY). Dedicated in 1965 to the memory of Kentucky's earliest pioneers, the park contains a 1907 Daughters of the American Revolution marker designating the site of the original fort. In addition, there is a self-guided historic walking tour of the area, dotted with numerous historical markers, and a reconstructed model of the fort, built in 1974, with a small museum and several arts and crafts shops. The park is open from April through October.

Mason County Museum (Maysville, KY). There are many Daniel Boone and Simon Kenton artifacts located here.

The Society of Boonesborough (Richmond, KY). This organization, primarily genealogical in nature, is dedicated to preserving the memory of the original settlers of Fort Boonesborough.

Other Sources

Beiting, Ralph W. *Soldier of the Revolution: A New View of Daniel Boone.* Jefferson City, MO: Modern Litho Print, 1977. Provides sources, photographs and other information on Daniel Boone's life and times, and locations of historical sites and museums devoted to Boone.

Clubbe, John. *Byron's Natural Man: Daniel Boone*. Lexington, KY: The King Library Press, 1980. This is an analysis of the eight cantos written about Daniel Boone in Lord Byron's poem, *Don Juan*. It examines why Byron selected Boone, the poet's attitude toward America and republican government, and which sources he used for the Boone passage.

Fishwick, M. W. "Daniel Boone and the Pattern of the Western Hero." *Filson Club History Quarterly* 27 (1953): 119-138. This study provides an examination of sources—Timothy Flint's biography of Boone, Horatio Greenough's ante-bellum painting of the struggle between Boone and an Indian, George C. Bingham's 1851 painting of Boone leading settlers into an Eden-like land, and Boy Scout leader Daniel Beard's use of Boone as an exemplar—which have contributed to Boone's enduring heroic image.

Kellogg, Louise P. "The Fame of Daniel Boone." *Register of the Kentucky Historical Society* 32 (July 1934): 185-197. This article attempts to correct Clarence W. Alvord's 1926 essay on the Boone myth. It analyzes traits—love of solitude, moderation and self-control, and integrity—that led to Boone's fame, and makes extensive use of the Draper manuscripts.

Kincaid, Robert L. *The Wilderness Road*. Harrogate, TN: Lincoln Memorial University Press, 1947. This scholarly account makes good use of primary source material on the history of the famous road, and contains numerous references to Boone.

Lofaro, Michael A. "The Eighteenth Century Autobiographies of Daniel Boone." *Register of the Kentucky Historical Society* 78 (Autumn 1978): 85-97. Using Henry Nash Smith's theory that Boone represents a duality between the agent of civilization and primitive man of nature, the author traces the similarities and differences between John Filson's and John Trumbull's biographies of Boone.

Moore, Arthur K. *The Frontier Mind: A Cultural Analysis of the Kentucky Frontiersman*. Lexington: University of Kentucky Press, 1957. An analysis of the negative forces working on the frontier. It is very critical of early Boone biographers' overemphasis of the natural man theme.

Ranck, George W. *Boonesborough: Its Founding, Pioneer Struggles, Indian Experiences, Transylvania Days, and Revolutionary Annals*. Louisville, KY: John P. Morton, 1901. This is the best book written on the history of Boonesborough. It makes extensive use of primary source material, much of which appears in the appendix, and clearly views Boone as a force which held the early community together.

Smith, Henry Nash. *Virgin Land: The American West as Symbol and Myth*. Cambridge, MA: Harvard University Press, 1950. This study is a brilliant intellectual history of how the nineteenth-century West influenced and shaped the life and character of American society. It views Boone as a product of the popular image of civilization's standard bearer on one hand, and child of nature on the other.

Walton, John. *John Filson of Kentucke*. Lexington, KY: University of Kentucky Press, 1956. Provides a careful analysis of the architect of the Boone legend, although some may question his contention that Boone was America's first hero, from which others have been modeled.

Young, Chester Raymond. *Westward into Kentucky: The Narrative of Daniel Trabue*. Lexington, KY: University Press of Kentucky, 1981. This is a well-edited work of primary source information about one of Boone's Kentucky contemporaries; it is especially useful for data about the frontiersman's 1778 court-martial trial.

Charles C. Hay III
Eastern Kentucky University

Daniel Boone, 1968

WILLIAM E. BORAH
1865-1940

Chronology

Born William Edgar Borah on June 29, 1865, in Fairfield, Illinois, the son of William N. Borah, a farmer, and Elizabeth West Borah; *1865-1883* is raised in Fairfield, where he attends Tom's Prairie School and Cumberland Presbyterian Academy; *1883* moves to Lyons, Kansas, where he becomes a teacher; *1885-1887* attends University of Kansas; *1887-1890* practices law in Lyons; *1890* moves to Boise, Idaho; *1891* marries Mamie McConnell; *1891-1903* is a partner in the Boise law firm of Stewart and Borah; becomes prominent as a trial lawyer; *1899-1907* as prosecutor of Idaho's law cases, he successfully prosecutes officials of Western Federation of Miners; *1907-1940* serves as a Republican senator from Idaho; gains a reputation for oratory, political independence, anti-interventionism, and domestic progressivism; *1924-1933* chairman of Senate Foreign Relations Committee; *1940* dies on January 19 in Washington, D.C.

Activities of Historical Significance

As senator, Borah was one of the most powerful legislators ever to frequent the halls of Congress. As chairman of the Senate Foreign Relations Committee, "Big Bill" could exercise more influence than the secretary of state. To liberals, he appeared as living proof that the Republican party embodied more than the forces of vested privilege. To intellectuals, he appeared as a voice of conscience in a political world governed by expediency. Borah possessed a rugged handsomeness, an eloquent speaking style, and an extraordinary ability to capture publicity.

Borah began his career as a vigorous expansionist, backing American participation in the Spanish-American War, the annexation of the Philippines, Theodore Roosevelt's foreign policy, a tough posture towards Mexico, and entry into World War I. The Great War challenged his imperialistic assumptions, and as it ended, Borah became a leading "Irreconcilable" who adamantly opposed American participation in the League of Nations.

He regained national visibility in 1921 by his call for the convening of the Washington Naval Conference. Once it assembled, however, he denounced it as a conspiracy to divide the spoils of China and entrench an aggressive Japan on the Asian mainland. He was most influential in securing adoption of the Kellogg-Briand Pact (1928), though at first he was suspicious of the agreement; he gave his backing only when he was assured there would be no provisions for enforcement. He fought American entry into the World Court with the same passion he exhibited in fighting banking and railroad "interests" in his native Idaho. In some ways, he was quite globally-minded, for he opposed America's Siberian intervention (1918-

1920), served as a leader in the movement to recognize the Soviet Union, and opposed American intervention in Central America.

In domestic politics, Borah was long known as a political maverick. He supported most of Theodore Roosevelt's domestic policies but was cool to those of Woodrow Wilson. In 1920, he was a major supporter of Hiram Johnson for president. An advocate of prohibition and the free coinage of silver, he sought federal licensing of all interstate corporations, profit sharing, and the outlawing of child labor and wage discrimination against women. He thought Franklin D. Roosevelt a genuine liberal, and he supported such New Deal measures as social security, while opposing the National Industrial Recovery Act (1933) and Supreme Court reorganization (1937).

Overview of Biographical Sources

For many years, journalists perceived Borah as a political "rogue elephant," the title given him in Ray Tucker and Frederick R. Barkley, *Sons of the Wild Jackass* (1932). Serious writing began with Claudius O. Johnson, *Borah of Idaho* (1936), a scholarly work by a political scientist. Within twenty years after Borah's death, professional historians produced monographs of high caliber, including J. Chalmers Vinson, *William E. Borah and the Outlawry of War* (1957); Robert James Maddox, *William E. Borah and American Foreign Policy* (1969); and Leroy Ashby, *The Spearless Leader: Senator Borah and the Progressive Movement in the 1920s* (1972). Marian C. McKenna, *Borah* (1961), is the only full-length biography; it makes excellent use of his unpublished papers.

Evaluation of Principal Biographical Sources

Ashby, Leroy. *The Spearless Leader: Senator Borah and the Progressive Movement in the 1920s*. Urbana: University of Illinois Press, 1972. **(A)** Centers on the disappointments many progressives felt with Borah's inability to offer them responsible leadership. Ashby interprets Borah's weaknesses as a progressive leader in terms of a rugged individualism rooted in a disappearing frontier.

Johnson, Claudius O. *Borah of Idaho*. New York: Longmans, Green, 1936. **(A, G)** Although this book is close to being an authorized biography, it is both solid and scholarly. Particularly helpful on details of the League fight, it notes that Borah held President Wilson's respect throughout the controversy.

Maddox, Robert James. *William E. Borah and American Foreign Policy*. Baton Rouge: Louisiana State University Press, 1969. **(A)** Maddox argues that Borah had a far more practical comprehension of foreign affairs than his often grotesque rhetoric and utopian peace plans indicate. Yet the book is revisionist only to a point: "Endlessly professing his yearning for international cooperation, he opposed every serious effort to bring it about."

McKenna, Marian C. *Borah*. Ann Arbor: University of Michigan Press, 1961. **(A, G)** A professional historian supplies the best complete life. In this sympathetic account that delves into the League issue, McKenna argues that he and President Wilson differed not on principle, but methods. Challenging the picture of Borah as a narrow isolationist, she writes, "The question with him was not withdrawal from world affairs, but when and where and how much to use the country's influence."

Vinson, J. Chalmers. *William E. Borah and the Outlawry of War*. Athens: University of Georgia Press, 1957. **(A)** Shows how an isolationist could be an active leader in working for peace. It also ably demonstrates the interaction between Borah and the burgeoning peace movement of the 1920s.

Overview and Evaluation of Primary Sources

Borah's own writings can be found in several collections. *American Problems: A Collection of Speeches and Prophecies by William E. Borah*, edited by Horace Green (New York: Duffield, 1924; **A, G**), includes his speeches on the League of Nations, Versailles, the Disarmament Conference of 1921, and recognition of the Soviet Union. *Bedrock*, edited by Horace Green (Washington: National Home Library Foundation, 1936; **A, G**), is another volume of Borah speeches.

The William E. Borah Papers at the Library of Congress consist of over 700 poorly organized boxes dealing mostly with routine matters.

Other Sources

Cooper, John Milton. "William E. Borah, Political Thespian." *Pacific Northwest Quarterly* 56 (October 1965): 145–158. A strong critique. Borah is seen as simplistically reducing political problems to moral absolutes. The article includes a rejoinder by Borah biographer Claudius O. Johnson.

Leuchtenberg, William E. "William E. Borah." In *Dictionary of American Biography*, supp. 2, edited by Robert Livingstone Schuyler. New York: Scribner's, 1958. A standard biographical sketch.

Toth, Charles W. "Isolationism and the Emergence of Borah: An Appeal to the American Tradition." *Western Political Quarterly* 14 (June 1961): 555–568. Asserts that Borah believed cooperation with other nations and complete independence in foreign policy were compatible.

Justus D. Doenecke
New College of the University of South Florida

LOUIS D. BRANDEIS
1856–1941

Chronology

Born Louis David Brandeis on November 13, 1856, in Louisville, Kentucky, the son of Adolph and Frederika Dembitz Brandeis, members of a prosperous and cultured family of Bohemian-Jewish immigrants who fled Europe after the failure of the liberal Revolutions of 1848; changes his middle name to Dembitz later in life; *1872* completes his early education in the public schools of Louisville; *1872–1875* the Brandeis family lives in Europe, and Louis attends schools in Dresden; *1875–1878* attends Harvard Law School (though he never attended an undergraduate institution) and compiles the best academic record in the history of the school; *1878* practices law in St. Louis; *1879–1916* is an attorney in Boston, and a leading, if somewhat controversial, figure in the Boston bar; *March 22, 1891* marries Alice Goldmark, a second cousin and the daughter of a prominent family of intellectuals and social activists—they remain married until Brandeis's death and have two daughters, Susan and Elizabeth; *1895–1916* becomes a leading progressive reformer on the municipal, the state, and finally on the national level; crusades for a dozen causes ranging from municipal reform to conservation of natural resources, from the rights of labor to the creation of a new form of life insurance, from scientific management of industry to the struggle against monopoly and big business; *1908–1915* argues a series of cases defending the right of states to protect workers by limiting hours of labor and setting a minimum wage; invents "the Brandeis brief," a form of argument that relies on sociological evidence rather than upon legal precedent in order to show the necessity for such social legislation; *1912* meets Woodrow Wilson during the presidential campaign and becomes his adviser, urging him to espouse positions that become known as "the new freedom"; *1913–1916* serves as an informal adviser to President Wilson and is the architect of several important pieces of progressive legislation; *1914–1941* takes an active interest and a leadership role in the American Zionist movement and helps to make that movement a major force in American-Jewish life; *January 28, 1916* Wilson nominates him to become an Associate Justice of the United States Supreme Court, and after a lengthy and bitter confirmation struggle, is confirmed and takes his seat in June; *1916–1939* serves as one of the most influential and illustrious justices in American history; *1919* visits Palestine in connection with his interest in Zionism; *1921–1931* the Brandeis faction of the American Zionist movement is ousted from power by a faction loyal to the English Zionist Chaim Weizmann, and Brandeis, while remaining a loyal and committed Zionist, has little to do with the day-to-day operations of the movement; *1933–1937* becomes involved in the New Deal administration of Franklin Roosevelt as an opponent of concentrated business, an advocate of conservation and workers' unemployment insurance, and, perhaps

176

most important, as a behind-the-scenes presence, with his friend Felix Frankfurter, in making executive appointments and in influencing the policies and programs of various executive departments; *February 13, 1939* resigns from the Supreme Court; *1941* dies on October 5 in Washington, D.C., following a heart attack.

Activities of Historical Significance

During his lifetime, Brandeis made genuinely significant contributions in several fields, but four areas of endeavor deserve special comment: progressive reform; social legislation; American Zionism; and the Supreme Court.

His work on behalf of progressive reform in the early twentieth century was notable, not only for his untiring energy, persistence, and effectiveness, but also for the way in which he exemplified and helped to define a particular kind of reform activity. His earliest efforts were in Boston, where he worked for honest government, public control of transportation facilities, and rationalization of the chaotic gas industry. In connection with the last effort, he invented the "sliding scale," which tied increasing corporate dividends for stockholders to lower gas prices for consumers. His two most important efforts on the state level were the creation of Savings Bank Life Insurance, a form of low-cost insurance sold in the Savings Banks of Massachusetts to low-income wage earners (a reform which he regarded as his most satisfying, and one to which he gave constant attention for a third of a century); and the ten-year struggle against the New York, New Haven & Hartford Railroad's attempt to secure a monopoly over New England transportation.

His fame as a local and state reformer inevitably drew him to the national arena. There he played an active part in the Pinchot-Ballinger conservation controversy in 1910; in settling the huge New York garment industry strike, and establishing influential innovations in labor-management relations (the "preferential union shop" and an arbitration mechanism within the industry); in the efforts of the Interstate Commerce Commission to set equitable railroad rates; and in early attempts by Senator Robert M. La Follette and others to make the Sherman Antitrust Act a more effective tool against the domination of big business. During the first years of the Wilson administration, he helped to prepare such crucial New Freedom legislation as the Federal Reserve Act, the Clayton Antitrust Act, and the Federal Trade Commission Act. By the time he was appointed to the High Court, Brandeis symbolized that sort of progressive reform that emphasized democratic control, a restoration of free competition, and a rigorous war against what he called "the curse of bigness." By 1916, he was well known across the country as "the people's attorney."

Brandeis's work on behalf of social legislation was also historically significant— both for the actual changes in the conditions of labor that he helped to bring about, and for the legal innovations he employed in order to achieve these changes. Beginning in 1908, when he defended an Oregon law for a ten-hour workday for women (*Muller v. Oregon*), until his appointment to the High Court in 1916, Brandeis defended various state laws designed to improve the lot of working people. His method of argument was to marshal large quantities of evidence—studies by social workers, sociologists, doctors, and others—which showed the harmful effects of low pay, long hours, and harsh working conditions. This method of arguing, which required judges to notice both the legal precedents involved in a dispute and the actual effects upon society of certain social arrangements, was part of the general movement toward a "sociological jurisprudence." Brandeis deserves some of the credit for this important change, which affected both social-industrial legislation and the right of individual states to experiment.

Brandeis has a secure place in the history of the Jewish people in America. Although not a religious man himself, and certainly never a "practicing" Jew, he became interested in Zionism in 1912 and, with the outbreak of World War I, accepted the leadership of the American Zionist movement. He poured himself into this work with his usual energy and literally built the movement from the ground up, until it was an extremely powerful part of American-Jewish life. He applied methods of efficiency, discipline, practicality, and attention to detail (methods so successful in his work as a progressive reformer) to this effort and can literally be regarded as the founding father of effective American Zionism. He resigned official leadership after appointment to the Court, but continued to informally direct affairs in the movement until 1921. He played a small, but important, part in the British decision to issue the Balfour Declaration, promising a "Jewish homeland" in Palestine.

From 1921 to 1931 the American Zionist movement was in the hands of his opponents, and his role was much reduced. With the return of his followers to power, he once again assumed an important, but informal, advisory position. He interceded several times with President Roosevelt on behalf of Jewish interests in Palestine.

Brandeis is also notable in American-Jewish history because his immense stature symbolized the growing acceptance of Jews in American culture. He was the first Jew ever appointed to the Supreme Court and, despite occasional brushes with anti-Semitism during his career, he encouraged by example many young Jews to enter into the political, social, and intellectual life of the United States. His own successes persuaded many—both Jews and non-Jews—that there was no contradiction in being a Jew and being a patriotic American, devoted to the service of the nation.

Finally, Brandeis's twenty-three year career as an Associate Justice was historically significant. He participated fully in the work of the Court and felt a great loyalty to it as an institution. He was a consistent "liberal" in his judicial decisions, and he frequently dissented from the majority opinions of the often conservative Court. Indeed, he was probably best known, in the popular mind, for joining with his longtime friend and colleague, Justice Oliver Wendell Holmes, in these dissents. He had the great satisfaction of seeing a number of these minority opinions—

including some on important matters of judicial policy—later become the opinion of the majority and the law of the land. Brandeis was an eloquent and persuasive spokesman for the protection of civil liberties, for the maintenance of competition in the face of big business, for the public regulation of public utilities, for the rights of organized labor, and for limiting the authority of the central government while protecting the rights of the individual states to undertake political and economic experiments.

Overview of Biographical Sources

Justice Brandeis steadfastly refused to cooperate with most of the people who wished to write about him. During his lifetime, studies were done by Jacob DeHass (1929), emphasizing Brandeis's Zionist work, by Alfred Lief (1936), and by Bernard Flexner (1938), covering the Judge's efforts on behalf of the University of Louisville; but their subject refused even to read or review these manuscripts before publication. He similarly had nothing to do with the celebratory collections of articles about himself edited by Felix Frankfurter (1932). He relented somewhat to Alpheus T. Mason, a Princeton professor. On the strength of earlier studies he had made of Brandeis's career, Mason was given access to the retired Justice's private papers and granted a series of interviews during the summer of 1940.

For more than twenty-five years, Mason's *Brandeis: A Free Man's Life* (1946) was the standard and definitive biography. Mason's work was characterized by warm praise for Brandeis's character, career, methods, and ideals; there are almost no negative judgments passed upon his subject. In the years after 1970, a flood of work about Brandeis has appeared: a number of excellent full-length biographies, and many studies of parts of his life and work.

The best full-length books have been done by Melvin I. Urofsky (1971; 1981), Allon Gal (1980), Nelson L. Dawson (1980), Lewis Paper (1983), and Philippa Strum (1984). On the whole, these tend to be more balanced in their approach, and, although demonstrating high regard for Brandeis's achievements and motives, each of these biographers is willing to discuss more questionable aspects of his life and character. The most penetrating critical studies have been done by Richard Abrams (1962), Bruce Allen Murphy (1982), and Thomas K. McCraw (1984; 1985). Each of these writers demonstrates superb scholarship, and none of them ignores Brandeis's many contributions. Thus, half a century after his death, some of the most extravagant evaluations of Brandeis's virtues have been tempered by recent scholarship, but he still enjoys an extremely high reputation among historians and the general public.

Evaluation of Principal Biographical Sources

Abrams, Richard M. "Brandeis and the New Haven-Boston & Maine Merger

Battle Revisited." *Business History Review* 36 (1962): 408–430. **(A)** Abrams challenges some of Brandeis's economic assumptions and defends his opponents in the merger battle, claiming that they were men deeply committed to improving Massachusetts's commercial position by consolidating the transportation system. Abrams succeeds in lifting the controversy from the simplistic tone of "good v. evil."

Dawson, Nelson L. *Louis D. Brandeis, Felix Frankfurter, and the New Deal.* Hamden: Archon, 1980. **(A, G)** A short, but thoroughly researched study of the activities of the two men during the New Deal. It gives the details of the behind-the-scene efforts of the pair to staff executive departments and to influence New Deal policy.

Frankfurter, Felix, ed. *Mr. Justice Brandeis.* New Haven: Yale University Press, 1932. **(A, G)** This is a collection of affectionate essays written to celebrate his seventy-fifth birthday. The essays are by Justice Holmes, Chief Justice Hughes, Max Lerner, Donald Richberg, Henry W. Bikle, Walton H. Hamilton, and Frankfurter. The book also lists Brandeis's opinions from the start of his service on the Court until the close of the October 1930 term.

Freund, Paul A. "Louis Dembitz Brandeis." In *The Dictionary of American Biography,* supplement 3. New York: Charles Scribner's Sons, 1973. **(A, G)** This concise, accurate, and thorough account is written by a former law clerk and a distinguished scholar of American constitutional law. It is probably the best biographical article of its length.

Gal, Allon. *Brandeis of Boston.* Cambridge: Harvard University Press, 1980. **(A, G)** This outstanding monograph by an Israeli scholar examines Brandeis's early life until 1916. Gal lays particular stress on Brandeis's "Jewishness" and on the anti-Semitism he encountered as a young Boston lawyer. The work is notable for Gal's meticulous digging into obscure sources, and for his sharp and sometimes striking insights.

Konefsky, Samuel J. *The Legacy of Holmes and Brandeis: A Study in the Influence of Ideas.* New York: Macmillan, 1956. **(A, G)** This is an illuminating summary and analysis of the judicial philosophies of Holmes and Brandeis, with attention given both to their similarities and differences. Konefsky admires both judges and does an excellent job of showing how two such differing temperaments could see eye to eye so often.

Levy, David W., and Bruce Allen Murphy. "Preserving the Progressive Spirit in a Conservative Time: The Joint Reform Efforts of Justice Brandeis and Professor Felix Frankfurter." *Michigan Law Review* 78 (1980): 1252–1304. **(A)** An attempt to detail both the controversial financial arrangement between Brandeis and Frankfurter and the numerous political, diplomatic, journalistic, Zionist, and personal "assignments" that Brandeis suggested to his young protégé over the years.

Mason, Alpheus T. *Brandeis: A Free Man's Life*. Princeton: Princeton University Press, 1946. **(A, G)** The definitive study for many years, this book is still valuable in some areas. The best parts of the book are Mason's accounts of Brandeis's reform crusades. The weakest parts are his chapters on Zionism and the Supreme Court. Unfortunately, Mason was denied access (by Felix Frankfurter) to the Court papers, making the story of that twenty-three year period of his subject's life superficial and much too brief.

————. *The Brandeis Way: A Case Study in the Workings of Democracy*. Princeton: Princeton University Press, 1938. **(A)** This careful study of Brandeis's work for the Savings Bank Life Insurance reform traces Brandeis's initial outrage over the evils of the insurance industry, his invention of this form of insurance, the legislative battles to establish the reform, and his constant nursing of the system to maturity. On this narrow topic, this is a very useful book.

McCraw, Thomas K. "Louis D. Brandeis Reappraised." *American Scholar* 54 (1985): 525–536. **(A, G)** This judicious reevaluation of Brandeis, conducted in the light of recent studies, finds that his economic views were faulty and that beneath his public image was a highly effective advocate, bent on winning his cases. McCraw also gives credit to Brandeis's integrity, character, and patriotism—thus providing an excellent introduction to the present state of his reputation.

————. *Prophets of Regulation: Charles Francis Adams, Louis D. Brandeis, James M. Landis, Alfred E. Kahn*. Cambridge: Harvard University Press, 1984. **(A, G)** An impressive study of the history of ideas of economic regulation in the United States. McCraw believes that many of Brandeis's economic views and assumptions have been proved wrong by time. This book won the Pulitzer Prize for History in 1985.

Murphy, Bruce Allen. *The Brandeis/Frankfurter Connection: The Secret Political Activities of Two Supreme Court Justices*. New York: Oxford University Press, 1982. **(A, G)** This book focuses on the extra-judicial activities of both men, showing both to be deeply involved in political and economic affairs while serving as Supreme Court justices. Murphy emphasizes the financial connection between Brandeis and Frankfurter—Brandeis paid his younger protégé considerable sums of money after 1916. Although Murphy based his book on prodigious research, he has been roundly criticized both for the conspiratorial tone he sometimes adopts, and for the sensational, and somewhat misleading publicity that accompanied the book's release.

Paper, Lewis. *Brandeis*. Englewood Cliffs, NJ: Prentice Hall, 1983. **(A, G)** One of the worthy new biographies. It is easy to read and contains many anecdotes, although the style sometimes seems excessively dramatic. Paper's book is based on extensive interviews with Brandeis's clerks and with other associates, and is most useful for the light it sheds on Brandeis's personal and family life.

Strum, Philippa. *Louis D. Brandeis: Justice for the People*. Cambridge: Harvard University Press, 1984. **(A, G)** A fine, balanced, thorough account of Brandeis's life. The author touches all aspects of his career, incorporates heretofore unused letters to members of his family, and is particularly valuable on Brandeis's ideological assumptions and philosophic beliefs. The book also has an excellent brief bibliography.

Todd, A. L. *Justice on Trial: The Case of Louis D. Brandeis*. New York: McGraw-Hill, 1964. **(A, G)** An engrossing and dramatic account of the fierce confirmation battle of 1916, when Brandeis's entire previous life was displayed before the Senate committee hearing testimony on his "fitness" for the office of Associate Justice.

Urofsky, Melvin I. *A Mind of One Piece: Brandeis and American Reform*. New York: Scribner's, 1971. **(A, G)** This book is a series of essays, each one examining a particular aspect of Brandeis's work. But each aspect, according to Urofsky, illuminates a life and a mind most notable for its unity of purpose. The essays are stimulating and valuable.

————. *Louis D. Brandeis and the Progressive Tradition*. Boston: Little, Brown, 1981. **(A, G)** An excellent short account of Brandeis's life, especially useful for readers who want a brief, but solid summary.

Overview and Evaluation of Primary Sources

The primary sources relating to Brandeis's life and career may be considered under two headings: personal papers, letters, and documents; and his writings and speeches.

He left behind a huge mass of personal papers, letters, and documents, which may be found in several places. Those relating to his Court work are at the Harvard Law School; those touching upon his non-judicial and reform activities, as well as his personal life, are at the Library of the Law School of the University of Louisville. Sixty-nine volumes of Brandeis's "Scrapbooks," containing mostly newspaper clippings, are also deposited there. An extensive group of papers relating to his legal practice are kept by his old law firm in Boston. The Zionist papers are at the Hebrew University in Jerusalem, although sizeable sections of them may also be found in Louisville, Harvard, and the American Jewish Archives in Cincinnati (which has thirty-two microfilm reels of Brandeis's Zionist correspondence). A large group of letters written to his wife and daughter Susan have been deposited at the Goldfarb Library of Brandeis University. These various depositories have arranged to exchange and share their holdings, so any one of them may have, on microfilm or by other means of reproduction, copies of materials deposited in the others.

In addition, Melvin I. Urofsky and David W. Levy have edited a five-volume collection of *The Letters of Louis D. Brandeis* (Albany: State University of New York Press, 1971–1978; **A**). They have also edited two additional volumes of letters: *"Half Brother, Half Son: The Letters of Louis D. Brandeis to Felix Frankfurter* (Norman: University of Oklahoma Press, 1989; **A**), and a forthcoming book of letters to members of his family. There are also two extensive microfilm editions of Brandeis papers: Abraham L. Sachar and William M. Goldsmith, eds., *A Microfilm Edition of the Public Papers of Louis Dembitz Brandeis in the Jacob and Martha Goldfarb Library of Brandeis University* (Cambridge: General Microfilm, 1978; **A**); and Thomas L. Owen and Janet Hodgson, eds., *The Papers of Louis Dembitz Brandeis at the University of Louisville* (Louisville: University of Louisville Law School, 1980; **A**). The latter edition runs to 184 reels of film.

The second major body of primary materials comes from his pre-Court career. Brandeis wrote a considerable number of articles on various topics related to his reform work and gave testimony to Massachusetts or Congressional bodies on a number of occasions. For a comprehensive listing of these published works see Roy R. Mersky, ed., *Louis Dembitz Brandeis, 1856–1941; a Bibliography* (New Haven: Yale Law School, 1958; **A**). Two collections of articles were supervised by the author: Louis D. Brandeis, ed., *Business—A Profession* (Boston: Small, Maynard, 1914; 1933; **G**), and Brandeis, ed., *Other People's Money and How the Bankers Use It* (New York: F. A. Stokes, 1914, 1932; **G**). A recent edition of *Other People's Money*, by Harper & Row (1967), contains a useful introduction by Richard M. Abrams.

In addition, there are valuable collections of Brandeis's writings, testimony, speeches, and letters: Osmond K. Fraenkel, ed., *The Curse of Bigness* (New York: Viking Press, 1934; **G**); two collections compiled by Rabbi Solomon Goldman, *Brandeis on Zionism* (Washington, DC: Zionist Organization of America, 1942; **G**), and *The Words of Justice Brandeis* (New York: Henry Schuman, 1953; **G**); and two collections by Alfred Lief, *The Social and Economic Views of Mr. Justice Brandeis* (New York: Vanguard Press, 1930; **G**), and *The Brandeis Guide to the Modern World* (Boston: Little, Brown, 1941; **G**). Another collection of his writings is Ervin H. Pollack, ed., *The Brandeis Reader: The Life and Contribution of Mr. Justice Brandeis* (New York: Oceana, 1956; **G**). Also noteworthy is Alexander M. Bickel, ed., *The Unpublished Opinions of Mr. Justice Brandeis* (Cambridge: Harvard University Press, 1957; **A, G**).

Museums, Historical Landmarks, Societies

Brandeis Plaque (St. Louis, MO). Marks the place where Brandeis was admitted to the bar.

Brandeis Summer Home (Chatham, MA). Located on Cape Cod, this home has been designated a National Historic Landmark.

Brandeis University (Waltham, MA). This institution, named in his honor, owns a collection of Brandeis memorabilia.

Ein HaShofet (Israel). A kibbutz named "Spring of the Judge" in recognition of Brandeis's financial contributions to its establishment.

Harvard Law School (Cambridge, MA). Owns a collection of memorabilia.

University of Louisville Law School (Louisville, KY). Brandeis's ashes, together with those of his wife, are here, accompanied by a simple marker. This institution houses a collection of memorabilia as well.

Other Sources

Abrams, Richard M. *Conservatism in a Progressive Era.* Cambridge: Harvard University Press, 1964. Abrams provides an able description of the setting of Massachusetts politics during Brandeis's time.

Bernard, Burton C. "Brandeis in St. Louis." *St. Louis Bar Journal* 11 (1964): 54–60. The article is a meticulous account of Brandeis's first year of legal practice.

Freund, Paul. "Mr. Justice Brandeis." *Harvard Law Review* 55 (1941): 195–196. This former clerk renders a particularly moving reminiscence. This issue, published at Brandeis's death, contains several such reminiscences.

Landis, James M. "Mr. Justice Brandeis and the Harvard Law School." *Harvard Law Review* 55 (1941): 184–190. Landis, a former clerk and the Dean of Harvard Law, tells about Brandeis's lifelong devotion to the school and his many contributions to its program.

Mann, Arthur. *Yankee Reformers in an Urban Age.* Cambridge: Harvard University Press, 1954. This is another fine account of Massachusetts political life at the turn of the century.

McClennen, Edward F. "Louis D. Brandeis as a Lawyer." *Massachusetts Law Quarterly* 33 (1948): 1–28. McClennen was the law partner who managed Brandeis's "case" before the Senate subcommittee hearing testimony on his 1916 nomination. This is an affectionate remembrance of Brandeis, the attorney.

Shapiro, Yonathan. *Leadership of the American Zionist Organization, 1898–1930.* Urbana: University of Illinois Press, 1971. This important study of the Zionist movement, and Brandeis's role in it, explores tensions between the "Americanized" leadership of Brandeis and his followers and the Eastern European rivals for control of the organization. He emphasizes anti-Semitism in accounting for Brandeis's turn to Zionism.

Urofsky, Melvin I. *American Zionism from Herzl to the Holocaust*. Garden City: Doubleday, 1975. A balanced and fascinating picture of the Zionist movement in America.

U.S. Congress, Committee on the Judiciary. *Hearings Before the Subcommittee on the Nomination of Louis D. Brandeis to be an Associate Justice of the Supreme Court of the United States*. 2 vols. 64th Congress, 2nd session, 1916. This official transcript of the Brandeis hearing still makes gripping reading and provides the best account of the dramatic ordeal that the nominee endured at his confirmation. The 1700 page record also contains many documents and testimonials, both for and against the nominee.

David W. Levy
The University of Oklahoma

JOSEPH BRANT
c.1742–1807

Chronology

Born Thayendanegea, probably in 1742, near the Ohio River, the son of Nickus Brant, a full-blooded Mohawk and chief of the Wolf clan, and an obscure Shawnee woman; *1742–1755* lives with his mother and stepfather after his father dies; he is an intelligent boy, but does not appear destined for greatness among his people because his father is dead and his mother is not a Mohawk; *1755–1761* his life is dramatically altered when one of his sisters, Molly Brant, becomes the common-law wife of Sir William Johnson, a wealthy and powerful trader and representative of the British government to the nations composing the Iroquois League; *1761–1763* supported by Johnson, he enrolls in Moor's Indian Charity School in Lebanon, Connecticut, and proves himself to be an apt student;*1763–1764* leaves Moor's school and serves in the war against Pontiac, marries in 1764, converts to the Anglican church, and settles into a routine of life befitting a promising young man; *1764–1774* assists Reverend John Stuart in missionary work among the Iroquois, translates religious materials into the Mohawks' tongue, and gradually asserts himself as one of the major leaders of his tribe; *1774–1776* Guy Johnson, who succeeds Sir William Johnson as Great Britain's agent to the Iroquois, appoints Brant as his secretary thereby guaranteeing Brant's rise to eminence; *1775–1776* as the political situation in America deteriorates, he is commissioned a Captain in the King's forces, travels to England where he is entertained by the elite of London's society, sits for a portrait done by George Romney and returns to America with a deepened commitment to Great Britain; *1776–1783* participates in the American Revolution opposing the rebelling colonists, and leads Indian troops in an abortive attack on Fort Schuyler, in the Battle of Oriskany, and in raids in the Lake Oswego area and the Cherry Valley in New York; *1783–1785* after the war journeys to Great Britain and seeks compensation for Mohawk losses in the war and obtains a grant of land along the Grand River in Ontario, Canada; *1785–1800* leads his people to the Grand River where they establish the village of Brantford and attempt to rebuild their society; *1800–1807* lives on his estate near Brantford, continues to lead his people, frequently travels abroad; *1807* dies on November 24 and is buried in the Grand River Cemetery in Brantford, Ontario.

Activities of Historical Significance

Joseph Brant was one of the dominant political and military leaders among the Iroquois during the era of the American Revolution. Prior to the war, he had steadily risen to prominence in the councils of the Iroquois League and had clearly demonstrated his skills as a wise politician and statesman. He was, for example, elevated to the status of a "Pine Tree Chief" among the Iroquois nations in 1774. A "Pine Tree Chief" was a man chosen for his honor, wisdom, and bravery and such a figure wielded great influence among the Iroquois. Except for brief service in the war against Pontiac in 1763, Brant's role among the Iroquois was that of a rising politician and Christian missionary. Then, when the American Revolution began, he assumed the mantle of soldier and led his people in the struggle to suppress the rebellion. In 1777, he participated in the assault upon Fort Schuyler in western New York, fought in the Battle of Oriskany, and, in 1778, led a series of raids in the vicinity of Lake Oswego and directed the attack into New York's Cherry Valley. Brant was a resourceful soldier who exhibited both courage and compassion on the battlefield, and his name inspired both fear and respect among his enemies.

When the American Revolution was formally concluded by the Treaty of Paris in 1783, the Mohawks found most of their homeland controlled by the United States, their erstwhile foe. In 1785, Brant decided to travel to England to seek compensation for the losses the Mohawks had suffered as a result of remaining faithful to the British government. His 1785 visit to England proved to be both pleasant and productive. Brant was warmly received by London's social elite that season, and, while enjoying his celebrity, he obtained land grants for his Mohawks along the Grand River in Ontario, Canada. Upon returning to America, Brant led his people to their new lands where they settled, established the town of Brantford, and reconstructed their lives. During this period of painful transition for the Mohawk nation, his abilities as a leader were frequently tested and he proved equal to the challenges. He spent vast amounts of energy protecting Mohawk lands from encroachment by land speculators who tried to victimize the émigrés. Brant also had to encourage his people to persevere and to ward off the political machinations of his old adversary Red Jacket, an influential Seneca leader who sought to discredit him among Indian councils. After the defeat of the Indian forces at Fallen Timbers in 1794, Brant became an advocate for peace with the United States. His peace policy was criticized by many, but he prevailed.

Brant frequently traveled abroad from his estate near the entrance to Burlington Bay on the western shore of Lake Ontario, and, by the time he died in 1807, he had become a grand, elder-statesman and legend. Brant was a capable soldier, but he was an outstanding political figure and deft diplomat who served his people with distinction and devotion.

Overview of Biographical Sources

Even though he lived an eventful life in an exciting time, Brant has been the subject of only two full-scale biographies. William L. Stone's two-volume *Life of Joseph Brant—Thayendanegea* (1838) is the earlier of the two studies of Brant's life. Stone's biography of Brant has several weaknesses but it is still worthwhile reading. Its great attraction lies in the fact that Stone interviewed many people who had first-hand recollections of Brant, and those efforts preserved many intriguing bits of information that would otherwise have been lost. Considering that Stone was doing pioneer work seeking the sources to underpin his examination of Brant's life, he performed a valuable service; but, in light of subsequent scholarship on Indian affairs, British policy in America, and the American Revolution, his work must be approached with caution. The better source for readers who want an up-to-date treatment of Brant's life and times is Isabel Thompson Kelsay's *Joseph Brant, 1743–1807, Man of Two Worlds* (1984). Kelsay's massive study draws heavily on all the scholarship concerning Brant and the Iroquois from Stone's work to the present. Moreover, Kelsay's book is well-written, well-organized, and well-documented.

Evaluation of Principal Biographical Sources

Kelsay, Isabel Thompson. *Joseph Brant, 1743–1807, Man of Two Worlds*. Syracuse, NY: Syracuse University Press, 1984. **(A)** This is the single best source of information concerning Brant. A comprehensive account of his life, it also incorporates modern scholarship concerning the Iroquois and their role in the Revolutionary era and its immediate aftermath.

Stone, William L. *Life of Joseph Brant—Thayendanegea*. 2 vol. New York: Blake, 1838. **(A)** The pioneer study of Brant's life. Stone's work is seriously dated in scope and content, but it must eventually be read by the serious student of this phase of American history. Stone wrote in a spirited fashion, and, while his biography has several serious flaws, it is enjoyable reading.

Overview and Evaluation of Primary Sources

Primary materials concerning Joseph Brant's life are not ample and those that do exist are widely scattered among many collections of manuscripts and published memoirs and diaries. The most impressive sources on the life and times of Joseph Brant may be located in the State Historical Society of Wisconsin's Draper Collection, located in Madison. This collection is named for Lyman Draper, who gathered this imposing mass of material with the intention of writing a biography of Brant. Draper never finished his original plan once William L. Stone's biography of Brant appeared in 1838, but his collection stands as a monument to his interest and diligence. Draper interviewed many of the participants in Brant's life and many more who had first-hand recollections of the circumstances of that complicated era. The major group of materials is entitled the Draper Collection, State Historical Society of Wisconsin, Series F., 22 vol. **(A)**. Contained within that source is the Brant Miscellanies, Draper Collection, 3 vol., State Historical Society of Wisconsin **(A)**. The Brant Miscellanies are a treasure of bits and pieces of information about Brant's life. Both of these sources are essential to the efforts of any researcher who wishes to master the primary materials related to Brant. Another valuable aid in understanding the forces that shaped Brant's destiny in his early years is *The Papers of William Johnson*, 14 vol., edited by James Sullivan, Alexander C. Flick, and Milton W. Hamilton (Albany, NY: State University of New York, 1921–65; **A**). Johnson had a profound effect on Brant's life, and many of the details of his impact on his protégé may be gleaned from this source. Then, there are numerous manuscript collections in such locations as the William L. Clements Library, Ann Arbor, Michigan, and the National Archives and the Library of Congress, both in Washington, D.C.

Fiction and Adaptations

Joseph Brant has not been the direct subject of either novels or films. Readers may, however, enjoy Walter Dumaux Edmond's *Drums Along the Mohawk* (1936). This novel is about American settlers living in the Mohawk River Valley who endure the rigors of war and Indian raids during the American Revolution. It is a readable, action-packed story of life and its uncertainties in a vulnerable settlement during a frontier Indian war. *Drums Along the Mohawk* is not about Brant *per se*, but it portrays the era in which he lived.

Museums, Historical Landmarks, Societies

Her Majesty's Chapel of the Mohawks (Brantford, Ontario). This chapel was built in 1785 with funds raised by Joseph Brant. It was the first Episcopal church in Upper Canada.

Woodland Indian Cultural Centre (Brantford, Ontario). This is an excellent museum in which visitors may learn a good deal about the Mohawks and their culture.

Other Sources

Flexner, James Thomas. *Mohawk Baronet, Sir William Johnson of New York*. New York: Harper and Brothers, 1959. This is the best work on Johnson and his life among the Iroquois.

Graymont, Barbara. *The Iroquois in the American Revolution*. Syracuse, NY: Syracuse University Press, 1972. The best study of the tangled politics surrounding the Iroquois and their role in the War of Independence.

Hamilton, Milton W. "Joseph Brant—'The Most Painted Indian'." *New York History* 39 (April 1958): 119–132. A noteworthy article concerning the portraits of Brant done by famous artists of his time.

Hunt, George T. *The Wars of the Iroquois: A Study in the Intertribal Trade Relations*. Madison: University of Wisconsin Press, 1940. The standard account of the complex relationships among the Iroquois.

Johnson, Charles M. "Joseph Brant, the Grand River Lands and the Northwest Crisis." *Ontario History* 55 (1963): 119–132. A good account of a phase of Brant's long struggle to protect the Mohawks' claims to the lands granted to them by Great Britain after the American Revolution.

Lydekker, John Wolfe. *The Faithful Mohawks*. New York: Macmillan, 1938. A useful and highly readable account of the Mohawks and their role in frontier politics and warfare.

Larry G. Bowman
University of North Texas

JOHN BROWN
1800–1859

Chronology

Born John Brown on May 9, 1800, in Torrington, Connecticut, to Owen Brown, a farmer, and Ruth Mills Brown; *1805* moves to Hudson, Ohio, where he receives his education, which consists primarily of reading (he receives no formal elementary education); *1812* drives cattle with his father to supply food for troops in the War of 1812; *1816–1817* attends formal school in Massachusetts and Connecticut; *1819–1825* works as a foreman in his father's tanning establishment; *June 21, 1820* marries Dianthe Lusk; *May 1825* moves to Randolph, later called New Richmond, Pennsylvania, establishing his own tannery; *1828–1832* serves as postmaster; *August 10, 1832* his wife dies; *July 11, 1833* marries Mary Ann Day; *1835* returns to Ohio and speculates in land; *1841* begins sheep-farming; *1842* declares bankruptcy; *1844–1851* works as a wool merchant with friend Simon Perkins; *1851–1855* farms land bought from Gerrit Smith, the nation's foremost philanthropist; *1855* travels to Kansas, arriving on August 7; *May 24–25, 1856* kills five supporters of slavery; *September 20, 1856* leaves Kansas for Massachusetts; *March–April 1857* tours New England, raising money; *March 1857* contracts for 1,000 pikes; *May 1857* travels west to Iowa; *December 1857* founds a military school in Iowa; *January 1858* returns to the East; *June 1858* returns to Kansas; *December 1858* conducts a raid into Missouri and frees eleven slaves; *May–June 1859* plots in Boston with the Secret Six; *July 3, 1859* arrives at Harper's Ferry, Virginia (now West Virginia); *October 16, 1859* foray against Harper's Ferry begins; *October 17, 1859* captures Harper's Ferry; *October 18, 1859* Brown is captured; *October 25–November 4, 1859* is tried, found guilty of treason against the state of Virginia, and sentenced to be hanged; *December 2, 1859* is executed by hanging at Charlestown, Virginia (now West Virginia).

Activities of Historical Significance

John Brown's historical significance lies primarily in his controversial activities as an abolitionist. He devoted a large portion of his life to the abolition of slavery and eventually gave his life for the cause he espoused. After spending his first fifty-five years working at numerous occupations in which he was unsuccessful, Brown entered the Kansas territory determined that it should join the Union as a free state, and to that end he worked tirelessly and ruthlessly. On May 21, 1856, the anti-slavery town of Lawrence was attacked, and John Brown retaliated under the pretext that he was working as an agent of God. During the night of May 24–25, 1856, this self-proclaimed avenging angel of the Lord killed five pro-slavery men in what history calls the "Pottawatomie Massacre." The troubles in the territory were henceforth known collectively as "Bleeding Kansas."

After securing support from leading abolitionists, a group of whom became known as the "Secret Six" for their covert assistance, Brown attempted his coup d'état. He devised a scheme to establish a place in the Appalachian Mountains where free blacks and escaped slaves could hide. Wishing to instigate a general slave uprising, he launched an attack upon the federal arsenal at Harper's Ferry. After capturing the armory on October 17, 1859, he was compelled to surrender to a force of marines under Colonel Robert E. Lee. Tried and convicted of treason against the state of Virginia, Brown was hanged in Charlestown on December 2, 1859.

The question of Brown's sanity has sparked a great deal of debate. Many historians accept at face value affidavits collected at the time of his trial attesting that he was insane and that insanity ran in the Brown family. Stephen B. Oates, in his magnificent biography of Brown, rejects psychology as an imprecise science and suggests that it is impossible to determine whether John Brown really was a crazed lunatic.

Overview of Biographical Sources

Nearly all of the biographies of John Brown are either sympathetic defenses or vicious attacks, and most works fall into the former category. The only biographies that attack Brown are Robert Penn Warren, *John Brown: The Making of a Martyr* (1929), and Hills P. Wilson, *John Brown, Soldier of Fortune: A Critique* (1913). Stephen B. Oates, *To Purge This Land With Blood: A Biography of John Brown* (1970), is the only objective and balanced biography.

The defenses of John Brown are numerous, and the best is Oswald G. Villard's meticulously researched *John Brown, 1800–1859; A Biography Fifty Years After* (1910). W. E. B. Du Bois, *John Brown* (1909), offers a sympathetic portrait focusing on Brown's relations with blacks. The earliest of the defenses include William E. Connelley, *John Brown* (1900); Joseph E. Chamberlin, *John Brown* (1899); Franklin B. Sanborn, *The Life and Letters of John Brown* (1885); and James Redpath, *The Public Life of Capt. John Brown* (1860).

Evaluation of Principal Biographical Sources

Connelley, William E. *John Brown*. Topeka, KS: Crane, 1900. **(A, G)** One of the early defenses of Brown, this work focuses on Brown's activities in Kansas and Harper's Ferry. Also included are discourses on slavery in America and politics in Kansas.

Du Bois, W. E. B. *John Brown*. Philadelphia: G. W. Jacobs, 1909. **(A, G)** This sympathetic biography relies on secondary sources. The analysis of Brown's relationship with black Americans is excellent.

Oates, Stephen B. *To Purge This Land With Blood: A Biography of John Brown*. New York: Harper and Row, 1970. **(A, G)** This accurate, complete, and objective treatment of Brown is the best to date.

Redpath, James. *The Public Life of Capt. John Brown, With an Auto-biography of his Childhood and Youth*. Boston: Thayer and Eldridge, 1860. **(A, G)** Although the author vehemently defends Brown throughout and refers to him as a "saint," this work is important and useful for the autobiography that is included.

Sanborn, Franklin B. *The Life and Letters of John Brown*. Boston: Roberts Brothers, 1885. **(A, G)** Another of the many unabashedly sympathetic biographies, this one is valuable for the personal letters it contains.

Villard, Oswald G. *John Brown, 1800–1859; A Biography Fifty Years After*. Gloucester, MA: P. Smith, 1910. **(A, G)** This is a laudatory, yet thoroughly researched, biography.

Warren, Robert Penn. *John Brown: The Making of a Martyr*. New York: Payson and Clark, 1929. **(A, G)** Warren writes a pro-Southern indictment of Brown, which presents him as a thief.

Wilson, Hill Peebles. *John Brown, Soldier of Fortune: A Critique*. Lawrence, KS: Hill P. Wilson, 1913. **(A, G)** Wilson offers an unfavorable portrayal of Brown that is meant to "correct" the sympathetic Villard biography.

Overview and Evaluation of Primary Sources

Although little primary source material has been published, a fine collection of letters, *John Brown Letters* (Wooster, OH: Bell and Howell, 1970; **A, G**), is available on microfilm. Other published primary sources are found in biographies or other monographs, including *The Life, Trial and Execution of Capt. John Brown* (1859. Reprint. New York: R. M. DeWitt, 1969; **A, G**), which contains a fine collection of materials on the raid and trial; the aforementioned Franklin B. Sanborn, *The Life and Letters of John Brown*; and Richard Warch and Jonathan F. Fanton, eds., *John Brown* (Englewood Cliffs, NJ: Prentice-Hall, 1973; **A, G**), a source of many primary documents.

A great deal of manuscript material is available and can be found at numerous repositories: Atlanta University Library; Boston Public Library; John Brown's Farm, Lake Placid, New York; Chicago Historical Society; Houghton Library of Harvard University; Henry E. Huntington Library, San Marino, California; Illinois State Historical Library; Kansas State Historical Society; Library of Congress;

Maryland Historical Society; Ohio Historical Society; Torrington Public Library, Torrington, Connecticut; Western Reserve Historical Society, Cleveland; and Yale University Library. Also useful is Louis Ruchames, ed., *A John Brown Reader* (New York: Abelard-Schuman, 1959; **A, G**), a collection that includes letters by Brown, essays written by people who knew him, and excerpts from a variety of other sources, ranging from the writings of Henry David Thoreau and Ralph Waldo Emerson to the historians of today.

Fiction and Adaptations

John Brown's dramatic raid on Harper's Ferry has inspired many literary works. Perhaps the most famous is Stephen Vincent Benét's classic book-length poem, *John Brown's Body* (1928), which presents the raid in the context of the Civil War. The partisan tone of William Channing's lengthy poem is evident in the title, *John Brown and the Heroes of Harper's Ferry* (1886). Elbert Hubbard's *Time and Chance* (1899) is a two-volume fictional and romanticized biography of Brown. Brown is also included in Truman J. Nelson's *The Surveyor* (1960), a fictional account of the activities in Kansas between March 1855 and October 1856, and in Thomas Dixon's *The Man in Gray: A Romance of North and South* (1921), a work of historical fiction focusing on the Civil War. John Brown has inspired two plays as well: Barrie Stavis's *Harper's Ferry: A Play About John Brown* (1967), and J. C. Swayze's *Osawatomie Brown: or, The Insurrection at Harper's Ferry* (1859).

Museums, Historical Landmarks, Societies

Harper's Ferry Armory (Harper's Ferry, WV). The site of John Brown's raid and the surrounding countryside is maintained by the National Park Service.

John Brown's Farm (Lake Placid, NY). Brown's burial place is maintained by the New York State Historic Trust and is open to the public.

John Brown Home Museum (Akron, OH). Brown lived in this house from 1842–1846, and his memory is preserved here with memorabilia and period pieces.

John Brown Memorial Museum (Osawatamie, KS). His headquarters from 1855–1858, this museum has a collection of guns and other artifacts of Brown's legacy.

Ohio Historical Society (Columbus, OH). Has a collection of artifacts related to Brown's life.

Todd House (Tabor, IA). Brown's headquarters for his raids into Kansas also served as a stop on the Underground Railroad; it has been restored by the Tabor Historical Society and is open to the public.

Other Sources

Abels, Jules. *Man on Fire: John Brown and the Cause of Liberty.* New York: Macmillan, 1971. The author, trained in the law, attempts to present another view of John Brown. Unfortunately, he offers nothing new.

Davidson, James W., and Mark H. Lytle. "The Madness of John Brown." In *After the Fact: The Art of Historical Detection.* New York: Alfred A. Knopf, 1982. This interesting article examines how psychohistory has been used to analyze John Brown.

Johnson, Allen. "John Brown." In *Dictionary of American Biography*, edited by Allen Johnson. Vol. 3. New York: Charles Scribner's Sons, 1929. This remarkably objective capsule sketch of Brown is a good place to start a study of the man.

Keller, Allan. *Thunder at Harper's Ferry.* Englewood Cliffs: Prentice-Hall, 1958. This account of the raid relies heavily on secondary sources and should not be consulted for a scholarly view of the incident.

Malin, James C. *John Brown and the Legend of Fifty-Six.* Philadelphia: American Philosophical Society, 1942. Condemns Brown for the 1856 Kansas massacre.

Quarles, Benjamin, ed. *Blacks on John Brown.* Urbana: University of Illinois Press, 1972. A collection of essays, all authored by blacks, spanning over a century of opinions of Brown.

Scott, Otto J. *The Secret Six: John Brown and the Abolitionist Movement.* New York: Times Books, 1979. Based on secondary sources, this book discusses the role of the Secret Six, Brown's inactive co-conspirators who supported him financially and morally.

Woodward, C. Vann. "John Brown's Private War." In *Burden of Southern History*, edited by Woodward. Baton Rouge: Louisiana State University Press, 1968. One of the best short interpretive essays on the Harper's Ferry raid.

Christopher C. Meyers

Kansas Territorial Centennial, 1954

WILLIAM JENNINGS BRYAN
1860–1925

Chronology

Born William Jennings Bryan on March 19, 1860, in Salem, Illinois, the oldest son of eight children of Judge Silas Bryan and Mariah Elizabeth Jennings Bryan; *1860–1881* is raised in strict accordance with Biblical principles and the tenets of the Democratic party; attends the local school, Whipple Academy, and Illinois College in Jacksonville, Illinois, and Union Law School, Chicago; *1881* marries Mary Elizabeth Baird, with whom he will have three children; *1890* following a six-year stint as a lawyer in Jacksonville, Bryan moves to Lincoln, Nebraska, and is elected to the 51st Congress, after a campaign based largely on the issue of tariff reform; *1892* is reelected to Congress; *1896* wins the Democratic presidential nomination, but loses the election to William McKinley; *1898* serves as the colonel of the Third Nebraska Volunteers during the Spanish-American War, but never sees action; *1900* again wins the Democratic presidential nomination but loses the election to Theodore Roosevelt; *1901–1923* publishes the *Commoner*, a journal that reflects his political, social, and religious views; earns a good deal of money as a lecturer, especially on the Chautauqua circuit; *1901* begins dealing increasingly in religious matters; *1904–1906* travels in Latin America and about the world; *1908* wins the Democratic presidential nomination for the third time, and loses the election to William Howard Taft; *1909–1920* encourages ratification of the Sixteenth, Seventeenth, Eighteenth, and Nineteenth Amendments by speaking, writing, and influencing his friends in Congress; *1912* supports Woodrow Wilson for the Democratic presidential nomination; when Wilson wins the election, he names Bryan as Secretary of State; *1913–1914* through his influence in Congress, he helps Wilson push through his New Freedom reforms; *1915* fearing that Wilson will lead the nation into the Great War, he resigns his secretaryship on June 9; *1916* campaigns for Wilson's reelection and supports the war effort; *July 1925* serves as a prosecutor in the famous Scopes trial, in Dayton, Tennessee, in which a biology teacher was accused of breaking a state law by teaching evolution; wins the Scopes case, but reveals an appalling lack of knowledge about history and science; dies on July 16 in Dayton of apoplexy and a cerebral hemorrhage connected with diabetes.

Activities of Historical Significance

Bryan's elections in 1890 and 1892 from the Republican State of Nebraska were outstanding as was his rarely matched record of three presidential nominations. A marvelous speaker whose rich baritone voice could be heard at a great distance, he reigned as one of the world's greatest orators for thirty-five years. "Special privilege for none, equal justice for all" well summarizes his political credo. A supporter of many reforms, Bryan sponsored changes in the tariff, banking and currency, and corporation control, as well as the establishment of a personal federal income tax, woman suffrage, conservation of national resources, regulation of campaign contributions, lesser penalties for labor injunctions, the direct election of senators, and guaranteed savings banks. In foreign affairs he opposed America's acquisition of empire in 1898 and persistently demanded that the Philippines be granted their independence (an early enunciation of the principle of national self-determination). However, while Secretary of State (1913–1915), he proved to be a realist by expanding American power in the Caribbean, seeking to teach Latin Americans how to govern themselves, stopping Japan from encroaching upon China, and achieving world peace by having nations sign "cooling off" treaties.

After 1900, in keeping with the Social Gospel movement, Bryan demanded a turning away from the crass materialism of his age, and a moral awakening that would result in the rule of love and The Brotherhood of Man. He was often a delegate to the annual conference of the Presbyterian Church of the United States of America. He wrote a syndicated Sunday school lesson and taught a large winter-time tourist Bible class in Miami. According to many critics, he countered progress with his support for Prohibition and defense of the literal interpretation of the Bible. Bryan's views of biblical teachings were challenged during the Scopes evolution trial, when the main defense attorney, Clarence Darrow, forced him to agree that the Bible could not be interpreted literally and that human civilization predated the writing of the Bible. He is probably best remembered for his role in the Scopes trial, and he was, in the end, more of a moralist and evangelist than a statesman.

Overview of Biographical Sources

Bryan has been the subject of many biographies. The earliest biographies, written during Bryan's lifetime, tended to be laudatory. Among the first were Albert Gale and George W. Kline, *An Appreciation from a Republican Viewpoint. Bryan the Man: The Commoner at Close Range* (1908), and Richard L. Metcalfe, comp., *The Real Bryan* (1908). The title of Gale and Kline's work speaks for itself, and Metcalfe's account is a campaign biography by a worker at the *Commoner* who was enamored of Bryan. Wayne C. Williams, *William Jennings Bryan* (1923), is partisan and uncritical. Eleven years after Bryan's death, Williams published another uncritical biography, *William Jennings Bryan* (1936).

The first Bryan biography to follow his death was a hurriedly produced, cut-and-paste work by Genevieve Forbes Herrick and John Origen Herrick, *The Life of William Jennings Bryan* (1925). It was followed by John C. Long, *Bryan: The Great Commoner* (1928), a sympathetic account of a man whom most Americans revered but would not elect. In 1929, two negative accounts appeared: Paxton Hibben and C. Hartley Grattan, *The Peerless Leader*, and M. R. Werner, *Bryan*. Hibben and Grattan's work criticizes Bryan from beginning to end, emphasizing the worst possible implications of all his actions. Werner states that, although Bryan often supported good causes, he was suspicious of education, inflexible in his opinions, and certainly not an intellectual. The other account of note that was written in the first ten years following Bryan's death, Charles M. Rossner, *The Crusading Commoner: A Close-up of William Jennings Bryan and His Times* (1932), is the work of an uncritical adviser who contends that his subject erred in becoming Secretary of State but that Bryan's willingness to fight for his convictions was commendable.

More recent studies tend to be more balanced. The most useful are: Robert W. Cherny, *A Righteous Cause: The Life of William Jennings Bryan* (1985); Kendrick A. Clements, *William Jennings Bryan: Missionary Isolationist* (1982); Paolo E. Coletta, *William Jennings Bryan*, 3 vols. (1964–1969); LeRoy Ashby, *William Jennings Bryan: Champion of Democracy* (1987); and Paul W. Glad, *The Trumpet Soundeth: William Jennings Bryan and His Democracy, 1896–1912* (1960). Glad also edited *William Jennings Bryan: A Profile* (1968), a collection of essays by more than a dozen contributors. Glad covers the election of 1896 in *McKinley, Bryan, and the People* (1964).

Evaluation of Principal Biographical Sources

Ashby, LeRoy. *William Jennings Bryan: Champion of Democracy.* Boston: Twayne, 1987. **(A, G)** Portrays Bryan as a political liberal but religious fundamentalist.

Cherny, Robert W. *A Righteous Cause: The Life of William Jennings Bryan.* Boston: Little, Brown, 1985. **(A, G)** Concentrates on Bryan's political and religious learnings at his parents' hands, and on his attempts to solve the problems of Western and Southern farmers.

Clements, Kendrick A. *William Jennings Bryan: Missionary Isolationist.* Knoxville: University of Tennessee Press, 1982. **(A, G)** States that Bryan believed that the United States should lead the world by setting a Christian example, a goal which he violated while serving as Secretary of State.

Coletta, Paolo E. *William Jennings Bryan: Political Evangelist, 1860–1908.* Lincoln: University of Nebraska Press, 1964. **(A, G)** Covers Bryan's antecedents, education, beginnings in politics, election to Congress and service therein, presidential candidacy in 1896, service in the Spanish-American War, renomination as presidential candidate in 1900, loss of prestige and power and turning toward religion between 1900 and 1904, and his resurgence, renomination, and defeat in 1908.

————. *William Jennings Bryan: Progressive Politician and Moral Statesman,* 1908–1915. Lincoln: University of Nebraska Press, 1969. **(A, G)** Deals with Bryan's testing of Democratic presidential candidates in 1912 and leaning toward Wilson, his granting of patronage as Secretary of State to "deserving Democrats," his influence in Wilson's New Freedom reforms, his problem solving with Mexico and Japan and China, his attempts to keep out of the Great War, and his resignation as Secretary of State.

————. *William Jennings Bryan: Political Puritan.* Lincoln: University of Nebraska Press, 1969. **(A, G)** Deals with Bryan's part in antipreparedness and peace crusades relevant to the Great War, his gradual loss of political power, the duel to the death at Dayton, and a summary of his contributions to history.

Glad, Paul W. *The Trumpet Soundeth: William Jennings Bryan and His Democracy, 1896–1912.* Lincoln: University of Nebraska Press, 1960. **(A, G)** Sees Bryan as a spokesman for rural American and revivalist religion, and a great opponent of Republican domination of national politics.

Overview and Evaluation of Primary Sources

Bryan's correspondence and many publications tell much about his personal accomplishments, beliefs, and values. A good source for his opinions on politics, diplomacy, and religion is *The Credo of the Commoner: William Jennings Bryan* (Los Angeles: Occidental College, 1968; **A, G**), compiled by William Jennings Bryan, Jr., and edited by Franklin Modisett. Still the best compilation on Bryan's first presidential campaign is his 2-volume *First Battle: A Story of the Campaign of 1896* (1896; Reprint. Port Washington, NY: Kennikat Press, 1971; **A, G**). For twenty-two years he aired his political, religious, economic, and social views in editorials in his personal journal, the *Commoner.* As a reporter, in *A Tale of Two Conventions* (1912; Reprint. New York: Arno Press, 1974; **A, G**), he reported on both the Democratic and Republican national conventions. After 1901, he devoted himself more to religion than to politics, and produced several works on religion in the last two decades of his life. Meanwhile, he published *The Life and Speeches of William Jennings Bryan* (New York: Ogilvie, 1901; **A, G**); *Under Other Flags: Travels, Lectures, Speeches* (Lincoln: Woodruff-Collins, 1904; **A, G**); and *The Old World and Its Ways* (St. Louis: Thompson, 1907; **A, G**). The latter two works contain observations stemming from his world tour of 1905–1906. Bryan completed two-fifths of the manuscript for his memoirs before his death. His wife wrote the remainder of the work, which was published as *The Memoirs of William Jennings Bryan* (1925; Reprint. Port Washington, NY: Kennikat Press, 1971; **A, G**).

Collections of Bryan papers are at the Manuscript Division, Library of Congress; Nebraska State Historical Society; Occidental College, Los Angeles; the estate of the late Mrs. Thomas Stinson Allen (Bryan's younger sister), Lincoln; and at the Illinois College Library and Archives, Jacksonville. These should be supplemented by the papers of Woodrow Wilson and of his cabinet members, many of them in the Manuscript Division, Library of Congress; the J. Sterling Morton Collection, University of Nebraska Library; the Henry Steele Commager Papers; the George S. Bixby Papers, New York State Library, Albany; the Silas Bryan Papers, invaluable for the correspondence between Bryan and his brother, Charles Wayland; the Mrs. Ruth Bryan Rohde (a daughter) papers; the John Peter Altgeld, Joseph G. Cannon, and Waldo R. Brown collections in the Illinois State Historical Society, Springfield; and the William Jennings Bryan-Samuel Untermyer Papers, American Jewish Archives, Cincinnati.

Fiction and Adaptations

Bryan's image was hurt less in the play by Jerome Lawrence and Robert E. Lee, *Inherit the Wind* (1950), than by the film of the same title (1960). In the play, which ran for two years on Broadway and has been offered many times since, Paul Muni as Darrow and Ed Begley as Bryan gave unforgettable performances. However, in the film Frederick March portrayed Bryan as a low-comedy stooge, Gene Kelly represented an unrecognizable Mencken, and Spencer Tracy, as Darrow, emerged the hero. The television production of December 6, 1968, by the Theater Company of Boston, entitled "A Celebration for William Jennings Bryan," showed Bryan to be a "good" man but was destructively critical of his political and his religious ideas.

Museums, Historical Landmarks, Societies

Bryan Birthplace (Salem, IL). This house has been made into a museum. Also located in Salem is a large statue of Bryan created by Gutzon Borglum in 1934. The statue rested in Washington, DC, until the mid-1960s.

Bryan College (Dayton, TN). A small private college, founded in 1930.

Capitol Building (Washington, DC). A bronze bust of Bryan is on display in the Rotunda.

Fairview (near Lincoln, NE). Bryan's home is now maintained as a National Historic Landmark. A large statue of Bryan that once rested on the statehouse grounds has been moved here in order to provide an unobstructed view of the state capital building.

Rhea County Courthouse (Dayton, TN). The site of the Scopes trial has been restored and, along with a museum in the basement, serves as a memorial to the infamous court case.

Other Sources

Ginger, Ray. *Six Days or Forever? Tennessee vs. John Thomas Scopes.* Boston: Beacon Press, 1958. An in-depth look at the Scopes trial.

Hollingworth, J. Rogers. *The Whirligig of Politics: The Democracy of Cleveland and Bryan.* Chicago: University of Chicago Press, 1963. Tells of the contest between Cleveland and Bryan for control of the Democratic party between 1890 and Cleveland's death in 1904.

Levine, Lawrence W. *Defender of the Faith. William Jennings Bryan: The Last Decade, 1915-1925.* 1965. Reprint. New York: Oxford University Press, 1987. The best portrayal of Bryan's relationship with American farmers.

Scopes, John T., and James Presley. *Center of the Storm: Memoirs of John T. Scopes.* New York: Holt, Rinehart, and Winston, 1967. An account from the perspective of the defendant in the Scopes trial.

Paolo E. Coletta
U.S. Naval Academy (Ret.)

JAMES BUCHANAN
1791–1868

Chronology

Born James Buchanan on April 23, 1791, near Mercersburg, Pennsylvania, to Elizabeth Speer Buchanan and James Buchanan, a storekeeper who immigrated to America in 1783; *1791–1807* grows up and attends school in Mercersburg; *1807* enters Dickinson College; *1809* graduates; *1812* admitted to the bar; *1814* elected to the Pennsylvania House of Representatives as a Federalist; *1815* reelected; *1820* elected to the U.S. House of Representatives and serves for ten years; *1831* made minister to Russia; *1834* elected U.S. senator to replace the deceased William Wilkins; *1837* wins reelection, and is again reelected in 1843; *1845* appointed secretary of state by President Polk; *1853* appointed minister to Great Britain by President Pierce; *1854* is a member of the triumvirate that drew up the "Ostend Manifesto"; *1856* nominated for president by the Democratic party; *November 1856* elected president; *March 4, 1857* inaugurated as the fifteenth president of the United States; *1857* the *Dred Scott* decision is made by the Supreme Court, which Buchanan accepts as final; *November 1860–March 1861* the secession crisis occurs; *December 20, 1860* South Carolina secedes from the Union and civil war is imminent; *March 4, 1861* retires to private life; *1866* publishes book entitled *Mr. Buchanan's Administration on the Eve of the Rebellion*; 1868 dies on June 1 at his Wheatland home in Lancaster, Pennsylvania.

Activities of Historical Significance

James Buchanan's chief historical significance lies in his lengthy public service. He entered politics as a Federalist and witnessed the political evolution of the National Republican, Democratic Republican (Jacksonian), Know-Nothing, Free Soil, Whig, and Republican parties. After becoming a Jacksonian Democrat he entered the House of Representatives and later the Senate. He served as President Polk's secretary of state, and in that capacity managed negotiations concerning Oregon and Texas. As President Pierce's minister to Great Britain he was part of the trio that drew up the "Ostend Manifesto." Buchanan was out of the country when the Kansas controversy was going on, so he was not identified with either side, making him the ideal Democratic candidate for president in 1856.

After taking the oath of office Buchanan began one of the most controversial and crucial administrations in American history. He supported, and may have even influenced, the Supreme Court's *Dred Scott* decision in 1857. Buchanan wished to admit Kansas as a state with its proslavery Lecompton Constitution. These two events illustrate his pro-southern beliefs that immediately earned him the label "doughface."

Throughout the secession crisis Buchanan maintained that secession was unconstitutional, but as president he had no constitutional authority to interfere and put down the rebellion. In January 1861, he sent a ship to supply Fort Sumter, but for the most part he did little, wishing to turn over a stable Union to Lincoln. During his last four months in office, Buchanan epitomized the "lame duck" president.

Overview of Biographical Sources

Despite the crucial nature of Buchanan and his administration, he has inspired few biographies. There are, however, several books about his administration. A couple of campaign biographies appeared in 1856, including R. G. Horton, *Life and Public Services of James Buchanan* (1856), and C. Jerome, *Life of James Buchanan* (1856). Like most campaign literature, these were hastily written and sympathetic to the subject. The first serious biography was George T. Curtis, *Life of James Buchanan* (1883), followed by John R. Irelan, *History of the Life, Administration and Times of James Buchanan* (1888). The next biography, however, did not appear until 1962; Philip S. Klein, *President James Buchanan: A Biography*, is the best, most comprehensive biography of Buchanan to date.

Evaluation of Principal Biographical Sources

Auchampaugh, Philip G. *James Buchanan and His Cabinet on the Eve of Secession*. Boston: J. S. Canner, 1965. (**A, G**) A well-written work that discusses Buchanan and his cabinet from the 1860 election to the close of his administration. It was intended as a supplement to George Curtis's biography, published in 1883. Sympathetic and partisan to Buchanan, the book offers an unbalanced judgment.

Curtis, George T. *Life of James Buchanan*. 2 vols. New York: Harper and Brothers, 1883. (**A, G**) The first serious biography of Buchanan. Although it contains much valuable information, it is poorly organized and full of gaps.

Irelan, John R. *History of the Life, Administration and Times of James Buchanan*. Chicago: A. C. McClurg, 1888. (**A, G**) One of the initial biographies of James Buchanan. It is sympathetic to the subject, and gaps are evident.

Klein, Philip S. *President James Buchanan: A Biography*. University Park: Pennsylvania State University Press, 1962. (**A, G**) This is a well-written, fair portrait of James Buchanan. President Buchanan has carried the stigma of being labelled a "doughface," but Klein portrays him as a firm and patriotic leader. He is shown as a conservative, middle-of-the-road politician who loathed abolitionists and disliked southern fire-eaters. This work is thoroughly researched and is the most comprehensive biography of Buchanan yet.

Smith, Elbert B. *The Presidency of James Buchanan*. Lawrence: University Press of Kansas, 1975. (**A, G**) A volume in the American Presidency series, this book covers the administration of one of the most significant presidencies in American history. The author states that Buchanan did much to create a political climate conducive to war, and charges Buchanan with a great deal of the responsibility for the political crisis of the late 1850s. Relying heavily upon previous works on Buchanan, Smith takes the stance that Buchanan was not a tool of southern leaders, but that he followed a pro-South policy from personal conviction.

Overview and Evaluation of Primary Sources

Although the number of Buchanan biographies is limited, a good deal of primary source material is available. Horatio King, who served for a brief time as Buchanan's postmaster general, wrote *Turning on the Light: A Dispassionate Survey of President Buchanan's Administration, from 1860 to Its Close* (Philadelphia: J. B. Lippincott, 1895; **A, G**). His work surveys the end of the administration and includes several letters written by Buchanan that had not been published, but King often strays from his subject. Buchanan penned a defense of his administration in *Mr. Buchanan's Administration on the Eve of the Rebellion* (New York: D. Appleton, 1866; **A, G**). This work is important in understanding his policies as president, though it deals with very little of the presidency except the events just prior to the Civil War. The publication of the *Works of James Buchanan*, edited by John Bassett Moore (1908–1911. Reprint. New York: Antiquarian Press, 1960; **A, G**), was a great contribution to the study of James Buchanan.

Manuscripts have been gathered in the Buchanan Collection at the Historical Society of Pennsylvania, and the James Buchanan Papers at the Library of Congress.

Fiction and Adaptations

John Updike produced a three-act play, *Buchanan Dying* (1974), about aspects of Buchanan's administration and his final days. He used Philip Klein's biography as his chief source and guide.

Museums, Historical Landmarks, Societies

Malcolm X Park (Washington, DC). A statue of a seated Buchanan graces this large, European-style park.

Wheatland (Lancaster, PA). James Buchanan's home is maintained by the James Buchanan Foundation for the Preservation of Wheatland and is open to the public.

Other Sources

Fish, Carl Russell. "James Buchanan." In *Dictionary of American Biography*, vol. 3. Edited by Allen Johnson. New York: Charles Scribner's Sons, 1929. A rather one-sided discussion, very sympathetic to Buchanan. The entry serves as a good overview of the subject, but some extreme statements are made, such as the declaration that as Polk's secretary of state, Buchanan shaped the policy of the administration.

Christopher C. Meyers

Wheatland, 1956

WILLIAM F. BUCKLEY, JR.
1925

Chronology

Born William Frank Buckley on November 24, 1925, in New York City, one of ten children of William Frank Buckley, Sr., a Texan who amasses considerable wealth in oil speculation before his death in 1958, and Aloise Steiner Buckley, a gentle woman of southern extraction; *1931* shows early signs of his brash personality by writing letter to the King of England demanding that Britain repay its war debts to the United States; *1943* enters the University of Mexico after graduating from Millbrook Academy in New York; *1944–1946* serves as second lieutenant in the U.S. Army; *1946–1950* attends and graduates from Yale University, where he serves as Chairman of the *Yale Daily News*; *1950* marries Maria Patricia Taylor; *1951* wins national attention with the publication of his book *God and Man at Yale*, a scurrilous attack on the liberal biases of the Yale curriculum; arranges for distribution of the book at Yale commencement exercises; *1951–1952* works for the CIA in Mexico; *1953* his son Christopher is born; *1954* with Brent Bozell, publishes *McCarthy and His Enemies*, a defense of the anti-Communist practices of Wisconsin Senator Joseph McCarthy; *1955* launches the conservative journal *National Review*; *1959* publishes *Up from Liberalism*; *1962* begins weekly newspaper column *On the Right*; *1965* runs on the Conservative party ticket in New York City mayoralty race in which he wins 13% of the vote in three-way race with John Lindsay and Abraham Beame; *1966* begins weekly television interview program *Firing Line*, which will become the longest continuing offering on the Public Broadcasting System; *1968* appears with Gore Vidal on ABC-TV as commentator for the Republican and Democratic National Conventions; *1970* his brother James is elected to the U.S. Senate from New York; *1973* is appointed by President Nixon to the U.S. delegation to the United Nations; *1976* begins a series of Cold War spy novels with publication of *Saving the Queen*, and a series of books recounting his sailing adventures with *Airborne*; *1978* debates future president Ronald Reagan on the merits of the United States's relinquishing control of the Panama Canal, and the debate shows a genuine rift in the Right as Buckley defends the treaties that propose to make that transfer while Reagan vehemently protests; *1978–present* continues to write fiction and political commentary.

Activities of Historical Significance

From the time of his first publication, Buckley has been one of the most widely known and outspoken conservative intellectuals in the United States. As author, syndicated columnist, and television personality, Buckley has advanced his conservative ideas in a forceful and engaging way. He has become famous for his highly stylized mannerisms, his prodigious vocabulary, his erudition, and his willingness to engage any opponent on any issue. By force of these qualities, Buckley has advanced a conservative intellectual movement that, although eloquent, seemed lifeless in the years after World War II.

God and Man at Yale (1951) effectively promoted the conservative point that America's institutions had succumbed to a dominant liberal ideology. Buckley argued that his alma mater's curriculum thoroughly discredited free market capitalism and ridiculed religion. The notoriety Buckley gained from *God and Man at Yale* made him the suitable person to launch *National Review*.

This publication brought together the voices of a diversified and sporadic conservative intellectual movement within the pages of one publication. Conservative intellectuals of all persuasions—Catholic traditionalists, anti-Communists, free-market economists and libertarians, Burkeans—found a place in *National Review*. Indeed, Buckley effectively organized a conservative "family" that gained a sense of common purpose in its efforts.

The idea of such a "family" has been an integral part of Buckley's conservatism. His books are full of personalities and a pervasive sense of tribalism. Clear delineations are made between friends and enemies, those who belong and those who do not. This peculiarity is probably derived from the influence of the flamboyant, irascible, and brilliant Yale conservative Willmoore Kendall, and the controversial Whittaker Chambers. Kendall, Buckley's mentor at Yale, had warned that a "liberal revolution" was advancing under the ideology of the "open society," threatening to dissolve the nation's cohesive value system. Chambers, Buckley's friend and correspondent, became well-known for his exposé of the Communist background of Alger Hiss, an act that perpetrated one of the most divisive and controversial trials of the Cold War era. But it was Chambers's powerful testimony, *Witness* (1952), that dramatized the Cold War as a spiritual struggle in which the fate of Western civilization was at stake. Likewise, Buckley's writings reflect this rigid division of the enemies of communism on the one hand and its sinister or foolish sympathizers on the other. *McCarthy and His Enemies* (1954) defends anti-communism as an exercise of the simple right of any society to protect majoritarian ideals from the threat of alien ideas. *Up from Liberalism* (1959), a book that is full of names, perpetuates the Buckley habit of seeing the dissenter as the outsider and enemy, an outcast of the tribe. When projected onto the world scene, this perspective renders the Soviet Union as a dark, sinister force in the world. Buckley has been uncompromising in advocating a hard and unyielding stance against the Soviet Union and its allies, outrightly rejecting policies of co-existence or accommodation.

Buckley's intellectual conservatism has never fallen into a single category. He has consistently espoused a free-market economy, but on issues of manners and morals his views have not been uniformly libertarian, and, on questions of Catholic worship and theology, he has been an outspoken traditionalist. He has opposed egalitarian social philosophies, vigorously defended the rights of property, and seemed quite comfortable with the disparities of rank and privilege in the United States that increasingly troubled liberals in the 1960s and 1970s. But the man who often assumed the posture of a conservative aristocrat has been at times forcefully populist in his attitudes. Buckley, like other conservative intellectuals, has vigorously attacked the entrenched bureaucratic elites whose power seems to betray the democratic principle that legitimate political power must rest with the people's elected officials, and he has further disparaged the mandarins of America's elite colleges and universities. Buckley's comment that he would rather be governed by the first one thousand names in the Boston phone book than by the entire Harvard faculty has been a favorite quotation among his enthusiasts.

Buckley's views have never been predictable and no consistent ideology has emerged over his long career. He has defended voting for black political candidates simply on the principle of race, championed the cause of a convicted criminal, endorsed a public program of free food for anyone who wants it, and spoken for the legalization of homosexual acts and prostitution.

Overview of Biographical/Critical Sources

To date, only two book-length works on Buckley have appeared. The most comprehensive biography of Buckley is John B. Judis, *William F. Buckley, Jr.: Patron Saint of the Conservatives* (1988). Judis's book is a chronological review, while Mark Royden Winchell's *William F. Buckley, Jr.* (1984) is more topical.

On the other hand, numerous assessments of Buckley's polemical writings have appeared in periodicals. As might be expected, Buckley usually inspires strong reactions from both supporters and detractors.

Evaluation of Principal Biographical/Critical Sources

Bundy, McGeorge. "The Attack on Yale." *Atlantic Monthly* (November 1951): 50–52. **(A, G)** Bundy scurrilously attacks Buckley for his indictment of Yale and labels his economic views reactionary.

[DuBois, L. Clayton]. "Sniper." *Time* (November 3, 1967): 70–72 **(A, G)** A many-faceted review of Buckley's career.

Eastman, Max. "Buckley Versus Yale." *American Mercury* (December 1951): 22–26. **(A, G)** Eastman, the radical turned libertarian conservative, renders a favorable review of *God and Man at Yale*.

Hart, Jeffrey. *The American Dissent: A Decade of Modern Conservatism.* Garden City, NY: Doubleday, 1966. **(A, G)** An excellent study of *National Review*, with intriguing suggestions as to why humor is more prevalent among conservative than among liberal writers.

Judis, John B., *William F. Buckley, Jr.: Patron Saint of the Conservatives*. New York: Simon and Schuster, 1988. **(A, G)** This book is a solid overview, full of anecdotal material and accounts of the people and personalities that have marked Buckley's career and controversies. It is an essential contribution to the intellectual history of American conservatism.

King, Larry L. "God, Man, and William F. Buckley." *Harper's* (March 1967): 53–61. **(A, G)** King finds that Buckley's likeable wit conceals a genuine contempt for the common person.

Leo, John. "Very Dark Horse in New York." *New York Times Magazine* (September 5, 1965): 8–9+. **(A, G)** A readable profile of Buckley as candidate for mayor of New York City.

MacDonald, Dwight. "Scrambled Eggheads on the Right." *Commentary* (April 1956): 367–373. **(A, G)** This prominent member of the leftist New York intellectuals denigrates Buckley and the group surrounding the newly organized *National Review*.

Wakefield, Dan. "William F. Buckley, Jr.: Portrait of a Complainer." *Esquire* (January 1961): 49–52. **(A, G)** This essay matches Buckley in wit.

Winchell, Mark Royden. *William F. Buckley, Jr.* New York: Twayne, 1984. **(A, G)** A comprehensive overview of Buckley's writings that is cleverly written but spoiled somewhat by the author's persistent interjection of editorial comments on Buckley's opinions. Contains a chronology and selected bibliography.

Overview and Evaluation of Primary Sources

The Buckley repertoire is extensive and diverse. He has written book-length polemical works, editorials, a syndicated column, personal memoirs, accounts of his sailing adventures, and spy fiction. He has also edited several works. A good place for the general reader to begin is *The Best of Bill Buckley* (*National Review*, n.p., n.d.; **G**), a compilation of notable quotations from "Chairman Bill."

Buckley's polemical works of the 1950s serve to illustrate why he was capable of rousing so much ire in his opponents. *God and Man at Yale: The Superstitions of "Academic Freedom"* (Chicago: Henry Regnery, 1951; **A, G**) is a major piece of literature in the conservative case against the liberal academic establishment in America. This work is intemperate, to be sure, but reflects a genuine wrath against the intellectual elite of the United States. *McCarthy and His Enemies: The Record and Its Meaning* (Chicago: Henry Regnery, 1954; **A, G**), written with R. Brent Bozell about a man that the intellectual community generally vilified, takes up the case for the anti-Communist movement and advances some persuasive theoretical points on the rights of society against the liberties of its enemies. *Up From Liberalism* (1959; New York: Stein and Day, 1984; **G**) is a collection of essays that bristles with attacks on people and personalities from the whole liberal spectrum in the U.S. It is especially controversial for Buckley's essay in defense of racial segregation.

For over thirty years Buckley editorialized in the *National Review*, and when he became a nationally syndicated writer, his essays appeared from time to time in books published by Putnam of New York City. These extremely valuable works chronicle the career of a conservative thinker as he confronts and comments on a host of issues, people, and events over decades of American history. One should begin with *The Jeweler's Eye: A Book of Irresistible Political Reflections* (1958; **A, G**), which contains an essay on *Playboy* and its moral philosophy; Buckley's libertarianism fades in the face of Hugh Hefner's individualistic ethos. *The Governor Listeth: A Book of Inspired Political Revelations* (1970; **A**) contains a notorious apology for the wanton murder of Vietnamese citizens by the American soldier, Lieutenant Calley. Buckley sees Calley as victim of the declining moral values of American public culture. *Inveighing We Will Go* (1972; **A, G**) contains a lengthy interview Buckley gave to *Playboy*; it is one of the most accessible summaries of Buckley's philosophy. *A Hymnal: The Controversial Arts* (1975; **A, G**) contains one of Buckley's most powerful essays, that on the Soviet writer Alexander Solzhenitsyn. And *Right Reason* (1985; **A**) brings Buckley into the 1980s and gathers his reflections on such events as the revolution in Iran, the shooting of the Korean airliner by the Soviets, and the American intervention in Grenada.

Buckley has also written three books of personal memoirs. *The Unmaking of a Mayor* (New York: Viking, 1966; **A, G**) recounts Buckley's adventure in election politics; it is long and detailed, but an interesting piece of New York City history. *Overdrive: A Personal Documentary* (Boston: Little, Brown, 1981; **A, G**) is a day-by-day account, but also includes reminiscences of Buckley's career at Millbrook prep school. This narrative angered Buckley's critics because Buckley tells unabashedly how he acquired his limousine. *United Nations Journal: A Delegate's Odyssey* (New York: Putnam, 1974; **A, G**) recounts an insider's frustration with the institution and offers many Buckley insights on world affairs. *Cruising Speed* (New York: Putnam, 1971; **A, G**) is a less engaging account of mundane affairs.

Among the works that Buckley has edited, two are significant. *Odyssey of a Friend: Whittaker Chambers' Letters to William F. Buckley, Jr. 1954–1961* (New York: Putnam, 1961; **A, G**) contains some of Chambers's important reflections on conservatism. *Did You Ever See a Dream Walking? American Conservative Thought in the Twentieth Century* (Indianapolis: Bobbs-Merrill, 1970; **A, G**) has a lengthy introductory essay by Buckley and contains his comments on many conservative thinkers.

In 1976 Buckley launched a new series of books. An avid sailor, Buckley began to recount his adventures on the brine with the publication of *Airborne: A Sentimental Journey* (New York: Putnam, 1976; **G**). There followed *Atlantic High* (New

York: Putnam, 1982; **G**) and *Racing Through Paradise: A Pacific Passage* (New York: Random House, 1987; **G**). Among a select set of Buckley followers, these books have been extremely popular. They do have interesting reflections on sundry matters, but the sailing enthusiast will enjoy them most.

Also in 1976, Buckley undertook a venture into fiction writing and the genre of Cold War storytelling. His spy novels feature the hero Blackford Oakes, who becomes involved in all kinds of improbable episodes, including a romp with the Queen of England in the first of the adventures, *Saving the Queen* (1976; **G**). Published by Doubleday of New York City, the series includes *Stained Glass* (1978; **G**), *Who's on First* (1980; **G**), *Marco Polo If You Can* (1982; **G**), *The Story of Henry Todd* (1983; **G**), *See You Later, Alligator* (1985; **G**), and *High Jinx* (1986; **G**). The books generally have received critical acclaim, due in part, one suspects, to the reputation of their author. But they are not literary classics, even in the spy genre of fiction. The characters are flat and the dialogue somewhat pedestrian.

Other Sources

DuBois, L. Clayton. "The First Family of Conservatism." *New York Times Magazine* (August 9, 1970): 10+. A generally favorable portrait of the large Buckley clan.

Markmann, Charles Lam. *The Buckleys: A Family Examined*. New York: William Morrow, 1973. This book has been called a "hatchet job." Read with caution.

Nash, George H. *The Conservative Intellectual Movement in America: Since 1945*. New York: Basic Books, 1976. This major work on the subject is indispensable for placing Buckley in the context of intellectual conservatism in the U.S.

Ross, Mitchell S. *The Literary Politicians*. Garden City, NY: Doubleday, 1978. A helpful essay on Buckley is included in this work that considers intellectuals who practice politics by writing books.

Wills, Garry. *Confessions of a Conservative*. Garden City, NY: Doubleday, 1979. Wills recalls his years with *National Review* and explains his departure.

Winfrey, Carey. "Buckley at Home." *New York Times Book Review* (May 14, 1978): 725–726. An interview.

J. David Hoeveler, Jr.
University of Wisconsin-Milwaukee

AARON BURR
1756–1836

Chronology

Born Aaron Burr on February 6, 1756, in Newark, New Jersey, to Reverend Aaron Burr and Esther Edwards Burr, daughter of Reverend Jonathan Edwards; *1758–1769* is orphaned and raised by his mother's oldest brother in a household of many children; *1769–1772* he attends Princeton; *1772–1775* considers a career in the ministry, but soon decides to practice law instead; *1775–1776* upon hearing news of Concord and Lexington, rushes to enlist and soon volunteers to serve under Colonel Benedict Arnold; takes part in Arnold's campaign against Canada, serving as an aide-de-camp for General Richard Montgomery; is at Montgomery's side when the general is fatally wounded; becomes a war hero; *1777–1778* joins Israel Putnam for the Battle of Long Island, the evacuation of Manhattan, and the encampments of Westchester; is promoted to Lieutenant Colonel, making him second in command of William Malcom's "additional" regiment; is placed in charge and clears Orange County of Loyalist raiders and then joins Washington's main army at Valley Forge; serves as an intelligence officer in the Hudson Valley until his health fails; meets Mrs. Theodosia Prevost; *1779* resumes his law studies; *1782* is admitted to the New York bar in January; marries the recently widowed Theodosia Prevost in July; moves with family to New York to establish law practice; *1783* his wife gives birth to a daughter, Theodosia; *1784–1785* serves in the New York Assembly; *1789* is appointed state's attorney general; *1791* is chosen to serve in the U.S. Senate; *1792* helps to create the Jeffersonian Republican Party in New York; *1794* his wife dies; *1796* is considered a potential candidate for the vice-presidency, but instead finishes his senate term and becomes a state assemblyman; *1800* is named as Thomas Jefferson's running mate in the presidential election; when the Electoral College vote finds Jefferson and Burr tied for the presidency, Burr is persuaded to seek the office for himself; Jefferson eventually wins a majority vote in the House; *1801–1805* serves as vice president, though the struggle for the presidency has alienated him from Jefferson; unsuccessfully campaigns for New York's gubernatorial seat; *July 11, 1804* fights a duel with Alexander Hamilton, with whom he has developed bitter personal and political antagonisms, and Hamilton is killed; following the duel, Burr flees West; *March 1, 1805* resigns from the vice-presidency; *1805–1806* supposedly attempts to create a separate nation out of the recently acquired Louisiana territory; *1807* because of his activities with the Louisiana Territory, is charged with treason; Supreme Court Justice John Marshall finds him not guilty; *1808–1812* travels abroad and unsuccessfully seeks citizenship in France and England; *1812* upon returning to New York, resumes his law practice and is plagued by financial difficulties that are never resolved; *1813* receives word that his daughter and grandchild have perished at sea;

1833 marries Madame Eliza Jumel, who will divorce him a year later; *1835* his health declines rapidly; *1836* dies on September 14 on Staten Island.

Activities of Historical Significance

A colorful and charismatic man, Aaron Burr is perhaps most commonly known as a political villain, the man who sought to steal the presidency from Thomas Jefferson, the murderer of Alexander Hamilton, a plotter against the national government in the Louisiana Territory, a man constantly in debt, a manipulator of land development, and a notorious womanizer. His service to his country began with his heroic efforts in the Revolutionary War and ended when he resigned from the vice-presidency from his self-imposed exile in the West which followed his killing Hamilton.

Burr's political career was launched with his election to the New York Assembly. After one year on the assembly, he concentrated on building his law practice but returned to the political arena a few years later when appointed Attorney General of New York. The appointment allied him with the dominant state political faction, the Clintonians. Burr assiduously threw himself into the work of his office and into that of the New York Land Office Commission, where he sat as an ex officio member. In recognition of his outstanding labors and talents, the legislature chose him to succeed Philip Schuyler in the U.S. Senate.

In this new position, Burr began to court politicians nationwide while distancing himself from the New York Clintonians. This coolness was clearly delineated when Burr agreed to be considered by the Hamiltonian forces as a possible candidate against George Clinton in the gubernatorial election of 1792. Burr's loss to the more widely known New York Federalist, John Jay, did not end his involvement in that gubernational election. Questions arose concerning the canvassing, transporting, and final counting of ballots from three counties. When called upon to provide an opinion regarding the disputed ballots, Burr provided a legal brief supporting Clinton's election. Such a stand helped to alienate Burr further from such Federalists as Alexander Hamilton and Philip Schuyler.

On a national level, Burr became involved in a scheme to unseat Vice President John Adams while his own name was being suggested by those interested in creating a Jeffersonian opposition to continued Federalist control. When this effort failed, Burr entered the New York lists once again by seeking nomination as a gubernatorial candidate in 1795. Immediately, his opponents raised the cry that he was spending more time politicking locally than attending to senatorial affairs. Burr believed that there was a strong chance of his being nominated, but he lost out to Robert Yates, who received George Clinton's endorsement.

In 1796, the national Jeffersonian Republican caucus nominated Burr as Jefferson's running mate. When the campaigning began in earnest, it became clear that the Republicans were divided, in New York and throughout the country, as to whether they would support Burr rather than Jefferson in the Electoral College. In the end, he did not receive a single electoral vote from New York. Burr began to prepare for a return to private life, but was soon nominated and elected as a member of the assembly. As a member of that body he ventured into many speculating endeavors. One of his most blatant schemes was the creation of the Manhattan Company, which was ostensibly to provide water for New York City, but was actually engaged in banking.

In 1800, Burr once again ran for the vice-presidency as Jefferson's running mate. The Electoral College vote found both Jefferson and Burr with seventy-three votes. The decision then rested with the Federalist-controlled House. On the thirty-sixth ballot, Jefferson received the requisite number of votes. This struggle over the presidency produced a lasting alienation between Jefferson and Burr. With Jefferson's open hostility, Burr recognized that his national career was at an end. He then entered the race for New York's gubernatorial position in 1804 by seeking to create a new local political coalition. His defeat marked his last effort at an elected position. During this campaign, Hamilton made public and private remarks that cast serious doubts upon Burr as a politician and as a person, leading directly to the duel in Weehawken, New Jersey. After Hamilton's death, Burr fled West and resigned from the vice-presidency.

During 1805–1806 Burr was supposedly engaged in a plot to create an independent nation carved from a portion of the recently acquired Louisiana Territory. It was assumed that Burr masterminded a scheme of military actions against the Mexicans. The Jefferson administration did not view Burr's activities lightly and instituted court proceedings against him for treasonable acts. Though his trial in Richmond, Virginia, ended in a decision of not guilty, Burr still faced bitter public sentiment, and litigation stemming from the Hamilton duel. He escaped to Europe.

He remained abroad from the summer of 1808 until February 1812. During that time he unsuccessfully sought citizenship in both England and France while attempting to win favor with leading politicians. These efforts were fruitless and Burr, in financial ruin, returned to New York to resume a career as a practicing attorney.

Like his public life, Burr's private life did not end happily. The tragedies began early. He was orphaned at the age of two and was sent to live with his maternal grandmother, who died soon after Aaron's arrival. He was raised by an uncle until he was accepted by Princeton at the age of thirteen. Later, the death of his wife was followed by the drowning of his daughter and grandchild. He sought refuge in women and cheerfully acknowledged fathering several children out of wedlock. His marriage to Madame Eliza Jumel when he was seventy-seven years old was commonly recognized as his means of settling many outstanding financial obligations. She divorced him on the grounds of adultery after one year. He died two years after his divorce in a hotel on Staten Island.

Overview of Biographical Sources

Aaron Burr's colorful life has attracted a great many biographers, ranging from his contemporaries to present-day historians. From the historian's perspective, it is unfortunate that a greater abundance of personal letters has not survived. Burr did entrust some personal materials to his political lieutenant and close friend Matthew L. Davis. Out of such personal memorabilia, Davis produced the two-volume *Memoirs of Aaron Burr: With Miscellaneous Selections From His Correspondence* (1836–1837) shortly after Burr's death. This was followed by his editing of *The Private Journal of Aaron Burr, During His Residence of Four Years in Europe; With Selections From His Correspondence*, issued in two volumes in 1838. The latter work contains some of Burr's correspondence with his daughter, Theodosia. These letters are most revealing of his inner thoughts as he tried desperately to create a new life for himself abroad.

The first scholarly work based upon the use of such published source material came from James Parton, who wrote *The Life and Times of Aaron Burr, Lieutenant Colonel in the Army of the Revolution, United States Senator, Vice-President of the United States, etc* (1858). At first criticized as being too partial toward its subject, this work is currently assessed as the first Burr biography to examine with psychological import the wheelings and dealings of this fascinating character. In 1892, Hamilton Bullock Tompkins published *Burr Bibliography: A List of Books Relating to Aaron Burr*, containing 119 separate titles which relate to some aspect of Burr's career. This may be supplemented by Samuel H. Wandell, *Aaron Burr in Literature: Books, Pamphlets, Periodicals, and Miscellany Relating to Aaron Burr and His Leading Political Contemporaries* (1936). This interesting compilation contains an appendix which includes a list of Burr's law cases. The most recent and all-inclusive biographical examination of Burr is Milton Lomask's two-volume study: *Aaron Burr: The Years from Princeton to Vice President, 1756–1805* (1979) and *Aaron Burr: The Conspiracy and Years of Exile, 1805–1836* (1982).

Works that deal with specific aspects of Burr's career include Francis P. Beirne, *Shout Treason: The Trial of Aaron Burr* (1959); Walter F. McCaleb, *The Aaron Burr Conspiracy and a New Light on Aaron Burr* (1966); and Jeannette C. Nolan, *Soldier, Statesman, and Defendant: Aaron Burr* (1972). Beirne's work is suitable for an academic or general audience; the latter two are suitable for a younger audience.

Evaluation of Principal Biographical Sources

Lomask, Milton. *Aaron Burr: The Years from Princeton to Vice President, 1756–1805* and *Aaron Burr: The Conspiracy and Years of Exile, 1805–1836*. New York: Farrar, Straus & Giroux, 1979 and 1982. (**A, G**) This two-volume work is the most recent and complete life of Aaron Burr, based to a great extent upon the twenty-seven microfilm reels of Burr Papers recently gathered under the sponsorship of the

New-York Historical Society. Likely to remain the definitive Burr biography for many years to come.

Parmet, Herbert, and Marie B. Hecht. *Aaron Burr: Portrait of an Ambitious Man*. New York: Macmillan, 1967. **(A, G)** The most up-to-date and well-rounded biography of Burr prior to the appearance of Lomask's work.

Schachner, Nathan. *Aaron Burr: A Biography*. New York: A. S. Barnes, 1937. **(A, G)** The twentieth century's second major study of Burr and still worthy of special notice.

Wandell, Samuel H., and Meade Minnigerode. *Aaron Burr: A Biography Compiled from Rare, and in Many Cases Unpublished, Sources*. New York: G. P. Putnam's Sons, 1927. **(A, G)** The first major study of Burr to appear in the twentieth century. The authors were described as having made "no attempt to hide or minimize Burr's personal faults or weaknesses."

Overview and Evaluation of Primary Sources

A large portion of Burr's personal papers were lost at sea along with his daughter, Theodosia, and her child. Many remaining papers were entrusted to the care of his political cohort, Matthew L. Davis, "to be disposed of at his discretion." Davis used the bulk of these papers to produce the *Memoirs of Aaron Burr*, 2 vols. (New York: Harper & Brothers, 1837; **A, G**). Davis also edited *The Private Journal of Aaron Burr* (New York: Harper & Brothers, 1838; **A, G**). Unfortunately, Davis expurgated material from the published items and eventually sold, scattered, or destroyed others.

Burr's legal papers eventually made their way to the New-York Historical Society. Under the auspices of this organization and the National Historical Publications Commission, a comprehensive microfilm edition of all extant Burr papers was undertaken by Mary-Jo Kline. The resulting twenty-eight reels of microfilm, *Papers of Aaron Burr* (Glen Rock, NJ: Microfilming Corporation of America, 1978; **A, G**), and the published two-volume collection, *The Political Correspondence and Legal Papers of Aaron Burr* (Princeton: Princeton University Press, 1983; **A, G**), place all previously scattered material into an accessible, organized body. The microfilm edition is available in over one hundred U.S. libraries.

Primary sources containing information relating to Burr's political career include the works of two of his political enemies: Harold Syrett, ed., *The Papers of Alexander Hamilton*, 26 vols. (New York: Columbia University Press, 1961–1979; **A, G**), and Paul L. Ford, ed., *The Writings of Thomas Jefferson*, 10 vols. (New York: G. P. Putnam's Sons, 1891–1899; **A, G**). Burr's activities in the Louisiana Territory are documented in William H. Safford, ed., *The Blennerhassett Papers* (Cincinnati: Moore, Wilstach, Keys, 1864; **A, G**), and David Robertson, ed., *The Trial of Aaron Burr for Treason* (New York: DaCapo Press, 1875; **A, G**). The latter contains the testimony from Burr's trial. Thomas P. Abernethy, *The Burr Conspiracy* (New York: Oxford University Press, 1954; **A, G**), uses documentary materials in an attempt to show that a conspiracy to wrest the Louisiana Territory from the U.S. did take place.

Fiction and Adaptations

Burr's career lends itself to fictionalized accounts. He appears as either the main character or the supporting character in many novels. For an overview, see Charles F. Nolan, Jr., *Aaron Burr and the American Literary Imagination* (1980). Perhaps the most famous novel featuring Burr is Gore Vidal's *Burr: A Novel* (1973). Mixing historical events with fictional whimsy, Vidal creates a lively account of events during Burr's lifetime. The author bases his work on a careful reading of Burr's published journal and memoirs. He seeks to make a case for Martin Van Buren being one of Burr's illegitimate children. While Burr readily admitted to having sired several children out of wedlock, this account is fictitious. The work is an extremely clever blend of historical fact and novelistic freedom.

Museums, Historical Landmarks, Societies

Morris-Jumel Mansion (New York, NY). The home of Burr's second wife is located on Edgecombe Avenue and West 160th Street.

New Jersey Historical Society (Newark, NJ). This organization's office at 230 Broadway houses Gilbert Stuart's portrait of Aaron Burr.

U.S. Senate Gallery (Washington, DC). A bust of Burr, modeled by Jacques Jouvenal, is housed here.

Other Sources

"Aaron Burr." In *Dictionary of American Biography*, edited by Allen Johnson. Vol. 3. New York: Charles Scribner's Sons, 1929. A seven-page entry with detailed material regarding Burr's political career and western ventures.

McDonald, Archie P., ed. *Encyclopedia U.S.A.* Vol. 8. Gulf Breeze, FL: Academic International Press, 1986. Contains brief essays and bibliographies on Burr, the conspiracy, the duel, and the treason trial.

Jacob Judd
Lehman College and the Graduate Center
of the City University of New York

BENJAMIN F. BUTLER
1818–1893

Chronology

Born Benjamin Franklin Butler on November 5, 1818, at Deerfield, New Hampshire, the third child of John Butler, an army captain in the War of 1812, and Charlotte Ellison Butler; *1819* father dies in the West Indies, never having seen his last son; *1828* moves with his mother to Lowell, Massachusetts, where she takes in factory girls as boarders; *1838* graduates from Waterville College, Maine, and returns to Lowell to study the legal profession; *1840* is admitted to the Massachusetts bar; *1841* opens his legal practice in Lowell, excelling in criminal defense; *1844* marries actress Sarah Hildreth; *1845* son Paul is born; *1847* daughter Blanche is born; *1850* son Paul dies; *1852* second son named Paul is born; *1853* is elected to the Massachusetts House of Representatives as a Democrat; *1854* son Benjamin Israel is born; *1859* is elected to the Massachusetts Senate; *1860* unsuccessfully runs for governor of Massachusetts, staunchly supports moderate Jefferson Davis for president at the divisive Democratic convention at Charleston, South Carolina, then withdraws from the reconstructed Baltimore Democratic convention and throws his support to John C. Breckinridge; *1861* is elected as a brigadier general of Massachusetts militia; secures Annapolis for the Union on his way to report to Washington, restoring communication to a beleaguered capital; peacefully occupies riot-torn Baltimore; President Lincoln appoints him as his first political major general of volunteer troops; while in command of Fort Monroe, Butler declares slaves fleeing from the south as "Contraband" of war, refusing to return them to slavery; is defeated in battle at Big Bethel, but captures Forts Hatteras and Clark, North Carolina; *1862* occupies the city of New Orleans and is appointed military governor of Louisiana, where his administration becomes known for questionable fiscal policy and corruption; hangs William Mumford for taking down a United States flag, and promulgates General Order No. 28, the infamous "Woman Order," ordering women who show disrespect to Union authority in the city to be treated as prostitutes, causing international comment; *1863* commands the Army of the James in Virginia and North Carolina; *1864* acts as Union commissioner for prisoner exchange, gaining Confederate recognition of the legitimate status of black Union soldiers; is corralled with his army in Bermuda Hundred and held there by a smaller force; in December, fails in attempt to take Fort Fisher, North Carolina, in concert with the Navy; *1865* Ulysses S. Grant orders him home to Lowell, where he joins with radical members of the Republican party; *1866* is elected to Congress, where he serves for nine years; *1868* takes an active part in Andrew Johnson's impeachment trial; *1871–1872* vainly seeks the Republican nomination for governor of Massachusetts; *1875* loses his congressional seat; *1876* wife Sarah dies; *1878* is reelected to Congress as a Greenbacker and again runs for governor;

1879 tries again for governor's seat; *1880* supports Winfield Scott Hancock for the Democratic presidential nomination; *1882* as a Democrat, is elected governor of Massachusetts and attempts humane reforms despite a hostile legislature; *1883* is denied reelection; *1884* announces bid for the presidency and is nominated by the Anti-Monopoly and National parties; *1892* writes his autobiography; *1893* dies on January 11 in Washington, D.C.

Activities of Historical Significance

A clever, combative Massachusetts lawyer with a flair for the sensational, Butler loved conflict, invited personal attacks and relished confrontations and controversy. He quickly made enemies in all political parties and among both the army and naval forces in the Civil War, yet his position as a Democratic politician in support of the Union cause gave him celebrity and soon landed him an appointment as one of Lincoln's ill-fated and equally ill-prepared political generals. Nonetheless, his early riot control activities helped keep Maryland in the Union. But his arbitrary and severe administration of New Orleans caused international controversy. He reformed sanitary conditions, restored order, armed free blacks and instituted a poor tax, executed and banned civilians, and seized supposedly Southern gold from the Dutch consulate. He ignored corruption in his own administration, leading his enemies to style him "Beast" and "Spoons" Butler for his actions and supposed theft, and Jefferson Davis to brand him an "outlaw." Militarily, he often proved inept, but Lincoln valued his loyalty to the Union, his encouragement of the use of black troops in battle, and his capture of the forts at Hatteras Inlet when little else was going well for the Union cause. His political power kept him in the army, but his inability to get along with other military commanders contributed to spectacular failures in battle.

Butler's advocacy of the politically and economically disadvantaged brought him into lifelong conflict with established parties. In Massachusetts politics he sought the secret ballot, the ten-hour work day, and reform of social programs, while nationally he called for equal rights and duties for all citizens. He was the first governor of Massachusetts to be denied an honorary degree by Harvard College, and his groundbreaking appointments of minorities to important positions in Massachusetts government were overshadowed by his limited state power. He is better known nationally for his wartime controversies, his political role in Reconstruction, and his leading role in Andrew Johnson's impeachment.

Overview of Biographical Sources

Due to his controversial life and political nature, Butler has rarely been a popular subject for unimpassioned study. His first biographies, notably James Parton's

Gen. Butler in New Orleans (1864) and T. A. Bland's *Life of Benj. F. Butler* (1879), were standard campaign biographies, intended to flatter their subject and to oppose regular Southern publications concerning his wartime administrations. Butler's unflattering postwar reputation, largely the outcome of his wartime actions, political leanings and pugnacious temperament, led him to write his own defensive autobiography.

Although scholars continued to study various aspects of Butler's career, not until after the Korean War did biographers reopen the subject of his life, beginning with Robert S. Holzman's sympathetic *Stormy Ben Butler* (1954). Hans L. Trefousse countered with an insightful analysis of Butler's public life, and an evenhanded analysis of his abilities and failures in his *Ben Butler: The South Called Him Beast!* (1957). Even this analysis proved too kind for Robert Werlich, who, inspired by stories of Butler and by the discovery of Butler's likeness on a chamber pot in a New Orleans antique store, determined to bring the "real" story of the infamous Butler to light in *"Beast" Butler: The Incredible Career of Major General Benjamin Franklin Butler* (1962). Never one to avoid controversial subjects, Richard Sedgewick West, Jr., tackled Butler shortly thereafter. West's *Lincoln's Scapegoat General: A Life of Benjamin F. Butler, 1818–1893* (1965) proved overly admiring, despite subtle acknowledgement of his real failures in battle, but it remains the best overall survey of his wartime career. Howard P. Nash, Jr.'s *Stormy Petrel: The Life and Times of General Benjamin F. Butler* (1969) defends Butler on all charges. Perhaps the best and most impartial assessment of both Butler's political and military life can be found by reading both West's and Trefousse's studies.

Evaluation of Principal Biographical Sources

Bland, T. A. *Life of Benj. F. Butler*. Boston: Lee and Shepard, 1879. **(G)** A laudatory campaign biography of Butler's political and military life to that point; of little value.

Holzman, Robert S. *Stormy Ben Butler*. New York: Octagon Books, 1954, 1978. **(G)** A highly sympathetic account of Butler's life, well-documented, but with little new material or incisive analysis.

Nash, Howard P., Jr. *Stormy Petrel: The Life and Times of General Benjamin F. Butler, 1818–1893*. Rutherford, NJ: Fairleigh Dickinson University Press, 1969. **(G)** A somewhat disjointed and anecdotal sketch, unabashedly defensive while it offers little new evidence, it does portray Butler's more humorous side.

Parton, James. *Gen. Butler in New Orleans*. New York: Mason Brothers, 1864. **(G)** A popular and admiring campaign biography of Butler's life to December 1862, written with Butler's assistance.

Trefousse, Hans Louis. *Ben Butler: The South Called Him Beast!* New York: Twayne, 1957. **(A, G)** The best one-volume biography of Butler, Trefousse provides a thorough analysis, revealing both Butler's strengths and failings as a politician and reformer.

Werlich, Robert. *"Beast" Butler: The Incredible Career of Major General Benjamin Franklin Butler*. Washington: Quaker Press, 1962. **(G)** This short study, designed for the general reading public, aims, in the author's words, to reveal Butler as a "psychotic," "unscrupulous," "incompetent," and "corrupt" Yankee "demagogue."

West, Richard Sedgewick, Jr. *Lincoln's Scapegoat General: A Life of Benjamin F. Butler, 1818-1893*. Boston: Houghton Mifflin, 1965. **(A, G)** Perhaps the most entertaining and readable of Butler's biographies, particularly concerning his Civil War career. The author provides a thorough analysis of crucial events at the battles of New Orleans and Fort Fisher. The book also explores Butler's personal life and family relationships, which are examined in a more balanced and authoritative way than in most studies, but West's work suffers from his attempt to resuscitate Butler's image as a misunderstood idealist and a scapegoat for Union failures.

Overview and Evaluation of Primary Sources

Butler's *Autobiography and Personal Reminiscences of Major General Benj. F. Butler: Butler's Book* (Boston: A. M. Thayer, 1892; **A, G**), written after the death of all his wartime enemies, contains several good maps and documents as well as his own personal defense of his actions. Although major portions of *Butler's Book* have since been revealed as significantly inaccurate, and should be used with care, it remains an interesting reflection of his personality. In an effort to revise his image as an effective Civil War leader, his family later edited several of his letters, publishing them in five volumes as the *Private and Official Correspondence of Gen. Benj. F. Butler, during the Period of the Civil War* (Privately printed, 1917; **A**). Still, the most valuable source of wartime Butler correspondence remains the 128-volume War Department series, *The War of the Rebellion: A Compilation of the Official Records of the Union and Confederate Armies* (Washington: Government Printing Office, 1880-1901; **A, G**). Several of Butler's addresses to Congress, speeches, letters, court arguments, eulogies, and legal opinions have been published in limited quantities and are listed in the *National Union Catalog, Pre-1956 Imprints* (London: Mansell, 1970; **A**) 87: 311-318.

Butler's personal collection of letters, over 275 boxes, resides at the Library of Congress, but many more letters and documents are scattered in various libraries. A small collection of Butler papers are at the Phillips Exeter Academy Library, Exeter, New Hampshire. Documents concerning his military governance of Virginia can be found in the Iveson L. Brookes Papers, Duke University Library. An interview with Butler, together with some of his correspondence, is in the James Parton Papers, Houghton Library, Harvard University. 1862–1864 documents concerning the investigation of Butler's wartime administrations are in the George H. Gordon Papers, Massachusetts Historical Society Library, Boston. Other Butler correspondence can be found in various collections at the Library of Congress; the University of Virginia Library; the Mississippi Department of Archives and History; the U.S. Naval Academy Museum; the Western Reserve Historical Society, Cleveland, Ohio; Boston University Library; the Massachusetts Historical Society Library; the Maryland Historical Society Library; the State Historical Society of Wisconsin, Madison; the New Hampshire Historical Society, Concord; Duke University Library, Durham, North Carolina; the U.S. Military Academy; the University of Iowa Library, Iowa City; the U.S. Army Military History Institute, Carlisle Barracks, Pennsylvania; and the Nebraska State Historical Society, Lincoln.

Other Sources

Crenshaw, William Vanderclock. "Benjamin F. Butler: Philosophy and Politics: 1866–1879." Doctoral Dissertation, University of Georgia, 1976. Examines and applauds Butler's national leadership of the reform faction of the Republican party in Reconstruction.

Fish, Carl Russell. "Benjamin Franklin Butler." In *Dictionary of American Biography*. New York: Charles Scribner's Sons, 1929. A short, authoritative review of Butler's life and political activity.

Harmond, Richard. "The 'Beast' in Boston: Benjamin F. Butler as Governor of Massachusetts." *Journal of American History* 55 (1968): 266–280. This brief chronicle of Butler's popular reform efforts during his year as Massachusetts governor argues that despite his uneven record, Butler seriously sought reform and instituted positive changes in Massachusetts leadership.

[Hudson, Henry Norman]. *A Chaplain's Campaign With Gen. Butler*. New York: n.p., 1865. Despite the obvious bitterness of this extended letter to Butler, outlining the author's arrest and imprisonment by Butler, and subsequent interviews with him, this recounting reveals some interesting aspects of Butler's military style.

Kallman, John D. "Benjamin Franklin Butler." In *Historical Times Illustrated Encyclopedia of the Civil War*, edited by Patricia L. Faust. New York: Harper & Row, 1986. A short review of Butler's wartime career and his importance to the Union cause.

Neely, Mark E., Jr. "Abraham Lincoln and Black Colonization: Benjamin Butler's Spurious Testimony." *Civil War History* 25 (1979): 77–83. A good exposition on one of the many inaccuracies in *Butler's Book*.

Weiss, Nathan. "The Political Theory and Practice of General Benjamin Franklin Butler." Doctoral Dissertation, New York University, 1961. A study of Butler's political philosophy and its applications in national and local politics.

Tamara Moser Melia
Naval Historical Center,
Washington, D.C.

WILLIAM BYRD II
1674–1744

Chronology

Born William Byrd on March 28, 1674, at his father's plantation on the James River in Virginia, the only surviving son of William Byrd I, an English-born goldsmith, Indian trader, planter, and head of the governor's Council in Virginia, and Mary Horsmanden Filmer Byrd, widow of Samuel Filmer and daughter of Warham Horsmanden, a Cavalier who had fled to Virginia; *1674–1681* grows up in Virginia, probably taking refuge with his mother near the coast during Bacon's Rebellion in 1676; *1681–1690* sent to England to live with his grandfather, who places him in the Felsted School in Essex, under the tutelage of Christopher Glasscock, where he discovers the classics and learns Latin, Greek, and Hebrew, as well as the modern languages; *1690–1692* goes to Holland to learn business practices; returns to England; enters the Middle Temple in London to study law; *1695* admitted to the bar; *1696* elected to the Royal Society; *1696–1697* returns to Virginia at the request of his father and enters the Virginia House of Burgesses; *1697–1703* returns to London representing his father and Virginia governor Sir Edmund Andros in a dispute with Virginia Commissary James Blair over ecclesiastical issues and educational control of the College of William and Mary; publishes a short description of an albino Negro, "An Account of a Negro Boy that is Dappled in Several Places of his Body with White Spots," in the *Philosophical Transactions of the Royal Society*; tries his hand at verse; moves in fashionable circles; unsuccessfully courts Lady Elizabeth Cromwell, an Irish woman of large fortune who inspires Byrd's "Facetia" letters in 1703; *1704* father dies; inherits his father's large estate, which totals more than 26,000 acres, and his lucrative post as receiver general for the colony; *1705* settles at the family estate of Westover, which he enlarges and improves in his new role as tidewater planter; begins gathering and arranging his library, which at his death numbers more than 3,600 volumes and rivals that of Cotton Mather and James Logan as the largest and best in the colonies; *May 4, 1706* marries Lucy Parke, daughter of Colonel Daniel Parke, a Virginia planter and erstwhile governor of the Leeward Islands, and with Lucy has four children, only two of whom survive infancy, Evelyn (1707) and Wilhelmina (1715); *1709* wins appointment to the governor's Council, a position he holds until his death; also around this time, begins keeping the first of his several diaries in cryptic shorthand; *1710* after the murder of his father-in-law in Antigua, agrees with Parke's heirs to assume Parke's debts in exchange for the Parke Virginia plantations, a bad bargain that nags Byrd almost until his death; *1715–1726* travels to London to represent members of the Virginia Council in a dispute with the governor, Alexander Spotswood, and to settle the Parke estate; *1716* sells office of receiver general; his wife joins him in London and dies of smallpox shortly thereafter; *1719* publishes several verses under the pseudonym "Mr. Burrand" in *Tunbrigalia: or Tunbridge Miscellanies, for the Year 1719* (London); *1720* during a brief visit home, reconciles with Spotswood; *1721* returns to England as agent for Virginia and appears before the Board of Trade several times; publishes *A Discourse Concerning the Plague, With Some Preservatives Against It. By a Lover of Mankind* (London), which has been attributed to Byrd by many scholars; *1722–1723* redrafts his self-portrait, "Inamorato L'Oiseaux," which in its raw form was probably first written some time before 1705; *May 1724* marries Maria Taylor, a young heiress of modest fortune from Kensington, with whom he will have four children; *1726–1744* with his wife and two daughters Evelyn and Wilhelmina, returns to Virginia; *1726* resumes seat on governor's Council; *1727* receives appointment as one of three commissioners to settle the Virginia boundary dispute with North Carolina; *1728* leads the combined Virginia and North Carolina surveying party and records his experiences in what will become his two most important works, *The Secret History of the Line* (1841) and *The History of the Dividing Line* (1929), both of which Byrd circulates privately, and from his notes also later drafts an engineering proposal and promotional piece, *A Description of the Dismal Swamp and a Proposal to Drain the Swamp* (1841); *1730–1731* builds his mansion at Westover; *1732* visits various iron mines at Germanna along the Rappahannock and records his account in what is later published as *A Progress to the Mines, Written from 1728 to 1736* . . . (1841); *1733* surveys his newly acquired lands, known as Eden, along the Dan River and records his observations in what is later published as *A Journey to the Land of Eden, A.D. 1733* (1841); *1735–1736* as king's commissioner, leads expedition to determine the true bounds of the Northern Neck proprietary in northern Virginia; *1736* arranges to bring German Swiss to settle his Land of Eden in Virginia; *1737* publishes tract, *Neu-gefundenes Eden* (Bern, Switzerland), signed Wilhelm Vogel and probably written by Samuel Jenner based on information only in part provided by Byrd, describing and promoting his land; founds Richmond; *1743* succeeds to presidency of governor's Council; *1744* finally discharges last of the Parke debt; dies on August 26 at Westover.

Activities of Historical Significance

Byrd's role as commissioner to run the boundary line between Virginia and North Carolina resulted in the exploration and settlement of a large area of the Virginia/North Carolina frontier. Typical of the great Virginia tidewater planters, Byrd established his financial competency in growing tobacco but achieved his wealth in land speculation. Byrd used his position to aggrandize large tracts of rich lands; at his death, he left an estate of more than 179,000 acres. In addition, his attempts to colonize his lands on the Dan River with Swiss Germans, though unsuccessful, reflected the recruitment policies of colonial southern proprietors who sought European and British settlers, and who experimented with a host of non-planting ventures, including mining. Byrd's travel accounts also reveal him to be a natural scientist, sharing his observations on American people, flora and fauna with such English correspondents as Peter Collinson. Natural history was the science of America, and Byrd, like other eighteenth-century American scientists, became a defender of the American environment against European charges that America was both hostile and lacking in "cultural" achievement. In time, he admitted his rusticity and turned it to moral advantage. Such a defense planted seeds of an American "national" identity.

Byrd's two travel accounts—the *Secret History* he wrote for friends, with its ribald humor and candid portrayals of other members of his party, and the more polished *History of the Dividing Line* which he intended for a wider audience, with its emphasis on the country—established his reputation as a man of letters. The publication of the histories in 1841 and 1929 first served to reinforce the Cavalier image of the Virginia gentleman, but recent scholars generally recognize them as major works of colonial American literature, linking them with the tradition of factual narrative and identifying them as a foundation of American frontier humor.

Byrd's overweening political ambition typified his class. It led him to scheme to gain the governorship of Virginia and, having failed, to use the governor's Council to check royal authority in Virginia whenever it clashed with his private interest. Byrd's magnificent mansion at Westover, which he built in early Georgian architectural style and furnished lavishly with English furniture, portraits, and other material objects, attested to his wealth and station and symbolized his claims to authority. The construction of Westover in 1730–1731, along with the completion of the Governor's Palace in Williamsburg in 1714, and the construction of other great Virginia houses, heralded the emergence of a self-conscious gentry culture along the eastern seaboard. Despite an admiration for London culture and society, a wide range of correspondents in England, and the formal English refinement he showed in his personal tastes and lifestyle, Byrd was a provincial. Like other "great planters" in the Chesapeake region, he sought autonomy on his plantation even as tobacco and purchases of English goods tied him to English creditors. Land grabbing, investment in mining, and attempts to diversify his agriculture typified his methods of advancement, but politics became both the indication and the instrument of his power. Byrd's lifestyle and behavior assume historical significance because they represented in bold relief the values and practices of the Virginia gentry.

Overview of Biographical Sources

Numerous short studies of Byrd exist, but it was not until the early twentieth century that he attracted serious scholarly attention. Early works on Byrd stressed his histories of the boundary dispute and regarded Byrd as a symbol for his age.

Nineteenth-century writers, led by the rabid southerner Edmund Ruffin who first published Byrd's major works in 1841, tended to be Virginians who depicted Byrd as the embodiment of the Cavalier type—a perception that still persists even among scholarly biographers. Until 1939 biographers were unaware of Byrd's secret diaries, and thus based their assessments of Byrd's character on his public papers, letters, and travel accounts. Byrd's handsome estate at Westover provided visual evidence of a "golden age" of Virginia gentry, and Byrd's lifestyle and his abundant correspondence with scientists and prominent families in England reinforced the image. His public poses were assumed to be his true self.

William K. Boyd's publication of Byrd's *Secret History* in *William Byrd's Histories of the Dividing Line Betwixt Virginia and North Carolina* (1929) encouraged much new work on Byrd, but critical opinion centered on Byrd as a historian and, still, as the quintessential Cavalier. Thomas Wertenbaker's sketch in *The Dictionary of American Biography* (1930) summed up prevailing judgments that Byrd was a wit who manifested the grace, charm, and culture of his age. Richmond Beatty's favorable biography, *William Byrd of Westover* (1932), admitted the hard edges of Cavalier Byrd, especially his indebtedness and his anglophilia, but dismissed Byrd the writer as a humorist. More modern scholars recognize the humor: in 1957 Kenneth Lynn, *Mark Twain and Southwestern Humor*, suggested that Byrd's *History* marks the beginning of southwestern humor. These scholars also relate Byrd's writings to pamphleteering and satirical styles of England's Augustan age.

The most important and widely accepted recent scholarly estimation of Byrd the writer remains that of Richard Beale Davis, who, in *Major Writers of Early American Literature* (1972), observed that Byrd "has been labelled belated Restoration cavalier and satirist, Queen Anne wit, pamphleteer, promoter, American Pepys, virtuoso, travel writer, and historian. He is most of these things in some degree, and more." In a host of works recovering the intellectual life of the colonial South, Davis established Byrd's literary preeminence among colonial American writers, ranking him with Franklin as an American writer in his interests and approach.

The discovery and decoding of the Byrd diaries, beginning in 1939, revealed a rakish private man that shocked conventions of a polite Cavalier grace. Byrd's diaries—with his matter-of-fact recordings of sexual activities with strumpets, chambermaids, and ladies (sometimes all on the same day) mixed with his litanies of prayers to God and details of a busy planter's life—confounded earlier one-dimensional views of Byrd and his class. With the publication of the diaries Byrd became, in the words of his editors, an American Pepys. But, more than that, the diaries invited new readings of Byrd the man.

Several different Byrds appeared. Interest in Byrd, for instance, grew at the same time that students of American slavery were recasting the images of planters and their world. Byrd emerged as a new archetype: the planter who would be a patriarch. This reading of Byrd's character was suggested by Gerald Mullin in *Flight and Rebellion: Slave Resistance in Eighteenth-Century Virginia* (1972) and soon became commonplace in descriptions of master-slave relations and planters' self-delusions in colonial America. Interest in family life among colonial Americans led other scholars to study Byrd. The most substantial treatment, which uses Byrd to trace kinship networks, the loss of mastery over one's family, and related themes of authority within the Chesapeake planter household, is found in Daniel Blake Smith, *Inside the Great House: Planter Family Life in Eighteenth-Century Chesapeake Society* (1980).

Byrd became another kind of metaphor as well. His ambivalence as a colonial torn between a sophisticated England and a rustic Virginia represents, for many recent writers, a microcosm of the agony of eighteenth-century Americans' struggle for self-identity. Finally, a revived interest in colonial American politics has brought attention to Byrd as a salient example of the ambitious colonial seeking preferment and a councilor intriguing against the royal governor. This view is exemplified by Warren Billings, John E. Selby, and Thad W. Tate, *Colonial Virginia: A History* (1986). Byrd's insatiable appetite for land and his constant jockeying for position and advantage bespoke a general American aggressiveness that unhinged the empire—or so recent histories suggest.

Evaluation of Principal Biographical Sources

Bassett, John Spencer, ed. *The Writings of Colonel William Byrd of Westover in Virginia, Esqr.* New York: Doubleday, 1901. **(A, G)** Drawn almost wholly from manuscript sources, including many personal letters, historian Bassett's eighty-page "Introduction" to *The Writings* is the first extensive scholarly treatment of Byrd's life and has remained a basic source for most later Byrd biographers. Set against the economic, social, and political development of Virginia and Byrd's family, the "Introduction" focuses primarily on political events, with only passing notice of the literary significance of Byrd's writings.

Beatty, Richmond Croom. *William Byrd of Westover*. Boston: Houghton Mifflin, 1932. **(A, G)** This first full-length biography stresses Byrd's English background and connections and views Byrd as an unhappy provincial yearning to return to England. Relying on Byrd's travel narratives, letters, and public documents, Beatty draws an overly sympathetic portrait of Byrd's character, but in light of the later discovery and deciphering of Byrd's shorthand diaries, Beatty's study suffers from an inaccurate reading of Byrd's private life.

Hatch, Alden. *The Byrds of Virginia*. New York: Holt, Rinehart, & Winston, 1969. **(A, G)** In "Book Two: The Black Swan of Virginia," Hatch provides an encyclopedic chronological description of Byrd's life, covering Byrd's political ambition and public service, debts, land hunger, relationships with various women, and writings.

Lockridge, Kenneth A. *The Diary, and Life of William Byrd II of Virginia, 1674–1744*. Chapel Hill: University of North Carolina Press, 1987. **(A)** A provocative and original reading of Byrd's inner self, based almost wholly on the diaries, Lockridge's "psychobiographical" essay analyzes Byrd as a man at war with himself, attempting to emulate a dead father he never really knew by achieving position in Virginia and connections in England, only to discover the dimensions of his provinciality, and finally, accommodating to this true identity as a tidewater Virginia gentleman. For Lockridge, Byrd's life represented a design for mastery over self and others that Byrd never fully achieved.

Marambaud, Pierre. *William Byrd of Westover, 1674–1744*. Charlottesville: University Press of Virginia, 1971. **(A, G)** Drawing on extensive research in manuscript collections and in published writings, the French historian Marambaud renders the fullest and best Byrd biography to date. Marambaud views Byrd as a perfectionist of limited intellectual originality who produced works of important consequence for the social historian, but of little literary merit. In his discussions of Byrd the planter and man of letters, Marambaud sees Byrd as a key transitional figure separating colonial from provincial Virginia.

Robertson, Henry Alphonso, Jr. "A Critical Analysis of William Byrd II and His Literary Technique in *The History of the Dividing Line* and *The Secret History of the Line*." Doctoral dissertation, University of Delaware, 1966. **(A)** Though focusing on Byrd's boundary line expedition, Robertson surveys Byrd's life, family background, and writings, and particularly measures Byrd as a naturalist.

Overview and Evaluation of Primary Sources

Byrd's significance derives from his writings, very few of which were published during his lifetime. His literary reputation largely rests on his histories of the 1728 expedition to resolve the Virginia-North Carolina boundary dispute, which are also valuable sources for natural and social history. Beginning in 1841, several editions of Byrd's travel accounts to the interior have been published. A useful and accessible edition is William K. Boyd, ed., *William Byrd's Histories of the Dividing Line Betwixt Virginia and North Carolina* (1929. Rev. ed. Mineola, NY: Dover Publications, 1967; **A, G**), which printed the *Secret History* for the first time. John Spencer Bassett, ed., *The Writings of Colonel William Byrd of Westover in Virginia, Esqr.* (1901. Reprint. New York: Burt Franklin, 1970; **A, G**), includes the *History of the Dividing Line*, "A Journey to the Land of Eden," "A Progress to the Mines," and miscellaneous letters. The best edition of Byrd's four principal writings is Louis B. Wright, ed., *The Prose Works of William Byrd of Westover: Narratives of a Colonial Virginian* (Cambridge: Harvard University Press, 1966; **A, G**), which contains *The Secret History of the Line*, *The History of the Dividing Line*, "A Progress to the Mines," and "A Journey to the Land of Eden." Wright's "Introduction: William Byrd as a Man of Letters" emphasizes Byrd's satirical humor and "idiomatic expression" in his extant writings, exclusive of the shorthand diaries.

Though he wore masks even for himself, the private Byrd (his courtships, quarrels and reconciliations with Lucy Parke Byrd, religious practices, dreams and superstitions, diet, work habits, public responsibilities, and relations with his family, slaves, and others) emerges most clearly in his diaries. The first diary that was discovered and decoded appeared as *The Secret Diary of William Byrd of Westover, 1709–1712*, edited by Louis B. Wright and Marion Tinling (Richmond: Dietz Press, 1941; **A, G**). An abridged paperback edition was published as *The Great American Gentleman: William Byrd of Westover in Virginia: His Secret Diary for the Years 1709–1712* (New York: Capricorn Books, 1963; **G**). The second decoded diary was published as *Another Secret Diary of William Byrd of Westover, 1739–1741. With Letters & Literary Exercises, 1696–1726*, edited by Maude H. Woodfin and Marion Tinling (Richmond: Dietz Press, 1942; **A, G**). This edition also reprints Byrd's poems from *Tunbrigalia* and his *A Discourse Concerning the Plague, With Some Preservatives Against It. By a Lover of Mankind* (originally published in London in 1721) and publishes "The Female Creed," and various letters, essays, literary pieces, and character sketches including Byrd's long self-analysis "Inamorato L'Oiseaux." A third diary was discovered, deciphered, and published as *The London Diary (1717–1721) and Other Writings, of William Byrd of Virginia*, edited by Louis B. Wright and Marion Tinling (New York: Oxford University Press, 1958; **A, G**), which includes extracts from Byrd's major prose works and an introduction by Wright that is the best short biography available. Of lesser interest are the very rare Thomas F. Ryan, ed., *William Byrd, Esq., Accounts as Solicitor General of the Colonies and Receiver of the Tobacco Tax 1688–1704 . . . Letters Writ to Facetia by Veramour* (Baltimore: privately printed, 1913; **A**), and Earl G. Swem, ed., *Description of the Dismal Swamp and a Proposal to Drain the Swamp, by William Byrd of Westover* (Metuchen: Printed for C. F. Heartman, 1922; **A**). Byrd's political and legal abilities are suggested in Louis B. Wright, ed., *An Essay Upon the Government of the English Plantations on the Continent of America (1701)* (San Marino, CA: The Huntington Library, 1945; **A**), which includes two Byrd memoranda to the Board of Trade: "Representation of Mr. Byrd concerning Proprietary Governments" (1699), and "Proposals humbly submitted to the Lords of the Council of Trade and Plantations for sending the French Protestants to Virginia" (1698). Byrd's tilt against Virginia governor Alexander Spotswood can be followed in R. A. Brock, ed., *The Official Letters of Alexander Spotswood*, 2 vols. (Richmond: Virginia Historical Society, 1882–1885; **A**). Many selected Byrd letters have been published in the *Virginia Magazine of History and Biography*, vols. 9 (1901–1902), 35 (1927), 36 (1928), and 37 (1929), and elsewhere, but all these works have been superseded by Marion Tinling, ed., *The Correspondence of the Three William Byrds of Westover, Virginia, 1684–1776*, 2 vols. (Charlottesville:

University Press of Virginia, 1977; **A, G**), a carefully annotated and comprehensive modern scholarly edition revealing Byrd's many and varied interests—natural history and science, surveying and land development, agriculture, political preferments in England and Virginia, family ties (with much on Byrd's efforts at male dominance), literature, and religion and more.

Byrd's most important writings are now available in print. The key manuscript collections are at the Virginia Historical Society, which holds Byrd's diary of 1717–1721, commonplace book, letterbooks, numerous letters (located in various manuscript collections), title book, public documents, and the famous "Westover Manuscripts" that contain all Byrd's travel accounts except *The Secret History*. The manuscript of *The Secret History* is held by the American Philosophical Society. The Huntington Library in San Marino, California, owns Byrd's diary of 1709–1712 and some pages of a Byrd letterbook, including the inventory of Byrd's estate in 1746, while the University of North Carolina at Chapel Hill has the diary of 1739–1741 and a small collection of letterbooks. Colonial Williamsburg houses two Byrd letterbooks. Byrd letters are in the British Library and the Public Record Office in England and in the Library of Congress, the Historical Society of Pennsylvania, the New York Public Library, the Harvard College Library, and private collections. Portraits of Byrd hang at the Virginia Historical Society and in the capitol building at Williamsburg.

Fiction and Adaptations

In 1892 Marion Harland [Mary Hawes Terhune] published a novel, *His Great Self*, based on the story of Byrd's supposed refusal to allow his daughter to marry an English baronet. The novel features a highly romanticized portrait of the Cavalier Byrd and his plantation world.

Museums, Historical Landmarks, Societies

Westover (Virginia). Byrd's brick mansion, one of the finest examples of early Georgian architecture in America, is on a bank of the James River about thirty miles from Williamsburg (on State Route 5) and stands pretty much as it did in the eighteenth century, despite being partly burned in 1749 and occupied during the Civil War. It was renovated in 1900–1905. Westover includes the gardens and various outbuildings recalling the eighteenth-century ambience of the Virginia gentry. Westover remains in private hands, but it is open to the public for tours during the spring.

Other Sources

Bain, Robert. "William Byrd of Westover." In *The History of Southern Literature*, edited by Louis Rubin, Jr., B. Jackson, R. S. Moore, L. Simpson, and T. D. Young. Baton Rouge: Louisiana State University Press, 1985. An excellent overview and concise analysis of Byrd's writings related to his life and his place in colonial American literature.

Boyd, William K., ed. *William Byrd's Histories of the Dividing Line Betwixt Virginia and North Carolina*. Raleigh: North Carolina Historical Commission, 1929. Boyd's "Introduction," which offers a history of Byrd's expedition, assays Byrd's character and compares the *History of the Dividing Line* with the *Secret History* (even setting them on parallel pages) and questions the accuracy of the former in light of the latter.

Cutting, Rose Marie. *John and William Bartram, William Byrd II and St. John de Crevecoeur: A Reference Guide*. Boston: G. K. Hall, 1976. In the most comprehensive and reliable bibliographical listing on Byrd, Cutting annotates the "Writings About William Byrd II, 1817–1974," including various editions of his works and secondary treatments.

Davis, Richard Beale. "William Byrd: Taste and Tolerance." In *Major Writers of Early American Literature*, edited by Everett Emerson. Madison: University of Wisconsin Press, 1972. In an important assessment of Byrd's life and writings, Davis characterizes Byrd as archetypal of both the society and literature of his time and region and, in his mature naturalistic American writings, as a "genuinely American" writer.

Hubbell, Jay B. *The South in American Literature, 1607–1900*. Durham, NC: Duke University Press, 1954. In his chapter on "William Byrd" and his "Bibliography" on Byrd, Hubbell evaluates Byrd's life and works, ranking him as a major colonial American writer. Hubbell provides summaries of the publication histories of Byrd's writings and lists sources for biographical information, criticism, and locations of manuscript materials on Byrd.

Preston, Richard M. "William Byrd II." In *Dictionary of Literary Biography*. Vol. 24, *American Colonial Writers, 1606–1734*, edited by Emory Elliott. Detroit: Gale, 1984. A good, concise recent summary of Byrd's life and principal writings.

Risjord, Norman. "William Byrd II, Virginia Gentleman." In *Representative Americans: The Colonists*. Lexington, MA: D. C. Heath, 1981. Risjord's chapter presents the most readable short account of Byrd's life, focusing on Byrd the colonial grandee who blended the cultures of London and tidewater Virginia.

Wright, Louis, B., and Marion Tinling. "William Byrd of Westover, an American Pepys." *South Atlantic Quarterly* 39 (July 1940): 259–274. A seminal article, based on the discovery of Byrd's secret diary, that introduces the private Byrd as diarist and social observer of his times.

Zuckerman, Michael. "William Byrd's Family." *Perspectives in American History* 12 (1979): 255–311. An important article that sets Byrd in the larger context of the unstable social and psychological self-identities of eighteenth-century New World "gentlemen" by arguing that Byrd sought to build an extended family of friends, slaves, governmental officials, and others in an effort to bind the plantation world together.

Randall M. Miller
Saint Joseph's University

JOHN C. CALHOUN
1782–1850

Chronology

Born John Caldwell Calhoun on March 18, 1782, at the Long Canes near present Abbeville, South Carolina, fourth of five children of Patrick Calhoun, an early Scotch-Irish settler of the South Carolina upcountry, Revolutionary leader, and Indian fighter, and of Martha Caldwell Calhoun; *1782–1802* grows up on his father's plantation, largely self-educated except for two years at a classical academy; *1802–1804* enters junior class of Yale College and graduates; *1804–1811* studies law at Charleston and at the Litchfield, Connecticut, Law School; practices law in the South Carolina upcountry and serves two terms in the state legislature; *January 8, 1811* marries a cousin, Floride Colhoun [sic], with whom he has ten children; *1811–1817* serves in the U.S. House of Representatives as a Jeffersonian Republican and is recognized as a leader of the "War Hawks" and an able debater; becomes chairman of the Foreign Relations Committee and is one of the ablest legislative leaders of the administration during the War of 1812; *1816* plays a leading role in legislation for a peacetime military establishment and the chartering of the Second Bank of the United States, and for a national plan of internal improvements which is vetoed by President Madison; *1817–1825* serves as Secretary of War in the Cabinet of President James Monroe, proving an able administrator; preserves an efficient professional officer corps in the face of severe retrenchment, strengthens West Point, improves Indian relations, and reorganizes administration and accountability; owns the Georgetown estate later known as "Dumbarton Oaks"; *1823* is one of five prominent men seeking the Presidency in a period with no clear-cut political parties; *1824* withdraws from Presidential consideration but is elected Vice-President by a large majority in the Electoral College; the Presidential election is bitterly divided between four candidates and has to be decided in the House of Representatives in favor of John Quincy Adams; *1825–1829* serves first term as Vice-President, during which he separates himself from Adams and throws his support to Andrew Jackson; *1826* settles permanently at "Fort Hill" near Pendleton, South Carolina; *1828* re-elected Vice-President on Jackson's ticket; *1829–1832* breaks with Jackson over a variety of matters and reluctantly takes the lead in the strong movement in South Carolina against federal tariff legislation; endorses and defends the idea of nullification, a suspensive state veto of federal laws deemed unconstitutional when all other remedies have failed; *1832* a South Carolina constitutional convention adopts nullification, Calhoun resigns as Vice-President and is appointed U.S. Senator; *1833* Calhoun joins the Senate, defends his state and nullification, but works to defuse the conflict by compromise; Congress affirms the right to enforce federal laws and collect the tariff duties but at the same time honors an arrangement worked out by Calhoun and Henry Clay to gradually reduce tariff duties; Calhoun returns to South Carolina and persuades the state to repeal nullification; armed conflict is avoided in this "Compromise of 1833"; *1833–1838* serves in the Senate and maintains a position independent of both Whig and Democratic parties; criticizes Whigs for their nationalist program and Democrats for spoilsmanship, jingoism, and bad fiscal management; *1836* begins to respond to a rising tide of militant abolitionism by insisting that the existing Southern system is the best possible under the circumstances, and that the "compromises of the Constitution" must be respected by Northerners in spirit as well as letter; *1838–1843* rejoins the Democratic party and regains considerable national influence and reputation; one of the leading members of the Senate, widely admired for principled, eloquent, and independent positions on all major issues of the day: banking and currency, public lands, internal improvements, territorial expansion, tarrifs, foreign relations; *1843* seeks the Democratic Presidential nomination; *1844–1845* withdraws from the Presidential campaign and is appointed Secretary of State by President John Tyler, in which position he serves a year; lays the groundwork for peaceful settlement of the Oregon question with Great Britain in the next administration; concludes a treaty of annexation with the independent Republic of Texas, which is rejected by the Senate; before Calhoun leaves office the same objective is accomplished by admission of Texas to the Union; *1846–1850* serves in the Senate; criticizes the Mexican War as unnecessary and claims it was brought on by unconstitutional executive action; spends his last years seeking to marshal the South to act with unanimity in defense of its sectional interests under the belief that only by unanimity can the minority section exercise enough power to defend itself and at the same time preserve the Union from a future breakup; *1850* dies in Washington on March 31 in the midst of the debates over the Compromise of 1850, which he opposed for not offering sufficient concessions to the South nor providing a lasting settlement; left manuscripts of *A Disquisition on Government* and *A Discourse on the Constitution and Government of the United States*, systematically setting forth his ideas on constitutional government and the concurrent majority, to be published after his death.

Activities of Historical Significance

The historical significance of Calhoun's career has two aspects—statesman and thinker. As one of the "Great Triumvirate," along with Henry Clay and Daniel Webster, he exercised a major, though never predominant, influence over American political life during the four decades from 1811 to 1850. His influence was not limited to the South, nor was it confined entirely to matters of states' rights and slavery, with which his name has most commonly been associated in recent times. For instance, a historian of American banking, after studying Calhoun's speeches of the 1830s, observed that his constructive proposals in regard to fiscal and monetary policies exceeded those of any other figure of the time.

Because Calhoun always cast his political positions and arguments in principled and philosophical terms, he has proved to be of continuing interest to later thinkers of widely diverse times and viewpoints. Since the 1940s, Calhoun has inspired a large body of scholarly literature, spanning disciplines and continents, devoted to the analysis of his political ideas. This literature concentrates primarily on his idea of the "concurrent majority" as an analysis of the shortcomings of unqualified majority rule and as a suggestive program for the defense of the rights of minorities. He has thus been seen by some observers as an invaluable contributor to the understanding of characteristic problems of democracies, and even as an early formulator of democratic pluralism. Others have found him interesting as a critic of industrial capitalism or an anticipator of theories of class conflict.

Overview of Biographical Sources

A considerable amount of biographical material appeared in books and periodicals during and immediately after Calhoun's lifetime, most of which was favorable in tone. After the Civil War, American historians tended to anticipate the treatment of Hermann E. von Holst, who saw Calhoun as an evil genius whose fanatical devotion to slavery was one of the chief causes of the war. This view was based upon ignorance of many important details of the broad span of Calhoun's life and political career. The turn of the twentieth century saw a number of attempts to treat Calhoun more objectively and to base views on serious research. This period saw the biographies of Hunt and Meigs, and the publication by a leading professional historian, J. Franklin Jameson, of an edition of Calhoun's correspondence, considered by the editor as one of the major lacunae in American historical sources.

The Depression and World War II brought a new interest in Calhoun from so many quarters that it amounted to a small movement in intellectual history. Biographies were undertaken by Styron, Wiltse, and Coit, along with a thorough study of Calhoun's political thought by Spain and the inauguration of a comprehensive edition of his papers. Calhoun was the subject of a flood of scholarly and popular articles analyzing every incident of his career, and every facet of his political thinking: a flood—international in scope—which has slowed but not abated. This body of literature is largely, though not entirely, sympathetic to Calhoun's political career, which is seen as a heroic and constructive effort to preserve the Union, and to his political thought, which is generally thought to be relevant to issues of later eras.

Major figures generate new biographical interest every generation, and, in the late 1980s at least three new biographies of John C. Calhoun were under way (by Irving Bartlett, John Nivens, and Merrill D. Peterson) that promised new perspectives on Calhoun's life and role in American history.

Evaluation of Principal Biographical Sources

Coit, Margaret L. *John C. Calhoun: American Portrait*. Boston: Houghton Mifflin, 1950. **(G, Y)** A colorful, dramatic, and intimate account. A fine example of biographical writing which received the Pulitzer Prize.

Holst, Hermann E. von. *John C. Calhoun*. Boston: Houghton Mifflin, 1881. **(A)** The first scholarly biography of Calhoun, this work was highly argumentative and is chiefly useful as an indicator of how Calhoun was viewed in the post-Civil War period.

Hunt, Gaillard. *John C. Calhoun*. Philadelphia: George W. Jacobs, 1908. **(A, G)** This is a reservedly sympathic and well-written life that is still worthy of interest for its interpretations.

[Hunter, Robert M. T.] *Life of John C. Calhoun, Presenting a Condensed History of Political Events from 1811 to 1843*. New York: Harper & Brothers, 1843. Reprinted in *The Papers of John C. Calhoun*, vol. 17. **(A, G)** This short work, often mistakenly thought to be an autobiography, was written anonymously by a close associate of Calhoun, Robert M. T. Hunter. It contains the first good account of Calhoun's early life, and a description of his career and the course of American history up to 1843.

Meigs, William Montgomery. *The Life of John Caldwell Calhoun*. 2 vols. New York: Neale, 1917. **(A, G)** Carefully researched and detailed on political events, this biography marked a substantial advance in knowledge of Calhoun's career, mostly but not entirely superseded by the work of Charles M. Wiltse.

Styron, Arthur M. *The Cast-Iron Man: John C. Calhoun and American Democracy*. New York: Longmans-Green, 1935. **(G, Y)** Though somewhat eccentric, this book is colorfully written and marks the beginnings of a renewed twentieth-century interest in Calhoun.

Wiltse, Charles M. *John C. Calhoun*. 3 vols. Indianapolis: Bobbs-Merrill, 1944–1951; Reprint, New York: Russell & Russell, 1968. **(A, G)** Wiltse's detailed, definitive, and sympathetic treatment of Calhoun is indispensable both for the subject and for his period of American history.

Overview and Evaluation of Primary Sources

The Papers of John C. Calhoun (Columbia: University of South Carolina Press, 1959–1987; A; Robert L. Meriwether, ed., vol. 1; W. Edwin Hemphill, ed., vols. 2–9; Clyde N. Wilson, ed., vols. 10–17) is a comprehensive edition currently in production, which includes correspondence, speeches, writings, and other papers. A total of twenty-five volumes are projected; each volume contains a substantial interpretive introduction.

The most important collection of correspondence and other papers of Calhoun and his immediate family is at Clemson University, which inherited Calhoun's house and lands. There is also a large collection at the South Caroliniana Library of the University of South Carolina. Many documents are found in the Library of Congress and the National Archives, in various collections. More are found in over a hundred manuscript repositories, and still others in newspapers and pamphlets contemporary to Calhoun's life. The total corpus is c.50,000 items. Besides these actual Calhoun documents, the amount of relevant material among the papers of his contemporaries is incalculable since he was a major and arresting figure for forty years.

Richard K. Crallé, ed., *The Works of John C. Calhoun*, (6 vols. Columbia, SC: A. S. Johnston, 1851, and New York: D. Appleton, 1853–1857; **A**) is still a useful and judicious selection of Calhoun's most important public papers. Volume 1 contains the original publication of *A Disquisition on Government* and *A Discourse on the Constitution and Government of the United States*, though the former has also been printed in paperback several times in the twentieth century. Volumes 2–4 contain the most important speeches from all parts of his Congressional career; volumes 5 and 6 contain a variety of official reports, public letters, and other documents.

John M. Anderson, ed., *Calhoun: Basic Documents* (State College, PA: Bald Eagle Press, 1952; **A**), which is widely available, contains a much smaller, but well-chosen, selection from Calhoun's most important speeches and writings. Two published collections of correspondence are still useful, pending the completion of *The Papers of John C. Calhoun*, which has so far reached the year 1843. These are J. Franklin Jameson, ed., *Correspondence of John C. Calhoun*, 2 vols. (Washington: U.S. Government Printing Office, 1900; **A**), and Chauncey S. Boucher and Robert P. Brooks, eds., *Correspondence Addressed to John C. Calhoun* (Washington: Government Printing Office, 1930; **A**).

Museums, Historical Landmarks, Societies

Dumbarton Oaks (Washington, DC). The gardens of Calhoun's Georgetown estate are open to the public daily. The grounds include a Byzantine museum, and the house is sometimes open to the public.

Fort Hill (Clemson, SC). The plantation house and detached office of Calhoun's home from 1826 to 1850 are preserved with many of the original furnishings and family possessions in the center of what is now the campus of Clemson University.

Other Sources

Coit, Margaret L., ed. *John C. Calhoun*. In *Great Lives Observed* series. Englewood Cliffs: Prentice-Hall, 1970. A vivid collection of contemporary and later observations and evaluations.

Cook, Harriet Hefner. *John C. Calhoun—The Man*. Columbia, SC: privately printed, 1965. A localistic and eulogistic treatment which is well illustrated and contains much material on Calhoun's home, family, and daily life.

Current, Richard N. *John C. Calhoun*. New York: Washington Square Press, 1963. Analyzes Calhoun's political thought in terms of class conflict and argues against its relevance for later times.

Drucker, Peter F. "A Key to American Politics: Calhoun's Pluralism." *Review of Politics* 10 (October 1948): 412–426. Describes Calhoun as a prophet of modern American democratic pluralism.

Hofstadter, Richard. "John C. Calhoun: The Marx of the Master Class." *The American Political Tradition and the Men Who Made It*. New York: Alfred A. Knopf, 1948. A famous analysis of Calhoun as a theorist of class conflict.

Kuic, Vukan. "John C. Calhoun's Theory of the 'Concurrent Majority.'" *American Bar Association Journal* 69 (April 1983): 482–486. An argument for the continuing relevance and broad applicability of the "concurrent majority" as exemplified in judicial decisions.

Lerner, Ralph. "Calhoun's New Science of Politics." *American Political Science Review* 57 (December 1963): 918–932. An analysis of Calhoun's contributions to political thought.

Phillips, Ulrich B. "John Caldwell Calhoun." In *Dictionary of American Biography* Vol. 3. A short account of Calhoun's career, packed with facts and astute judgments.

Spain, August O. *The Political Theory of John C. Calhoun*. New York: Octagon Books, 1951. The most thorough and objective analysis of the sources and nature of Calhoun's ideas.

Thomas, John L., ed. *John C. Calhoun: A Profile*. New York: Hill and Wang, 1968. A substantial collection of evaluative articles from the nineteenth and twentieth centuries.

Wilson, Clyde N. "John Caldwell Calhoun." In *Antebellum Writers in New York and the South*, ed. by Joel Myerson. Vol. 3 of *Dictionary of Literary Biography*. Detroit: Gale Research, 1979. A good brief biography and evaluation.

Clyde N. Wilson
University of South Carolina

AL CAPONE
1899–1947

Chronology

Born Alphonse Capone on January 17, 1899, in Brooklyn, New York, the fourth of nine children of Neapolitan-born barber Gabriel Capone (originally Caponi) and Teresa Riolia Capone; *1899–1917* grows up in Brooklyn; after quitting school in sixth grade, joins the notorious Five Points Gang and becomes involved in menial jobs and petty crime, notably as a bartender/bouncer for Brooklyn racketeer Frank Yale; *1918* marries Mae Coughlin, sales clerk and daughter of a construction laborer; *1919* moves to Chicago at invitation of rising gang chief Johnny Torrio; *1920–1924* aids Torrio's consolidation of the Chicago underworld, meanwhile advancing to role of chief lieutenant and number-one enforcer in the new crime syndicate; *1925–1928* succeeds the wounded Torrio as syndicate head and continues the expansion of the criminal empire; *1929* orders "St. Valentine's Day Massacre" of rival gang; *1929–1930* serves ten months on weapons conviction in Pennsylvania, a maneuver probably orchestrated for self-protection; *1931* sentenced to eleven years imprisonment on federal income tax evasion charges, serves at Atlanta Penitentiary and later Alcatraz; *1939* released from prison on medical grounds and for good behavior; retires to Florida home; *1947* dies on January 25 of advanced syphilis and bronchial pneumonia in Miami.

Activities of Historical Significance

Capone has become the legendary epitome of the American gangster. The recognition is not based mainly on his historical accomplishment. Such men as Charles "Lucky" Luciano and Meyer Lansky are generally considered as having had the greatest influence on the development of a national crime syndicate. Even in Chicago, Johnny Torrio played the main role in originating a consolidated criminal organization. Yet it is Capone's image of a ganglord that triumphed and has endured—the dark, beefy figure dressed in a double-breasted pinstripe suit, diamonds on fingers, panama hat on head, seven-inch cigar in mouth, perhaps with a sinister scar down one cheek. This is what a racketeer looks like, a picture that has lasted into the 1980s and has meanwhile spread around the world. Probably the man's natural flamboyance contributed much to making Capone a pop-cultural icon. On a deeper level, he can be viewed as operating in the "beloved rogue" tradition that produced such figures as Robin Hood and Jesse James. The vicious hoodlum who personally executed three traitors with a baseball bat was also known to give hundred-dollar tips to newsboys and operated a soup-kitchen for the needy. The fact that Capone was providing alcoholic beverages to quench the thirst of a Prohibition-dried populace likewise enhanced his popularity. "I give the public what they want," Capone is quoted as saying. During his heyday he was a favorite subject of the media and even appeared on the cover of *Time* magazine. The federal government's decision to "get" Capone as an object-lesson for other racketeers also suggests his prominence. The public fascination with this figure from the Roaring Twenties continues to the present day—the recent discovery of Capone's "secret vault" under the Lexington Hotel led to an astonishing amount of news hype and a prime-time television special.

Overview of Biographical Sources

Much has been written about Capone, from his own time up to the present. Numerous books deal with organized crime in Chicago; since Capone was the most visible of the city's racketeers, he figures prominently in these works. Personal biographies of the man himself are rarer. Discounting the various sensationalized "dime-store" periodicals of the era, Pasley's 1931 book was the first complete account of Capone's career. It remained the standard biography for the next forty years; though, obviously, it did not carry the story through to its conclusion. Gangster sagas never seem to go out of fashion, and the bibliography of Capone-related books continued to expand during the 1940s and 1950s. However, the publication of Eliot Ness's memoir, *The Untouchables* (1957), appears to have sparked a revival of popular interest in Capone the individual. There were new movies, television programs, and magazine articles, and Pasley's biography was reissued with an up-to-date epilogue. John Kobler tied all the strands together in his excellent 1971 book, which has become the closest thing to a comprehensive account of Capone's "life and world." All of these works are more narrative than analytical, and Capone awaits a scholarly biographer.

Evaluation of Principal Biographical Sources

Elliott, Neil. *My Years With Capone: Jack Woodford-Al Capone, 1924-1932.* Seattle: Woodford Memorial Editions, 1985. **(G)** This short book transcribes journalist Woodford's reminiscences of Life With Al in a breezy, intimate style. However, since the preface admits that Woodford was "a born BS artist" and "a fictioneer, not a historian," it should be approached with caution.

Kobler, John. *Capone: The Life and World of Al Capone.* New York: Putnam, 1971. **(G)** Well-written, thorough account of Capone's career from childhood through death. The definitive biography.

Landesco, John. *Organized Crime in Chicago.* Reprint edition. Chicago: University of Chicago Press, 1968. **(A, G)** Originally published as part of a 1929 study, this is a detailed description and analysis of the city's underworld in the late

1920s, as well as an exploration of its ethnic and social context. Not specifically a biography of Capone, it is a valuable work for understanding his milieu.

Pasley, Fred D. *Al Capone: The Biography of a Self-Made Man.* London: Faber & Faber, 1931. **(G)** The earliest full-scale biography of Capone. Written by a journalist during the high-days of Prohibition, it is somewhat haphazard in organization and sketchy at points. However, it has the advantage of being a contemporary piece and has obviously influenced later accounts.

Ross, Robert. *The Trial of Al Capone.* Chicago, 1933. **(A, G)** Concentrating on the legal proceedings, Ross's self-published work is the most accessible source for testimony and appeals in the Capone tax case.

Spiering, Frank. *The Man Who Got Capone.* Indianapolis: Bobbs-Merrill, 1976. **(G)** The story of Frank Wilson, the treasury agent who built the tax case against Capone. Some good details on specific events in Capone's prosecution, though much of the general material is available elsewhere.

Overview and Evaluation of Primary Sources

Primary sources are extremely limited. Capone himself wrote no memoirs, and the gangland code of silence restrained his associates and adversaries from recording their reminiscences. However, Eliot Ness, the Prohibition agent who battled Capone, did write a memoir, *The Untouchables* (New York: Julian Messner, 1957; **G**). This is a key document in the development of the Capone mystique, though other observers have questioned Ness's own importance in the downfall of the gang leader. Most of the other primary source material on Capone's activities rests in government documents relating to his legal matters. The Treasury Department file is available; Kobler drew on it heavily for his biography. Since that time, the FBI files have also been opened. Aside from the scattered newspaper interviews with Capone, nothing else of value survives.

Fiction and Adaptations

Capone has been a popular subject of feature films since his own day. Such early gangster portrayals as Edward G. Robinson in *Little Caesar* (1930) and Paul Muni in *Scarface: The Shame of the Nation* (1932) are clearly patterned on aspects of Capone's career and persona. Ben Hecht, who was a Chicago journalist during the 1920s, wrote the screenplay for the latter film. Legal cautions dictated that these contemporary stories be presented as fictional accounts. However, when Hollywood finally got around to addressing Capone by name, the films still contained large doses of make-believe. The first of these newer treatments was *Al Capone* (1959), an excellent film starring Rod Steiger that also did well at the box office. John Roeburt's novel *Al Capone* (1959) is based on this film. It was followed by

The Scarface Mob (1962), a theatrical release assembled from episodes of the popular "The Untouchables" television series; Neville Brand played the Capone role. Roger Corman's *St. Valentine's Day Massacre* (1967) related the story of the title-event, as well as the familiar episodes of the Capone saga, in a downbeat, semi-documentary style that drew mixed reviews and poor business; Jason Robards, Jr., starred. Ben Gazzara next played the lead in *Capone* (1975), a violent film scorned by critics and public. Most recently, Brian De Palma's *The Untouchables* (1987) retold the tale of Eliot Ness and Capone's tax downfall in rousing fashion; Robert De Niro played Capone with a bit more humor than is usual in the role, suggesting the personal charisma that undoubtedly contributed to the gangster's popularity.

Museums, Historical Landmarks, Societies

Alcatraz Prison (Alcatraz, CA). Capone was "sent up the river" for tax evasion to this notorious prison island, known as "the rock," where he occupied a cell in the B Block from 1934–1939. Alcatraz is now part of the Golden Gate National Park, and the Park Service gives tours of the prison.

Chicago Historical Society (Chicago, IL). This organization has a clipping file on Capone, as well as a comprehensive collection of books and magazines.

The Hideout (Couderay, WI). Now a resort/restaurant complex, Capone's 400-acre retreat is still reminiscent of his lavish lifestyle.

Lexington Hotel (Chicago, IL). Site of Capone's headquarters and location of the famous "secret vault." Currently undergoing restoration, with a suggestion that part of the building will be a gangland museum.

Other Sources

Haller, Mark H. "Alphonse Capone." In *Dictionary of American Biography,* Sup. 4, edited by John A. Garraty and Edward T. James. New York: Charles Scribner's Sons, 1974. Interpretive biographical sketch on the man and his career by a respected scholar.

Mitchell, John G. "Said Chicago's Al Capone: 'I Give the Public What the Public Wants . . . .' " *American Heritage* 30 (February/March 1979): 82–93. Well-written, popular account of Capone's rise and fall.

John R. Schmidt

ANDREW CARNEGIE
1835-1919

Chronology

Born Andrew Morrison Carnegie on October 25, 1835, in Dunfermline, Scotland, the eldest of three children of William Carnegie, a handloom linen weaver, and Margaret Morrison Carnegie; *1848* immigrates with his family to the United States, arriving at Castle Garden in the New York harbor, on July 15, and moving on to Pittsburgh, Pennsylvania; *1849* works in a textile mill; *1849-1853* works for a telegraph company; *1853* begins work as personal secretary and private telegraph operator for Thomas A. Scott of the Pennsylvania Railroad; *1859-1865* superintends the western division of the Pennsylvania Railroad; *1861* works for the War Department, overseeing military transportation and telegraph communications, notably at Bull Run; *1861-1872* manages or invests in telegraph, oil, iron, bridge, and railroad concerns, and sells bonds in Europe; *1862* returns in triumph to Scotland with mother; *1867* moves to New York City where he joins Anne Lynch Botta's circle of intellectuals and the Nineteenth Century Club, and embraces the writings of Herbert Spencer; *1872-1901* organizes and runs (as controlling partner) the Carnegie Steel company; *1886* publishes *Triumphant Democracy*; *1887* marries Louise Whitfield on April 22; *1892* incurs public criticism in the wake of bloody labor conflict at Carnegie Steel's plant in Homestead, Pennsylvania; *1897* his only child, Margaret, is born; *1898-1900* becomes involved in the effort to keep the U.S. from taking possession of the Philippine Islands; *1900* publishes *The Gospel of Wealth*; establishes the Carnegie trade schools (which will become Carnegie Institute of Technology in 1912, and later be incorporated into Carnegie Mellon University); *1901* sells his steel business to what becomes the United States Steel Corporation; *1905* publishes *James Watt* and establishes the Carnegie Foundation for the Advancement of Teaching; *1908* publishes *Problems of Today*; *1910* creates the Carnegie Endowment for International Peace; *1911* establishes the Carnegie Corporation of New York; *1919* dies on August 11 at his summer home in the Berkshires, in Lenox, Massachusetts, and is buried in Sleepy Hollow Cemetery in North Tarrytown, New York.

Activities of Historical Significance

Some of Carnegie's accomplishments are of historical importance not merely in and of themselves, but also because of the heritage he shared with so many other immigrants. Like millions of other Europeans in the nineteenth century, Carnegie's parents decided to leave their homeland for the greater opportunities that the New World seemed to offer. Like most immigrants of their time, his family followed relatives and neighbors who gave them some idea of what to expect in the U.S., and helped with shelter and work when they arrived.

The Carnegie family typified immigrants in many ways, but Andrew was unique in the enormous success he achieved in America. He embodied the myth of "rags to riches," the vision that with hard work one could start at the bottom and work up to the top. Unlike most big businessmen of his day, who began the climb already well up the ladder, Carnegie started near the bottom. Unlike most immigrant children, he got much farther than from "rags to respectability."

Carnegie's career mirrored, as it promoted, the development of the nineteenth-century American economy. He began work as a bobbin boy in a cotton mill. Thus the mechanization of textile production, which had cost his father his job in Scotland, supplied young Andrew his first employment in America, in the first industry of the industrial revolution. In the 1850s, he worked at jobs in the communications and transportation revolution, first in the telegraph business, then in the nation's "first big business," the railroad (the Pennsylvania). Finally, he rose to greatness, along with the American economy, as he led the new steel industry into the twentieth century.

Carnegie was a leader in the late-nineteenth-century process of "vertical integration," an effort to bring under one company's control all the major components of a business, including the raw materials to be processed, the various stages of the production process itself, and the marketing. By the 1890s, his steel company operated its own coal mines, iron fields, shipping and railroad lines, and steel mills. The central concern in such an enormous business was cutting costs through efficient management, the latest technology, and large-scale operations—"big trains, loaded full, and run fast," as Carnegie put it.

As the railroad system reached relative completion, Carnegie turned to the cities as the next major source of demand for his product. He successfully sought contracts to supply the steel for the Brooklyn Bridge, America's first skyscraper office building (Chicago's Home Insurance Building), the Washington Monument, and the elevated railroads of Chicago and New York City.

The strike at the Homestead, Pennsylvania, steel plant in 1892 resulted in bloodshed and a public outcry. It also revealed Carnegie's successful intent to destroy the Amalgamated Association of Iron and Steel Workers so that Carnegie Steel could operate without unions.

Carnegie spent the first half his adult life making a fortune, and the second half giving that fortune away. Believing that "he who dies rich dies disgraced," he converted philanthropy into a big business with an investment of about $350,000,000. His legacy provided thousands of library buildings and church organs, with millions of dollars going to higher education or to the cause of peace. He remembered the city of his greatest economic triumphs with gifts to establish the Carnegie Institute of Pittsburgh and the schools that are now part of Carnegie Mellon University, and he contributed lavishly to education and other causes in his native Scotland. With the bulk of his fortune, he founded the Carnegie Corporation of New York, the largest of its kind until the Ford Foundation was established.

Carnegie had a profound impact on higher education in America. He contributed funds to several southern black or Appalachian schools, including Hampton Institute, Tuskegee Institute, and Berea College, and also operated at wholesale through the Carnegie Foundation for the Advancement of Teaching. In 1905 he inaugurated the first pension fund for college and university teachers, which became TIAA (Teachers Insurance and Annuity Association) in 1918. Instituting qualifications criteria for beneficiaries of the fund led to an accreditation procedure that resulted in the upgrading of many schools nationwide. After the "Flexner Report" (1910), the Carnegie Foundation also had a great impact on medical education.

Carnegie developed a profound aversion to war. In the great days of the international peace movement that preceded World War I, he worked to promote arbitration as a nonmilitary way to resolve international disputes. He created the Carnegie Endowment for International Peace and financed construction of three "temples of peace"—the Hague Peace Palace in the Netherlands, a Central American Court of Justice in Costa Rica, and the Pan American Union Building in Washington, D.C. The catastrophe of World War I devastated Carnegie's optimism, crushing his belief that war had become avoidable, even outmoded. No longer could he assume that "all is well since all grows better."

Overview of Biographical Sources

Carnegie has been the subject of study primarily as an industrialist but also as a philanthropist, pacifist, writer, and immigrant. Many studies of his life emphasize his seemingly contradictory roles as steelmaker and philanthropist. The first generation of writings about Carnegie, dating through the 1930s, reflects the immediacy of people's acquaintance with him and of the issues that his public career intersected. These works either revere him or revile him. In recent decades, by contrast, writers have tended to be more dispassionate.

The legacy of Carnegie's contributions to libraries, museums, schools, and other institutions can be traced in various works. A summary, though dated, is Robert M. Lester, *Forty Years of Carnegie Giving: A Summary of the Benefactions of Andrew Carnegie and of the Work of the Philanthropic Trusts Which He Created* (1941). Another such work is Howard J. Savage, *Fruit of an Impulse: Forty-Five Years of the Carnegie Foundation, 1905–1950* (1953). A more recent survey of Carnegie's philanthropic legacy is Simon Goodenough, *The Greatest Good Fortune: Andrew Carnegie's Gift for Today* (1985). The major studies of his libraries are George S. Bobinski, *Carnegie Libraries: Their History and Impact on American Public Library Development* (1969), and David I. Macleod, *Carnegie Libraries in Wisconsin* (1968). Carnegie Hall is the subject of two books by Richard Schickel, *The World of Carnegie Hall* (1960) and *Carnegie Hall: The First One Hundred Years*

(1987), and of Theodore O. Cron and Burt Goldblatt, *Portraits of Carnegie Hall: A Nostalgic Portrait in Pictures and Words of America's Greatest Stage and the Artists Who Performed There* (1966). Ellen Condliffe Lagemann has written *Private Power for the Public Good: A History of the Carnegie Foundation for the Advancement of Teaching* (1983).

Evaluation of Principal Biographical Sources

Alderson, Bernard. *Andrew Carnegie: The Man and His Work.* New York: Doubleday, Page, 1902. **(G)** An early celebration of Carnegie the industrialist and the philanthropist.

Beisner, Robert L. *Twelve against Empire: The Anti-Imperialists, 1898–1900.* New York: McGraw-Hill, 1968. **(A, G, Y)** Includes a chapter on Carnegie, who, like other anti-imperialists at the time, displayed much more concern about the Philippines than about places that were closer to North America and easier to pacify.

Bridge, James Howard. *The Inside History of the Carnegie Steel Company: A Romance of Millions.* New York: Aldine, 1903. **(G)** A spirited deprecation of Carnegie, still useful for one version of "the inside history."

Fabian, Larry L. *Andrew Carnegie's Peace Endowment: The Tycoon, the President, and Their Bargain of 1910.* Washington, DC: Carnegie Endowment for International Peace, 1985. **(A, G, Y)** A sprightly account of Carnegie's involvement in the world peace movement, looking back on 75 years of the Endowment.

Hacker, Louis M. *The World of Andrew Carnegie: 1865–1901.* Philadelphia: J. B. Lippincott, 1968. **(A, G)** The life and times of Andrew Carnegie. Hacker, an economic historian, is intent on dispelling the image of "robber barons." He highlights the constructive role played by men like Carnegie ("the greatest entrepreneur of the period") between the end of the Civil War and the organization of U.S. Steel.

Hendrick, Burton J. *The Life of Andrew Carnegie.* 2 vols. Garden City, NY: Doubleday, Doran, 1932. **(A, G)** A work of affection, it quotes copiously from Carnegie's letters and other writings.

Hughes, Jonathan. *The Vital Few: The Entrepreneur and American Economic Progress.* Rev. ed. New York: Oxford University Press, 1986. **(A, G)** History through biography by an economist, with a chapter on Carnegie the entrepreneur. No footnotes.

Josephson, Matthew. *The Robber Barons: The Great American Capitalists, 1861–1901.* New York: Harcourt, Brace, 1934. **(G)** A Depression-era treatment in which Carnegie figures prominently.

Livesay, Harold C. *Andrew Carnegie and the Rise of Big Business*. Boston: Little, Brown, 1975. **(A, G, Y)** Evokes the social process of immigration to America, but focuses on Carnegie's work life in his new country. Livesay emphasizes Carnegie's successful application to the steel industry of the managerial techniques he learned with the Pennsylvania Railroad.

Lynch, Frederick. *Personal Recollections of Andrew Carnegie*. New York: Fleming H. Revel, 1920. **(G)** A tribute by a clergyman who knew Carnegie from the peace movement.

McCloskey, Robert Green. *American Conservatism in the Age of Enterprise: A Study of William Graham Sumner, Stephen J. Field, and Andrew Carnegie*. Cambridge: Harvard University Press, 1951. **(A, G)** An analysis of the growth of "laissez faire" thought and an indictment of "the sterile pursuit of a materialist ideal." Carnegie is viewed as an ambivalent figure who sought to justify in his writings the new industrial world that his actions did so much to create.

Swetnam, George. *Andrew Carnegie*. Boston: Twayne, 1980. **(A, G, Y)** This volume's inclusion in Twayne's United States Author Series is an indication of Carnegie's importance as a writer. A concise and readable treatment.

Tiple, John. *Andrew Carnegie / Henry George: The Problems of Progress*. Cleveland: Howard Allen, 1960. **(A, G)** A brief comparison of two of the leading writers on "progress" in late-nineteenth-century America, one of whom emphasized the benefits, the other the costs.

Wall, Joseph Frazier. *Andrew Carnegie*. New York: Oxford University Press, 1970. **(A, G)** This is the definitive biography: detailed, and lengthy, and based on work in sources that have been unavailable to other writers. Wall does justice to Carnegie's personal life as well as to his deeds as a captain of the steel industry and an investor in philanthropy. Extensive documentation, but no bibliography.

Williams, Haley. *Men of Stress: Three Dynamic Interpretations—Woodrow Wilson, Andrew Carnegie, William Heskith Lever*. London, England: Jonathan Cape, 1948. **(G)** Evokes the two opposing sides of Carnegie, manifested as steelmaker and philanthropist, each following one of his parents.

Winkler, John K. *Incredible Carnegie: The Life of Andrew Carnegie (1835–1919)*. New York: Vanguard Press, 1931. **(G)** An attack on the "greediest little gentleman ever created."

Evaluation of Biographies for Young People

Henry, Joanne Landers. *Andrew Carnegie: Young Steelmaker*. Indianapolis: Bobbs-Merrill, 1966. Emphasizes Carnegie's childhood. A good introduction for young readers.

Judson, Clara Ingram. *Andrew Carnegie*. Chicago: Follett, 1964. For younger readers.

Kurland, Gerald. *Andrew Carnegie, Philanthropist and Early Tycoon*. Charlotteville, NY: SamHar Press, 1973. A brief but comprehensive, fact-filled survey.

Lavine, Sigmund A. *Famous Industrialists*. New York: Dodd, Mead, 1961. One chapter gives a sketch of the life and times of Andrew Carnegie.

Leipold, L. Edmond. *Founders of Fortunes*. 2 vols. Minneapolis: T. S. Denison, 1967. A chapter in the first volume offers a biographical sketch of "A Rich Man Who Wanted To Be Poor."

Malone, Mary. *Andrew Carnegie: Giant of Industry*. Champaign, IL: Garrard, 1969. An illustrated biography for younger readers.

Shippen, Katherine B. *Andrew Carnegie and the Age of Steel*. New York: Random House, 1958. A comprehensive, readable biography; perhaps the best introduction to Carnegie for most high school students.

Simon, Charlie May. *The Andrew Carnegie Story*. New York: E. P. Dutton, 1965. Emphasizes the first half of Carnegie's life.

Weisberger, Bernard A. *Captains of Industry*. New York: American Heritage, 1966. Includes chapter on "The Happiest Millionaire."

Overview and Evaluation of Primary Sources

Carnegie left his imprint by his words as well as his actions, churning out letters, essays, and books that were marked not only by their impressive quantity but also by their enormous energy and distinctive style.

A large collection of Carnegie's business and personal papers are located in the Manuscript Division of the Library of Congress. Another collection, concentrating on Carnegie as industrialist and manager, are held by USX (United States Steel) Corporation in Pittsburgh, but are generally unavailable to scholars (though Joseph Frazier Wall was permitted to use them extensively for his biography). Smaller collections are available in the Carnegie Library in Pittsburgh, the Carnegie Library in Dunfermline, and the New York Public Library.

Many of Carnegie's writings have been published and are widely available. His first two books, *An American Four-in-Hand in Britain* (New York: Charles Scribner's Sons, 1883; **G, Y**) and *Round the World* (New York: Charles Scribner's Sons, 1884; **G, Y**), report on his travels and reflect, as do his later works, his belief that the United States offered a "freer atmosphere" than any other country. Four of Carnegie's next five books offer reflections on many of the central issues of his time and consist of essays on the possibilities, and responsibilities, of political democracy and economic opportunity: *Triumphant Democracy, or Fifty Years'*

March of the Republic (New York: Charles Scribner's Sons, 1886; **A, G**); *The Gospel of Wealth, and Other Timely Essays* (New York: Century, 1900; **A, G**); *The Empire of Business* (New York: Doubleday, Page, 1902: **A, G**); and *Problems of Today: Wealth, Labor, Socialism* (New York: Doubleday, Page, 1908; **A, G**). In a biography, *James Watt* (New York: Doubleday, Page, 1905; **A, G**), Carnegie tells the story of a fellow Scotsman who had had, a century earlier, a comparable impact on the economic patterns of his time.

All of Carnegie's writings tell the saga of his life and times, but none more than his final book, *Autobiography of Andrew Carnegie* (Boston: Houghton Mifflin, 1920; **A, G, Y**), which John C. Van Dyke edited and published after Carnegie's death. A number of writers have warned that Carnegie cannot be trusted to get the story right; nonetheless, his account of his life before 1901 is of some value. Though he is said to have made self-serving amendments to the truth about his life, in his fullest autobiographical effort he deemphasizes the post-retirement, philanthropic phase, on which some of his admirers have focused, and offers his own version of the period about which there has been most controversy.

Other examples of Carnegie's writing can be found in Helen H. Dow, ed., *Letters of Andrew Carnegie and Louise Whitfield* (New York: n.p., 1956; **A, G**), tracing their relationship from courtship to marriage.

Fiction and Adaptations

Two short films on Carnegie are available. The Encyclopedia Brittanica's black and white film, "Andrew Carnegie" (1951), surveys his life; and Robert Saudek Associates' color film "Andrew Carnegie: The Gospel of Wealth" (1973), starring Bramwell Fletcher, is a dramatization of Carnegie's life.

Museums, Historical Landmarks, Societies

The Carnegie Institute of Pittsburgh (Pittsburgh, PA). "The Carnegie" has a library, an art gallery, a music hall, and a museum of natural history. The museums of art and natural history, in particular, are introduced in Agnes Dodds Kinard, *Celebration of Carnegie in Pittsburgh: The Man, the Institute and the City* (1982).

Carnegie Mansion National Historic Landmark (New York, NY). More well known as the Cooper-Hewitt Museum (the Smithsonian Institution's National Museum of Design), Carnegie lived here from 1901.

Other Sources

Brody, David. *Steelworkers in America: The Nonunion Era.* Cambridge: Harvard University Press, 1960. The first few chapters cover labor and management during and after Carnegie's involvement in the steel business.

Fine, Sidney. *Laissez Faire and the General-Welfare State: A Study of Conflict in American Thought, 1865–1901*. Ann Arbor: University of Michigan Press, 1956. The author writes that, like other big businessmen of the era, Carnegie borrowed only theories of laissez-faire economists and Social Darwinists that served his purposes.

Heilbroner, Robert L. "Epitaph for the Steel Master." In *Great Stories of American Businessmen*. New York: American Heritage, 1972. Interpretive summary.

Hendrick, Burton J., and Daniel Henderson. *Louise Whitfield Carnegie: The Life of Mrs. Andrew Carnegie*. New York: Hastings House, 1950. A sensitive and knowledgeable biography of Andrew Carnegie's wife.

Ingham, John N. "Andrew Morrison Carnegie." In *Biographical Dictionary of American Business Leaders*. Vol. 1. Westport, CT: Greenwood Press, 1983. Summary.

Leichtman, Robert R. *From Heaven to Earth: Carnegie Returns*. Columbus, OH: Ariel Press, 1982. This small book seems less what it purports to be, a conversation between Leichtman and Carnegie (by means of a medium, six decades after Carnegie's death), than a conversation between Leichtman and Leichtman.

Livesay, Harold C. *American Made: Men Who Shaped the American Economy*. Boston: Little, Brown, 1979. One chapter offers a summary of the author's book on Carnegie.

Temin, Peter. *Iron and Steel in Nineteenth-Century America: An Economic Inquiry*. Cambridge: M.I.T. Press, 1964. An analysis of the development of the steel industry offering a brief, thoughtful consideration of Carnegie's role.

Wall, Joseph Frazier. "Carnegie." In *The Encyclopedia of American Biography*, edited by John A. Garraty and Jerome L. Sternstein. New York: Harper & Row, 1974. An interpretive summary by Carnegie's major biographer.

————. *Skibo*. New York: Oxford University Press, 1984. An engaging history of Skibo Castle, Carnegie's summer home in Scotland, through several periods: before Carnegie, during his tenure, in his wife's hands, and then in his daughter's.

Wyllie, Irvin G. *The Self-Made Man in America: The Myth of Rags to Riches*. New Brunswick, NJ: Rutgers University Press, 1954. An essay in intellectual (not social) history, this study scrutinizes the myth that Carnegie embodied.

Peter Wallenstein
Virginia Polytechnic Institute and
State University

KIT CARSON
1809-1868

Chronology

Born Christopher Houston Carson on December 24, 1809, on Tate's Creek, Madison County, Kentucky, one of many children born to Lindsey Carson, a frontiersman who was first involved in settling the Boonesborough area of Kentucky with the Transylvania Company, and his second wife, Rebecca Robinson Carson, a native of Virginia; *1809-1811* lives in Kentucky in a three room log cabin; *1811-1826* moves with family to Boonslick region of Missouri, works with father clearing land and farming, receives virtually no education and goes through life essentially illiterate; *1824* apprentices to saddler in Franklin, Missouri, but hates the work; *1826-1841* travels with a caravan to Santa Fe, New Mexico; traps with a series of companies in California and throughout the Rocky Mountains; *1841-1842* works as a hunter for Bent's Fort, Colorado; *1842* guides John C. Frémont's first expedition to the Rocky Mountains from June through September; *1843-1844* guides Frémont's second expedition to Great Salt Lake and the Great Basin region of the central Rockies before returning to Bent's Fort; *1845-1846* guides Frémont's third expedition to California via the Nevada desert, where Frémont participates in the Bear Flag Revolt during the Mexican War; *1846-1853* guides wagon trains, traps in mountains, and acts as detective to apprehend bandits operating along the Santa Fe Trail; *1854-1861* acts as Indian Agent from his home in Taos, New Mexico, and serves periodically as guide for federal troops policing the frontier; *1861-1867* becomes Colonel (later brevetted to Brigadier General) in New Mexico Volunteer Regiment; *1868* serves as superintendent of Indian affairs for Colorado Territory from January to May; dies on May 23, at Fort Lyon, Colorado, and is buried at Boggsville; *1869* body is reinterred in Taos, New Mexico.

Activities of Historical Significance

Carson leapt to prominence as the guide of John C. Frémont during his first three expeditions to explore the Trans-Mississippi West. His importance as an essential ingredient in the success of these missions should not be underestimated; he brought to Frémont's expeditions a knowledge of the West and its inhabitants, an innate sensibility about possibly difficult situations, and the savvy to work well with the ambitious Frémont. But Carson also came to the public attention through Frémont's post-expedition reports, in which the frontiersman is always portrayed as a trustworthy and admirable assistant. Carson became a symbol of self-reliance and courage, action, and reason for an entire nation.

Because of the initial fame he won with Frémont, Kit Carson emerged as a mythical frontiersman in the literary world of the East during the late 1840s. As a successor to Leatherstocking in the James Fenimore Cooper stories, Carson embodied all that was commendable in the adolescent nation as it expanded to the West. A whole genre of fiction used Carson as a character of heroic proportions.

As an Indian agent and military officer in New Mexico during the 1850s and 1860s, Carson achieved additional success in settling the region. This aspect of his career, although significant, has not received as much emphasis as his earlier exploits.

Overview of Biographical Sources

Kit Carson has probably received more than his share of biographers. This has been due, perhaps, as much to the subject's genuinely humble and open persona as to his event-filled life. Although there were earlier accounts of Carson's exploits, especially those written in John C. Frémont's reports, the first full-blown biographical study of Carson was DeWitt Peters, *Life and Adventures of Kit Carson* (1858), based on stories Carson told the author. This biography, which casts Carson as a modern knight of the prairies defending virtue and civilization, set the style and provided raw material for several other biographies that appeared from 1860 to 1914. In 1914, Edwin L. Sabin published *Kit Carson Days*, which became the standard nonfiction work on Carson until 1962. It offered much additional information and a depiction of its subject that toned down his heroic proportions and placed him in the context of the western historical setting.

Major biographies by Bernice Blackwelder, *Great Westerner* (1962), and M. Marion Estergren, *Kit Carson* (1962), superseded Sabin's work. These books add substantial amounts of fugitive information and present a reasonable portrait of the westerner as an agent of civilization, yet one with human failings.

The most recent biography by Thelma S. Guild and Harvey L. Carter, *Kit Carson* (1984), clearly establishes Carson's importance in the American westward movement and argues that his long-term significance is not a heroic figure, but as a guide for expeditions in the Trans-Mississippi West and as an expert on Indian affairs.

An outstanding discussion of Carson as a figure in American literature can be found in Henry Nash Smith, *Virgin Land* (1950); valuable discussions of his role in the mid-1860s Navajo War are available in Clifford E. Trafzer, *The Kit Carson Campaign* (1982).

Evaluation of Principal Biographical Sources

Abbott, John S. C. *Christopher Carson, Known as Kit Carson*. 1873. Reprint. New York: Dorchester Publishing, 1977. **(A, G)** This life of Carson partakes, without guile, of the heroic image of the westerner. The author's intent seems to have been to make Carson a strong moral example; he does not drink or swear, and he resists temptation of all types.

Blackwelder, Bernice. *Great Westerner: The Story of Kit Carson*. Caldwell, ID: Caxton Printers, 1962. **(A, G)** The product of many years of research by a Taos resident, this book makes important contributions to knowledge about Carson. Genuinely sympathetic to the subject, the author avoids the heroic and adventure-some image of Carson and concentrates on his tangible accomplishments.

Burdett, Charles. *The Life of Kit Carson, the Great Western Hunter*. Philadelphia: n.p., 1860. **(A, G)** A work of limited value which used the DeWitt Peters biography as the sole source of information about Carson.

Carter, Harvey L., and Guild, Thelma S. *Kit Carson: A Pattern for Heroes*. Lincoln: University of Nebraska Press, 1984. **(A, G)** A fine recent biography of Carson that incorporates all of the best scholarship on the subject. While the authors admire Carson, they never slump into hero-worship.

Ellis, Edwin S. *The Life and Times of Christopher Carson, the Rocky Mountain Scout and Guide*. New York: n.p., 1861. **(A, G)** A solid historical work that emphasizes the adventure of Carson's life, written by a professional who specialized in fiction. Even so, he does not mix truth with tale. In 1889 a revised edition of this biography appeared that contained letters solicited from several individuals who had known Carson. These additions presented some new information about Kit Carson.

Estergren, M. Morgan. *Kit Carson: A Portrait in Courage*. Norman: University of Oklahoma Press, 1982. **(A, G)** Another able and positive biography that explicitly deals with the details of his life. The author avoids the hero-worshiping attitude of other biographers, but does perpetuate some of the myths surrounding his image.

Gerson, Noel B. *Kit Carson: Folk Hero and Man*. Garden City, NY: Doubleday, 1964. **(G)** One of the worst books ever written by this able historical fiction author, this work is a morass of misinformation, overgeneralization, and poor interpretation.

Hafen, LeRoy R., ed. *The Mountain Men and the Fur Trade of the Far West*. 10 vols. Glendale, CA: Arthur H. Clark, 1965–1972. **(A, G)** A monumental collection of essays on the Trans-Mississippi western fur trade and the men who made it. The essay on Kit Carson, written by Harvey L. Carter, is a succinct and useful discussion of the subject's career.

Hough, Emerson. *The Way to the West, and the Lives of These Early Americans: Boone, Crockett, Carson*. Indianapolis: Bobbs-Merrill, 1903. **(A, G)** A general explanation of westward expansion using the representative lives of Boone, Crockett, and Carson.

McClung, Quantrille D. *Carson-Bent-Boggs Genealogy*. Denver: Denver Public Library, 1962. **(A)** A most useful reference work, this book details the genealogical ties of the three families, all of whom were significantly involved in important western issues.

Peters, DeWitt C. *The Life and Adventures of Kit Carson, the Nestor of the Rocky Mountains.* New York: N. R. C. Clark and Meeker, 1858, 1859, 1874. **(A, G)** Written by an army surgeon who was stationed at Taos in 1854–1856, this account contributes both to the historic and legendary Kit Carson. It uses facts related by Carson, as well as some embellishments, but provides, for the first time, the basic materials of Carson's life and set the tone for several biographies published later. It is monumental in scope and heroic in proportions, presenting Carson as an exemplar, while stressing his adventures.

Pettis, Captain George H. *Kit Carson's Fight with the Comanche and Kiowa Indians, November 1864.* Albuquerque: New Mexico Historical Society Publication 12, n.d. **(A, G)** A short study of one aspect of Carson's career.

Sabin, Edwin Legrand. *Kit Carson Days (1809–1868).* 1914. Rev. ed. 2 vols. New York: Press of the Pioneers, 1935. **(A, G)** Although written by a fiction writer, this book presents extremely valuable research. The author made extensive use of firsthand accounts and interviews with people who knew Carson.

Trafzer, Clifford E. *The Kit Carson Campaign: The Last Great Navajo War.* Norman: University of Oklahoma Press, 1982. **(A, G)** An able and useful study of the Navajo Indian Campaign in which Carson was involved during 1863–1864, written from the Navajo perspective.

Vestal, Stanley [Walter S. Campbell]. *Kit Carson, the Happy Warrior of the Old West.* Boston: Little, Brown, 1928. **(G)** The author, an English professor at the University of Oklahoma, was a widely-renowned western authority during this period. This book, however, is disappointing, for it relies almost solely upon folklore to create a Carson of epic proportions.

Evaluation of Biographies for Young People

Boesch, Mark J. *Kit Carson of the Old West.* New York: Farrar, Straus, 1959. One of many biographies written for a youthful audience, this work simplistically recounts the heroic and adventuresome life of Carson, extolling him as a paragon of virtue warranting emulation.

Bryant, Will. *Kit Carson and the Mountain Men.* New York: Grossett, Dunlap, 1960. Similar to Boesch's work, it praises Carson's lifestyle and suggests that readers emulate him.

Moody, Ralph. *Kit Carson and the Wild Frontier.* New York: Random House, 1955. This biography portrays an individual who overcomes tremendous hardship as a boy to achieve outstanding success in every aspect of his life. Accordingly,

Carson becomes a heroic figure through hard work and persistence. Contains illustrations by Stanley W. Galli.

Stevenson, Augusta. *Kit Carson: Boy Trapper*. Indianapolis: Bobbs-Merrill, 1962. One of many biographers in the heroic westerner mold, this work explains its subject's virtues and accentuates his adventures.

Worcester, Donald E. *Kit Carson: Mountain Scout*. Boston: Houghton Mifflin, 1960. Like Stevenson, Worcester portrays his subject as a hero of the West and an agent of civilization.

Overview and Evaluation of Primary Sources

Carson became a national hero upon the publication of Frémont's widely read reports on their expeditions to the West. The latest and most authoritative edition of these reports is Donald Jackson and Mary Lee Spence, eds., *The Expeditions of John Charles Frémont*, 3 vols. (Urbana: University of Illinois Press, 1970–1984; **A, G**). Volume 1 of this set is particularly relevant.

Another important work written by a fellow adventurer is George Douglas Brewerton, *Overland with Kit Carson: A Narrative of the Old Spanish Trail in 1848* (1853; Reprint edited by Stall Vinton. New York: Coward McCann, 1930; **A, G**). During Carson's second transcontinental journey as a dispatch bearer, he was accompanied as far as Santa Fe by Lieutenant Brewerton, who originally published this detailed, interesting, and truthful account in *Harper's Magazine*. It is one of the most well written and most penetrating analyses of Carson.

Carson also plays a role in W. F. Cody (Buffalo Bill), *The Story of the Wild West and Camp-Fire Chats; A Full and Complete History of the Renowned Pioneer Quartette, Boone, Crockett, Carson, and Buffalo Bill* (New York: Ayer, 1888; **A, G**). This self-serving work suggests that western expansion in America was the result of four individuals, one of whom was Carson, but the most important of whom was Buffalo Bill.

Kit Carson's autobiography originally appeared as Blanche C. Grant, ed., *Kit Carson's Own Story of His Life; As Dictated to Col. and Mrs. D. C. Peters about 1856–57, and Never Before Published* (Taos, NM: Kit Carson Memorial Foundation, 1926, 1955; **A, G**). This book presents the original manuscript that provided the basis for DeWitt Peters's biography of Carson, but which had been lost. Discovered among the effects of Peters's son, the work contains very little in the way of editorial comment or alteration to the manuscript. Another version of this manuscript was published as Milo M. Quaife, ed., *Kit Carson's Autobiography* (1935; Lincoln: University of Nebraska Press, 1965; **A, G**). Quaife has edited the work for spelling and clarity, and provides useful editorial comments. The best rendition of the autobiography is found in Harvey L. Carter, *"Dear Old Kit": The Historical Christopher Carson* (Norman: University of Oklahoma Press, 1968; **A, G**). Carter's work includes extensive annotations, as well as the finest set of essays relating to the subject's life. Especially useful is a discussion of the development of the Carson legend.

Another valuable primary source is Lawrence C. Kelley, ed., *Navajo Roundup: Selected Correspondence of Kit Carson's Expedition Against the Navajo, 1863– 1865* (Boulder: Pruett, 1970; **A, G**). This source contains documents originating from the Navajo campaign; all are generally favorable portrayals of Carson's activities.

Fiction and Adaptations

Carson has inspired several works of fiction. The first two were published in 1849, shortly after Carson's participation in the Frémont expeditions. Charles Averill portrays Carson as a young, handsome frontiersman of Herculean stature in *Kit Carson: Prince of the Gold Hunters*. Carson is depicted fighting Indians, injustice, and crooks, and is credited with discovering gold in California. Emerson Bennett's 1849 work, *The Prairie Flower; or Adventures in the Far West*, is a rather blustery novel of adventure and intrigue. Carson is chiefly an Indian fighter who moves across the narrative to rescue heroines and avenge evil. The sequel to this novel, *Lenni-Leoti; or Adventures in the Far West* (1850), depicts Carson in a similar light. Writing under the pseudonym J. F. C. Adams, Edward S. Ellis produced *The Fighting Trapper; or Kit Carson to the Rescue* (1879), a lurid piece of fiction that casts its hero as a romantic western figure and glories in his adventuresome life. Claude Gentry's historical fiction, *Kit Carson* (1956), is poor history, but it adds to the legend. Carson is once again a paragon of virtue and a man of action who can snatch victory out of seemingly impossible situations.

Museums, Historical Landmarks, Societies.

Bent's Old Fort National Historic Site (La Junta, CO). This fine reconstruction of a southwestern adobe fort was a frequent stopping point for Carson and many others on the Santa Fe trail. For a time, Carson was employed at the fort as a hunter. Each year the site hosts a Mountain Man Rendezvous which offers valuable insights into the west of Kit Carson.

Kit Carson Memorial Foundation, Inc. (Taos, NM). An excellent house museum, this organization maintains the Carson home in Taos. Most collections relate directly to the westerner's life and experiences in the West. Carson is buried near this site.

Kit Carson Museum and Historical Society (Las Animas, CO). This local museum has some exhibits built around Kit Carson and the frontier experience in Colorado.

Other Sources

Koskinen, M. S. "Kit Carson." In *Cavalcade of Young Americans*, edited by Carl L. Carmer. New York: Lothrop, 1958. A simple discussion of Carson's accomplishments with the emphasis on his greatness. Written for boys.

Lavender, David. *Bent's Fort*. Lincoln: University of Nebraska Press, 1972. This excellent portrait of the history of one of the most important outposts of civilization on the Santa Fe trail has very little direct information about Kit Carson. It is more important as an outstanding description of the era and the lifestyle of the frontiersman.

Nevins, Allan. *Frémont, Pathmarker of the West*. New York: D. Appleton, 1939. A warmly written and passionately sympathetic portrait of the individual who, more than any other, ensured Kit Carson's fame.

Smith, Henry Nash. "Kit Carson in Books." *Southwest Review* 28 (Winter 1943): 164–190. This study assesses the importance of Carson as a literary type. His arguments have also been reiterated in *Virgin Land: The West in Myth and Symbol*. New York: Alfred A. Knopf, 1950. Reprint. Cambridge: Harvard University Press, 1970.

Steckmesser, Kent Ladd. *The Western Hero in History and Legend*. Norman: University of Oklahoma Press, 1965. A lucid and absorbing analysis of the cult of the western hero in America.

Weber, David J. *The Taos Trappers: The Fur Trade in the Southwest, 1540–1846*. Norman: University of Oklahoma Press, 1971. A readable and trustworthy account of the fur trade of the southwestern frontier. It details the exploits of the traders and trappers who operated from New Mexico.

Roger D. Launius
Department of the Air Force

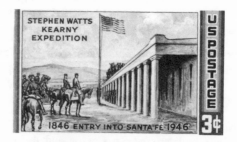

Kearny Expedition, 1947

RACHEL CARSON
1907-1964

Chronology

Born Rachel Louise Carson on May 27, 1907, in Springdale, Pennsylvania, the youngest of three children of Robert Warden Carson, an insurance and real estate salesman, and Maria McLean Carson, a graduate of the Female Seminary in Washington, Pennsylvania, and a schoolteacher who is musically talented and devoted to nature; *1907–1925* grows up on sixty-five acres at the edge of Springdale, where her mother encourages her love for books, nature, and her ambition to be a writer; publishes three stories in *St. Nicholas* magazine; attends Springdale High School, graduates from Parnassus High School, and wins partial scholarship to Pennsylvania College for Women (later Chatham College); *1925–1929* excels as an English, then science, major; graduates magna cum laude; awarded summer fellowship at Woods Hole Marine Biological Laboratory and a scholarship for graduate study in zoology at Johns Hopkins University; *1929–1936* works as lab assistant to Dr. Raymond Pearl, geneticist, and as teaching assistant in biology summer courses at Johns Hopkins; *1932* receives M.A., works as a part-time assistant in zoology at the University of Maryland, and lives with family who have moved to Baltimore; *1935* father dies suddenly; *1936* sister dies, leaving two young daughters to be brought up by Rachel and her mother; scores first in civil service examination; earns appointment as junior aquatic biologist at Bureau of Fisheries; writes occasional articles for the *Baltimore Sunday Sun*; *1937* publishes "Undersea" in *Atlantic Monthly*, and gains wide acclaim; *1941* publishes first book, *Under the Sea Wind*; *1942–1949* works as assistant to the chief of the Office of Information of United States Fish and Wildlife Service, writing government booklets on conservation of resources and gathering materials; *1951* publishes *The Sea Around Us*, which wins the National Book Award; *1955* publishes *The Edge of the Sea*; *1957* her niece Marjorie dies, leaving a five-year-old son whom Carson adopts; *1958* her mother dies; *1962* publishes *Silent Spring* and is personally and professionally attacked, especially by members of the chemical industry, but is soon vindicated by her own careful evidence; *1964* dies on April 14 of cancer at her home in Silver Spring, Maryland.

Activities of Historical Significance

One of the first and the most eloquent of writers to sound the alarm of the hazard of pesticides to natural life cycles, Rachel Carson, in her book *Silent Spring*, prompted national and international awareness of the environment. Because her last angry indictment may well have changed the course of history, readers sometimes forget the importance of her earlier trilogy of books on the sea: *Under the Sea*

259

Wind, *The Sea Around Us*, and *The Edge of the Sea*. These remain the record of a best-selling and distinguished writer whose love of nature, scientific knowledge, and writing talent merged to recreate a sense of wonder at the intricate and delicate balance of life on earth. Without the respect and admiration of a wide audience established by these books, Carson's *Silent Spring* might not have had the same explosive and lasting impact.

Overview of Biographical Sources

Rachel Carson remained a very private person in her lifetime, and she did not come from a family of writers who might have left some detailed record of her life. Since her death, three biographies have begun to establish a framework of information about the quiet life of this best-selling writer. Philip Sterling, *Sea and Earth* (1970), composed for young readers, carefully describes Carson's upbringing, schooling, and employment, emphasizing her last famous years as scientist-writer. Paul Brooks, her friend and editor at Houghton Mifflin Company, probes her talent, skill and training as a writer by showing her at work and giving excerpts of her unpublished and published writing in *The House of Life* (1972). Carol Gartner, *Rachel Carson* (1983), demonstrates the literary quality of Carson's work in interpretive analyses of each of Carson't books. Interesting details about the difficulties surrounding her last book make Frank Graham, Jr., *Since Silent Spring* (1970), an important source for the wider context of the concluding chapter of Carson's life.

Evaluation of Principal Biographical Sources

Brooks, Paul. *The House of Life: Rachel Carson at Work*. Boston: Houghton Mifflin, 1972. **(A, G)** In his insightful, professional biography, Brooks shows the fragile, even torturous process by which a book is actually formed in the author's mind before it becomes pages of print. His story of Carson's process of gathering and sifting expert information, revision, and rewriting is interwoven with details from her personal life and extensive quotations from her published and unpublished writing. Includes sources listed by chapter and page, a complete bibliography of Carson's work, photographs, and an index.

Gartner, Carol B. *Rachel Carson*. New York: Frederick Ungar, 1983. **(A, G)** A yearly chronology of Carson's life and a brief biography introduce this scholarly study of the literary qualities of Carson's books. Gartner presents Carson as an artist who clearly communicates sounds, rhythms, images, and forms of nature. Originally a doctoral dissertation with a concise, often abrupt style, Gartner's study provides detailed footnotes, a complete bibliography, and an index.

Graham, Frank Jr. *Since Silent Spring*. Boston: Houghton Mifflin, 1970. **(A, G)** Graham places *Silent Spring* in the context of Carson's life and its time. He tells the progress of the pesticide controversy since the publication of the book, with descriptions of environmental poisoning scandals and tragedies, and of government investigations pinpointing the culprits who continue to use such poisons. Lists safe and unsafe pesticides, federal registration requirements, references by chapter and page, and includes an index.

Sterling, Phillip. *Sea and Earth: The Life of Rachel Carson*. New York: Thomas Y. Crowell, 1970. (**A, G, Y**) Careful, if not exhaustive, research informs this biography composed for young readers. Carson's old classmates, family members, employer, friends, school records, and correspondence give substantial details to a life sensitively told by a journalist-biographer. Sterling quotes from Carson's earliest childhood publications, summarizes her college papers, and includes childhood drawings. Includes an extensive source list, a bibliography, photographs, and an index.

Overview and Evaluation of Primary Sources

Although not autobiographical, Carson's books reveal a good deal about their author's personality. Her love and concern for nature are most poignantly expressed in her trilogy of books on the sea, particularly her first and personal favorite *Under the Sea Wind* (New York: Simon and Schuster, 1941; **A, G, Y**). In this series of descriptive narratives, the poet-scientist recreates the remarkable adventures of sea life in such creatures as Scomber the mackerel and Anquilla the eel. Well-reviewed but not widely read, the book was reissued and became a best seller at the height of the popularity of *The Sea Around Us* (New York: Oxford University Press, 1951; **A, G, Y**).

Established as a first-rate popular writer and naturalist, Carson has more authority of tone and focus in her second book. She freely quotes the authority of voyagers and scientists while giving a history of the study of the sea, including recent discoveries. She also includes an extensive, annotated list of suggestions for further reading.

If she seems to be the hidden observer in her first two books, Carson comes out to find a place on the pages of *The Edge of the Sea* (Boston: Houghton Mifflin, 1955; **A, G, Y**). Her scientific knowledge still informs her passionate love of the sea and its creatures, but she now seems more relaxed and confident. She feels free to express pleasure, to help an octopus in distress, and wonder at the mystery of life on the shore.

The posthumous republication of her essay "The Sense of Wonder" (New York: Harper & Row, 1965; **A, G, Y**) comes closest among her published works to being autobiographical in nature. First printed in *Woman's Home Companion* (1956) as "Teach Your Child to Wonder," this essay instructs by example. Carson describes how she taught her own adopted son, Roger, to feel, as well as to know, nature.

The least autobiographical but most passionate of her books is *Silent Spring* (Boston: Houghton Mifflin, 1962; **A, G**), for which she is most famous. Written in anger and alarm at the increasing contamination of the environment by poisonous chemicals, the book documents the chain of death that breaks down the delicate balance achieved by evolution. Carson raises the scientific and moral questions then unasked by users of pesticides. She suggests another road: biological control of and accommodation with insects.

Other papers may be found at the Rachel Carson Council, Washington, D.C., and in the Rachel Carson Papers at Yale University Library.

Fiction and Adaptations

RKO's 1953 film adaptation of Carson's *The Sea Around Us* won an Oscar for feature-length documentary, but Carson was displeased with the liberties that the film took with her work. On April 3, 1963, Carson debated one of her harshest critics, Dr. Robert White-Stevens of the American Cyanamid Company, on a CBS News Special entitled "The Silent Spring of Rachel Carson." Carson also appeared on CBS television in an interview on May 15, 1963, "The Verdict on the *Silent Spring* of Rachel Carson," after the Report of the President's Science Advisory Committee confirmed her thesis.

Museums, Historical Landmarks, Societies

Rachel Carson Childhood Home (Springdale, PA). This site is now an ecological center and museum.

Rachel Carson Council (Washington, DC). Originally called the Rachel Carson Trust for the Living Environment, this council is managed by Carson's friend and colleague, Shirley Briggs. The council holds published and unpublished papers by and about Carson. The board of directors is composed of prominent scientists and conservationists who have been active in the struggle for a clean environment.

Rachel Carson Memorial Fund (New York, NY). Administered by the National Audobon Society, with the advice of the Rachel Carson Council, this fund is used to review and evaluate government policies and programs of industry, and to encourage safe methods of pest control. This was the source of a large part of the money used to fight the use of DDT in New York, Michigan, and Wisconson during the late 1960s.

Rachel Carson National Wildlife Refuge (Coastal marshes of Maine). On the fifth anniversary of Carson's death, public demand that the government designate a fitting memorial to Carson resulted in this refuge.

Rachel Carson Seacoast Fund (Washington, DC). Managed by Nature Conservancy, this fund began with money left by Carson to preserve natural areas along the New England coast.

Other Sources

Brooks, Paul. "Rachel Carson." In *Speaking for Nature: How Literary Naturalists from Henry Thoreau to Rachel Carson Have Shaped America*. Boston: Houghton Mifflin, 1980. Perspective on Carson's place in the tradition of literary naturalists from Thoreau to present.

————. "Rachel Carson." In *Notable American Women: The Modern Period*. Cambridge: Harvard University Press, 1980. Concise interpretive essay by Carson's editor-biographer.

Norman, Geoffrey. "The Flight of Rachel Carson." *Esquire* (December 1983): 472–479. Succinct estimate of Carson's eloquent, influential place in the environmental movement.

Whorton, James. *Before Silent Spring: Pesticides and Public Health in Pre-DDT America*. Princeton: Princeton University Press, 1974. Further scholarly information on the wider context of Carson's *Silent Spring*.

Gretchen Sutherland
Cornell College

JIMMY CARTER
1924

Chronology

Born James Earl Carter on October 1, 1924, in Plains (Sumter County), Georgia, the oldest of four children born to James Earl Carter, Sr., a farmer and small businessman, and Lillian Gordy Carter, a nurse; *1928* family moves to Archery, Georgia; works on the family farm and attends public school in nearby Plains; *1941* enters Georgia Southwestern College, Americus; *1942* receives an appointment to the United States Naval Academy; *1943* enters Annapolis after completing needed mathematics courses at Georgia Institute of Technology, Atlanta; *1946* graduates from the Naval Academy fifty-ninth out of a class of 820; marries Rosalynn Smith; *1948* completes submarine training school and is assigned to the USS *Pomfret*; *1950* is reassigned to the USS *K-1*; *1952* joins a select group of naval officers in the development of the first nuclear powered submarine and serves as engineering officer on the nuclear submarine *Sea Wolf* commanded by Captain Hyman G. Rickover; *1953* resigns from the Navy after his father's death and returns home to Plains to manage family business; *1955-1962* serves on Sumter County Board of Education; *1962-1966* serves two terms in the Georgia State Senate; *1966* is defeated for the Georgia Democratic gubernatorial nomination; *1966-1970* travels state of Georgia extensively, making approximately 1,800 speeches; *1970* wins Georgia Democratic gubernatorial nomination and defeats Republican Party opponent in the general election by 200,000 votes; *1971-1975* serves as governor of Georgia; *1972* heads Democratic Governors' Campaign Committee; *1974* becomes chairman of the Democratic National Campaign Committee; *1975* announces his candidacy for President of the United States and begins national campaign for the Democratic Party nomination; *1976* wins party presidential nomination and defeats incumbent president Gerald R. Ford by a narrow 1,600,000 popular votes; *1977-1981* serves as the nation's thirty-ninth president; *1980* renominated for president by the Democratic Party, but is defeated by Republican Ronald Reagan; *1981* returns to Plains; *1982* publishes presidential memoirs; *1984* establishes Carter Center of Emory University, Atlanta; *1987* opens Carter Presidential Library, Atlanta.

Activities of Historical Significance

James Earl "Jimmy" Carter, Jr., came into national political prominence in 1971 when he succeeded arch-segregationist Lester G. Maddox as governor of Georgia and declared in his inaugural address that the time for racial injustice was over. His four-year term as Georgia's chief executive was marked by reforms in state budgetary procedures, by the passage of environmental protection legislation, and by an affirmative action program that increased minority employment within state government by forty per cent.

In 1975, when Carter stepped down as governor and announced plans to run for the office of President of the United States, few political observers gave him much chance of success. In the wake of the Watergate scandal and Vietnam War, however, the distrust many Americans felt for their national leaders worked to Carter's advantage. Exploiting the fact that he was an outsider to Washington and not tied to any special interest groups, the Plains native scored early victories in the Iowa caucuses and New Hampshire primary and went to the 1976 National Democratic Convention with enough committed delegates to win the presidential nomination on the first ballot. In November he outpolled incumbent President Gerald R. Ford by a narrow 1,600,000 votes to become the nation's thirty-ninth president.

During his presidency, Carter gave great emphasis to worldwide human rights, negotiated a treaty with Panama ceding control of the canal to the Panamanian government, acted as a mediator in the Israeli-Egyptian peace negotiations, and inaugurated full diplomatic relations with the People's Republic of China. Questions concerning national defense, however, plagued his administration, and Carter acquired the image of a weak president. His decision not to build either the super-sonic B-1 Bomber or the "Neutron" Bomb lent credence to arguments by critics who claimed he was soft on defense. A sluggish, high-interest-rate economy, together with a year-long unsuccessful effort to gain the release of American Embassy personnel taken hostage in Teheran, Iran, on November 4, 1979, contributed to his defeat in 1980 when he sought re-election.

Overview of Biographical Sources

A major definitive study of Jimmy Carter and scholarly interpretation of his presidential administration has not yet been written. This is due primarily to the current unavailability of his personal White House papers which are in the process of being organized for research purposes. To date, the most studious treatment of Carter is *Jimmy Carter: In Search of the Great White House* (1980) by Professor Betty Glad, an experienced biographer and political scientist. Although her evaluation of Carter ends shortly after he became president, Glad includes an excellent examination of his gubernatorial administration and an interesting assessment of the popular notion that what the federal bureaucracy needs to "clean things up" is an outsider. Haynes Johnson also addresses this perception. *In the Absence of Power* (1980) documents the difficulties Carter had with Congress, the national press, as well as the federal bureaucracy.

Several other biographies—those by Kucharsky, Miller, and Wooten—were written following Carter's 1976 victory and in the glow of the populist image that he enjoyed. Although these journalistic accounts portray Carter with little criticism, they do provide an understanding of the importance of religion in his life and how much the South shaped his politics. Wooten's *Dasher* (1978) (the code name given Carter by the Secret Service) is particularly insightful regarding Carter, the southerner and the compulsive politician. Wooten paints a good picture of the superhuman campaign effort Carter made in 1976.

The most critical current biography, *Jimmy Carter: The Man and the Myth* (1979) by Victor Lasky, attempts to explode the myth that Carter is basically a Populist and to reveal how this image was really the result of a carefully planned publicity campaign.

Evaluation of Principal Biographical Sources

Fink, Gary M. *Prelude to the Presidency: The Political Character and Legislative Leadership Style of Governor Jimmy Carter*. Westport: Greenwood, 1980. **(A, G)** Examines Carter's reorganization of the executive branch of the state of Georgia while he was governor.

Glad, Betty. *Jimmy Carter: In Search of the Great White House*. New York: Norton, 1980. **(A, G)** Argues that Carter's political style proved well suited for the immediate post-Watergate era. This book is both thorough and critical.

Johnson, Haynes. *In the Absence of Power: Governing America*. New York: Viking, 1980. **(A, G)** A very readable analysis of the Carter presidency by a veteran Washington reporter who views his subject with little subjectivity.

Kucharsky, David. *The Man from Plains: The Mind and Spirit of Jimmy Carter*. New York: Harper, 1976. **(G)** The author of this rather abbreviated and subjective biography attempts to explain Carter from an evangelical point-of-view.

Lasky, Victor. *Jimmy Carter: The Man and the Myth*. New York: Marek, 1979. **(A, G)** Lasky paints the picture of a politician driven more by ambition than by principle.

Mazlish, Bruce, and Edwin Diamond. *Jimmy Carter: A Character Portrait*. New York: Simon and Schuster, 1979. **(A, G)** The authors of this biography relied mainly upon interviews with members of Carter's family and staff. The conclusions are psychoanalytical and are not based on the kind of scholarship needed to understand someone as complex as Carter.

Miller, William L. *Yankee from Georgia: The Emergence of Jimmy Carter*. New York: Time Books, 1978. **(G)** Casts Carter in the image of an old-time New England Puritan as opposed to a twentieth-century southern demagogue. This book is generally readable, even if Miller's findings are somewhat questionable.

Shogan, Robert. *Promises to Keep: Carter's First Hundred Days*. New York: Crowell, 1977. **(G)** Shogan was a *Los Angeles Times* political reporter at the time he wrote this book. He gives attention to Carter's first days in office, his cabinet and staff appointments, and his early dealings with Congress.

Shoup, Laurence H. *The Carter Presidency, and Beyond: Power and Politics in the 1980s*. Palo Alto: Ramparts, 1980. **(A, G)** An interesting examination of Carter's political ascendancy. Shoup argues that America's "Eastern Ruling Establishment" played a major role in his political success.

Smith, Betsy C. *Jimmy Carter, President*. New York: Walker, 1986. **(Y)** Smith's biography of Carter was written for younger readers, but in places her analysis seems more appropriate for adults. She examines Carter's involvement in human rights, the Bert Lance fiasco, and the Iranian hostage crisis.

Stroud, Kandy. *How Jimmy Carter Won: The Victory Campaign from Plains to the White House*. New York: Morrow, 1977. **(G)** An insightful and detailed look at Carter and his presidential campaign. The author includes many revealing anecdotes about the president that lay readers may find interesting.

Wooten, James. *Dasher: The Roots and the Rising of Jimmy Carter*. New York: Summit, 1978. **(A, G)** A very readable account of Carter and his bid for the presidency in 1976 written by a *New York Times* correspondent who covered the South while Carter was governor of Georgia and the White House during Carter's first year in office.

Overview and Evaluation of Primary Sources

When Jimmy Carter left the White House in 1981, he took some twenty-seven million documents which are housed in the Carter Presidential Library in Atlanta. Although only six million of these documents are presently open to the public for research, the Library, which is run by the National Archives and Records Center, plans to have more available within a short time. There is also a large archive of audio-visual materials in the Carter Library which includes video tape recordings and photographs covering Carter's political career from the time he ran for the Georgia State Senate through his White House years.

The National Archives in Washington has the departmental records of the Carter presidency, and the Georgia State Archives in Atlanta holds the records of his gubernatorial administration. The nine-volume set of *Public Papers of the Presidents of the United States* (Washington: Government Printing Office, 1977–1982; **A, G**) contains all of Carter's public messages, statements and speeches arranged chronologically. Volume 1, parts 1 and 2, of *The Presidential Campaign, 1976*, edited by Faye M. Padgett and Earl Mazo (Washington: Government Printing Office, 1978; **A, G**), concerns Carter, and volume 3 deals with the 1976 presidential debates.

Several other available sources comprise selected speeches and public statements Carter made. *"I'll Never Lie to You,"* compiled by Robert L. Turner (New York: Ballantine, 1976; **G**), contains selected statements Carter made during the 1976 campaign; *A Government as Good as Its People* (New York: Simon and Schuster, 1977; **G**) is a compilation of sixty-two speeches and interviews given by Carter between the time he became governor of Georgia and when he took the presidential oath of office; *The Wit and Wisdom of Jimmy Carter* (Secaucus: Citadel, 1977; **G**) is also a selection of Carter quotations; and *The Spiritual Journey of Jimmy Carter*, compiled by Wesley G. Pippert (New York: Macmillan, 1978; **G**), includes statements Carter made about religion during his first six months in office.

Jimmy Carter has written several books about himself and his presidency. *Why Not the Best?* (New York: Bantam, 1976; **G**) is a brief autobiography published during the 1976 campaign to gain him greater public recognition. It is laced with liberal doses of Carter's personal morality as well as his plans for the White House. *Keeping the Faith: Memoirs of a President* (New York: Bantam, 1982; **A, G**) is Carter's official account of his term of office. He devotes lengthy attention to his frustrating attempt to negotiate the release of the American hostages in Iran in 1979–1980. *The Blood of Abraham* (Boston: Houghton Mifflin, 1984; **A, G**) is about the Middle East, and while it offers little that is new in the area of Arab-Israeli affairs, the book reveals a great deal about its author. Finally, Carter and his wife, Rosalynn, have written *Everything To Gain: Making the Most of the Rest of Your Life* (New York: Random House, 1987; **G**). In it the Carters discuss their changing marital relationship, address current health issues in the United States, and offer advice to older Americans about living fulfilling lives.

Following his term of office, a number of Carter's closest White House associates and cabinet members wrote accounts of his administration. These books provide an invaluable perspective on the Carter presidency and its times of turmoil. *Taking Care of the Law* (New York: Morrow, 1982; **A, G**) by Carter's attorney general, Griffin B. Bell, is a candid and opinionated recollection of Bell's experiences as a member of Carter's cabinet. Bell openly discusses some of the mistakes he believes his boss made. *Power and Principle: Memoirs of the National Security Advisor, 1977–1981* (Scranton: Farrar, Straus, and Giroux, 1983; **A, G**) by Zbigniew Brzezinski is unhesitatingly critical and contains highlights of many of Carter's personal triumphs as well as failures. Joseph A. Califano, Jr., wrote *Governing America: An Insider's Report from the White House and Cabinet* (New York: Simon and Schuster, 1981; **A, G**) shortly after he resigned from the Carter cabinet in 1979. This book addresses issues Califano confronted as secretary of the Department of Health, Education, and Welfare and tells of the tenuous relationship he had with Carter that eventually led to his resignation.

First Lady From Plains (Boston: Houghton Mifflin, 1984; **A, G**) is Rosalynn Carter's autobiography. She chronicles her life and marriage and reveals the role she played as her husband's personal ambassador and valued adviser. Of special interest is her inside account of the Iran hostage debacle.

In *American Hostages in Iran: The Conduct of a Crisis* (New Haven: Yale, 1985; **A, G**), Warren Christopher, Robert Carswell, Harold H. Saunders, Oscar Schachter, and Abraham A. Ribicoff offer a definitive history of the Iranian hostage crisis from legal, economic, and diplomatic points of view. As a deputy secretary of state in the Carter State Department, Christopher's account is particularly insightful. Another perspective of the Iranian crisis is offered by Hamilton Jordan, Carter's chief of staff and close political adviser. *Crisis: The Last Year of the Carter Presidency* (New York: Putnam, 1982; **A, G**) documents Carter's weaknesses as president, and in diary format, reflects on his frustrating last year in office. The most critical view of the way Carter handled the Iranian hostage crisis is by his secretary of state, Cyrus Vance. *Hard Choices: Critical Years in American Foreign Policy* (New York: Simon and Schuster, 1983; **A, G**) presents Vance's case against Carter's abortive attempt to rescue the embassy hostages. This is a very honest, personal account of his tenure on the Carter cabinet.

Panama Odyssey (Austin: University of Texas Press, 1984; **A, G**) by William J. Jorden, United States Ambassador to Panama from 1974 to 1978, is the definitive study of the evolution of the treaty which returned control of the canal to the Panamanian people. As a principal participant in the negotiation of the final treaty, Jorden's recollections are invaluable. Foreign policy under Jimmy Carter is the concern of Gaddis Smith, *Morality, Reason, and Power: American Diplomacy in the Carter Years* (New York: Hill and Wang, 1986; **A, G**). Smith argues that foreign policy during Carter's four-year term of office was carried on with unusual morality. Carter's press secretary, Jody Powell, has written *The Other Side of the Story* (New York: Morrow, 1984; **A, G**) which implies that the press, not Carter himself, was responsible for his 1980 election defeat. William B. Quant, a senior Middle East Staff member on the National Security Council from 1977 to 1979, in his book *Camp David: Peacemaking and Politics* (Washington: Brookings Institution, 1986; **A, G**), focuses on President Carter's catalytic role in the 1979 Israeli-Egyptian peace treaty process. This book is invaluable in its descriptive account of the delicate steps taken to reach a successful agreement. Another version of the Iranian hostage crisis is provided by Gary Sick, who served the Carter Administration as a principal aide for Iranian Affairs on the National Security Council. His book *All Fall Down: America's Tragic Encounter with Iran* (New York: Random House, 1985; **A, G**) depicts the major American figures involved in the attempt to gain the freedom of the American embassy personnel held hostage in Teheran.

The role of the Central Intelligence Agency under Carter is considered by Stansfield Turner, *Secrecy and Democracy: The CIA in Transition* (Boston: Houghton Mifflin, 1985; **A, G**). Turner outlines the problems a democratic society encounters when it sanctions clandestine intelligence operations.

Museums, Historical Landmarks, Societies

Jimmy Carter Library Museum (Atlanta, GA). Houses photographs, official state gifts, and mementoes of the Carter White House. The museum contains a replica of the oval office as it looked when Carter occupied it, and a display which presents an interpretation of American history from the perspective of the nation's first thirty-nine presidents.

Plains, Georgia Carter Museum (Plains, GA). Memorabilia of Carter's early life and political career are displayed in the town's old railroad depot.

Other Sources

Germond, Jack W. and Jules Witcover. *Blue Smoke and Mirrors: How Reagan Won and Why Carter Lost the Election of 1980.* New York: Viking, 1981. Two veteran political journalists account for Carter's loss because the American people lost faith in his ability to govern.

Schram, Martin. *Running for President, 1976.* Briarcliff Manor: Stein and Day, 1977. Schram, *Newsday*'s Washington Bureau Chief, blueprints how Carter, the from-out-of-nowhere candidate, managed to win the 1976 presidential election.

Talbott, Strobe. *Endgame: The Inside Story of SALT II.* New York: Harper and Row, 1979. An interesting chronicle of how SALT II was negotiated and the role Carter and his advisers played.

Witcover, Jules. *Marathon The Pursuit of the Presidency, 1972–1976.* New York: Viking, 1977. An exhaustively detailed account of the important political events leading up to the presidential election of 1976. Witcover addresses both the issues and nonissues of the campaign and tells the story of the army of workers who made Carter's victory possible.

Howard L. Preston

GEORGE WASHINGTON CARVER
c.1864–1943

Chronology

Born George Washington Carver in Spring 1864 or 1865 in Diamond, Missouri, the son of a slave named Mary, who was owned by Moses and Susan Carver; *1865–1875* is raised by the Carvers after mother's disappearance; *1875–1890* wanders around in Missouri, Kansas, and Iowa seeking an education while supporting himself doing laundry, cooking, and homesteading; *1890–1896* enters Simpson College and then transfers to Iowa State College, where he receives bachelor's and master's degrees in agriculture; *1896* accepts an offer by Booker T. Washington to work at Tuskegee Normal and Industrial Institute in Tuskegee, Alabama; *1896–1925* serves in various capacities in the Agricultural Department at Tuskegee and operates Tuskegee Agricultural Experiment Station; *1916* becomes member of the Royal Society for the Arts; *1920* testifies before a congressional tariff committee on the value of peanuts and begins to receive national publicity as the "Peanut Man"; *1923* some Atlanta businessmen found the Carver Products Company to market Carver's various peanut products and paints made from native clays, but the company flounders; other unsuccessful companies follow; *1923–1936* lectures in white colleges under the auspices of the Commission on Interracial Cooperation and the Young Men's Christian Association; *1923–1943* receives numerous awards and honorary degrees, including the Spingarn Medal from the National Association for the Advancement of Colored People and a Roosevelt Medal; *1925–1943* remains at Tuskegee but ceases teaching and agricultural field work, concentrating instead on laboratory work and lecturing nationally; *1933–1941* engages in physical therapy work with infantile paralysis patients, using peanut oil massages; *1940* donates his life's savings to establish the George Washington Carver Foundation to support scientific research; *1943* dies on January 5 in Tuskegee, following an extended illness.

Activities of Historical Significance

Although Carver became famous as a "creative chemist," his hundreds of products from peanuts, sweet potatoes, native clays, and other southern resources were neither original nor commercially successful. In some ways the commercialization efforts represented a perversion of Carver's original aims. When he came to Tuskegee in 1896, his primary goal was to alleviate the crushing cycle of debt and poverty suffered by many landless black farmers in the South. Without land for collateral, sharecroppers borrowed against future crops for such necessities as food and fertilizers, frequently carrying debts from season to season. As the director of the only all black-staffed agricultural experiment station, Carver practiced and

271

advocated what has come to be called "appropriate technology," seeking to exploit available resources to replace expensive, purchased items. For over twenty years Carver used such innovative agricultural education techniques as farmers' institutes and a movable school to take his message of self-reliance directly to those who needed it most. His efforts enriched the lives of hundreds of people, even if they failed to avert the decline of the small-scale, black farm. At the same time, he helped a number of peanut and other food processors to solve technical problems and to publicize their crops—all without accepting compensation from them.

Carver's renown grew dramatically as a myriad of groups found his life and work symbolically useful. Advocates of racial equality, segregation, the "New South," the religious approach to science, and the "American Dream" appropriated Carver as a folk hero. Distortions crept into the story of his life. Some of the mythology that developed was destructive, but he served as a positive role model to numerous black men and women. His warm, compelling personality became a great asset in his interracial work and helped to convert many white college students to the cause of racial justice. He related well to young people and became a friend and mentor to a number of Tuskegee students as well.

With his gift of $60,000 to found the George Washington Carver Foundation at Tuskegee University, Carver also left a living legacy. Since the 1940s, the Foundation has provided funds and facilities to numerous blacks engaged in research.

Overview of Biographical Sources

The romance of Carver's life story and the eccentricities of his personality are very appealing and have led to the publication of numerous biographies. Only two of these were written before his death: one by a former Tuskegee student, Raleigh Merritt, which appeared in 1938, and one by Rackham Holt that was published the year Carver died. Both were "authorized biographies," and their authors received some degree of help from their subject. Merritt's book is limited in scope but is helpful in determining what Carver actually said about his past. Holt's book greatly benefitted from extensive interviews of Carver contemporaries, many of whom had died before later biographies were undertaken. It is marred, however, by occasional fictionalization by the author. Because of such liberties and the lack of documentation, one frequently has difficulty determining exactly what Holt's sources told her.

Two other books of limited scope are useful for specific aspects of Carver's career. Alvin D. Smith, *George Washington Carver: Man of God* (1954), is an account of Carver's Bible class at Tuskegee. Ethel Edwards, *Carver of Tuskegee* (1971), is invaluable for understanding his impact in interracial relations.

Many other popular biographies of varying merit have appeared since Carver's death. These, as well as biographies written for children, frequently provide interesting insight into the making of the Carver myths. Gary R. Kremer, *George Washington Carver in His Own Words* (1987), provides selections from Carver's personal and published papers to illumine various aspects of his life and personality. Louis R. Harlan's two-volume biography of Booker T. Washington is very useful to understanding the environment in which Carver worked. The only full-scale, documented biography is Linda O. McMurry, *George Washington Carver: Scientist and Symbol* (1981). It explores both the myth and reality of his life.

Evaluation of Principal Biographical Sources

Bontempts, Arna Wendell. *The Story of George Washington Carver*. New York: Grosset & Dunlap, 1954. **(G, Y)** A well-written account, this book is an example of the retelling of the Carver story marred by the inclusion of mythological stories that cannot be documented.

Edwards, Ethel. *Carver of Tuskegee*. Cincinnati: Psyche Press, 1971. **(A, G)** Drawn from extensive interviews of whites with whom Carver came into contact during his interracial work. This is one of the best sources on that aspect of Carver's career and contains material not found in earlier biographies.

Elliott, Lawrence. *George Washington Carver: The Man Who Overcame*. Englewoods Cliffs, NJ: Prentice-Hall, 1966. **(G)** One of the better popular biographies, this book is more balanced than most but still contains some of the errors that crept into the story of Carver's life story as he became famous.

Graham, Shirley, and George D. Lipscomb. *Dr. George Washington Carver, Scientist*. New York: J. Messner, 1944. **(Y)** Written primarily for young people, this extremely laudatory book is one of the better works of this genre.

Holt, Rackham. *George Washington Carver: An American Biography*. Garden City, NY: Doubleday, Doren, 1943. **(G)** Written while Carver was still alive and with the close cooperation of several of his key colleagues, this book contains much valuable information but is marred by a lack of objectivity and some degree of fictionalization. It and a second edition have been extremely popular and a source for many other accounts of Carver's life.

Kremer, Gary R. *George Washington Carver in His Own Words*. Columbia: University of Missouri Press, 1987. **(A, G)** A selection of Carver's letters and writings with commentary. This book provides interesting insights into Carver's personality and certain aspects of his career.

McMurry, Linda O. *George Washington Carver: Scientist and Symbol*. New York: Oxford University Press, 1981. **(A, G)** The only full-scale, documented biography, this book seeks to separate the man and the myth, explores the significance of both the man and his career, and discusses the symbolic uses of Carver's life.

Merritt, Raleigh Howard. *From Captivity to Fame; or The Life of George Washington Carver*. Boston: Meador Publishing, 1938. **(G)** Written by a former Tuskegee student, this book is somewhat limited in scope and very laudatory but contains a number of useful documents and is helpful in determining what Carver actually said about his past.

Smith, Alvin D. *George Washington Carver: Man of God*. New York: Exposition Press, 1954. **(G, Y)** Written from notes taken by the author during Carver's Bible class at Tuskegee, the book is a valuable source on Carver's impact on students and his religious beliefs.

Toogood, Anna Coxe. *George Washington Carver National Monument, Diamond Missouri; Historic Resource Study and Administrative History*. Denver: Denver Service Center, Historic Preservation Team, National Park Service, 1973. **(A)** The first attempt to document fully Carver's early life, it is the most valuable source on his activities prior to his arrival in Tuskegee.

Overview and Evaluation of Primary Sources

Carver was a prolific correspondent and saved most of the letters he received as well as many carbons of his replies. These were preserved first in the George Washington Carver Museum on the campus at Tuskegee, where some were destroyed by a fire. Surviving papers were then housed and organized in the Tuskegee University Archives along with copies of Carver's lectures, articles, agricultural bulletins, and miscellaneous other materials, including typescripts of interviews of Carver contemporaries conducted by Tuskegee personnel in the 1950s. In the 1970s, the National Historical Publication Center provided funds to obtain copies of Carver materials in other archives and to microfilm the entire collection. Both the microfilm edition of the papers and a guide to the collection are available for purchase. Included in the microfilm are copies of most Carver-related items from such repositories as the National Archives, the Library of Congress, the George Washington Carver National Monument, and the archives of Simpson College and Iowa State University as well as letters donated by individuals.

Certain materials were unknown or unavailable at the time of the publication of the *Microfilm Edition of the George Washington Carver Papers*. Three small, but rich, collections of Carver papers were not included. The first is located in the Michigan Historical Collections at Ann Arbor, Michigan, and consists of miscellaneous items contributed by Carver's research assistant, Austin Curtis. The second collection is the Lucy Cherry Crisp Papers at East Carolina University in Greenville, North Carolina. Crisp was a woman whom Carver met in his interracial work, and her papers included valuable information she collected when writing a biography of Carver that has never been completed. Also, two document boxes of significant Carver materials collected by Jessie P. Guzman were not filmed but can be found in the Tuskegee Archives.

Since the microfilm project has been completed, several individuals have also donated letters to the George Washington Carver National Monument and to Tuskegee University. The National Monument also has tapes of interviews of Carver contemporaries made by Park Service personnel after Carver's death. Finally, the Tuskegee Archives contains several sources not directly related to Carver but still useful. These include minutes of the school's Executive Council and General Faculty meetings—some of which are also found in the Booker T. Washington Papers in the Library of Congress.

Fiction and Adaptations
The Pete Smith Specialty Company of Hollywood, California produced a short feature film of Carver's life in 1932. It features Carver playing himself in his later years.

Museums, Historical Landmarks, Societies
George Washington Carver Museum (Tuskegee, AL). Now run by the National Park Service as a national historic site, it was originally organized by Carver himself just prior to his death. It includes materials from the original museum such as several of Carver's paintings as well as other items reflecting on the black experience.

George Washington Carver National Monument (Diamond, MO). The site of Carver's birth and childhood, it houses various memorabilia, manuscripts, and tape collections as well as a museum.

Other Sources
Fuller, Robert P., and Merrill J. Mattes. "The Early Life of George Washington Carver." Typescript at the George Washington Carver National Monument, Diamond, Missouri.

Mackintosh, Barry. "George Washington Carver: The Making of a Myth." *Journal of Southern History* 42 (November 1976). A debunking article highly critical of Carver and his work.

Linda O. McMurry
North Carolina State University

WHITTAKER CHAMBERS
1901-1961

Chronology

Born Jay Vivian Chambers on April 1, 1901, in Philadelphia, the son of Jay Chambers, a newspaper artist, and Laha Whittaker Chambers, a retired actress; *1902-1920* spends an unhappy childhood in Lynbrook, New York; parents separate; takes name of David Whittaker Chambers, the first of eleven names he will use during his tumultuous political and literary career; *1920* briefly enrolls at Williams College, then enrolls at Columbia College, and is influenced by Mark Van Doren; *1923* leaves Columbia; works at New York Public Library; *1924-1925* returns to Columbia; *1925* joins the Communist party and begins working for the *Daily Worker*; wins acclaim as translator and linguist; *1929-1931* breaks with Communist party over Stalinist policies; *1931* marries Esther Shemitz, a Socialist; *1931-1938* rejoins Communist party and serves as a spy for the Soviet Union in Washington, D.C.; *1938* breaks with the Communist party and Soviet spy network; *1938-1939* translates Gustav Regler's *The Great Crusade*; *1939-1948* works as a book reviewer, senior editor, and special projects editor for Henry Luce's *Time* magazine; becomes vehement anti-Communist; *1948-1950* appears as a witness for the House Committee on Un-American Activities and the subsequent trials of Alger Hiss; *1950* retires to his farm in Westminster, Maryland; *1952* publishes his autobiography, *Witness*; *1957-1959* serves as an editor of *National Review*; *1961* dies on July 9 in Westminster, Maryland.

Activities of Historical Significance

Whittaker Chambers was involved in the development of the Communist party during its formative period in the 1920s and 1930s. As a well-connected party member and activist, Chambers had access to the highest levels of the Communist party. During the 1930s, he participated in a Soviet espionage network in Washington directed against the American government. But after his final break with communism in 1938, Chambers reverted to the conservatism of his youth. In 1948, he was subpoenaed to testify before the House Committee on Un-American Activities. In his testimony, Chambers asserted that many officials in the government were Communist party members or sympathizers during the 1930s, and suggested that some of these individuals were still supportive of Soviet-backed communism.

In the environment of the Cold War, Chambers's allegations resulted in a national hysteria. Chambers charged that Alger Hiss, who had served with distinction in the Departments of Agriculture, Justice, and State during the Roosevelt administration, and who was serving as president of the Carnegie Endowment for World Peace, had been involved in spying for the Soviet Union during the mid-1930s. Chambers produced a quantity of documents, the "pumpkin papers," and revealed a complex tale of conspiracy that implicated Hiss, who was indicted and tried twice; the jury in the 1949 trial could not reach a verdict, but the next year he was found guilty of perjury and sentenced to a five-year prison term.

Chambers became a hero to the developing New Right in America whose leaders included William F. Buckley, Jr., William Rusher, and Ralph de Toledano. In 1952, Chambers published his widely acclaimed autobiography, *Witness*. He remains a hero to conservatives, as evidenced by the Medal of Freedom which he was posthumously awarded in 1984 by President Reagan.

Overview of Biographical Sources

No full-scale biography of Whittaker Chambers has been written, but the Chambers-Hiss controversy continues to factionalize scholars and journalists. Allen Weinstein, *Perjury: The Hiss-Chambers Case* (1978), presents the most exhaustive scholarly analysis of the famous case, concluding that Hiss was indeed guilty.

Though many scholars consider Weinstein's work the definitive assessment, Victor Navasky, "Allen Weinstein's 'Perjury': The Case Not Proven Against Alger Hiss," *Nation* (April 8, 1978), refutes Weinstein's arguments, faulting his methodology, questioning the validity of quotations from key sources, and challenging the application of the data. These partisan interpretations characterize the highly emotional arguments that have been voiced on the issue since 1948.

Evaluation of Principal Biographical Sources

Burnham, James. *The Web of Subversion: Underground Networks in the U.S. Government*. New York: John Day, 1954. **(G)** This book, a contemporary defense of Chambers, advances a thesis that emphasizes the seriousness of the Communist infiltration of the American government.

de Toledano, Ralph. *Lament for a Generation*. New York: Farrar, Straus, and Cudahy, 1960. **(G)** An account of the case and the era which is sympathetic to Chambers and critical of Hiss and the leftists of the post-war period.

de Toledano, Ralph, and Victor Lasky. *Seeds of Treason*. New York: Funk and Wagnalls, 1950. **(G)** A popular right-wing partisan account supportive of Chambers.

Smith, John Chabot. *Alger Hiss: The True Story*. New York: Holt, Rinehart, and Winston, 1976. **(G)** An analysis of the case which asserts that Chambers fabricated an elaborately documented case against an innocent Alger Hiss.

Weinstein, Allen. *Perjury: The Hiss-Chambers Case*. New York: Alfred A. Knopf, 1978. **(A, G)** Examines and advances the theory of Hiss's guilt.

Overview and Evaluation of Primary Sources

The writings of Whittaker Chambers constitute a valuable resource for the study of the man and his period. Chambers's major works were his autobiography, *Witness* (New York: Random House, 1952; **A, G**), and two posthumously published works, *Cold Friday* (New York: Random House, 1964; **G**), and *Odyssey of a Friend*, edited by William F. Buckley, Jr. (New York: Putnam, 1969; **G**). These works portray Chambers as a serious-minded individual who experienced intellectual crises and shifts of allegiance on several occasions. He claims to have broken with communism because he found it devoid of intellectual substance and moral value. In addition to his numerous essays for *Time* and other Luce publications, Chambers wrote essays for such journals as *News Magazine Supplement*, the *Morningside*, *New Masses*, *National Review*, the *Nation*, *Poetry*, *Two Worlds*, *American Mercury*, and *Commonweal*. As a leftist writer early in his career, Chambers was recognized as a talented literary artist who advanced proletarian values. His translations of Felix Salten's *Bambi*, Heinrich Mann's *Mother Mary*, Franz Werfel's *Class Reunion*, and Gustav Regler's *The Great Crusade* merited him acclaim as a scholarly linguist.

Among the more pertinent contemporary memoirs are works by Mark Van Doren, Richard Nixon, Arthur Koestler, Dean Acheson, and Alger Hiss. Mark Van Doren's *The Autobiography of Mark Van Doren* (New York: Harcourt, Brace, 1958; **A, G**) provides firsthand insights into Chambers's life as a student at Columbia and his shift from conservatism to communism. Richard M. Nixon's *Six Crises* (New York: Pocket Books, 1962; **G**) discusses the political crisis of the post-war era in light of the Chambers-Hiss case. In *The Invisible Writing* (London: Collins, 1954; **A, G**), Arthur Koestler expresses support for Chambers, while Dean Acheson's *Present at the Creation* (New York: Norton, 1969; **A, G**) addresses the case and the era in a more dispassionate fashion, from the perspective of national power. Until recently, Alger Hiss's *In the Court of Public Opinion* (New York: Alfred A. Knopf, 1957; **A, G**) constituted his fullest statement on the case and his professed innocence; but his recently published autobiography, *Recollections of a Life* (New York: Seaver/Henry Holt, 1988; **A, G**), goes into even greater detail, providing a convincing case for his innocence, and characterizing Chambers as a "possessed man and a psychopath."

The manuscript collections relating to Chambers's testimony in the Hiss case and to his earlier life are substantial. The papers of Herbert Solow relating to his 1938 discussions with Chambers are deposited at the Hoover Institute in Stanford, California. Private collections of letters and notes relating to Chambers held by Isaac Levine, Meyer Schapiro, and Sidney Hook were used extensively by Allen Weinstein for his research on *Perjury*. The Time Incorporated Archive in New York City holds records on Chambers's career with Time and on the case. The Random House manuscripts on Chambers and relevant oral history transcripts are available at Columbia University. Other noteworthy depositories include the Karl E. Mundt Library, Princeton University (oral history transcripts by Allen Dulles and Richard

M. Nixon), and Yale University (the Josephine Herbst and Jerome Frank collections). Among the significant federal government sources are the case files of the Federal Bureau of Investigation and the Central Intelligence Agency, and the trial exhibits and case files of the Department of Justice and the United States Attorney's Office, Southern District of New York. Further, the records of the House Committee on Un-American Activities and the Senate Committees on the Judiciary and Government Operations are essential sources for information on the case.

Other Sources

Aaron, Daniel. *Writers on the Left.* New York: Avon, 1961. An adequate introduction to leftist literary contributions in the United States during the mid-twentieth century.

Belfrage, Cedric. *The American Inquisition, 1945–1960.* Indianapolis: Bobbs-Merrill, 1973. A critical assessment of the reactionary sentiment in the United States during the period under review. Advances the thesis that anti-intellectualism dominated the era.

Buckholder, Roger Glen. "Whittaker Chambers: The Need to Believe." Bowdoin Prize, Harvard University, 1965. Available on file in the Widener Library, Harvard, this is a perceptive and provocative study of Chambers and the case by a younger scholar.

Buckley, William F. *The Committee and Its Critics: A Calm Review of the House Committee on Un-American Activities.* New York: Putnam, 1962. This analysis is sympathetic to the committee's purposes and to the individuals who led and served on it.

Buckley, William F., and L. Brent Bozell. *McCarthy and His Enemies.* Chicago: Regnery, 1954. The apology for McCarthy and the conservative reaction of the post-war period which has maintained the support of the Chambers partisans for over thirty years.

Carr, Robert Kenneth. *The House Committee on Un-American Activities, 1945–1950.* Ithaca: Cornell University Press, 1952. A contemporary analysis of the committee's activities and philosophy.

Castellain, J. *L'Espionage Sovietique aux Etats-Unis: L'Affaire Alger Hiss.* Lausanne, France: Jaunin, 1950. A European analysis of the case which raises questions of legal procedures and of the credibility of the evidence in the case.

Fund for the Republic. *Bibliography on the Communist Problem in the United States.* New York: Fund for the Republic, 1955. A biased but useful bibliography of books and articles published to 1954.

Harper, Alan D. *The Politics of Loyalty: The White House and The Communist Issue, 1946–1952.* Westport, CT: Greenwood Press, 1969. An analysis of the policy and conduct of the Truman administration during the period of the Chambers-Hiss case.

Kirkendall, Richard S., ed. *The Truman Period as a Research Field.* Columbia: University of Missouri Press, 1967. A dated but still useful resource.

Nash, George. *The Conservative Intellectual Movement in America Since 1945.* New York: Basic Books, 1975. The standard study of conservative intellectualism with a discussion of the influence of the Chambers-Hiss case on its development.

William T. Walker
Philadelphia College of Pharmacy and Science

SALMON P. CHASE
1808-1873

Chronology

Born Salmon Portland Chase on January 13, 1808, in Cornish, New Hampshire, one of eleven children of Ithamar Chase, a farmer and politician, and Janet Ralston Chase; *1818* father dies; moves to Ohio, where he is raised by uncle, Bishop Philander Chase; *1823-1826* returns to New Hampshire; attends and graduates from Dartmouth College; *1826-1830* moves to Washington, D.C.; directs a private boys' school while reading law under Attorney General William Wirt; *1830* moves to Cincinnati to establish law practice; *1830-1836* is active in community and cultural affairs while rising in legal profession; *1834* marries Catherine Jane Garniss; *1835* Catherine dies; *1836-1844* becomes active defender of fugitive slaves; *1839* marries Eliza Ann Smith; *1841* joins recently formed Liberty party; advocates a merger with antislavery elements of major parties; *1845* second wife dies; *1846* marries Sarah Dunlop Ludlow; *1848* helps found the Free-Soil party and helps write its platform advocating the containment of slavery; *1849* is elected senator when Free-Soilers secure a balance of power in the Ohio legislature; *1852* third wife dies; *1854* joins Charles Sumner and Joshua Giddings in calling for a new party following the introduction of the Kansas-Nebraska Bill; *1855-1859* serves as the first Republican governor of Ohio, using the post as a stepping-stone to presidential nomination; *1860-1861* fails to secure the Republican nomination; is appointed by Lincoln as secretary of the treasury; *1861-1864* serves as treasury secretary during the Civil War years, managing the Union's finances while seeking further political leverage; *1862* helps persuade Lincoln to issue the Emancipation Proclamation; *1864* resigns as treasury secretary; is appointed Chief Justice of the United States Supreme Court; *1864-1873* continues to seek presidential nomination, in 1868 as a Democrat, and in 1872 as a Liberal Republican; *1868* presides over Andrew Johnson's impeachment trial; *1873* dies on May 6 in New York City after suffering his second stroke.

Activities of Historical Significance

Chase's forty-year political career spanned a broad spectrum of parties, elected and appointed offices, and unfulfilled ambitions. He gained initial prominence as "the Attorney General for Runaway Negroes" when he unsuccessfully challenged the fugitive slave laws of Ohio and the United States in the late 1830s and 1840s. Active in thirty-party politics during the 1840s, he developed the "freedom national" concept, arguing that the federal government must divorce itself from support or responsibility for the state institution of slavery. Using this argument, he wrote numerous party platforms for the Liberty and Free-Soil parties as he at-

281

tempted to arrange third-party union with Democratic and Whig antislavery politicians.

Elected to the United States Senate in 1849, Chase joined a small group of Northern lawmakers in resisting the Compromise spirit in Congress in 1850. His goal of a broader-based antislavery party was realized with the formation of the Republican party in 1854, an organization he helped to create.

Chase's election as governor of Ohio in 1855 gave him a base from which to pursue his twin goals of antislavery and a presidential nomination. His attempts to gain the presidential nomination at the Republican conventions in 1856 and 1860 proved disappointing, since his party chose candidates who took a more moderate stance on slave-related issues. But as a result of his support of Abraham Lincoln in the 1860 election, he was rewarded with the key cabinet post of secretary of the treasury.

Chase's most significant contributions were made during the Civil War. He developed financial policies to guide the Union through the turmoil of war, a process that led to banking, currency, and debt management policies of permanent importance. Never confining himself to Treasury duties, Chase also used his position to influence Lincoln toward emancipation and more liberal racial politics, even as he sought to unseat the president for the 1864 Republic nomination. Following his third and final attempt to secure the Republican nomination, Chase resigned his cabinet position, loyally supported Lincoln's reelection, and was named Chief Justice of the United States Supreme Court in December of that year.

Chase's remaining years were spent as Chief Justice, but he continued to combine politics with official duties. As the nation's top jurist, he was increasingly at odds with more radical Republicans, but avoided an open confrontation with Congress over its Reconstruction policies. At the same time, he helped to strengthen the Court's independence and prestige. His political goals still paramount, he broke with the Republican party and, at the insistence of his ambitious daughter, Kate Chase Sprague, sought the Democratic nomination in 1868. But his devotion to progressive principles remained strong, and his advocacy of black suffrage helped to deny him his new party's nomination as well.

Chase's quixotic career revealed his belief that political parties were never ends in themselves, but rather a means to attain his own personal and political goals. His ambition was so overwhelming that his enemies were many, and constant friends few. Yet he maintained a moral courage that helped push the country toward eventual emancipation and equality for blacks.

Overview of Biographical Sources

Although several biographies of Chase were written in the nineteenth century, he has only recently received the scholarly treatment he deserves. Two highly laudatory biographies were published in the year after his death. Both included many of his letters: Jacob W. Schuckers, *The Life and Public Services of Salmon Portland Chase* (1874), and Robert B. Warden, *An Account of the Private Life and Public Services of Salmon Portland Chase* (1874). The first interpretation of Chase's life by an historian was Albert B. Hart's *Salmon P. Chase* (1899), which objectively describes and analyzes Chase's multi-faceted career. Although numerous articles on specific aspects of Chase's career have appeared, no modern biography was published until Frederick J. Blue's *Salmon P. Chase: A Life in Politics* (1987). Blue had access to numerous sources not available to Hart, and deals with questions of historical interpretation not addressed by earlier historians. The long gap between biographies was due in part to Chase's tremendously varied career, and to the difficulty of deciphering his horrendous penmanship.

Evaluation of Principal Biographical Sources

Belden, Thomas G., and Marva R. Belden. *So Fell the Angels*. Boston: Little, Brown, 1956. (**A, G**) The Beldens offer a highly critical study of the Chase-Sprague families during the Civil War and Reconstruction years. This well-written account uses circumstantial evidence to support a claim that Chase's son-in-law, William Sprague, was involved in corrupt trade practices with the Confederacy which Chase knew of and did little to stop. Kate Chase Sprague is portrayed as both overly ambitious and conniving in her attempts to place her father in the White House.

Blue, Frederick J. *Salmon P. Chase: A Life in Politics*. Kent: Kent State University Press, 1987. (**A, G**) The first twentieth-century biography of Chase is based on primary sources and the most recent secondary accounts. Blue describes Chase as both politically-motivated and dedicated to racial equality.

Hart, Albert B. *Salmon P. Chase*. 1899. Reprint. New York: Chelsea House, 1980. (**A, G**) A well-written and scholarly biography which lacks the benefit of later research.

Schuckers, Jacob W. *The Life and Public Services of Salmon Portland Chase*. New York: D. Appleton, 1874. (**A, G**) Schuckers, a close associate of Chase, was chosen by Kate Chase Sprague to write the kind of eulogy she desired. Although not totally uncritical, Schuckers met Kate's wishes.

Sokoloff, Alice H. *Kate Chase for the Defense*. New York: Dodd, Mead, 1971. (**G**) Sokoloff's popularized biography is a useful account of Chase's ambitious daughter Kate, and includes much material on Chase himself.

Warden, Robert B. *An Account of the Private Life and Public Service of Salmon Portland Chase*. Cincinnati: Wilstach, Baldwin, 1874. (**A, G**) Warden's study is a verbose but insightful view of Chase. The author served briefly as his private secretary and was chosen by Chase to write a biography. Although more critical than Schuckers, Warden nonetheless reveals himself as a fierce Chase partisan.

Overview and Evaluation of Primary Sources

Two major twentieth-century compilations of letters and diaries have been published: Edward G. Bourne *et al.*, eds., "Diary and Correspondence of Salmon P. Chase," in *Annual Report of the American Historical Association, 1902* 2 (Washington, DC: Government Printing Office, 1903; **A**), includes letters to and from Chase throughout his career, and David Donald, ed., *Inside Lincoln's Cabinet: The Civil War Diaries of Salmon P. Chase* (New York: Longmans Green, 1954; **A**), provides insight into the secretary's war policies and politics, and includes an effective analysis of Chase's Civil War-era achievements and failures. Two important sources of many Chase letters are Jacob W. Schuckers, *The Life and Public Services of Salmon Portland Chase* (New York: D. Appleton, 1874; **A, G**), and Robert B. Warden, *An Account of the Private Life and Public Service of Salmon Portland Chase* (Cincinnati: Wilstach, Baldwin, 1874; **A, G**).

Collections of Chase's letters are located in various historical societies and archives, including the Cincinnati Historical Society; the Ohio Historical Society (in Columbus), which has much of his correspondence from his years as governor of Ohio; the Historical Society of Pennsylvania (in Philadelphia), which has his letterbooks; and the Library of Congress and the National Archives in Washington, D.C.

Fiction and Adaptations

During the presidential campaign of 1864, John Trowbridge wrote an idealized campaign biography of Chase, *The Ferryboy and the Financier* (1864). The best-selling historical novel by Gore Vidal, *Lincoln: A Novel* (1984), presents an unflattering portrayal of the politically-ambitious secretary of the treasury.

Other Sources

Foner, Eric. *Free Soil, Free Labor, Free Men: The Ideology of the Republican Party Before the Civil War*. New York: Oxford University Press, 1970. An insightful study of Chase's advocacy of the federal government's divorce from slavery.

Gerteis, Louis. "Salmon P. Chase, Radicalism and the Politics of Emancipation, 1861–1864." *Journal of American History* 60 (1973): 42–62. Gerteis traces Chase's racial policy and strategy during the Civil War, and his efforts to convince Lincoln of the wisdom of emancipation and black land ownership.

Hughes, David. "Salmon P. Chase, Chief Justice." *Vanderbilt Law Review* 18 (1965): 569–614. Hughes gives an evenhanded and competent analysis of Chase's Supreme Court role in the most critical issues of Reconstruction.

Randall, James G. "Salmon Portland Chase." In *Dictionary of American Biography*. Vol. 4, edited by Allen Johnson and Dumas Malone. New York: Scribners, 1933. A concise and scholarly article that includes a bibliography.

Walker, Peter. *Memory, Desire and Imagination in Nineteenth Century American Abolition*. Baton Rouge: Louisiana State University Press, 1978. Analyzes how Chase's upbringing led to his interest in the plight of the fugitive slave.

Frederick J. Blue
Youngstown State University

GEORGE ROGERS CLARK
1752–1818

Chronology

Born George Rogers Clark on November 19, 1752, in Albemarle County, Virginia, on the family farm near the Rivanna River, the second son of John Clark and Ann Rogers Clark, both descendants of old Virginia families; *1757* moves with family to a plantation in Caroline County on the Rappahannock River, where he grows up and briefly attends Donald Robertson's local school, where he proves an apt pupil in mathematics but indifferent in classics, languages, and English; *1772* leaves home after learning surveying and makes first trip to the Ohio country, where he floats down the Ohio River with land seekers, stakes out a claim some forty miles below Wheeling, clears land and surveys plots for other settlers; *1774* participates in Dunmore's War as militia captain, and gains valuable experience in militia command and wilderness warfare; *1775–1776* explores and surveys in central Kentucky, where he takes up land, becomes a militia major and commands Kentucky defense forces; works for the extension of Virginia jurisdiction over Kentucky settlements, and on December 7, 1776, sees this effort crowned with success when Virginia extends legal claims to Kentucky, an action that earns him the title of "Founder of the Commonwealth"; *1777* as war with Native Americans in the West intensifies under British leadership from Detroit, he leads Kentucky defensive efforts and conceives a plan to ease Native American pressures on Kentucky settlements by seizing British posts in the Illinois country; *1778* his plan for a campaign against the British posts is a secret known to few, but the Virginia Assembly authorizes Governor Patrick Henry and the Council to mount an offensive "and attack any of our western enemies"; by late spring, he, as a commander with rank of lieutenant colonel, gathers a force of approximately 175 men at the falls of the Ohio and from there moves to the Illinois country, where on July 4–5 his troops take Kaskaskia and shortly thereafter all other forts in the area as well as Vincennes on the Wabash; *1779* after an incredibly difficult march conducted in mid-winter over flooded terrain with his force from Kaskaskia, he attacks and retakes Vincennes from Lieutenant Governor Henry Hamilton, who had taken it the previous December with a force from Detroit; the surrender takes place on February 25 and is the high point of Clark's career, allowing United States control of the Illinois country until the end of the Revolutionary War; *1780–1791* hopes for an opportunity to attack Detroit that never materializes; at the end of the war, settles in Louisville; leads an unsuccessful expedition against the Native Americans in 1786; suffers repeated failure in his efforts to receive compensation from Virginia for his Revolutionary War efforts and campaign expenses; *1792–1818* lives in financial straits; for a brief period enters the service of the French Republic for a proposed Mississippi campaign against the Spanish; has troubles with alcohol dependency and other health problems, suffering a stroke in 1809 and amputation of a leg; *1818* dies on February 13 of a stroke at his sister's home in Louisville.

Activities of Historical Significance

George Rogers Clark performed services for his country during the era of the American Revolution in a largely unknown and undeveloped area, the trans-Allegheny region. He had been attracted to the western country as a young man, and it is not the least of his claims to historical significance that he soon saw the importance of Kentucky and the Ohio and Illinois country. After living on the Kentucky frontier only a short time, he was convinced of its future, and, though he was only twenty-four, he played a leading role in the movement to extend Virginia's jurisdiction to the Kentucky settlements. Then, as British-supported Native American raids increased, Clark found himself publicly acknowledged as the primary leader, a major of militia, in the defense of Boonesborough, Harrodsburg, Logan's Station, and other settlements.

Clark became convinced that the pressure from Native American raids on Kentucky could be eased considerably by capture of the British-held posts in the old French settlements in the Illinois country and on the Wabash. Early in 1778, his plans received backing from the Virginia Assembly, and on June 24 Clark and his men left their training camp at the falls of the Ohio and set out for the Illinois country. By early July his forces had taken Kaskaskia, Cahokia, and Vincennes. When Vincennes was retaken by Lieutenant Governor Henry Hamilton from Detroit that December, Clark decided on a surprise winter attack, and by February 25, 1779, Vincennes was again in American hands and Hamilton a prisoner. This magnificent campaign put most of the western frontier area under American control, paving the way for Clark to crown his efforts with an attack on Detroit, the real center of British power in the West. But neither Virginia nor Congress was able to provide troops or funds for such an attack, and the Kentucky-Ohio borders remained subject to British-led Native American raids until the end of the Revolutionary War.

For many years after the American Revolution, a number of American historians attributed to Clark's campaigns the British cession of the western country up to the Mississippi, and he was acclaimed as the "Conqueror of the West." To a great extent, this belief continues to shape the popular image of Clark, but professional historians have generally accepted the view that Clark's efforts were not primary in the cession. Still, George Rogers Clark merits recognition as a highly skilled and inspirational leader, a shrewd strategist and an able diplomat. Without doubt, some historians and others will continue to see Clark's campaigns against Kaskaskia and Vincennes as "the most brilliant single military accomplishment of the Revolution."

Overview of Biographical Sources

George Rogers Clark did not begin to attract biographical attention until relatively late in the nineteenth century, long after numerous of his contemporaries had found chroniclers in plenty. There are several explanations for Clark's relative failure to attract biographical attention from his own generation. Among these are his inability to build a stable personal life once peace came to the frontier and the efforts of James Wilkinson to discredit him. But perhaps the most important reason was that his major feats during the Revolutionary War, although important and dramatic, were performed in an area remote from the main military theaters. Because Clark operated in a region geographically remote from most Americans, it was left to later generations, secure and proud of the growth and vitality of their new West, to look back over the region's history and discover Clark's role. Hailed as the "Conqueror of the West," "The Winner of the Old Northwest," and the "archetype of Western hero," he inspired a number of biographical studies and articles detailing his accomplishments.

This view of Clark as a prime architect of a western empire was reflected in early accounts, which were not biographies *per se*, but did include much biographical material and also made use of Clark's own writings. Examples here are Mann Butler, *History of the Commonwealth of Kentucky* (1834), and John B. Dillon, *History of Indiana* (1859). Theodore Roosevelt also devoted considerable space to Clark in the second volume of *The Winning of the West* (1889). By the 1890s, more scholarly works appeared, such as a two-volume account by William H. English, *Conquest of the Country Northwest of the River Ohio, 1778–1783, and Life of General George Rogers Clark* (1896). This work posited that Clark's western campaigns had influenced the British decision to cede the western country to the United States at the Peace of Paris in 1783. For the next thirty-odd years, works on the subject either directly or implicitly advanced English's view that Clark's victories won the West for the U.S.

By the middle 1930s, however, many American scholars, especially diplomatic historians such as Samuel Flagg Bemis, believed that Clark's dramatic feats had not been a major factor in the British cession. Even J. Alton James, author of the definitive Clark biography, *The Life of George Rogers Clark* (1928), had come to occupy a more moderate position on the question of Clark's influence.

Growing acceptance of other reasons for Britain's generous territorial settlement may or may not have been the major factor in the lack of serious biographical studies of Clark, but it was not until the 1950s that other biographies, such as those by John Bakeless (1957) and Walter Havighurst (1952), were published. Interest in the frontier, however, did not show great decline, and in 1962 Dale Van Every followed Bakeless's work with *A Company of Heroes: The American Frontier, 1775–1783*, which devoted several chapters to Clark, depicting him as responsible for United States possession of the West. The bicentennial of the American Revolution revived some interest in Clark and his western campaigns, but none of the work thus stimulated made extreme claims for Clark. An excellent example of these books is Lowell H. Harrison, *George Rogers Clark and the War in the West* (1976).

Evaluation of Principal Biographical Sources

Bakeless, John. *Background to Glory: The Life of George Rogers Clark*. New York and Philadelphia: J. B. Lippincott, 1957. (**A, G**) This is possibly the most readable and also the best known Clark biography. Bakeless believed Clark a forgotten hero and clearly intended this book to help establish Clark's place in United States history. Thus, he credits Clark's campaigns with winning the West. Unfortunately, Bakeless is not always careful or critical of the sources he uses. An unorthodox style of notes makes it difficult to check references, but all major collections of Clark manuscripts have been used.

Bodley, Temple. *George Rogers Clark, His Life and Public Services*. Boston and New York: Houghton Mifflin, 1926. (**A, G**) After years of study and collecting Clark manuscripts, Bodley was determined to write a volume that would bring Clark the attention and credit he felt was due. Primary materials are extensively quoted, but the book is too obviously eulogistic and fails to deal insightfully with Clark's character and personality. For Bodley, Clark is clearly responsible for winning the West.

English, William H. *Conquest of the Country Northwest of the River Ohio, 1778–1783, and the Life of General George Rogers Clark*. 2 vols. 1896. Reprint. New York: Arno Press and The New York Times, 1971. (**A, G**) The author makes use of a vast number of primary sources and prints a number of them in full, including all four accounts of the campaigns against the British posts in the West that Clark is known to have written. Because much of the text consists of long quotations from Clark and his acquaintances, these two volumes are as much source books as biography. English plainly admires but does not eulogize Clark, and obviously believes that Clark's campaigns were responsible for the "Conquest of the Country Northwest of the River Ohio."

Harrison, Lowell H. *George Rogers Clark and the War in the West*. Lexington: University Press of Kentucky, 1976. (**A, G**) This book focuses on Clark's efforts in defense of Kentucky and on the Illinois campaigns as part of that effort. Shorter than other Clark studies and thus not as detailed, it is still an accurate, well researched, and highly readable work by a professional historian. Clark's work is judged important to the West but the author does not make extravagant claims in terms of its impact on the Peace of Paris of 1783.

Havighurst, Walter. *George Rogers Clark: Soldier in the West*. New York: McGraw-Hill, 1952. (**G, Y**) By a skilled and prolific writer, this highly readable book is an accurate portrayal of Clark as the conqueror of the Old Northwest for the United States. Although relatively brief, it presents an insightful and believable portrait of the frontier leader. Well-suited for high school and some junior high readers.

James, James Alton. *The Life of George Rogers Clark.* 1928. Reprint. New York: Greenwood Press, 1969. (**A, G**) This is the most thorough, reliable, and scholarly of all Clark biographies. The tone is not defensive or eulogistic, but Clark still emerges an extraordinary individual. A major strength of the book is that Clark and his activities are always placed in the context of the frontier. Although James clearly believes Clark's work did affect the peace settlement of 1783, he does not make extreme claims.

Van Every, Dale. *A Company of Heroes: The American Frontier 1775–1783.* New York: William Morrow, 1962. (**A, G**) This book, by an accomplished author, is not a biography of Clark but does have four well-written and informative chapters dealing with him. The strength of Van Every's contribution is a sound characterization of Clark and an excellent exposition of his milieu. A reasonable case is also made for Clark's campaigns influencing the British cession of western lands.

Overview and Evaluation of Primary Sources

Among libraries, historical societies, and archives holding George Rogers Clark materials are the State Historical Society of Wisconsin at Madison, the Library of Congress, and the Virginia State Library. Smaller collections of Clark manuscripts and related materials are held by the Chicago Historical Society, the Missouri Historical Society in St. Louis, and the Filson Club, Louisville, Kentucky. Fortunately, many important Clark papers, particularly for the era of the American Revolution, have been published in J. A. James, ed., *George Rogers Clark Papers,* 2 vols. (Springfield, IL: State Historical Library, 1912–1926; **A, G**). Edited by the foremost authority on Clark, these volumes are the basis for most published studies and include useful and well-written introductions. Other published sources are Julian P. Boyd, ed., *The Papers of Thomas Jefferson,* 21 vols. to date (Princeton: Princeton University Press, 1950– ; **A, G**); John C. Fitzpatrick, ed., *The Writings of George Washington,* 39 vols. (Washington: Government Printing Office, 1931–1944; **A, G**); Milo M. Quaife, ed., *The Conquest of The Illinois* (Chicago: Lakeside Press, 1920; **A, G**), a carefully edited and accurate printing of Clark's famous "Memoir" written in 1789 and 1790; John D. Barnhart, ed., *Henry Hamilton and George Rogers Clark in the American Revolution with the Unpublished Journal of Lieut. Gov. Henry Hamilton* (Crawfordsville, IN: R. E. Banta, 1951; **A, G**), a journal by the British commander who opposed Clark at Vincennes that is a useful counterbalance to the accounts from Clark's side; and William H. English's aforementioned volumes containing Clark's accounts of the western campaigns.

Fiction and Adaptations

Clark is portrayed in two fictional works: Winston Churchill's *The Crossing* (1904), which deals with his Kentucky and Ohio frontier adventures, and Maurice Thompson's *Alice of Old Vincennes* (1900), a romance centered around his taking of Vincennes.

Museums, Historical Landmarks, Societies

Cave Hill Cemetery (Louisville, KY). George Rogers Clark's grave is in a family plot. His remains were moved here in 1869 from his original burial site at Locust Grove, near Louisville.

George Rogers Clark National Historical Park (Vincennes, IL). Maintains an extensive collection of early American West artifacts, as well as maps, letters, and other materials relevant to the life of Clark. A bronze statue of Clark is also on display.

George Rogers Clark Park (Louisville, KY). The site of the Clark family homestead, Mulberry Hill, is now a city park. Although the original buildings are gone, part of the original property has been preserved.

Locust Grove National Historic Site (Louisville, KY). The home of Clark's sister and brother-in-law, to which he retired in 1809, has been restored and is open to the public.

Monument Square (Indianapolis, IN). Statue of Clark sculpted by J. H. Mahoney, placed February 25, 1895.

Other Sources

Higginbotham, Don. "George Rogers Clark." In *The Encyclopedia of American Biography*, edited by John A. Garraty and Jerome L. Sternstein. New York: Harper & Row, 1974. Brief sketch by an expert on military aspects of the American Revolution, which states that no hard evidence exists to show Clark's campaigns had effect on British land cessions.

Smith, Dwight L. "The Old Northwest and the Peace Negotiations." In *The French, The Indians, and George Rogers Clark in the Illinois Country: Proceedings of an Indiana American Revolution Bicentennial Symposium*. Indianapolis: Indiana Historical Society, 1977. An excellent article that gives extensive documentation on the effect of Clark's campaigns on the peace settlement at Paris.

Alan S. Brown
Western Michigan University

HENRY CLAY
1777–1852

Chronology

Born Henry Clay on April 12, 1777, in Hanover County, Virginia, to John Clay, a Baptist minister and farmer, and Elizabeth Hudson Clay; *1781–1791* is reared by his mother and stepfather, Henry Watkins, after the death of his father; attends local schools; *1791* goes to work in a retail store in Richmond, Virginia; *1792* becomes deputy clerk in Virginia's High Court of Chancery at the time his parents emigrate to Versailles, Kentucky; *1793–1796* serves as amanuensis for George Wythe, Chancellor of the High Court; *1796–1797* studies law under former governor, Robert Brooke; *1797* moves to Lexington, Kentucky, and opens law practice; *1799* marries Lucretia Hart, daughter of Lexington merchant Thomas Hart; advocates gradual emancipation of Kentucky slaves during election of delegates to a state constitutional convention; *1803–1806* serves in the lower house of the state legislature as a Jeffersonian Republican; *1806* serves a brief, uncompleted term in the U.S. Senate, although he is under the constitutional age requirement; *1807* is reelected to the Kentucky legislature and is chosen speaker of the general assembly; *1809* fights duel with Humphrey Marshall; *1810* is elected to fill an unexpired term in the U.S. Senate; *1811–1814* serves in the U.S. House of Representatives as leader of the War Hawks and as Speaker of the House; *1814–1815* acts as one of the U.S. peace commissioners negotiating the Treaty of Ghent; *1815–1821* returns to the U.S. House and the Speakership; *1821* emerges as leader of the "Second Missouri Compromise," then resigns from the House to resume law practice; *1823* returns to U.S. House and to the Speakership; *1824* wins 39 electoral votes in the presidential contest to James K. Polk; *1848* hopes for Whig presidential election; *1825* supports John Quincy Adams in the presidential election in the U.S. House; *1825–1829* serves as Secretary of State; *1826* fights duel with John Randolph; *1829–1831* resumes law practice and farming at his estate, "Ashland," near Lexington; *1831* returns to the U.S. Senate; *1832* runs for president as the National Republican party candidate and loses to Andrew Jackson; *1833* proposes and successfully negotiates the passage of the Compromise Tariff of 1833; *1839* loses the Whig presidential nomination but continues as party leader in the Senate; *1842* resigns from the Senate; *1844* loses presidential contest to James K. Polk; *1848* hopes for Whig presidential nomination which goes instead to General Zachary Taylor; *1849–1852* serves in U.S. Senate where he introduces the Compromise of 1850; *1852* dies on June 29 of tuberculosis in Washington, D.C.

Activities of Historical Significance

Although he had previously served for two brief periods in the U.S. Senate, Clay first emerged as a significant national figure when he entered the House of Representatives in 1811 and immediately was elected Speaker. He became a leader of the "War Hawks"—a group of Southern and Western congressmen who advocated war with Great Britain for violating the rights of the U.S. as a neutral nation and for inciting Indian attacks on the American frontier. Clay's support for the War of 1812 was an aberration in a career otherwise devoted to preserving peace at home and abroad.

In 1814 President James Madison appointed Clay as one of the five commissioners to negotiate a peace treaty. As a member of the U.S. delegation, he served as a spokesman for the interests of the West, a role he had assumed since his first entry into the Senate, and was frequently at odds with John Quincy Adams, a commissioner who represented the interests of New England. Clay reluctantly signed the Treaty of Ghent although it was silent on virtually all issues over which the war had been fought.

In 1815 Clay was reelected to the House. Again chosen as Speaker, he became a leading spokesman for a national economic program he called the "American System." Consisting of federal aid to internal improvements, a national bank, and a protective tariff, the American System became the central theme of his political platform. In 1818 he also became a champion for the cause of South American independence.

Clay first began to earn the title "The Great Compromiser" during the Missouri controversy of 1820–1821. He supported but did not take a leading role in developing the compromise which allowed Missouri to be admitted to the Union as a slave state but otherwise prohibited slavery north of the 36° 30' line of latitude. When Missouri's new provisional constitution attempted to prohibit the immigration of free blacks, a furor in Congress threatened the granting of statehood. Clay then proposed the so-called "Second Missouri Compromise" that forced the legislature of Missouri to agree not to deprive citizens from another state of equal rights and privileges.

In the presidential election of 1824, Clay won only 39 electoral votes to 41 for William H. Crawford, 84 for John Quincy Adams, and 99 for Andrew Jackson. Since no candidate held a majority, the House of Representatives had to choose among the three top candidates. Speaker Clay, now out of contention, ignored the instructions of the Kentucky legislature to vote for Jackson and threw his support to Adams. When he became president, Adams appointed Clay Secretary of State. Jackson and Crawford followers charged that Clay and Adams had made a "corrupt bargain," an accusation which dogged Clay for the rest of his life and seriously impeded his presidential prospects.

Following his tenure as secretary of state, Clay returned in 1831 to the Senate, where he led opposition to the Jackson administration. Running as the candidate of the National Republican party, he lost the 1832 presidential election to Jackson by an electoral vote of 219 to 49. During this campaign he had promoted the passage of the Tariff of 1832. When South Carolina nullified that act and threatened secession if it were enforced, Clay successfully proposed a compromise to reduce gradually the tariff rates in exchange for repeal of the nullification ordinance.

Clay became the leader of the newly-formed Whig party during the late 1830s but lost its 1840 presidential nomination to war hero William Henry Harrison. After John Tyler succeeded Harrison, Clay attempted to push the Whig party's nationalistic legislative program through the Senate, repeatedly clashing with the president, who strongly advocated states' rights. Concluding that further attempts to enact the Whig program were futile, Clay resigned from the Senate on March 31, 1842, and returned home to prepare for the 1844 election. Easily winning the Whig nomination, he struggled through a bitter campaign, fighting against revived charges of his "corrupt bargain" with Adams and ultimately floundering on the issue of the annexation of Texas. His "Raleigh" letter of April 17, 1844, appeared to oppose annexation and cost him his Southern support, while his two "Alabama" letters in July seemed to hedge his opposition to annexation and cost him significant support in the North. Nevertheless, he lost to Democrat James K. Polk, an ardent annexationist, by only 38,000 popular votes and by an electoral vote of 170 to 105.

Opposing the declaration of war against Mexico but supporting the war once it began, Clay still hoped to win the presidency in 1848 but was passed over for the nomination. Nonetheless, with his reputation as "The Great Compromiser" intact, he returned to the Senate in 1849 as the debate over the question of the extension of slavery into the territories acquired from Mexico began to threaten the Union. He proposed the series of resolutions which ultimately became known as the Compromise of 1850. These proposals, which Congress passed one-by-one and not as a single comprehensive piece of legislation, included admission of California as a free state, provided that the people in the territories of New Mexico and Utah would decide the status of slavery in their constitutions when they applied for statehood, adjusted the Texas-New Mexico boundary, provided for assumption of the Texas debt by the U.S., abolished the slave trade in the District of Columbia, and included a strengthened fugitive slave law. This compromise, which was Clay's last major public act, postponed the Civil War for a decade.

Overview of Biographical Sources

Biographies of Henry Clay abound, yet surprisingly few are of recent origin. Many of the nineteenth-century works were written by Clay partisans and were intended as campaign literature. The first of these was George D. Prentice's *Biography of Henry Clay* (1831). Also notable in this group is Epes Sargent's *The Life and Public Services of Henry Clay* (1842); Daniel Mallory's *The Life and Speeches of the Hon. Henry Clay* (1843–1844); James B. Swain's *The Life and Speeches of Henry Clay* (1843); William G. Brownlow's *A Political Register, Setting Forth the Principles of the Whig and Locofoco Parties in the United States with the Life and Public Services of Henry Clay . . .* (1844). While all of these extol Clay's virtues as a man and his sagacity as a politician, they nevertheless provide significant information which is not available elsewhere, especially about his early life. The Mallory and Swain editions each provide a collection of speeches in addition to biographical material. Nathan Sargent's thirty-two page pamphlet, *Life of Henry Clay* (1844), which sold for three cents a copy, was intended to be the campaign biography for the masses. Clay's premier biographer during the antebellum era was Calvin Colton, who first published *The Life and Times of Henry Clay* (1846) with Clay's cooperation and then, after Clay's death, substantially extended the work.

A number of biographies appeared during the latter half of the nineteenth and early twentieth centuries. Of these, Carl Schurz's *Henry Clay* (1887) is the outstanding example. Its assessment of Clay's strengths and weaknesses is still valid, although it reflects Schurz's strong anti-slavery and nationalist biases. Joseph M. Rogers's *The True Henry Clay* (1904) attempted to rectify some myths but contains significant errors of its own. Its interpretation, however, is quite balanced. Clay's grandson, Thomas Hart Clay, began *Henry Clay* (1910), which ultimately was finished by Ellis P. Oberholtzer. This work contains many of the traditional stories handed down in the family.

The most comprehensive, scholarly works to date were completed in the 1930s. Glyndon G. Van Deusen's *The Life of Henry Clay* (1937) utilized the manuscript sources available at the time, and it remains the most thorough account of Clay's personal and political life. Equally scholarly is Bernard Mayo's *Henry Clay: Spokesman of the New West* (1937) which covers in detail his career up to 1812. George R. Poage's *Henry Clay and the Whig Party* (1936) focuses primarily on the period from 1840–1852, emphasizing his role as leader of the Whig party.

Perhaps the best overall interpretative biography is Clement Eaton's *Henry Clay and the Art of American Politics* (1957). Although brief, this work provides the best insight into the contradictions and dilemmas which pervaded Clay's career. Also significant is Merrill D. Peterson's composite study, *The Great Triumvirate: Webster, Clay, and Calhoun* (1987) which provides a brilliant analysis of Clay's American System.

Evaluation of Principal Biographical Sources

Brownlow, William G. *A Political Register, Setting Forth the Principles of the Whig and Locofoco Parties in the United States with the Life and Public Services of Henry Clay . . . .* Jonesborough, TN: Office of Jonesborough *Whig,* 1844. **(A, G)** This work was written as a campaign tract for the 1844 presidential election. It provides a brief biography of Clay, testimonials to him, and a number of letters and documents.

Clay, Thomas Hart, and Ellis Paxson Oberholtzer. *Henry Clay.* Philadelphia: George W. Jacobs, 1910. **(G)** This work was begun by Clay's grandson, who died in 1907; it was completed by Oberholtzer as a volume in the American Crisis

Biography Series. It emphasizes Clay's oratorical skills as a key to his success and presents the view that his reputation has suffered because the Civil War changed attitudes and obscured the reputation of those men who tried to avert it.

Eaton, Clement. *Henry Clay and the Art of American Politics*. Boston: Little, Brown, 1957. **(A, G)** This brief work provides the best interpretative analysis of Clay's career and the dilemmas he attempted to solve through compromise.

Gantz, Richard Alan. *Henry Clay and the Harvest of Bitter Fruit: The Struggle with John Tyler, 1841–1842*. Ann Arbor: University Microfilms International, 1986. **(A)** This work, which was completed as a doctoral dissertation at Indiana University in 1986, presents the most balanced view of the Clay-Tyler struggle available.

Mallory, Daniel. *The Life and Speeches of the Hon. Henry Clay . . . .* 2 vols. New York: Van Amringe and Bixby, 1843–1844. **(A)** This campaign biography praises Clay and attacks the Jacksonians. The larger portion of it is devoted to speeches.

Maness, Lonnie E. *Henry Clay and the Problem of Slavery*. Ann Arbor: University Microfilms International, 1982. **(A)** This 1980 Ph.D. dissertation from Memphis State University analyzes both the role slavery played in Clay's career and Clay's role in the sectional controversy developing over that issue. The author contends that Clay committed himself to compromise and Unionism during the Missouri controversy and never deviated from it.

Mayo, Bernard. *Henry Clay: Spokesman of the New West*. Boston: Houghton Mifflin, 1937. **(A, G)** This work is the best and most complete description of Clay's early life and career to 1812. It is especially strong in its presentation of the cultural and political milieu which influenced Clay's developing nationalism.

Poage, George R. *Henry Clay and the Whig Party*. Chapel Hill: University of North Carolina Press, 1936. **(A)** This work focuses on the period 1840–1852 but gives an overview of Clay's career up to that time. Although adequately supplied with footnotes, it does contain some errors in chronology.

Prentice, George D. *Biography of Henry Clay*. Hartford, CT: S. Hanmer, Jr. & J. J. Phelps, 1831. **(A, G)** The first biography of Clay, this work served as a campaign document for the 1832 presidential election. It contains an appendix of anecdotes, letters, and testimonials. The author became editor of the Whig newspaper, the Louisville *Journal*.

Sargent, Epes. *The Life and Public Services of Henry Clay Down to 1848; edited and completed at Mr. Clay's death by Horace Greeley*. 2 vols. New York: C. M. Saxton, Barker, 1852. **(A, G)** Published first in 1842, enlarged and reissued in 1844, this biography pleased Clay more than any other completed during his lifetime. While not an exhaustive study in itself, it provides much information. The 1852 edition contains eulogies given in Congress at the time of his death.

Sargent, Nathan (Oliver Oldschool). *Life of Henry Clay*. Philadelphia: R. G. Berford, 1844. **(A, G)** This pamphlet provides a brief summary of Clay's career and refutes at length the corrupt bargain charge. A campaign document for the masses, it sold for three cents a copy.

Schurz, Carl. *Life of Henry Clay*. 2 vols. Boston: Houghton Mifflin, 1887. **(A)** The most thorough and balanced of the nineteenth-century works, this study appeared in the American Statesmen Series. It provides an excellent analysis of Clay's strengths and weaknesses as a leader and rejects many of the myths found in the campaign biographies.

Swain, James B. *The Life and Speeches of Henry Clay*. 2 vols. New York: Greeley & McElrath, 1843. **(A)** The biographical section of this work ends in 1842 with Clay's resignation from the Senate, but does not really cover anything in detail after 1840. Speeches comprise the remainder of the volumes.

Van Deusen, Glyndon G. *The Life of Henry Clay*. Boston: Little, Brown, 1937. **(A)** This work is the most thorough, scholarly study to date.

Van Deusen, Glyndon G. and Editors of Silver Burdett. *Illustrious Americans: Henry Clay*. Morristown, NJ: Silver Burdett, 1967. **(G)** This work is one in a series in which great men and women are studied in three ways—biography, pictures, and his/her own words. In this volume Van Deusen has written the biographical section, while the editors have chosen illustrations and excerpted some 60,000 of Clay's own words. It provides an excellent chronology, index, and annotated bibliography.

Evaluation of Biographies for Young People

Caldwell, Howard W. *Henry Clay: The Great Compromiser*. Chicago: Frederick J. Drake, 1898. This work, written for a general audience of high school level, includes some speeches, letters, and a section called "The Story of Henry Clay, For a School or Club Programme." It contains several errors, such as the first name of Clay's father.

Life of Henry Clay: The Statesman And The Patriot. Boston: Lee and Shepard, 1868. Aimed at the junior high level, this selection in the Young American's Library Series presents Clay as a national hero. It is long on anecdotes and quotations but short on accuracy. No author is given.

Mayo, Barbara. *Henry Clay*. New York: Farrar & Rinehart, 1943. This lively, well-authenticated study stresses Clay's public career rather than his personal life. It is written for the junior high school level.

Wilkie, Katharine E. *The Man Who Wouldn't Give Up: Henry Clay*. New York: Julian Messner, 1961. This biography, written for elementary school children, dwells at length on Clay's early years and skims over his life after 1829. It is, however, historically accurate.

Overview and Evaluation of Primary Sources

Henry Clay manuscripts abound in virtually every major repository in the United States and can be found in many small libraries, archives, and private collections as well. The Papers of Henry Clay editorial project at the University of Kentucky is attempting to acquire copies of all Clay correspondence and speeches for publication in a comprehensive, letterpress edition. Nine volumes have been published to date in *The Papers of Henry Clay*, edited by James F. Hopkins, Mary W. M. Hargreaves, Robert Seager II, and Melba Porter Hay (Lexington, KY: University Press of Kentucky, 1959–; A). When completed, the ten volumes plus supplement will include all known Clay letters in either complete, summarized, or calendared form, along with the location of the original document. The largest collection of original Clay documents is in the Library of Congress.

The earliest attempts to compile and publish primary materials on Clay were Calvin Colton's two works, *The Private Correspondence of Henry Clay* (New York: A. S. Barnes, 1856; A) and his six-volume *The Life, Correspondence, and Speeches of Henry Clay* (New York: A. S. Barnes, 1857; A). Later, Colton's various works were combined into a ten-volume federal edition, *The Works of Henry Clay, Comprising His Life, Correspondence, and Speeches . . .* (New York: G. P. Putnam's Sons, 1904; A), which also included an introduction by Thomas B. Reed and a history of tariff legislation by William McKinley.

In addition to these published sources, Clay's speeches can be found in *Annals of Congress, Register of Debates*, and the *Congressional Globe*.

Fiction and Adaptations

The major fictional biography of Clay is Alfred L. Crabb's *Home to Kentucky, A Novel of Henry Clay* (1953). It begins with Clay's move to Kentucky and includes numerous samples of his oratory. Another work of fiction for elementary school children is Regina Z. Kelly's *Henry Clay: Statesman and Patriot* (1960). This work, which emphasizes his early years, is not always historically accurate.

The National Information Center For Educational Media has produced a number of videotapes dealing with specific aspects of Clay's career. Among these are: "Americans All—A Series," which includes a twenty-minute tape concerning Clay that attempts to deal with his leadership ability and his personal drive and ambition; "Era of Good Feeling—1817–1828," which reviews the stands of such leaders as Clay, Webster, Calhoun, and Monroe on important contemporary issues, including the protective tariff, the national bank, and internal improvements; "John

Quincy Adams, President—1825–1829, parts 1 & 2," both of which deal in part with the corrupt bargain charge against Clay and Adams.

Museums, Historical Landmarks, Societies

Ashland, the Estate of Henry Clay (Lexington, KY). The house, rebuilt by Clay's son James in 1852 on the same foundation and with the same floor plan as the original, sits on twenty acres that were once a part of Clay's six hundred-acre estate. Now owned and operated by the Henry Clay Memorial Foundation, the house and grounds are open for tours. Among the original outbuildings is a pair of early nineteenth-century ice houses.

Other Sources

Coleman, Mrs. Chapman, ed. *The Life of John J. Crittenden with Selections from His Correspondence and Speeches*. 2 vols. Philadelphia: J. B. Lippincott, 1871. **(A)** This work contains many letters between Crittenden and other Whigs discussing party matters and Clay's role in them.

Hamilton, Holman. *Prologue to Conflict: The Crisis and Compromise of 1850*. **(A)** Lexington: University of Kentucky Press, 1964. This work details the congressional history of the Compromise but emphasizes the role of Stephen A. Douglas, not Clay, in its passage.

Hargreaves, Mary W. M. *The Presidency of John Quincy Adams*. Lawrence: University Press of Kansas, 1985. **(A)** This work considers Clay's role as Secretary of State in the Adams administration. The author emphasizes the spirit of nationalism that Clay and Adams shared as they attempted to increase foreign and domestic markets.

Heale, Michael J. *The Presidential Quest: Candidates and Images in American Political Culture, 1787–1852*. London and New York: Longman, 1982. **(A)** This study focuses primarily on presidential elections from 1832 to 1852, comparing the emerging campaign styles of the Democrats and Whigs, as well as the differing popular image each party was attempting to project of its candidates.

McCormick, Richard P. *The Second American Party System: Party Formation in the Jacksonian Era*. Chapel Hill: University of North Carolina Press, 1966. **(A)** This study concludes that the development of the two-party system which emerged between 1824 and 1840 stemmed from the heated presidential contests that took place during the period. McCormick deals with the role Clay played as leader of the faction that became the Whig party.

Moore, Glover. *The Missouri Controversy, 1819–1821*. Lexington: University of Kentucky Press, 1953. **(A)** This work is the most complete account of the sectional controversy which helped give Clay the title of "The Great Compromiser."

Peterson, Merrill D. *Olive Branch and Sword—The Compromise of 1833*. Baton Rouge: Louisiana State University Press, 1982. **(A)** This book presents the best analysis available of Clay's Compromise Tariff of 1833 (the olive branch), as well as Jackson's Force Bill (the sword). Peterson concludes that together the two approaches to the problem of nullification preserved the peace, the Constitution, and the Union in 1833.

Shanks, Henry T.,ed. *The Papers of Willie Person Mangum*. 5 vols. Raleigh: North Carolina State Department of Archives and History, 1953. **(A)** This work includes many references about Clay written by or to his close friend and associate in the Senate.

Melba Porter Hay
The Papers of Henry Clay
University of Kentucky

GROVER CLEVELAND
1837–1908

Chronology

Born Stephen Grover Cleveland on March 18, 1837, in Caldwell, New Jersey, the fifth child of Richard Cleveland, a Presbyterian minister, and Ann Neale Cleveland; *1853* his father dies, and Cleveland is forced to rely upon his own resources until going to live with an uncle in Black Rock, New York; *1855–1859* reads law and is admitted to the bar; serves as a ward supervisor and then as assistant district attorney of Erie County; *1863* purchases a substitute for his military service in order to stay home and support his family; *1871–1873* serves as sheriff of Erie County; *1873* returns to law practice; *1881* wins a sweeping victory when Democrats nominate him for reform mayor of Buffalo to attack graft and corruption; *1882* though relatively unknown, is nominated for reform governor of New York against opposition from New York City's powerful Tammany Hall; *1883* as governor, vetoes what he considers to be fraudulent bills; *1884* selected as a presidential candidate; is the first Democratic president elected since the Civil War; *1886* marries Frances Folsom, with whom he will have five children; *1888* reformism and misunderstanding of a diplomatic affair result in his defeat for reelection; *1889–1892* practices law in New York City and befriends many influential men; *1892* is renominated and reelected for president, becoming the only U.S. president to serve two nonconsecutive terms; *1897–1908* retires to Princeton, New Jersey, where he writes a book about the problems he faced while president; advises against the election of William Jennings Bryan in 1900 and 1908; serves in the reorganization of an insurance company; *1908* dies on June 24, in Princeton, New Jersey, of gastro-intestinal disease complicated by heart and kidney ailments.

Activities of Historical Significance

During his meteoric rise in politics, Cleveland was the essential reformer. Stubbornly honest and independent of judgment, he refused to use his elected positions to reward the "faithful." For this reason, he supported the Civil Service Act of 1883; indeed, in 1885 he refused even to grant interviews to office seekers. He pressured Congress to repeal the Tenure of Office Act of 1867, which restrained presidential power over appointments.

During his first term, he vetoed what he considered fraudulent pension bills and western land claims, and informed supporters of silver coinage that he would use both gold and silver. By signing the Dawes Act, he disestablished the reservation system, which had treated Native Americans as wards of the government. Because of railroad strikes, he urged Congress to give workers greater benefits and rights.

In 1888, a Department of Labor was established. His signing of the Interstate

Commerce Bill introduced the first independent regulatory agency. Although protective tariff rates were sanctioned by most Republicans and some Democrats, he courageously delivered his annual message of 1887 on the need to reduce rates to a tariff-for-revenue only. A rugged individualist, he declined to approve a bill that would provide seeds to drought-stricken farmers, yet he signed the Hatch Act, which provided federal subsidies for the creation of agricultural experiment stations.

The only nationally known member of his first term cabinet was Secretary of State Thomas F. Bayard, but he gave southerners two cabinet posts and put still another southerner on the Supreme Court. This ended northern predominance that had continued since the Civil War. Through William C. Whitney, he reformed and strengthened the "steel" Navy.

During his second term he again opposed some Democrats and most Republicans on tariff reform. He considered the Wilson-Gorman tariff act (1894) so unacceptable that he let it become law without his signature.

Although most Democrats and Populists and some Republicans were opposed, he favored retaining the gold standard rather than adopting free silver. Despite the severe depression that rocked the nation beginning in May 1893, he succeeded in stopping governmental purchase of silver; by selling bonds for gold, he upheld the gold standard, called "sound money." This meant that debtors would have to repay creditors in appreciated money.

On the grounds that order must be maintained and "the mails must go through," in 1894 he used federal troops to stop the Pullman strike that threatened rail service. Eugene V. Debs went to jail for violating an injunction to end this strike.

A noninterventionist and anti-imperialist in foreign affairs, Cleveland rejected a treaty which provided for the acquisition of the Hawaiian Islands and another that would have acquired a canal route through Nicaragua. The Senate obstructed his attempts to settle fisheries' problems with Great Britain, but when the parties involved failed to arbitrate the British Guiana-Venezuela boundary line (1893–1895), he invoked the Monroe Doctrine, adding that if the British did not comply with his wishes he would have the boundary surveyed and, if necessary, fight to uphold the line. Faced with many other problems, the British caved in. His Senate then rejected a general arbitration treaty with Britain (1897). With respect to those who desired him to go to war or to at least recognize the Cuban revolt against Spain, Cleveland rejected intervention, but enforced America's neutrality laws and warned Spain that war would ensue if she did not stop her "senseless slaughter."

At the Democratic national convention of 1896, the Cleveland administration was repudiated, and William Jennings Bryan was named to face his Republican opponent, William McKinley. His second term finished, Cleveland decided to live in Princeton, New Jersey. There his last two children were born, and he was elected as trustee of Princeton University. Toward the end of his life, he rejected demands that he run again for president and served as one of the three trustees to supervise a reorganization of the Equitable Life Assurance Company. Not tall, he weighed about 250 pounds and in his last years suffered from gastro-intestinal disease and heart and kidney ailments. He died in Princeton, where he was buried.

Overview of Biographical Sources

The first works on Cleveland were quickly written campaign biographies: Chauncey F. Black, *Life and Public Services of Grover Cleveland and Thomas A. Hendricks* (1884); Herman Dieck, *Life and Public Services of Our Great Reform President, Grover Cleveland* (1888); William Forsheimer, *Life and Public Services of Grover Cleveland* (1888); Frederick E. Goodrich, *Life and Public Services of Grover Cleveland* (1884); William U. Hensel and George F. Parker, *Life and Public Services of Grover Cleveland* (1892); Pendleton King, *Life and Public Services of Grover Cleveland* (1884); J. B. McClure, ed., *The Life of Honorable Grover Cleveland* (1884); W. P. Nixon, ed., *A Man of Destiny* (1885); William O. Stoddard, *Grover Cleveland* (1888); and Deshler Welch, *Stephen Grover Cleveland* (1884). Stoddard's biography is the best of this group.

An extended biographical sketch appears in volumes 3 and 4 of D. A. S. Alexander, *Four Famous New Yorkers: The Political Careers of Cleveland, Platt, Hill, and Roosevelt* (1923). A very favorable evaluation which stresses the human side of his subject is found in Richard Watson Gilder, *Grover Cleveland: A Record of Friendship* (1910). A short, laudatory piece is Ronald Hugins, *Grover Cleveland: A Study in Political Courage* (1922); another is Denis Tilden Lynch, *Grover Cleveland: A Man Four-Square* (1932), which contains end notes but no bibliography. A longer work is Robert McElroy, *Grover Cleveland: The Man and Statesman* (1923). Samuel Merrill has written *Bourbon Leader: Grover Cleveland and the Democratic Party* (1957), yet the best biography is that by Allan Nevins, *Grover Cleveland: A Study in Courage* (1932). Nevins also wrote the biographical sketch for the *Dictionary of American Biography*. Much on Cleveland appears in George F. Parker, *Recollections of Grover Cleveland* (1909); Parker was closely associated with Cleveland during his last years. Rexford Tugwell, *Grover Cleveland* (1968), is a laudatory and undocumented biography: Richard E. Welch, Jr., *The Presidencies of Grover Cleveland* (1988), concentrates on Cleveland's two presidential terms.

Cleveland is frequently mentioned in Oscar Straus, *Under Four Administrations: From Cleveland to Taft* (1922), and William Allen White devotes four unflattering chapters to him in *Masks in a Pageant* (1928). His times are covered in H. J. Ford, *The Cleveland Era* (1921), J. Rogers Hollingsworth, *The Whirligig of Politics: The Democracy of Cleveland and Bryan* (1963), and James K. McGuire, ed., *The Democratic Party of the State of New York* (1905).

Evaluation of Principal Biographical Sources

Lynch, Denis Tilden. *Grover Cleveland: A Man Four-Square.* New York: Horace Liveright, 1932. **(A, G)** The author proceeds chronologically with Cleveland's ancestry and schooling; reform activities in his first political offices; battles with Tammany Hall in both New York State and national politics; narratives of the national conventions of 1884–1904; domestic and foreign problems and accomplishments of his first administration; his marriage; activities while a New York lawyer; domestic and foreign problems and the accomplishments of his second administration; and his last years at Princeton. The book contains letters to and from Cleveland that illuminate many subjects. Lynch sees President Cleveland as a courageous reformer, particularly in civil service, currency, and tariff matters, and as a noninterventionist in foreign affairs. Capable of close friendship with a few, especially those who liked to fish, he remained steadfastly opposed to the liberal and progressive ideas of the Bryan wing of Democracy and Populism.

McElroy, Robert. *Grover Cleveland, The Man and Statesman: An Authorized Biography*. New York: Harper and Brothers, 1923. **(A, G)** Traces Cleveland's early environment and heredity; his activities as reform mayor of Buffalo and governor of New York; the national conventions, campaigns, and elections of 1884; and the problems and accomplishments of his first term as president. McElroy sees Cleveland as a rugged and courageous man who dared to disregard party in the service of principle.

Nevins, Allan. *Grover Cleveland: A Study in Courage*. New York: Dodd, Mead, 1932. **(A, G)** Like Lynch and McElroy, Nevins proceeds chronologically. He covers the same subjects but adds materials unavailable to earlier biographers, and makes greater use of official documents. He sees Cleveland as a ruggedly honest man of dual personalities—the jovial man of leisure, and the stern man of duty. He deals skillfully with the Mugwump campaign of 1884 and subsequent campaigns in which Cleveland was involved. More than others, Nevins is aware of the changing times in which Cleveland lived.

Welch, Richard E., Jr. *The Presidencies of Grover Cleveland*. Lawrence: University Press of Kansas, 1988. **(A, G)** For Cleveland's first term, Welch deals with his handling of three major subjects: labor, silver, and the tariff. He follows with two chapters on Cleveland's direction of foreign affairs, then proceeds to the second term, where again the issues of labor, silver, and the tariff predominate. Welch notes the contradictions in the philosophy and personality of Cleveland and offers a critique of his political leadership.

Overview and Evaluation of Primary Sources

During his retirement, Cleveland wrote about his years as chief executive in *Presidential Problems* (New York: Century, 1904; **A, G**), which includes his version of the Venezuela boundary controversy, Pullman strike, and independence of the president. The essays contained in *Presidential Problems* were also published separately as magazine articles and booklets.

A microfilm version and an index of Cleveland's papers are in the Manuscript Division of the Library of Congress. Fortunately, Allan Nevins succeeded in deciphering Cleveland's almost illegible handwriting and edited the most pertinent letters in *The Letters of Grover Cleveland, 1850–1908* (1933. Reprint. New York: Da Capo Press, 1970; **A, G**). His messages to Congress and other pronouncements may be found in volumes 8 and 9 of James D. Richardson, comp., *Messages and Papers of the Presidents of the United States* (Washington: Government Printing Office, 1896; **A**). Robert I. Vexler, ed., *Grover Cleveland, 1837–1908* (Dobbs Ferry, NY: Oceana Publications, 1968; **A**), contains many important documents. Other notable published primary sources are *The Public Papers of Grover Cleveland, Twenty-Second President of the United States, March 4, 1885, to March 4, 1889* (Washington: Government Printing Office, 1889; **A**); *The Public Papers of Grover Cleveland, Twenty-Fourth President of the United States, March 4, 1893, to March 4, 1897* (Washington: Government Printing Office, 1897; **A**); *The Public Papers of Grover Cleveland as Governor* (Albany: Argus, 1883–1884; **A**); Albert Ellery Bergh, ed., *Letters of Grover Cleveland* (New York: Unit Book Company, 1909; **A**); and George F. Parker, ed., *Writings and Speeches of Grover Cleveland* (New York: Cassell, 1892; **A**). The last contains topically arranged documents from 1881 to 1892.

Most relevant among the papers of his acquaintances are several collections in the Library of Congress—William Jennings Bryan, Walter Q. Gresham, Charles Hamlin, Daniel S. Lamont, Richard Olney, Joseph Pulitzer, William C. Whitney, and Woodrow Wilson—and those of John Peter Altgeld (Illinois State Historical Society, Springfield); George S. Bixby (New York State Library, Albany); and J. Sterling Morton (University of Nebraska-Lincoln).

Museums, Historical Landmarks, Societies

Cleveland Birthplace (Caldwell, NJ). On Cleveland's seventieth birthday, friends placed a bronze tablet in the room where he was born, which also contains artifacts of his life and times.

Cleveland Gravesite (Princeton, NJ). Above his grave at the "old Princeton Cemetery," an engraved granite shaft has been erected.

Cleveland Memorial Tower (Princeton, NJ). Paid for by public subscription, this national memorial rests about a mile from Cleveland's home.

Other Sources

Ashby, LeRoy. *William Jennings Bryan and His Democracy*. Boston: Twayne,

1987. A very readable condensation of Bryan's life that emphasizes the contrast between the political ideas of Bryan and Cleveland.

Blodgett, Geoffrey. "The Political Leadership of Grover Cleveland." *South Atlantic Quarterly* 82 (Summer 1983): 288–299. A good short analysis.

Calhoun, Charles C. "Rehearsal for Anti-Imperialism: The Second Cleveland Administration's Attempt to Withdraw from Samoa, 1893–1895." *Historian* 48 (February 1986): 209–224. Cleveland's stand on Samoa typified his anti-imperialist and noninterventionist ideals.

Campbell, Charles S., Jr. *The Transformation of American Foreign Relations, 1865–1900*. New York: Harper & Row, 1976. Includes extensive information on foreign policy during Cleveland's administration.

Coletta, Paolo. *William Jennings Bryan: Political Evangelist, 1860–1908*. Lincoln: University of Nebraska Press, 1964. Much on the Bryan-Cleveland battle for control of the Democratic party, with heavy emphasis on their differing view on the currency question.

Ginger, Ray. *The Bending Cross: A Biography of Eugene Victor Debs*. Brunswick: Rutgers University Press, 1949. Excellent on the Pullman strike and Debs's presidential campaigns.

Glad, Paul W. *The Trumpet Soundeth: William Jennings Bryan and His Democracy*. Lincoln: University of Nebraska Press, 1960. A good deal of coverage of the Bryan-Cleveland conflict.

Gompers, Samuel. *Seventy Years of Life and Labor*. 2 vols. New York: Dutton, 1925. Gompers discusses Cleveland's lack of sympathy for labor.

Hirsch, Mark D. *William C. Whitney: Modern Warwick*. New York: Dodd, Mead, 1948. On Whitney's influence on Cleveland's political career and his work as reform secretary of the Navy.

White, William Allen. *Masks in a Pageant*. New York: Macmillan, 1928. White's animus is clear from the titles of the four chapters he devotes to Cleveland: "His Accidency," "His Excellency," "His Obstinacy," and "His Complacency."

Paolo E. Coletta
U.S. Naval Academy (Ret.)

CHRISTOPHER COLUMBUS
1451-1506

Chronology

Born Cristoforo Colombo between August 25 and October 31, 1451, in the Olivella district of Genoa, Italy, the eldest of five children of Domenico Colombo, a wool weaver, and Susanna Fontanarossa Colombo, daughter of a wool weaver; *mid-1470s* appears in Lisbon, where his brother Bartholomew keeps a shop which sells charts and nautical instruments; *c.1479* marries a Portuguese lady of lesser nobility, Felipa de Perestrello, daughter of one of Prince Henry the Navigator's captains; *c.1480* birth of his son Diego; *1482* King John II of Portugal refuses his proposition for a westward expedition to Japan; *1485-1486* arrives in Spain and first meets with Ferdinand and Isabella of Spain, who are too busy fighting the Moors of Granada to support his proposal; *1488* in Cordoba, Columbus, now a widower, takes as his mistress Beatriz Enríquez de Haraña, who bears his son Fernando; *January 2, 1492* Ferdinand and Isabella capture Granada from the Moors and can now afford to support Columbus; *August 3, 1492* sails from Palos in the three caravels provided by the Spanish monarchs; *October 12, 1492* lands on an island of the Bahamas, which he names San Salvador; *March 1493* arrives triumphant in Spain and prepares for his second voyage with 17 ships and 1,200 men; *November 3, 1493* reaches the West Indies, passing Dominica, the Virgin Islands, Puerto Rico, and Haiti; *1498* on his third voyage, discovers Trinidad and the Gulf of Paria; *1500* is arrested in Santo Domingo by the royal emissary, Francisco de Bobadilla and returned to Spain in chains; *1502* his fourth expedition reaches Martinique, Honduras, and Panama, where he learns that another ocean lies a few days' march across the mountains; *1504* returns to Spain, but Queen Isabella dies before he can meet with her; *1506* dies on May 20 at Valladolid.

Activities of Historical Significance

As the first European who brought Europe to the Western hemisphere and opened it to European influence and colonization, Columbus had one of the most unique experiences in the history of mankind. The romantic element in his story is enhanced by the fact that he never realized the magnitude of his accomplishment. Also legendary is his remarkable persistence in the face of adversity, epitomized in the final lines of Joaquin Miller's famous poem, "Columbus": "He gained a world; he gave that world / Its greatest lesson: 'Oh! sail on!' "

The demands that Columbus made in exchange for his voyage of discovery were great; they included an admiralty and noble rank to be inherited by his sons. When Queen Isabella at long last acceded to his demands, no discoverer had ever been promised so much before proving his worth. But in the proving never had a discoverer's worth so greatly exceeded his promise.

Columbus had a sense of divine mission and was fully aware of the etymological implications of the name Christopher ("bearer of Christ across the area"). His monogram, combining both Latin and Greek initials, read, "I am Christopher, servant of the Most High Saviour, Christ, Son of Mary."

As a colonial administrator he was inept and mistrustful of anyone except the members of his own family. Yet while Queen Isabella was alive, he was always able to convince the court to side with him. He even managed to benefit from his arrest in Santo Domingo and his return to Spain in chains; and even after the death of his benefactress, he lived without financial difficulty. But he was deeply unhappy, seeking to secure his family's future to the fullest, and especially resentful of younger mariners who continued to make astounding discoveries. The chain of events that made up his life served to usher in a new, unforeseen age of hope, enterprise, and renewed human self-esteem.

In his 1978 book, *The 100: A Ranking of the Most Influential Persons in History*, Michael H. Hart ranked Columbus ninth, immediately following Johann Gutenberg and preceding Albert Einstein.

Overview of Biographical Sources

As the nations of the Americas became independent entities, growing interest was accorded to the figure of Christopher Columbus. Washington Irving, intending originally only to translate Martin Fernández de Navarrete's collected materials on Columbus, decided instead to research his own full-length biography that ran well over a thousand pages. For more than a century following its appearance in 1828, Irving's *The Life and Voyages of Christopher Columbus* was the definitive biography of Columbus in the English-speaking world. Samuel Eliot Morison, the naval historian of World War II, superseded Irving in 1942 with his two-volume *Admiral of the Ocean Sea*, adapted to one volume (minus its wealth of bibliographic material) the same year with the same title. This was further abridged for younger readers as *Christopher Columbus: Mariner* (1955). Paolo Emilio Taviani, an Italian senator and professor at the University of Genoa, was equally devoted to the study of Columbus. Morison himself earlier awaited the appearance in Italy of Taviani's three-volume biography, which was reduced to a single volume when translated into English as *Christopher Columbus: The Grand Design* (1985). In this country, Morison's work has yet to be superseded, although in 1986 Joseph Judge, the senior associate editor of *National Geographic*, claimed to have improved upon the trajectory of the first Columbus voyage as tracked by Morison in "Our Search for the True Columbus Landfall," *National Geographic* (November, 1986).

Evaluation of Principal Biographical Sources

Granzotto, Gianni. *Christopher Columbus*. Translated by Stephen Sartarelli. New York: Doubleday, 1985. (G) Written like a novel, this work is filled with unverifiable details that drive scholars mad. Nonetheless, Granzotto takes a firm stand against the Madariaga theory that Columbus was Jewish, claiming that for Madariaga the history of Spain's Jews is like a spiderweb that extends everywhere.

Guardini, Cesare. *The Life and Times of Columbus*. Translated by Frances Lanza. New York: Curtis Books, 1967. (G, Y) Only 75 pages but lavishly illustrated in color with a gallery of Columbus portraits. An appendix provides a chronology of Columbus's life.

Irving, Washington. *The Life and Voyages of Christopher Columbus*. 1828. Reprint. Boston: Twayne, 1981. (G) Although demonstrating craftsman-like historiography, much of the writing is sentimental and idealized, and Irving chooses to perpetuate some of the more fanciful myths about Columbus.

Landström, Björn. *Columbus*. Translated by Michael Phillips and Hugh W. Stubbs. New York: Macmillan, 1966. (G) Copiously illustrated with maps and drawings, and particularly strong on the subject of Columbus's ships, their provisions and equipment.

Madariaga, Salvador de. *Christopher Columbus*. New York: Macmillan, 1940. (G) Relentlessly pursuing the case for a Jewish Columbus, this author maintains that the admiral was born in Genoa of Spanish Jewish parents (his mother's name was the Hebrew Susanna). In Spain, Colón was a Jewish surname, and a Jewish ancestry would explain why Columbus so readily abandoned the Italian form Colombo and reverted to what he may have conceived as an earlier form.

Morison, Samuel Eliot. *Admiral of the Ocean Sea*. Boston: Little, Brown, 1942. (G) Unsurpassed as a biography, and especially strong on navigational detail since its author followed most of the admiral's journals from port to port in his own yacht. Unfortunately, the single-volume version that is most readily available is shorn of all bibliography.

―――――. *The European Discovery of America: The Southern Voyages, 1492–1616*. New York: Oxford, 1974. (A) Contains the exhaustive bibliographical notes necessary to complement the single-volume version of the previously cited work.

Taviani, Paolo Emilio. *Christopher Columbus: The Grand Design*. London: Orbis, 1985. (G) Lavishly illustrated in color, this truncated masterpiece in its English version offers ample bibliography after each chapter.

Evaluation of Biographies for Young People

Ceserani, Gian Paolo, and Piero Ventura. *Christopher Columbus*. New York:

Random House, 1978. The familiar story is here told brightly and with good humor. Colorful sketches appear on each page. For elementary school students.

Dalgliesh, Alice. *The Columbus Story*. Color illustrations by Leo Politi. New York: Charles Scribner's Sons, 1955. The book is intended to be read aloud, and it uses the Admiral's own words as refrains in the text. For elementary school students.

Foster, Genevieve. *The World of Christopher Columbus and Sons*. Illustrated by the author. New York: Charles Scribner's Sons, 1965. This substantial (406 pages) treatment of the age of Columbus includes an index and numerous sketches, diagrams and signature facsimiles. For high school students.

Fritz, Jean. *Where Do You Think You're Going, Christopher Columbus?* Illustrated by Margot Jones. New York: Putnam, 1980. An interesting account of Columbus and his voyages. For elementary school students.

McGovern, Ann. *The Story of Columbus*. Illustrations by Joe Lasker. New York: Random House, 1962. A standard retelling of the Columbus story for young children.

Showers, Paul. *Columbus Day*. Illustrated by Ed Emberley. New York: Thomas Y. Crowell, 1965. Tells the story of Columbus with special attention to why and how the holiday is celebrated in various locales. For elementary school students.

Sperry, Armstrong. *The Voyages of Christopher Columbus*. New York: Random House, 1950. Illustrated by the author. Beginning with the arrival of Columbus at Palos in the mid–1480s, the story is told from the point of view of his young son Diego. For junior high and high school students.

Weil, Lisl. *I, Christopher Columbus*. Illustrated by the author. New York: Atheneum, 1983. A basic biography for elementary school students. For an older audience, Weil wrote an earlier work, *Columbus: Founder of the New World* (New York: Morrow, 1952).

Overview and Evaluation of Primary Sources

The most accessible assemblage of original materials in English translation is *The Journals and Other Documents on the Life and Voyages of Christopher Columbus*, translated and edited by Samuel Eliot Morison (New York: Heritage Press, 1963; **A, G**). This includes the all-important journal of the first voyage, documents on the early life of Columbus, the Toscanelli correspondence, his first Letter to the Spanish Sovereigns, and narratives and documents of the other three voyages. Also included are passages from the biography of Columbus written by his illegitimate son Fernando Colón (1488–1539), the text of which survived only in its Italian version *Historie del S. D. Fernando Colombo; nelle quali s'ha particolare, & vera relatione della vita, & de' fatti dell'Ammiraglio D. Christoforo Colombo, suo padre* (1571). This work, translated and annotated by Benjamin Keen as *The Life of the Admiral Christopher Columbus* (New Brunswick, NJ: Rutgers University Press, 1959; **A, G**), is one of the most important sources on the life of Columbus. Certainly Colón exaggerated many facts, but as Samuel Eliot Morison sagely observed, the book "needs no more discounting than does any biography of a distinguished father by a devoted son."

Long sections from the Fernando Colón biography are excerpted in J. M. Cohen's *The Four Voyages of Christopher Columbus: Being His Own Log-Book, Letters and Dispatches with Connecting Narrative Drawn from the Life of the Admiral by His Son Hernando Colón and Other Contemporary Historians* (Baltimore: Penguin Books, 1969; **A, G**). A bilingual edition of *The Journal of the First Voyage*, translated and edited by Barry Ife of Birkbeck College, London, is scheduled for publication in 1990 by Aris and Phillips Ltd., London.

Several important works have not been translated from the Spanish or Italian, and are not readily available in the U.S. Bartolomé de las Casas (1474–1566), called the Apostle of the Indians, was the first to edit the now lost journals of Columbus, and these appear in his *Historia de las Indias*, mostly written between 1550 and 1563 but not published for over 300 years (Madrid; n.p., 1875; **A**). Las Casas, the son and nephew of Columbus's shipmates on the second voyage, criticized him for his enslavement of the Indians and for his imperfect command of both written and spoken Spanish, but nonetheless basically admired the admiral. Gonzalo Fernández de Oviedo y Valdés, who witnessed the triumph of Columbus in Barcelona in 1493, wrote *Historia general y natural de las Indias* (n.p., 1535; **A**), which includes an account of Columbus and his voyages as well.

The beginning of all source collections for the maritime aspect of Columbus's life is by Martin Fernández de Navarrete, *Colección de los viages y descubrimientos que hicieron por mar los Españoles desde fines del siglo XV*, 5 vols. (Madrid: n.p., 1825–1837; **A**). The best texts of almost all sources are included in the 14 volumes of the *Raccolta di documenti e studi pubblicati della R. Commissione Columbiana* (Rome: n.p., 1892–1894; **A**), which was compiled by the classical scholar Cesare di Lollis in preparation for the Italian government's celebration of the 400th anniversary of the discovery of America.

Fiction and Adaptations

Columbus is the subject of well-known poems by James Russell Lowell, "Columbus" (1847); Walt Whitman, "The Prayer of Columbus" (1874); Joaquin Miller, "Columbus" (1896); and Franklin Pierce Adams, whose "Christopher Columbus" (1931) begins, "In Fourteen Hundred and Ninety-Two / Columbus sailed the ocean blue." In 1927, plays about Columbus were written by both Paul Claudel and Michel de Ghelderode. Other writers who have treated the Columbus legend in their works include Lope de Vega, Jakob Wassermann, Riccardo Bacchelli, Massimo Bontempelli and Alejo Carpentier. Literally hundreds of juvenile books on Columbus have appeared in English, Spanish, and Italian.

In 1987 Stephen Marlowe wrote *The Memoirs of Christopher Columbus*, a novel which presents an omniscient Columbus poking fun at his own biographers, even quoting from the polemic between Morison and Madariaga over his alleged Judaism. Significantly, in the Marlowe novel the Judaism of Columbus is accepted as factual.

In 1949, the biographical film *Christopher Columbus* was released in Great Britain. Directed by David MacDonald and starring Frederic March and Florence Eldridge, it was lavish but otherwise unremarkable. Three decades later, Italian and American television collaborated on a splashy six-hour television mini-series, also titled *Christopher Columbus*, which aired over CBS on May 19 and 20, 1985. It cost $15 million to produce, was filmed in Malta, Spain, and the Dominican Republic, and involved 46 major roles, 82 minor ones and more than 200 speaking parts by actors from 10 different countries. Nicol Williamson and Faye Dunaway portrayed the King and Queen of Spain, and Irish actor Gabriel Byrne played Columbus; the cast also included Virna Lisi, Eli Wallach, Rossano Brazzi, Oliver Reed, Raf Vallone and Max Von Sydow. The film was directed by Alberto Lattuada with the assistance of Italian scholar Paolo Emilio Taviani.

Museums, Historical Landmarks, Societies

Christopher Columbus Family Chapel (Boalsburg, PA). The interior of the sixteenth-century Christopher Columbus Chapel was brought to the U.S. from Spain in 1919, and is now housed at the Boal Mansion and Museum.

Christopher Columbus Monument (Genoa, Italy). Located opposite the Principe Railway Station.

Columbus Day (October 12). In the U.S., the day was first celebrated in New York in 1792. In 1892 President Benjamin Harrison asked that Columbus Day be made a national holiday, and it has been celebrated officially since 1920. In most of the Latin American countries, October 12th is designated as Día de la Raza.

Columbus Door (Washington, DC). Located in the central portico of the United States Capitol, with eight panels and a semi-circular transom depicting scenes from the life of Columbus.

Columbus Fountain (Washington, DC). A semi-circular fountain in front of Union Station.

Columbus Statue (Liverpool, England). Located on the portico of the Exchange Building.

Columbus Statue and Santa Maria Replica (Barcelona, Spain). At the end of the Ramblas in the Plaza de la Puerta de la Paz there is a bronze statue of Columbus mounted on a huge column that may be climbed for a fine view of the harbor. Anchored in the water nearby is a reconstruction of the Santa Maria, the flagship of Columbus.

House of Columbus (Genoa, Italy). A modest, vine-covered building on the Piazza Dante, off the Vico Dritto Ponticello. The eighteenth-century reconstruction at the site of what may have been the home of Christopher Columbus is not open to the public.

Knights of Columbus. A society devoted to promoting friendship between Catholics and non-Catholics, charity and education. Founded in New Haven, Connecticut, in 1882, the society helped to establish October 12th as Columbus Day in many states.

Other Sources

Curtis, William Eleroy. *Christopher Columbus: His Portraits and His Monuments*. Chicago: W. H. Lowdermilk, 1893. A valuable catalogue of Columbus portraits and memorials up to the end of the nineteenth century.

Judge, Joseph. "Our Search for the True Columbus Landfall." *National Geographic* 170 (November 1986): 564–605. Maintains that if the Columbus track is retraced with allowance for current and leeway, the end point falls about 60 miles to the south of Watling Island at Samana Cay. This is the first major contradiction to the Morison canon of Columbus studies.

Menéndez Pidal, Ramón. *La lengua de Cristóbal Colón*. Buenos Aires: Espasa Calpe, 1942. Analyzing the Spanish writings of Columbus as transcribed by las Casas, Pidal concludes that Columbus was probably a speaker of Portuguese and rejects the possibility of a Jewish background on linguistic evidence alone. The article has not been translated, but a summary of Pidal's conclusions can be found in Steven Hess, *Ramón Menéndez Pidal* (Boston: Twayne, 1982).

Roth, C. "Columbus, Christopher." In *Encyclopedia Judaica Jerusalem*, edited by C. Roth. Vol. 5. New York: Macmillan, 1971. This controversial article, blasted by Samuel Eliot Morison as ponderous and riddled with innuendo, concludes that it is impossible to exclude or confirm the hypothesis that Columbus descended from a Jewish family.

Stewart, George R. *Names on the Globe*. New York: Oxford University Press, 1975. The chapter "Columbus and Revolution" examines the toponymic legacy of Columbus in the New World. Because Columbus appears to have been a man of "considerable egotism," according to Stewart, it is remarkable that he named no site after either himself or any of his comrades.

Jack Shreve
Allegany Community College

Landing of Columbus, 1893

CALVIN COOLIDGE
1872–1933

Chronology

Born John Calvin Coolidge on July 4, 1872, in Plymouth Notch, Vermont, to John Calvin Coolidge, who runs a general store and post office, and Victoria Josephine Moor Coolidge; *1872–1895* grows up in Plymouth Notch and is educated in local schools; his mother dies in 1885 following childbirth; his father remains a widower for seven years before remarrying; attends Amherst College; *1895* graduates cum laude and as class orator; *1896* speaks in favor of the gold standard during this critical election year; *1897* reads law and is admitted to the bar; begins law practice in Northampton, Massachusetts; becomes a member of the city council; *1899–1902* serves as city solicitor; *1904* chairs the Republican City Committee; *1905* marries Grace Anna Goodhue, a teacher of the deaf, on October 4; *1906–1910* serves in the Massachusetts House of Representatives; his sons John and Calvin are born; *1910–1911* serves as mayor of Northampton; *1911* elected to the state senate; *1915* elected lieutenant governor; *1918* elected governor; *1919* attains national recognition when he opposes a Boston police strike in a letter to Samuel Gompers, head of the American Federation of Labor; *1920* is soundly defeated by Warren G. Harding in bid for the Republican presidential nomination; wins the vice-presidency; *1923* assumes the presidency upon Harding's death on August 2; quickly restores honesty and integrity to an administration plagued by rumors of corruption; *1924* his son Calvin dies of a blood infection; easily wins presidential election; *1928–1933* spends his last years in Northampton; writes his autobiography; writes a syndicated column extolling the virtues of laissez-faire and rugged individualism; serves as a lifetime trustee of Amherst College; *1933* dies on January 5 in Northampton of a coronary thrombosis.

Activities of Historical Significance

Coolidge climbed every rung of the political ladder, but he cannot be rated as a strong president; he administered rather than led and often failed to direct events, or even to respond to them effectively. In proclaiming treaties written at the Washington Naval Disarmament Conference of 1921–1922, he merely formalized work accomplished by Harding. Nothing came of the naval disarmament conference held in Geneva in 1927, and the Kellogg-Briand peace pact of 1928 was also ineffectual. With respect to the repayment of war debts, he made the cryptic remark, "They hired the money, didn't they?" By signing the Immigration Act of 1924, which excluded Asians, he greatly offended the Japanese.

On the other hand, he wisely chose his Amherst College classmate, Dwight Morrow, to head an investigation into the correct employment of air power, and later to handle the volatile Mexican problem that in part grew out of Mexico's expropriation of oil properties. Assigning Henry L. Stimson to handle problems in Nicaragua was another good decision. Also commendable were Coolidge's withdrawal of Marines from the Dominican Republic, and his approval of a bill that granted Native Americans citizenship and of the Rogers Act to reorganize the Department of State.

Coolidge was considered "the high priest of prosperity." During his administration, lack of regulation led to unwieldy big business growth and uncontrolled speculation on a stock market that rocketed upward. Such supposedly regulatory bodies as the Federal Trade Commission and the Tariff Commission were encouraged to support rather than control big business. Suffering farmers, miners, and other workers received no assistance. While Coolidge approved raising protective tariff rates, lower taxes for the wealthy, and reducing the national debt, he vetoed measures that would support farm prices (McNary-Haugen bills, 1927, 1928) and build a hydroelectric dam at Muscle Shoals, Alabama. Perhaps an intuition that an economic depression impended led to his August 1927 announcement: "I do not choose to run for President in 1928."

Overview of Biographical Sources

Very little was written about Coolidge outside of Massachusetts until, as governor, he intervened in the Boston police strike of 1919. This incident boosted him into consideration for the presidency, and several ephemeral campaign biographies appeared: Horace Green, *The Life of Calvin Coolidge* (1924); M. E. Hennessey, *Calvin Coolidge: From a Green Mountain Farm to the White House* (1924); Roland D. Sawyer, *Cal Coolidge: President* (1924); and R. M. Washburn, *Calvin Coolidge: His First Biography* (1924).

Various aspects of his life and ideas are covered in several other books written before his death: Ernest C. Carpenter, *The Boyhood Days of Calvin Coolidge* (1925); Duff Gilfond, *The Rise of Saint Calvin* (1932); Thomas T. Johnson, *Have Faith in Calvin Coolidge* (1925); Edward Elwell Whiting, *Calvin Coolidge: His Ideas of Citizenship* (1924); and Robert A. Woods, *The Preparation of Calvin Coolidge* (1924).

Assessments of Coolidge and his administration by contemporaries and associates are found in Edward Connery Latham, *Meet Calvin Coolidge: The Man Behind the Myth* (1960); C. Bascom Slemp, ed., *The Mind of the President* (1926); Henry L. Stoddard, *As I Knew Them: Presidents and Politics from Grant to Coolidge* (1927); Charles W. Thomson, *Presidents I've Known and Two Near-Presidents* (1929); and James Watson, *As I Knew Them* (1936).

The most valuable biography is Donald R. McCoy, *Calvin Coolidge: The Quiet President* (1967). Also noteworthy are Claude M. Fuess's official biography, *Calvin Coolidge: The Man from Vermont* (1940), and William Allen White's two works, *Calvin Coolidge: The Man Who Is President* (1925) and *A Puritan in Babylon: The Story of Calvin Coolidge* (1938).

Evaluation of Principal Biographical Sources

Fuess, Claude M. *Calvin Coolidge: The Man from Vermont*. Boston: Little, Brown, 1940. (**A, G**) The official biography is the product of several years' extensive research. One-half of the account is devoted to Coolidge's antecedents and career in Massachusetts; the other half addresses his experiences in national politics. Despite his defensive tone, Fuess acknowledges that Coolidge accomplished little of value.

McCoy, Donald R. *Calvin Coolidge: The Quiet President*. New York: Macmillan, 1967. (**A, G**) This comprehensive and valuable work covers its subject's personal and public life. A specialist on the 1920s and 1930s, McCoy seeks to reassess Coolidge and his administration, striking a balance between Coolidge worshippers and those who saw him as a "know-nothing, do-nothing" president.

White, William Allen. *Calvin Coolidge: The Man Who Is President*. New York: Macmillan, 1925. (**A, G**) Writing as a journalist rather than as a historian, White seeks "to find the man behind his mask of protective modesty."

―――. *Masks in a Pageant*. New York: Macmillan, 1928, pp. 435–462. (**A, G**) An essay on Coolidge, asserting that he was "divinely fitted for the job" but "exhibited absolutely no initiative."

―――. *A Puritan in Babylon: The Story of Calvin Coolidge*. New York: Macmillan, 1938. (**A, G**) In this fuller study, the author relates Coolidge to his times, especially during the years 1923–1929, and bases his text upon personal interviews with Coolidge and men who knew him, such as Dwight W. Morrow and Herbert Hoover.

Overview and Evaluation of Primary Sources

Upon leaving the presidency, Coolidge wrote his *Autobiography* (New York: Cosmopolitan, 1929; **A, G**). Although characterized as bland and unrevealing, the work is of some value to readers already familiar with Coolidge's era. Coolidge published three other works before and during his presidency: *Have Faith in Massachusetts: A Collection of Speeches and Messages by Calvin Coolidge* (Boston:

Houghton Mifflin, 1919; **A, G**); *The Price of Freedom* (New York: Charles Scribner's Sons,1924; **A, G**); and *Foundations of the Republic: Speeches and Addresses* (New York: Charles Scribner's Sons, 1926: **A, G**).

A collection of Coolidge papers, including official papers, family photographs, and memorabilia, is in the Calvin Coolidge Memorial Room of Forbes Library, Northampton, Massachusetts. The largest collection of Coolidge Papers can be found in the Manuscript Division, Library of Congress, but because Coolidge ordered his personal papers destroyed the value of this collection is limited. A microfilm copy and index are available. Small collections exist in the libraries of Amherst and Holy Cross Colleges.

Philip R. Moran, ed., *Calvin Coolidge, 1872–1933: Chronology, Documents, Bibliographical Aids* (Dobbs Ferry, NY: Oceana Publications, 1970; **A, G**), contains the most important presidential documents.

Other documents, messages, and speeches can be found in the *Congressional Record*, in the appropriate volumes of the *Papers Relating to Foreign Affairs of the United States*, in reports made by cabinet members either to the president or to Congress, and in printed versions of presidential messages provided by the Government Printing Office. For Coolidge's press conferences, see Howard H. Quint and Robert H. Ferrell, eds., *The Talkative President: The Off-the-Record Press Conferences of Calvin Coolidge* (Amherst: University of Massachusetts Press, 1964; **A, G**); and *Press Conferences: August 21, 1923–March 1, 1929*, 2 reels (Willon, CT: International Microfilming, 1971; **A, G**).

For Coolidge's post-presidential years, the following collections in the Manuscript Division of the Library of Congress are important: Edward T. Clark, a secretary; Theodore Roosevelt, Jr.; Elihu Root; Charles Evans Hughes; Charles L. McNary; Henry T. Rainey; Walter L. Fisher; and George Sutherland, especially valuable for the campaign of 1920.

Among the transcripts of oral interviews conducted by the Oral History Program of Columbia University are those of John W. Davis, Claude M. Fuess, Albert D. Lasker, and James W. Wadsworth.

Museums, Historical Landmarks, Societies

Calvin Coolidge Memorial Room, Forbes Library (Northampton, MA). Collection includes the personal and professional artifacts and documents relating to Coolidge's life and presidency.

Coolidge Homestead National Historic Landmark (Plymouth Notch, VT). The site of Coolidge's birth and childhood home maintains a collection of artifacts relating to his life. Coolidge was sworn into the presidency on August 3, 1923, in the homestead's parlor, after learning of President Harding's sudden death. Coolidge's mother was born next door, at the Wilder House.

State Game Lodge (Game Lodge, SD). Coolidge's rustic residence, now a resort, was the site of his famous surprise announcement that he would not seek the presidency in 1928.

Other Sources

Abel, Jules. *In the Time of Silent Cal*. New York: Putnam, 1969. A concise, analytical and well-balanced account of the era.

Abrams, Richard M. *Conservatism in a Progressive Era: Massachusetts Politics, 1900–1912*. Cambridge: Harvard University Press, 1964. Good on Coolidge's early career.

Feis, Herbert. *The Diplomacy of the Dollar: First Era, 1919–1931*. Baltimore: Johns Hopkins Press, 1950. Recounts errors that the U.S. made as a creditor nation.

Hicks, John D. *Republican Ascendancy, 1921–1933*. New York: Harper, 1960. Especially good on the politics and foreign policies of the period covered.

Leuchtenburg, William E. *The Perils of Prosperity, 1914–1932*. Chicago: University of Chicago Press, 1958. Excellent economic and social history.

McCoy, Donald R. *Coming of Age: The United States during the 1920s and 1930s*. Baltimore: Penguin Books, 1973. Describes the environment in which Coolidge lived.

Murray, Robert K. *The Politics of Normalcy: Governmental Theory and Practice in the Harding-Coolidge Era*. New York: W. W. Norton, 1973. Analyzes the impracticality of Coolidge's administration and the results of his mismanagement.

Slosson, Preston W. *The Great Crusade and After, 1914–1928*. New York: Macmillan, 1930. Great social history.

Starling, Edmund W., as told to Thomas Sugrue. *Starling of the White House*. New York: Simon & Schuster, 1946. By a Secret Service operative who was close to Coolidge.

Sullivan, Mark. *Our Times: The United States, 1900–1925*. 6 vols. New York: Charles Scribner's Sons, 1926–1935. Vol. 6, *The Twenties*. Excellent on the social and literary aspects of the decade.

Paolo E. Coletta
U.S. Naval Academy (Ret.)

JAMES FENIMORE COOPER
1789–1851

Chronology

Born James Cooper on September 15, 1789, in Burlington, New Jersey, the twelfth of thirteen children to William Cooper, a landowner, judge and congressman, and Elizabeth Fenimore Cooper, both of Quaker ancestry; *1790–1803* grows up in Cooperstown, a settlement in central New York State established by his father on a large tract of wilderness land; spends much of boyhood outdoors, exploring the woodlands surrounding the village and canoeing; *1803–1806* attends Yale University but is a poor student and is finally expelled in his junior year for committing a series of pranks, including allegedly tying a donkey to a professor's chair; *1806–1810* pursues a naval career, first as a sailor aboard a merchant vessel in the Atlantic trade, then as a U.S. Navy officer stationed at Fort Oswego and New York City; *1811* marries Susan Augusta De Lancey, member of a wealthy and socially prominent New York family; daughter Elizabeth is born, the first of seven children, five of whom survive to adulthood; *1811–1820* pursues a generally unsuccessful career as a gentleman farmer and small-time speculator in Westchester County and Cooperstown, New York, while taking an active role in local Clintonian Republican party and New York State militia; his mother, four brothers, and a daughter die, while his inheritance from his father's estate is steadily eroded by poor management and adverse economic conditions; *1820–1851* publishes his first novel, *Precaution*, which brings him to the attention of the New York literary world; over the next thirty-one years he produces a staggering total of thirty-two novels, and fourteen volumes of social commentary, biography, drama, history, and travel, plus numerous shorter pieces on literature, politics, constitutional philosophy, public finance, and even horse racing; *1826–1833* is assigned to largely ceremonial post of U.S. Consul to Lyons, France, and moves his family to Europe, living principally in Paris with extended stays in Italy and Switzerland; resigns his Consular post in 1828 to spend most of his time socializing, writing, and traveling extensively; *1833* returns to New York; his homecoming is, for complex reasons, chilly, and the phenomenal popularity that he enjoyed with his early fiction steadily dwindles over the remainder of his life; *1837* becomes involved in a controversy with residents of Cooperstown over the public use of some family land; argument grows into a series of libel suits filed against the principal newspaper editors of the state and is argued until 1842; *1838–1850* involves himself conspicuously in a number of public controversies argued in various journalistic and legal forums, including the debate over the role of Commodore Perry at the Battle of Lake Erie, the *Somers* mutiny case of 1842, and the so-called Anti-Rent War in upstate New York; continues to publish novels at the rate of about one a year; *1850* publishes his last novel, *The Ways of the Hour*; health begins to deteriorate rapidly; *1851* dies on September 14 in Cooperstown, and is buried in the family plot.

Activities of Historical Significance

Cooper is, in many respects, the father of the American novel. His novels, more than those of any of his contemporaries or predecessors, defined for later writers the subjects, themes, and genres that addressed themselves specifically to American conditions and reflected the preoccupations of the American imagination. He was the first American novelist to make a career of his art, and the enormous domestic and international popularity that made that career possible provided American writers with a model for literary success in a republic more concerned with commerce than art. His critical acclaim abroad created respect for American literary culture in European artistic circles that had previously given only condescending notice to New World writers.

If he had written nothing else, Cooper's Leatherstocking novels—*The Pioneers* (1823), *The Last of the Mohicans* (1826), *The Prairie* (1827), *The Pathfinder* (1840), and *The Deerslayer* (1842)—would secure his prominence in American literary history. The main character of the series, Nathaniel Bumppo, better known as Leatherstocking, Deerslayer, or Hawk-eye, still captures the American imagination as a symbol of self-reliance and the conflict between the conscience of the individual and the demands of social conformity and law. The Leatherstocking novels thus stand at the head of a major tradition in American popular and literary fiction in which the hero, ranging from the cowboy of the dime-store Western to Mark Twain's Huckleberry Finn, would rather "light out for the territories" than be suffocated by the trappings of civilization.

The enduring relevance of the Leatherstocking series is also shown by its recent recognition as an early argument for both the environmental and Native American movements. Leatherstocking's numerous complaints about the "wasty ways" of the settlers who exploit the land's resources are a reminder that the conflict between the gospel of progress and the lure of the wilderness has been present since the nation's earliest days. And, while Cooper was not by any means free of the prejudices of his day concerning Native Americans, his novels, especially *The Last of the Mohicans*, speak eloquently of the tragedy of a people decimated and broken by the march of white civilization. The characters of Uncas and Chingachgook stand as the first sympathetically portrayed Native Americans in American popular literature.

But Cooper's historical significance does not rest on the Leatherstocking books alone. With *The Pilot* (1824) he published the first serious American novel of the sea and provided, in this and subsequent nautical fiction, a model for later ocean-going writers like Herman Melville. With *The Spy* (1821) he established the historical novel in America; this book, and later novels dealing with various aspects of America's short but rich national past, helped create a context for the work of Nathaniel Hawthorne and other historical romanticists. With *Homeward Bound* (1838) he invented the international novel of the sort that Henry James would master, in which American and European manners are consciously contrasted. His social commentaries, like *Notions of the Americans* (1828) and the more acerbic *The American Democrat* (1838), provided the young nation with an image of itself which was not always flattering. Such works nevertheless contributed significantly to the efforts of nineteenth-century writers to explore the possibilities and limitations of artistic expression in a democracy. In short, Cooper was America's literary "pioneer" and "pathfinder"; his prodigious and diverse canon opened the major avenues of aesthetic and intellectual exploration that would guide the nation's fiction to maturity.

Cooper's significance as an historian must also be mentioned. His *History of the Navy of the United States of America* (1839) was a landmark in its field and remained the standard study of the Navy's early history for many years. More broadly, though, Cooper believed that an important part of his mission as America's first professional novelist was to tell tales about America that would teach its citizens about their past and remind them of the principles on which the country had been founded. Many of his books are based on original, if often limited and erroneous, historical research into matters as diverse as the American Revolution, the history of Indian culture under European domination, the evolution of law in the New World, and colonial military history. If he was a decided amateur, and if he often bent historical fact to suit the needs of his novelist's imagination, his role in turning the nation's attention to its past as a way of understanding its present and future should not be underestimated.

Overview of Biographical Sources

The first full-length biography of Cooper was Thomas R. Lounsbury's *James Fenimore Cooper* (1882). This scholarly and entertaining book remained the standard biography for nearly seventy years, despite the early twentieth century publication of several less distinguished biographies, most notably Mary E. Phillips, *James Fenimore Cooper* (1913), and Henry Walcott Boynton, *James Fenimore Cooper* (1931). Two specialized biographies published during this period remain useful. Robert Spiller, *Fenimore Cooper, Critic of his Times* (1931), covers the ground broken by Lounsbury with an emphasis on Cooper's political and social thought. Marcel Clavel's biography of Cooper's youth, *Fenimore Cooper: Sa vie et son oeuvre: La jeunesse (1789–1826)* (1938), is an extremely detailed look at Cooper's life from birth through the height of his early popularity.

Cooper biography was greatly advanced in 1949 with the publication of James Grossman, *James Fenimore Cooper: A Biographical and Critical Study*. Grossman's intelligent handling of the connections between Cooper's life and art, and his sensitive readings of the novels established this relatively short book as the standard general biography, a position it still retains. A more recent full-length biography that similarly focuses on the relationship between Cooper's life and his published work is George Dekker's *James Fenimore Cooper: The American Scott* (1967).

In 1979, Stephen Railton published a psycho-biography of Cooper, *Fenimore Cooper: A Study of his Life and Imagination*. The book remains very controversial in its conclusions about Cooper's emotional life and the way his internal conflicts are manifested in his fiction. Whether or not one agrees with Railton's conclusions, there is no doubt that the book is one of the two most significant Cooper biographies, and is perhaps the book most responsible for the recent surge of interest in Cooper among historians of American literature.

Evaluation of Principal Biographical Sources

Boynton, Henry Wolcott. *James Fenimore Cooper*. New York: The Century Company, 1931. **(G)** This is the first biography of Cooper written with access to the family collection of manuscripts and letters. It remains one of the most complete narratives of Cooper's life.

Dekker, George. *James Fenimore Cooper: The American Scott*. New York: Barnes and Noble, 1967. **(A, G)** An overview of Cooper's career that focuses on his position in literary history.

Grossman, James. *James Fenimore Cooper: A Biographical and Critical Study*. Stanford, CA: Stanford University Press, 1949. **(A, G)** An excellent critical biography that skillfully weaves intelligent, well-focused discussions of the author's life together with illuminating interpretations of his works. A very readable book that remains, after nearly forty years, the best introduction to Cooper's life and work.

Lounsbury, Thomas R. *James Fenimore Cooper*. Boston: Houghton Mifflin, 1882. **(A, G)** A fine example of the genteel tradition of literary biography, Lounsbury's book is witty, mildly opinionated, elegantly written, and generally accurate. This biography was originally written as part of the distinguished American Men of Letters series, to which a number of America's best writers of the late nineteenth century contributed.

Phillips, Mary E. *James Fenimore Cooper*. New York: John Lane, 1913. **(G)** An unsatisfying and often inaccurate work which is nevertheless well-written and contains a number of fine illustrations.

Railton, Stephen. *Fenimore Cooper: A Study of His Life and Imagination*. Princeton, NJ: Princeton University Press, 1979. **(A, G)** A very intelligent and provocative psychological study of Cooper and his art. Railton is principally concerned with Cooper's relationship with his father and the way that relationship is manifested in his life and art. While many have taken exception to Railton's Freudian perspective and the conclusions about the novels to which it leads, the argument is rigorously pursued, consistently stimulating, and gracefully articulated.

Spiller, Robert. *Fenimore Cooper, Critic of His Times*. New York: Minton, Balch, 1931. **(A, G)** Spiller's biography focuses on the author's role, in his life and in his work, as a social critic. The book describes in detail Cooper's ideas about politics and culture, and pays particular attention to his extensive involvement in public controversies. Spiller's work remains useful to those interested in Cooper as a commentator on antebellum America.

Overview and Evaluation of Primary Sources

Most of Cooper's letters, manuscripts, and journals, are in the Yale University Library. Smaller collections can be found at the New York State Historical Association in Cooperstown, the New-York Historical Society in New York City, the New York Public Library, and in the Houghton Library of Harvard University.

Every student of Cooper's career owes a tremendous debt to Professor James Franklin Beard, who has collected *The Letters and Journals of James Fenimore Cooper*, 6 vols. (Cambridge: Harvard University Press, 1960–1968; **A, G**). The title of the collection does not quite describe its contents since Beard includes many of Cooper's major journalistic pieces. Beard's introductory remarks on each chronological or topical section offer excellent summaries of Cooper's activities and opinions, as well as valuable contextual information. The footnotes are generous, providing not merely biographical descriptions of Cooper's correspondents and the nature of their relationship with the author, but extensive quotations from historical documents of all sorts elucidating material found in Cooper's writings. For the scholar, the footnotes alone are worth the price of the set.

Beard's collection supersedes the only other collection of Cooper's letters, *Correspondence of James Fenimore-Cooper*, edited by James Fenimore Cooper (New Haven, CT: Yale University Press, 1922; **A, G**). Edited by Cooper's grandson, this two-volume set contains some interesting peripheral material, most notably "Small Family Memories," reminiscences written by the author's daughter, Susan Fenimore Cooper, in 1883.

Susan Cooper also provides some useful primary accounts of her father's life in *Pages and Pictures from the Writings of James Fenimore Cooper* (New York: W. A. Townsend, 1861; **A, G**). She splices extracts from her father's novels with recollections and observations—some quite perceptive—about his life and works.

Another interesting source of observations about Cooper by those who knew him is the *Memorial of James Fenimore Cooper* (New York: Putnam's, 1852; **A, G**), a collection of speeches and letters offered in honor of the author after his death. Items by William Cullen Bryant, Washington Irving, George Bancroft, and Francis Parkman, among others, are included.

Cooper's fiction is, of course, an important source of information on his experiences and opinions. Several complete editions of his fiction were published in the nineteenth century. For many years, the standard edition for scholarly work has been *Cooper's Novels*, 32 vols. (New York: W. A. Townsend, 1859–1861; **A, G**). This is the so-called "Darley" edition, featuring illustrations by the ubiquitous nineteenth-century artist, F. O. C. Darley. Most modern printings of his novels are based on the "Darley" edition. The "Darley" is currently being replaced as the standard edition by *The Writings of James Fenimore Cooper*, published by the State University of New York Press, and under the general editorship of James Franklin Beard. This series, when complete, will contain not only the fiction but the major works of non-fiction. The volumes published to date are a model of textual scholarship and contain extremely valuable historical and textual commentary by leading Cooper scholars.

Readers unfamiliar with Cooper's extensive canon may find a short guide to his fiction useful. The following guide identifies some of the major categories into which the novels may be arranged, and names two or three books in each category that are most likely to interest students of history. This guide is provided with the caveat that any list of this sort is artificial, and that many of the books mentioned might reasonably be placed in several categories. Novels of the American Revolution: *The Spy* (1821), *The Pilot* (1824), *Lionel Lincoln* (1825), *Wyandotté* (1843); Novels of the Sea: *The Pilot* (1824), *The Red Rover* (1827), *The Wing-and-Wing* (1842), *The Sea-Lions* (1849); Novels of Social Criticism: *The Monikins* (1835), *Homeward Bound* (1838), *Home as Found* (1838), *The Crater* (1847); The Anti-Rent Novels (New York History): *Satanstoe* (1845), *The Chainbearer* (1845), *The Redskins* (1846); Novels of the Frontier: the Leatherstocking Tales, *The Oak Openings* (1848); Novels of British and European History and Culture: *The Bravo* (1831), *The Headsman* (1833), *The Two Admirals* (1842), *The Wing-and-Wing* (1842); Novels of Colonial American History: *The Last of the Mohicans* (1826), *The Wept of Wish-ton-Wish* (1829), *Satanstoe* (1845).

Fiction and Adaptations

Several films have been based on Cooper's novels, although very few have done justice to their subject. The best is, unfortunately, an old and rare film: French director Maurice Tourneur's 1920 version of *The Last of the Mohicans*, starring Henry Lorraine and Barbara Bedford. Film historians agree that Tourneur's fairly free adaptation of the novel is one of the greatest films of the silent era.

The Last of the Mohicans has been filmed less successfully by several other directors, beginning with a 1909 D. W. Griffith movie titled *Leatherstocking*. In 1932, Mascot Studios released a version directed by Reeves Easton and Ford Beebe and starring Harry Carey as Hawk-eye. The extent to which this production deviates from the novel may be judged by the fact that Uncas is portrayed as being thirteen years old. The best sound version of the book is a 1936 production directed by George B. Seitz and starring Randolph Scott. This version is fairly faithful to the novel, although Seitz adds an inexplicable romance between Hawk-eye and

Alice Munro. The last American filming of the novel was the 1947 Columbia Pictures production *The Last of the Redskins*, produced by Sam Katzman and starring Michael O'Shea and Buster Crabbe, which distorts the novel almost beyond recognition. A 1965 German version, *Der Letzte Mohikaner*, was produced by Harald Reinl.

Mohicans has been produced for television twice, first in a Canadian series of the mid-1950s starring Lon Chaney, Jr., and again in the 1970s in a thirteen-part BBC series.

The Deerslayer has been filmed four times, three of which are forgettable. These three—a 1913 Vitagraph production starring Hal Reid, a 1924 Pathe version titled *Leatherstocking*, and a Twentieth Century-Fox release in 1957 starring Lex Barker and Cathy O'Donnell—are poorly made and corrupt Cooper's narrative. The film that is generally thought to be the best production of a Cooper novel is a 1943 Republic picture produced by P. S. Harrison and E. B. Deer and starring Bruce Kellogg. The settings are excellent, the acting good, and the plot and characterizations faithful to the original.

The Pioneers, The Prairie, and *The Pathfinder* have each been filmed once, and poorly. *The Pioneers* was released by Monogram in 1941, starring Tex Ritter and Wanda McKay; *The Pathfinder* was filmed in 1952 by Sam Katzman for Columbia Pictures; and *The Prairie* was liberally adapted and produced by Frank Wisbar in 1947.

Museums, Historical Landmarks, Societies

Cooper Convention (Oneonta, NY). There is no formal Cooper Society, but there is a bi-annual gathering of Cooper scholars and other interested persons at SUNY-College at Oneonta, which is about thirty miles from Cooperstown. The program is administered by the English Department at the college.

Fenimore House (Cooperstown, NY). Contains a good deal of material relating to Cooper and his family, as well as exhibits illustrating other aspects of life in the region. It also serves as the office of the New York State Historical Association. In a sense, the entire town of Cooperstown and the surrounding areas constitute a Cooper museum. Cooper set *The Pioneers* and *The Deerslayer* in landscapes that resemble closely the Lake Otsego region. The novelist and many of his relations are buried there, and several of the homes in town are connected with the Cooper family.

Other Sources

Clavel, Marcel. *Fenimore Cooper: Sa vie et son oeuvre: La jeunesse (1789–1826)*. Aix-en-Provence: Imprimerie Universitaire de Provence, 1938. A doctoral thesis that provides an immensely detailed study of the author's early life; it is scholarship on a monumental scale. Anyone interested in this period of Cooper's life will not find a more minute account.

Dekker, George, and John P. McWilliams, eds. *Fenimore Cooper: The Critical Heritage*. London and Boston: Routledge and Kegan Paul, 1973. A very useful compendium of critical responses to Cooper, including both contemporary reviews of his publications and modern evaluations of his works and career.

Elliot, Emery, ed. *Columbia Literary History of the United States*. New York: Columbia University Press, 1988. A general survey of American literature that helps put Cooper's work in cultural, historical, and literary context.

McWilliams, John P. *Political Justice in a Republic: James Fenimore Cooper's America*. Berkeley: University of California Press, 1972. A very intelligent analysis of Cooper's political and social opinions as revealed in his novels.

Smith, Henry Nash. *Virgin Land: The American West as Myth and Symbol*. Cambridge: Harvard University Press, 1950. A landmark study of the West which treats Cooper's Leatherstocking books as the forerunner of the popular Western novel.

Charles H. Adams
University of Arkansas

James Fenimore Cooper, 1940

CORONADO
c.1510–1554

Chronology

Born Francisco Vásquez de Coronado about 1510 in Salamanca, Spain, into a family that originally took its name from the village of Cornado (sic) in Galicia; *1535* comes to Mexico in the entourage of Antonio de Mendoza, first viceroy of New Spain; *1537* marries Beatriz de Estrada, daughter of the former treasurer of New Spain, and receives as dowry an estate near Mexico City said to consist of "half of Tlalpa"; *1538* becomes *regidor* (governor) of New Galicia on the nomination of Mendoza; *July 15, 1539* writes to the king mentioning the discovery of the wealthy cities of Cibola by Fray Marcos de Niza, and is subsequently made commander of an expedition to follow up the friar's explorations; *February 1540* Coronado's army sets out from Compostela on a march northward; *July 6, 1540* comes to Hawikuh, the first of the seven "golden cities of Cibola," but finds no gold; *August 1540* Hernando de Alvarado sets out from Cibola to find Tiguex (between Albuquerque and Bernalillo) and Cicuye; extravagant claims about a "Gran Quivira" to the northeast revive languishing hopes of finding gold; *November 1540* reaches Tiguex, where he winters; *April 23, 1541* in search of Gran Quivira; *July 1541* arrives at Quivira in eastern Kansas, is disappointed, and returns to Tiguex within a month; *December 1541* falls from his horse and is seriously injured; *April 1, 1542* his army abandons Tiguex and starts for Mexico, leaving behind three missionaries who are soon martyred; *August 8, 1544* faces an inquiry into the conduct of his office; *September 17, 1544* is found guilty of charges and fined six hundred gold pesos; *February 19, 1545* is absolved of all charges against him by five judges of the Royal Audiencia in Mexico City; *1545–1554* lives in his castle-like home on the southern side of the Zócalo in Mexico City; *1549* receives a small *encomienda* (grant of land with Indians residing on it) for meritorious service in discovery and conquest; dabbles in breeding merino sheep; *1554* dies on September 22 in Mexico City; is probably buried in the Church of Santo Domingo, the oldest church in Mexico City.

Activities of Historical Significance

Coronado, the last of the great Spanish conquistadors, was a loyal and competent officer who carried out a difficult mission to the best of his abilities. Pedro de Castañeda, member and chronicler of the expedition, called this army of eager soldiers and Indian allies "the most brilliant company ever assembled in the Indies to go in search of new lands." For nearly three years Coronado's army explored the American Southwest, a strange and often hostile land. Coronado noted the customs of the native peoples and the resources of the land; Indian tribes were identified and pacified.

So formidable was this task that forty years elapsed before anyone else dared to re-enter what came to be called "Coronado country." A major deterrent was Coronado's report on the severity of the winter weather. In comparison with the acts of aggression and war committed by such conquistadors as Cortez, De Soto, or the Pizarros, the Coronado expedition was mild on atrocities. The Indian allies who accompanied the expedition were so well treated that none deserted during the entire three-year period.

Coronado's expedition discovered the Continental Divide, and one of his lieutenants, García López de Cárdenas, exploring west of the Colorado River, was the first white man to witness the majesty of the Grand Canyon of Arizona. Another branch of the expedition was led by Hernando de Alarcón, who kept a parallel course along the Pacific coast searching for a water route to the Seven Cities. While traversing the Colorado River, he may have been the first Spaniard to reach California. Pedro de Tovar was the first white man to see the Hopi towns of northeastern Arizona. Still another officer, Hernando de Alvarado, went eastward and discovered the "sky city" pueblo of Acoma; heading southeast along the Pecos River, Alvarado and his troops were the first white men to see the American bison. Coronado himself crossed the panhandles of Texas (probably through Canyon City, Borger, Amarillo and Spearman) and Oklahoma (probably through Hardesty and Tyrone) and penetrated into eastern Kansas (probably through Liberal, Meade, Fowler and Ford). In the Texas panhandle he discovered Palo Duro Canyon.

The Coronado expedition solved the "mystery of the north" and gave the Spaniards a fairly accurate concept of the southern half of the present United States. Coronado found no great cities, no new empires, and no gold, but he did return with an appreciation for the great expanse and power of the land through which he had passed.

Overview of Biographical Sources

A burst of interest in Coronado occurred around the time of the expedition's *cuarto centennial* in 1940; the decade saw the appearance of the two major biographies: *Coronado: Knight of Pueblos and Plains* (1949) by Herbert Eugene Bolton, and *Coronado's Quest: The Discovery of the Southwestern States* (1940) by A. Grove Day. These biographies have not yet been superseded. Of the two, Bolton's work is the more complete because he covers Coronado's entire life, not merely the expedition, and because he was privy to crucial information assembled and published in 1940. Within the field of American historiography, Bolton is noteworthy as a pioneer who viewed American history holistically in relation to French and Spanish activities on the continent. He was one of the first scholars of American history to make use of archival materials available in Madrid, Paris, and Mexico City.

Evaluation of Principal Biographical Sources

Bolton, Herbert Eugene. *Coronado: Knight of Pueblos and Plains*. New York: McGraw-Hill, 1949. **(A, G)** The finest single work on Coronado, this biography includes chapters on the legal investigations that followed his return to Mexico. These chapters are based on primary sources first revealed in the Hammond and Rey materials. The book has an appendix on Pueblo society, a page of bibliographical acknowledgments, and a statement about the author's own retracing of the Coronado trail from Compostela to central Kansas. Bolton includes an exhaustive chapter-by-chapter listing of references and a 25-page bibliography that is divided into manuscript materials, printed materials, and lost documents.

Day, A. Grove. *Coronado's Quest: The Discovery of the Southwestern States*. Berkeley: University of California Press, 1940. **(A, G)** Concentrates on the expedition rather than on the life of its subject. The bibliography is 14 pages, but does not list the crucial Hammond-Rey materials published in 1940.

————. *Coronado and the Discovery of the Southwest*. New York: Meredith Press, 1967. **(Y)** This book for younger readers is Day's updating of the previous work. Includes attractive graphics but no bibliography. Especially noteworthy is the additional material included about the criminal charges brought against Coronado on his return to Mexico. There is an index, and the end papers show a map of the Coronado trail.

Hammond, George P. *Coronado's Seven Cities*. Albuquerque: United States Coronado Exposition Committee, 1940. **(G)** Called by its author a "booklet" rather than a book, it is an occasional treatment of the Coronado expedition written by one of the compilers of original materials relating to the expedition. It is interesting for its many direct quotations from the original accounts. A history of the Coronado celebrations is included as an afterword.

Horgan, Paul. *Conquistadors in North American History*. New York: Farrar, Straus, 1963. **(G)** The 30-page section "To the North" describes the search for the Seven Cities of Cibola with the author's inimitable flare for storytelling. Includes a bibliography and an index.

Norman, Charles. *Discoverers of America*. New York: Thomas Y. Crowell, 1968. **(G)** Norman spends nearly 30 pages on the Coronado expedition, especially availing himself of long passages taken from the Castañeda account.

Sauer, Carl Ortwin. *Sixteenth Century North America: The Land and the People as Seen by the Europeans*. Berkeley: University of California Press, 1971. **(A, G)** Sauer here pays more attention to flora and fauna and other external phenomena of the Coronado expedition than most accounts. The tortillas of the Yumas, for example, are noted as being poorly made (citing Alarcón), in reference perhaps (ventures Sauer) to the meal ground of dry grain instead of the wet-ground hominy used in Central Mexico. Jaramillo was struck by the "fine appearance" of the Kansas plains, and also by the plums, which he said must have originated in Castile. Castañeda is quoted as noting that the men ate buffalo meat "until they were sick of it." A valuable discussion of bibliographic material is included within the text, as well as a final bibliography.

Overview and Evaluation of Primary Sources

The best primary source available for the history of the Coronado expedition is the *Relación de la jornada de Cibola compuesta por Pedro de Castañeda de Naçera donde se trata de todos aquellos poblados y ritos y costumbres; la cual fue el año de 1540*, written in the years following the expedition's return by one of Coronado's men. More than 300 years later, this narrative was published in both English and Spanish, with an introduction by George Parker Winship as "The Coronado Expedition, 1540–1542," *Fourteenth Annual Report of the Bureau of Ethnology* (Washington: U.S. Bureau of American Ethnology, 1896; A). Castañeda's narrative, along with a terser report written by another soldier, Juan Jaramillo, was published in English by Winship, *The Journey of Coronado, 1540–1542* (New York: Trail Makers Series, 1904; A). Castañeda was reprinted in *Spanish Explorers in the Southern United States, 1528–1543*, edited by Frederick W. Hodge and Theodore H. Lewis (New York: Original Narratives of Early American History, 1907; A).

As it related to his work on Viceroy Mendoza, Arthur S. Aiton discovered and published *The Muster Roll and Equipment of the Expedition of Francisco Vasquez de Coronado* (Ann Arbor: University of Michigan Press, 1939; A). The report made to Viceroy Mendoza by Coronado's lieutenant Hernando de Alarcón was preserved in its 1556 Italian translation, *Terzo volume delle navigationi e(t) viaggi* under the authorship of Giovanni Battista Ramusio.

In addition, Pedro de Tovar left behind some sort of narrative to which Matias de la Mota Padilla apparently had access. His *Historia de la conquista de la provincia de Nueva Galicia, escrita en 1742* appeared in the *Boletín de la Sociedad Mexicana de Geografía y Estadística* (1870). A relevant portion was translated for the article by A. Grove Day, "Mota Padilla on the Coronado Expedition," *Hispanic American Historical Review* (February 1940): 88–110 (A).

George P. Hammond and Agapito Rey's *Narratives of the Coronado Expedition 1540–1542* (Albuquerque: Coronado Cuarto Centennial Publications, 1940; A) includes in translation extensive selections from the formerly little used records of the *residencia* of Coronado's administration as governor of *Nueva Galicia* and of the criminal trials of both Coronado and his lieutenant Cárdenas. The narratives also include translations of the Castañeda and Jaramillo narratives, and of the Alarcón report.

Fiction and Adaptations

Coronado's expeditions have inspired artists in various genres. Pearl Rosencrans Casey's 95-page poem, *Coronado* (1940), was published in time for the *cuarto centennial*. The poem "Quivira," by Arthur Guiterman, is anthologized in Burton Egbert Stevenson, ed., *Poems of American History* (1922). J. Frank Dobie's classic work, *Coronado's Children: Tales of Lost Mines and Buried Treasures of the Southwest* (1931), depicts hoaxes subsequent to the one that inspired Coronado's men.

Scott O'Dell's novel for younger readers, *The King's Fifth* (1966), is the story of a young mapmaker named Esteban de Sandoval who marches in the Coronado expedition and whose genuine desire to chart the immense new territory is over-shadowed by his lust for gold.

N. C. Wyeth produced an illustration titled "Coronado searches for the riches of the Seven Cities of Cibolo" (sic) that appeared first in color for the 1940 "America in the Making" calendar produced by John Morrell and Company. A black-and-white version of this illustration appears in many history textbooks and in the *World Book Encyclopedia*.

Museums, Historical Landmarks, Societies

Coronado Borderlands Festival (Hereford, AZ). Sponsored by the Coronado National Memorial, the festival celebrates the region's Spanish/Mexican heritage and culture, as originated by Coronado's travels through the region.

Coronado National Memorial (Hereford, AZ). Preserves the history of Coronado's expedition through the Sonora and San Pedro Valleys, with a museum collection of sixteenth century Spanish costumes and other historical artifacts.

Coronado State Monument (near Bernalillo, NM). Created in 1935, this landmark consists of a museum on the site of two Tiguex pueblo ruins. The 400th anniversary of Coronado's arrival here was celebrated in 1940.

Kansas State Historical Society and Museum (Topeka, KS). Houses a sword that may have belonged to one of Coronado's men.

Nebraska Knights of Ak-Sar-Ben (Omaha, NE). Although historians no longer believe that Coronado marched through Nebraska, the Knights of Ak-Sar-Ben crown the King and Queen of Quivira each fall in the state's most elaborate social occasion.

Other Sources

Bannon, John Francis. *The Spanish Borderlands Frontier, 1513–1821*. New York: Holt, Rinehart and Winston, 1963. Chapter 2 deals with the conquistadors.

The extensive bibliography is useful since it includes some more recent works, particularly journal articles that touch upon the Coronado expedition.

Bartlett, Richard A. "Coronado, Francisco Vasquez de." In *The Reader's Encyclopedia of the American West*, edited by Howard R. Lamar. New York: Thomas Y. Crowell, 1977. Special emphasis on Coronado's contribution to western American history.

Bolton, Herbert Eugene. "Coronado, Francisco Vazquez." In *The Dictionary of American Biography*, edited by Allen Johnson. New York: Scribner's, 1927, 1964. Noteworthy encyclopedic treatment, especially strong on bibliography.

Jack Shreve
Allegany Community College

Coronado Expedition, 1940

CHARLES E. COUGHLIN
1891–1979

Chronology

Born Charles Edward Coughlin on October 25, 1891, in Hamilton, Ontario, the son of Thomas J. Coughlin, an American and former merchant seaman, and Amelia Mahoney Coughlin, a Canadian; *1891–1903* grows up in Hamilton as the family's sole surviving child; *1903–1911* receives secondary and college education at St. Michael's College in Toronto, where he is class valedictorian; *1913–1916* trains for the priesthood and is ordained on June 29, 1916; *1916–1926* teaches for a few years at Assumption College in Sandwich, Ontario, and serves as a priest in various dioceses in Ontario and Michigan; *1926* receives the pastorate of the Shrine of the Little Flower in Royal Oak, Michigan, a stronghold of the anti-Catholic Ku Klux Klan; delivers first radio broadcast on WJR, Detroit, on October 17; *1926–1929* organizes Radio League of the Little Flower; his popular weekly sermons, largely on religious and moral topics, bring in substantial contributions from audiences; *1929–1936* speeches become more politically and economically oriented during the Great Depression, as he denounces the machinations of communists and bankers, as well as the failure of President Hoover to end the depression; *1934* forms the National Union for Social Justice; *1936* breaks with President Franklin D. Roosevelt, whom he initially supported with great enthusiasm; creates the Union Party, but its presidential candidate, Representative William Lemke of North Dakota, is defeated; *1938–1942* moves to the extreme right of the political spectrum, denouncing Roosevelt, communists, and Jews for America's problems; opposes America's entry into World War II before Pearl Harbor and then criticizes the war effort; *1942* government invokes the Espionage Act to bar Coughlin's *Social Justice* magazine from the mails; Church bans him from speaking on political matters; *1943–1966* completes 50 years of service as a priest before retiring in 1966; later years find him still vigorously denouncing communism, as well as liberal changes in the Church; *1979* dies on October 27 in Bloomfield Hills, Michigan.

Activities of Historical Significance

During both his college years and his training for the priesthood, Father Coughlin became exposed to Catholic teachings on social justice, notably to the philosophy embodied in Pope Leo XIII's encyclical *Rerum Novarum* (1891). These teachings stimulated his sense of reform and helped to mold his life-long concern for the worker and his detestation of communism and the excesses of capitalism. As a crusader for social justice, the "Radio Priest" foreshadowed the widespread social activism among the clergy during the 1960s.

Father Coughlin's involvement in American political life proved exceedingly controversial. An outspoken critic of those whom he deemed parasites or corrupters of the nation's economic structure and social system, he turned to mass politics in an attempt to remedy matters. He predicted that Congressman Lemke would poll 9 million votes in the 1936 presidential election; Lemke garnered less than a million. Afterward Coughlin moved to the far right, finding words of praise for Hitler and Mussolini and vilifying Roosevelt and communism with increased fervor. Though denying he was anti-Semitic, he strongly criticized Jews and identified with the fascist, anti-Semitic Christian Front organization.

Finally, Charles E. Coughlin represented one of the first examples of the successful use of the media as a force for political persuasion and the dissemination of ideas. At times his radio sermons, which were broadcast nationally during much of the 1930s, reached a greater audience (estimated at 30 to 45 million) than did the famous "fireside chats" of President Roosevelt. For a while, this compelling orator was one of the most popular and admired figures in the United States.

Overview of Biographical Sources

Sheldon Marcus, one of Father Coughlin's major biographers, has claimed that he was "the most revered, the most loved, the most hated and the most feared American of his time. He was Christ; he was Hitler; he was savior; he was destroyer; he was patriot; he was demagogue." Whatever hyperbolic element the statement may contain, it does accurately point to the widely divergent views of Coughlin held by his contemporaries, especially during the 1930s and early 1940s. Writers, too, reflected this broad spectrum of opinion. Hardly anything written about the Radio Priest at that time escaped the bias of either wild adulation or fierce vilification.

Once Coughlin passed from the public limelight, biographical writings achieved more balance, while not avoiding distinct points of view. That only two serious Coughlin biographies have been published since 1960—one by Charles J. Tull and one by Sheldon Marcus—reflects a lack of Coughlin's personal papers, rather than a sharply diminished interest in the subject. To date there has been no full-length life of Coughlin since his death nearly a decade ago. However lacking in biographers, Coughlin has provided a focus for other studies, notably those dealing with the politics of the 1930s. Two noteworthy examples of the latter have been David H. Bennett, *Demagogues in the Depression* (1969), and Alan Brinkley, *Voices of Protest* (1982).

Evaluation of Principal Biographical Sources

Bennett, David H. *Demagogues in the Depression: American Radicals and the Union Party, 1932–1936.* New Brunswick, NJ: Rutgers University Press, 1969. **(A, G)** This study presents the ideas of Coughlin, the Reverend Gerald L. K.

Smith, Dr. Francis E. Townsend, and Representative William Lemke. Noting both their similarities and differences, the author examines how and why these opponents of the New Deal forged the Union Party that went down to crushing defeat in the 1936 election. Though the bulk of the book covers the years from 1932 to 1936, the author also provides appropriate background information as well as a thoughtful epilogue. Despite its animus against these "demagogues," the book is moderate and generally fairminded in presentation.

Brinkley, Alan. *Voices of Protest: Huey Long, Father Coughlin, and the Great Depression*. New York: Alfred A. Knopf, 1982. **(A, G)** Winner of the American Book Award for History, this is a major contribution to the literature on Father Coughlin, who, along with Huey Long, was the most powerful rallying point for political dissent during the depression. Brinkley rejects two widely-held views that these figures were leaders either of a darkly irrational mass movement or of a grass-roots groundswell for popular reforms. Instead, he interprets their appeal as having stemmed from "the urge to defend the autonomy of the individual and the independence of the community against encroachments from the modern industrial state." Brinkley also offers an interesting appraisal of Coughlin's anti-Semitism and alleged support for fascism.

Kernan, William C. *The Ghost of Royal Oak*. New York: Free Speech Forum, 1940. **(G)** This is a strongly anti-Coughlin work written by a clergyman at a time when Coughlin had embraced the politics of the extreme right. The author condemns his subject for lacking true Christian spirit. Written for a general audience rather than for scholars, it warns of Coughlin as "the symbol of danger to America."

Marcus, Sheldon. *Father Coughlin: The Tumultuous Life of the Priest of the Little Flower*. Boston: Little, Brown, 1973. **(A, G)** As one of only two biographies of Coughlin to appear during the past quarter of a century, this study is both scholarly and readable. Having secured an interview with his subject in 1970, the author attests to his "charisma." Nonetheless, he views Coughlin's ideas and career as antecedents for the McCarthyism of the 1950s and for the left-wing and right-wing extremism of the following decade.

McCoy, Donald. *Angry Voices: Left of Center Politics in the New Deal Era*. Lawrence, KS: University of Kansas Press, 1958. **(A, G)** This is a useful study of radical figures during the Great Depression by an accomplished political historian. The section on Coughlin is illuminating, despite his arguable inclusion in a work dedicated to "left of center politics."

Mugglebee, Ruth. *Father Coughlin of the Shrine of the Little Flower*. Garden City, NY: Garden City Publications, 1933. **(G)** This is a largely uncritical, highly favorable early biography of the Radio Priest at the height of his popularity. Its pro-Coughlin bias epitomizes the difficulty writers of that era had in displaying objectivity toward their subject. It does, however, draw on some interesting interviews the author had with Coughlin.

Spivak, John L. *Shrine of the Silver Dollar*. New York: Modern Age Books, 1940. **(G)** This work represents the reverse image of the Mugglebee book. If the latter can find no fault with Coughlin, this one can find nothing but faults. The author presents Coughlin as a virulent anti-Semite and as a liar whose fund-raising activities for his church were dubious if not fraudulent.

Swing, Raymond Graham. *Forerunners of American Fascism*. New York: Julian Messner, 1935. **(A, G)** According to Swing, who was a journalist at the time, Coughlin, among others, took advantage of those who were "ready to believe the impossible." The priest was "one of the most talented fomenters of hatred ever to have addressed an American crowd." Unfortunately, the section on Coughlin, though usefully provocative, is much too brief to be of any real significance.

Tull, Charles J. *Father Coughlin and the New Deal*. Syracuse, NY: Syracuse University Press, 1965. **(A, G)** This is a balanced biography that does not assess Coughlin as ever being a truly serious threat to democracy, his ominous pronouncements notwithstanding. He was not, according to the author, a "fascist," a word that, like "communist," all too frequently simply represented an epithet. This study has benefited from cogent personal interviews and correspondence.

Ward, Louis B. *Father Charles E. Coughlin: An Authorized Biography*. Detroit: Tower Publications, 1933. **(G)** Like most other authorized biographies, this one casts its subject in positive relief. Praising Coughlin for following the precepts of Pope Leo XIII, the author portrays him as a leader of global dimensions, contending that had Coughlin lived in Russia before the Bolshevik Revolution, communism and atheism "probably" would not have taken root there.

Overview and Evaluation of Primary Sources

Regrettably, Father Coughlin never wrote his memoirs. Nor did he leave behind a collection of manuscripts for interested scholars. Coughlin letters are extant in various collections, as in the Franklin D. Roosevelt Papers (Hyde Park, NY), but they are scattered and not easily accessible.

Coughlin did, however, author a series of works during the 1930s, most of which represent his radio addresses and deal primarily with economic and social issues, but also with foreign policy as the decade drew to a close. There is a certain overlap of material in these books, all of which were published by the Radio League of the Little Flower. Of interest to scholars and interested laypersons alike, they include: *By the Sweat of Thy Brow* (1931); *Radio Discourses, 1931–1932* (1932); *The New Deal's Money* (1933); *Eight Discourses on the Gold Standard* (1933); *Eight Lectures on Labor, Capital and Social Justice* (1934); *A Series of Lectures on Social Justice, 1935–1936* (1936); *Radio Addresses, January 12,*

1936–April 21, 1940 (1940). Those interested in Coughlin should also see his *Am I an Anti-Semite?* (Detroit: Condon Printing, 1939).

Museums, Historical Landmarks, Societies
Shrine of the Little Flower Church (Royal Oak, MI). Though not preserved as a landmark per se, the church tower, which served as his study, may be of interest to the student of Coughlin.

Other Sources
Bennett, David H. "Charles Edward Coughlin." In *The Encyclopedia of American Biography*, edited by John A. Garraty and Jerome L. Sternstein. New York: Harper & Row, 1974. Useful entry by one of Coughlin's chief biographers.

Social Justice (1936–1942). In its half-dozen years of existence, this weekly journal served as a primary vehicle for conveying Coughlin's views.

Robert Muccigrosso
Brooklyn College, City University of New York

CRAZY HORSE
c.1841–1877

Chronology

Born in the Autumn of 1841 or 1842 (sources cite dates from 1839 to 1849), in what is now South Dakota, the second of three children of Crazy Horse (Tashunca-Uitco), an Oglala Sioux medicine or holy man, and his Brule bride, who is the sister of Spotted Tail; *c.1841–1851* is called Curly in his youth; his mother dies sometime after 1843; cholera, smallpox, and other heretofore unknown diseases are spread by white travelers on the Oregon Trail during the late 1840s; *1851* Fort Laramie Treaty Council establishes temporary peace on the Oregon Trail; *1854* witnesses the "Grattan Massacre"; experiences a life-guiding vision; participates in his first buffalo hunt; *1855* participates in his first war party and kills an Omaha woman; Spotted Tail's camp at Bluewater is destroyed by Colonel William Harney; *1857* his father bestows the name Crazy Horse on his son and changes his own name to Worm; *1861–1865* the Native American tribes of the northern Plains fight mainly among themselves while the U.S. Army is busy fighting the Civil War; *November 1864* Sand Creek Massacre of Cheyenne village by whites; *1865* participates in the Platte Bridge fight; *1866–1868* serves as a key leader under Red Cloud, who has organized various Sioux tribes to attack forts that the U.S. Army has constructed in an attempt to keep the Bozeman Trail open; *1869* returns to raiding Crows and other traditional enemies after Red Cloud signs a treaty because he believes it will exclude whites from the Powder River country and the Black Hills; *1870* breaks with Red Cloud, who has become a peace advocate following a trip to Washington and New York; *1873* encounters General George Custer at Yellowstone; *1874–1876* Custer leads expedition to the Black Hills, and "treaty Sioux" sell the territory to the government; *June 25, 1876* Crazy Horse, with Sitting Bull and Gall, leads Sioux and Cheyenne forces in the Battle of the Little Big Horn, where Custer and more than 200 of his men are killed; *1876–1877* is relentlessly pursued by the U.S. Army; *1877* surrenders on May 6 at Camp Robinson; on September 5, is stabbed while under arrest and dies around midnight; his parents secretly bury the body in an unknown location.

Activities of Historical Significance

Crazy Horse represents one of the finest examples of the strength and skill of the Plains Indians. Throughout his life, his main contact with whites was on the battlefield, where he was uncompromising in his resistance to the encroachment of Native American lands by whites. Participating in nearly every major engagement between the Sioux and the U.S. Army, few other warriors could match his individual skill and courage in battle.

Nonetheless, this individual skill and daring that was his strength was also the weakness of his people. Personal freedom to choose how and when a man would fight was an accepted part of the cultures of the Sioux and many other tribes. The Native Americans of the Plains were not united and spent as much time fighting among themselves as they did with the whites. Even a tribe like the Sioux was fractured into numerous branches, bands, and sub-units. It was difficult to gain cooperation in fighting even a common foe. Rarely was there central leadership to the tribe. The Bozeman Trail fights and the Battle of the Little Big Horn represent some of the few times when a large portion of the Sioux were united for action.

It is difficult to determine how much actual influence Crazy Horse had over his people's day-to-day life, for he was primarily a war leader. Whatever power he possessed, it was earned through his reputation on the battlefield. Until the very end of his life, he had little contact with whites except in battle.

Crazy Horse often stressed the need for greater cooperation among the Sioux in their engagements with the whites, but he was rarely successful in convincing them to act together. As the leader of war parties, he had few equals. For the Sioux and all Native Americans, Crazy Horse was an outstanding leader.

Overview of Biographical Sources

Crazy Horse has had many biographers and his story is also covered, in part, in many of the biographies of his principal military adversaries. Unfortunately, few, if any, of these sources are without some bias. There are relatively few primary sources available portraying the Native Americans' viewpoint.

Of all the sources on Crazy Horse, one of the best is Mari Sandoz's *Crazy Horse* (1942). Her work benefits from the extensive interviews she and Eleanor Hinman conducted among members of the Oglala Sioux who had known Crazy Horse, including He Dog (a lifelong friend) and the daughter of Chief Red Cloud. For accounts of the events surrounding the death of Crazy Horse, see E. A. Brininstool's *Crazy Horse* (1949), Robert A. Clark's *The Killing of Chief Crazy Horse* (1976), and Edward and Mabell Kadlecek's *To Kill an Eagle* (1981).

Evaluation of Principal Biographical Sources

Ambrose, Stephen E. *Crazy Horse and Custer: The Parallel Lives of Two American Warriors*. Garden City, NY: Doubleday, 1975. (A, G) An excellent work that traces the rise and fall of two of the most interesting military leaders of the mid nineteenth century. The work is richly illustrated.

Brininstool, E. A., ed. *Crazy Horse: The Invincible Ogalla* [sic] *Sioux Chief, The "Inside Stories," by Actual Observers, of a Most Treacherous Deed Against a Great Indian Leader*. Los Angeles: Wetzel, 1949. (A, G) Accounts from the white observers of the events surrounding the death of Crazy Horse.

Brown, Vinson. *Great Upon the Mountains: The Story of Crazy Horse, Legendary Mystic and Warrior*. New York: Macmillan, 1971. (**A, G**) This slender work details the major events in the life of Crazy Horse. Of importance is the description of the vision that guided his life. Useful features include the "Map of Major Events" and a glossary of Lakota terms.

Clark, Robert A., ed. *The Killing of Chief Crazy Horse: Three Eyewitness Views by the Indian, Chief He Dog; The Indian-White, William Garnett; The White Doctor, Valentine McGillycuddy*. Glendale, CA: Arthur H. Clark, 1976. (**A, G**) A fascinating account of Crazy Horse's death given by contemporaries. He Dog provides a "history" of Crazy Horse. The volume also includes a foreword by Carroll Friswald.

Kadlecek, Edward, and Mabell Kadlecek. *To Kill an Eagle: Indian Views on the Death of Crazy Horse*. Boulder, CO: Johnson Books, 1981. (**A, G**) Using interviews with elderly Native Americans, the authors detail the life and events of the death of Crazy Horse.

Moeller, Bill, and Jan Moeller. *Crazy Horse: His Life, His Lands*. Wilsonville, OR: Beautiful America Publishing, 1987. (**A, G**) A beautifully illustrated work that provides a chronology of Crazy Horse's life. Includes a present-day photograph of the location of each event.

Sandoz, Mari. *Crazy Horse, the Strange Man of the Oglalas: A Biography*. New York: Hastings House, 1942. (**A, G**) Perhaps the best biography, this work is often cited by later writers on Crazy Horse's life. Contains a good bibliography of sources.

Evaluation of Biographies for Young People

Benchley, Nathaniel. *Only Earth and Sky Last Forever*. Boston: G. K. Hall, 1973. This is a first-person fictional biography told by "Dark Elk." Grades six to twelve.

Dines, Glen. *Crazy Horse*. New York: Putnam, 1966. This work is part of the See and Read Beginning to Read Biography series. The work is written for second grade readers.

Garst, Doris Shannon. *Crazy Horse, a Great Warrior of the Sioux*. Boston: Houghton Mifflin, 1950. A fictionalized biography for readers grades seven to nine. The work is illustrated by William Moyers.

Grant, Matthew G. *Crazy Horse, War Chief of the Oglala*. Mankato, MN: Creative Education, 1973. This short work is part of the Gallery of Great Americans series. It is illustrated by John Keely and Dick Brude. Grades two to four.

Kotzwinkle, William. *Return of Crazy Horse*. New York: Farrar, Straus and Giroux, 1971. A brief picture-book portraying the efforts of Korczak Ziolkowski to create the Crazy Horse Monument at Thunderhead Mountain in South Dakota.

Meadowcroft, Enid La Monte. *Crazy Horse, Sioux Warrior*. Champaign, IL: Garrard, 1965. A fictionalized biography written for readers in grades two and three.

Milton, John R. *Crazy Horse*. Minneapolis, MN: Dillon Press, 1974. This short work is part of the Story of an American Indian series.

Rothaus, James R. *Crazy Horse*. Mankato, MN: Creative Education, 1987. This work is part of the We the People series.

Overview and Evaluation of Primary Sources

Very few if any Native American leaders have depositories of written materials. As a result, a researcher is often dependent upon other contemporary accounts for information about these leaders. Very few collections provide direct information about Crazy Horse's life. Probably the most important information is in the Nebraska State Historical Society Collection, Lincoln. This archive includes Eleanor Hinman's interviews of Sioux contemporaries of Crazy Horse, and the Judge E. S. Ricker papers, which also include interviews with various Plains Indians. Also in the archive are the papers of Susan Bettelyoun, a teacher on the Rosebud Indian Reservation.

For the Battle of the Little Big Horn, one should also consult the collection at the U.S. Army Military History Institute (Carlisle Barracks, Pennsylvania). This collection includes transcripts of reminiscences of Crow scouts and Sioux warriors concerning this famous engagement. At the University of North Dakota Libraries, the Sioux Indian Papers Collection includes a manuscript in Teton Sioux written in 1931 by White Bull. This Oglala chief claimed to have killed Custer.

Nearly every collection for any of the major military figures involved in the campaigns against the northern Plains Native Americans may have information of importance concerning the events in the life of Crazy Horse.

Fiction and Adaptations

The events surrounding Crazy Horse's resistance to the coming of the white man have served as the background for countless novels, short stories, and other literary treatments. He has served as the offscreen nemesis in many "wagontrain/settler/ prospector" movies as well. Perhaps the best known portrayals of Crazy Horse are in four Hollywood films: *They Died with Their Boots On* (1941), a highly fictionalized epic account of the life of Custer, released by Warner Brothers, directed by Raoul Walsh, and starring Errol Flynn as Custer and Anthony Quinn as Crazy

Horse; *Chief Crazy Horse* (1955), an account of the final years of Crazy Horse's life, released by Universal, directed by George Sherman, and starring Victor Mature in the title role; *Sitting Bull* (1954), another adaptation of the events of 1876, released by United Artists, and starring Iron Eyes Cody as Crazy Horse and J. Carrol Nash as Sitting Bull; and *The White Buffalo* (1977), another totally fictional depiction of events on the northern Plains, released by United Artists starring Will Sampson as Crazy Horse and Charles Bronson as Wild Bill Hickok.

Museums, Historical Landmarks, Societies

Crazy Horse Memorial (Crazy Horse, SD). Korczak Ziolkowski began working on this memorial in 1949, and his family continues to work on it. The project will include most of the 600-foot Thunderhead Mountain in the Black Hills. For more information, see *Crazy Horse and Korczak: The Story of an Epic Mountain Carving* (1982) or Robb Dewall's *Korczak, Storyteller in Stone: Boston to Crazy Horse, September 6, 1908–October 20, 1982* (1984), both published by Korczak's Heritage of Crazy Horse, South Dakota.

Custer Battlefield National Monument (Big Horn Country, MT). The site of the Battle of Little Big Horn includes a museum.

Other Sources

Dockstader, Frederick J. *Great North American Indians: Profiles in Life and Leadership*. New York: Van Nostrand Reinhold, 1977. Contains a useful biographical sketch.

Grinstead, Wren Jones. "Crazy Horse." In *Dictionary of American Biography*, edited by Allen Johnson and Dumas Malone. Vol. 4. New York: Charles Scribner's Sons, 1930. A highly academic review of the principal events in Crazy Horse's life. The bibliography is good for older materials and accounts of some of the principal military leaders.

Josephy, Alvin M., Jr. *The Patriot Chiefs: A Chronicle of American Indian Resistance*. New York: Viking Press, 1958. Includes an excellent, highly readable, biographical sketch. This work helps to place Crazy Horse in context with other Native American leaders.

Matthiessen Peter. *In the Spirit of Crazy Horse*. New York: Viking, 1983. Traces U.S. government-Native American (particularly Oglala) relations, concentrating on the twentieth century. The first chapter includes information on Crazy Horse, and many chapters begin with quotations from Crazy Horse.

Whitaker, Jane. *Patriots of the Plains: Sitting Bull, Crazy Horse, Chief Joseph.* New York: Scholastic Book Services, 1973. This work is part of the Firebird Books series and is written for a high school audience.

Maurice G. Fortin
University of North Texas

DAVY CROCKETT
1786–1836

Chronology

Born David Crockett on August 27, 1786, in Greene County, Tennessee, to John Crockett, a farmer and tavern-keeper, and Rebecca Hawkins Crockett; *1798–1803* works at several trades to help settle his father's debts; starts school but quits and runs away from home; works for nearly three years before returning; *1805* rejected by the girl he intends to marry; *August 14, 1806* marries Mary (Polly) Finley; *1811* moves to Lincoln County, in western Tennessee; *1813* moves to Franklin County, near the Alabama border; *1813–1815* during the Creek War, enlists in the Tennessee militia and serves under Andrew Jackson for ninety days; reenlists after nine months and serves until the end of the war; *1815* his wife dies; *1816* marries Elizabeth Patton, a widow; *1817–1821* moves to Lawrence County and serves as justice of the peace, magistrate, and colonel in the militia; *1821* runs for election as a state representative and wins a seat in the Tennessee House; *1821–1824* serves as a representative; is reelected in 1823; *August 1825* is defeated in an election for the House of Representatives; *1827* wins election to Congress; *1827–1831* serves in the House; is reelected in 1829; votes against many of President Andrew Jackson's policies, including a proposed bill for removal of Native Americans; *1831* James Kirke Paulding's play *The Lion of the West*, whose Nimrod Wildfire is based on Crockett, is a popular success; Crockett is defeated for his third term in Congress; *1833* Crockett wins reelection to the House; *Life and Adventures of Colonel David Crockett of West Tennessee*, purported to be an accurate biography, is published; *1834* with Thomas Chilton, Crockett writes and publishes his autobiography, *A Narrative of the Life of David Crockett of the State of Tennessee*; makes a celebrated political tour of the North; *1835* publication of *Davy Crockett's Almanack, of Wild Sports in the West, And Life in the Backwoods*; the Whig Party publishes two books under Crockett's name for political purposes; Crockett is defeated in his bid for reelection; leaves Tennessee with three others to go to Texas; *1836* signs an oath of allegiance to the Texas government and joins the small garrison at the Alamo; is captured and executed on March 6 while fighting to defend the Alamo.

Activities of Historical Significance

The historical David Crockett was a frontiersman, Congressman, and author of a lively autobiography, who died at the Alamo. The legendary "Davy" Crockett was "half-horse, half-alligator," or "King of the Wild Frontier," a superman, folk philosopher, and man of the people. The legendary Davy has tended to overshadow the historical David to the extent that Crockett is often dismissed as a myth and nothing more. Crockett's public life was brief but significant in the context of Tennessee politics. His service in the House of Representatives was undistinguished but his outspoken opposition to Andrew Jackson was notable.

The mythologizing began during Crockett's lifetime; indeed, he contributed to the tall tales. Perhaps the historical David's significance lies primarily in his contemporary celebrity as a frontiersman and as a friend of the common folk. His death at the Alamo, which has even sparked a controversy over whether he died swinging his rifle or was executed as a prisoner, was only the beginning. After his death he was increasingly known as Davy Crockett, the central character of incredible tales about the American frontier, and it is as Davy that he is best remembered today.

Overview of Biographical Sources

A problem obviously central to any study of Crockett is separating the historical David from the legendary Davy, often a difficult task and sometimes an impossible one. James A. Shackford, *David Crockett: The Man and the Legend* (1956), is essential for the facts of Crockett's life; it should be supplemented by Crockett's own *Narrative of the Life of David Crockett of the State of Tennessee* (1834), an authentic, if exaggerated, autobiography. The autobiography should be followed by Michael A. Lofaro, et al., *Davy Crockett: The Man, The Legend, The Legacy 1786–1986* (1986), and Richard Boyd Hauck, *Crockett: A Bio-Bibliography* (1982); these two last works will refer the interested reader to the books and films which created the Crockett of myth.

Evaluation of Principal Biographical Sources

Hauck, Richard Boyd. *Crockett: A Bio-Bibliography.* Popular Culture Bio-Bibliographies. Westport, CT: Greenwood Press, 1982. **(A)** Hauck's study is a bibliography that brilliantly evaluates the massive body of Crockett literature. A fine study for those wanting further information.

Lofaro, Michael A., ed. *Davy Crockett: The Man, The Legend, The Legacy 1786–1986.* Knoxville: University of Tennessee Press, 1986. **(A, G)** This collection of essays, written by several notable scholars, discusses Crockett's image from the nineteenth-century almanacs to twentieth-century film. Although the essays are of varying quality, this excellent collection is the best synthesis of Crockett scholarship available.

Shackford, James Atkins. *David Crockett: The Man and The Legend.* Edited by John B. Shackford. Chapel Hill: University of North Carolina Press, 1956. **(A, G)** This is the definitive biography of the historical Crockett and the necessary starting point for reading about him. Shackford succeeded in uncovering the most reliable information about Crockett's life, and his interpretation, though somewhat dated, is quite valuable.

Evaluation of Biographies for Young People

Holbrook, Stewart H. *Davy Crockett: From the Backwoods of Tennessee to the Alamo*. Landmark Books. New York: Random House, 1955. Detailed and entertaining, this book focuses on the historical Crockett more than do many of the children's biographies.

Moseley, Elizabeth R. *Davy Crockett: Hero of the Wild Frontier*. A Discovery Book. Champaign, IL: Garrard Publishing, 1967. A study that includes many of the Crockett legends; though somewhat fictionalized, a good first biography for young children.

Parks, Aileen Wells. *Davy Crockett: Young Rifleman*. Childhood of Famous Americans Series. Indianapolis: Bobbs-Merrill, 1949. One in a popular series of American biographies, Parks's book details Crockett's childhood and youth. Interesting, though generalized and fictionalized.

Overview and Evaluation of Primary Sources

The best primary source for David Crockett's life is his autobiography, *A Narrative of the Life of David Crockett of the State of Tennessee* (1834; A Facsimile Edition with Annotations and an Introduction by James A. Shackford and Stanley J. Folmsbee, Knoxville: University of Tennessee Press, 1973; **A, G**). Written after the appearance of a spurious biography in 1833, Crockett's book claims to be an attempt to correct the earlier book's errors. Written with assistance from Thomas Chilton, it is actually an attempt to enlarge his reputation as a backwoodsman and to help him win reelection to Congress. Though often exaggerated and sometimes misleading, the autobiography is generally accurate and is considered an early masterpiece of American humor. It is the only genuine autobiography of several attributed to Crockett.

The extant Crockett manuscript collections are small, containing from one to five letters, but many contain valuable material. Collections with more than one letter include the Historical Society of Pennsylvania; the Tennessee State Library and Archives; the State Historical Society of Wisconsin; Yale University; the Chicago Historical Society; Indiana University; and the New-York Historical Society.

Fiction and Adaptations

Tall tales, legends, and myths are crucial to an understanding of David Crockett. The most lasting images of Crockett are as Davy, the frontiersman, the joking Congressman, and the hero of the Alamo; both the printed word and the motion picture helped to establish and confirm this Crockett. Some of the earliest tales were the most influential ones, appearing in several popular series of almanacs supposedly written by Crockett. The first two series, published in Nashville from 1835 to 1841, have been reprinted in Franklin J. Meine, ed., *The Crockett Alma-*

nacks: Nashville Series, 1835-1838 (1955), and Michael A. Lofaro, ed., *The Tall Tales of Davy Crockett: The Second Nashville Series of Crockett Almanacs 1839-1841* (1987). Particularly significant modern collections include Walter Blair, *Davy Crockett—Frontier Hero: The Truth as He Told It—The Legend as His Friends Built It* (1955); Richard M. Dorson, ed., *Davy Crockett: American Comic Legend* (1939); and Constance Rourke, *Davy Crockett* (1934). Dorson reprinted some of the best stories from the almanacs; Blair and Rourke adapted the stories and retold them imaginatively.

Perhaps the most enduring David Crockett appeared on television and in film. Walt Disney, looking for an American folk hero to feature on his television series *Disneyland*, decided on Crockett and aired three episodes in late 1954 and early 1955. Starring Fess Parker as Crockett, Disney's series was wildly successful, starting a Davy Crockett fad that became a phenomenon of American popular culture. Coonskin caps were perhaps the most obvious result of the craze, and the series' theme song, "The Ballad of Davy Crockett," sold over four million records. Disney's three television episodes were soon combined and released as a feature film, *Davy Crockett: King of the Wild Frontier*. Though the third episode depicted Crockett at the Alamo, the demand was so great that another two episodes, detailing earlier adventures, were filmed. They too were released as a feature film. Disney's Crockett is humorous, practical, and, when necessary, heroic—a role model for children. The fad died out by the end of 1955, but its impact on the popular perception of Crockett was enormous and lasting. Another notable film version of Crockett is portrayed by John Wayne in *The Alamo*, (1960). Wayne's Crockett is more understated than Disney's and more conscious of his own stature as a popular hero.

Museums, Historical Landmarks, Societies

The Alamo (San Antonio, TX). The site of the famous siege in which Crockett and some 150 others died.

David Crockett Cabin (Rutherford, TN). A cabin in which the young Crockett lived, with the grave of his mother Rebecca nearby.

David Crockett Tavern and Museum (Morristown, TN). A reproduction of the 1795 tavern operated by Crockett's father.

Davy Crockett Birthplace State Historic Area (Greene County, TN). A replica of the cabin in which Crockett was born.

Tennessee State Museum (Nashville, TN). Houses exhibits on Crockett's life, including his rifles and a bench he made.

Other Sources

Kilgore, Dan. *How Did Davy Die?* College Station: Texas A&M University Press, 1978. A short synthesis of the accounts of Crockett's death, Kilgore's book concludes that he survived the battle at the Alamo only to be captured and executed.

Lord, Walter. *A Time to Stand.* New York: Harper and Row, 1961. Though written for a popular audience, this is well-written and based on solid research; it is the single best account of the Alamo, placing the battle in the context of Texas's fight for independence.

Schoelwer, Susan Prendergast. *Alamo Images: Changing Perceptions of a Texas Experience.* Vol. 3 of the DeGolyer Library Publications Series. Dallas: DeGolyer Library and Southern Methodist University Press, 1985. Schoelwer's study, the catalog for an exhibit at Southern Methodist University, is a fascinating assessment of changing American perceptions of the Alamo since 1836.

J. Tracy Power
South Carolina Department of Archives and History

Davy Crockett, 1957

GEORGE A. CUSTER
1839–1876

Chronology

Born George Armstrong Custer on December 5, 1839, in New Rumley, Ohio, the eldest son of Emanuel Custer, the town blacksmith, and Maria Kirkpatrick Custer, who is Emanuel's second wife; *1836–1856* spends his formative years living on his father's small farm near New Rumley and in Monroe, Michigan, in the home of one of his half-sisters; attends Boys and Young Mens Academy in Monroe and McNeeley Normal school in Hopedale, Ohio, and briefly teaches school; *1857* appointed to the United States Military Academy by Congressman John A. Bingham of Ohio; *1857–1861* attends U.S. Military Academy and graduates with an undistinguished record as the Civil War begins; *1862* attracts the attention of General George B. McClellan, who appoints him to his staff; *1863* moves to staff of General Alfred Pleasonton, who commands the Army of the Potomac Cavalry Corps; determined to improve the Union cavalry, Pleasonton promotes Custer to Brigadier General of Volunteers, and Custer's rise to prominence as a twenty-three-year-old general is assured; *1863–1865* gains fame as an aggressive cavalry officer on Pleasonton's staff and later as Major General of Volunteers commanding the Third Cavalry Division under General Philip Sheridan, who assumes command of Army of the Potomac's cavalry; *1864* marries Elizabeth Bacon, a member of a prominent family in Monroe, Michigan, and distinguishes himself as a successful cavalry leader to the war's end; *1865–1866* serves in post-war army as a Captain in the United States Fifth Cavalry in Texas; *1866* commissioned Lieutenant Colonel in newly forming Seventh Cavalry and becomes actual commander as the Seventh's Colonel remains on detached duty; *1867* leads an unsuccessful campaign against the Southern Cheyenne and is court-martialed and suspended from duty for being absent without permission while at his ailing wife's side; *1868* returns to the Seventh Cavalry and leads an attack on Black Kettle's camp on the Washita River in Indian Territory, dealing a heavy blow to the Cheyenne and also advancing his name as an aggressive frontier soldier; *1869–1873* serves on Kansas frontier and in Kentucky, then leads the expedition to explore the Black Hills in Dakota Territory; *1873–1876* posted with Seventh Cavalry at Fort Abraham Lincoln in Dakota Territory; leads his unit into battle at the Little Bighorn River on June 25, 1876, where his forces, which he divides to attack the Sioux and Cheyenne camped along the Little Bighorn, are defeated; dies with five companies of his men, who are annihilated by an Indian force of greater numbers than anyone in the army thought possible to assemble.

Activities of Historical Significance

Custer's enduring notoriety sadly rests upon the military debacle he led his troops into that fateful Sunday afternoon in 1876 on the Little Bighorn River in modern-day Montana. Until the disaster on the Little Bighorn, Custer was not a national figure, but those who were familiar with his exploits recognized him as an aggressive, somewhat vain and eccentric soldier whose bravery and stamina were unquestionable. Some of his critics, and he had many, believed Custer frequently failed to think carefully before he acted, while his many admirers viewed him as a daring, decisive, and ideal cavalryman. He was a decidedly controversial figure who provoked strong reactions to his personality, style of life, and leadership traits.

From the days of his victories in the Civil War to his death at the age of thirty-six, Custer constantly sought command and combat and, for the most part, acquitted himself well. Between 1862 and 1876, he earned the reputation of being a dashing cavalryman and acquired a bit of celebrity in the process. Nevertheless, he was nowhere as well known prior to 1876 as he became after his downfall in the campaign against the Sioux and Cheyenne.

He nearly wrecked his career in 1876 and missed his rendezvous with destiny when he testified in the investigation about the management of Indian affairs and antagonized President Ulysses S. Grant. Custer's testimony, which seemed to implicate one of Grant's relatives in the growing scandal, angered the President, who ordered that Custer not take part in the upcoming 1876 campaign. General Alfred Terry wanted Custer to be in the campaign, intervened on Custer's behalf, and got him reinstated even though the President remained unmollified. Custer then led the Seventh Cavalry to the Little Bighorn and into legend. Had Custer not been defeated so dramatically, he and his exploits prior to 1876 would probably have drawn scant attention. He was a competent soldier who won immortality from his single worst blunder.

Overview of Biographical Sources

Readers will have no difficulty locating biographical sources related to Custer's life and role in the army. In fact, more has probably been written about him than has been written about any other American military figure. No other American soldier's life has prompted a fiercer debate, and the outpouring has continued almost from the day of Custer's defeat to the present time. Some of the more important accounts are Frederick Whittaker's *A Complete Life of Gen. George A. Custer* (1876); Frederick Van De Water's *Glory-Hunter, A Life of General Custer* (1931); Edgar I. Stewart's *Custer's Luck* (1955); Jay Monaghan's *Custer: The Life of George Armstrong Custer* (1959); Lawrence A. Frost's *The Custer Album* (1964) and *General Custer's Libbie* (1976); Stephen E. Ambrose's *Crazy Horse and Custer: The Parallel Lives of Two American Warriors* (1975); Brian W. Dippie's *Custer's Last Stand: The Anatomy of an American Myth* (1976); and Gregory J. W.

Urwin's *Custer Victorious: The Civil War Battles of General George Armstrong Custer* (1983). These secondary works illuminate Custer's strengths and weaknesses and clearly illustrate the vast difference of opinion concerning his merit as a military commander.

Evaluation of Principal Biographical Sources

Ambrose, Stephen E. *Crazy Horse and Custer: The Parallel Lives of Two American Warriors*. Garden City, NY: Doubleday, 1975. (A, G) Written by an American author who has written on a variety of subjects. This book provides an amazing insight into the personalities of the two men who were destined to clash on the Little Bighorn.

Connell, Evan S. *Son of the Morning Star*. San Francisco: North Point Press, 1984. (A, G) Connell explores deeply the personalities of Custer and other federal and Indian leaders while attempting to explain how the complete tragedy of the Little Bighorn evolved.

Dippie, Brian W. *Custer's Last Stand: The Anatomy of an American Myth*. Missoula: University of Montana Publications in History, 1976. (A, G) This study, as its title clearly implies, deals with the question of why and how the Custer "massacre" became such a large issue in American military history. It is an excellent account of this aspect of the Custer legend.

Frost, Lawrence A. *The Custer Album: A Pictorial Biography of General George A. Custer*. Seattle, WA: Superior Publishing, 1964. (A, G) Frost, who was a practicing physician in Monroe, Michigan, and curator of the Custer Museum, has assembled in this volume some of the best Custer photographs to be found anywhere.

————. *General Custer's Libbie*. Seattle, WA: Superior Publishing, 1976. (A, G) In this volume, Frost examines the life of Elizabeth Bacon Custer and her positive impact on the General's life. It, like Frost's *Custer Album*, contains an excellent array of photographs depicting Libbie's life.

Monaghan, Jay. *Custer: The Life of George Armstrong Custer*. Boston: Little, Brown, 1959. (A, G) This is the best overall biography of Custer's life. Monaghan is sympathetic to Custer, yet he maintains a good balance when judging his subject's deeds. This book is the best source for the beginner to read. It is a fairly comprehensive, thorough account of Custer's life and times.

Stewart, Edgar I. *Custer's Luck*. Norman: University of Oklahoma Press, 1955. (A, G) The best study of the events of the 1870s leading to the battle on the Little Bighorn. Stewart deals with Indian policy, the peace policy, and the gathering storm of the 1870s. He does not place a great emphasis on the personality of Custer.

Urwin, Gregory J. W. *Custer Victorious: The Civil War Battles of George Armstrong Custer*. London and Toronto: Associated University Presses, 1983. **(A, G)** There is nothing better than this account of Custer's feats as a cavalryman in the Civil War. Urwin has carefully studied Custer's rise in the Union cavalry and he also provides some important insights into the General's personality, habits, and battlefield traits. An outstanding piece of scholarship.

Van De Water, Frederick F. *Glory-Hunter: A Life of General Custer*. Indianapolis: The Bobbs-Merrill Company, 1931. **(A, G)** The title of this book clearly describes the author's attitude toward his subject. This biography has several serious flaws, but it is representative of how some writers have positioned themselves as open, vigorous critics of Custer.

Whittaker, Frederick. *A Complete Life of Gen. George A. Custer, Major-General of Volunteers, Brevet Major-General U.S. Army, and Lieutenant Colonel Seventh U.S. Cavalry*. New York: Sheldon and Company, 1876. **(A, G)** The first Custer biography, this work has many flaws, but, once a reader gains some understanding of Custer and the issues of his day, it is worth reading.

Overview and Evaluation of Primary Sources

There are a good many sources readers may consult to gain a first-hand understanding of the events surrounding much of Custer's life. One of the first volumes a reader may wish to consult is George A. Custer's *My Life on the Plains*, edited by Milo Milton Quaife (New York: The Citadel Press, 1962; **A, G**). This was written and originally issued in 1874, and obviously does not deal with some of the more fateful events of the last few years of his life. Elizabeth Bacon Custer published three interesting books, *Books and Saddles* (New York: Harper and Brothers, 1885; **A, G**), *Following the Guidon* (New York: Harper and Brothers, 1890; **A, G**), and *Tenting on the Plains* (New York: C. L. Webster, 1893; **A, G**). All three describe the life of a frontier soldier's wife and, at the same time, provide a lovingly biased view of Custer as a man and husband. Mrs. Custer was a good writer and her books are pleasant reading. An excellent source to use to understand George and Elizabeth is Marguerite Merington, ed., *The Custer Story: The Life and Intimate Letters of General Custer and His Wife Elizabeth* (New York: Devin-Adair, 1950; **A, G**). Another good source to use to gain an insight into life in the Seventh Cavalry is Robert M. Utley, ed., *Life in Custer's Cavalry: Diaries and Letters of Albert and Jennie Barnitz, 1867–1868* (New Haven: Yale University Press, 1977; **A, G**). Also see Brian W. Dippie, ed., *Nomad: George A. Custer in Turf, Field, and Farm* (Austin, TX: University of Texas Press, 1980; **A, G**). "Nomad" was Custer as he moved about and wrote of his experiences for a popular magazine. In the process of relating some of "Nomad's" experiences, Custer reveals a good deal about himself.

In addition to the works relating to the Custers' lives, there are autobiographies and memoirs that will help a reader understand the 1860s and 1870s. These writings include Philip H. Sheridan, *Personal Memoirs*, 2 vols. (New York: Charles L. Webster, 1888; **A, G**); Martin F. Schmitt, ed., *General George Crook: His Autobiography* (Norman: University of Oklahoma Press, 1960; **A, G**); George B. McClellan, *McClellan's Own Story* (New York: Charles L. Webster, 1887; **A, G**); Nelson A. Miles, *Personal Recollections and Observations* (New York: Werner, 1896; **A, G**); Anson Mills, *My Story* (Washington, D.C.: privately printed, 1918; **A, G**); and John M. Carroll, ed., *Custer in the Civil War: His Unfinished Memoirs* (San Rafael, CA: Presidio Press, 1977; **A, G**).

The Western Collection of the Billings, Montana, Public Library contains the Custer Files and the Custer Scrapbooks. The files include a mass of miscellaneous material dealing with Custer's "Last Stand," and the scrapbooks are a semi-useful collection of newspaper clippings relating to the Custers. The Elizabeth B. Custer Papers are held at Eastern Montana College.

Fiction and Adaptations

Custer's life and his defeat at the Little Bighorn have been the subjects of two films. The earlier of the two films was entitled *They Died with Their Boots On*. This film, which was released in 1941, features Errol Flynn, Olivia de Havilland, and Anthony Quinn and tells a heavily fictionalized account of Custer's life from West Point to the Little Bighorn. A second feature film on Custer's life, entitled *Custer of the West*, was released in 1968. This film, starring Robert Shaw, Mary Ure, and Robert Ryan, was filmed in Spain and concentrated on Custer and his last battle. Other films, such as *Little Big Man* (1970), have Custer as a part of their plots. In *Little Big Man* Custer is portrayed as being mad. To date, an accurate, historically sound film of Custer's life has not been produced. One interesting novel, Douglas C. Jones, *The Court-Martial of George Armstrong Custer* (1976), deserves mention. Jones's novel develops from the premise that Custer was found alive on the battlefield among his slain men and the army has to decide what to do with him.

Museums, Historical Landmarks, Societies

Custer Battlefield National Monument (Crow Agency, MT). The site where Custer and his forces were obliterated is preserved. Markers indicate where the last of Custer's men fell, and a visitor center features exhibits that reenact the confrontation.

Custer Memorial State Park (near New Rumbley, OH). The site of Custer's birth and childhood home is preserved here with a statue, monument, and collection of artifacts from his life.

Fort Abraham Lincoln State Historical Park (Mandan, ND). The fort from which Custer led his men to defeat at Little Bighorn is now a state park. The site houses Mandan Indian artifacts and memorabilia from Custer, the Seventh Cavalry, and the 1870s military.

Way Park Museum (Custer, SD). Located in the Way City Park, this museum has a collection of artifacts from Custer's Seventh Cavalry.

Other Sources

Garland, Hamlin. "General Custer's Last Fight as Seen by Two Moon." *McClure's* 9 (September 1898): 443–448. The Indians' point of view.

Gibbon, Colonel John. "Last Summer's Expedition against the Sioux." *American Catholic Quarterly Review* 2 (April 1877): 271–304. A good account of the 1876 campaign written by an eyewitness right after the events in question.

Graham, William A. *The Custer Myth: A Source Book of Custeriana*. Harrisburg, PA: Stackpole, 1953. This volume contains an array of Custer materials. Several eyewitness accounts of the Little Bighorn battle are reproduced here.

———. *The Reno Court of Inquiry*. Harrisburg, PA: Stackpole, 1954. Major Marcus Reno was in command of one part of the attack on the Sioux and Cheyenne on the Little Bighorn in 1876 and, after considerable investigation of his conduct in that battle, he was acquitted of any charge of wrongful action.

Kidd, James H. *Personal Recollections of a Cavalryman with Custer's Michigan Cavalry Brigade in the Civil War*. Ionia, MI: The Sentinel Press, 1908. An interesting memoir by a man who served with Custer in the glory days of the Civil War.

Larry G. Bowman
University of North Texas

RICHARD J. DALEY
1902-1976

Chronology

Born Richard Joseph Daley on May 15, 1902, in Chicago, Illinois, the only son of Irish-American Catholics Michael Daley, a sheet-metal worker, and Lillian Dunne Daley; *1902-1920* grows up in Southside Chicago where he attends a Roman Catholic elementary school, serves as an altar boy, and then graduates from Christian Brothers De LaSalle High School; *1920-1933* works as a stockyard "cowboy," clerks in the Cook County controller's office, and enrolls at DePaul Law School at night, where he earns a law diploma; *1933-1946* works his way up through the precinct and ward organization and is elected Illinois state representative in 1936, and two years later, to the Illinois state senate, where he serves until 1946; *1936* marries Eleanor Guilfoyle, with whom he will have four sons and three daughters; *1946-1953* suffers his only election loss in 1946 as a Democratic candidate for Cook County Sheriff; appointed state revenue director by Illinois Governor Adlai Stevenson; returns to Chicago as elected clerk of the Cook County Board of Commissioners; *1953* elected chairman of the Cook County Democratic Central Committee, which becomes the springboard for his mayoral candidacy; *1955-1975* defeats incumbent Democratic Mayor Martin H. Kennelly in a primary election and then wins over a Republican challenger in the general election of that year; reelected mayor five consecutive times, and establishes an all-time record of mayoral office holding for twenty-one years; *1976* dies on December 20 in Chicago, early in his sixth term and is buried in Worth, Illinois.

Activities of Historical Significance

Daley's twenty-one-year tenure established a record among Chicago's mayors. In that office, he helped to reverse a downward trend in the central business district, renewing it with a building boom, professionalizing the police force, and upgrading the fire department's services. Daley solved a Chicago Transit Authority cash crisis by creating a Regional Transit Authority which broadened the tax base and brought more resources to transportation. During his career Daley expanded city services while deftly shifting a large measure of the costs onto the state, the county, and the Chicago-area suburbs. An astute financial manager, the mayor pushed the state legislature to pass a measure that transferred the cost of administering welfare programs from the city and county to the state, and helped form a Public Building Commission to finance public construction through the use of revenue bonds while protecting the city's bond rating. He also prodded the state to form a Metropolitan Fair and Exposition Authority which built a convention center in the city at little cost to the Chicago taxpayers. Finally, he persuaded the state to build a University of Illinois campus in Chicago, at state taxpayers' expense, which has served primarily Chicago area students. Daley's superior ability as a budget manager and an expert on public finance became clearer in the mid-1970s when bankruptcy threatened cities such as New York, Cleveland, and Detroit, while Chicago retained a top-grade, gilt-edged credit and bond rating with the two major public credit rating services.

Politically, Richard Daley was known as the last of the big city machine bosses and probably the most powerful mayor of his time. He was credited by many pundits with having helped elect John F. Kennedy president in 1960, and was one of the premier power brokers in Democratic politics during the 1960s. His reputation among liberal Democrats suffered grievously as a result of his "shoot to kill" order during the riots following Martin Luther King Jr.'s murder, and his rough handling of street and anti-war protesters at the 1968 Democratic National Convention held in Chicago. Media liberals predicted that Daley's public career was finished, and the lockout of the Daley delegation by the liberal McGovern wing from the 1972 Democratic National Convention seemed to clinch that view. Yet the naysayers proved wrong, for Daley went on to win his largest mayoral victory ever in 1975, securing an unprecedented sixth term to that office.

Daley was also criticized for his unwillingness to reach out to the suburbs and recruit new voters, for his slow accommodation of newcomer blacks and Hispanics in the party, and for his stormy relations with the press and news media. Yet most voters were pleased to have a steady hand steering the city through the turbulent and riot-ridden 1960s and a traditionalist reassuring them that their world would not be turned upside-down. The city's building boom, along with its solid financial base and strong credit ratings, also improved Daley's image. Daley's public reputation had ridden a political roller coaster, but recovered in time for a glorious obituary at his death in 1976.

Overview of Biographical Sources

Richard J. Daley has been the subject of much newspaper reportage, many scholarly articles, and several biographies, including Mike Royko's *Boss: Richard J. Daley of Chicago* (1971), which New York writer Jimmy Breslin described as a book "which does more written damage to a man than perhaps anything I have ever read." A more balanced view, although equally incomplete, is Bill Gleason's *Daley of Chicago* (1970), which does not cover the mayor's fifth term in office. Surprisingly, very few of the ex-mayor's principal aides have published reminiscences, although many have made themselves available for interviews by the media and scholars. Scholars have written more about the constituent issues of Daley's Chicago, such as race, patronage, and elections, than about Daley himself. One notable work that does attempt to probe the inner workings of the man is Eugene Kennedy's *Himself: The Life and Times of Mayor Richard J. Daley* (1978), which deals with Daley's Irish heritage. The best single work on how the Daley political machine operated is Milton Rakove's *Don't Make No Waves—Don't Back No Losers: An Insider's Analysis of the Daley Machine* (1975).

Evaluation of Principal Biographical Sources

Gleason, Bill. *Daley of Chicago: The Man, the Mayor, and the Limits of Conventional Politics*. New York: Simon and Schuster, 1970. **(A, G)** Provides balanced coverage of the mayor as politician through Daley's difficult fourth term which included the convention and King riots.

Kennedy, Eugene. *Himself: The Life and Times of Mayor Richard J. Daley*. New York: Viking, 1978. **(A, G)** Seeks to probe the inside workings of the man, and treats the mythic and Irish dimension of Daley the urban chieftain with insight and imagination.

O'Connor, Len. *Clout: Mayor Daley and His City*. Chicago: Regnery, 1975. **(G)** A knowledgeable and veteran city watcher and newspaperman, Len O'Connor provides insight into Daley's power base and political style.

―――. *Requiem: The Decline and Demise of Mayor Daley and His Era*. Chicago: Contemporary Books, 1977. **(A, G)** Written after Daley's death, O'Connor takes a second look at the Daley machine, its steady decline before the mayor's demise, and Daley's legacy to the city.

Rakove, Milton. *Don't Make No Waves—Don't Back No Losers: An Insider's Analysis of the Daley Machine*. Bloomington: Indiana University Press, 1975. **(A, G)** The single best account of how the Daley political machine accumulated and used power.

Royko, Mike. *Boss: Richard J. Daley of Chicago*. New York: Dutton, 1971. **(A, G)** A highly entertaining, wickedly clever, and often illuminating look at the frailties and strengths of Richard Daley and his long-lived political machine. The author, a long time critic of Chicago's Democratic machine politics, catapulted himself to national fame with this book.

Overview and Evaluation of Primary Sources

No comprehensive archive of Daley's manuscripts or papers exists, but items relating to his public career can be found in several repositories. The Chicago Historical Society has some limited material, including a video tape collection of the mayor's news conferences and public appearances. The University of Illinois at Chicago's manuscripts division has an incomplete file of Daley's typed speech transcripts through his third term. Some of the mayor's speech "bloopers" were compiled and published by Peter Yessne in *Quotations from Mayor Daley* (New York: Putnam, 1969; **A, G**).

Fiction and Adaptations

Daley's life has not been the subject of a feature-length movie or television series, although Chicago's local television stations have produced "specials" on the former mayor. In 1986, on the tenth anniversary of his death, WBBM-TV produced "The Daley Years," WMAQ-TV showed "Hizzoner," and WTTW-TV aired a two-hour special entitled "Daley."

Museums, Historical Landmarks, Societies

Daley Center (Chicago, IL). A plaza and public office building named in honor of the former mayor.

Daley College (Chicago, IL). A junior college named after the late mayor.

Other Sources

Green, Paul M., and Melvin G. Holli, eds. *The Mayors: The Chicago Political Tradition*. Carbondale: Southern Illinois University Press, 1987. Places Daley in historical perspective with Chicago's other elected mayors, and polls experts who rank Daley as the city's best chief executive.

Rakove, Milton. *We Don't Want Nobody Nobody Sent*. Bloomington: Indiana University Press, 1979. An engaging collection of oral histories on how precinct captains and ward bosses kept the machine running.

Melvin G. Holli
University of Illinois at Chicago

CLARENCE DARROW
1857–1938

Chronology

Born Clarence Seward Darrow on April 18, 1857, in Farmdale, Ohio, the fifth of eight children of Amirus Darrow, furniture-maker, undertaker, and bookish agnostic, and Emily Eddy Darrow, a woman's rights advocate; *1863–1873* grows up in Kinsman, Ohio, learning to speak in public from an early age; attends Presbyterian church with mother, who dies when he is fourteen; loves baseball but is an indifferent student in the public schools; *1873–1874* attends preparatory department at Allegheny College in Meadville, Pennsylvania; *1874–1877* drops out of school in the aftermath of the Panic of 1873; teaches school in Vernon, Ohio; joins in local Saturday night debates and begins to read law; *1877–1878* attends University of Michigan Law School in Ann Arbor; *1878* clerks in Youngstown, Ohio, law office; is admitted to state bar and returns to Kinsman; *1880* marries high school sweetheart Jessie Ohl, whose prosperous mill-owning family supplies him with law books; *1880–1883* practices law in Andover, Ohio; becomes involved in Democratic politics; only child, Paul, is born; *1884–1887* moves to Ashtabula, the county seat; is mentored by Judge Laban Sherman, and is elected borough solicitor; reads Henry George and John Peter Altgeld's *Our Penal Machinery and Its Victims*; *1887–1888* moves to Chicago to practice law; joins Haymarket Amnesty Association, Henry George Single Tax Club, and the Sunset Club, and mingles with political and reform leaders, attracting recognition as a public speaker and debater; *1889–1892* appointed special assessment attorney, and later, Chicago corporation counsel; successfully represents city to gain right-of-way from railways for construction of roads to the World's Fair; becomes Judge John Peter Altgeld's confidant and political agent in gubernatorial race; *1892–1894* hired by legal department of Chicago and North Western Railway; *1893–1897* is partner in firm of Collins, Goodrich, Darrow and Vincent; in 1893, works with S. S. Gregory (later American Bar Association president) in unsuccessful defense appeal for Patrick Eugene Prendergast, assassin of Chicago Mayor Carter Harrison; first literary essay, "Realism in Literature and Art," published in *Arena*; *1894–1913* begins phase as a labor lawyer, resigning as railroad attorney to defend Eugene Debs and the American Railway Union in the aftermath of the Pullman strike, although the conspiracy case is eventually dismissed when a juror becomes ill; *1895* loses federal injunction case against Debs, who is convicted of contempt of court and sent to jail; *1896* runs unsuccessfully as Democratic candidate for the 3rd congressional district seat; *1897* divorces wife; *1897–1903* draws lucrative business to new firm of Darrow, Thomas and Thompson; takes model tenement apartment near Hull House, which becomes center of circle of "new women" and literary figures; *1898* successfully defends Thomas I. Kidd, general secretary of Amalgamated Woodworkers International Union, against conspiracy charges in strike against Paine

360

Lumber Company; *1899* publishes *A Persian Pearl and Other Essays*; Altgeld joins law firm as a senior partner; *1902* writes series of stories for the Hearst papers about common law defenses used against workers seeking compensation for industrial accidents; Altgeld, his close friend and mentor, dies an impoverished, embittered and discredited man, and Darrow joins Jane Addams in giving a memorial oration; is elected to Illinois House of Representatives as an independent from the 17th district; publishes pacifist essays as *Resist Not Evil*; *1902–1903* appointed counsel for the United Mine Workers, representing the union's strike position at hearings of the U.S. Anthracite Coal Commission; *1903–1911* establishes new firm of Darrow, Masters and Wilson; marries Ruby Hammerstom, a journalist, in 1903; honeymoons in Europe, where he becomes friends with George Bernard Shaw; *1904* nominates William Randolph Hearst for president at Democratic National Convention in St. Louis; fictionalized childhood reminiscences are published as *Farmington*; *1905* signs call to establish Intercollegiate Socialist Society; appointed Chicago traction counsel; his naturalist novel dealing with capital punishment, *An Eye for an Eye*, is published; *1906–1908* successfully defends officials of the Western Federation of Miners Union against charges of conspiracy to murder former Idaho Governor Steunenberg; nearly dies from an ear infection; *1910* represents labor on arbitration panel to settle Chicago garment workers strike; *1911–1913* persuaded by Samuel Gompers to defend McNamara brothers in Los Angeles *Times* bombing case, and angers organized labor and Socialists when he changes plea to guilty to save the brothers' lives; exhausts funds and self in successful defense against charges of juror bribery; *1913–1925* enters criminal defense practice with new firm of Darrow, Sissman, Holly, and Carlin; begins national lecture and debate circuit to repay debts; *1916* ignores hostile poem, "On a Bust," written by former law partner Edgar Lee Masters; *1917–1918* casts aside Tolstoyan pacifism, regaining some respectability as supporter for American entry into World War I; *1919–1920* defends Communists in free speech cases around the country; extends First Amendment free speech guarantees in Gitlow cases; *1922* publishes *Crime: Its Cause and Treatment*; *1924* saves lives of Leopold and Loeb in Bobby Frank murder case after a guilty plea, by convincing judge to accept mental illness as a defense; *1925* participates in famous "monkey trial," defending Tennessee schoolteacher John Scopes who is charged with violating state anti-evolution laws by teaching Darwinian theory, although he loses the trial (a higher court later overturns the ruling); puts prosecuting attorney William Jennings Bryan on the witness stand, and Bryan defends the Biblical story of creation; *1925–1926* acts as defense lawyer for the NAACP in the racially heated Sweet case in Detroit; *1927* is defense attorney in New York's Greco–Carillo murder case; *1928* name appears in *Red Network*, published by the DAR; *1929–1930* retires; loses wealth in stock-market crash; reenters public life; *1931* declines to join the Scottsboro defense; *1932* defends Lt. Massie, a naval officer, and a southern family in murder of a Hawaiian; publishes autobiography, *The Story of My Life*; *1934–1935* chairs President Franklin Roosevelt's National Recovery Administration Review Board; *1938* dies on March 13 in Chicago, following a long, debilitating illness; his ashes are scattered from the Jackson Park bridge.

Activities of Historical Significance

In an era of rapid social change, Clarence Darrow's courtroom defenses of persons and causes that challenged the old paradigms educated the general public about the common humanity of all of society, and contributed to a climate in which experts and reformers crafted Progressive Era political solutions, including state workmen's compensation laws, union recognition, collective bargaining, and expansion of constitutional free speech protections.

Darrow's existential hacking away at chaos, chance and free will to reveal fixed environmental and biological systems governing behavior resulted case by case in new understandings of the human condition. Ordinary jurors and consumers of the popular media came to understand and identify with the disenfranchised, the oppressed, the sick, and the poor as victims of society or of their own natures. The free will assumptions implicit in Anglo-American theories of law and punishment were called into question by Darrow, who pleaded for tolerance and mercy, cure and treatment, seeking societal transformation rather than retribution and punishment. Students of radical criminology and critical legal studies take up many of these themes today, while the oppressed or exploited groups whom Darrow defended have gradually been incorporated into a range of rights, entitlements, and protections through federal statutes or landmark court cases in the half century since Darrow's death.

Finally, Darrow left a legacy of tactical brilliance in controversial cases that has captured the popular imagination, and has turned many a precocious adolescent to a legal career. His extraordinary skills in interrogation and selection of jurists, in cross-examination, and in summation, continue to serve as textbook exemplars for lawyers, rhetoricians, and political scientists.

Overview of Biographical Sources

Darrow has been the subject of popular full-length biographies such as Charles Yale Harrison, *Clarence Darrow* (1931), Irving Stone, *Clarence Darrow for the Defense* (1941), Kevin Tierney, *Darrow: A Biography* (1979), and Arthur and Lila Weinberg, *Clarence Darrow, A Sentimental Rebel* (1980). He has also been the subject of many scholarly, legal, historical, and psychological treatises, articles, essays, and personal reminiscences.

Alan Hynd's vignette in *Defenders of the Damned* (1960) portrays Darrow the trickster, scowling, shuffling, unkempt, and magnetic in the courtroom. On the other hand, Charles True Wilson, a Methodist minister who debated Darrow on the meaning of life, praises him for his personal warmth and candor in "Darrow, Friendly Enemy," in John A. Beckwith and Geoffrey Coope, eds., *Contemporary American Biography* (1941).

Indeed, many of Darrow's contemporaries were transfixed by his forceful, complex character, and boundless energy. Attempts to decode the mystery of the man, as evidenced through their diaries, letters, and memoirs, can be found in William Ryan, "The Later Years: Radical Energy and Stormy Seas," in *Humanist* (1967), and in the writings of co-counsel Arthur Garfield Hays, *Let Freedom Ring* (1928), *Trial by Prejudice* (1933), and *City Lawyer* (1942), and in the scattered references in correspondence and autobiographies by Lincoln Steffens, Brand Whitlock, H. L. Mencken, George Jean Nathan, Hamlin Garland, and Hutchins Hapgood. The poet Edgar Lee Masters, who was Darrow's partner during the Western Federation of Miners trials, sketches a dark portrait of Darrow in *Across Spoon River: An Autobiography* (1936), as does Adela Rogers St. John (whose father defended Darrow in the first bribery trial in Los Angeles) in *Final Verdict* (1962).

Darrow's connection with Altgeld, labor, and Hull House is richly woven in Ray Ginger, *Altgeld's America: The Lincoln Ideal Versus Changing Realities* (1958). In an earlier article, "Darrow," in *Antioch Review* (1953), Ginger stresses the discontinuities in Darrow's career, and the sources of his contradictory mechanistic-individualism.

Darrow's use of psychology to outmaneuver his opponents has been discussed in a number of works. "The goat theory"—Darrow's singling out of a prosecution attorney or opposing witness for personal humiliation and destruction in summation—is analyzed by Jacob A. Stein in "Great Arguments: Haywood Found Not Guilty," in *Litigation* (1986).

Darrow's tactical brilliance in jury selection and use of ethnic, religious, and psychological profiles is discussed in numerous articles, notably Matilda Fenberg, "I Remember Clarence Darrow," in *Chicago History* (1973), and Ann Fagan Ginger, "Watching Darrow Work a Jury," in *Criminal Justice Journal* (1985). His views on capital punishment are examined in James Edward Sayer, *Clarence Darrow: Public Advocate* (1978).

Although Darrow's legal legend now overshadows his literary legacy, there have also been several works produced about his writing. Donald Pizer, *Twentieth Century Literary Naturalism: An Interpretation* (1982), places Darrow's *An Eye for an Eye* and his short stories in the context of naturalism, in which thwarted potential defines the American sense of the tragic. In a book-length study, Abe C. Ravitz's *Clarence Darrow and the American Literary Tradition* (1962), Darrow is seen as "a conscious artist writing in the genre which was to become prominent a few years later with the publication of Upton Sinclair's *The Jungle*."

A comprehensive bibliography by Willard D. Hunsberger, *Clarence Darrow: A Bibliography* (1981), covers contemporary and secondary sources on trials with which Darrow was associated, as well as biographical writings through 1979.

Evaluation of Principal Biographical Sources

Harrison, Charles Yale. *Clarence Darrow*. New York: Jonathan Cape and Harrison Smith, 1931. (**A, G**) A sympathetic biography written with the cooperation of his subject. An American-born Canadian journalist, Harrison vividly evokes the public Darrow in the Haymarket-Pullman Strike decade telling Irish nationalists in a Chicago speech "obedience to the law is not the highest virtue." Interviews with Darrow admirers provide the principal source and slant on the famous trials. Omitted are unromanticized accounts of the first marriage, the political work for Altgeld, the corporate law phase. Harrison repeats the contemporary view that Darrow was not a great lawyer, but a "very effective jury lawyer and pleader."

Stone, Irving. *Clarence Darrow for the Defense*. Garden City, NY: Doubleday, 1941. (**A, G**) Stone, a prolific writer of best sellers, published this work three years after the lawyer's death, and it has become the source of much of the enduring hero legend. Like Harrison, Stone's biography is rich in uncritically retold interview material; Stone's visualizations of Darrow scenes, anecdotes, philosophical stances, mental agility, and opportunism provide insights not to be overlooked. Unlike some other writers, he credits Darrow with enormous preparation time, writing and memorizing, before delivering his addresses, "full of striking, original statements, in simple language, punctuated with shafts of wit and sarcasm . . . . "

Tierney, Kevin. *Darrow: A Biography*. New York: Thomas Y. Crowell, 1979. (**A, G**) Critical use of sources, a glimpse of Darrow's dark side, and elegantly written accounts of the famous trials rank this book by an English-born, Yale-educated lawyer among the best. Tierney constructs the case for Darrow as Altgeld's political agent in Chicago. He discerns a relation between Darrow's need for advocacy and iconoclasm manifested by frenetic work and speech schedules, and its function in warding off underlying depression. He brings to life the Hull House connection in the 1890s and "new women," such as Gertrude Barnum and Helen Todd, and explores Edgar Lee Masters's destructive dependence and Darrow's social marginality. He questions whether Darrow's social justice summations— repertoires of "original ploys, usuable and reusable . . . with only a minimum of modification"—really benefitted his clients, or merely represented a philosophical indulgence. His ambivalence and skepticism about his complex subject mark Tierney's study as a refreshing change in the biographical landscape.

Weinberg, Arthur, and Lila Weinberg. *Clarence Darrow: A Sentimental Rebel*. New York: G. P. Putnam's Sons, 1980. (**A, G**) The Weinbergs, students of Darrow's writings and related manuscript collections, have made many of his summations and debates accessible in published form. This full-length tribute to Darrow, a "folkhero in his own lifetime," revisits the Stone template and adds to it an extended discussion on the McNamara brothers' case and the bribery trials. Mary Field, a "new woman" omitted from other biographies, appears at critical junctures in Darrow's life. Further, the Weinbergs interpret the Los Angeles cases as crucial societal events leading to the investigations by Taft's Commission on Industrial Relations and to the passage of the Clayton Act in 1915 which recognized the right of labor to organize.

Overview and Evaluation of Primary Sources

Darrow's first articles were published in the newspapers. His literary and political addresses to the clubs of the 1890s were reworked, and some later appeared in *The Persian Pearl and Other Essays* (1899. Reprint. New York: Haskell House, 1974; **A**) as short pieces on secrets ("skeleton in the closet") and literary realism, and as interpretive sketches of Omar Khayyam, Walt Whitman, and Robert Burns. His Tolstoyan pacifism phase finds outlet in *Resist Not Evil* (1902. Reprint. Montclair, NJ: Patterson Smith, 1972; **A, G**). Powerful short stories and a naturalistic novel, *An Eye for an Eye* (1905. Reprint. Durham, NC: Moore, 1969; **A, G**), follow in a sustained period of creative achievement.

His theory of crime and human nature, expounded in jury summations, appeared in book form as *Crime: Its Cause and Treatment* (New York: Crowell, 1922; **A**). With Victor Yarros, he wrote *The Prohibition Mania* (New York: Boni and Liveright, 1927; **A, G**), and with Wallace Rice compiled *Infidels and Heretics: An Agnostic's Anthology* (1929. Reprint. New York: Gordon Press, 1975; **A, G**).

Darrow's perceptive fictionalized account of childhood in northeast Ohio, written in Europe during his honeymoon, is entitled *Farmington* (Chicago: A. C. McClurg, 1904; **G**). A philosophical autobiographical reflection, written almost thirty years later, was published as *The Story of My Life* (New York: Scribner's, 1932; **A, G**). Both are enduring.

Among the most often cited of Darrow's works are the jury summations, which contemporaries like William Dean Howells thought Darrow raised to a subliterary art form. Although still available in many libraries in the original Kerr or Haldeman-Julius format ("corrected" by Darrow from court transcripts), they are also accessible in Arthur Weinberg, ed., *Attorney for the Damned* (New York: Simon and Schuster, 1957; **A, G**). This collection includes excerpts from summations in the Haywood, bribery, Communist Labor party, Loeb-Leopold, Scopes, Sweet and Massie trials, excerpts from the Anthracite Coal Commission hearings, and the complete "Address to the Prisoners in the Cook County Jail." Debates, addresses, short stories, and most of the essays from *The Persian Pearl* comprise another book edited by Arthur Weinberg, with Lila Weinberg, *Clarence Darrow: Verdicts Out of Court* (Chicago: Quadrangle, 1963; **A, G**). To track Darrow's writings in the *Chicago American, Rubric, Pilgrim, Everyman, International Socialist Review, Liberal Review, American Mercury, Vanity Fair, Scribner's, Christian Century, Forum,* and *Esquire,* Willard D. Hunsberger, *Clarence Darrow: A Bibliography* (Metuchen, NJ: Scarecrow, 1981; **A, G**), is useful. A comprehensive bibliography, it covers contemporary and secondary sources on trials with which Darrow was associated, as well as biographical writings up to 1979.

Darrow correspondence and privately collected material from the famous trials are stored in manuscript collections in the Midwest and the East Coast. The Library of Congress contains some correspondence and copies of speeches, articles, and books in the Darrow papers; additional materials are found in the Horne, Lindsey, Russell, and Whitlock papers. Chicago houses Darrow material in the Newberry Library (the Binder and O'Brien papers), the Chicago Historical Society (Sunset Club proceedings) and the University of Chicago Regenstein Library (Darrow and Farrell papers). The University of Illinois/Illinois Historical Survey Collections at Urbana include Darrow correspondence in the Illinois State Politics and Government papers, and in the Germer papers. The Trumbull papers are at the Illinois State Historical Society, Springfield. The University of Michigan Bentley Historical Library contains a rich vein on the Sweet Trial, traceable in the Asher, Baskin, Baumgardner, Gomon, Murphy, and Walker papers. Wisconsin State Historical Society yields material on the Kidd case in the Germer papers, and more broadly in the Lloyd papers (on microfilm) and Ross papers. In Ohio, the American Jewish Archives in Cincinnati includes Loeb-Leopold material in the Cronbach papers; the Toledo Public Library has the Cochran papers, and the Ohio Historical Society in Columbus has the Fitch papers. Yale's Beinecke Library contains the Johnson, Palmer, Weinberger and White papers. The Liveright papers at the University of Pennsylvania contain Darrow correspondence, as do the Bascom papers at the University of Virginia and the Barnes papers at the University of Wyoming. Columbia (Brown papers), Syracuse University (Parsons papers) and Radcliffe's Schlesinger Library (Van Waters papers) also contain Darrow correspondence.

Fiction and Adaptations

Darrow starred in a film on the theory of evolution, *The Mystery of Life*, in 1931. His "whimsical, pessimistic remarks" were complemented by zoologist H. M. Parshley's script and scientific narration.

Hollywood has produced two major motion pictures on the most famous 1920s Darrow trials. The Leopold and Loeb trial was portrayed in *Compulsion* (1959), based on a book by Meyer Levin (a contemporary of Darrow). Produced under the taut, restrained direction of Richard Fleischer, this was Richard Zanuck's first film for Twentieth Century-Fox. The three male leads captured the best actor award at the Cannes Film Festival: Orson Welles as the fictionalized Darrow character, Dean Stockwell as Leopold, and Bradford Dillman as Loeb.

In 1960, Stanley Kramer produced and directed *Inherit the Wind* for United Artists, in Nathan Douglas's adaptation of a Jerome Lawrence and Robert E. Lee play. The Scopes trial drama, richly allegorical in post-McCarthy America, gained its title from the biblical rebuke attributed to William Jennings Bryan in a prayer meeting: "He that troubleth his own house shall inherit the wind." Some critics consider the Spencer Tracy (Darrow) and Frederich March (Bryan) performances the finest in the two actors' careers. The original play opened on Broadway in 1955 with Paul Muni and Ed Begley. A television adaptation in 1965 starred Melvin Douglass and Ed Begley. In 1988, NBC-TV aired a new production with Jason Robards as Darrow and Kirk Douglas as Bryan.

In 1974–1975, Henry Fonda portrayed a complex, brooding Darrow in David Rintels' one-man, two-act play, *Clarence Darrow*. A 16-mm color film version was produced in 1979, and distributed by Twyman Films. Documentary footage of Darrow and his contemporaries is available in two 16-mm films: *The Inheritence* (1964) and *Clarence Darrow* (1965). *The Inheritence* was produced by Mayer-Sklar and distributed by Harold Mayer. *Clarence Darrow* was produced by Wolper Productions, and Sterling Educational Films controls its distribution.

Museums, Historical Landmarks, Societies

National Portrait Gallery (Washington, DC). A bust of Darrow, created in bronze by renowned sculptor Jo Davidson, is housed here among a collection of some twenty-five portrait sculptures donated to the Gallery in 1978.

Rhea County Courthouse (Dayton, TN). The courtroom where the explosive Scopes trial took place has been restored to its 1925 appearance as a memorial to the event. A museum in the building's basement houses artifacts from the trial and its participants.

Other Sources

Fenberg, Matilda. "I Remember Clarence Darrow." *Chicago History* 2 (Fall/Winter 1973). A reminiscence of Darrow's courtroom technique.

Ginger, Ann Fagan. "Watching Darrow Work a Jury." *Criminal Justice Journal* 8 (Winter 1985): 29–46. An examination of Darrow's talent for swaying and influencing jurors.

Ginger, Ray. *Altgeld's America: The Lincoln Ideal versus Changing Realities.* 1958. Reprint. New York: New Viewpoints, 1973. A look at John Peter Altgeld and the progressive labor movement, this work includes discussions of Darrow's friendship with Altgeld and his involvement in the movement.

———. "Darrow." *Antioch Review* 13 (Spring 1953): 52–66. Examines the contradictions in Darrow's life and work.

———. "Darrow, Clarence Seward." In *Dictionary of American Biography.* Vol. 11, Supp. 2. New York: Scribner's, 1958. A good thumbnail sketch by an eminent Darrow scholar.

Maloney, Martin. "Clarence Darrow." In *A History and Criticism of American Public Address*, edited by Marie Kathryn Hochmuth. New York: Longmans, Green, 1955. Explores the broader implications of Darrow's conscious mythmaking, and the resonance between the elements of his own life and the structure of American society.

Mosk, Edward. "Darrow on Trial." *California Lawyer* 3 (March 1983): 32–34, 64. A look at Darrow's summation strategy in his own defense, its analogue in the Angela Davis trial of 1970, and the logical options an apologia can take.

Rabitz, Abe C. *Clarence Darrow and the American Literary Tradition*. Cleveland: Western Reserve University Press, 1962. This critical analysis of Darrow's literary work places him at the forefront of the naturalist, progressive movement that was soon to spawn such authors as Upton Sinclair and Theodore Dreiser.

Ryan, William. "Shades of Darrow." *New Jersey Lawyer* (February 1981): 38–41. A window on the pop-cultural heroism of Darrow's legend.

Sayer, James Edward. *Clarence Darrow: Public Advocate*. Port Washington, NY: Kennikat Press, 1978. Discusses Darrow's views on capital punishment.

Weinberg, Arthur, and Lila Weinberg. "Darrow: Scopes Revisited." *Trial Diplomacy Journal* 8 (Winter 1985): 14–17. A look back on the methods, madness, and implications of the Scopes trial.

Jacqueline K. Parker
Cleveland State University

JEFFERSON DAVIS
1808–1889

Chronology

Born Jefferson Davis on June 3, 1808, near Fairview, Kentucky, the tenth and last child of Samuel Emory Davis, a farmer and veteran of the American Revolution, and Jane Cook Davis; *1810–1815* lives in Woodville, Mississippi, where the family settles about 1810; attends local schools; *1816–1822* attends St. Thomas College in Bardstown, Kentucky, and Jefferson College in Washington, Mississippi; *1823–1824* attends Transylvania University, Lexington, Kentucky; *1824–1828* attends and is graduated from the U.S. Military Academy; *1828–1835* serves as a lieutenant on the Northwestern frontier and in what is now Oklahoma; *1835* resigns from the First Dragoons and marries Sarah Knox (c.1814–1835), daughter of Zachary Taylor; *1835–1843* following death of his wife, travels to Havana to recuperate from malaria; establishes himself as a planter at "Brierfield" near Vicksburg, Mississippi; *1843* runs unsuccessfully for state legislature; *1844* is chosen presidential elector for the Democratic party in Mississippi; *1845* marries Varina Banks Howell (1826–1906) of Natchez; *1845–1846* serves in U.S. House of Representatives; *1846–1847* elected colonel of the First Mississippi Regiment; sees action at the battles of Monterrey and Buena Vista; *1847* declines appointment as brigadier general of volunteers; *1847–1851* appointed, then elected, to the U.S. Senate; *1851* runs unsuccessfully for governor of Mississippi as a State Rights Democrat; *1851–1853* works as a planter; *1853–1857* serves as secretary of war in Franklin Pierce's cabinet; *1857–1861* returns to U.S. Senate; *1861–1865* serves as president, Confederate States of America; *1865–1867* imprisoned at Fort Monroe, Virginia; *1867–1869* joins family in Montreal, and travels to Europe; *1869–1877* lives in Memphis, where he is president of the Carolina Life Insurance Co.; travels abroad and in the West; *1876* is president of the American branch of the Mississippi Valley Society; *1877–1889* retires to "Beauvoir" near Biloxi, Mississippi, where he writes his memoirs (1881) and a history of the Confederacy (1889); *1889* dies on December 6 of bronchitis in New Orleans; *1893* reinterred at Hollywood Cemetery, Richmond.

Activities of Historical Significance

Known mainly as chief executive of the Confederacy, Davis's presidency capped a twenty-year public career. His service in the House and Senate centered on his chairmanship of the Committee on Military Affairs and his role as a southern spokesman, particularly during the crisis over the Compromise of 1850, the re-alignment of political parties in the late 1850s, and secession. But he was also keenly interested in the establishment of the Smithsonian Institution, of which he was an original trustee, government-sponsored scientific endeavors such as the Coast Survey, and the extension of the Capitol and improvement of other public properties. As secretary of war, he displayed exceptional skill as an administrator: supervising the Pacific Railroad surveys; directing expeditions to secure camels for use by the army in the West; expanding the line of frontier forts; winning from Congress a long overdue increase in the army and better pay for men and officers; securing appropriations for the Capitol extension and Washington Aqueduct; overseeing numerous nationwide rivers and harbors projects directed by army engineers; spearheading improvements in the curriculum and establishing a five-year course of study at the Military Academy; adopting new models of military equipment and weaponry; appointing official observers to the Crimean War with directions to report on military education, equipment, and strategy. As a personal friend of the president, he was a trusted adviser on important issues such as the acquisition of Cuba and the admission of Kansas as a state. In the Senate, Davis was the voice of southern moderation, working tirelessly to maintain the Union and resigning reluctantly when Mississippi seceded.

As a Mexican War officer, Davis led a regiment that distinguished itself at Monterrey and Buena Vista. In Mexico he quickly became Zachary Taylor's confidant, led some daring sorties, and was named one of three commissioners to arrange the capitulation at Monterrey. At the Battle of Buena Vista, he was conspicuous for gallantry and was seriously wounded.

His military background and devoted service to his adopted state led to Davis's appointment as major general of Mississippi troops in 1861. Within a month, however, he was elected president of the Confederacy. He immediately assumed the burdens of office and became the new nation's chief crusader.

Davis's tenure as president is the best documented portion of his life. Some of the major themes are his direction of the war effort, organization of the central government, struggles with the Confederate Congress, role as commander-in-chief of the armies, diplomatic initiatives, and peace negotiations. When Richmond fell in April 1865, Davis escaped and for a month made valiant efforts to reestablish the government. He was captured in Georgia on his way to the West and for two years was imprisoned at Fort Monroe, Virginia.

Released on bail, he was never tried for treason. He rejoined his family, who had been living in Canada, traveled abroad, worked for some years in Memphis as president of an insurance company, then retired to the Mississippi Gulf Coast. He wrote his memoirs, undertook some speaking tours for Confederate causes, and pursued a lawsuit for recovery of his plantation.

Overview of Biographical Sources
    Published during his lifetime, the earliest biographical sketches were campaign pamphlets and entries in biographical dictionaries of prominent Americans; for some of the latter Davis himself provided the data. Soon after the war several

polemics appeared, followed by Davis's *The Rise and Fall of the Confederate Government* (1881) and Varina Davis's memoir of her husband (1890). Scholarly and popular biographies are numerous. The three-volume set by Hudson Strode (1955–64) is the best-known general work; Clement Eaton's *Jefferson Davis* (1977) is the most recent scholarly study covering Davis's whole life. Virtually all studies of the immediate prewar period and the Confederacy examine Davis. The following specialized works, while not full biographies, are helpful for various aspects of his life: Michael B. Ballard, *A Long Shadow: Jefferson Davis and the Final Days of the Confederacy* (1986); Albert T. Bledsoe, *Is Davis A Traitor?* (1866); John J. Craven, *Prison Life of Jefferson Davis* (1866); Paul D. Escott, *After Secession: Jefferson Davis and the Failure of Confederate Nationalism* (1978); Frank E. Everett, *Brierfield* (1971); Burton J. Hendrick, *Statesmen of the Lost Cause: Jefferson Davis and His Cabinet* (1939); Stanley Kimmel, *Mr. Davis's Richmond* (1958); Frederick B. Maurice, "Jefferson Davis and Joseph E. Johnston" and "Jefferson Davis and Lee," in *Statesmen and Soldiers of the Civil War* (1926); Rembert W. Patrick, *Jefferson Davis and His Cabinet* (1944); Russell H. Quynn, *Constitutions of Abraham Lincoln and Jefferson Davis* (1959); and Frank E. Vandiver, *The Making of a President* (1962).

Evaluation of Principal Biographical Sources

Alfriend, Frank H. *The Life of Jefferson Davis*. Philadelphia: National, 1868. (A) One of the earliest studies, by the former editor of the *Southern Literary Messenger*. Alfriend's perspective is that of a friendly fellow southerner.

Cutting, Elisabeth Brown. *Jefferson Davis, Political Soldier*. New York: Dodd, Mead, 1930. (A, G) Journalist Cutting's book is well-written and utilizes European sources that were new at the time; she emphasizes Davis's personality flaws and military failures.

De Grummond, Lena Young, and Lynn de Grummond Delaune. *Jeff Davis, Confederate Boy*. Indianapolis: Bobbs-Merrill, 1960. (Y) By well-known writers of juvenile fiction, this book centers on Davis's childhood in Mississippi.

Dodd, William E. *Jefferson Davis*. Philadelphia: George W. Jacobs, 1907. (A, G) Somewhat dated but still reliable and based on primary sources, Dodd describes Davis's pro-Union sentiment and assigns much of the blame for Confederate defeats to the actions of Congress, the vice-president, and the governors.

Eaton, Clement. *Jefferson Davis*. New York: Free Press, 1977. (A) The most recent full biography by an eminent historian of the South. More than others, Eaton illuminates Davis's formative years, praises his dedication to the Confederate cause, analyzes his personal faults and relationships, but devotes almost no attention to Davis's postwar activities.

Eckenrode, Hamilton J. *Jefferson Davis, President of the South*. New York: Macmillan, 1923. **(A)** Utilizing a "scientific" approach to examine political and military topics, Eckenrode critically describes Davis as a "tropic Nordic" and concentrates on his actions as president.

Gordon, Armistead C. *Jefferson Davis*. New York: Charles Scribner's Sons, 1918. **(A, G)** Similar to Dodd's biography, Gordon's is a straightforward account emphasizing the importance of economic forces in the coming of the Civil War.

Knight, Landon. *The Real Jefferson Davis*. Battle Creek, MI: Pilgrim Magazine, 1904. **(G)** A Georgia newspaperman who turned several magazine articles into an undocumented biography, Knight was primarily interested in the forces responsible for the war, particularly state rights and slavery.

McElroy, Robert M. *Jefferson Davis: The Unreal and the Real*. 2 vols. New York: Harper and Brothers, 1937. **(A)** A complete biography but working mostly from secondary and printed primary sources, McElroy's major theme is Davis's strict constitutionalism and devotion to state rights.

Pollard, Edward A. *Life of Jefferson Davis, with a Secret History of the Southern Confederacy, Gathered "Behind the Lines in Richmond."* Philadelphia: National, 1869. **(A)** Pollard published several "histories" of the war before writing this biography; the bitter proprietor of the Richmond *Examiner* established the durable image of Davis as the scapegoat for Confederate defeat and popularized the "southern conspiracy" theory for the coming of the war.

Schaff, Morris. *Jefferson Davis, His Life and Personality*. Boston: John W. Luce, 1922. **(G)** Imbued with the patriotic fervor of World War I and, like Davis, a graduate of West Point, Schaff argues for reconciliation and emphasizes Davis's service to the Union, particularly as secretary of war.

Strode, Hudson. *Jefferson Davis*. 3 vols. New York: Harcourt, Brace, 1955–64. **(A, G)** Written by an English professor, this popular Davis biography seeks to counter the stereotypical image of Davis as cold and austere; commendable for the use of Davis family materials and a detailed chronicle of the postwar years, Strode's work lacks objectivity and often loses historical perspective.

Tate, Allen. *Jefferson Davis, His Rise and Fall: A Biographical Narrative*. New York: Minton, Balch, 1929. **(A)** Interesting for its "Nashville Agrarian" viewpoint, Tate's portrait shows that Davis's pride, inflexibility, and indecisiveness led to crucial errors in his administration as president.

Winston, Robert W. *High Stakes and Hair Trigger: The Life of Jefferson Davis*. New York: Henry Holt, 1930. **(A, G)** A North Carolina judge, Winston is extremely critical of Davis as a southern spokesman, believing that secession was always his goal.

Overview and Evaluation of Primary Sources

In the last year of his life Davis began dictating his autobiography. A concise version was published in *Belford's Magazine* 4 (January 1890): 255–266; a more detailed account, but ending with his Military Academy experiences, is included in his wife's reminiscences. Varina Howell Davis's *Jefferson Davis, Ex-President of the Confederate States of America: A Memoir* (2 vols., New York: Belford, 1890; **A, G**) is vital to any study of Davis. It includes valuable descriptions of the Davises' friends and family, many letters, and her colorful narrative of their life together. Davis's own reminiscences, incorporated in *The Rise and Fall of the Confederate Government* (2 vols., New York: D. Appleton, 1881; **A**) are disappointing and incomplete; the book is a general defense of the constitutional arguments for secession and Confederate goals. Davis's papers were first collected in a ten-volume set, *Jefferson Davis, Constitutionalist*, edited by Dunbar Rowland (Jackson: Department of Archives and History, 1923; **A**). A new edition, in preparation at Rice University, looks toward the publication of fourteen volumes; six volumes of *The Papers of Jefferson Davis* are in print (Baton Rouge: Louisiana State University Press, 1971–88; **A**), covering Davis's career through 1860.

Some other printed works contain even more of Davis's writings and correspondence: A. Dudley Mann, *"My Ever Dearest Friend": The Letters . . . to Jefferson Davis, 1869–89*, edited by John Preston Moore (Tuscaloosa, AL: Confederate Publishing, 1960; **A**); *Lee's Dispatches: Unpublished Letters of General Robert E. Lee, C.S.A., to Jefferson Davis and the War Department . . . 1862–1865*, edited by Douglas Southall Freeman (New York: Putnam, 1957; **A**); and *Private Letters*, edited by Hudson Strode (New York: Harcourt, Brace & World, 1966; **A, G**). For Davis's prewar career, contemporary newspapers are often the only sources for speeches; see also the record of debate and Senate and House reports in the *Congressional Globe* and in the serial set of government documents; for the Confederate period, see *The War of the Rebellion: Official Records of the Union and Confederate Armies* (128 vols., Washington: Government Printing Office, 1880–1901; **A**), *Official Records . . . Navies* (30 vols., Washington: Government Printing Office, 1894–1922; **A**), and *A Compilation of the Messages and Papers of the Confederacy* (2 vols., Nashville: United States Publishing, 1905; **A**).

Shortly after Davis's death two large books appeared containing tributes by his friends. Uneven in quality, they do provide important details of his life, as well as of his personal and political relationships: *Life and Reminiscences of Jefferson Davis* (Baltimore: R. H. Woodward, 1890; **A, G**); and J. William Jones, *The Davis Memorial Volume; or, Our Dead President, Jefferson Davis, and the World's Tribute to His Memory* (Richmond: B. F. Johnson, 1890; **A, G**). See also the reminiscences and diaries of Davis's contemporaries, for example: *Mary Chesnut's Civil War* (New Haven: Yale University Press, 1981; **A**); John B. Jones, *Rebel War Clerk's Diary* (New York: Sagamore, 1958; **A, G**); Robert G. H. Kean, *Inside the Confederate Government* (New York: Oxford University Press, 1957; **A**); Henry S. Foote, *War of the Rebellion* (New York: Harper, 1866; **A**); Joseph E. Johnston,

Narrative of Military Operations (New York: D. Appleton, 1874; **A**); Alexander H. Stephens, *A Constitutional View of the Late War Between the States* (2 vols., Philadelphia: National, 1868-70; **A**).

Manuscript sources are vast and scattered. No one collection adequately spans Davis's entire career. The collections of the National Archives contain most of Davis's correspondence for the years of his public service, 1845-51, 1853-61; the Davis collection at the Library of Congress is almost entirely prewar documents, although several hundred Davis letters are found in other Library of Congress collections; Transylvania University holds a small but important collection of personal material and notes for speeches; the University of Alabama, Tulane University, and the Museum of the Confederacy preserve large collections from Davis's heirs; Duke University and Miami University have substantial holdings of mainly Civil War materials; the Mississippi Department of Archives and History owns a wide variety of Davis and Howell family documents.

Fiction and Adaptations

Several historical novels have been written about the Davises: James B. Agnew, *Eggnog Riot* (1979), concerns Davis's West Point career and is based on primary sources; Thomas Dixon, *The Victim* (1914), is about Davis as president; Harnett T. Kane, *Bride of Fortune* (1948), is mainly on Varina Davis; Theodore V. Olsen, *There Was a Season* (1972), portrays Davis as a young army officer and is suitable reading for adolescents as well as adults; and Shirley Seifert, *The Proud Way* (1948), describes Davis's courtship of Varina Howell.

In the movies, longtime character actor Erville Anderson gave a credible performance as Davis in *Santa Fe Trail* (1940), about the coming of the war. On television, Davis was portrayed in one segment of the Du Pont-sponsored "Cavalcade of America" series in the early 1950s and more recently by television stalwart Lloyd Bridges in the 1986 miniseries, "North and South."

Museums, Historical Landmarks, Societies

Beauvoir (Biloxi, MS). Davis's last home on the Mississippi Gulf Coast. Willed by Varina Davis to the Sons of Confederate Veterans and still maintained by them, the house and grounds contain numerous family artifacts, a small museum, Confederate cemetery, and restored gardens.

Confederate Memorial Hall (New Orleans, LA). Contains an impressive array of Davis memorabilia—"from cradle to war boots"—donated by his widow, along with numerous Confederate military items.

First White House of the Confederacy (Montgomery, AL). A house museum across from the capitol where Davis took the oath as president. It has many personal articles belonging to the Davises, some furniture, and Confederate mementos.

Fort Davis National Historic Site (Fort Davis, TX). Established in 1854 and named for Davis, this is a prime example of the many frontier posts sited during the years he was chairman of the Senate Military Affairs Committee and secretary of war.

Hollywood Cemetery (Richmond, VA). Includes the impressive Davis Circle, where Davis and his immediate family are buried; has noteworthy bronze statuary.

Jefferson Davis Monument Shrine (Fairview, KY). Marks Davis's birthplace. There is a replica of the log house where he was born, an obelisk, and a small museum.

Museum of the Confederacy (Richmond, VA). Has the largest collection of Confederate memorabilia and many Davis family items. The complex includes a museum, library and manuscript collection, and the Robert Mills-designed Brockenbrough mansion, where the Davises lived, 1861–65.

Old Court House Museum (Vicksburg, MS). Contains a large roomful of Davis items and much vital information about his nearby plantation (no longer extant).

Rosemont (Woodville, MS). Davis's modest and impeccably preserved boyhood home and site of the biennial meetings of the Davis Family Association. There is some Davis furniture, personal items, and a private cemetery.

Other Sources

Beringer, Richard E., et al. *Why the South Lost the Civil War*. Athens: University of Georgia Press, 1986. Provides a controversial analysis of Davis's contribution to the Southern failure of will which resulted in defeat.

Connelly, Thomas L., and Archer Jones. *The Politics of Command*. Baton Rouge: Louisiana State University Press, 1973. Concentrates on Confederate strategy in the West, Davis's relationships with his generals, and the department command system.

Johnson, Ludwell H. "Jefferson Davis and Abraham Lincoln as War Presidents." *Civil War History* 27 (March 1981): 49–63. Rejecting the traditional contrast of Davis and Lincoln, documents in detail the author's belief that Davis was "clearly superior".

Jones, Archer. *Confederate Strategy from Shiloh to Vicksburg*. Baton Rouge: Louisiana State University Press, 1961. Faults Davis for his lack of a comprehensive plan and the policy of defensive resistance.

McWhitney, Grady. "Jefferson Davis and the Art of War." *Civil War History* 21 (June 1975): 101–112. Terming Davis a "military mystic," chronicles Davis's faults as a military leader, emphasizing personality flaws.

————. "Jefferson Davis and His Generals." In *Southerners and Other Americans*. New York: Basic Books, 1973. Concentrates on the influence that Davis's physical frailties and character defects played in the choice of field commanders.

Patrick, Rembert W. *Jefferson Davis and His Cabinet*. Baton Rouge: Louisiana State University Press, 1944. Portrays Davis favorably in virtually a composite portrait of the Confederate civilian leadership.

Potter, David M. "Jefferson Davis and the Political Factors in Confederate Defeat." In *Why the North Won the Civil War*, edited by David Donald. Baton Rouge: Louisiana State University Press, 1960. An overwhelmingly critical summary of Davis's failures in politics, diplomacy, and domestic and military matters of all sorts.

Thomas, Emory. "Jefferson Davis and the American Revolutionary Tradition." *Journal of the Illinois State Historical Society* 70 (February 1977): 2–9. Finds that although Davis skillfully used rhetoric and symbolism from the American Revolution, he did not succeed as a leader.

Vandiver, Frank E. "Jefferson Davis—Leader Without Legend." *Journal of Southern History* 43 (February 1977): 3–18. Reviews the Davis historiography, focusing on Davis's talents as an innovator, at his best in crisis.

————. *Rebel Brass*. Baton Rouge: Louisiana State University Press, 1956. Shows Davis as an essentially cautious executive confronting revolutionary issues with little support from Congress, the press, and state leaders.

————. *Their Tattered Flags*. New York: Harper's Magazine Press, 1970. Places Davis at center stage of the Confederate experience, a hero with some flaws who was willing to hazard controversial actions to achieve independence.

Wiley, Bell I. "Jefferson Davis, Reluctant Helmsman." In *The Road to Appomattox*. Memphis: Memphis State College Press, 1956. Gives Davis high marks for his courage and experience but is critical of his administrative skills and failure to conceive a overarching strategy.

Lynda Lasswell Crist
The Papers of Jefferson Davis, Rice University

EUGENE V. DEBS
1855-1926

Chronology

Born Eugene Victor Debs on November 5, 1855, in Terre Haute, Indiana, of Alsatian immigrants Jean Daniel Debs, a small businessman, and Marguerite Marie Debs; *1855-1870* grows up in Indiana and attends school until age 15; *1870-1875* employed by the Terre and Indianapolis Railway as a locomotive cleaner and fireman; *1875-1878* serves three years as secretary of the Brotherhood of Locomotive Firemen in Terre Haute; *1878* becomes associate editor of the union's national *Locomotive Firemen's Magazine*; *1879-1883* elected to two terms as Terre Haute city clerk as a Democrat; also becomes treasurer and national secretary of the Brotherhood and editor of the *Fireman's Magazine* in 1880; *1884* elected to the state legislature as a Democrat; *1885* marries Katherine Metzel, daughter of the town's leading druggist; *1892* resigns from the Brotherhood to assist railroad laborers to organize the American Railway Union, but remains on as editor of the *Fireman's Magazine*; *1893* Railway Union formed with Debs as President; *1894* Debs successfully leads a strike of unskilled workers against the Great Northern Railroad, but sees the Union crushed in a strike against the Pullman Palace Car Company; arrested during the Pullman strike and sentenced to six months in prison; *1897* instrumental in founding the Social Democratic Party of America; *1900* runs for President and receives 97,000 votes; *1901* helps merge the Social Democratic party with a faction of the Socialist Labor party to form the Socialist Party of America; *1904* receives 402,000 votes as party candidate for president; also helps edit the Kansas Socialist newspaper, *Appeal to Reason*; *1905* active in the founding of the Industrial Workers of the World (IWW); *1908* polls 421,000 votes as Socialist presidential candidate; *1912* receives almost a million votes in the presidential campaign; *1918* arrested for speaking out against United States involvement in World War I and sentenced to 10 years in prison; *1920* runs for president while in jail in an Atlanta federal penitentiary, again winning nearly a million votes as a Socialist; *1921* pardoned by President Warren Harding; *1922* prepares a series of articles about his prison experiences, later published as *Wars and Bars*; *1922-1926* rejects the entreaties of American communists and continues to work for Socialist party causes; *1926* dies on October 20 in Elmhurst, Illinois.

Activities of Historical Significance

As a five-time Socialist candidate for president, Debs was a leading critic of industrial capitalism in the late nineteenth and early twentieth centuries. He was a powerful speaker who appealed to tens of thousands of workers and farmers under the Socialist banner. Under his leadership the Socialist movement stressed democratic and egalitarian principles and gained its greatest popularity. Twelve hundred Socialists were elected to local government during the Progressive era, including seventy-nine socialist mayors.

Debs was a small-town boy who rose to national fame as a leader in the labor struggles of the 1890s. During the 1894 Pullman strike, he was arrested and served a six-month jail term. After that experience, Debs went on to found the first mass-based Socialist party in the United States. Though both applauded and attacked by contemporaries, the issues he raised about the impact of industrial capitalism on American society were debated by Americans of all social classes. Many of the reforms the Socialist party advanced under Debs were enacted by the major parties in later years. These reforms include old-age and unemployment insurance, munic-ipal regulation of utilities, and public works projects for the unemployed.

Debs's approach to the labor movement also distinguished him from mainstream labor leaders. As head of the American Railway Union, he was an early advocate of industrial unionism. His subsequent efforts on behalf of the IWW, in opposition to the American Federation of Labor (and numerous Socialists), were an important precedent for the establishment of the Congress of Industrial Organizations in the 1930s.

Overview of Biographical Sources

Until recently the literature on Debs was more celebratory than analytical. The first two substantial biographical studies to appear—McAlister Coleman's *Eugene V. Debs* (1930) and Ray Ginger's *The Bending Cross* (1949)—depicted Debs as a heroic figure who stood on the perimeters of American society. In contrast, a definitive study by Nick Salvatore, *Eugene V. Debs* (1983), places Debs in a fuller social context. Salvatore stresses Debs's American roots and his central place in American political culture. Accordingly, he reinterprets Debs's 1894 prison experi-ence. In contrast to Coleman and Ginger, who argue that Debs experienced a "conversion" to socialism while in jail, Salvatore stresses the continuity in Debs's thought over time. He links Debs's transition from conservative trade unionist in the 1870s to a left-wing Socialist in the 1890s to changes in the economy.

An older historiographical debate explores Debs's status as either a humanitarian democrat in the liberal tradition or a militant revolutionary in opposition to that tradition. Both liberal and radical writers have claimed Debs as one of their own. (No conservative has broached the subject.) The former view is advanced by H. Wayne Morgan, *Eugene V. Debs* (1962), and in essays by Charles Madison and Arthur M. Schlesinger, Jr. Meanwhile, David Herreshoff, *American Dis-ciples of Marx* (1967), and Bert Cochran argue for the revolutionary Debs. So does Ginger, but in a less partisan fashion. He criticizes Debs's revolutionary politics as ineffective.

Evaluation of Principal Biographical Sources

Cochran, Bert. "The Achievement of Debs." In *American Radicals: Some Problems and Personalities*, edited by Harvey Goldberg. New York: Monthly Review Press, 1957. **(A, G)** Stresses Debs's militant and revolutionary program.

Coleman, McAlister. *Eugene V. Debs: A Man Unafraid*. New York: Greenberg, 1930. **(A, G)** The first full-length biography of Debs, published four years after his death. Although dated, the book nicely captures Debs's humanitarian spirit.

Currie, Harold W. *Eugene V. Debs*. Boston: Twayne, 1976. **(A, G)** An analysis of Debs's writings and speeches, with greatest attention to his Socialist years. The author discusses Debs's attitudes toward violence, religion, and education.

Ginger, Ray. *The Bending Cross: A Biography of Eugene Victor Debs*. New Brunswick: Rutgers University Press, 1949. **(A, G)** For many years this dramatic biography by an eminent historian was the most popular book on Debs. Its main deficiency is that it minimizes Debs's conservative beginnings.

Herreshoff, David. *American Disciples of Marx: From the Age of Jackson to the Progressive Era*. Detroit: Wayne State University Press, 1967. **(A, G)** The author offers the unorthodox view that Debs was an ally of Daniel De Leon, founder of the Socialist Labor party.

Hyfler, Robert. "Socialism in the Working Class: Debs and the Wobblies." In *Prophets of the Left: American Socialist Thought in the Twentieth Century*. Westport, CT: Greenwood Press, 1984. **(A, G)** Treats Debs's views toward industrial unionism.

Karsner, David F. *Debs: His Authorized Life and Letters*. New York: Boni and Liveright, 1919. **(A, G)** Written while Debs was in jail in 1918, by a reporter and friend who covered his trial. Half of the book details Debs's arrest, conviction, and first months of imprisonment. The other half outlines his life.

Madison, Charles. "Eugene Victor Debs: Evangelical Socialist." In *Critics and Crusaders: A Century of American Protest*. New York: Henry Holt, 1947. **(A, G)** The author believes that Debs represents the Socialist aspect of Jeffersonian democracy.

Morgan, H. Wayne. *Eugene V. Debs: Socialist for President*. Syracuse: Syracuse University Press, 1962. **(A, G)** This study focuses on Socialist efforts in national politics between 1900 and 1920. Most attention is given to the presidential campaigns. The author notes how Debs's third-party campaigns influenced mainstream parties.

Salvatore, Nick. *Eugene V. Debs: Citizen and Socialist*. Urbana: University of Illinois Press, 1983. **(A, G)** The stress on Debs as a product of American political culture opens the way to view the Debsian Socialist movement as an indigenous response to American industrialization. The discussion of the importance of republicanism in Debs's thought breaks new ground.

Overview and Evaluation of Primary Sources

Debs's experience in labor journalism early in his career served him well later on. He authored hundreds of articles and speeches, many of which have been collected in book form. Some of the better collections include Alexander Trachtenberg, ed., *Speeches of Eugene Debs* (New York: International Publishers, 1928; **A, G**); Arthur M. Schlesinger, Jr., ed., *Writings and Speeches of Eugene V. Debs* (New York: Hermitage Press, 1948; **A, G**); Gene Tussey, ed., *Eugene V. Debs Speaks* (New York: Pathfinder Press, 1970; **A, G**); and Ronald Radosh, ed., *Debs* (Englewood Cliffs, NJ: Prentice-Hall, 1971; **A, G**).

A series of articles Debs wrote about his prison experience were published in book form a year after his death. *Walls and Bars* (Chicago: Charles H. Kerr, 1973; **A, G**) is an attack on the degrading elements of prison life, which Debs witnessed in an Atlanta penitentiary.

Accounts by Debs's contemporaries include Max Eastman, "Greek Drama in Cleveland: The Trial of Eugene Debs" in his *Heroes I Have Known* (New York: Simon and Schuster, 1942; **A, G**). The literary radical and former editor of the *Masses* offers a tender, sentimental portrait of Debs. In contrast, Elizabeth Gurley Flynn, who worked with Debs in the IWW, describes him as a firebrand and agitator in *Debs, Haywood, Ruthenberg* (New York: International Publishers, 1937; **A, G**). The journalist Lincoln Steffens offers an insightful interview and profile of Debs in "Eugene V. Debs on What the Matter is in America and What to Do About It," *Everybody's* (October, 1908): 455–469 (**A, G**).

Unfortunately, a large correspondence between Debs and his brother Theodore was destroyed by members of Kate Debs's family after her death in 1937. However, a wealth of material on Debs is available. The most important collection is at the Cunningham Library, Indiana State University, Terre Haute, which includes some 5,000 letters relevant to Debs's public and private life. Other material in Terre Haute is found at the Debs Foundation and the Fairbanks Memorial Library. The Indiana State Library, the Indiana Historical Society, and the Lilly Library at Indiana University, Bloomington, also contain important materials. For Debs's Socialist activity, the collection of the Socialist party at the William R. Perkins Library, Duke University, is essential, as are numerous collections at the Tamiment Institute, Bobst Library, New York University, and at the Wisconsin State Historical Society in Madison.

Fiction and Adaptations

Debs is the subject of two novels. The most successful is Irving Stone's *Adversary in the House* (1947), which is closely based on Debs's life. A less satisfying work is Aaron Nissenson's *Song of Man: A Novel Based on the Life of Eugene V. Debs* (1964).

When Debs was in prison in 1918, some two dozen writers offered him praise in a collection of poems edited by Ruth Le Prade, *Debs and the Poets* (1920). The writers include George Bernard Shaw, Upton Sinclair, H. G. Wells, and Carl Sandburg. Debs's imprisonment is also the subject of a scene in Lucy Robins's out-of-print novel, *War Shadows* (n.d.). Debs figures in John Dos Passos's *The 42nd Parallel* (1937). For Dos Passos, Debs represents the "lover of mankind."

Other Sources

Buhle, Mari Jo. *Women and American Socialism, 1870–1920*. Urbana: University of Illinois Press, 1981. An important study of American women Socialists. Debs is a marginal figure in the study.

Green, James R. *Grass-Roots Socialism: Radical Movements in the Southwest 1895–1943*. Baton Rouge: Louisiana State University Press, 1978. This book explores the appeal of socialism among farmers and landless tenants in the Southwest. Its geographic focus is a needed counterpoint to studies of urban workers and intellectuals in the Northeast.

Shannon, David A. *The Socialist Party of America: A History*. New York: Macmillan, 1955. A standard history of the party.

Weinstein, James. *The Decline of Socialism in America, 1912–1925*. New York: Monthly Review Press, 1967. Challenges the view that the Socialist movement declined after 1912; attributes the movement's decline to the rise of factionalism within the Left after World War I.

Ivan Greenberg
Graduate School and University Center
City University of New York

GEORGE DEWEY
1837–1917

Chronology

Born George Dewey on December 26, 1837, in Montpelier, Vermont, to Dr. Julius Yemans Dewey, a descendant of a French Huguenot family that settled in Massachusetts in 1634, and Mary Perrin Dewey; *1837–1854* grows up in Vermont, attending schools in Montpelier and at Jamestown; *1854* enters the Naval Academy at the age of sixteen; *1858* ranks fifth among the academy's fifteen graduates; *1861* after his first sea duty, on the steam frigate *Wabash*, he passes his examination for lieutenant, just as the Union needs naval officers; is detailed as the executive officer on the steam frigate *Mississippi* and serves under David Glasgow Farragut, who becomes his role model; *1862* participates in the Battle of New Orleans in April, and in the investment of Port Hudson in July; *December 1864* takes part in the attack on Fort Fisher; *1865* participates in another attack on Fort Fisher in January; *1865–1866* serves as lieutenant commander on the sloop-of-war *Kearsarge* and then on the flagship *Colorado* on the European Station; *1867* returns to the U.S. to marry Susan Boardman Goodwin; *1867–1872* serves a tour of duty at the Naval Academy; *1872* his wife dies five days after giving birth to a son; *1872–1875* commands the fourth-rate *Narragansett*; engages in a survey of the Gulf of California waters; *1876–1877* serves as lighthouse inspector out of Boston; *1878–1882* serves as secretary of the Lighthouse Board in Washington, D.C.; *1882–1883* commands the *Juanita* on the Asiatic Station; *1885–1888* returns to the Asiatic Station as commander of the *Pensacola*; *1889–1893* serves as chief of the Bureau of Equipment; *1895–1897* serves as president of the Lighthouse Board and of the Board of Inspection and Survey; *1896* is promoted to the rank of commodore; *November 1897* using political influence and enlisting the aid of Assistant Secretary of the Navy Theodore Roosevelt, he obtains the billet of chief of the Asiatic Station; *1898* becomes the hero of the Battle of Manila Bay following his May 1 destruction of the Spanish fleet; *1899* Congress makes him the third admiral in American history; marries wealthy socialite widow, Mildred McLean Hazen, and loses popularity by transferring ownership of a house in Washington, D.C., bought by public subscription, to her; *1900–1917* serves as president of the General Board of the Navy; *1902* commands the concentrated fleet designed to dissuade Germany from breaching the Monroe Doctrine; *1914* World War I breaks out, but he is unable to persuade the Wilson administration to prepare for war; *1917* dies on January 16 of arteriosclerosis in Washington, D.C.

Activities of Historical Significance

Dewey's outstanding contribution to history was his defeat of Admiral Montojo's squadron in the Battle of Manila Bay on May 1, 1898, for it proved to be the first step in the United States acquiring the Philippines and becoming one of the principal powers in the Far East. Using tactics learned from Admiral David G. Farragut during the Civil War, he stymied Spain's attempt to retain the Philippines.

After proving his tactical abilities at Manila Bay, Dewey then contributed to the growth and efficiency of the U.S. Navy as an elder statesman. Official and popular acclaim for his victory led him to consider seeking the 1900 Democratic presidential nomination, but he settled for the position of president of the General Board of the Navy. In that billet, he was authorized to offer advice to the secretary of the Navy on policy, development, and a multitude of other issues. In addition, beginning in 1903, he served as president of the Joint Board of the Army and Navy, precursor of the Joint Chiefs of Staff. President Theodore Roosevelt held Dewey in such high esteem that he directed him to command the fleet during the winter of 1902 when Germany's activities in Venezuela threatened to violate the Monroe Doctrine. Dewey was also consulted during the 1903 and 1906 crises with Japan, and during the Mexican civil war, but his recommendations were not implemented. In retrospect, one of his most important contributions was his advice in 1903 that the U.S. build a Navy "second to none" which would include forty-eight battleships by 1925.

Overview of Biographical Sources

Dewey's Manila Bay victory on May 1, 1898, stimulated the production of a number of quickly written biographies, mainly by journalists, that have not stood the test of time. Among these are John Barrett, *Admiral George Dewey: A Sketch of the Man* (1899); William M. Clemens, *The Life of Admiral Dewey* (1899); Murat Halstead, *Life and Achievements of Admiral Dewey from Montpelier to Manila* (1899); Margherita Hamm, *Dewey, the Defender: A Life Sketch of America's Great Admiral* (1899); Frederick Palmer, *George Dewey, USN* (1900); Thomas J. Vivian, *With Dewey at Manila* (1899); Louis S. Young, *Life and Heroic Deeds of Admiral Dewey* (1899); and Edward S. Ellis, *The Life Story of Admiral Dewey, Hero of Manila, for Boys and Girls* (1899). Slightly better biographies were written by Dewey's son Adelbert M. Dewey, *The Life and Letters of Admiral Dewey* (1909), and Laurin Hall Healy and Luis Kutner, *The Admiral* (1944). A long-time aide, Nathan Sargent, produced a very sympathetic tale in *Admiral Dewey and the Manila Campaign* (1947). By far the best biography is Ronald Spector, *Admiral of the New Empire: The Life and Career of George Dewey* (1974). An excellent sketch is found in Richard S. West, *Admirals of American Empire: The Combined Story of George Dewey, Alfred Thayer Mahan, Winfield Scott Schley, and William Thomas Sampson* (1948). Unfortunately, *The Autobiography of George Dewey, Admiral of the Navy* (1913), largely written by journalist Frederick Palmer, is far from being a completely candid or reliable work, and says little about Dewey's work on the General Board.

Evaluation of Principal Biographical Sources

Spector, Ronald. *Admiral of the New Empire: The Life and Career of George Dewey.* Baton Rouge: Louisiana State University Press, 1974. **(A, G)** In about two hundred pages Spector develops the theme that, although Dewey served well during the Civil War, he did little of special note while in command of ships engaged in routine duties and in shore billets until he won the Battle of Manila Bay and became an instant folk hero. Meanwhile, in administrative capacities he did not prove to be a great thinker or brilliant innovator, but was wise enough to select bright officers to serve with him on the General Board. He was thus able to competently advise three presidents and eight secretaries of the Navy. Spector makes good use of official records and of manuscript collections, including the Dewey family papers and the diary of the admiral's second wife.

West, Richard S. *Admirals of American Empire: The Combined Story of George Dewey, Alfred Thayer Mahan, Winfield Scott Schley, and William Thomas Sampson.* Indianapolis: Bobbs-Merrill, 1948. **(A, G)** As the title indicates, the author offers only a partial biography which centers upon Dewey's command of the Asiatic Station, the Battle of Manila Bay, and his year of fighting Filipino insurgents. A naval historian, West offers excellent analyses of the tactics of Manila Bay and Dewey's role in the ensuing Spanish-American diplomacy.

Overview and Evaluation of Primary Sources

Dewey was extremely careful to hide the fact that he had used political influence to become chief of the Bureau of Equipment and commander of the Asiatic Station, and was similarly close-mouthed in his personal papers and ghost-written autobiography about his work on the General Board. Further, one can rarely tell if he created the official papers he signed or merely signed those prepared for him. However, the diary of his second wife contains interesting recordings of his opinions and conversations. The Dewey Papers in the Manuscript Division of the Library of Congress, though extensive, contain little of value. The Dewey Papers at the Vermont Historical Society are helpful for his early life, but do not go much beyond the Civil War. More informative is his correspondence with his son, George Goodwin Dewey, who published many of the letters in his biography.

Judgments about Dewey appear in his contemporaries' papers available in the Manuscript Division, Library of Congress. Useful papers include those of Josephus Daniels, Secretary of the Navy, 1913–1921; Bradley A. Fiske, who served on the General Board in 1910 and was Secretary Daniels's Aide for Operations, 1913–1915; elder naval statesman Stephen B. Luce; naval officer and historian A.T. Mahan; Secretary of the Navy John D. Long, 1897–1902; Secretary of the Navy William H. Moody, 1902–1904; Secretary of the Navy George Lengerke von Meyer, 1909–1913; Theodore Roosevelt, which deal in part with the defense of the Philippines, the imbroglio in Venezuela in the winter of 1902, and the Japanese crisis of 1906; Nathan Sargent, a trusted assistant; William S. Sims, who wished that Dewey would be more innovative; William Howard Taft, Roosevelt's secretary of war and then president, which are useful for the Philippine base controversy; Admiral Henry C. Taylor, which foreshadow the creation of the General Board; and Woodrow Wilson, who rejected Dewey's advice to prepare for war between 1914 and 1917.

Other autobiographies and diaries of contemporaries that comment upon Dewey as president of the General Board include E. David Cronon, ed., *The Cabinet Diaries of Josephus Daniels, 1913-1921* (Lincoln: University of Nebraska Press, 1963; **A, G**), and Bradley A. Fiske, *From Midshipman to Rear-Admiral* (New York: Century, 1919; **A, G**). Fiske, *Wartime in Manila* (Boston: Gorham, 1913; **A, G**), contains the weekly letters home written by a member of Dewey's squadron in the Philippines. The letters provide a realistic portrayal of naval duty in Philippine waters and show Fiske's high regard for Dewey.

Dewey's service during the Civil War may be followed in *Official Records of the Union and Confederate Navies in the War of the Rebellion*, 31 vols. (Washington: Government Printing Office, 1894-1927; **A**), his service as president of the court of inquiry requested by Schley in the National Archives' 2-volume *Record of Proceedings of a Court of Inquiry in the Case of Rear Admiral Winfield Scott Schley, USN*. Dewey's reports while he served with the Lighthouse Board, Board of Inspection and Survey, Bureau of Equipment, the Asiatic Station, and General Board are found in *Annual Report of the Secretary of the Navy* (Washington: Government Printing Office, 1861-1917; **A**).

Museums, Historical Landmarks, Societies

Dewey Arch (New York, NY). An arch costing one million dollars, financed by public subscription, was built across Fifth Avenue in honor of Dewey's Manila Bay triumph.

Olympia (Philadelphia, PA). Dewey's flagship at Manila Bay is on public display near Independence Hall.

Other Sources

Beale, Howard K. *Theodore Roosevelt and the Rise of America to World Power.* Baltimore: Johns Hopkins Press, 1956. A masterful survey of Roosevelt's diplomacy and navalism.

Braisted, William R. In *Dictionary of American Military Biography*, edited by Roger J. Spiller and Joseph G. Dawson III. Vol. 1. Westport, CT: Greenwood Press, 1984. A concise sketch.

―――――. *The United States Navy in the Pacific, 1897–1909*. Austin: University of Texas Press, 1958. Contains excellent coverage of Dewey at Manila Bay, fighting Filipino insurgents, and handling the Japanese crisis of 1906.

―――――. *The United States Navy in the Pacific, 1909–1922*. Austin: University of Texas Press, 1971. Covers Dewey's work in the General Board with respect to Pacific affairs until his death in 1917, with much emphasis on providing defense for the Philippines, and on the Japanese crisis of 1913.

Chadwick, French Ensor. *The Relations between the United States and Spain: The Spanish-American War.* 2 vols. New York: Charles Scribner's Sons, 1911. Chadwick graduated from the Naval Academy in 1864, and his career continued until 1906. The commander of Admiral Sampson's flagship and his chief of staff during the Caribbean campaign of 1898, he offers firsthand observations. Also an acquaintance of Dewey, he covers his campaign in the Philippines.

Challener, Richard. *Admirals, Generals and American Foreign Policy, 1898–1914.* Princeton: Princeton University Press, 1973. Assesses Dewey's impact upon American foreign policy during the period covered.

Coletta, Paolo E. *French Ensor Chadwick: Scholarly Warrior.* Lanham, MD: University Press of America, 1980. Relates Dewey's relations with Chadwick, president of the Naval War College and charter member of the General Board, who helped organize the board into committees and established its record-keeping system.

Grenville, John A., and George B. Young. *Politics, Strategy, and American Foreign Diplomacy: Studies in Foreign Policy.* New Haven: Yale University Press, 1966. In part, traces the rapprochement between the United States and Great Britain, and the worsening German-American relations during Dewey's service on the General Board.

Morgan, H. Wayne. *William McKinley and His America.* Syracuse: Syracuse University Press, 1963. Covers Dewey's role in the Battle of Manila Bay and the Filipino insurrection, his membership on the first Philippine Commission, his naiveté as a politician, and his becoming president of the General Board.

Trask, David F. *The War with Spain in 1898.* New York: Macmillan, 1981. Chapters 1–5 tell of the origins of the war with Spain and the Battle of Manila Bay and its aftermath. Chapters 16–20 deal with the Philippine insurrection and the signing of the peace treaty with Spain.

Paolo E. Coletta
U.S. Naval Academy (Ret.)

JOHN DEWEY
1859-1952

Chronology

Born John Dewey on October 20, 1859, in Burlington, Vermont, to Archibald Sprague Dewey, a small business owner and member of the First Vermont Cavalry during the Civil War, and Lucina Rich Dewey, daughter of a Vermont General Assemblyman; *1864–1867* lives with family in Virginia during father's time in the cavalry; *1867–1875* spends rest of childhood in Burlington, graduating from Burlington High School; *1879* graduates Phi Beta Kappa from the University of Vermont, with an A.B.; *1879–1880* teaches high school in Oil City, Pennsylvania; *1881–1882* teaches at Lake View Seminary in Charlotte, Vermont, and studies philosophy privately with Professor H. A. P. Torrey; *1882–1884* studies at Johns Hopkins University and earns his Ph.D.; *1884–1888* serves as an instructor, and then assistant professor, of philosophy at the University of Michigan; marries Harriet Alice Chipman on July 28, 1886; *1888–1894* after a year as a full professor at the University of Minnesota, returns to the University of Michigan, where he is promoted to the same rank; *1894–1904* teaches at the University of Chicago, where he chairs the Department of Philosophy, Psychology, and Education; *1899* is elected first president of the American Psychological Association; *1904–1930* teaches philosophy at Columbia University; *1905* is elected president of the American Philosophical Association; *1910* becomes a member of the National Academy of Sciences; *1915* founds and is first president of the American Association of University Professors; *1919–1921* lectures at Imperial University, Tokyo, and at National Universities of Peking and Nanking; *1923* is a corresponding member of the Academy of Moral and Political Sciences of the Institut de France; *1924–1928* takes educational surveys of Turkey, Mexico, and Soviet Russia; *1926* his wife dies; *1929* serves as a Gifford Lecturer, University of Edinburgh; *1930–1952* is Professor Emeritus of Philosophy at Columbia University; *1937* chairs the Commission of Inquiry into the Charges Made against Leon Trotsky in the Moscow Trials; *1946* marries Roberta Grant on December 11; *1952* dies on June 1 at his home in New York City.

Activities of Historical Significance

Dewey's founding of the Laboratory School at the University of Chicago in 1894 marked the beginning of the scientific study of education in the U.S. His book describing the early years of the school, *The School and Society* (1899; rev. ed. 1915), has been reprinted many times and is still read today. His lifelong interest in the philosophy and practice of education permeates his philosophical writings.

387

Among his works specifically treating education, *Democracy and Education* (1916) and *Experience and Education* (1938) are the best known.

Throughout his life, John Dewey actively supported liberal, democratic causes at home and abroad. As a consultant, he visited developing nations all over the world—China, Mexico, Turkey, Russia—and wrote extensively about his experiences. His reputation continues to derive from his social and political involvement as well as from his philosophical innovation. Dewey's most widely read and translated writings in this area are *The Public and its Problems* (1927); *Impressions of Soviet Russia and the Revolutionary World—Mexico, China, Turkey* (1929); *Freedom and Culture* (1939); and *Problems of Men* (1946).

Overview of Biographical Sources

The only full-scale biography of Dewey is George Dykhuizen's *The Life and Mind of John Dewey* (1973). A number of other works treat aspects or periods of Dewey's life, and he appears as an important figure in the biographies and autobiographies of contemporaries as well as protégés. Among the most important partial or particular biographical treatments are Neil Coughlan's *Young John Dewey* (1975), Jo Ann Boydston's Introduction to *The Poems of John Dewey* (1977), and articles by Lewis Feuer, Sidney Hook, Max Eastman, and Jane Dewey.

Evaluation of Principal Biographical Sources

Boydston, Jo Ann. Introduction to *The Poems of John Dewey*. Carbondale and Edwardsville: Southern Illinois University Press, 1977. **(A)** This close study of the years 1915–1925, when Dewey wrote a number of poems not published during his lifetime, presents many previously unknown biographical facts and insights. Relating the poems' content to events in Dewey's life, notably his relationship with the novelist Anzia Yezierska, provides a number of new perspectives on Dewey's personality.

Coughlan, Neil. *Young John Dewey: A Study in Early American Intellectual History*. Chicago: University of Chicago Press, 1975. **(A)** Coughlan provides a penetrating and comprehensive look at the early formative years of his subject's life with detailed, perceptive sketches of a number of persons who influenced Dewey's development. This is a scholarly, humane study of the intellectual era and environment that molded Dewey, replete with illuminations of Dewey's personality.

Dewey, Jane Mary, ed. "Biography of John Dewey." In *The Philosophy of John Dewey*. Library of Living Philosophers series. Vol. 1. Evanston and Chicago: Northwestern University, 1939. **(A)** Written by John Dewey's eldest daughter from material provided by the philosopher himself, this is an intimate glimpse into Dewey's life written when he was almost 80.

Dykhuizen, George. *The Life and Mind of John Dewey.* Carbondale and Edwardsville: Southern Illinois University Press, 1973. **(A, G)** This thorough and straightforward chronicle of Dewey's life, which includes a detailed analysis of all his writings, should serve as the basic factual reference for a more intimate, full-scale biography yet to be written.

Eastman, Max. "John Dewey: My Teacher and Friend." In *Great Companions.* New York: Farrar, Straus and Cudahy, 1959. **(A)** Eastman presents a lively, entertaining, sometimes controversial view of Dewey and his family, based on long personal acquaintance.

Feuer, Lewis. "H. A. P. Torrey and John Dewey: Teacher and Pupil." *American Quarterly* 10 (1958): 34–54; "John Dewey's Reading at College." *Journal of the History of Ideas* 19 (1958): 415–421; "John Dewey and the Back-to-the-People Movement in American Thought." *Journal of the History of Ideas* 20 (1959): 545–568. **(A)** In several thorough, interesting articles, this eminent sociologist and Dewey scholar traces the origin and impact of many of Dewey's ideas.

Hook, Sidney. *John Dewey: An Intellectual Portrait.* New York: John Day, 1939. **(A)** An objective study of the links between events in Dewey's life and the development of his philosophy; this is not a biography in the usual sense but exactly what the title implies.

————. "Portrait of John Dewey." *American Scholar* 17 (1947–1948): 105–110; "Some Memories of John Dewey." *Commentary* 14 (1952): 245–253; "John Dewey—Philosopher of Growth." *Journal of Philosophy* 56 (1959): 1010–1018. **(A)** Dewey's friend and protégé, sometimes called "Dewey's left Hook," writes with authority, charm, and characteristic flair about the man he has called a "secular saint." Hook's long association with Dewey and his admiration of him do not distort his analysis of Dewey's thought and character.

Overview and Evaluation of Primary Sources
The Collected Works of John Dewey, 1882–1953 **(A)**, the definitive edition of all Dewey's writings, will be completed in thirty-eight volumes (including cumulative short-title and subject indexes) in 1991. Thirty-three of the volumes are currently available. This collection is being edited by the Center for Dewey Studies and is published by the Southern Illinois University Press.

M. Halsey Thomas has compiled a thorough bibliography of Dewey's works, *John Dewey: A Centennial Bibliography* (Chicago: University of Chicago Press, 1962; **A)**. Addenda to the Thomas bibliography are included in the twelve subject bibliographies accompanying analytical essays on Dewey's thought in Jo Ann Boydston, ed., *Guide to the Works of John Dewey* (Carbondale and Edwardsville: Southern Illinois University Press, 1970; **A)**.

The only published autobiographical statement by John Dewey is his "From

Absolutism to Experimentalism," published in volume 2 of George Plimpton Adams and William Pepperell Montague, eds., *Contemporary American Philosophy: Personal Statements* (New York: Macmillan, 1930; **A**). Dewey describes in connected fashion the persons and events that influenced his intellectual development and evaluates the relative impact of various forces on him. Other less personal firsthand philosophical accounts appear in various essays such as "My Philosophy of Law," in *My Philosophy of Law: Credos of Sixteen American Scholars* (Boston: Boston Law, 1941; **A**); "What I Believe," in Clifton Fadiman, ed., *I Believe: The Personal Philosophies of Certain Eminent Men and Women of Our Time* (New York: Simon and Schuster, 1939; **A**); and "Experience, Knowledge and Value: A Rejoinder," in Paul A. Schlipp, ed., *The Philosophy of John Dewey* (Evanston and Chicago: Northwestern University, 1939; **A**).

Museums, Historical Landmarks, Societies

John Dewey Foundation (New York, NY). In cooperation with the Center for Dewey Studies, this organization promotes research on Dewey's life and writings through an annual Essay Project, small research grants, and Senior Fellowships.

John Dewey Memorial (Burlington, VT). Dewey's ashes are interred at this site, located on the campus of the University of Vermont.

John Dewey Society for the Study of Education and Culture (location varies). Engages in various research and publication projects "in the spirit of John Dewey." This organization meets regularly and sponsors a John Dewey Lecture, which is published. The location of the organization's offices varies, moving with the secretary of the society. The present secretary is Robert Morris, School of Education, Northern Illinois University, DeKalb, IL.

Other Sources

Boydston, Jo Ann, and Kathleen Poulos, eds. *Checklist of Writings about John Dewey.* 2nd ed. Carbondale and Edwardsville: Southern Illinois University Press, 1978. Complete information on secondary sources. A third edition is scheduled for 1988 publication.

Edman, Irwin. *John Dewey: His Contribution to the American Tradition.* Indianapolis: Bobbs-Merrill, 1955. A former student and colleague of Dewey's, Edman writes with characteristic lucidity and charm.

Flower, Elizabeth, and Murray G. Murphey. *A History of Philosophy in America.* 2 vols. New York: G. P. Putnam's Sons, 1977. A crisp, comprehensive view of Dewey and his contemporaries as well as predecessors.

Geiger, George R. *John Dewey in Perspective*. New York: Oxford University Press, 1958. As his title implies, Geiger provides insight into Dewey's contributions to contemporary American philosophy, from the point of view of Dewey's last doctoral student.

Hook, Sidney, ed. *John Dewey: Philosopher of Science and Freedom. A Symposium*. New York: Dial Press, 1950. Wide-ranging series of essays from differing points of view.

Kennedy, Gail, ed. *Pragmatism and American Culture*. Boston: D. C. Heath, 1950. Scholarly, readable treatment of the development of the only truly American philosophy, with emphasis on Dewey's influence on the movement.

Rorty, Richard. *Consequences of Pragmatism*. Minneapolis: University of Minnesota Press, 1982. This recent discussion of pragmatism has sparked a revival of interest in contemporary American philosophy and considerable discussion in the philosophical community.

Sleeper, Ralph. *The Necessity of Pragmatism: John Dewey's Conception of Philosophy*. New Haven and London: Yale University Press, 1986. The most thorough, and the latest, discussion of Dewey's reconstruction of pragmatism. A powerfully argued reassessment of Dewey's total work, showing how pragmatism as a philosophy has the power to effect social change through criticism and inquiry.

Smith, John E. *Purpose and Thought: The Meaning of Pragmatism*. New Haven: Yale University Press, 1978. Elegant elucidation of pragmatism's significance in the history of American thought.

Thayer, Horace Standish. *Meaning and Action: A Critical History of Pragmatism*. Indianapolis: Bobbs-Merrill, 1968; rev. ed., 1973. Thorough, insightful, beautifully organized and articulated overview of this philosophical movement and its roots.

Jo Ann Boydston
Center for Dewey Studies
Southern Illinois University, Carbondale

THOMAS E. DEWEY
1902-1971

Chronology

Born Thomas Edmund Dewey on March 24, 1902, in Owosso, Michigan, the son of George Martin Dewey, Jr., a local newspaper editor, postmaster, and Republican county chairman, and Annie Louise Thomas Dewey; *1919-1923* attends and graduates from University of Michigan; *1923-1925* attends and graduates from Columbia University Law School; *1925-1927* is associated with law firm of Larkin, Rathbone and Perry; *1926* is admitted to New York bar; *1927-1931* is associated with law firm of McNamara and Seymour; *1928* marries singer Frances Eileen Hutt; *1931-1933* is chief assistant to George Z. Meladie, United States attorney, Southern District of New York; *1933* is appointed United States attorney; *1934-1935* becomes special assistant attorney general; *1935-1937* works as special prosecutor, Investigation of Organized Crime, New York; *1937-1941* serves as district attorney, New York County; *1938* is Republican candidate for governor, New York State; *1940* makes unsuccessful bid for Republican presidential nomination; *1942-1954* serves as governor of New York State; *1944, 1948* is Republican nominee for president; *1955-1971* is partner in law firm of Dewey, Ballantine, Bushby, Palmer and Wood; *1971* dies on March 16 of heart attack in Bal Harbour, Florida.

Activities of Historical Significance

Dewey made his national reputation as the "racket-buster" of "Murder, Inc." and other underworld groups. Appointed special investigator of organized crime in 1935 by New York Governor Herbert H. Lehman, who was acting at the insistence of the city's famed "runaway grand jury," Dewey obtained 72 convictions in 73 prosecutions. Among those sent to prison were such criminals as "Lucky" Luciano, Irving Wechsler ("Waxey" Gordon), "Legs" Diamond, and Louis Lepke. His indictment of the powerful Tammany leader Jimmy Hines, reputed dispenser of state patronage for the Roosevelt administration and court fixer for gangster "Dutch" Schultz, brought nationwide headlines. In 1940, he made a strong showing as contender for the Republican president nomination, even drawing support from conservative and isolationist leaders.

As governor of New York from 1942 to 1954, he gained a reputation as a tough-minded modernizer, an official administrator who did not sacrifice humane considerations. While always submitting a balanced budget, Dewey established a state university, built a thruway (which was named after him), promoted the first civil rights laws in America, and fostered programs against tuberculosis and cancer.

As a presidential candidate in 1944 and 1948, Dewey was less successful. Though his first defeat by the popular Roosevelt was expected, most commentators found his 1948 loss to Truman a major upset—in fact one of the great political surprises of American history. Among the causes of his defeat were a bland campaign, aimed at offending the least number of people, and, more important, the surprising survival of the old Roosevelt voting coalition, including the all-important farm vote. Nor was he helped by his cold and taciturn personality. Only five-foot-eight and wearing a dark smear of a mustache, he was uncomfortable with strangers, impatient with admirers, and spoke in a resonant, studied, unctuous tone. Dewey remained in Republican politics, leading the internationalist wing against Senator Taft. Because he played a major role in the 1952 nomination of Eisenhower and Nixon, he was admired by liberal Republicans, and detested by conservative ones.

Overview of Biographical Sources

For eulogistic campaign biographies, see Rupert Hughes, *Attorney for the People* (1940), which focuses on Dewey's role as prosecutor; Hughes's *The Story of Thomas E. Dewey: Attorney for the People* (1944), an obvious updating of his previous volume; and Stanley Walker, *Thomas E. Dewey: An American of This Century* (1944). The last third of Walker's book contains Dewey speeches delivered between 1937 and 1944. Serious scholarship begins with Barry K. Beyer, *Thomas E. Dewey, 1937–1947: A Study in Political Leadership* (1979). Richard Norton Smith's *Thomas E. Dewey and his Times* (1982) is the only major full-length biography.

Evaluation of Principal Biographical Sources

Beyer, Barry K. *Thomas E. Dewey, 1937–1947: A Study in Political Leadership*. New York: Garland, 1979. **(A, G)** Essentially a doctoral dissertation completed in 1962 and slightly updated, it offers valuable material on Dewey's rivals in New York State politics, but otherwise provides little that is new.

Smith, Richard Norton. *Thomas E. Dewey and His Times*. New York: Simon and Schuster, 1982. **(A, G)** A well-written, thorough account based upon the Dewey papers, oral history projects, and interviews. Shows Dewey as a much misunderstood man, a youthful genius pressed too far too fast, with an almost tragic element lying behind his trim, dapper exterior.

Overview and Evaluation of Primary Sources

Dewey's *The Case Against the New Deal* (New York: Harper and Row, 1940; **G**), timed for the 1940 campaign, consists of his speeches delivered from December

1939 to June 1940. His *Journey to the Far Pacific* (New York: Doubleday, 1952; **G**), based upon a sixty-day trip, presented a "domino theory" concerning Indochina and called for a Pacific mutual defense treaty. *On the Two-Party System* (New York: Doubleday, 1966; **G**), a series of lectures delivered at Princeton in 1950, covers the decline of the two-party system, a growing imbalance in federal-state relations, and foreign policy. *Twenty Against the Underworld*, edited by Rodney Campbell (New York: Doubleday, 1975; **G**), based upon his memoirs, details his fight with the underworld.

The Papers of Thomas E. Dewey are located in the University of Rochester's Rush Rhees Library. This is a major collection, consisting of 1,500 boxes and 300 thick scrapbooks. Also at Rochester are the notes and interviews compiled in the late 1950s by Harlan Phillips, a scholar at Columbia University hired to research a Dewey memoir.

Fiction and Adaptations

Two grade-B movies were produced in 1938, based upon Dewey's battles against the underworld: *Racket Busters* and *Smashing the Rackets*. Both are highly speculative.

Other Sources

Abels, Jules. *Out of the Jaws of Victory*. New York: Holt, 1959. Former *Newsweek* editor claims that Dewey threw away a sure victory by such errors as choosing Earl Warren as his running mate. Typical of the worst in romantic history.

Kirkendall, Richard S. "Election of 1948." In *History of American Presidential Elections, 1789–1968*, edited by Arthur M. Schlesinger, Jr. and Fred L. Israel. Vol. 4. New York: Chelsea House, 1971. The best account of the 1948 race. Challenges traditional view that the election was an upset, in which Truman single-handedly secured victory.

Ross, Irwin. *The Loneliest Campaign: The Truman Campaign of 1948*. New York: New American Library, 1968. Sounder than Abels but containing little fresh insight and still stressing individual heroics.

Justus D. Doenecke
New College of the University of South Florida

JOHN DICKINSON
1732–1808

Chronology

Born John Dickinson on November 2, 1732, in Talbot County, Maryland, to Mary Cadwalader Dickinson and Samuel Dickinson, a wealthy lawyer who has large land holdings in Maryland, Delaware, and Pennsylvania; *1740–1754* moves to Kent County, Delaware; is tutored at home; reads law with John Moland in Philadelphia; *1754–1757* completes legal education at the Middle Temple, one of the Inns of Court in London; *1757–1758* becomes a successful lawyer in Philadelphia; *1759* is elected member of Delaware assembly, and serves as speaker for one term; *1762–1765* is elected to Pennsylvania's unicameral assembly; opposes Benjamin Franklin and Joseph Galloway in their attempt to end the Penn proprietorship; writes assembly's "Resolves against the Stamp Act"; attends Stamp Act Congress in New York and writes "Declaration of Rights and Grievances"; writes *The Late Regulations Considered; 1767–1768* in response to the Townshend Acts, publishes twelve essays as *Letters of a Pennsylvania Farmer*, which makes him the most popular and influential American speaking out against British actions; *July 19, 1770* marries Mary Norris, an heiress and devout Quaker, with whom he will have five children, although only two, Sara (1771) and Maria (1783), will survive; *1774–1781* represents Pennsylvania at First Continental Congress; writes *Petition to King* asking for relief from ministerial oppression; attends Second Continental Congress, where he writes the *Olive Branch Petition* and *Causes and Necessity of Taking Up Arms*, both of which are approved by Congress; writes first draft of the Articles of Confederation, the nation's first constitution; refuses to sign the Declaration of Independence; serves as colonel in the First Philadelphia Batallion; *1781* elected president (governor) of Delaware; *1782* elected president of Pennsylvania, and resigns his Delaware office two months later; *1787* serves as a delegate from Delaware to the Constitutional Convention; *1791* helps write the Delaware Constitution; *1808* dies on February 14 in Wilmington, Delaware.

Activities of Historical Significance

Dickinson was among the most influential founding fathers in the American colonies, earning the title of "Penman of the Revolution" with his essays attacking the constraints of British rule. During a career that spanned four decades, he served in the Delaware and Pennsylvania legislatures, the Stamp Act Congress, both Continental Congresses, and at the Constitutional Convention. No founding father wrote as many influential essays, or participated in as many congresses and conventions. Yet, he remains almost unknown except among historians.

Already a practical, polished propagandist in 1767, Dickinson made his reputation with the *Letters of a Pennsylvania Farmer*. This collection of twelve essays, which first began appearing in the *Pennsylvania Chronicle* in December 1767, protested the passage of the British Parliament's Townshend Acts, which placed taxes on some consumer goods, restructured the Vice Admiralty Courts, and established an American Board of Customs Commissioners. Few pamphlets in Revolutionary War literature compare with the letters in style, quality, cogency, and depth. With the exception of Thomas Paine's *Common Sense*, the letters' circulation surpassed all other publications in the Revolutionary War era. They were immediately reproduced in 19 of the 23 colonial newspapers, quickly collected and printed in pamphlet form, and at least eight editions were circulated in the colonies, two appeared in London, and one in Dublin.

Overview of Biographical Sources

Despite his remarkable contributions to the American revolutionary cause, Dickinson has received little attention from biographers. Charles Stillé's *The Life and Times of John Dickinson* (1891) was the first biography to attempt to resurrect Dickinson's legacy. Accordingly, Stillé tends to overstate his subject's achievements and excuse his shortcomings. In contrast, Milton Flower's thoroughly researched *John Dickinson, Conservative Revolutionary* (1983) points out some character flaws—hypochondria, acute sensitivity to criticism—but offers little analysis.

Another worthwhile work is David L. Jacobson's *John Dickinson and the Revolution in Pennsylvania, 1774–1776* (1965), which explores Dickinson's early life and provides a careful analysis of Pennsylvania politics. A superb appraisal of Dickinson's ideas can also be found in Bernard Bailyn, ed., *Pamphlets of the American Revolution* (1965).

Evaluation of Principal Biographical Sources

Flower, Milton. *John Dickinson, Conservative Revolutionary*. Charlottesville, VA: University Press of Virginia, 1983. **(A, G)** An excellent portrait, based on original sources, but lacking in analysis.

Jacobson, David L. *John Dickinson and the Revolution in Pennsylvania, 1764–1776*. Berkeley, CA: University of California Press, 1965. **(A)** Examines Dickinson's role in Pennsylvania politics and involvement in the American Revolution.

Stillé, Charles. *The Life and Times of John Dickinson*. 1891. Reprint. New York: B. Franklin, 1969. **(A, G)** This first major biography of Dickinson is solid, if overly appreciative. Contains Dickinson's "Vindication."

Overview and Evaluation of Primary Sources

The Logan Collections of Dickinson's papers, located at both the Historical Society of Pennsylvania, and the Library Company of Philadelphia, are invaluable resources for students and scholars. Both libraries are also repositories for the related collections of Gratz, McKean, Dreer, and Loudon, all of which include materials on Dickinson. Dickinson College (Carlisle, Pennsylvania) also has some useful materials, as do the Historical Society of Delaware and the Delaware State Archives in Wilmington.

Many of Dickinson's writings can be found in Paul Leicester Ford, ed., *The Writings of John Dickinson, 1764–1774* (Philadelphia: Historical Society of Pennsylvania, 1895; A). A collection published during his lifetime is Dickinson's *The Political Writings of John Dickinson* (1801. Reprint. New York: Da Capo Press, 1970; A).

A good primary source that also offers a fine dose of analysis is H. Tevor Colbourn's study, "A Pennsylvania Farmer in the Court of King George: John Dickinson's Letters, 1774–1776," in *Pennsylvania Magazine of History and Biography* 86 (1962; A), which offers a superb biographical sketch along with Dickinson's letters to his family which he wrote while studying law at the Inns of Court.

Museums, Historical Landmarks, Societies

Dickinson Birthplace Marker (near Trappe, MD). Although "Crosiadore," the Dickinson ancestral estate where he was born, no longer exists, an historical marker designates the site.

Dickinson College (Carlisle, PA). Named for Dickinson, this institution also houses a collection of materials relating to his life and career.

Dickinson Mansion National Historic Landmark (near Dover, DE). Dickinson's childhood home contains furnishings and a few artifacts from his life. Open to the public.

Other Sources

Bailyn, Bernard, ed. *Pamphlets of the American Revolution*. Cambridge, MA: Belknap Press, 1965. Includes a fine examination of Dickinson's literary talents as a propagandist and essayist.

Boyd, Julian. "The Disputed Authorship of the 'Declaration of Causes of Taking Up Arms.'" *Pennsylvania Magazine of History and Biography* 74 (1950): 51–73. Examines the controversy over the true writer of Dickinson's famous "Declaration."

Gummere, Richard M. "John Dickinson, the Classical Penman of the Revolution." *Classical Journal* 52 (1960): 81–88. An appreciation of Dickinson's life as a man of revolutionary letters.

Holder, Jean. "The Historical Misrepresentation of John Dickinson." *Journal of Historical Studies* 1 (1976): 1–20. A look at why and how Dickinson has been ignored or misunderstood by historians.

Kaestle, Carl. "The Public Reaction to John Dickinson's Farmers' Letters." *Proceedings of the American Antiquarian Society* 78 (1969): 323–353. A discussion of the incendiary effects of Dickinson's infamous letters about the Townshend Acts.

Knollenberg, Bernard. "John Dickinson vs. John Adams, 1774–1776." *Proceedings of the American Philosophical Society* 197 (1962): 135–144. Relates the enmity between Dickinson and Adams that climaxed with Dickinson's refusal to sign the Declaration of Independence.

Powell, John H. "Speech of John Dickinson Opposing the Delaware State." *Pennsylvania Magazine of History and Biography* 65 (1941): 458–481. An examination of Dickinson's oratorical stand against the Declaration of Independence.

————. "John Dickinson, President of the Delaware State, 1781–1782." *Delaware History* 1 (1946): 1–54. Relates Dickinson's short but important tenure as president (governor) of Delaware.

————. "John Dickinson as President of Pennsylvania." *Pennsylvania History* 28 (1961): 254–267. An examination of Dickinson's governance of Pennsylvania that is particularly valuable when read in conjunction with Powell's aforementioned examination of Dickinson's Delaware presidency.

Robert J. Chaffin
University of Wisconsin—Oshkosh

Drafting the Articles of Confederation, 1977

DOROTHEA DIX
1802–1887

Chronology

Born Dorothea Lynde Dix on April 4, 1802, in Hampden, Maine, the oldest of
three children and only daughter of Joseph Dix, itinerant preacher, and Mary
Bigelow Dix, and granddaughter of Dr. Elijah Dix, a prominent Boston physician,
merchant, and land speculator; *1814* flees from the increasingly impoverished and
unhappy household of her parents to her widowed paternal grandmother in Boston;
1816 at age fourteen, opens a day school in Worcester, Massachusetts; *1821* opens
Dix Mansion School in her grandmother's Orange Court home in Boston; *1824–
1832* publishes a series of children's books and collections of devotions, one of
which, *Conversations on Common Things*, will go through sixty editions by 1869;
1827 is invited by Dr. William Ellery Channing, the eminent Boston Unitarian
minister and humanitarian, to serve as his children's tutor during a six-month
family vacation on Narragansett Bay; *1830–1831* spends the winter with the Channings on St. Croix in the Danish West Indies; *April 1836* having been forced
periodically since the mid-1820s to give up her teaching and most other activities
because of a respiratory illness, departs for Europe to regain her health, spending
almost the entire eighteen months with friends of the Channings, the William
Rathbones, at their home near Liverpool; *1837* returns to Boston healthy and also
financially independent because her grandmother has died and left a modest be-
quest; *March 28, 1841* while teaching Sunday school to women inmates in the East
Cambridge, Massachusetts, jail, she is shocked to discover several insane women
in unheated cells; *1841–1842* visits jails, correction houses, asylums and poor-
houses in Massachusetts, investigating the care of the insane; *January 1843* submits *Memorial to the Legislature of Massachusetts*, a detailed description of the
shocking conditions she has found; *1843–1861* using her successful Massachusetts
strategy, visits virtually every state east of the Mississippi River, plus Louisiana,
Arkansas, Missouri, and eastern Canada, to investigate the housing and care of the
insane, making public her findings through letters and editorials as well as memorials to state legislatures; *March 25, 1845* is informed that the New Jersey legislature
has approved construction of the New Jersey State Lunatic Asylum at Trenton
which, because it is the first new hospital for the insane that owes its existence to
her efforts, she will always refer to as "my first-born child"; *May 1854* is shocked
and dismayed by President John Tyler's veto of a bill to distribute millions of acres
of public land among the states to provide for the indigent insane, having campaigned for such a reform since proposing it to Congress in 1848; *1854–1856* takes
her campaign on behalf of the insane to Europe; *June 10, 1861* Secretary of War
Cameron appoints her superintendent of women nurses, a position she will hold,
refusing compensation, for the duration of the Civil War; *1865–1882* after the war,

returns to her work for the insane, revisiting hospitals and asylums constructed, enlarged, or remodeled largely as a result of her efforts, and carrying her campaign to other states, including California and Oregon, for the first time; *1882–1887* in declining health, retires to the apartment set aside for her use in the hospital for the insane in Trenton, New Jersey; *1887* dies on July 17 at the Trenton hospital, and is buried in Mt. Auburn Cemetery in Cambridge, Massachusetts.

Activities of Historical Significance

Unquestionably, Dorothea Dix is one of the greatest figures in the history of humanitarian reform in the United States. If her work is measured simply in terms of physical endurance—the thousands of miles she traveled and the hundreds of institutions she visited despite the opposition she encountered, the restricted status of women, and the limited means of transportation available—then she may have been the nation's most determined and tireless reformer. By the spring of 1848, according to one of her biographers, "she had traveled 60,000 miles, visiting over 9,000 insane, epileptic, and idiotic persons, besides thousands in prisons and other detention houses."

Equally impressive was the degree of her success, especially if the ignorance about insanity and indifference about its victims among the general public at the time are considered. Whereas, when she launched her campaign, there were only thirteen asylums or hospitals for the insane in the U.S., forty years later, according to the 1880 census, there were close to 140, both public and private. Of the public ones, Dix was directly involved in the establishment of thirty-two, and indirectly involved in many others. Henry M. Hurd, a leading scholar on the history of the care and treatment of the insane in the U.S. and Canada, writing in 1916, reported that "this remarkable woman contributed more to the general awakening of the country to the needs of the insane than all other agencies combined," her efforts advancing "the general care of the insane in America fully a quarter of a century." Gerald N. Grob, also a leading scholar in the field, who describes Dix as the "most famous and influential psychiatric reformer of the nineteenth century," has suggested that "in many ways Dix's most important contribution was to stimulate the thrust toward broadening the role of government in providing institutional care and treatment of the mentally ill."

Her four years as superintendent of women nurses during the Civil War are a very different story. "This is not the work I would have my life judged by," she later told a friend. The great frustrations she encountered as superintendent were inevitable considering the fact that she had to carry out her responsibilities in a war-time civil and military administrative system that was chaotic and totally male-dominated. Nonetheless, her biographers are in agreement that she must assume at least part of the responsibility for the obstacles, hostility, and criticism she encountered from hospital administrators, surgeons, and members of the U.S. Sanitary

Commission. Apparently, the almost fanatical determination that had served her so well in the crusade on behalf of the insane now worked against her. According to Francis Tiffany, her first biographer, the fault was "an overwrought zeal precipitating her at times into intemperate action." Nevertheless, her superintendency of women nurses is an important, though rather neglected, chapter in the medical history of the Union Army, as well as in the history of the emergence of nursing as a profession in the United States.

Overview of Biographical Sources

Surprisingly, considering the historical importance of Dorothea Dix and the dramatic nature of her life, the number of book-length biographies is relatively small. During the century since her death, only seven works have appeared, and four of these are for young readers. Furthermore, all three substantial biographies are deficient for one reason or another.

Because of the general historical importance of the two activities that are the basis for her reputation as one of the greatest reformers in U.S. history—her prominence in the campaign to improve the care and treatment of the mentally ill, and her role in the Civil War as superintendent of women nurses—considerable biographical information may be found in both primary and secondary sources relating to these events. Invaluable sources for a historical assessment, as well as a description of Dix's work on behalf of the mentally ill, are the scholarly accounts of the evolution of knowledge about, and care and treatment of, the mentally ill in the United States. These sources are particularly useful in evaluating the work of Dix in the context of the most advanced knowledge of insanity during her lifetime and her influence on later developments. Although there is some disagreement among these authorities on the degree of Dix's interest in the treatment as well as the care of the insane, most are as favorable in their assessment of her efforts as are her more general biographers.

All of the secondary sources on Dix's performance as superintendent of women nurses during the Civil War, including her most sympathetic biographers, are in agreement that she encountered much opposition in that role, and that she was at least partially responsible for that opposition. However, none of these sources provides sufficient evidence of the extent of that opposition, or produces adequate explanations for it. That she made such mistakes as initially setting screening criteria for her volunteer nurses that were too restrictive, and refusing to accept nuns as nurses because of her anti-Catholic sentiments, is easily documented. But little or no evidence has been provided to support suggestions that she was a poor administrator and too emotional, quarrelsome, pious, or opinionated. Moreover, there also is little evidence of this behavior in primary sources. It is true that George Templeton Strong, a top official in the U.S. Sanitary Commission, for example, referred to her in his diary as "that philanthropic lunatic, Miss Dix" and

that even such admirers as Samuel Gridley Howe and Louisa May Alcott acknowledged that she could be quite difficult (she was "very queer and arbitrary," Alcott
wrote in her Civil War journal). However, among the most valuable primary
sources are letters, diaries and memoirs of nurses who were appointed by and
worked closely with her, and they are virtually unanimous in their praise of her.

Evaluation of Principal Biographical Sources

Brooks, Gladys. "Dorothea Lynde Dix." In *Three Wise Virgins*. New York:
E. P. Dutton, 1957. (**A, G**) This is the best of the shorter biographies. It is beautifully written but lacks footnotes and a bibliography.

Grob, Gerald N. *Mental Institutions in America: Social Policy to 1875*. New
York: Free Press, 1973. (**A**) Grob includes many references to Dix plus a biographical sketch several pages in length. The book is particularly valuable in assessing
the work of Dix in the larger context of the efforts to improve the care and treatment of the insane during the first two centuries of U.S. history. Grob, in assessing
Dix's contributions to these efforts, concludes that she was "the most famous and
influential psychiatric reformer of the nineteenth century."

Hathaway, Marion. "Dorothea Dix and Social Reform in Western Pennsylvania,
1845–1875." *Western Pennsylvania Historical Magazine* 17 (December 1934):
247–258. (**A, G**) Hathaway presents a detailed account of Dix's campaign on behalf of the insane in western Pennsylvania that led to the construction of Western
Pennsylvania Hospital and Dixmont Hospital. This article is also important in
illustrating Dix's involvement in the ongoing administration of the hospitals that
she had helped to establish or expand.

Hurd, Henry M., ed. "Dorothea Lynde Dix and Her Work." In vol. 1 of *The
Institutional Care of the Insane in the United States and Canada*. 4 vols. Baltimore: Johns Hopkins University Press, 1916. (**A**) This thirty-eight-page chapter
appears to be based exclusively on Tiffany's biography. The other volumes in the
work describe the development of institutional care of the insane in each state in the
U.S. and province in Canada, and there are many references to Dix in the sections
on those states (and Nova Scotia) in which she was active.

Marshall, Helen E. *Dorothea Dix: Forgotten Samaritan*. Chapel Hill: University
of North Carolina Press, 1937. (**A, G**) Probably the most satisfactory of the three
major biographies, this includes numerous footnotes and a detailed bibliography.
Also very valuable is the inclusion of a chapter on the history of the care and
treatment of the mentally ill prior to 1840. However, when lacking biographical
fact, Marshall too often offers fictionalized accounts: faced, as all Dix biographers
have been, with very meager information about her personal life (especially during

her childhood and early womanhood), Marshall presents what she surmises Dix may have done or what her thoughts, impressions and motives may have been.

Tiffany, Francis. *Life of Dorothea Lynde Dix*. Boston: Houghton Mifflin, 1890. (**A, G**) Francis Tiffany, a Unitarian minister, is the most important of Dix's biographers for two related reasons: because he wrote the biography only a few years after her death and was invited to undertake it by her friends, he was provided with information about her family and personal life that otherwise would have been lost; similarly, in conducting his research, he was successful in locating and preserving invaluable collections of her private correspondence. The significance of these contributions is made clear by Tiffany in the Preface, where he describes and attempts to explain Dix's "positive refusal to permit anything to be written of her." He also includes a brief chapter on the history of the treatment of the insane. Although Tiffany quotes extensively from Dix's letters and public papers, he does not include footnotes or a bibliography.

Wilson, Dorothy Clarke. *Stranger and Traveler: The Story of Dorothea Dix, American Reformer*. Boston: Little, Brown, 1975. (**G, Y**) This is a particularly disappointing biography considering that it is the most recent, and, thus, that Wilson had access to all previous scholarship and to primary sources not available to Marshall. The major problem with the biography is that Wilson, more so than Marshall, often relies on her own imagination, even going so far as to invent dialogue. Furthermore, there are no footnotes, and, although the bibliography is almost as detailed as Marshall's, it is rather carelessly compiled (one of the biographies of Dorothea Dix listed is actually a biography of "Dorothy Dix" a.k.a. Elizabeth M. Gilmer, the popular journalist and advice-to-the-lovelorn columnist).

Evaluation of Biographies for Young People

Lowe, Corinne. *The Gentle Warrior: A Story of Dorothea Lynde Dix*. New York: Harcourt, Brace, 1948. This is a rather melodramatic biography for young teenage readers.

Malone, Mary. *Dorothea L. Dix: Hospital Founder*. Champaign, IL: Garrard, 1968. This is a very brief biography in the Discovery Books series for very young readers.

Melin, Grace Hathaway. *Dorothea Dix: Girl Reformer*. Indianapolis: Bobbs-Merrill, 1963. This relatively brief biography is a volume in the Childhood of Famous Americans series for young readers.

Norman, Gertrude. *Dorothea Lynde Dix*. New York: G. P. Putnam's Sons, 1959. This is a volume in the Lives to Remember series of biographies for young readers.

Overview and Evaluation of Primary Sources

In the 1820s, both while teaching and, more often, during those intervals when she was forced to temporarily close Dix Mansion School because of her ill health, Dorothea Dix published a series of small volumes for children and books of devotions. Several proved to be extremely popular at the time, but all are now long-forgotten. They include *Conversations on Common Things, Guide to Knowledge With Questions* (Boston: Munroe & Francis, 1824; **Y**); *Evening Hours* (Boston: Munroe & Francis, 1825; **G, Y**); *The Garland of Flora* (Boston: S. G. Goodrich and Carter and Hendee, 1829; **G**); *Hymns for Children, Selected and Altered* (Boston: Munroe & Francis, 1825; rev. ed., 1833; **Y**); *Meditations for Private Hours* (Boston: Munroe & Francis, 1828; **G, Y**); *The Pearl, or Affection's Gift; A Christmas and New Year's Present* (Philadelphia, 1829; **G, Y**); and *Ten Short Stories for Children* (Boston, 1827–1828; **Y**), reprinted as *American Moral Tales for Young Persons* (Boston: Leonard C. Bowles and B. H. Greene, 1832). Of these publications, perhaps the most revealing is *The Garland of Flora* because of the impressive variety of selections of poetry she included.

Of her published writings, certainly the most important are the memorials she submitted to state legislatures and to Congress which were such a crucial part of her campaign on behalf of the mentally ill. Copies of ten of her memorials (those for Massachusetts, New York, New Jersey, Pennsylvania, Kentucky, Tennessee, North Carolina, Mississippi and Maryland, plus the one she submitted to the U.S. Congress in 1848), are readily available in Dorothea L. Dix, *On Behalf of the Insane Poor: Selected Reports* (New York: Arno Press & The New York Times, 1971; **A, G**). This is one of forty-four volumes in the Arno Press/New York Times Series *Poverty, U.S.A.: The Historical Record*, advisory editor David J. Rothman. These state memorials, plus those not included (e.g., those for Alabama and Illinois), are also available in the public archives of each state. The memorial that Dix submitted to the legislature in Nova Scotia has been reprinted as appendix A in volume 1 of Henry M. Hurd, ed., *The Institutional Care of the Insane in the United States and Canada* (Baltimore, MD: Johns Hopkins University Press, 1916; **A, G**).

Considering the number of state prisons and penitentiaries she visited, it should not be surprising that Dix became involved in the prison reform movement that was underway at the time. In 1845, she published *Remarks on Prisons and Prison Discipline in the United States* (Boston: Munroe and Francis, 1845; **A, G**), which has been reprinted as Publication No. 4 in the Patterson Smith Reprint Series in Criminology, Law Enforcement, and Social Problems (Montclair, NJ: Patterson Smith, 1967; **A, G**) with an "Introduction" by Leonard D. Savitz.

The other primary sources, in addition to Dix's published writings, are considerably more numerous than she intended. In addition to being an extremely private person ("notoriety is my special aversion"), she believed that for women to permit "unnecessary publicity" was "at variance with the delicacy and modesty which are the most attractive ornaments of their sex." As a result, she not only refused to provide any written autobiographical information, in spite of the entreaties of her friends and admirers, but also, in what her biographer Francis Tiffany described as "a mistaken sense of duty of self-effacement," instructed her friends to destroy all her letters. Fortunately, most of them refused to do so, and Francis Tiffany was able to locate and assure the preservation of most of her correspondence. Virtually all of the most important Dix papers, with the exception of one crucial collection of letters, are housed at the Houghton Library at Harvard University. The twenty-nine boxes in this collection include manuscripts, clippings, pictures, personal mementos and other effects, and thousands of letters. Of this collection, without doubt the most important are the Heath-Dix Papers, the correspondence of Dix and her most intimate friend, Ann Heath, from 1825–1878. A second very important source for Dix's correspondence are the Papers of William Rathbone V in Liverpool, England, that include many letters from Dix to the Rathbones from 1837 to 1875.

Primary sources that provide valuable glimpses of Dix's conduct as superintendent of women nurses during the Civil War are found in a number of published diaries, journals, and recollections of nurses and others who had contact with her during that time. Among the most compelling of these are the reminiscences of Louisa May Alcott, one of Dix's nurses who went on to considerable fame herself. Alcott's views of Dix are presented in her *Hospital Sketches* (1863. Reprint. Cambridge, MA: Belknap Press of Harvard University Press, 1960; **A, G**), and in *Louisa May Alcott: Her Life, Letters, and Journals*, edited by Ednah D. Cheney (1889. Reprint. Boston: Little, Brown, 1928; **A, G**). Although there are only single references to Dix in these works, they are of special interest because of the two very different descriptions of Dix that Alcott provides. Also of note is the "Introduction" by Bessie Z. Jones in the 1960 edition of *Hospital Sketches*, which includes a detailed description of nursing during the Civil War, and offers a sympathetic discussion of Dix's difficulties.

A variety of other primary sources from the Civil War also shed light on Dix's involvement with nursing. In volume 3 of *The Diary of George Templeton Strong*, edited by Allan Nevins and Milton Thomas (New York: Macmillan, 1952; **A, G**), a top official of the U.S. Sanitary Commission, with which Dix was involved in jurisdictional disputes, is highly critical of her work. Sophronia E. Bucklin's *In Hospital and Camp: A Woman's Record of Thrilling Incidents Among the Wounded in the Late War* (Philadelphia: John E. Potter, 1869; **A, G**) probably includes the most numerous and positive firsthand accounts of Dix's conduct. *Our Army Nurses*, compiled by Mary A. Gardner Holland (Boston: N. Wilkins, 1895; **A, G**), includes the accounts of more than ninety Civil War nurses. In addition to a seven-page biography of Dix based on the Tiffany biography, this work offers numerous references to Dix in the recollections of her former nurses.

Museums, Historical Landmarks, Societies

Dorothea Dix Park (Hampden, ME). This park near the site of her birth was established in 1899 as a result of the efforts of the Dorothea Dix Memorial Association in Hampden.

Other Sources

Adams, George W. *Doctors in Blue: The Medical History of the Union Army in the Civil War*. New York: Henry Schuman, 1952. Adams briefly discusses the controversy over the use of woman nurses in the army hospitals and refers to Dix several times. He discusses critically the administrative problems she experienced, referring to her as a "muddled executive."

Baker, Christina H. "Dorothea Lynde Dix." In *The Dictionary of American Biography*, edited by Allen Johnson and Dumas Malone. Vol. 3. New York: Charles Scribner's Sons, 1959. Considering its relative brevity, this is a surprisingly detailed sketch of Dix's life. The bibliography is too brief and selective to be very useful.

Barton, William E. *The Life of Clara Barton, Founder of the American Red Cross*. 2 vols. 1922. Reprint. New York: AMS Press, 1969. In the first volume of this biography, Barton provides a biographical sketch of Dix and an enlightening description of some of the difficulties she encountered.

Brockett, L.P., M.D., and Mrs. Mary C. Vaughan. *Woman's Work in the Civil War: A Record of Heroism, Patriotism and Patience*. Philadelphia: Zeigler, McCurdy, 1867. Published shortly after the close of the Civil War, this book overuses superlatives in describing the contributions of women, most of them nurses, to the Union cause. Included is a rather detailed biographical sketch of Dix, concentrating on her performance as superintendent of women nurses and sympathetically describing the difficulties she encountered.

Dain, Norman. *Concepts of Insanity in the United States, 1789–1865*. New Brunswick, NJ: Rutgers University Press, 1964. Dain includes numerous references to Dix. He reports that those scholars and other writers concerned about the scientific treatment of the insane have been critical of Dix for seeming to concentrate on the custodial care of the insane rather than on their treatment. Dain discusses in considerable detail Dix's knowledge and understanding of the psychiatric ideas of her day and her resulting interest in forms of treatment, concluding that her concerns did include cure as well as care and that her "psychiatric views resembled those of most psychiatrists of her day."

Leech, Margaret. *Reveille in Washington, 1860–1865*. New York: Harper & Brothers, 1941. This superb account of the nation's capital during the Civil War includes a brief but balanced description and assessment of Dix's activities.

Maxwell, William Q. *Lincoln's Fifth Wheel: The Political History of the United States Sanitary Commission*. New York: Longmans, Green, 1956. Because members of the U.S. Sanitary Commission were among those most critical of Dix, most of the references to her in this history of the commission are critical.

Stimson, Julia C., and Miss Ethel C. Thompson. "Women Nurses With the Union Forces During the Civil War." *Military Surgeon* 62 (January and February 1928): 1–17, 208–230. The authors of this two-part article describe the experiences of women nurses during the Civil War, relying primarily on the accounts of nurses such as those compiled by Mary Holland. In discussing Dix, they also rely on Tiffany.

Tyler, Alice Felt. *Freedom's Ferment: Phases of American Social History From the Colonial Period to the Outbreak of the Civil War.* Reprint ed. New York: Harper & Brothers, 1962. In discussing humanitarian reform in the pre-Civil War period, Tyler describes Dix's national campaign on behalf of the insane and also presents a brief historical summary of the care and treatment of the insane in America prior to 1840.

Willard, Frances E. "Dorothea Dix." *Chautauquan* 10 (October 1889): 61–65. This is an interesting biographical sketch because it was written before Tiffany's biography had been published, and thus Willard had to rely on conversations and correspondence with Dix's friends and associates for biographical information. Among the correspondence is a long and informative letter on Dix from Dr. John W. Ward of the New Jersey State Lunatic Asylum (Dix's "first-born child"), who was with Dix when she died, a letter that Willard includes in her article.

Thomas C. McClintock
Oregon State University

STEPHEN A. DOUGLAS
1813-1861

Chronology

Born Stephen Arnold Douglas on April 23, 1813, in Brandon, Vermont, to Stephen Arnold Douglas, Sr., a local physician, and Sarah Fisk Douglas; *1833* seeks his fortune in the West and migrates to Illinois, where he studies law and gains admission to the bar; *1836* is elected to the Illinois legislature as a Democrat; *1840* becomes a member of the Illinois Supreme Court; *1842-1846* is elected to the U.S. House of Representatives and serves two terms; *1846-1861* serves in the U.S. Senate; *1847* marries Martha Denny Martin, with whom he will have two sons; *1852* unsuccessfully seeks his party's nomination for the presidency; *1853* his wife dies; *1854* is the principal author of the controversial Kansas-Nebraska Act; *1856* makes another unsuccessful bid for a presidential nomination; marries Adele Cutts, grand-niece of Dolley Madison; *1858* successfully defends his Senate seat against Republican Abraham Lincoln in a campaign that produces a series of famous debates; *1860* runs for the presidency on the Northern Democratic ticket, but loses to Lincoln; *1861* dies on June 3 in Chicago of typhoid fever.

Activities of Historical Significance

Stephen A. Douglas achieved national prominence in 1854, while serving as Chairman of the Senate Committee on Territories, when he proposed that Kansas and Nebraska be granted territorial status in anticipation of statehood, and that the issue of slavery in the newly organized area be resolved by "popular sovereignty." Although he had a personal distaste for slavery, Douglas championed the principle of popular sovereignty because he regarded the people's right to resolve the issue on the local level to be of greater importance. His solution became law in the Kansas-Nebraska Act, but angered Northern abolitionists and moderates, who were opposed to the extension of slavery into the Western territories. The measure also appeared to abrogate a portion of a federal statute of 1820, the Missouri Compromise, which had proclaimed the region "forever free" of slavery.

Three years later, in the *Dred Scott Decision*, the Supreme Court ruled that neither the Missouri Compromise nor popular sovereignty would prevail, as the Court guaranteed the right of owners to take their slave property into the Kansas Territory. Despite this ruling, Douglas insisted upon popular sovereignty, and consequently lost much of his party's support in the South. Southerners refused to accept his presidential nomination in the 1860 Democratic National Convention and chose a rival candidate. This split virtually assured Republican Abraham Lincoln's victory in the presidential election. Thus, the principle of popular sovereignty, which probably would have garnered wide support in almost any other period of American history, led to Douglas's political demise.

Overview of Biographical Sources

Although an abundance of biographical information on Douglas is available, most of it portrays him in an unflattering light. Douglas is often viewed as a well-intentioned blunderer or as a foil to Lincoln. The earliest biography written by a professional historian is Allen Johnson, *Stephen A. Douglas: A Study in American Politics* (1908). Recent works are more likely to be balanced and objective, a change that began with the publication of George Fort Milton, *The Eve of Conflict: Stephen A. Douglas and the Needless War* (1934), a work that goes somewhat too far in its unqualified praise of Douglas.

Among the early and now badly dated biographies, are Robert B. Warden, *Stephen Arnold Douglas* (1860); Henry Flint, *Life of Stephen Douglas* (1863); William G. Brown, *Stephen A. Douglas* (1902); William Gardner, *Stephen A. Douglas* (1905); Henry P. Willis, *Stephen A. Douglas* (1910); Louis Howland, *Stephen A. Douglas* (1920); Frank E. Stevens, "Life of Stephen A. Douglas," *Journal of the Illinois State Historical Society* 16 (October 1923-January 1924): 247–673. While often inaccurate, these works may be consulted in order to trace how portrayals of Douglas have changed over the years. A more accurate early biography is James W. Sheahan, *The Life of Stephen A. Douglas* (1860). As a campaign biography, this work is, of course, biased in favor of its subject.

Almost any account of pre-Civil War, Civil War, or Reconstruction politics includes information on Douglas. His prominence in the argument between state and human rights, and his consistent opposition to Lincoln's policies, secured him a central, though not popular, role in the politics of his era.

Evaluation of Principal Biographical Sources

Capers, Gerald M. *Stephen A. Douglas: Defender of the Union*. Boston: Little, Brown, 1959. **(A, G, Y)** Though brief, this work is significant as a balanced and sympathetic account that exposes the many earlier writers who saw little good in Douglas's ideas and actions.

Johannsen, Robert W. *Stephen A. Douglas*. New York: Oxford University Press, 1973. **(A, G)** The most comprehensive and respected study of the life of Douglas. Interesting and fully documented, this biography discounts Douglas's image as Lincoln's foil and portrays him as the dominant political figure of his day.

Johnson, Allen. *Stephen A. Douglas: A Study in American Politics*. New York: Macmillan, 1908. **(A, G)** The first biography written by a professional historian.

Although somewhat dated, it remains a good survey of Douglas as a politician. Also valuable in tracing the origin of "popular sovereignty" in America.

Milton, George Fort. *The Eve of Conflict: Stephen A. Douglas and the Needless War*. Boston: Houghton Mifflin, 1934. **(A, G)** Inspired by the surfacing of many of Douglas's papers and memorabilia, this book was the first serious study that found much virtue in the man. The admiration appears excessive as the author suggests that Douglas almost managed, singlehandedly, to prevent the Civil War.

Sheahan, James W. *The Life of Stephen A. Douglas*. New York: Harper and Brothers, 1860. **(A)** A notable campaign biography, authored when Douglas was a candidate for the presidency. Sheahan, editor of the pro-Douglas *Chicago Times*, was among his closest confidants.

Wells, Damon. *Stephen A. Douglas: The Last Years, 1857–1861*. Austin: University of Texas Press, 1971. **(A, G)** In this valuable study, Wells laments that Douglas held on to his supposed cure-all, popular sovereignty, instead of addressing the issue of slavery. On the other hand, Wells points out that Douglas became a skilled statesman in the last year or two of his life.

Overview and Evaluation of Primary Sources

Many of Douglas's letters, speeches, and assorted memorabilia have yet to resurface, or have been destroyed. One rich collection of those extant is in the possession of Douglas's descendants, the Martin F. Douglas family of Greensboro, North Carolina. Also, a large collection of materials is located in the University of Chicago library, but here, as with some of the other collections, the materials center upon the last four years of his life. These letters are largely to Douglas, not by him, and many are highly sympathetic to his cause. Other collections worthy of note are located at the Illinois State Historical Library (Springfield), Chicago Historical Library, National Archives, and Library of Congress.

The most comprehensive and convenient printing of Douglas's papers is found in Robert W. Johannsen, ed., *The Letters of Stephen A. Douglas* (Urbana: University of Illinois Press, 1961; **A, G**). This ambitious single-volume work, however, does not include his speeches. Also, letters written to Douglas are excluded.

Douglas endeavored to explain the Kansas dilemma and his proposed solutions in "The Dividing Line Between Federal and Local Authority: Popular Sovereignty in the Territories," *Harper's New Monthly* 19 (September 1839; **A**).

Douglas composed a brief "autobiography" of his early life, written in his twenties, which may be found in the *Journal of the Illinois State Historical Society* 5 (1912; **A**). His major speeches were usually printed in the *New York Times*, which gave him good, and fair, coverage. In Illinois, the *Chicago Times* and *Illinois State Register* (Springfield), both Democratic papers, gave him faithful coverage. Of course, the many and varied speeches Douglas made in the House and Senate over a twenty-year period are reported in the *Congressional Globe*.

The primary materials that best illustrate Douglas's views on his Kansas-Nebraska Bill, his "popular sovereignty" principle, and his reaction to the *Dred Scott Decision* consist of his debate speeches with Abraham Lincoln in the 1858 U.S. senatorial campaign. In the semi-centennial year of the debates, Edwin Erle Sparks edited a complete printing of the speeches of both protagonists: *The Lincoln-Douglas Debates of 1858* (Springfield: Illinois State Historical Library, 1908; **A**). A centennial edition appeared in 1958, edited by Paul M. Angle: *Created Equal? The Complete Lincoln-Douglas Debates of 1858* (Chicago: University of Chicago Press, 1958; **A, G**).

The most primary of sources on the "debates" campaign are found in the original scrapbook Lincoln compiled of Douglas's speeches, clipped from the *Chicago Times*, a newspaper committed to Douglas's political fortunes, and his own speeches, cut from the Republican paper, the *Chicago Press and Tribune*. This scrapbook became the printer's copy for the Ohio Republican party publication of the "debates" as a campaign document in 1860. The original is now in the Alfred Whital Stern Collection of Lincolniana in the Library of Congress. A facsimile of this scrapbook (comprising photographs of the newspaper clippings) was published by the Library of Congress in 1958 as *The Illinois Political Campaign of 1858*.

Fiction and Adaptations

Few literary interpretations of history feature Douglas as a principal character, but many adaptations of Lincoln's life include an interplay with Douglas. A good novel in this vein is Gore Vidal's *Lincoln* (1984). Robert Sherwood offers a play about the two Illinois politicians, *Abe Lincoln in Illinois* (1939). Adele Cutts, Douglas's second wife, narrates Shirley Seifert's novel *The Senator's Lady* (1967).

Museums, Historical Landmarks, Societies

Old State Capitol National Historic Landmark (Springfield, IL). Douglas delivered his famous address here in 1861, rallying citizens behind the Union.

Stephen A. Douglas Birthplace (Brandon, VT). Douglas's birthplace contains his cradle and other original furnishings, and is operated by the Daughters of the American Revolution. Open by appointment.

Stephen A. Douglas State Memorial (Chicago, IL). Douglas is buried here, in a tomb designed by Leonard Volk.

Other Sources

Fehrenbacher, Don E. *Prelude to Greatness: Lincoln in the 1850s*. Stanford: Stanford University Press, 1962. A good study chronicling the emergence of Lincoln to power, and the parallel fortunes of Douglas.

Graebner, Norman A., ed. *Politics and the Crisis of 1860*. Urbana: University of Illinois Press, 1961. A collection of five scholarly essays on political problems preceding the Civil War.

Hamilton, Holman. *Prologue to Conflict: The Crisis and Compromise of 1850*. Lexington: University of Kentucky Press, 1964. Good background on Douglas's rise to power.

Heckman, Richard Allen. *Lincoln vs. Douglas: The Great Debates Campaign*. Washington, DC: Public Affairs Press, 1967. This monograph examines the roles of Douglas and Lincoln in the 1858 senatorial campaign. The only study to analyze all aspects of the race, rather than simply printing the debates with editorial comment, this is particularly helpful on the allure and pageantry of "stump speaking" on the Illinois prairie.

Jaffa, Harry V. *Crisis of the House Divided: An Interpretation of the Issues in the Lincoln-Douglas Debates*. New York: Doubleday, 1959. An in-depth analysis from a political scientist's perspective.

Nevins, Allan. *The Emergence of Lincoln*. 2 vols. New York: Scribner's, 1950. This study of the 1850s portrays Douglas as a Machiavellian character and attacks his efforts to compromise with the South during the secession crisis.

Randall, James G., and David Donald. *The Civil War and Reconstruction*. Lexington, MA: D.C. Heath, 1969. A good comprehensive view of mid-nineteenth-century America, with an annotated bibliography in excess of 100 pages. Douglas is viewed as well-intentioned but blundering.

Sandburg, Carl. *Abraham Lincoln: The Prairie Years*. New York: Harcourt, Brace, 1926. A popular literary study that sheds light on Douglas as well.

Stampp, Kenneth M. *And the War Came: The North and the Secession Crisis, 1860–1861*. Baton Rouge: Louisiana State University Press, 1950. Analysis of political problems leading to the Civil War, with some discussion of Douglas's influence.

Richard Allen Heckman
California State Polytechnic University

FREDERICK DOUGLASS
c.1817–1895

Chronology

Born Frederick Augustus Washington Bailey, c.1817, in Talbot County on Maryland's Eastern Shore, the son of a black slave mother and a white father; *1817–1838* lives in slavery, working as a house servant and as an unskilled laborer in Baltimore and on the Eastern Shore; *1836* makes an unsuccessful attempt to escape and is sent to work in Baltimore's shipyards; *1838* escapes from slavery by borrowing a black sailor's "protection" papers and impersonating him; marries Anna Murray, a free black, in New York; moves to New Bedford, Massachusetts, changes his surname to Douglass, and works for four years at odd jobs; *1841* attends an abolitionist meeting at Nantucket, Massachusetts, and is asked to speak of his slavery experiences and to join as a full-time antislavery lecturer; *1845–1847* publishes his *Narrative of the Life of Frederick Douglass*; tours the British Isles, making speeches on abolition; moves to Rochester, New York, and begins publishing his reformist weekly, the *North Star*; *1848* is one of the few men to play a prominent role in the women's equal rights convention held at Seneca Falls, New York; *1855* publishes his second autobiography, *My Bondage and My Freedom;* *1858* entertains John Brown for three weeks as a houseguest while Brown plans his raid on Harpers Ferry; *1863* recruits black troops for the Union army; *1864* meets with President Lincoln concerning black soldiers in the Union army; *1865* leads a delegation of blacks to visit President Andrew Johnson to ascertain the chief executive's views on matters relating to the recently freed slaves; *1870* is the featured speaker at celebrations of the ratification of the Fifteenth Amendment; *1876* is orator of the day at the April 14 unveiling of the freedman's memorial monument to Lincoln in Washington, D.C.; *1877* President Rutherford B. Hayes appoints him U.S. marshal for the District of Columbia; *1881* publishes his final autobiography, *Life and Times of Frederick Douglass*; President James Garfield appoints him recorder of deeds for the District of Columbia; *1882* his wife dies; *1883* leads the denunciations of the Supreme Court for declaring unconstitutional the Civil Rights Act of 1875; President Benjamin Harrison appoints him minister-resident and consul-general to the Republic of Haiti and charge d'affaires for Santo Domingo; *1884* stirs controversy by marrying Helen Pitts, a white woman; *1895* dies on February 25 of a heart attack at his Washington, D.C., home after speaking at a women's rights meeting.

Activities of Historical Significance

The nineteenth-century's preeminent black abolitionist and equal rights advocate, Frederick Douglass was born into slavery. Separated from his mother as an infant,

413

he saw her only four or five times before her death when he was about seven. Douglass was sent to Baltimore, where he learned to read and write while working as a house servant. When his owner found that his wife was teaching Douglass, he said that if she continued her instruction, "there would be no keeping [Douglass]. It would forever unfit him to be a slave." His owner's words had a great impact on Douglass; from that moment, he understood that the pathway from slavery to freedom was education.

Although Douglass was forbidden to continue his education, he did not abandon his desire to read. When he went on errands in the neighborhood, he took food from his owner's house and exchanged it with hungry white children for reading lessons. He later wrote, "This bread I used to bestow upon the hungry little urchins, who, in return, would give me that more valuable bread of knowledge."

Douglass's mastery of the language enabled him to eloquently express the oppressive effects of slavery. The view from his owner's house, of ships sailing the Chesapeake Bay, later inspired him to write a famous passage:

> You are loosed from your moorings and are free. I am fast in my chains, and am a slave. You move merrily before the gentle gale, and I sadly before the bloody whip! You are freedom's swift-winged angels, that fly round the world. I am confined in bonds of iron! O that I were free! . . . only think of it; one hundred miles straight north, and I am free! Try it? Yes! Meanwhile, I will try to bear up under the yoke. There is a better day coming.

After an unsuccessful attempt in 1836, Douglass succeeded in escaping to New York City in 1838. He remained in New York only long enough to marry Anna Murray, then the couple went to New Bedford, Massachusetts. While attending a Nantucket abolitionist meeting in 1841, Douglass delivered an extemporaneous speech about his recollections of slavery. His passionate words inspired the Massachusetts Anti-Slavery Society to engage him as a full-time lecturer. For the next four years, the young ex-slave was one of the society's star speakers.

The 1845 publication of the *Narrative of the Life of Frederick Douglass* brought him widespread publicity in America and the British Isles. After spending two years in Britain, where he denounced American slavery before large sympathetic audiences, Douglass moved to Rochester and launched the *North Star*, a high standard, well-edited abolitionist weekly that continued publication until 1863. In addition to abolition, the *North Star* supported education for blacks, woman suffrage, and abstinence from alcoholic beverages.

During the 1840s, Douglass identified with the Garrisonian principles of the American Anti-Slavery Society. By the end of the decade, however, his own quest for leadership and his growing doubts about the practicality of William Lloyd Garrison's exclusive reliance upon moral suasion produced tensions between the two men that culminated in a complete break in 1851. Thereafter, Douglass associated with the causes of the Liberty and Radical Abolition parties, and often endorsed Free Soil and Republican candidates.

Douglass saw the Civil War as a milestone, a crusade for freedom, pure and simple. Because he believed that the war's purpose was the emancipation of slaves, he was anxious that blacks be involved. He successfully recruited black troops for the Union, had several meetings with President Lincoln regarding black soldiers, and grew increasingly critical when he felt the president was moving too slowly.

After the war, Douglass became a staunch supporter of the Republican party, though he did not hesitate to criticize its shortcomings. He continued to protest growing patterns of segregation, disfranchisement, and mob violence. Yet his adolescent vision that a better day would come remained alive, and his belief that he could influence both blacks and whites was supported by the numerous presidential appointments he received.

Championing the cause of the downtrodden is one of Douglass's major contributions to American democracy. Also significant was his ability to vividly demonstrate human beings' inhumanity to others and to illustrate that individuals can succeed in the face of dire adversity.

Overview of Biographical Sources

Several extensive studies of Douglass's life and times have been published, including Frederick May Holland, *Frederick Douglass* (1891); Charles W. Chestnutt, *Frederick Douglass* (1899); Booker T. Washington, *Frederick Douglass* (1906); Shirley Graham, *There Was Once a Slave* (1948); Philip Foner, ed., *The Life and Writings of Frederick Douglass*, 5 vols. (1950–1975); Dickson J. Preston, *Young Frederick Douglass* (1985); and Waldo E. Martin, Jr., *The Mind of Frederick Douglass* (1984). Holland, Chestnutt, and Washington were contemporaries of Douglass; their studies, along with Graham's, tend to cast him in a heroic mold and are rather short on historical interpretation.

Evaluation of Principal Biographical Sources

Foner, Philip S., ed. *The Life and Writings of Frederick Douglass*. 5 vols. New York: International Publishers, 1950–1975. (**A, G**) Foner's studies, based on extensive research, provide excellent details on Douglass's later career and perform a valuable service by printing in text form hundreds of Douglass's letters, speeches, and writings.

Martin, Waldo E., Jr. *The Mind of Frederick Douglass*. Chapel Hill: University of North Carolina Press, 1984. (**A, G**) This engrossing intellectual biography also provides a meaningful view of nineteenth-century American and Afro-American social and intellectual history.

Preston, Dickson J. *Young Frederick Douglass: The Maryland Years.* Baltimore: Johns Hopkins University Press, 1985. (**A, G**) Preston's study substantiates much of the material in Douglass's autobiographies. It deals almost exclusively with Douglass's life as a slave and is highly sympathetic to Maryland's nineteenth-century social patterns.

Quarles, Benjamin. *Frederick Douglass.* 1948. Reprint. New York: Atheneum, 1974. (**A, G**) This remains the best biography of Douglass. Quarles brings to his task the insight and balance of an excellent historian and portrays his subject as a human being with faults as well as virtues.

Overview and Evaluation of Primary Sources

Two invaluable sources for the researcher are John W. Blessingame, ed., *The Frederick Douglass Papers*, 2 vols. (New Haven: Yale University Press, 1979–1982; **A, G**), and the aforementioned Philip S. Foner, ed., *Life and Writings of Frederick Douglass*, 5 vols. (1950–1975). Douglass was a prolific writer, and most of his speeches, personal letters, formal lectures, editorials, and magazine articles have been brought together in these works.

Douglass's three autobiographies—*Narrative of the Life of Frederick Douglass: An American Slave* (Boston: Anti-Slavery Society, 1845; **A, G**), *My Bondage and My Freedom* (New York: Miller, Orron and Mulligan, 1855; **A, G**), and *Life and Times of Frederick Douglass* (Hartford: Park, 1881; **A, G**)—are generally reliable sources.

Yale University holds the most comprehensive collection of Douglass material. Preserved copies of the Frederick Douglass Papers are available in the Boston Public Library's Anti-Slavery Collection; the New York Public Library's Arthur A. Schomburg Center for Research in Black Culture; the Library of Congress; the National Archives; Howard University's Moorland-Spingarn Collection; and the Morgan State University Library in Baltimore.

Douglass' Monthly (New York: Negro Universities Press, 1969; **A, G**) for the years 1858–1863 is available in most research libraries. The five volumes contain Douglass's original publications in unabridged form.

Fiction and Adaptations

The House on Cedar Hill (1982), a film produced by the Schomburg Center in New York, highlights Douglass's house, an historical landmark. A film starring Ossie Davis, *Frederick Douglass* (1986), was produced by William Greaves Productions of New York City.

Museums, Historical Landmarks, Societies

Frederick Douglass Home (Washington, DC). Douglass's home has been pre-served, and houses documents, furnishings, and other artifacts.

Other Sources

Kraditor, Aileen. *The Means and Ends in American Abolitionism: Garrison and His Critics on Strategy and Tactics, 1834–1850.* New York: Pantheon, 1967. A brilliant study focusing on the factions within the anti-slavery movement.

Melvin R. Williams
Brooklyn College,
City University of New York

Emancipation Proclamation, 1963

W. E. B. DU BOIS
1868–1963

Chronology

Born William Edward Burghardt Du Bois on February 23, 1868, in Great Barrington, Massachusetts, the son of Alfred Du Bois, of French Huguenot and African descent, and Mary Sylvina Burghardt Du Bois, of Dutch and African descent; *1868–1884* father deserts family, and Du Bois is reared by his mother; grows up one of about fifty blacks in a town of 5,000 people and is the only black student in his high school's graduating class; *1885–1888* studies at Fisk University in Nashville, where he finds racism overwhelming, and receives a B.A. degree; *1888–1892* enters the junior class at Harvard, earns his B.A. in philosophy *cum laude*, then takes an M.A. in American history; *1892–1895* studies for two years at the University of Berlin, then teaches Latin, Greek, German, and English at Wilberforce University; becomes the first Afro-American to receive a Ph.D. from Harvard; *1896* his dissertation, *The Suppression of the African Slave Trade to the United States, 1638–1870*, is published; marries Nina Gomer, a Wilberforce student of German and African parentage; leaves Wilberforce for the University of Pennsylvania, where he researches his pioneering sociological study, published in 1899 as *The Philadelphia Negro*; *1897–1910* serves as professor of economics and history at Atlanta University, where he organizes the university's annual conferences for the study of "Negro problems" and edits their proceedings; publishes *The Souls of Black Folk* in 1902, one of the most insightful and influential books ever written about Afro-Americans; organizes the Niagara Movement in 1905 to oppose the views of Booker T. Washington, and is active in it until 1909; founds two short-lived magazines, *Moon* and *Horizon*; joins with liberal whites to found the National Association for the Advancement of Colored People (NAACP) in 1909 and takes a position as the organization's director of publications and research; *1911–1934* founds and edits *Crisis*, the NAACP's monthly magazine; organizes Pan-African Congresses in 1919, 1921, 1923 and 1927; *1934–1944* leaves his NAACP position to become chairman of the sociology department at Atlanta University; founds *Phylon*, a social science journal, and writes a weekly column for black newspapers; *1944–1948* returns to the NAACP as director of special research; produces several studies; attends the San Francisco Conference as a representative of the NAACP and presides over the Fifth Pan-African Congress; *1948–1951* leaves the NAACP in a dispute over his support for Henry Wallace; co-chairs the Council on African Affairs; chairs the Peace Information Center circulating the Stockholm Peace Appeal against nuclear proliferation; runs for U.S. Senate on the American Labor party ticket; is acquitted on charges of being an unregistered agent of a foreign power; marries Shirley Lola Graham in 1951 after the death of his first wife; *1951–1961* writes, lectures, and travels worldwide, visiting several Communist nations; receives Lenin Peace Prize; *1961–1963* joins the Communist party of the United States and becomes a citizen of Ghana; *1963* dies on August 27 in Accra, Ghana.

Activities of Historical Significance

Du Bois's lifelong, prolific writings embrace history, sociology, journalism, and belles lettres. The product of brilliant, often pioneering scholarship, they are sometimes enhanced and more often diminished by polemics, but always communicate a coherent, complex, insightful analysis of the meaning of the black experience in America. Together they constitute a major interpretation that changed the ways Americans think about race, and inspired numerous scholars and activists in their work.

Beyond theory, Du Bois was an organizer and activist particularly effective in developing and promoting Pan-African Congresses and in supporting a broad variety of pan-African activities. His celebrated disagreement with Booker T. Washington's conservative approach to winning acceptance and civil rights for blacks in American society generated important intellectual, social, and political debate. His less well-known disagreement with Marcus Garvey over Garvey's planned relocation of American blacks in Africa was very significant in that it coincided with Du Bois's intense pan-African organizing activities and provided a clear, if complex, analysis of the relationships of Afro-Americans with African realities and culture, and American realities and culture.

The highly controversial ideological evolution of his later years deprived Du Bois of much of the influence he might have had upon the civil rights struggle of the 1950s and 1960s. He has been called a "leader without followers," and at no time was that more true than in the years after his 1948 break with the NAACP.

Overview of Biographical/Critical Sources

Despite his protean career and enormous intellectual influence, there is less biographical literature on Du Bois than one would assume. In part this may be due to the large number of autobiographical pieces he himself wrote and in which he carefully constructed his persona. In part it has probably been the result of the unavailability of his papers for twenty years after his trial in 1951. In any event, most studies of Du Bois analyze his thought and miss or avoid the quality of his personality. Even the best biographical studies, those by Francis Broderick (1959) and Elliot Rudwick (1960), are scholarly analyses and evaluations of Du Bois's work more than they are actual biographies. In all the works about Du Bois, the most often slighted aspect is his strictly literary work; but this is admirably covered in Arnold Rampersad's *The Art and Imagination of W. E. B. Du Bois* (1976), and in William Andrews's *Critical Essays on W. E. B. Du Bois* (1985).

Evaluation of Principal Biographical/Critical Sources

Andrews, William L. *Critical Essays on W. E. B. Du Bois*. Boston: G. K. Hall, 1985. (A) Part of a series on literary figures, this contains both original and republished essays evaluating Du Bois's contributions to American literature.

Broderick, Francis L. *W. E. B. Du Bois: Negro Leader in a Time of Crisis*. Palo Alto, CA: Stanford University Press, 1959. (A, G) Based on Du Bois's papers up to 1910, this is a very careful study that is critical and illuminating with regard to Du Bois's ideological inconsistencies. Still essential despite its age.

De Marco, Joseph P. *The Social Thought of W. E. B. Du Bois*. Lanham, MD: University Press of America, 1983. (A) An intellectual portrait that gives little attention to Du Bois's personal life, this work examines his views in chronological order and from a philosophical perspective.

Horne, Gerald. *Black and Red: W. E. B. Du Bois and the Afro-American Response to the Cold War, 1944–1963*. Albany, NY: SUNY Press, 1986. (A, G) Deals with the most complex and difficult to understand part of Du Bois's life in a clear and scholarly fashion.

Logan, Rayford W., ed. *W. E. B. Du Bois: A Profile*. New York: Hill & Wang, 1971. (A, G) This volume, part of the American Profiles series, presents ten essays by well-known Du Bois scholars, carefully and critically edited by one of his former colleagues at Atlanta University.

Marable, Manning. *W. E. B. Du Bois: Black Radical Democrat*. Boston: Twayne, 1986. (A, G) In covering Du Bois's life, this work depends uncritically on his self-portraiture. Only in the last section is it critical, and then rather harshly.

Moore, Jack B. *W. E. B. Du Bois*. Boston: Twayne, 1981. (A, G) After a brief biographical sketch, this work presents five chapters of clear and insightful analysis of Du Bois's writings and concludes with an annotated select bibliography. An excellent summary of Du Bois's thought.

Rampersad, Arnold. *The Art and Imagination of W. E. B. Du Bois*. Cambridge, MA: Harvard University Press, 1976. (A) This fine analytic biography focuses on Du Bois's intellectual development with major emphasis on his fictional works.

Rudwick, Elliot. *W. E. B. Du Bois: A Study in Minority Group Leadership*. 1960. Reprinted as *W. E. B. Du Bois: Voice of the Black Protest Movement*. Chicago: University of Chicago Press, 1982. (A, G) Based on the author's doctoral dissertation, this work sets Du Bois's thought and activity in the context of various crises in American race relations and treats the last years of his life summarily, as having little bearing on the main theme. Objective and rigorous, it remains one of the best books on Du Bois.

Tuttle, W. M., ed. *W. E. B. Du Bois*. Englewood Cliffs, NJ: Prentice-Hall,

1973. (**A, G**) Selections from Du Bois's writings are included, along with articles by his contemporaries and essays by historians.

Evaluation of Biographies for Young People

Hamilton, Virginia. *W. E. B. Du Bois: A Biography*. New York: Thomas Y. Crowell, 1972. Tailored to high school readers, this is more admirable for its factual coverage than for its style.

Lacy, Leslie A. *Cheer the Lonesome Traveler*. New York: Dial, 1970. Although prone to factual errors, this biography is sympathetic and complex in approaching Du Bois's personality. Makes his life work understandable to junior and senior high school students.

Sterne, Emma Gelders. *His Was the Voice: The Life of W. E. B. Du Bois*. New York: Cromwell-Collier, 1971. A highly readable introduction to Du Bois for junior high school students, this work reconstructs dialogue and is a bit too worshipful.

Overview and Evaluation of Primary Sources

In the course of a long life, Du Bois made many autobiographical statements, all of them highly interesting, all of them so cannily conceived and executed as to leave many pitfalls for the unwary. The last to appear was the posthumously published *The Autobiography of W. E. B. Du Bois: A Soliloquy on Viewing My Life from the Last Decade of Its First Century* (New York: International Publishers, 1968; **A, G**). Completed in 1960, about one-third of its length is devoted to Du Bois's youth in Great Barrington, with the greater part of the book constituting a synthesis of his thought and activity from the 1930s onward. The careful reader will note whole sections taken from a 1940 autobiography, *Dusk of Dawn: An Essay Toward an Autobiography of Race Concept* (New York: Shocken, 1968; **A, G**), which achieved great circulation when republished in the 1960s. Still an earlier work of autobiographical significance is Du Bois's 1920 work, *Darkwater: Voices from Within the Veil* (New York: Schocken, 1969; **A, G**). Two important shorter autobiographies are *A Pageant in Seven Decades* (Atlanta: Atlanta University, 1938; **A, G**), which was reprinted in Philip S. Foner, ed., *W. E. B. Du Bois Speaks: Speeches and Addresses, 1890–1919* (New York: Pathfinder, 1970; **A, G**), and *In the Battle for Peace: The Story of My Eighty-Third Birthday* (New York: Masses and Mainstream, 1952; **A, G**). Folkways issued a 1961 recording of an interview with Du Bois by Moses Asch, "W. E. B. Du Bois: A Recorded Autobiography."

All of Du Bois's approximately 2,000 published works are being reissued in the projected forty-volume *The Complete Published Works of W. E. B. Du Bois*, edited

by Herbert Aptheker (White Plains, NY: Kraus-Thomson, 1973– ; **A, G**). Herbert
Aptheker has also edited some of Du Bois's heretofore unpublished writings: *The
Correspondence of W. E. B. Du Bois*, 3 vols. (Amherst: University of Massachu-
setts Press, 1973–1978; **A, G**); *The Education of Black People: Ten Critiques,
1906–1960* (Amherst: University of Massachusetts Press, 1973; **A, G**); *Prayers for
Dark People* (Amherst: University of Massachusetts Press, 1980; **A, G**); and
Against Racism: Unpublished Essays, Papers and Addresses, 1887–1961 (Am-
herst: University of Massachusetts Press, 1985; **A, G**).

In addition to those by Foner, several other anthologies of Du Bois's writings
exist. John Henrik Clark, et al., eds., *Black Titan: W. E. B. Du Bois* (Boston:
Beacon Press, 1971; **A, G**), anthologizes some of Du Bois's lesser-known speeches
and articles, and includes a selected bibliography of his published writing and a
collection of tributes that followed his death. The Library of America has published
a superbly edited volume in its series Literary Classics of the United States,
W. E. B. Du Bois, *Writings*, edited by Nathan Huggins (New York: Viking, 1986;
A, G), containing *The Suppression of the African Slave Trade, The Souls of Black
Folk, Dusk of Dawn*, and some of his essays and articles. Julius Lester, ed., *The
Seventh Son: The Thoughts and Writings of W. E. B. Du Bois*, 2 vols. (New York:
Random House, 1971; **A, G**), contains a lengthy and very valuable introduction by
the editor. Henry E. Moon, ed., *The Emerging Thought of W. E. B. Du Bois* (New
York: Simon and Schuster, 1972; **A, G**), presents essays and editorials from *Crisis*.
W. E. B. Du Bois: A Reader (New York: Harper & Row, 1970; **A, G**), antholo-
gizes magazine articles by Du Bois. Virginia Hamilton, ed., *The Writings of
W. E. B. Du Bois* (New York: Crowell, 1975; **Y**), is the best selection for young
readers.

There are also two extensive bibliographies that are invaluable for their listings of
Du Bois's works: Herbert Aptheker, *Annotated Bibliography of the Published Writings of W. E. B. Du Bois* (White Plains: Kraus-Thomson, 1973; **A, G**), presents
nearly 2,000 annotated entries in eight major sections, and includes title and subject entries; Paul G. Parrington, *W. E. B. Du Bois: A Bibliography of His Published Writings* (Whittier, CA: The Author, 1977; **A**), although not annotated,
contains some 400 more citations than Aptheker, including works Du Bois published in languages other than English.

Du Bois's wife, Shirley Graham Du Bois, also published two works containing
valuable firsthand information: *His Day Is Marching On: A Memoir of W. E. B.
Du Bois* (Philadelphia: Lippincott, 1971; **A, G**) and *Du Bois: A Pictorial Biography* (Chicago: Johnson Publishing, 1978; **A, G**). The 1971 work is the most illuminating portrait of his later days, although it is respectful rather than intimate and
does not adequately analyze his motivations.

Du Bois's extensive collected papers are housed at the University of Massachusetts Library in Amherst. A microfilm version is available in eighty-nine reels,
together with a printed introduction, *The Papers of W. E. B. Du Bois: 1803 (1887–
1963) 1965*, edited by Robert W. McConnell (Sanford, NC: Microfilms Publishing

of America, 1980–1981; **A, G**). Another significant collection can be found in the Du Bois Papers, James Weldon Memorial Collection, Yale University.

Museums, Historical Landmarks, Societies

Du Bois Boyhood Homesite National Historic Landmark (Great Barrington, MA). Located in the Du Bois Memorial park, the site preserves the ruins of the home of Du Bois's grandparents, where he lived from 1868–1873.

Other Sources

Bracey, John H., Jr. "William Edward Burghardt Du Bois." In *The Encyclopedia of American Biography*, edited by John A. Garraty and Jerome L. Sternstein. New York: Harper & Row, 1974. A concise but very useful sketch based on Lester's introduction to *The Seventh Son*.

Logan, Rayford W., and Michael R. Winston. "William Edward Burghardt Du Bois." In *Dictionary of American Negro Biography*, edited by Logan and Winston. New York: Norton, 1982. A sound biographical sketch with a thoughtful interpretation of Du Bois by a former colleague.

Rampersad, Arnold. "William Edward Burghardt Du Bois." In *Dictionary of American Biography*, edited by John A. Garraty. Supp. 7. New York: Scribner's, 1981. An excellent short article with more insight into Du Bois's literary achievements than is usual in biographical summaries.

Joseph M. McCarthy
Suffolk University

Register and Vote, 1968

JOHN FOSTER DULLES
1888–1959

Chronology

Born John Foster Dulles on February 25, 1888, in Washington, D.C., to the Reverend Allen Macy Dulles, a Presbyterian minister, and Elizabeth Foster Dulles, daughter of President Benjamin Harrison's secretary of state; *1888–1904* moves with family to Watertown, New York, where he attends public schools, except for a six-month stay in Lausanne, Switzerland, where he concentrates upon learning French and German; *1904–1907* attends Princeton University, but in his junior year his grandfather, representing the Chinese government at the Second Hague Peace Conference, arranges to have him serve as secretary to the Chinese; *1908–1911* originally devoted to the ministry, he changes his mind in favor of a career in the public service; spends a year studying at the Sorbonne in Paris; studies law at Georgetown University; passes his bar examinations without completing the formal requirements for a degree; through his grandfather's influence, obtains a clerkship in the New York law firm Sullivan and Cromwell; *June 26, 1912* marries Janet Pomeroy Avery, with whom he will have three children; *1912–1917* becomes an expert in problems of international law; contracts malaria while on a business trip in British Guiana and is left with slightly impaired vision and a tic in his left eye; *1917–1918* President Woodrow Wilson sends him to Panama, Costa Rica, and Nicaragua to persuade the Central American countries to join the U.S. in declaring war on Germany; Dulles's success launches his public service career; serves on the War Trade Board, presided over by Bernard Baruch; *1919–1924* serves in Europe as counsel to the Reparations Section of the American Commission to Negotiate Peace; becomes a partner of Sullivan and Cromwell; *1924–1927* works in Europe as special counsel to the bankers who drafted the Charles G. Dawes Plan; represents the Polish government in negotiations to stabilize that country's finances; is made a senior partner of Sullivan and Cromwell; *early 1930s* works in Berlin, trying to salvage the Dawes plan; *1939* writes his first book, *War, Peace and Change*, which criticizes the Treaty of Versailles; *1940* chairs the Commission on a Just and Desirable Peace established by the Federal Council of Churches; *1943* publishes the pamphlet *Six Pillars of Peace*; *1944* is regarded as a leading Republican spokesman in foreign affairs; *1945* member of the American delegation to the San Francisco Conference; *1945–1949* under President Harry S Truman, serves on special delegations to assist the secretary of state at meetings of the Council of Foreign Ministers; *1946–1950* serves intermittently in the United States delegation to the U.N. General Assembly, and generally supports Truman; *1949* Governor Thomas E. Dewey appoints him to serve out the term of the late New York Senator Robert Wagner; *1950* loses state senate election; publishes his second book, *War or Peace*, in which he criticizes the containment policy; participates in Senator Arthur Vandenberg's attempt to move the Republican party toward bipartisanship and a tougher stance on communism; *1950–1951* Truman asks Dulles to negotiate a peace treaty with Japan and security treaties with Australia, New Zealand, and the Philippines; joins General Douglas MacArthur in asking Truman to aid South Korea in the Korean conflict; *1952* drafts the foreign policy planks for presidential candidate Dwight D. Eisenhower's platform; *1953* President Eisenhower appoints him secretary of state; *1954* negotiates the South East Asia Treaty Organization as a means to encircle the Soviet Union to the south; refuses to accept Geneva Conference accords with respect to Southeast Asia, fearing that "loss" of Indochina has foretold loss of the entire area in keeping with the "domino theory"; *1956* supports Eisenhower's call for the retirement of British, French, and Israeli forces that have invaded Egypt in an attempt to deny Nasser of Egypt control over the Suez Canal; *1958* seeks to defuse the Taiwan-Mainland China feud by restraining Chiang Kai-shek, but refuses to recognize Mainland China; *1959* resigns as secretary of state; dies on May 14 of cancer in Washington, D.C., and is buried at Arlington National Cemetery.

Activities of Historical Significance

John Foster Dulles's influential family, and his legal training in international economic affairs, launched his career in missionary diplomacy. Family influence helped to bring about his first diplomatic experience, as secretary to the Chinese delegation to the Second Hague Peace Conference, as well as a position with the prestigious law firm of Sullivan and Cromwell, which had many foreign clients. After proving his diplomatic abilities, Dulles served President Woodrow Wilson as a member of the War Trade Board and in solving European reparations questions. Seeing war as the result mainly of economic competition, he criticized the Versailles Treaty as too restrictive on "the dynamic forces" of the "have-not" nations.

Although he believed that what was good for the United States was also good for the rest of the world, Dulles held that a world federal system should replace the sovereign national state, and he bolstered his conclusion with much religious pontification. He forwarded this view while a delegate to both the San Francisco Conference of 1945 and the U.N. General Assembly.

Dulles's support of many diplomatic accomplishments of the Truman administration—the containment strategy, Truman Doctrine, Marshall Plan, and philosophy of foreign economic and military aid—fulfilled the Democratic president's need for bipartisan support. In 1952, however, Dulles drafted the foreign policy planks of the Republican national platform, proposing to replace containment with a more aggressive Cold War strategy that would "liberate" countries dominated by Communists.

As secretary of state, Dulles cemented his position with Congress by following the philosophy of its right wing, dismissing from the Foreign Service those (often incorrectly) believed to have been soft on communism, and instituting stringent security regulations for employment, promotion, and surveillance. He intended to support a dynamic foreign policy, a "new look" to counter Communist ideology, expansionism, and repression. (With respect to the East German uprising of 1953 and the brutally repressed Hungarian revolt of 1956, however, he did nothing.) Whereas some domestic spokesmen and West Europeans sought an accommodation with the Soviets and "Red" China, especially after Stalin's death, Dulles pursued a policy of "brinkmanship" (i.e., deterrence verging on war) to obtain the settlement of disputes in America's favor. Because of Eisenhower's reduction of conventional armed forces, he supported exploiting the threat of nuclear weapons as a means of "diplomacy."

Dulles appeared to many to be an inflexible moralist incapable of dealing with a complex and rapidly changing world. When the French objected to the creation of the European Defense Community because Germany would be re-armed, he threatened to undertake an "agonizing reappraisal" of American participation in West European security and perhaps leave West Europe to its own fate. His unilateral approach was distasteful to his allies in NATO and in the United Nations. Objecting to China's presence at the 1954 Geneva talks about Southeast Asia, he did not sign the ensuing agreement and spoke of the domino theory, asserting that the "loss" of South Vietnam would lead to the Communist takeover of the rest of Southeast Asia.

Important political changes of the 1950s were the growing economic and military power of the Soviet Union and the ferment of nationalism in the Third World. Dulles sought to enhance the West's encirclement of the U.S.S.R. with the South East Asia Treaty Organization. While abhorring their neutralism, he did little to help Third World countries escape from colonialism. Nor did he succeed in getting Arabs and Israelis to agree to American policy. He pushed Egypt, economically at least, toward Moscow when he refused to finance its projected high-rise Aswan Dam. Dumbfounded by the collusive Anglo-French-Israeli invasion of Egypt in 1956, he lost credibility with the attackers by calling for their withdrawal and seeking to internationalize the Suez Canal. He lost additional favor by supporting Chiang Kai-shek against Mainland China.

A keen lawyer and logician, Dulles concentrated upon putting out immediate brushfires rather than seeking solutions to global war. Instead of opening means of communications with Communist states, he would deny them normal commercial and diplomatic intercourse and even cultural exchanges. In the end, he remains an outstanding symbol of the cold warrior and conservative statesman who let the initiative pass to the other side.

Overview of Biographical Sources

Dulles's controversial career has spawned a good number of biographies; interestingly, the favorable portrayals greatly outnumber the critical. The first, John Robinson Beal's commendatory *John Foster Dulles* (1957), was published while its subject was still in office and revised in 1959, the year of his death. In 1960, two positive accounts appeared: Deane Heller, *John Foster Dulles: Soldier for Peace*, and Roscoe Drummond and Gaston Coblentz, *Duel at the Brink: John Foster Dulles's Command of American Power*. The first negative portrayal was Hans J. Morgenthau's twenty-page essay in Norman A. Graebner, ed., *An Uncertain Tradition: American Secretaries of State in the Twentieth Century* (1961). Several favorable accounts followed: Richard Goold-Adams, *John Foster Dulles: A Reappraisal* (1962); Eleanor Lansing Dulles, *John Foster Dulles: The Last Year* (1963); Louis L. Gerson, *John Foster Dulles* (1967); and Michael A. Guhin, *John Foster Dulles: A Statesman and His Times* (1972). Since 1972, however, a more critical view of Dulles has emerged: negative portrayals by Townsend Hoopes, *The Devil and John Foster Dulles* (1973), and Ronald W. Pruessen, *John Foster Dulles: The Road to Power* (1982), have been countered by only one favorable depiction, Leonard Mosely, *Dulles: A Biography of Eleanor, Allen and John Foster Dulles and Their Family Network* (1978).

Evaluation of Principal Biographical Sources

Beal, John Robinson. *John Foster Dulles, 1888–1959*. 1957. Rev. ed. New York: Harper & Brothers, 1959. (A, G) Written by a fine journalist while Dulles was still in office, with help from the Dulles family, the fast-paced narrative remains useful.

Gerson, Louis L. *John Foster Dulles*. Vol. 17 of *The American Secretaries of State and Their Diplomacy*. New York: Cooper Square Publishers, 1967. (A, G) In this standard account, Gerson praises Dulles as the only religious leader, lay or clerical, ever to become secretary of state, and tells how Dulles tried to translate his ideals into American foreign policy. To insure that godless Soviet policy would not rule the world, the "Iron Secretary" stood ready to go to the brink of war. The author contends that Dulles was both the architect of foreign policy and its chief negotiator, who became the scapegoat for all unresolved ills.

Dulles, Eleanor Lansing. *John Foster Dulles: The Last Year*. New York: Harcourt, Brace & World, 1963. (A, G) Eleanor judges her brother's record not merely from the closeness of family relations but from her long years of experience in the Department of State.

Goold-Adams, Richard. *John Foster Dulles: A Reappraisal*. New York: Appleton-Century-Crofts, 1962. (A, G) A judicious and objective, if undocumented, account that balances praise with criticism. The author asserts that Dulles's style stirred people as much as his actions. He credits Dulles with helping the Republican party to face international realities of the modern world, but asserts that he was too rigid to understand world developments after Stalin's death. Obsessed with morality rather than political problems, he opposed peaceful coexistence and had no genuine understanding of neutralism.

Guhin, Michael A. *John Foster Dulles: A Statesman and His Times*. New York: Columbia University Press, 1972. (**A, G**) A relatively favorable and well-documented account that disputes the generally accepted picture of Dulles as "a cold war ideologue with a distorting pair of moral spectacles." According to Guhin, he was a cold warrior until 1958, but he became more flexible, during his last year of life. Guhin supports his assertion by pointing to Dulles's hope for rapprochement with the People's Republic of China and his handling of the Taiwan Straits crisis of 1958.

Morgenthau, Hans J. "John Foster Dulles (1953–1959)." *An Uncertain Tradition: American Secretaries of State in the Twentieth Century, edited by Norman A. Graebner. New York: McGraw-Hill, 1961.* (**A, G**) A pejorative evaluation which tells how Dulles, fully supported by President Eisenhower, refused to delegate responsibility in the State Department, muzzled the Foreign Service, got rid of those in the department who disagreed with him, and, though proclaiming that he offered new and dynamic policies, failed to put them into practice. Morgenthau contends that, in the end, his attachment to old policies supported the status quo and prevented accommodation to many new circumstances short of resorting to all-out war.

Pruessen, Ronald W. *John Foster Dulles: The Road to Power*. New York: Free Press, 1982. (**A, G**) In this critical account, Dulles's antecedents, Pruessen traces education, services at the Paris Peace Conference, work as a lawyer in the 1930s, his seeking to use the church in foreign affairs, his work for the Truman administration, and his governing belief as secretary of state—that what was good for the United States was good for the world.

Overview and Evaluation of Primary Sources

Several of Dulles's own publications are worth reading in order to follow the development of his thoughts on diplomacy. In *War, Peace, and Change* (New York and London: Harper & Brothers, 1939; **A, G**), he sought to apply Wilsonian ideas to the 1940s, especially the concept that war can be avoided by international institutions that run on abstract principles. He attributed current crises in large part to the Versailles Treaty, in which the victors too greatly limited the aspirations of the defeated powers. Dulles asserts in *War or Peace* (New York: Macmillan, 1950; **A, G**) that he would not try to start a revolt in the Soviet Union or fight a preventive war. To replace the Truman policy of containment, he offered a vague mixture of "moral offensive" and simplistic anti-communism. In a two-part article for *Life*, "Thoughts on Soviet Foreign Policy and What To Do About It" (May 3 and 10, 1946), he proposed a supposed "policy of boldness" which boiled down to a mixture of moralism and politics that would aid the Republican party in the presidential election of 1948.

Dulles's personal papers are housed in the Princeton University Library. The collection includes drafts of printed works, speeches, statements, press releases, press conferences and interviews, press clippings, articles, reports, notes, memoranda, correspondence, and films. Janet Avery Dulles's papers in the Princeton library reveal a very submissive, supportive, devoted, and suffering wife. The Princeton library is also the repository for the Dulles Oral History Collection, 300 tape-recorded and transcribed interviews with men and women who had worked with Dulles. Also useful are the Truman Papers in the Truman Presidential Library (Independence, Missouri) and the Eisenhower Papers in the Eisenhower Presidential Library (Abilene, Kansas).

For an unflattering look at Dulles by one of his contemporaries, see John Emmet Hughes's polemical memoir, *The Ordeal of Power: A Political Memoir of the Eisenhower Years* (New York: Atheneum, 1963; **A, G**). Hughes was a former presidential speechwriter and formidable journalist who had few uncritical words for Eisenhower's secretary of state. On the other hand, Truman's forthright autobiography, *Memoirs by Harry S Truman*, 2 vols. (Garden City, NY: Doubleday, 1955–1956; **A, G**), credits Dulles with working well with the administration. Eisenhower's memoirs, *The White House Years*, 2 vols. (Garden City, NY: Doubleday, 1963–1965; **A, G**), contain a good deal of information on his first secretary of state's philosophy and techniques. Arthur Vandenberg, Jr., ed., *The Papers of Senator Vandenberg* (Boston: Houghton Mifflin, 1952; **A, G**), shows Dulles's relationship with the senator who helped push the Republican party from isolationism to bipartisanship in foreign affairs.

Dulles's diplomatic record has been captured in a number of works. Basic are the pertinent years of *Papers Relating to the Foreign Relations of the United States*. Also useful is the Department of State's series, *American Foreign Policy*. Dulles's testimony before Congress is contained in the *Congressional Record*. Major private documentary collections are *Documents on Foreign Relations*, published annually by the Council on Foreign Relations, and the accompanying *United States in World Affairs*. *Documents on International Affairs*, published annually by the British Royal Institute.

Museums, Historical Landmarks, Societies
Dulles Family Home (Watertown, NY). A marker merely designates this as one of the oldest houses in Watertown, but it was also Dulles's childhood home.

Other Sources
Acheson, Dean G. *Present at the Creation: My Years at the State Department*. New York: W. W. Norton, 1969. Dulles supported the Truman-Acheson foreign policies while cooperating with their administration.

Dunn, Frederick S. *Peace-making and the Settlement with Japan*. Princeton: Princeton University Press, 1963. Heavy on Dulles's work in drafting the treaty and also the security arrangements with Australia, New Zealand, and Japan.

Finer, Herman. *Dulles over Suez: Theory and Practice of His Diplomacy*. Chicago: Quadrangle Books, 1964. A critical account.

Stone, Irving F. *The Haunted Fifties*. New York: Vintage Books, 1969. Stone sees Dulles as "A lifelong servant of the most materialistic forces in our society. A Big Lawyer for the Big Money, a pre-War apologist for Japanese aggression and Nazi expansion, an exponent of Machiavellianism so long as the Axis was winning, and advocate of a Christian peace as soon as its defeat was foreseen."

Paolo E. Coletta
U.S. Naval Academy (Ret.)

MARY DYER
?–1660

Chronology

Born Mary Barret; *1633* marries milliner William Dyer in London, on October 27; *1635* the couple arrives in Boston, Massachusetts; enroll as members of Rev. John Wilson's "First Church" of Boston on December 13; *1637* Mary miscarries and, in light of her sympathy for Anne Hutchinson during the Antinomian Controversy, is alleged to have borne a monster; William is disfranchised as a member of the pro-Hutchinson faction; *1638* Mary follows Anne Hutchinson out of the church when the latter is excommunicated; the Dyers accompany the Hutchinson party to what is now Portsmouth, Rhode Island; William is elected clerk of the new colony; *1639* the Dyers abandon Portsmouth and help establish Newport; *1643* Mary delivers a funeral oration at Providence for Anne Hutchinson; *1651* the Dyers return to England; *1657* Mary returns to Boston, having converted to Quakerism while in England, and is promptly imprisoned; *1657–1658* Massachusetts denounces the Quakers as blasphemers and passes a series of severe anti-Quaker laws, culminating in a law imposing death upon those who return after banishment; *1658* is expelled from New Haven for missionary work; *October 1659* is sentenced to be hanged for returning to Massachusetts after banishment, along with fellow-Quakers William Robinson and Marmaduke Stephenson; is suddenly and theatrically reprieved at the gallows on October 27, whereupon she refuses to cooperate unless the law itself is revoked; *1660* returns to Boston and is once again arrested; her husband, by now one of the foremost citizens of Rhode Island, pleads for her life; is hanged until dead on June 1, and her body is thrown into an unmarked grave; *1661* King Charles II ends the death penalty for being a Quaker in Massachusetts.

Activities of Historical Significance

Mary Dyer's death was soon viewed, even within Massachusetts, as a catalyst in the struggle for religious toleration. Although one more Quaker was yet to be hanged in Boston (William Leddra on March 14, 1661), the newly restored Charles II of England sent a mandamus the following year to the Bay Colony removing the power to execute anyone merely for professing Quakerism.

Within a year of Dyer's death, George Bishop wrote triumphantly, "Your bloody laws were snapt asunder by a woman who, trampling upon you and your laws and your halter and your gallows and your priests, is set down at the right hand of God." In an 18-stanza poem called "The King's Missive, 1661" (1880) John Greenleaf Whittier paid tribute to Mary Dyer as one of the "fourfold chain"

431

of Quaker martyrs: "Not in vain / have ye borne the Master's cross of pain; / Ye have fought the fight, ye are victors crowned, / With a fourfold chain ye have Satan bound."

The casual remark made by a witness at the hanging that Mary Dyer's lifeless body wavered in the wind like a flag ironically became a token of her real contribution to the cause of religious freedom. Stories circulated that one of the officers of her guard, like the centurion at the crucifixion, thereafter resigned his military commission to embrace his victim's religion. A martyr in the most literal sense, Mary Dyer drew outside attention to the problem of religious bigotry in Massachusetts and marked the beginning of an end to religious persecution in America.

Mary Dyer continues to be relevant today. She was a feminist who also managed to raise seven children, and an evangelist whose inner light drove her to witness for God in the most uncomfortable of places. She stands out as the first woman put to death on American soil for a "crime" that is no longer considered "criminal."

Overview of Biographical Sources

After the Puritan ethic was discredited at the hands of such writers as Nathaniel Hawthorne and Charles Francis Adams in the nineteenth century, Mary Dyer and Anne Hutchinson were hoisted high as champions of the freedoms of religion and speech. Her still standard biography was written by Horatio Rogers, then an associate justice of the Rhode Island Supreme Court, *Mary Dyer of Rhode Island, the Quaker Martyr that was Hanged on Boston Common* (1896).

Even more than Anne Hutchinson, the image of Mary Dyer has endured untarnished as one who selflessly fought injustice, and whose death influenced social change. Her sense of mission was likened to that of the civil rights leaders, and in 1966 a fictionalized biography by Ethel White, *Bear His Mild Yoke*, portrayed her in this light.

Evaluation of Principal Biographical Sources

Bacon, Margaret H. *The Quiet Rebels. The Story of the Quakers in America.* New York: Basic Books, 1969. (G) A modern presentation of the facts of Mary Dyer's life, but since the author uses *Bear His Mild Yoke* as her primary source, some of Ethel White's fictional liberties are here given as fact.

Deen, Edith. *Great Women of the Christian Faith.* New York: Harper and Brothers, 1959. (G) This three-page profile emphasizes Mary Dyer's faith even unto death, her fearlessness at the gallows, and her total submission to the will of God, depicting her throughout as one who greatly helped the cause of religious toleration in America.

Hodges, George. *The Apprenticeship of Washington and other Sketches of Significant Colonial Personages*. New York: Moffat Yard, 1909. **(G)** Chapter 2 of this book, titled "The Hanging of Mary Dyer," includes a thorough chronicle of the Quaker movement in America from 1656–1661. The treatment is dated by the rhetoric of the times: the entrance of the Quakers into Boston is likened to the entrance of Paul and Silas into Philippi, and Mary Dyer is unabashedly compared to both St. Perpetua and Iphigenia.

Howe, M. A. DeWolfe. *Boston Common. Scenes From Four Centuries*. Boston: Atlantic Monthly Press, 1921. **(G)** Includes a description of Mary Dyer's hanging as well as an interesting and informed discussion as to whether the execution took place on the Common or elsewhere. There is an index and a meticulous bibliography.

Newman, Daisy. *A Procession of Friends*. Garden City, NY: Doubleday, 1972. **(G)** This fresh retelling of the Quaker story contains some new material about Mary Dyer and is thoroughly footnoted. It is especially valuable for the information it provides on the Mary Dyer statue in Boston.

Rogers, Horatio. *Mary Dyer of Rhode Island, the Quaker Martyr that was Hanged on Boston Common*. Providence: Preston and Rounds, 1896. **(G)** Still the only full-length biography of Mary Dyer available. There is an index, some limited bibliographic material given only in a preface, and four appendices that include some of Mary Dyer's letters and her husband's letter to Governor Endicott pleading for the life of his wife.

West, Jessamyn, ed. *The Quaker Reader*. New York: Viking Press, 1962. **(G)** Six pages of abridged passages culled from the Rogers biography are reprinted here under the title, "Mary Dyer Did Hang as a Flag."

Overview and Evaluation of Primary Sources

Contemporary physical descriptions of Mary Dyer use the word "comely," and even John Winthrop, in his 1638 journal, included in James K. Hosmer, ed., *The History of New England* (New York: Scribner's, 1908; **A, G**), wrote that she was a "very proper and fair woman." A Dutch writer named Gerard Croese, in *The General History of the Quakers* (London, 1696; microfilm 1980) as cited by Rogers, wrote of her as a "person of no mean extract and parentage, of an estate pretty plentiful, of a comely stature and countenance, of a piercing knowledge in many things, of a wonderful sweet and pleasant discourse, so fit for great affairs . . . "

The primary original source is George Bishop, *New England Judged, Not by Man's but by the Spirit of the Lord* (London, Part 1, 1661; Part 2, 1667; Reprint. Philadelphia: Thomas W. Stuckney, 1885; **A**). This inclusive martyrology is supposed to have been read by Charles II and is therefore claimed as influential in halting the subsequent persecution of Quakers in Massachusetts. For a study of inherent legal considerations, see G. P. Gooch and H. J. Laski, *English Democratic Ideas in the Seventeenth Century*, 2nd ed. (Cambridge: Cambridge University Press, 1927; **A**).

A graphic and lengthy description of Mary Dyer's 1637 miscarried fetus occurs in John Winthrop's *A Short Story of the Rise, Reign and Ruine of the Antinomians, Familists and Libertines* (**A**), published anonymously in 1644, and then almost immediately thereafter reissued with a new preface by Thomas Weld. According to this account, the Dyers are listed as "familists" who are very active in maintaining their party allegiances, and the birth is "so monstrous and misshapen, as the like hath scarce been heard of: it had no head but a face, which stood so low upon the brest, as the eares (which were like an Apes) grew upon the shoulders." Elsewhere he writes that it was a "woman child, a fish, a beast, and a fowle, all woven together in one, and without an head." The entire manuscript is reprinted in David D. Hall, ed., *The Antinomian Controversy, 1636–1638: A Documentary History* (Middletown, CT: Wesleyan University Press, 1968; **A**).

Fiction and Adaptations

Michael Colacurcio examines the influence of Anne Hutchinson on the writings of Nathaniel Hawthorne in his essay "Footsteps of Anne Hutchinson," included in the anthology *Anne Hutchinson: Troubler of the Puritan Zion* (1981). He points out, as well, that Mary Dyer, whom he calls Anne Hutchinson's strongest female ally, is the model for the Hawthorne character Quaker Catherine in "The Gentle Boy."

The melodrama of Mary Dyer taking the arm of her friend Anne Hutchinson as she leaves the scene of her Boston excommunication as a virtual pariah has been put to good use in many historical novels. The incident serves as the stopping point ("Mary Dyer's hand tightened on mine . . .as Winthrop read the sentence") between Parts 1 and 2 in *Witnesses* by Marcy Moran Heidish (1980); Anne Hutchinson is made to utter the words, "Mary Dyer has not deserted me" in *The Winthrop Woman* by Anya Seton (1958); and the scene serves as an effective closing for *Covenant of Grace* by Jane Gilmore Rushing (1982): "Then the two women moved on together out into the sunshine of that cold and cloudless day."

Deborah Crawford, *Four Women in a Violent Time* (1970), interweaves the lives of four early women of courage—Anne Hutchinson, Mary Dyer, Lady Deborah Moody, and Penelope Stout—who represent for her the finest strains that early American womanhood had to offer. Crawford takes novelistic liberties, assuming, for instance, a pre-existing London friendship between Anne Hutchinson and Mary Dyer. She also assumed that the two women were the same age, when actually Mary Dyer was considerably younger.

Caroline Dale Snedeker, *Uncharted Ways* (1935), features the fictional Quakeress, Margaret Stevenson, who is reprieved from execution for her missionary zeal on Nantucket. She is obviously based on the model of Mary Dyer, as is made very clear by her answers at the trial and her letter from prison, taken verbatim from the record of Mary Dyer, as is the melodramatic scene of her reprieve at the gallows. The debt to the historical personage of Mary Dyer is recognized by the author in an epilogue.

Bear His Mild Yoke (1966), by Ethel White, tells the story of Mary Dyer in journal form, preserving the "plain" language of the times as used in the subject's actual correspondence. When the facts of the case were lacking, White "imagined what might have been logical and appropriate." Her bibliography lists 19 items.

Museums, Historical Landmarks, Societies

Mary Dyer Statue (Boston, MA). Flanking the entrance of the State House in Boston are twin statues of Mary Dyer and Anne Hutchinson. Mary Dyer is seated on the right with her hands in her lap, wearing a simple seventeenth-century dress and a small cap. Funded by Zenos Ellis of Fairhaven, Vermont, and sculpted by Sylvia Shaw Judson of Lake Forest, Illinois, it was presented on July 9, 1959. Since no portrait of Mary Dyer exists, the statue is wholly original; the plaster model was then sent to Italy to be cast in bronze and the resultant sculpture, with its high cheekbones, resolute chin, and total simplicity, radiates the courage, compassion, and peace that characterized the life of its subject. Beneath the statue are carved the words, "My life not availeth me in comparison to the liberty of the Truth."

Society of Friends (Boston, MA). Once a year, the society holds a silent vigil upon the site where Mary Dyer is presumed to have been hanged on Boston Common and makes a visit to the statue on the State House grounds nearby.

Other Sources

Adams, James Truslow. "Dyer, Mary." In *The Dictionary of American Biography*, edited by Allen Johnson. New York: Scribner's, 1927; reprint, 1964. A noteworthy encyclopedia treatment, especially strong on primary and genealogical bibliography.

"Dyer, Mary." In *Webster's American Biographies*, ed. by Charles Van Doren. Springfield, MA: G. & C. Merriam, 1974. A concise biographical sketch especially strong on chronology. No bibliography.

Jones, Rufus. *The Quakers in the American Colonies.* 1911. Reprint. New York: W. W. Norton, 1966. Has a 28-page chapter, "The Martyrs," that includes some of Mary Dyer's correspondence, as well as the principal details of her tragic career. Extensive footnotes.

Jack Shreve
Allegany Community College

AMELIA EARHART
1897–1937

Chronology

Born Amelia Earhart on July 24, 1897, in Atchison, Kansas, the elder of two daughters of Amy Otis Earhart and Edwin Stanton Earhart, a railroad attorney and claims agent; *1897–1908* grows up with her sister Muriel, often in the care of wealthy maternal grandparents, Judge Alfred Otis and Amelia Harres Otis, while their parents must travel for railroad business; *1908–1916* moves with parents to Des Moines, where Edwin Earhart advances in his work while succumbing to alcoholism that eventually destroys his career and his marriage; family moves three times; Amelia graduates from Hyde Park High School in Chicago; *1916–1918* attends the Ogontz School, a woman's college near Philadelphia, and leaves just before graduating; *1918* serves as Voluntary Aid Detachment (VAD) nurse in Toronto where Muriel attends St. Margaret's College; a stunt pilot makes a profound impression on Amelia; *1919–1920* takes auto repair class at Smith College and begins pre-med at Columbia University; travels to Los Angeles where her parents reunite briefly before their divorce; takes her first flight with Frank Hawks; flies solo after lessons from Neta Snook, first woman graduate of Curtiss School; *1920–1928* qualifies for pilot's license, buys own plane, and sets women's altitude record; becomes social worker at Denison House in Boston; *1928* becomes first woman passenger to fly across the Atlantic; propelled to international celebrity as "Lady Lindy" because she has the Lindbergh look, modesty, interest in aviation; writes *20 Hrs. 40 Min.*; *1931* marries George Palmer Putnam, publisher, promoter and manager of her career; *1932* flies solo transatlantic; writes *The Fun of It*; *1935* flies from Hawaii to California; *June–July 1937* attempts flight around the world at the equator, disappears, and is presumed dead.

Activities of Historical Significance

Earhart's flight records, beginning with her altitude record in 1922, were a series of "firsts" for a woman. She wanted to prove that "women will know no restrictions because of sex, but will be individuals free to live their lives as men are free . . ." After her self-described "false heroine" celebrity as the first woman passenger to cross the Atlantic by air, she wanted to earn fame by setting speed records for women (1929 and 1930) and flying solo across the Atlantic Ocean (1932); her flight from Honolulu to Oakland (1935) made her the first person to fly from Hawaii to California, first person to fly solo anywhere in the Pacific, and first person to solo over both the Atlantic and Pacific Oceans. She left the records of her historic flights in three books: *20 Hrs. 40 Min.* (1928), *The Fun of It* (1932) and *Last Flight* (1937), arranged by G. P. Putnam. Both her well-publicized flights and

her books helped promote the aviation industry and her feminist ideas. Her founding membership in the Ninety-Nines, an association of women pilots, and her work
with women students at Purdue University were to further those causes.

Overview of Biographical Sources

Earhart's life and her mysterious disappearance have been the subject of many
books but the definitive scholarly biography has not been written. George Putnam's
biographical memoir of Amelia, *Soaring Wings* (1939), and his autobiographical
Wide Margins (1942) provided most early biographers with a framework of material. Paul Briand, Jr., used these sources and extensive interviews for his doctoral
dissertation later published as *Daughter of the Sky* (1960). More recently, Muriel
Earhart Morrissey—author of *Courage is the Price* (1963) and *Amelia, My Courageous Sister* (with Carol Osborne; 1987)—assisted the later, noteworthy biographers, Burke (1970) and Backus (1982).

Earhart's last flight and disappearance have been the subject of continuing, often
sensationalistic, controversy by journalists. Among books published on this topic is
the fast-moving, early book by newsman Fred Goerner, *The Search for Amelia
Earhart* (1966), supplying hearsay evidence that she died a Japanese prisoner in
Saipan after flying a spy mission over the Marshall Islands. Several later books
extend and correct the Earhart disappearance theories proposed by Briand and
Goerner. At least two books insist that Amelia Earhart survived her 1937 crash in
the Marshall Islands to return to the United States to live under another name.

Evaluation of Principal Biographical Sources

Backus, Jean L. *Letters from Amelia 1901–1937*. Boston: Beacon Press, 1982.
(A, G) The most thorough analysis of Amelia Earhart's character, this biography
uses many recently discovered letters to her mother dated from 1901 until her
disappearance. Earhart's private writing reveals a crisp, good-humored style of a
very busy woman who is sometimes playful but often demanding in her letters to
her family. By developing insights into Earhart's character not previously made
public, Backus wishes to correct the idealized image and render a less heroic, more
human biographical portrait. She succeeds in finding faults and virtues in Amelia's
self-revealing letters. Short, incomplete source list.

Briand, Paul L., Jr. *Daughter of the Sky*. New York: Duell, Sloan and Peace,
1960. **(A, G, Y)** Extensive interviews, letters, and photos collected by Air Force
Academy Professor Briand give drama and substance to his life of Earhart, enlarg-
ing the portrait left by Putnam. Briand's theory of the last flight, based upon the
account of a Marshallese woman, Josephine Blanco Akiyama, was the first published theory that Earhart ended up on Saipan. His theory has been corrected by

later research. There are no footnotes in this published version of his dissertation, but the bibliography is helpful.

Burke, John. *Winged Legend*. New York: G. P. Putnam's Sons, 1970. **(G)** Readable, probing, mildly psychobiographical, this study builds upon information by Putnam, Briand, Goerner and Morrissey to give reasons Earhart took such risks, thus deemphasizing Putnam's role in pushing her career and his possible complicity in a government spy mission for her last flight. Burke (a pseudonym for writer Richard O'Connor) examines Earhart's directness, extraordinary drive for fame and recognition, her modesty, candor, and compulsion to prove women could compete on equal terms with men. To show her life counted more than the moment of her death, Burke probes how her possible motivations are linked to the culture of her upbringing and ancestry. It regrettably lacks footnotes and a bibliography.

Goerner, Fred. *The Search for Amelia Earhart*. New York: Doubleday, 1966. **(G, Y)** Exciting, intense but hurriedly inaccurate report of a journalist's six-year investigation, Goerner leaves many questions unanswered and, final proof unfound, demands the government end its alleged cover-up that Earhart flew a spy mission over Japanese facilities. Index but no footnotes or bibliography.

Klaas, Joe, and Joseph Gervais. *Amelia Earhart Lives*. New York: McGraw-Hill, 1970. **(G)** A report of the seven-year, unofficial "Operation Earhart" led by pilot Joe Gervais and assisted by writer-pilot Joe Klaas to prove by curious evidence that Amelia did not perish in 1937 but was picked up by the Japanese after she crashed on Hull Island, imprisoned as a spy, released to play Tokyo Rose, then given anonymity in return for her services. This book indicates the strength of a continuing Amelia Earhart cult.

Loomis, Vincent, and Jeffrey Ethell. *Amelia Earhart: The Final Story*. New York: Random House, 1985. **(G)** Undoubtedly not the final story, another Air Force pilot re-examines old evidence, denies the "spy mission" theory, and debunks the theory that Earhart returned alive from her last flight. It presents a new look at technical data, including Japanese ship logs and a recreation of her supposed last flight course. Based on evidence given by Elinor Smith in her autobiography, *Aviatrix* (1981), and by other expert navigator-pilots who knew her, Loomis and Ethell dramatize that Earhart was neither an expert pilot nor a very responsible one. The bibliography is helpful. Includes photographs.

Myers, Robert H. *Stand By To Die*. Pacific Grove, CA: Lighthouse Writer's Guild, 1985. **(G)** Myers reports forty years later what he thinks happened to his friend based upon radio transmissions he says he received from Earhart, July 1 through July 11, 1937. Before she left, Earhart told him she was flying a secret mission and made him promise he would tell someone if something happened to her. He watched her plane being equipped with Naval cameras, boxes of film and ping pong balls for flotation. He is convinced she assumed another identity and returned to the U.S. Some of his evidence is corroborated. Photographs and bibliography.

Evaluation of Biographies for Young People

Blau, Melinda. *Whatever Happened to Amelia Earhart?* Milwaukee: Raintree Children's Books, 1977. Concise biography also discusses the mystery of Amelia's disappearance based on recently published evidence. Includes photographs and illustrations.

de Leeuw, Adele. *The Story of Amelia Earhart.* New York: Grosset and Dunlap, 1955. Beautifully written, complete and straightforward account for children and young adults based upon Putnam's *Soaring Wings.* Illustrated.

Howe, Jane Moore. *Amelia Earhart: Kansas Girl.* New York: Bobbs-Merrill, 1950, 1961. Dramatic and imaginary recreation of Amelia's childhood for younger children. Illustrated.

Parlin, John. *Amelia Earhart: Pioneer in the Sky.* Illinois: Garrard, 1962. For very young readers, a complete biography. Illustrated.

Overview and Evaluation of Primary Sources

Amelia Earhart's books contain only brief mention of her life before flight; they were produced hurriedly between an active flying and speaking schedule, to finance her flights and to promote interest in aviation, particularly for women. Conversational in tone and loose in construction, her books reveal candor, stamina, and strong convictions as well as intelligence and modesty. They also give evidence of undeveloped literary interest and talent. *20 Hrs. 40 Min.* (New York: G. P. Putnam's Sons, 1928; **A, G, Y**) quickly tells of her initial training but is chiefly based upon her log book from the *Friendship* flight across the Atlantic. Her sense of humor and restless desire for adventure permeate this account. A second book, a collection of essays entitled, *The Fun of It* (New York: Harcourt, Brace, 1932; **A, G, Y**), tells her feelings and facts about the trans-Atlantic flight. The posthumous *Last Flight* (New York: Harcourt, Brace, 1937; **A, G, Y**) contains more detailed logs of flights across the Pacific (1935), her solo flight from Burbank to Mexico City returning directly across the Gulf of Mexico to New York (1935), and finally notes describing the flight around the equator before her disappearance (1937).

Other primary material may be found in Amelia Earhart's column for *Cosmopolitan* from November 1928 through November 1929; in an article for *National Geographic Magazine* in May 1935, "My Flight from Hawaii"; in the Amelia Earhart and Amy Otis Earhart collections (the latter contains letters to her mother) in the Schlesinger Library at Radcliffe College; in the Purdue University Library

Earhart Collection; and in the Earhart files at the National Air and Space Museum, Smithsonian Institution.

Muriel Earhart Morrissey wrote about her sister in *Courage is the Price* (Wichita: McCormick-Armstrong, 1963); and in the revised version, *Amelia, My Courageous Sister* (Santa Clara: Osborne, 1987; **A, G**). "Pidge," Amelia's nickname for her younger sister, provides a detailed account of their childhood, their father's devotion and his alcoholism, their intermittent schooling. She gives sisterly details of major public and private events in "Meely's" adult life, balancing and correcting accounts by other biographers. After a hurried and incomplete analysis of many published theories, she concludes that no one has produced a convincing solution to Amelia's disappearance. Includes a list of citations, awards, gifts and memorials.

Ann Holtgren Pellegreno, *World Flight* (Ames, IA: Iowa State University Press, 1971; **A, G**), is written by a schoolteacher-pilot, who flew approximately the same air route around the equator in June and July, 1967, to complete the flight plan Amelia Earhart failed to finish in 1937. Pellegreno was accompanied by a co-pilot, a navigator, and the pilot-mechanic who had reconditioned their old Lockheed Electra, a sister ship of Earhart's plane. Pellegreno and her crew experienced some difficulty in finding Howland Island beneath the clouds but they did find it and dropped a wreath from the air. Pellegreno provides summaries of other published and unpublished theories of Earhart's disappearance. Photographs and bibliography.

The husband of Amelia Earhart, George Palmer Putnam, in *Soaring Wings* (New York: Harcourt, Brace and World, 1939; **A, G**), provides an informal and self-described "often unorderly" biography. This work memorializes her spirit and expands upon newspaper accounts of big events in her life with personal details from her correspondence and their life together. Uncharacteristically self-deprecating, Putnam gives center stage to "AE" (his name for her), elaborates on and clarifies her opinions of marriage, of women and equality, of careers in flight, and of famous people. This book forms the basis of most earlier biographical material on Earhart, especially biographies for young people. Recent publications may provoke substantial skepticism about Putnam's literary self-portrait as well as his view of Earhart.

Fiction and Adaptations

An NBC-TV movie, *Amelia Earhart*, first aired October 25, 1976, starring Susan Clark as Earhart. This production sometimes tediously dramatizes the new evidence concerning Earhart's life and last flight, and emphasizes her navigator's alcoholism, her lack of expertise, and the confusion of search missions.

Two novels give fictional accounts of Earhart's last flight based on the most recently uncovered evidence. Peter Tanous in *The Earhart Mission* (1978) weaves dramatic moments from Earhart's life with his fictional version of her disappearance and return. James Stewart Thayer in *The Earhart Betrayal* (1980) dramatizes the government's alleged complicity in Earhart's disappearance, her survival, and return to the U.S.

Sterling Educational Films made a twenty-five-minute black and white documentary film, *Amelia Earhart* (1962), of Earhart's public life by splicing newsreel filmstrips.

An RKO movie, *Flight for Freedom*, starring Rosalind Russell and Fred MacMurray, was released in April 1943. The movie proposes that the last flight was a government spy mission. Several biographers, including Morrissey, believe this movie served as inspiration for the "secret mission" theorists.

Museums, Historical Landmarks, Societies

Earhart Monument (Burry Point, Wales). Salutes "the first woman to fly over the Atlantic Ocean."

Franklin Institute (Philadelphia, PA). *Lockheed*, the airplane that Earhart flew across the Atlantic, is on display here.

National Air and Space Museum (Washington, DC). Holds display of Earhart's medals.

Ninety-Nines, Inc. (Oklahoma City, OK). Awards an annual Amelia Earhart Scholarship for women students in any branch of aeronautics.

United States Air Force Academy (USAF Academy, CO). Presents an annual Amelia Earhart Memorial Award to a graduate for excellence in social sciences.

Zonta International (Chicago, IL). Awards an annual Amelia Earhart Memorial Scholarship for women graduate students in the field of aeronautic sciences.

Other Sources

Douglas, George H. *Women of the 20s*. Dallas: Saybrook, 1986. In his book describing how successful women achieved new ground in the 1920s through their own accomplishments and talents, Douglas provides a chapter on Earhart, putting her in the context of her times.

Starr, Louis M. "Amelia Mary Earhart." In *Dictionary of American Biography*. New York: Scribner's, 1958. Concise, interpretive biographical sketch by a distinguished educator, oral historian, and journalist at Columbia University.

Gretchen R. Sutherland
Cornell College

MARY BAKER EDDY
1821-1910

Chronology

Born Mary Anne Morse Baker on July 16, 1821, in Bow, New Hampshire, the sixth and youngest child of Mark Baker and Abigail Barnard Ambrose Baker, strict Congregationalists; *1821-1836* grows up on the Baker farm; *1836* moves with her family to Sandbornton Bridge, New Hampshire; raised in an arduous religious environment, she is prone to nervous "fits" that leave her weakened and unable to attend school regularly; *1843* marries George Washington Glover and moves to Charleston, South Carolina; *1844* widowed, returns to Sandbornton Bridge, and gives birth to her only natural-born son, George Glover; *1851* unable to care for herself and her son, she gives him up; *1853* marries Dr. Daniel Patterson and moves to North Groton, New Hampshire; *1861* weak and unable to walk, contacts a "mental healer," Dr. Phineas Parkhurst Quimby; *1862* is treated at a water cure sanitarium; travels to Maine to work with Dr. Quimby; returns to New Hampshire stronger and committed to Dr. Quimby's "mental healing"; *1867* separates from Dr. Patterson and is later divorced; *1867-1870* continues her work on mental healing while moving from house to house; writes her first book; *1870* relocates to Amesbury, Massachusetts, and enters a "mental healing" partnership with Dr. Richard Kennedy which lasts until 1872; *1875* purchases a home in Lynn, Massachusetts, and establishes the first center for Christian Scientists; publishes *Science and Health*; *1877* marries Dr. Asa Gilbert Eddy, who dies in 1882; moves periodically between Massachusetts and New Hampshire; *1910* dies on December 3 of pneumonia and renal calculi at her home in Chestnut Hill, Massachusetts.

Activities of Historical Significance

Mary Baker Eddy worked tirelessly to establish the Christian Science Church as a legitimate religious body. Despite controversy throughout her life about the originality of her thoughts in *Science and Health*, Eddy's efforts resulted in a church still vital to its membership today.

Emerging during a time of great social upheaval, her religious beliefs, grounded in Christianity, proposed a view that healing, truth, life, and love are spiritual states of being: one can achieve understanding of God through right thinking; heaven is a spiritual state; material or sensual consciousness is mortal and, therefore, unreal. In this view, each individual has the power, through proper understanding, to overcome wrong thinking which results in sin and poor health. Although this is an oversimplification, her concept reflects a desire to gain control of her own life and to help others do the same.

In her lifetime, society was changing rapidly from agrarian to industrial, causing feelings of displacement and alienation. Spiritualists, mental healers, mesmerists, and other occult groups attracted many followers, yet only Eddy's movement survived.

The origins of the Christian Scientist movement can be traced to 1866, when, shortly after Dr. Quimby's death, Mary Baker Eddy experienced a "fall on the ice," interpreted by her and her followers as the crystalization of Christ's message and the power of healing. With her followers in 1875 and 1876, she established the foundations of the Church of Christ Scientist with the publication of *Science and Health* (now known as *Science and Health with the Key to the Scriptures*) and by formally chartering the Christian Science Association. In 1883, the first edition of the *Journal of Christian Science* was published to keep members in touch; this journal was to become known as the *Christian Science Journal*. Dissension in the Boston Church resulted in a reorganization of the Church structure in the 1890s; her creation of the *Manual of the Mother Church*, still the rule of the Church, and the establishment of the "Mother Church" in Boston were the outcome of this restructuring. Her last major accomplishment was the publication, in 1908, of the first edition of the *Christian Science Monitor*.

Overview of Biographical Sources

Although biographical sketches of Mary Baker Eddy exist, a consistent and reliable picture is difficult to obtain because of the protective attitude of current church leaders. The Mother Church possesses a great deal of primary source material, and although access to the material is possible, a researcher must receive permission from the Publication Committee, which must approve all uses of the material.

Several books have been published by the Christian Science Publishing Society that are heavily slanted: William Dana Orcutt, *Mary Baker Eddy and Her Books* (1950); Lyman P. Powell, *Mary Baker Eddy: A Life Size Portrait* (1930. Reprint, 1950); and Irving C. Tomlinson, *Twelve Years With Mary Baker Eddy Recollections and Experiences* (1945).

Sources available outside of the Church archives should be consulted to gain a fuller picture of her life and context.

Evaluation of Principal Biographical Sources

Bates, Ernest Sutherland, and John V. Dittemore. *Mary Baker Eddy: The Truth and The Tradition*. London: George Routledge & Sons, 1933. **(A, G)** Of great value since the author knew Mrs. Eddy, served as the Trustee of her estate, and as the Director of the Mother Church. These roles gave him access to many documents, including the diary of Calvin Frye, Mary Baker Eddy's secretary for twenty-eight years. This book attempts to give an in-depth look at the personal Eddy and protests the Mother Church's effort to create "a legend" of its founder.

Beasley, Norman. *Mary Baker Eddy*. New York: Duell, Sloan and Pearce, 1963. **(G)** Views her from the start as a "miracle worker." Not as informative or probative as other biographies.

Dakin, Edwin Franden. *Mrs. Eddy: The Biography of a Virginal Mind*. New York: Charles Scribner's Sons, 1929. **(A, G)** This was the first attempt to evaluate Eddy's life objectively through the use of letters and primary source material. It contains a detailed bibliography.

Milmine, Georgine. *The Life of Mary Baker G. Eddy and the History of Christian Science*. 1909. Reprint. Grand Rapids: Baker Book House, 1971. **(A, G)** The earliest comprehensive evaluation of her life, written while she was alive. Based on a series of articles in *McClure's Magazine* (1907–1908), it adopts a negative view, but significantly includes a number of affidavits from people involved with Eddy during various stages of her life. Many of these testimonies contradict her portrayal in later biographies.

Peel, Robert. *The Years of Discovery*. New York: Holt, Rinehart and Winston, 1966. *Mary Baker Eddy: The Years of Trial, 1876–1891*. New York: Holt, Rinehart and Winston, 1971; *Mary Baker Eddy: The Years of Authority*. New York: Holt, Rinehart and Winston, 1977. **(A, G)** This series of books is scholarly in scope and attempts to understand Eddy's religious ideas in relation to the ideas of her time.

Silberger, Julius J. *Mary Baker Eddy: An Interpretive Biography of the Founder of Christian Science*. Boston: Little, Brown, 1980. **(A, G)** Attempts to understand Eddy not only in the context of her time but in the context of those life experiences which contributed to her emergence as a woman of significance.

Wilbur, Sibyl. *The Life of Mary Baker Eddy*. Boston: The Christian Science Publishing Society, 1907. **(A, G)** The first authorized biography by the Mother Church. Most of the data comes from the subject herself. This book partially addresses controversies later ignored or minimized by the Mother Church.

Overview and Evaluation of Primary Sources

The overriding purpose of Mary Baker Eddy's works is to promote her religious concept and views. These works have been heavily edited since they were first written. Her autobiography, *Retrospection and Introspection* (Boston: The Trustees under the Will of Mary Baker G. Eddy, 1891; Reprint, 1920; **G**), is not very detailed and is simple in scope. *Prose Works Other than Science and Health with the Key to the Scriptures* (Boston: First Church of Christ, Scientist, 1953; **G**) contains a compilation of her letters, essays, sermons, and excerpts from various pamphlets, books, and testimonials, all relating to her religious and philosophical views. *Science and Health with the Key to the Scriptures* (Boston: The First Church of Christ, Scientist, 1875; Reprint, 1971; **G**) is used as one of the Church's "aids to the bible." *Manual of the Mother Church* (Boston: The First Church of Christ Scientist, 1936; **G**) was written to set down governing rules for all church-related administrative issues. Other volumes and pamphlets contain a sampling of her thoughts on the meaning of Christmas, her poetry, and lyrics for hymns.

Museums, Historical Landmarks, Societies

Mary Baker Eddy Home (Lynn, MA). One of her residences, maintained by the Mother Church and open to the public.

Mary Baker Eddy Home (Chestnut Hill, MA). Her last home and place of death, maintained by the Mother Church and open to the public.

Mary Baker Eddy Museum (Brookline, MA). Celebrates Eddy's life and accomplishments through displays of her writings and artifacts.

The Mother Church (Boston, MA). Established by Eddy, this organization holds many of her personal papers, works to protect her reputation, and maintains her residences.

Other Sources

Dickey, Adam. *Memoirs of Mary Baker Eddy*. Boston: Merrymount Press, 1927. Written by one of Eddy's administrators. Although she "authorized" Dickey to write her biography, she did not "authorize" him to publish it. The church managed to gain all but a few copies after its publication; though not readily available, this work can be found in the Library of Congress.

Dresser, Annetta G. *The Philosophy of P. P. Quimby*. Boston: George H. Ellis, 1895. Relates to the Quimby/Eddy controversy. Because Eddy's teachings had roots in Quimby's teachings to an extent, some tried to discredit her. The relationship of Quimby's teachings to Eddy's is important for an understanding of her early development.

Dresser, Horatio W., ed. *The Quimby Manuscript*. New York: Thomas Y. Crowell, 1921. A compilation of Quimby's writings. The Phineas Parkhurst Quimby Papers are housed in the Library of Congress.

Linda Firestone

THOMAS EDISON
1847-1931

Chronology

Born Thomas Alva Edison on February 11, 1847, in Milan, Ohio, the youngest of seven children to Canadian-born Samuel Edison, a fairly prosperous shingle manufacturer and businessman, and American-born Nancy Eliott Edison, a former school teacher; *1854* moves to Fort Huron, Michigan, with family; *1855–1861* educated by his mother after his public school teachers deem him slow; *1862* having developed an interest in chemistry at an early age, sets up a laboratory in basement when he is 15 years old; suffers partial hearing loss when a brakeman pulls him onto a moving train by his ears; *1863–1868* works as a telegraph operator throughout the Midwest, and begins inventing such electrical machines as a vote recorder, pen, and stock printer, and improves the stock ticker and the typewriter; *1869* works as a partner of an electrical engineering company in New York; *1870* establishes his own business and improves upon automatic telegraph; *1871* marries Mary G. Stilwell with whom he will have three children; *1874* makes duplex and quadruplex telegraphy possible; *1875* discovers alternating current but does not see advantage over direct current and discards the "Edison effect," which later becomes the vacuum tube essential to radio-telephony; *1876* devises carbon transmitter, improving Alexander Graham Bell's original telephone; *1877–1881* expands from invention to development, bringing to his credit the phonograph (1877), incandescent lamp (1879), and first central electric station in New York City (1881); *1884* wife dies; *1886* marries Mina Miller with whom he will have three children; *1887* builds large plant in West Orange, New Jersey, and guides a host of inventions while promoting sales of his products; *1889* consolidates the Edison General Electric Company; *1890–1900* works mainly on making a motion picture machine, a fluoroscope, and on devising a processing method for iron ore by the use of magnetic separation; manufactures Portland cement, which he uses to build highways and houses, his process inspiring Henry Ford's mass production automobile assembly line; produces the alkaline, nickel-iron storage battery, a dictating machine, a mimeograph machine, disk records, and electrified trains; devises processes for producing his own synthetic phenol and benzol; *1892* in need of finances, sells out Edison General to General Electric Company; *1901–1903* creates a battery-operated automobile, but advises Henry Ford that internal combustion engine will work better; *1915* becomes president of the Naval Consulting Board but works independently on problems of submarine and torpedo detection and periscopes; uses operations analysis to find sunken ships; improves batteries to increase submarine range; *1927* works with Ford and Harvey S. Firestone to produce rubber from domestic plants; *1929* begins suffering from Bright's disease and gastric ulcers; *1931* collapses in laboratory on August 1; dies on October 18 in Orange, New Jersey, where he is buried.

Activities of Historical Significance

Edison applied science, especially the principles of chemistry and electricity, to industry in order to provide items of commercial use that would streamline labor; improve communications, transportation, and housing; and, in the case of the incandescent lamp, eliminate dangers associated with petroleum or gas lighting. He invented the poured stressed concrete house and anticipated the all-electric house of later years. Having applied for an average of two patents per week for a total of 1,093, his genius began to waver after age 40, though his only hobby was more work.

Edison's dictaphone and phonograph made possible recordings that could be used for communicating, education, or listening pleasure, and his mimeograph machine and talking dolls are still in use. By teaming up with George Eastman of the Kodak Company, he proceeded from the kinetoscope, which could be viewed by only one person, to the moving, and later the talking, picture. His fluoroscope is still used daily by the medical community.

During World War I he greatly improved the operation of submarines and methods of torpedo detection. In a poll taken in 1913 on the ten most useful Americans, his name appeared in 87 percent of the lists. In 1923, the commercial value of his inventions was set at almost $16 billion. His philosophy of life was "work . . . Bringing out the secrets of nature and applying them for the happiness of man." He described genius as "one per cent inspiration and ninety-nine per cent perspiration."

Overview of Biographical Sources

More than eighty books have been written about Thomas Edison. Although the majority of publications prior to 1950 are little more than glorified caricatures, several substantive studies are available. Robert E. Conot, *A Streak of Luck: The Life and Legend of Thomas Alva Edison* (1979), is the most complete and authoritative biography to date. Conot based his research on the papers and artifacts in the Edison Archives as well as on secondary sources. Matthew Josephson, *Edison: A Biography* (1959), is also a scholarly account written by a skilled historian. William A. Simonds spent several years visiting Edison's haunts and interviewing his associates before he completed the detailed *Edison: His Life, His Work, His Genius* (1935).

Evaluation of Principal Biographical Sources

Bryan, George Sands. *Edison: The Man and His Work*. New York: Alfred A. Knopf, 1926. (**A, G**) A generally sympathetic account that also shows Edison's faults. Includes a chronology and samples from his employment questionnaire.

Burlingame, Roger. *Engines of Democracy: Inventions and Society in Mature America*. New York: Arno Press, 1976. (**A, G**) Condenses Edison's contributions in chapters 11 and 14.

Clark, Ronald W. *Edison: The Man Who Made the Future*. New York: Putnam, 1977. (**A, G**) A well-researched and well-written biography that even-handedly bestows praise and blame on Edison. One essay indicts him for failing to convert to alternating current earlier, and for overlooking the possibilities of the vacuum tube. Includes passages from Edison's writings and statements.

Conot, Robert E. *A Streak of Luck: The Life and Legend of Thomas Alva Edison*. New York: Seaview Books, 1979. (**A, G**) A 565-page biography, well-balanced and well-illustrated.

Dyer, Frank Lewis, and Thomas Commerford Martin. *Edison: His Life and Inventions*. 2 vols. New York and London: Harper's, 1910. (**A, G**) Regarded as the official biography, this detailed account includes oral and written statements furnished by Edison. The story is complete only to 1909, and most of the book was actually written by William Meadowcroft, author of *The abc of Electricity*.

Jones, Francis Arthur. *The Life Story of Thomas Alva Edison*. Rev. ed. New York: Grosset and Dunlap, 1931. (**A, G**) A complete biography concentrating on 1870–1890, Edison's most productive inventive decades.

Josephson, Matthew. *Edison: A Biography*. New York: McGraw-Hill, 1959. (**A, G**) Written by a skilled historian, this 511-page biography is the one to read after Conot. It proceeds chronologically from Edison's ancestry to his death.

Miller, F. T. *Thomas Alva Edison: Benefactor of Mankind*. Philadelphia: John C. Winston, 1931. (**G**) A sympathetic and laudatory account with illustrations.

Simonds, William Adams. *Edison: His Life, His Work, His Genius*. London: Allen & Unwin, 1935. (**A, G**) Simons visited every place Edison had lived and worked, enjoyed access to Edison's laboratory for three years, and interviewed as many Edison associates as he could. He stresses his subject's work and character and sees two Edisons: the benign, saintly figure pictured to the public, and the man doomed at the age of thirty to become the lion of his day and to live in the public spotlight for fifty years. Contains illustrations, documents, and letters.

Vanderbilt, Byron Michael. *Thomas Edison: Chemist*. Washington, DC: American Chemical Society, 1971. (**A**) Concentrates on Edison's industrial application of chemical research.

Wachhorst, Wyn. *Thomas Alva Edison: An American Myth*. Cambridge, MA: MIT Press, 1980. (**A, G**) The author concentrates on those factors in Edison's life and character that transformed him into myth. In Edison he finds a superb illustration of the Horatio Alger image and of the Puritan ethic of individualism, hard work, optimism, and anti-intellectualism.

Overview and Evaluation of Primary Sources

Dagobert D. Runes edited Edison's *Diary and Sundry Observations of Thomas Alva Edison* (New York: Philosophical Library, 1948; **A, G**), which contains observations about motion pictures and the arts, war and peace, education and work. A section about "The Realms Beyond" deals with Edison's fascination with the mystery of life and spiritualism. The entry dated July 12, 1885, captures the essence of Edison's musings quite effectively.

Science, Technology, and the Human Prospect: Proceedings of the Edison Centennial Symposium, edited by Chauncey Starr and Philip C. Ritterbush (New York: Pergamon Press, 1980; **A, G**), records the proceedings of a symposium held to observe the 100th anniversary of Edison's electric lighting system. Included in this volume are the original Edison papers read during sessions such as "Judging the Costs and Benefits of Technology," "Adapting the Institutional Frame of Technology," and "Human Needs and the Future of Inventions."

Over half a million Edison papers, notebooks, letters, and drawings are held in the Edison Laboratory, maintained by the National Park Service in West Orange, New Jersey. The Charles Edison Fund contains his family correspondence and provides insight into his relations with his second wife and children. Reese Jenkins of Rutgers University initiated a twenty-year project in 1978 intended to publish Edison's principal papers.

Henry Ford wrote *Edison As I Know Him* with Samuel Crowther (New York: Cosmopolitan Book Corporation, 1930; **A, G**), offering an interesting reflection on the relationship between these two industrial giants.

Museums, Historical Landmarks, Societies

The Charles Edison Fund (Orange, NJ). Contains Edison's family correspondence and provides an intimate picture of Edison's relations with his second wife and his children.

Edison Laboratory (West Orange, NJ). Maintained by the National Park Service, the lab contains more than half a million Edison papers, notebooks, letters, and drawings.

Edison National Historic Site (West Orange, NJ). Built around Edison's second research and development plant.

Edison Tower (Menlo Park, NJ). A 131-foot tower with a thirteen-foot bulb on top.

Edison Winter Home and Museum (Fort Myers, FL). Edison's winter home, the first pre-fabricated house built in Maine (and shipped down to Florida), has a collection of Edison's inventions, manuscripts, and other materials.

Henry Ford Museum of History (Village Green, MI). Contains a replica of Menlo Park.

Pageant of Light (Fort Myers, FL). A ten-day, combination Mardi Gras/sports festival/fair has been held annually since 1975. A Thomas Edison Great American Award is given every year.

The Thomas Alva Edison Foundation (West Orange, NJ). Founded in 1946, this non-profit organization is supported almost entirely by contributions from industry. The foundation functions to stimulate youths toward careers in science and technology.

Thomas Edison Birthplace Museum (Milan, OH). Edison's birthplace houses collections of family mementos, along with Edison's inventions, documents, and other artifacts.

Thomas Edison House (Louisville, KY). Edison's home has a large collection of memorabilia from his life.

The William Hammer Collection (Smithsonian Institution, Washington, DC). Sheds much light on the history of electric light and power, and on Edison's relations with Henry Ford and other friends and associates.

Other Sources

Ackerman, Carl W. *George Eastman*. London: Constable, 1930. An account of Eastman's collaboration with Edison on the motion picture.

Cronon, E. David, ed. *The Cabinet Diaries of Josephus Daniels, 1913-1921*. Lincoln: University of Nebraska Press, 1963. A study of Edison's relations with the Navy during World War I.

Crowther, James Gerald. *Famous American Men of Science*. New York: W. W. Norton, 1937. Includes a discussion of Edison.

Daniels, Josephus. *The Wilson Era: Years of War, 1917-1923*. Chapel Hill: University of North Carolina Press, 1946. Discusses Daniels, Edison, and the Naval Consulting Board.

Friedel, Robert D., Paul Israel, and Bernard S. Finn. *Edison's Electric Light: Biography of an Invention*. New Brunswick: Rutgers University Press, 1986. A study of Edison's work leading to the invention of electric light.

Hammond, John Winthrop. *Men and Volts: The Story of General Electric*. New York: J. B. Lippincott, 1941. A history of the company Edison founded.

Lesley, R. W., J. B. Lober, and G. S. Bartlett. *History of the Portland Cement Industry*. 1924. Reprint. New York: Arno Press, 1972. A history of an industry sprung from Edison's invention.

Ramsaye, Terry. *A Million and One Nights: A History of the Motion Picture*. 2 vols. New York: Simon and Schuster, 1926. Discusses Edison's sometimes aggressive involvement in the film industry.

Scott, Lloyd N. *Naval Consulting Board of the United States*. Washington, DC: Government Printing Office, 1920. A history of the board Edison headed during World War I.

Paolo E. Coletta
U.S. Naval Academy (Ret.)

Thomas A. Edison, 1947

JONATHAN EDWARDS
1703–1758

Chronology

Born Jonathan Edwards on October 5, 1703, in East Windsor, Connecticut, the fifth of eleven children, and the only son, of the Reverend Timothy Edwards, minister to the East Windsor congregation, and prep schoolmaster and Esther Stoddard Edwards; *1703–1716* grows up in East Windsor; is educated at his father's school, where he exhibits his early genius, probably writing his essay "On Insects" as early as 1715, and his essays on the rainbow and on colors in 1716; *1716* enters Yale College; *1720–1722* finishes college work, but remains at Yale to study theology and prepare for the ministry; in August of 1722, becomes minister to a rather impoverished Presbyterian church in New York City; *1723* accepts an invitation to serve as pastor to the congregation at Bolton, Connecticut, but, before filling this position, he is elected to a tutorship at Yale and accepts that post instead; *1724–1726* serves as senior tutor at Yale; *1726–1727* is invited to preach at the Presbyterian church at Northampton, Massachusetts, where his maternal grandfather, Solomon Stoddard, is the minister; takes position as Stoddard's assistant minister; *July 1727* marries Sarah Pierrepont, and takes up residence in Northampton; *1729* Solomon Stoddard dies in February; Edwards accepts post as Northampton's pastor, a position he holds until 1750; *1731* preaches the Thursday lecture at the First Church in Boston, the text of which is published as *God Glorified in the Work of Redemption, by the Greatness of Man's Dependence on Him, in the Whole of It*, establishing his fame as a theologian; *1741* preaches his sermon *Sinners in the Hands of an Angry God*; *mid-1740s–1750* Edwards and his congregation become embroiled in a long theological controversy concerning eligibility for church membership that results in an overwhelming vote for his dismissal as pastor in 1750; refuses an offer made by a friendly minority to establish a second congregation in Northampton; *1751* goes to Stockbridge, Massachusetts, as missionary and pastor to the Native Americans and the few white settlers there; *1757* is chosen to succeed his son-in-law Aaron Burr as president of the College of New Jersey (later called Princeton); *1758* goes to Princeton in January; dies on March 22 of a fever following a smallpox inoculation, in Princeton, and is buried there.

Activities of Historical Significance

Edwards played a major role in the revivalist phenomenon, now referred to as the Great Awakening, that swept the American colonies in the mid-eighteenth century. In 1734, Edwards's parish of Northampton experienced a revival that foreshadowed the Great Awakening of 1740. Edwards documented these events in his *Narrative of Surprising Conversions*, a work that began as a letter to Dr. Benjamin Coleman, pastor of the Brattle Street Church in Boston. Coleman had requested an account of the Northampton revival from Edwards and was so impressed by Edwards's response that he had the letter published in 1736, and sent copies to colleagues in London. The work became extremely popular in England, and Edwards was persuaded to expand upon it; the expanded version went through three editions and twenty printings between 1737 and 1739, and was also translated into German and Dutch.

Edwards became a very influential Great Awakening preacher, although he did not indulge in the pulpit histrionics of some of his revivalist colleagues. By all accounts, he delivered his terrifying sermons in a calm, low voice. It is reported that when he preached his most famous (or infamous) sermon, *Sinners in the Hands of an Angry God* (1741), he had to ask the Enfield, Connecticut, congregation to be still so that they could hear him speak.

Edwards was not merely a revivalist preacher; he represented one pole in the controversy between the Calvinist traditionalists who strongly opposed the presumably leveling aspects of the Great Awakening, and the revivalists who welcomed all who would regenerate church membership. Edwards was himself a strict Calvinist, a firm believer in predestination. In the end, he restricted church membership to those who could profess to having had an experience of saving grace—a policy which was the root cause of his disagreement with his Northampton congregation.

Overview of Biographical Sources

Most of the abundant works about Edwards are analyses or criticism of his philosophy; relatively little has been written about Edwards the man. This may be because he left behind little to document his day-to-day life: his voluminous correspondence is primarily on theological matters, and his diary is mainly a record of his progress (or lack thereof) in living a Christian life.

Edwards's first biographer was Samuel Hopkins, whose *The Life and Character of the Late Reverend Mr. Jonathan Edwards, President of the College of New Jersey* was published in Boston in 1765. Hopkins had studied theology with Edwards, and they were friends and fellow ministers in the Connecticut Valley. The next important biography was Sereno Edwards Dwight, *Life of President Edwards* (1829), the first volume in an edition of Edwards's works. The standard biography of Edwards is Ola Elizabeth Winslow's well-researched and well-written *Jonathan Edwards, 1703–1758: A Biography* (1940). Perry Miller's *Jonathan Edwards* (1949) is an intellectual biography, although it is interspersed with brief chapters on what Miller calls "The External Biography."

Evaluation of Principal Biographical Sources

Dwight, Sereno Edwards. *Life of President Edwards.* Vol. 1 of *The Works of Jonathan Edwards.* New York: S. Converse, 1829. (**A, G**) Dwight draws upon earlier biographies and includes selections from Edwards's writings. He covers Edwards's dismissal by the Northampton congregation at some length.

Hopkins, Samuel. *The Life and Character of the Late Reverend Mr. Jonathan Edwards, President of the College of New Jersey.* 1765. Reprint. New York: AMS Press, 1976. (**A, G**) Written by a friend and colleague, this is a highly laudatory account of Edwards's life. Reprinted numerous times, it was often used, with and without attribution, by other early biographers, and continues to be a useful biographical resource. It includes lengthy extracts from Edwards's "Resolutions," "Diary," and "Personal Narrative."

Miller, Perry. *Jonathan Edwards.* 1949. Reprint. Cleveland: World, 1959. (**A**) Miller states in the foreword to this work, "The real life of Jonathan Edwards was the life of his mind," and then proceeds to prove his point. The work is fascinating, but rather difficult to grasp without some background in New England Congregational Church history.

Parkes, Henry Bamford. *Jonathan Edwards, The Fiery Puritan.* New York: Minton, Balch, 1930. (**A, G**) An interesting, but not very sympathetic biography; Parkes concludes that Edwards was "a living and baneful influence."

Winslow, Ola Elizabeth. *Jonathan Edwards, 1703–1758: A Biography.* New York: Macmillan, 1940. (**A, G**) Winslow's work remains the standard biography. She does not focus on his thought (or, as with Parkes, on his influence on the development of American attitudes); she attempts to do no "more than indicate the chronology and general impact of his ideas, particularly with respect to his changing fortunes." A very readable biography.

Overview and Evaluation of Primary Sources

The first edition of a collection of Edwards's work, edited by Edward Williams and Edward Parsons, was published in eight volumes in England in 1806–1811. The first American edition, also in eight volumes, was edited by Samuel Austin, *The Works of President Edwards* (Worcester, MA: Isiah Thomas, 1808–1809; A). This was followed by Sereno Dwight's ten-volume New York edition in 1829–1830, and by E. Hickman's two-volume London edition of 1833. In 1957, the first volume of the Yale University Press edition of *The Works of Jonathan Edwards* appeared. The Yale edition, begun under the general editorship of Perry Miller, will be the standard edition upon its completion; until that time, the Austin edition is preferred.

An excellent selection from Edwards's work is *Jonathan Edwards: Representative Selections*, edited by Clarence H. Faust and Thomas H. Johnson (New York: Hill and Wang, 1962; A, G). The volume includes a lengthy introduction, an annotated bibliography, and notes on the selections. The Edwards archive is housed in Yale University; Princeton also has some Edwards manuscripts.

Museums, Historical Landmarks, Societies

Edwards Birthsite (New Haven, CT). Although the original birthplace and childhood home was destroyed in the early nineteenth century, a marker designates the site.

Edwards Hall (Stockbridge, MA). A sundial marks the location where Edwards's residence once stood, now the site of the Austen Riggs Psychiatric Center.

Mission House National Historical Landmark (Stockbridge, MA). Edwards's writing desk is on display here.

Other Sources

Lesser, M. X. *Jonathan Edwards: A Reference Guide*. Boston: G. K. Hall, 1981. An extensive annotated bibliography of works about Edwards.

Lowance, Mason I., Jr. "Jonathan Edwards." In *Dictionary of Literary Biography*. Vol. 24. Detroit: Gale, 1984. Examines Edwards's literary style with special emphasis on *Sinners in the Hands of an Angry God*.

Miller, Perry. "Jonathan Edwards and the Great Awakening." In *Errand into the Wilderness*. Cambridge, MA: Harvard University Press, 1956. Edwards's foreshadowing of the Great Awakening is analyzed.

Joan Marshall
Brooklyn College, CUNY (Ret.)

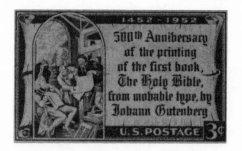

Gutenberg Bible, 1952

ALBERT EINSTEIN
1879–1955

Chronology

Born Albert Einstein on March 14, 1879, in Ulm, Germany, the only son of Hermann Einstein, a chemical engineer and a nonpracticing Jew, and Pauline Koch Einstein, a patron of musical arts; *1880–1894* family moves to Munich where father and uncle open a small electrical equipment factory; *1895* family moves to Milan, Italy; refuses to complete his Gymnasium studies; renounces his German citizenship; follows his family to Italy; *1896* after initially failing his entrance exam, he finally gains admission to the Zurich Eidgenössiche Technische Hochschule (Federal Polytechnic School); *1900* graduates without distinction; *1901* becomes Swiss citizen; *1902* accepts position at the Swiss Patent Office in Bern due to his failure to obtain a university appointment in physics; *1903* marries Mileva Marić, a former student he met at the Federal Polytechnic School; they have two sons; *1905* publishes a series of papers in *Annalen der Physik* that profoundly alters man's view of the universe and surpasses any scientific writings since the time of Sir Issac Newton; "A New Determination of Molecular Dimensions" is submitted and accepted for the Ph.D. degree at the University of Zurich; *1909* is appointed a professor at University of Zurich; and at Eidgenössiche Technische Hochschule; *1913–1933* serves as director of scientific research at the Kaiser Wilhelm Institute for Physics in Berlin; completes his work on the general theory of relativity; *1919* divorces first wife and marries his widowed cousin, Elsa Einstein; becomes active in social causes, especially pacifism and Zionism; *1921* receives the Nobel Prize in Physics; *1923* publishes *The Principle of Relativity*; *1926* publishes *Investigations on the Theory of the Brownian Movement*; *1933* opposes the rise to power of Nazi party in Germany and emigrates to United States; becomes a professor of physics at Institute for Advanced Study in Princeton, New Jersey, remains there for rest of his life; *1934* publishes *The World as I See It* and is formally deprived of German citizenship by the Nazis; *1938* co-authors with Leopold Infeld, *The Evolution of Physics*; *1939* dismayed by fascist militarism, he sends a letter to President Roosevelt that ultimately leads to the formation of a study committee in the United States for the development of an atomic bomb; plays no role in actual work on developing atomic weapons, but the bomb itself sustains his theories about matter and energy; *1940* becomes a United States citizen; *1940–1945* demonstrates interest and active support for the promotion of international government; *1950* publishes *Out of My Later Years*; expands upon his unified field theory describing the relationship between gravitations and electromagnetism; *1955* dies on April 18 in his sleep at Princeton.

Activities of Historical Significance

Einstein's research in the field of physics ranks him as one of the most creative intellects in human history. The special theory of relativity, the equivalence of mass and energy, the theory of Brownian motion, and the photon theory of light all represent great discoveries in physics. His 1905 paper "On the Electrodynamics of Moving Bodies," in which he presents the special theory of relativity, is considered his most significant contribution in the field of science. The concept of the relativity of time and space—previously unimaginable ideas—changed the Newtonian "common sense" view of time and motion. It became the basis of twentieth-century physics. Based on his special theory of relativity, Einstein also discovered an interrelationship between mass and energy, from which he developed his famous equation $E = mc^2$ (energy equals mass times the velocity of light squared). The formula postulated that very small amounts of mass could produce large amounts of energy. His theory became the basis for the development of atomic energy.

In scientific terms, Einstein's theory of relativity was contingent upon two closely linked interrelationships: the equivalence of mass and energy, and the special limiting character of the velocity of light. His famous formula provided the theoretical expression of the enormous energies locked in the atom. At the same time, by showing that all velocities are relative, Einstein was able to explain that, in spite of continuous acceleration, no particle could travel faster than the critical velocity of light. As a particle approached that velocity, its energy and mass increased simultaneously so that it became harder and harder to make it go faster.

His theory also included gravitation in the domain of the measurement of space and time. He postulated that when a body was "free" (not in physical contact with other bodies), it was unacted on by forces, and then its mode of motion simply expressed the quality of space-time at the places through which it passed. This approach explained the apparent shift of the position of the stars near the sun as well as irregularities in the motion of the planet Mercury. Einstein's expression for gravitation significantly improved upon Newton's theory of the solar system.

His involvement in the peace movement stemmed from his disillusionment with the prevailing political ideology in his native Germany and the strong sense of nationalism felt throughout Europe during World War I. The war crystallized his commitment to antimilitarism and internationalism. Einstein's opposition to war was tied to the concept that the killing of any human being, even as an instrument of state policy, was tantamount to murder.

Between the World Wars, Einstein was active in numerous peace causes. In 1922, he joined the Committee on Intellectual Cooperation of the League of Nations, through which he hoped to foster global understanding. He made a demonstrative visit to the world disarmament conference held in Geneva in 1932, cooperated in efforts to establish an international peace center, and participated in a famous public exchange of letters with Sigmund Freud on the cause and cure of war. By the end of the decade, disillusioned at the current state of global affairs, he became a reluctant proponent of collective security against fascism.

In a famous letter, he called to the attention of President Franklin D. Roosevelt the possibility of developing an atomic bomb, though he himself had no knowledge of the subsequent Manhattan Project and was dismayed by the American government's deployment of atomic weapons against Japan to end the Second World War. In 1946, Einstein and other prominent Americans organized the Emergency Committee of Atomic Scientists to call attention to the threat of atomic holocaust and the need to develop a transnational authority. In the final months of his life he worked closely with the renowned British mathematician and philosopher Bertrand Russell to develop a public appeal by the world's most eminent scientists for the abolition of war. Second only to his scientific work, Einstein's desire for world peace dominated his public activities.

His interest in socialism was tied closely to his belief in the dignity of free men. His socialist views resulted from his opposition to capitalist class division and to the exploitation of man by man; his belief that a capitalist economy could not adequately perform for the welfare of all the people and that the resulting economic anarchy was the source of society's contemporary evils; and his conviction that under socialism the individual had a greater possibility to attain the maximum degree of individual freedom compatible with the public welfare. Einstein's socialism was not the result of methodical study or a clearly defined ideological creed. It was a personal reaction to the inequities of the world in which he lived.

In his numerous writings on economics and society he advocated the necessity of a centrally planned economy to provide orderliness in production and distribution and to utilize the labor power of workers in the interests of the entire society. He always insisted that "an exaggerated competitive attitude is inculcated into the student, who is trained to worship acquisitive success as a preparation for his future career." Einstein encouraged the establishment of an educational system oriented toward social goals. "The education of the individual . . . would attempt to develop in him a sense of responsibility for his fellow-men in place of the glorification of power and success in our present society."

Politically, he considered true democracy an indispensable antidote for the misuse of economic power; such misuse, he maintained, was a constant threat to the welfare of society. His commitment to socialism, unlike his public actions on behalf of world peace and Zionism, was characterized by unattachment to political movements and associations. He preferred to write about, rather than participate in, socialist causes. The fear of concentrated power and the ambitions and drives to which such power might give rise was a central tenet of his social justice writings.

Einstein's support for Zionism and a Jewish state also proved both historically significant and controversial. His enthusiasm for Zionism and the cause of a Jewish homeland in Palestine developed as early as 1919, prompted by the anti-Semitism he observed in Berlin during the Great War. Judaism had played little part in his life, but he insisted that, "as a snail can shed his shell and still be a snail, so a Jew can shed his faith and still be a Jew." Einstein was sensitive quite early to the apparent contradiction between his view of nationalism as one of modern man's

great curses and his support for Zionism. He explained his competing commit-
ments in the following way: "When a man has both arms and he is always saying I
have a right arm, then he is a chauvinist. However, when the right arm is missing,
then he must do something to make up for the missing limb. Therefore I am, as a
human being, an opponent of nationalism. But as a Jew I am from today a supporter of the Jewish Zionist efforts." He was especially attracted to the idea of
establishing a university in Jerusalem that would belong to Jews and where Jewish
students and professors could pursue their intellectual interests free from European
anti-Semitic tensions. The systematic destruction of European Jews intensified his
support for the establishment of a Jewish state.

He welcomed with genuine happiness the United Nations resolution in 1948
establishing the State of Israel. When war broke out immediately between Israel
and its Arab neighbors, Einstein was willing to support the Israeli cause, but urged
the government of Israel to accommodate the Arab states and to work out a peaceful
agreement. In 1952, he was offered the presidency of Israel, but turned it down due
to ill health and lack of political inclination.

Overview of Biographical Sources

Einstein's eclectic interests, including pacifism, socialism, and Zionism, have
attracted numerous writers and scholars from all fields. His popularity as a subject
of historical significance began with his Nobel Award and interwar peace activism.
His private papers, opened to scholars in the 1960s, also increased the number of
biographical essays and portraits. To date, there are some thirty-five biographical
works, a few of which are edited compilations honoring his scholarly and public
activities.

Among the more notable works illuminating his personal and professional activities are: Jeremy Bernstein, *Einstein* (1973); Salomon Bochner, *Einstein Between
Centuries* (1979); Ronald W. Clark, *Einstein: The Life and Times* (1971), a work
that stresses the scientific isolation of Einstein's later years; Philipp Frank, *Einstein: The Life and Times* (1949), the most reliable biography written by an eminent European physicist; Lewis Feuer, *Einstein and the Generations of Science*
(1982); William Hermanns, *Einstein and the Poet: In Search of the Cosmic Man*
(1983), a philosophical treatise on Einstein's poetry as it relates to science; Banesh
Hoffmann and Helen Dukas, *Albert Einstein: Creator and Rebel* (1972), and their
edited volume based on further research in the Einstein Papers, *Albert Einstein:
The Human Side* (1979); Abraham Pais, *'Subtle is the Lord . . .': The Science and
Life of Albert Einstein* (1982); Jamie Sayen, *Einstein in America: The Scientist's
Conscience in the Age of Hitler and America* (1985), a work that is narrow in
scope, but historically important in its efforts to examine and explain Einstein's
contradictory positions on nationalism and Zionism; and Carl Seelig's European
perspective, *Albert Einstein: A Biographical Documentary* (1954). The best ac-

count of Einstein's opposition to war is Otto Nathan and Heinz Norden, eds., *Einstein on Peace* (1960).

Works delineating Einstein's scientific life and theories include Lincoln Barnett, *The Universe and Dr. Einstein* (1957); Peter Bergmann, *The Riddle of Gravitation: From Newton to Einstein to Today's Exciting Theories* (1968); J. D. Bernal, volume three of *Science in History* (1965); Nigel Calder, *Einstein's Universe* (1979); Aaron Bunsen Lerner, *Einstein and Newton* (1973); Elma Levinger, *Albert Einstein* (1949), useful for its description of his early years; and Barry Parker, *Einstein's Dream* (1986). There is universal agreement among his scientific biographers regarding the monumental discovery he made in the field of relativity; however, many part with him over his failed attempt to link gravity with electromagnetism and over his differences with Niels Bohr in the area of quantum mechanics.

Notable edited works, particularly helpful to scholarly audiences, include A. P. French, *Einstein: A Centenary Volume* (1979); Maurice Goldsmith, Alan McKay, and James Woudhuysen, *Einstein: The First Hundred Years* (1980); Gerald Holton and Yehuda Elkana, *Albert Einstein: Historical and Cultural Perspectives* (1982); Paul Schilpp, *Albert Einstein: Philosopher-Scientist* (1951); and G. J. Whitrow, *Einstein: The Man and His Achievement* (1973). The Goldsmith, McKay, and Woudhuysen volume and the Holton and Elkana book are most helpful in presenting scholarly observations of Einstein; the Schilpp work remains the standard edited reference, essential for understanding and appreciating Einstein the thinker.

Evaluation of Principal Biographical Sources

Barnett, Lincoln. *The Universe and Dr. Einstein*. New York: Sloane, 1957. **(A, G)** A revised edition of a 1948 work updating recent discoveries in atomic science and scientific hypotheses. Although intended for a scientific audience, the book presents a clear discussion of modern scientific theories about the universe for laypersons.

Bergmann, Peter. *The Riddle of Gravitation: From Newton to Einstein to Today's Exciting Theories*. New York: Charles Scribner's Sons, 1968. **(A)** A technical exposé of Einstein's theory of gravitation by a former student and professor of physics. It contains a brief reading list but no scholarly documentation, and is suitable for readers with a strong science background.

Bernal, J. D. *Science in History*. 4 vols. Cambridge: MIT Press, 1965. **(A, G)** The author, a noted historian of science, devotes considerable attention to Einstein's contributions in the realm of science. The third volume, *The Natural Sciences in Our Time*, is particularly useful and can be read by a general audience.

Bernstein, Jeremy. *Einstein*. New York: Viking Press, 1973. **(A, G, Y)** A work that can be read by anyone wishing to know more about Einstein's theory of relativity and his contributions in the field of quantum physics. This is not a full-scale biography though it deals well with Einstein the scientist.

Bochner, Salomon. *Einstein Between Centuries*. Houston: Rice University Studies, 1979. **(A)** A scholarly pamphlet assessing Einstein's scientific and public contributions on the 100th anniversary of the year of his birth.

Calder, Nigel. *Einstein's Universe*. New York: Viking Press, 1979. **(A)** A scholarly treatment of relativity, astrophysics, and cosmology. Suitable for those interested in physics.

Clark, Ronald W. *Einstein: The Life and Times*. New York and Cleveland: World Publications, 1971. **(A, G)** A popular, full-scale biography by a practiced biographer. It is superficial in its knowledge of modern physics and misses the point of the heroic debates between Einstein and Bohr over the interpretation of quantum mechanics. The strength of the book lies in the author's analysis of Einstein's personal life and the bibliography. Clark somewhat exaggerates the scientific isolation of Einstein in later years. It is well illustrated.

Feuer, Lewis S. *Einstein and the Generations of Science*. New Brunswick: Transaction Books, 1982. **(A, G)** A well-illustrated and popular book describing Einstein's contributions in the history of science.

Frank, Philipp. *Einstein: The Life and Times*. Munich: Paul List Verlag, 1949. **(A, G)** A thorough and scholarly analysis of Einstein's scientific, political, and social views written by an associate of Einstein and eminent European physicist. This, the best biography, is filled with pertinent biographical and personal detail.

French, A. P., ed. *Einstein: A Centenary Volume*. Cambridge: Harvard University Press, 1979. **(A)** A compilation of scholarly assessments by internationally famous scientists. The contributors examine the philosophical, educational, and cultural impact of his ideas. The work is supplemented with long extracts of his writings. A reliable and accurate reference source.

Goldsmith, Maurice, Alan McKay, and James Woudhuysen, eds. *Einstein: The First Hundred Years*. New York: Pergamon Press, 1980. **(A)** An important scholarly compilation honoring Einstein's centennial birth year, similar to the French volume in scope and analysis. Contains an excellent article by Joseph Rotblat, "Einstein the Pacifist Warrior."

Hermanns, William. *Einstein and the Poet: In Search of the Cosmic Man*. Brookline Village, MA: Branden Press, 1983. **(G)** A literary and philosophical exposé linking Einstein's poetry to a scientific understanding of the universe.

Hoffmann, Banesh, and Helen Dukas. *Albert Einstein: Creator and Rebel*. New York: New American Library, 1972. **(A, G)** A favorable account of the scientist and activist by close associates at Princeton. One of the three best biographies that competently explains Einstein's role and purpose as a physicist.

Hoffman, Banesh, and Helen Dukas, eds. *Albert Einstein: The Human Side*. Princeton: Princeton University Press, 1979. **(A, G, Y)** A nontechnical compilation that presents new glimpses of the scientist based on discoveries in the archives at the Institute for Advanced Study. Younger students can appreciate the personal side of Einstein.

Holton, Gerald, and Yehuda Elkana, eds. *Albert Einstein: Historical and Cultural Perspectives*. Princeton: Princeton University Press, 1982. **(A, G)** An invaluable scholarly compilation that is particularly strong in its coverage of the historical importance of Einstein's public activities. It contains some worthwhile personal reminiscences. Two interesting articles are Paul Doty, "Einstein and International Security," and Bernard T. Feld, "Einstein and the Politics of Nuclear Weapons."

Lerner, Aaron Bunsen. *Einstein and Newton*. New York: Lerner, 1973. **(A, G)** This comparative biography intelligently discusses the lives, attitudes, and contributions of two of the world's most renowned scientists.

Levinger, Elma. *Albert Einstein*. New York: Messner, 1949. **(G, Y)** Tells the story of the boy who hated school because he could not ask "why" and of the man who, when asked to explain his theory of relativity, offered to play the violin which he believed his questioner would appreciate and understand much better. The book captures the spirit of Einstein's youthful rebelliousness.

Pais, Abraham. *'Subtle is the Lord . . .': The Science and Life of Albert Einstein*. New York: Oxford University Press, 1982. **(A, G)** Provides valuable scholarly interpretations based on Einstein's personal papers. Especially interesting is the author's discussion of Einstein's pacifist views and his support for Zionism. Contains the best annotation of bibliographical sources published since 1960.

Parker, Barry. *Einstein's Dream*. New York: Plenum Press, 1986. **(A)** Although not a complete biography, the author thoroughly examines Einstein's attempt to unify quantum theory and relativity. Contains a sound discussion on the theories of space and gravity. A book suitable for a sophisticated audience.

Sayen, Jamie. *Einstein in America: The Scientist's Conscience in the Age of Hitler and America*. New York: Crown Publishers, 1985. **(A, G)** Sayen's historical account of Einstein's feelings regarding Zionism and the persecution of Jews in Europe is based on numerous interviews with Einstein's relatives, friends, and colleagues. Though limited in scope, the book is historically accurate.

Schilpp, Paul A., ed. *Albert Einstein: Philosopher-Scientist*. New York: Tudor Publishing, 1951. **(A, G)** Contains an insightful introductory analysis of Einstein the thinker by a noted writer on philosophers. Schilpp's intention is to introduce readers into the life and mind of Einstein. This compilation contains some of

Einstein's most important writings, numerous commentaries on the scientist, and a complete listing of his writings to 1949. It is the most complete Einstein bibliography to 1950.

Seelig, Carl. *Albert Einstein: A Biographical Documentary*. Zurich: Europa Verlag, 1954. **(A, G)** An uncritical portrait that contains a compilation of some of Einstein's scientific writings. The book reflects the admiration European scientists had for Einstein.

Whitrow, G. W., ed. *Einstein: The Man and His Achievement*. New York: Dover, 1973. **(A, G)** Another compilation written mainly by scientists who concentrate on Einstein's famous theories.

Overview and Evaluation of Primary Sources

Einstein's forgetfulness, eccentricities, and his refusal to adjust to the common conventions of modern life—his refusal to wear socks, his long white hair, and his unkempt appearance, for example—are far removed from the seriousness of his personal writings. Although treated by both public and the press as a celebrity rather than a scientist, Einstein was a person driven by deep convictions.

The most important autobiographical accounts are *Mein Weltbild* (1934; reprinted and expanded as *The World as I See It* [New York: Philosophical Library, 1949; **A, G**]) and *Out of My Later Years* (New York: Philosophical Library, 1950; **A, G**). In these books Einstein richly details his scientific views of the universe as well as his own personal philosophy respecting social and political issues. Laced with candid opinions, Einstein's autobiographical triology details the realities of twentieth-century life and what humankind must do to preserve its posterity. Also illuminating, especially for his childhood views and early education, is his "Autobiographical Notes" published in Schilpp's *Albert Einstein: Philosopher-Scientist*.

Einstein's early pacifist views have been conveniently compiled and edited by Alfred Lief in *The Fight Against War* (New York: John Day, 1933; **A, G**). Updating his views on freedom, Zionism, politics, education, Nazism, Russia, American customs, women, pacifism and war, atoms, and science is the rich collection that has been revised and edited by Sonja Bargmann, *Ideas and Opinions* (New York: Crown, 1954; **A, G**).

Einstein's major scientific works include *Investigations on the Theory of the Brownian Movement* (Munich: List Verlag, 1926; **A**), an attempt to explain a "unified field theory" linking gravity and electromagnetism, an unsuccessful search he continued until the end of his life; *Relativity, The Special and General Theory: A Popular Exposition* (London: Methuen, 1954; **A**); and *The Meaning of Relativity* (Princeton: Princeton University Press, 1923; reprint 1955; **A**). These last two works contain Einstein's principal ideas on the electrodynamics of moving bodies and explain the theory of relativity of a nonsymmetric field. *The Evolution of*

Physics (New York: Simon and Schuster, 1938; **A**), co-authored with Leopold Infeld, expands his ideas on relativity and his differences of opinion on the probablistic predictions raised by quantum mechanics. The narrative contains no mathematical computations.

A twenty-year legal battle over the publication of Einstein's private papers has been resolved with the appearance of volume 1 of *The Collected Papers of Albert Einstein* (Princeton: Princeton University Press, 1987; **A, G**), edited by Dr. John Stachel. This projected multivolume collection will shed new light on Einstein's life, his theory of relativity and other contributions to physics. Much of the emphasis is on scientific matters.

Beyond his own published writings, the collected material pertaining to Einstein is enormous in scope. Fortunately, all his manuscripts and thousands of documents and memorabilia have been preserved at the Institute for Advanced Study at Princeton, New Jersey. The Princeton University Library has also placed on microfilm his personal papers. Many of his earlier papers and documents left in Berlin were destroyed by the Nazis in 1934. When Einstein died in 1955, his will provided that all of his papers go to the Hebrew University of Jerusalem. In agreement with the Institute for Advanced Study and Einstein's executor Dr. Otto Nathan, most of the collection has been delivered.

Fiction and Adaptations

Though Einstein's life was the focus of considerable attention, he has not been the subject of Hollywood movie makers or television movie producers. However, three scholarly documentaries have been made that discuss the "superstar" of modern science. In 1974, Time-Life Films released "The Ascent of Man" series, narrated by philosopher Jacob Bronowski. Part 7, "The Majestic Clockwork—The Evolution of Einstein and Newton," presents a thorough explanation of the two noted scientists and their understanding of the universe. In 1985, the Public Broadcasting Service Network aired a thoughtful documentary entitled, "Einstein," narrated by actor Peter Ustinov. It discusses Einstein's theory of relativity and its mathematical derivations. Ustinov is entertaining and engaging in describing Einstein's personality and quixotic nature. Also in 1985, Government and Industrial Films for Teaching produced a 30-minute documentary, "From Kepler to Einstein," as part of the Mechanical Universe Series. It discusses how the law of gravity leads to Einstein's general theory of relativity which leads to the mysteries of the black hole.

Museums, Historical Landmarks, Societies

Einstein Statue (Washington, D.C.). A bronze statue by Robert Berks on the grounds of the National Academy of Sciences building on Constitution Avenue.

The statue captures the informal essence of Einstein's dress and manner, yet has him peering down into a correctly scaled map of the night sky, done with bronze pins on black marble.

Institute for Advanced Study, Princeton University (Princeton, NJ). Houses information on Einstein's scientific experiments as well as numerous photographs. The Institute's major focus is to preserve his scholarly research.

National Academy of Sciences (Washington, D.C.). Promotes academic debate and discussion of Einstein's accomplishments.

Other Sources

Cole, K. C. "A Theory of Everything." *The New York Times Magazine* (October 18, 1987): 20–28. Though the author focuses on Princeton University physicist Edward Witten's String Theory, he briefly mentions how Einstein's theory of relativity grew out of efforts to reconcile electromagnetism with classical mechanics. Cole also notes Einstein's unsuccessful struggle to unite gravity with electromagnetism to explain all of nature in terms of one "unified field."

Feinberg, Gerald. "Albert Einstein." In *Dictionary of American Biography*, supp. 5, edited by John A. Garraty. New York: Charles Scribner's Sons, 1977. An excellent analytic study of the scientific work with some discussion of Einstein's interest in world peace.

Josephson, Harold. "Albert Einstein: The Search for World Order." In *Peace Heroes in Twentieth Century America*, edited by Charles DeBenedetti. Bloomington: Indiana University Press, 1986. A superb study of Einstein's contributions to peace activism by a historian of American peace movements. It also contains an examination of Einstein's socialist feelings and beliefs.

Sullivan, Walter. "Einstein Letters Tell of Anguished Love Affair." In *New York Times* (May 3, 1987). A discussion of fifty letters uncovered between Einstein and his Serbian-born first wife, Mileva Marić. The letters reveal the family's disdain for Marić. Einstein's sister and close companion over the years, Maja, conveyed to him the family's belief that the marriage would ruin his future.

———. "West Berlin Reaches for Old Glory in Science." In *The New York Times* (December 1, 1987). Discusses the city of Berlin which for half a century, ending in the 1930s, was the scientific capital of the world. It was the place where Max Planck and Albert Einstein helped lay the foundation of modern physics.

Weiner, Charles. "New Site for the Seminar: Refugees and American Physics in the Thirties." In *Perspectives in American History*. Vol. 2, edited by Donald Flemming and Bernard Bailyn. Cambridge: Charles Warren Center for American History, 1968. A short monograph examining the historical impact that European scientists fleeing Nazi persecution had on the development of American physics. Einstein is the subject of considerable attention. An important article for the historian of science.

Wittner, Lawrence S. "Albert Einstein." In *Biographical Dictionary of Modern Peace Leaders*, edited by Harold Josephson. Westport: Greenwood Press, 1985. A concise, interpretative sketch of Einstein's views and activities on behalf of anti-militarism and internationalism.

Charles F. Howlett

DWIGHT D. EISENHOWER
1890–1969

Chronology

Born David Dwight Eisenhower on October 14, 1890, in Denison, Texas, the third of six surviving sons of David Jacob Eisenhower and Ida Elizabeth Stover Eisenhower; later reverses his given names; *1891* moves with his family to Abilene, Kansas; his father takes a position as a mechanic at the Belle Springs Creamery, while his mother uses the land from their rented house to grow food for all the family and to provide a surplus for sale; *1891–1911* grows up with the work ethic of his mother, separating his day into segments of chores, school, recess, study, part-time work at the creamery, and sleep, with some time for playing Wild West fantasies; *1911–1915* despite his mother's pacifist religious views, enters the United States Military Academy at West Point; injures his knee in a game on November 9, 1912, ending his football career and bringing a decline in his academic and disciplinary standing; *1915* graduates West Point, ranked 61st in academic and 125th in discipline in a graduating class of 164; commissioned as a second lieutenant in the U.S. Army; reports for active duty at Fort Sam Houston; *July 1, 1916* marries Mamie Geneva Doud, daughter of John Sheldon David and Elivera Carlson Doud, in her hometown, Denver, after meeting her in San Antonio; *1917* has a son, David Dwight; *1917–1918* proves so good at training troops in the U.S. that he is denied permission to join combat in World War I; *1918* commands a task corps training center at Camp Colt in Gettysburg, Pennsylvania, advancing to the temporary rank of lieutenant colonel; *1920* reverts to permanent rank of captain and then major, but will remain a major for fifteen years as he serves at Camp Dix and Fort Benning and then graduates from the Tank School at Camp Meade, Maryland; *1921* his son dies of scarlet fever; *1922* a second son, John Sheldon David, is born; *1922–1924* serves in the Panama Canal Zone as executive officer of the 20th Infantry Brigade under General Fox Conner, who believes that Eisenhower will be a top commander; *1924–1925* serves as recreation officer for Third Corps Area in Baltimore, and then as recruiting officer at Fort Logan, Colorado; *1925–1926* attends and graduates from the Command and General Staff School at Fort Leavenworth, as first in a class of 275 of the best officers in the Army; *1926* serves on the staff of the American Battle Monuments Commission under General John J. Pershing, who commanded the Allied Expeditionary Force in World War I; *1927–1928* attends and graduates from the National War College in Washington, D.C.; *1928–1929* serves again with the Battle Monuments Commission, this time in Paris; *1929–1932* serves as assistant executive in office of the deputy secretary of war; *1933–1939* serves as assistant to Chief of Staff General Douglas MacArthur, and then as senior assistant when MacArthur goes to the Philippines in 1935 as military adviser to the Philippines; *1939–1941* returns as lieutenant colonel from the Philippines to become executive officer of the 15th

Infantry Regiment at Fort Ord, California, and then chief of the 9th Army Corps at Fort Lewis, Washington; *1941* reports for duty on War Plans Division as a Brigadier General one week after the Japanese attack Pearl Harbor; *1942* in February, becomes assistant chief of staff for war plans, working directly under Chief of Staff General George C. Marshall; in June, becomes commanding general of U.S. forces training for Europe; in August, becomes commander of the Allied Force that invades North Africa on November 7; *1943* in July, commands invasion of Sicily; in September, commands Italian invasion; in December, becomes commanding general of "Overlord," the invasion of Normandy, France, which will take place six months later; *1944* on June 6, commands the actual invasion; in December, becomes General of the Army; *1945* on May 8, accepts the German unconditional surrender to the Allies; in November, is named U.S. Army chief of staff, a post he will hold for two and a half years; *1948* leaves chief of staff position in May; serves as president of Columbia University of New York City, a post he will hold until January 1950; *1950–1952* serves in Paris as commanding general of the NATO military forces; returns to U.S. in July 1952 to campaign for the presidency; defeats Adlai Stevenson to win the election on November 4, 1952; *1953–1961* serves as president; *1961–1969* retires to farm in Gettysburg, Pennsylvania; *1969* dies on March 28 of a heart attack at Walter Reed Hospital in Washington, D.C.

Activities of Historical Significance

Eisenhower was at the center of American life for over twenty-five years. He was, in turn, a leading military commander of combat forces in World War II; chief of staff of the U.S. Army from 1945 to 1948, at the outset of the cold war; president of Columbia University; commander of the military forces of the North Atlantic Treaty Organization (NATO); U.S. president from 1953–1961; and elder statesman from 1961 until his death in 1969. The impact of such a dynamic life cannot easily be assessed; one can only touch upon his most significant contributions.

As commander of the campaign against Nazi Germany and Fascist Italy, Eisenhower organized a unified war effort that encompassed the diverse political and military goals of the Allied nations. He faced open opposition from above and below in executing the campaign in Europe, but was able to maintain enough control to implement even his most controversial decisions. One of the strategies that caused the most consternation was his plan to attack on a broad front, rather than risking a single thrust that might have shortened the war. His decision not to race the Russians to Berlin also caused an uproar, as some politicians wanted to use the German capital as leverage to establish democratic governments in the Eastern European countries they had conquered. In both of these decisions, Eisenhower revealed a cautious nature that would later characterize his presidency.

Despite his original plans to retire from the military at the end of the war, Eisenhower felt the Army still needed him, and chose to stay on in a leadership position. As the nation moved toward a formal policy of containing communism around the world, many felt that they could rely on the atomic bomb alone for this purpose. But such a policy would have negated the need for a conventional army, and Eisenhower again ignored his critics, joining with the other chiefs of staff to forge common policies to ensure the continued maintenance of adequate conventional defenses (although this was a policy he would back away from when president).

Eisenhower was uncomfortable with the academic world of Columbia University, and was no doubt happy when asked to head the NATO forces. As NATO commander, he faced the double duty of garnering popular support in America while persuading diverse European nations to band together for a common defense. Despite his success in this arena, he was soon wooed back to the U.S. when the Republican party enticed him with the prospect of a presidential candidacy. Out of power for twenty years and fearful of remaining the minority party, the Republicans were eager to head their ticket with such a successful warrior.

As president, Eisenhower faced a Democratic Congress at a time when the American public was restless for serenity after two decades of national crisis. Eisenhower's self-restraint and apparent decency helped create an "era of consensus." Nonetheless, events of great import took place during this seemingly placid period: the civil rights movement erupted, and the Supreme Court followed suit by handing down such revolutionary decisions as *Brown v. Board of Education*; three serious economic recessions rocked the country; the space race and the cold war merged when the Soviets launched Sputnik; and tests of authority swept the world, from the dance floors of America, filled with gyrating adolescents, to the fields of Korea, filled with soldiers fighting a non-war.

Amidst such social chaos, Eisenhower's leadership helped bring the Republican party forward into the modern era. Yet, he moved with characteristic slowness to solve the nation's problems, and many of the great questions were still unanswered when he left office, paving a troubled, ambiguous path of discord for his successor, John F. Kennedy.

Once out of office, Eisenhower continued to be a major political force, rallying to President Kennedy's side during the crisis in Cuba, endorsing Richard Nixon for the 1968 presidential election, and keeping in the public eye through various appearances and advisory positions.

Overview of Biographical Sources

The evaluation of Eisenhower's military career has not changed much over the years. Critics continue to characterize his approach as political, compromising, and cautious. Supporters defend him, portraying him as a commander who allowed necessary latitude to his subordinates.

Eisenhower's presidency, however, has come under more evolutionary scrutiny over the past three decades. William Appleman Williams, often a critic of American presidents, said of Eisenhower, "He turns out to have been saner than either his immediate predecessors or successors in the White House." This assessment found many adherents in the years following 1971; it differs vastly from the negative evaluation of Eisenhower's performance given by most historians during the 1950s and 1960s. Contemporary liberal critics of Eisenhower's presidency attack both the 1950s and its president as being blind and passive to the nation's growing problems.

Critics complained of Eisenhower's failure to resist the harm and hysteria of the Red Scare, to support the civil rights movement, and to respond to the economic recessions. Beyond moral aphorisms and generalities, he seemed indifferent to the political process, too often passively allowing his corporate-dominated cabinet to take the initiative and make decisions. In foreign policy matters, his critics denounced a defense policy that seemed to rely exclusively on the threat of nuclear weapons—a threat which, although too often exposed as a bluff, was still potent enough to allow cut-backs in conventional military spending.

The 1950s are described as a decade of rest for the apathetic majority, wearied by twenty years of turmoil (although later scholars have also noted the country's developing progressivism, as epitomized by the evolution of the civil rights movement). But by and large, the dominant mood of the 1950s America was one of political paralysis, a tone that colored early evaluations of Eisenhower's presidency.

That history has been kinder to Eisenhower's memory than were contemporary analysts is apparent in the reversal of the opinions of historians over the past twenty years: when Arthur M. Schlesinger, Jr., surveyed historians in 1962, Eisenhower was rated as the tenth worst president in American history, but by 1982, a similar survey conducted by the *Chicago Tribune* ranked him the ninth best.

Stephen E. Ambrose has written the definitive biography in two volumes. After looking at an unprecedented amount of material on Eisenhower, Ambrose writes that he approves of Eisenhower's handling of war scares, defense budgets, and the Berlin crisis, although he criticizes his failures in combatting the Red Scare, segregation, and the nuclear menace. In the end, Ambrose concludes, "Whether as President, friend, elder statesman, or family man, he remained what he had always been, a great and good man."

Evaluation of Principal Biographical Sources

Ambrose, Stephen E. *Eisenhower: Soldier, General of the Army, President-Elect, 1890–1952* and *Eisenhower: The President*. New York: Simon and Schuster, 1983, 1984. (**A, G**) Written by someone who has studied Eisenhower for twenty-five years, this sympathetic but critical biography is the best available.

————. *Ike: Abilene to Berlin*. New York: Harper and Row, 1973. (**G, Y**) This work traces Eisenhower's life from his childhood through victory in Europe in World War II. The volume is intended for grades seven and up.

————. *The Supreme Commander: The War Years of Dwight D. Eisenhower*. Garden City, NY: Doubleday, 1970. **(A, G)** The best treatment of Eisenhower's military career.

Childs, Marquis. *Eisenhower—Captive Hero: A Critical Study of the General and the President*. New York: Harcourt, Brace, 1958. **(A, G)** Many were impatient with Eisenhower by the middle of his second term; this volume reflects that attitude.

Davis, Kenneth S. *Soldier of Democracy: A Biography of Dwight Eisenhower*. New York: Doubleday, Doran, 1945. **(A, G)** This well-written book gives the best account of Eisenhower's early life.

Henderson, Phillip G. *Managing the Presidency: The Eisenhower Legacy from Kennedy to Reagan*. Boulder: Westview Press, 1988. **(A)** The author argues that Eisenhower's most important contribution to the presidency was his organizational and management strategy and structure. Henderson believes that ignoring such ordered procedures has hurt succeeding presidents.

Kempton, Murray. "The Underestimation of Dwight D. Eisenhower." *Esquire* 68 (September 1967). **(A, G)** This article is generally viewed as the start of the modification of liberal critics' positions.

Krieg, Joann, ed. *Dwight D. Eisenhower: Soldier, Preacher, Statesman*. New York: Greenwood Press, 1987. **(A)** A collection of twenty-four papers presented at the Dwight D. Eisenhower Conference held at Hofstra University, reflecting the current assessment of Eisenhower's presidency.

Lyon, Peter. *Eisenhower: Portrait of the Hero*. Boston: Little, Brown, 1974. **(A)** Newly available documentation adds weight to Lyon's depiction of Eisenhower as too cautious.

McLanson, Richard A., and David Mayers, eds. *Reevaluating Eisenhower: American Foreign Policy in the 1950s*. Urbana and Chicago: University of Illinois Press, 1987. **(A)** This collection of articles draws heavily on recently declassified materials both to support the notion that Eisenhower's foreign policy was dynamic and defensible, and to point to the possibilities for monographic studies of specific foreign policy programs.

Miller, Merle. *Ike the Soldier: As They Knew Him*. New York: G. P. Putnam's Sons, 1987. **(A, G)** Miller draws on thousands of interviews conducted over a five year period in the 1980s, with those who knew Eisenhower. The author concludes that these reminiscences result in a portrait of the man that is more human, and therefore more revealing.

Reichard, Gary W. *The Reaffirmation of Republicanism: Eisenhower and the Eighty-Third Congress*. Knoxville: University of Tennessee Press, 1975. **(A)** A case study of Eisenhower's successful legislative dealings. This is a good example of many such studies that focus on a particular aspect of Eisenhower's presidency.

Rovere, Richard. *Affairs of State: The Eisenhower Years*. New York: Farrar, Straus, and Cudahy, 1956. (**A, G**) A collection of columns written for the *New Yorker* depicting Eisenhower as a passive but lucky president.

Sixsmith, E. K. G. *Eisenhower as Military Commander*. New York: Stein and Day, 1972. (**A, G**) A balanced account of the British view of Eisenhower's strengths and weaknesses.

Williams, William A. "Officers and Gentlemen." *New York Review of Books* (May 6, 1971). (**A, G**) Williams, the founding father of a new generation of historians critical of American foreign policy as imperialistic, nevertheless finds Eisenhower to have been a better president than many others.

Overview and Evaluation of Primary Sources

Eisenhower was an excellent writer, and left behind several published books and thousands of documents that have been collected and published in various forms.

His own books span his career. In *Crusade in Europe* (Garden City, NY: Doubleday, 1948; **A, G**), Eisenhower gives his own account of the campaign to defeat the European Axis powers of Germany and Italy. In *At Ease: Stories I Tell to Friends* (Garden City, NY: Doubleday, 1967; **A, G**), Eisenhower reminisces about life before he became president. For the presidency, he wrote two volumes, each covering four years of his administration: *Mandate for Change* (Garden City, NY: Doubleday, 1963; **A, G**) and *Waging Peace* (Garden City, NY: Doubleday, 1965; **A, G**).

Eisenhower started painting during World War II, and took it up seriously after becoming president of Columbia University. *The Eisenhower College Collection— the Paintings of Dwight D. Eisenhower* (Los Angeles: Nash, 1972; **A, G**), contains fifty reproductions of his artwork and features a text by Kenneth S. Davis and a critique by Frieda Kay Hall.

Several bibliographic essays in published works provide a comprehensive account of the primary and secondary materials available. In *The Presidency of Dwight D. Eisenhower* (Lawrence: The Regents Press of Kansas, 1979; **A, G**), Elmo Richardson observes that the Eisenhower papers "occupy more than a mile of shelf space" at the Eisenhower Library in Abilene. He advises the reader to obtain a guide to the materials by writing the Director of the Dwight D. Eisenhower Library, Abilene, Kansas 67410. Richardson provides a survey of published primary materials as well as an analysis of the major biographies and other studies of Eisenhower as president. Robert E. Burk, in *Dwight D. Eisenhower: Hero and Politician* (Boston: Twayne, 1986; **A, G**), provides a bibliographic essay that complements Richardson, and a useful chronology of Eisenhower's life. He includes an examination of material both on Eisenhower's military career and his presidency.

Fortunately, many scholars have not only ventured into all these archives and libraries but have evaluated, edited, and collected many materials in published form. The most comprehensive collection on Eisenhower's life from 1941 to 1950 is *The Papers of Dwight David Eisenhower* (Baltimore: Johns Hopkins University Press, 1970–; **A, G**). To date, eleven volumes have been published: Alfred D. Chandler, et al., eds. *The War Years*, 5 vols., which includes an excellent bibliographic essay describing the great mass of primary sources from this era; Alfred D. Chandler, Jr., and Louis Galambos, et al., eds., *Occupation*; and Louis Galambos, et al., eds., *The Chief of Staff*, 3 vols., and *Columbia University*, 2 vols. Many of the official documents are available in one form or another. Ralph J. Shoemaker, *The President's Words: An Index*, 7 vols. (Louisville: E. and R. Shoemaker, 1954–1961; **A, G**), and Robert Vexler, ed., *Dwight D. Eisenhower, 1890–1969, Chronology, Documents, Bibliographical Aids* (Dobbs Ferry, NY: Oceana Publications, 1970; **A, G**), are two excellent guides that should be available at larger libraries. Robert L. Branyan and Lawrence H. Larson, eds., *The Eisenhower Administration, 1953–1961: A Documentary History*, 2 vols. (New York: Random House, 1971; **A, G**), provides a good introduction. The eight volumes of the *Public Papers of the Presidents of the United States: Dwight D. Eisenhower 1953–1961* (Washington: Government Printing Office, 1958–1961; **A, G**) contain speeches and transcripts of press conferences.

Many documents are available to libraries on microfilm. Catalogs of microfilm collections are available from Scholarly Resources (Wilmington, Delaware), which has microfilmed several research collections on World War II; and from University Publications of America (Frederick, Maryland), which has microfilmed several research collections on the presidential years.

In addition to these official aids and materials, there are memoirs by family members, friends, staff, associates, and contemporaries of Eisenhower. His son, John S. D. Eisenhower, edited *Letters to Mamie* (Garden City, NY: Doubleday, 1978; **A, G**) and wrote his own memoir, *Strictly Personal* (Garden City, NY: Doubleday, 1974; **A, G**). The president's brother and advisor, Milton Eisenhower, published two volumes of memoirs: *The Wine is Better* (Garden City, NY: Doubleday, 1963; **A, G**), and *The President is Calling* (Garden City, NY: Doubleday, 1974; **A, G**). Eisenhower's grandson John, in the first of three projected volumes, *Eisenhower: At War, 1943–45* (New York: Random House, 1986; **A, G**), emphasizes the dilemma posed to Allied strategy by the alliance with the Soviets.

Memoirs by those who served with Eisenhower during World War II are numerous. Eisenhower's naval aid Harry C. Butcher wrote *My Three Years With Eisenhower* (New York: Simon and Schuster, 1946; **A, G**). Michael McKeogh, Eisenhower's orderly, wrote, with Richard Lockridge, *Sergeant Mickey and General Ike* (New York: Putnam's Sons, 1946; **A, G**). Kay Summersby, Eisenhower's chauffeur and secretary, wrote *Eisenhower Was My Boss* (New York: Prentice Hall,

1948; **A, G**) and, as Kay Summersby Morgan, *Past Forgetting: My Love Affair with Dwight D. Eisenhower* (New York: Simon and Schuster, 1976; **A, G**), in which she says that she and Eisenhower were in love during the war.

Many of Eisenhower's immediate subordinates also wrote memoirs. For example, Bernard L. Montgomery, commander of British forces, wrote *Memoirs* (Cleveland: World, 1958; **A, G**). Omar N. Bradley wrote *A Soldier's Story* (New York: Henry Holt, 1951; **A, G**) and, with Clay Blair, *A General's Life* (New York: Simon and Schuster, 1983; **A, G**). Few of Eisenhower's cabinet officers have published memoirs.

Fiction and Adaptations

Aside from the numerous newsreels in which Eisenhower appeared during the 1940s and 1950s, his persona has rarely been captured on celluloid. The only feature-length motion picture about his life was the ABC-TV movie *Ike: The War Years* (1978), starring Robert Duvall as Eisenhower, which is now available on videocassette. Two documentary films that can sometimes be found in libraries are *Ike* (1963), a fifty-minute black and white film produced by Hearst, and *Eisenhower: Years of Caution* (1980), a twenty-four-minute black and white video, available from the Learning Corporation of America.

Museums, Historical Landmarks, Societies

Dwight D. Eisenhower Library (Abilene, KS). Also known as the Eisenhower Center, this memorial complex covers twenty-two acres of landscaped grounds and buildings, including a museum, presidential library, the Eisenhower family home, and Eisenhower's grave.

Eisenhower Birthplace State Historic Site (Denison, TX). The house where Eisenhower was born is preserved, along with period furnishings and artifacts.

Eisenhower National Historic Site (Gettysburg, PA). The farm to which Eisenhower retired following his presidency includes original furnishings, equipment, and other items relating to the estate and the Eisenhowers.

Mamie Doud Eisenhower Birthplace (Boone, IA). The site of Mamie Eisenhower's birth is filled with memorabilia from her life and marriage, and has a collection of historical materials relating to the Doud, Carlson, and Eisenhower families.

Other Sources

Irving, David. *The War Between the Generals*. New York: Congdon and Larrés,

1981. Relying almost entirely on primary archival materials, this account focuses on the debates among the Allied commanders in World War II.

Larrabee, Eric. *Franklin Delano Roosevelt, His Lieutenants and Their War*. New York: Harper and Row, 1987. This outstanding work includes an extensive analysis of Eisenhower's role in World War II.

Leuchtenburg, William E. *In the Shadow of FDR: From Harry Truman to Ronald Reagan*. Ithaca, NY: Cornell University Press, 1983. Leuchtenburg, an admirer of Franklin Delano Roosevelt, examines the presidents who followed him and concludes that Eisenhower may have been more active than previously depicted, but that he worked for conservative policies.

Neustadt, Richard. *Presidential Power: The Politics of Leadership*. New York: John Wiley and Sons, 1960. In assessing Eisenhower's lack of leadership in budget matters, Neustadt gives the best expression of the prevailing liberal view of Eisenhower's caution.

Pogue, Forrest. *The Supreme Command*. Washington, DC: U.S. Department of the Army, 1954. Details events and personalities in Eisenhower's command in Europe. This account is one of the so-called "green books," a series of official books prepared by the military historians of the U.S. Army during World War II.

Weigley, Russell. *Eisenhower's Lieutenants: The Campaigns of France and Germany, 1944–1945*. Bloomington: Indiana University Press, 1981. A definitive account by one of the best military historians in the world.

Wills, Garry. *The Kennedy Imprisonment: A Meditation on Power*. Boston: Little, Brown, 1981. Wills contrasts Eisenhower's caution with Kennedy's recklessness, adding to the favorable view of Eisenhower's shrewdness that Wills wrote about in his earlier work, *Nixon Agonistes* (Boston: Houghton Mifflin, 1969).

Joseph P. Hobbs
North Carolina State University

Dwight D. Eisenhower, 1969

CHARLES W. ELIOT
1834-1926

Chronology

Born Charles William Eliot on March 20, 1834, in Boston, Massachusetts, the only son of Mary Lyman Eliot, daughter of a successful Boston merchant, and Samuel Atkins Eliot, who serves during the course of his life as mayor of Boston, member of the United States House of Representatives, and treasurer of Harvard College; *1834-1849* grows up in Boston, completing the rigorous Boston Latin School curriculum at age 15; enters Harvard College, favoring English, math, and science; *1849-1869* participates in laboratory and field work under Josiah Parsons; *1853* graduates second in his class of eighty-eight and begins tutoring in mathematics at Harvard; *1857* appointed assistant professor of mathematics and chemistry; *1861* placed in charge of chemistry at the Lawrence Scientific School; *1863-1865* failing to receive tenure, spends two years abroad studying public education institutions; *1865-1867* is professor of chemistry at the newly organized Massachusetts Institute of Technology; *1867* takes second study trip to Europe; *1869* two articles on "The New Education—Its Organization," which attract wide attention, and his successful administrative record lead to his consideration by the Harvard Corporation for the presidency; inaugurated as president of Harvard on October 15, after a negative and then two divided affirmative votes; *1869-1909* proves an activist president of Harvard University, instituting and supporting many important reforms in electives, admissions, professional education, and other issues which have a profound effect on American education; *1892* chairs and writes the very influential National Education Association's Committee of Ten report; *1909-1926* during retirement, oversees the publication of *The Harvard Classics*, travels, writes, and speaks widely and influentially on diverse topics such as education, labor/management strife, peace, sexual hygiene, and conservation, becoming, in Ralph Barton Perry's phrase, "advisor-at-large to the American people on things-in-general"; *1926* dies on August 22 in Northeast Harbor, Maine.

Activities of Historical Significance

Eliot's historical significance results from his activities over a forty-year tenure as president of Harvard. Through his leadership, Harvard established a Graduate School of Arts and Sciences, and a Graduate School of Applied Science and Business Administration; the university grew from 1,000 students and 60 teachers to 4,000 students and 600 teachers; the endowment increased from $2,225,000 to $20,000,000; admission requirements were toughened; undergraduate instruction was greatly strengthened; Radcliffe College came into existence; the Medical School was greatly improved; the case method was developed in the Law School;

research became a focus for faculty; foreign faculty exchanges were inaugurated; the sabbatical leave was instituted; unique and enduring graduate programs were formulated; the Divinity School became non-sectarian; undergraduate disciplinary regulations were liberalized; required chapel attendance was rescinded; and the elective system was initiated and popularized.

Eliot's ideas and Harvard's success influenced higher education and, subsequently, secondary education as well. His work as chairperson of the National Education Association Committee of Ten led to a report that influenced debate and change in secondary education curricula. The report's call for standardization provided the impetus for college entrance examinations, long advocated by Eliot as a democratizing plan.

In his post-Harvard years, Eliot supported various elements of "progressivism," including better training for teachers, hygienic classrooms, and a more varied curriculum. Retirement also provided him the opportunity to popularize other issues beyond traditional educational concerns (which he continued to influence as a member of the General Education Board) through extensive work with the Carnegie Endowment for International Peace and support for the League of Nations. Eliot's impact was guaranteed to continue for generations through another of his retirement activities, the editorship of the *Harvard Classics*, which brought great literary works, especially Eliot's favorites, to many who were not able to attend college.

Overview of Biographical Sources

There are two important biographical sources on Eliot: Henry James, *Charles W. Eliot: President of Harvard University, 1869–1909* (1930), providing 770 pages of great personal detail; and Hugh Hawkins, *Between Harvard and America: The Educational Leadership of Charles W. Eliot* (1972), which places Eliot more in the developing university culture of America. Of lesser importance are German exchange professor Eugene Kuehnemann's *Charles W. Eliot: President of Harvard University* (1909), which provides a view from abroad; Edward H. Cotton's *The Life of Charles W. Eliot* (1926), which provides more coverage on Eliot's important work on pre-collegiate questions; and Henry Hallam Saunderson's *Charles W. Eliot: Puritan Liberal* (1928), which attempts to connect Eliot to New England intellectual roots. Citations to a dozen chapter-length or short essays on Eliot can be found in appendix 1 of the James volumes.

Evaluation of Principal Biographical Sources

Hawkins, Hugh. *Between Harvard and America: The Educational Leadership of Charles W. Eliot*. New York: Oxford University Press, 1972. (**A, G**) In an analysis of how universities have originated, survived, and sometimes thrived in American society, Hawkins provides an in-depth look at the growing influence of Charles W. Eliot and Harvard during the crucial decades closing the nineteenth and opening the twentieth century. Thus, the work is a combination institutional/personal biography that draws heavily on the Harvard context. Less celebratory than other works and more historical in nature.

James, Henry. *Charles W. Eliot: President of Harvard University, 1869–1909.* 2 vols. 1930. Reprint. New York: AMS Press, 1988. (**A, G**) In Hawkins's words, "this is one of the finest examples of the life-and-letters form of biography." James had strong Harvard connections through family and as a student during Eliot's years, and makes wide use of manuscript sources provided by the Eliot family to, in his words, "delineate Eliot's character, not to hallow his memory or to chronicle all his achievements." James's work is somewhat lax in critical analysis and lower school concerns. He provides an extensive bibliography of Eliot's writings.

Overview and Evaluation of Primary Sources
Although they are not autobiographical, Eliot's writings on education provide valuable insights into the perspectives that shaped his life's work. The bibliography of his works in volume 2 of James's biography is over twenty pages long. Among the most important and enduring of Eliot's works are *American Contributions to Civilization* (New York: Century, 1898; **A**), *Educational Reform* (New York: Century, 1905; **A**), *The Road Toward Peace* (Boston: Houghton Mifflin, 1915; **A**), *The Durable Satisfaction of Life* (1910. Reprinted by Ayer of Salem, NH; **A**), and *A Late Harvest* (1924. Reprinted by Ayer of Salem, NH; **A**). Two brief autobiographical statements can be found in *Educational Review* (1911): 346, and *Harvard Graduates Magazine* (1926): 224.

Manuscript collections pertaining to Eliot are extensive. The Harvard University Archives has nearly 500 boxes, as well as newspaper files and a collection of 900 articles and addresses in the Eliot Papers. In addition, Harvard holds a variety of other important collections containing material relevant to Eliot (see the Bibliographical Note in Hawkins's work). Various official Harvard University publications are also useful: *Annual Report of the President of Harvard University, Harvard University Catalogue, Harvard Graduates Magazine, Harvard Monthly,* and records of the *Harvard Overseers.*

Other Sources
Morrison, Samuel Eliot. *Three Centuries of Harvard, 1636–1936.* Cambridge: Harvard University Press, 1936. Because Eliot's life was so intrinsically linked with Harvard, this is a useful biographical source.

Perry, Ralph Barton. "Charles William Eliot." In *Dictionary of American Biography*. Vol. 3, edited by Dumas Malone. New York: Charles Scribner's Sons, 1959. This brief biographical essay provides an excellent summary of the successful and unsuccessful reform that Eliot attempted at Harvard during his forty-year presidency.

J. Christopher Eisele
Illinois State University

RICHARD T. ELY
1854–1943

Chronology

Born Richard Theodore Ely on April 13, 1854, in Ripley, New York, to Ezra
Sterling Ely, a farmer, and Harriet Gardner Mason Ely, an art teacher and amateur
artist; *1854–1872* grows up in Fredonia, New York; *1872* enters Dartmouth; *1876*
completes his undergraduate education at Columbia; *1876–1879* studies in Europe
and receives a doctorate from the University of Heidelberg; *1881* appointed as the
first economist at the Johns Hopkins University, where he remains for eleven
years; *1884–1897* gives yearly summer courses on economics at Chautauqua, New
York; *1884–1943* writes prolifically on political economy and Christian Socialism;
1885–1888 serves on tax commissions in Maryland; *1886* organizes the American
Economics Association and serves as its secretary until 1892; *1892* becomes Professor of Political Economy and Director of the School of Economics, Political
Science, and History at the University of Wisconsin, where he helps establish the
Wisconsin Idea; *1893* serves as the secretary of the American and Canadian branch
of the Christian Social Union, and as president of the American Institute of Sociology; *1894* wins an academic freedom trial; *1895* serves on the executive committee
of the Wisconsin State Conference on Charities and Corrections; *1900* serves as
president of the American Economics Association, and town supervisor of Madison, Wisconsin; *1918* opposes LaFollette progressivism; founds the Wisconsin
Loyalty Legion and a branch of the League to Enforce the Peace; *1920* creates the
Institute for Research in Land Economics in Wisconsin; *1925* moves the Institute to
Northwestern University; *1932* establishes the Institute for Economic Research in
New York City; *1937* named an Honorary Associate at Columbia University; *1943*
dies on October 4 after returning in poverty to his ancestral home of Lyme, Con-
necticut.

Activities of Historical Significance

Richard T. Ely was an outspoken and controversial academic who believed that
politicians, academicians, and religious leaders should work for social reform. As
political economist, Christian Socialist, teacher, organizer, and author, he was
widely influential. Through the formation of the American Economic Association,
Ely led the effort to professionalize the study of economics and to modify the
traditional concepts of laissez faire that dominated classical economics. His books
on the labor movement and political economy were pathbreaking because they
sympathized with the workers' struggles and called for active governmental involvement in solving industrial problems.

In his lifetime, Ely wrote 26 books and over 300 articles about economic conditions and ideas, including monopoly, taxation, the land, and socialism. As an academic at Johns Hopkins and the University of Wisconsin, he played an important role in the development of American higher education, the modernization of economics, and the emergence of the social sciences. His academic freedom trial established the right of professors to be controversial and to become involved in public affairs. Similarly, the Wisconsin Idea encouraged universities to play a practical role in community affairs as the impartial provider of data and trained personnel to facilitate reform.

Ely was also a prominent proponent of Christian Socialism, a movement that called upon the churches to become active agents of social reform and to reach out to the poor. He viewed problems of industrialization as social problems, not individual failings, in an era when such notions were not widely accepted. While advocating practical policies for change, Ely consistently pursued visions of a humane, Christian world; thus, his economics and ethics were closely intertwined. He played an important role in the modernization and humanization of economic, social, and religious ideas at a time when the industrialization of America was challenging many pre-Civil War assumptions.

Overview of Biographical Sources

Only one major biography of Richard T. Ely has been published, which is surprising considering his importance in American intellectual history. Fortunately, this study by Benjamin Rader is comprehensive and solid. In addition, Ely has been discussed by other historians concerned with the development of ideas during the Gilded Age. Major works by Joseph Dorfman, Sidney Fine, and David Noble contain chapters on Ely that examine his contribution to economic and social thought.

Evaluation of Principal Biographical Sources

Coats, A. W. "The First Two Decades of the American Economics Association." *American Economic Review* 50 (September 1960): 555–572. **(A)** Useful data.

Dorfman, Joseph. *The Economic Mind in American Civilization, 1865–1918*, vol. 3. New York: Viking, 1959. **(A)** One chapter in this multi-volume study of American economic ideas depicts Ely as the leader of the new economics movement in the 1880s and suggests that, despite his support for labor, factory legislation, and the regulation of public utilities, Ely was not really a radical.

Everett, John R. *Religion in Economics: A Study of John Bates Clark, Richard T. Ely, Simon Nelson Patten*. New York: King's Crown, 1946. **(A)** Assesses Ely's contributions to Christian Socialism by emphasizing the religious content of his economics and his role as "preacher" of the Social Gospel through economics.

Fine, Sidney. *Laissez-Faire and the General Welfare State*. Ann Arbor: University of Michigan, 1957. **(A)** In one of the most influential studies of intellectual history in the late-nineteenth and early twentieth centuries, Ely emerges as a prominent figure. Chapters on the Social Gospel and the New Political Economy place Ely at the center of efforts to confront industrialism through the agency of both state and church.

Groves, Harold M. "Richard T. Ely: An Appreciation." *Journal of Land Economics* 45 (February 1969): 1–9. **(A)** Brief homage to Ely as founder of the field and the journal of land economics. This study disagrees with Rader's claim that Ely became conservative after 1894. For a vitriolic attack on Ely and land economics, see Emil O. Jorgenson, *False Education in Our Colleges and Universities. An Exposé of Professor Richard T. Ely and his Institute for Research in Land Economics and Public Utilities*. Chicago: Manufacturers and Merchants Federal Tax League, 1925 **(A)**.

Hoeveler, J. David, Jr. "The University and the Social Gospel: The Intellectual Origins of the Wisconsin Idea." *Wisconsin Magazine of History* 59 (1976): 282–298. **(A)** An examination of the Wisconsin Idea as it reflected Ely's blend of Christian ethics and social science.

Morehouse, Edward W. "Richard T. Ely: A Supplement." *Journal of Land Economics* 45 (February 1969): 10–18. **(A)** Identifies Ely's contribution as a teacher.

Noble, David W. *The Paradox of Progressive Thought*. Minneapolis: University of Minnesota, 1958, pp. 157–173. **(A)** Presents Ely as a complex thinker influenced by the major currents of late-nineteenth century intellectual history, especially the German historical school, Social Darwinism, English liberalism, and Christian Socialism.

Rader, Benjamin G. *The Academic Mind and Reform*. Lexington: University of Kentucky, 1966. **(A)** A thorough assessment of Ely's life and contribution as a reformer. Suggests that Ely was not a radical and that he provided a bridge between old and new ideas. To Rader, Ely was an optimist and a humanitarian who became increasingly conservative after his 1894 academic freedom trial.

Schlabach, Theron F. "An Aristocrat on Trial: The Case of Richard T. Ely." *Wisconsin Magazine of History* 47 (1963–1964): 146–159. **(A)** This sympathetic study of Ely's academic freedom trial argues that Ely was misrepresented as a radical when he was really a moderate blend of conservative and progressive.

Overview of Primary Sources

Richard T. Ely was a prolific writer, and any analysis of his contribution must begin with his autobiography, *Ground Under Our Feet* (1938). Ely's manuscript collection is available on microfilm through the Wisconsin State Historical Society. It includes personal correspondence, lecture notes, pamphlets, scrapbooks, and background essays by members of his family. Information on the American Economics Association can be found in the publications of that group, and material concerning his work on land economics appears in the *Journal of Land Economics* as well as in several of his books. At all times, Ely's writing style was lively and lucid, making him a less formidable subject for research than his academic label and quantity of works would suggest. For a full listing of Ely's books and articles see his autobiography, pp. 309–323, and Rader, pp. 237–253. A convenient selection of his writings on Social Christianity coupled with useful introductions both to the subject and the man appear in Robert T. Handy, ed., *The Social Gospel in America 1870–1920* (1966). Selected letters can be found in Sidney Fine, "The Ely-Labadie Letters," *Michigan History* (March 1952); Joseph Dorfman, "The Seligman Correspondence," *Political Science Quarterly* (June 1941); and Benjamin G. and Barbara K. Rader, "The Ely-Holmes Friendship," *Journal of American Legal History* (April 1966).

Evaluation of Primary Sources

Ely, Richard T. *Ground Under Our Feet*. New York: Macmillan, 1938. **(A, G)** Ely's strong personality is evident in this comprehensive, but easily read autobiography. Ely is outspoken about the various contributions he made throughout his long life.

————. *An Introduction to Political Economy*. New York: Chautauqua, 1889. **(A, G)** This book was widely used and, consequently, had a major impact on late-nineteenth-century thought. It was the first political economy text to openly support the new economics and to advocate state action to address industrial problems.

————. *The Labor Movement in America*. New York: Macmillan, 1886. **(A, G)** In this pathbreaking work, Ely suggested that the efforts to organize labor were necessary to, not destructive of, democracy and capitalism.

————. *Monopolies and Trusts*. New York: Macmillan, 1900. **(A, G)** Along with three articles in the May, June, and July 1887 issues of *Harper's New Monthly Magazine*, this study represents Ely as part of the anti-monopoly movement and the growing support for state regulation of monopolies during Progressivism.

————. *The Past and Present of Political Economy*. Baltimore: Johns Hopkins University Press, 1889. **(A, G)** Ely wrote this book to distance himself from the traditional school of classical economics and to call for a new economics with a nationalist and historical, rather than a universal and theoretical, thrust.

————. *Problems of To-Day*. New York: Thomas Y. Crowell, 1890. **(A, G)** Actually a compilation of newspaper articles written in 1888, this book focuses on the tariff question, the major issue of that election year. It touches upon a variety of problems related to industrialism and reveals that Ely was not a protectionist.

————. *Social Aspects of Christianity*. New York: Thomas Y. Crowell, 1889. **(A, G)** Explains the connection between ethics and economics, religion and social activism.

————. *Socialism*. New York: Thomas Y. Crowell, 1894. **(A, G)** One of several works that Ely wrote on this subject in which he consistently advocated immediate social reform in order to avoid radical social revolution.

Museums, Historical Landmarks, Societies

American Economic Association (Nashville, TN). This flourishing association has established an annual Ely lecture by a prominent economist.

Richard T. Ely House (Madison, WI). His home in Madison is considered a local historical site. At the nearby University of Wisconsin, a plaque on the main academic building commemorates Ely's 1894 trial. The *Journal of Land Economics*, founded by Ely, is still published by the university.

Other Sources

Curti, Merle, and Vernon Carstensan. *The University of Wisconsin: A History, 1848–1925*. Madison: University of Wisconsin Press, 1949. Discusses Ely's contributions to the university.

Haskell, Thomas L. *The Emergence of Professional Social Science: The American Social Science Association and the Nineteenth Century Crisis of Authority*. Urbana: University of Illinois Press, 1977. Examines Ely's role in establishing the American Economic Association as part of the development of the social sciences.

May, Henry F. *Protestant Churches and Industrial America*. New York: Harper and Row, 1949. Provides background on Christian Socialism and the Church's response to industrialism.

White, Ronald C., Jr., and Howard C. Hopkins. *The Social Gospel: Religion and Reform in Changing America*. Philadelphia: Temple University, 1976. A comprehensive view of how the Social Gospel developed and how it was applied.

Joanne Reitano
Fiorello H. LaGuardia Community College,
City University of New York

RALPH WALDO EMERSON
1803–1882

Chronology

Born Ralph Waldo Emerson on May 25, 1803, in Boston, Massachusetts, to the Reverend William Emerson and Ruth Haskins Emerson; *1811* his father dies; *1803–1817* grows up in Boston, attending the local grammar school and then the Boston Latin School; *1817* enters Harvard College at the age of fourteen, the youngest member of his class; *1821* graduates from Harvard as class poet; *1821– 1825* teaches school; *1826* approbated to preach in the Unitarian Church; *1827* graduates from Harvard Divinity School; *1829* marries Ellen Tucker; *1831* wife dies from tuberculosis; *1832* resigns from the ministry, citing his rejection of the Lord's Supper; travels to Europe where he meets Walter Savage Landor, Samuel T. Coleridge, Thomas Carlyle, and William Wordsworth; *1834* returns to Boston; begins a new career as a public lecturer; *1835* marries Lydia (Lydian) Jackson and settles in Concord; *1836* publishes first book of essays, *Nature*; attends a first meeting of the Hedge Club, whose membership includes prominent transcendentalists; first child, Waldo, is born; *1838* begins a long friendship with Henry David Thoreau; rejects orthodox Christianity in an address at the Harvard Divinity School; *1839* preaches his last sermon but expands public lecture circuit; *1840– 1844* co-edits with Thoreau and Margaret Fuller a transcendentalist magazine, the *Dial*; *1842* his son Waldo dies; *1846* publishes *Poems*; *1847* lectures in London and Paris; *1849* publishes *Nature, Addresses, and Lectures*; *1851* speaks out against slavery and becomes involved in the abolition movement; *1856* publishes *English Traits*; *1860* publishes *Conduct of Life*; *1862* meets with President Lincoln to discuss slavery; *1867* publishes *May-Day and Other Poems*; *1870* publishes *Society and Solitude*; *1871–1873* travels to California, then extensively in Europe; *1875* publishes *Letters and Social Aims*; *1882* dies quietly on April 27 in Concord and is buried there.

Activities of Historical Significance

Ralph Waldo Emerson's influence on society was primarily achieved through his writings and lectures. He toured extensively and published lectures, commenting on the public controversies and issues of his day as a concerned private citizen, expressing strong personal views. Indeed, because he believed that the insight of the individual and the dictates of a person's conscience were paramount, he felt compelled to speak out on the issue of slavery, on America's expansionism, and, to a certain extent, on women's rights. In his essays he expressed the tenets of a philosophy called transcendentalism.

Emerson's involvement in the abolitionist movement was sparked by an attempt to enforce the fugitive slave law in New England. Although at first reticent, he conceded that events surrounding this law demanded that he become more politically involved. "These events," he asserted, "have forced us *all* into politics." Emerson went so far as to suggest that the United States imitate Britain's action of buying slaves to free them. He argued against the Kansas-Nebraska bill of 1854 that would have extended the slave trade into a vast territory, hitherto free under the Missouri Compromise. By nature not a "joiner," he nevertheless became a member and outspoken advocate of the Anti-Slavery Society.

Emerson's sentiments made him an enthusiastic admirer of John Brown, whom he received as a house guest and lauded as "a new saint" who was to "make the gallows glorious like the cross." Brown was tried and executed in 1859 after attempting to raid the federal arsenal at Harper's Ferry, Virginia. He had hoped to touch off a slave rebellion.

Emerson's opposition to American expansionism after the war with Mexico (1848) was based on the slavery in Texas. He felt that annexation of Texas further committed the federal government to protecting the rights of slaveholders. He wrote that "swallowing Texas will poison the United States."

When Lincoln issued the Emancipation Proclamation in 1863, Emerson marked the day with a Jubilee Concert in Boston, where he delivered a stirring anti-slavery poem, "Boston Hymn."

Emerson's pronouncements on women's rights were sweeping, yet in some ways contradictory. In an address before a Boston convention for women's rights in 1855, he supported suffrage, the rights of women to own property, to be educated, to pursue a career, and to be elected to public office. However, he idealized the "frailty" and "etherealness" of his first wife as the perfect expression of femininity and showed a marked preference for dealing with timid and unaggressive women. He took it for granted that most women would not want to participate in public life or to pursue an independent career. In his view, "man is the Will, and Woman the Sentiment; for the ship of humanity, Will is the rudder and Sentiment the sail. . . ."

Emerson spoke of the rise of industrial society as a mixed blessing. He was aware of the possible abuses of wealth and power, yet he was optimistic that democracy would eventually check these extremes; he admired the ingenuity of industrialists but could not condone the oppression of the lower classes that he witnessed in England. Although hesitant to participate directly in politics, he was very much concerned with formulating political theory in the hope of influencing his society. In his opinion, scholars were responsible for fomenting an intellectual revolution to jolt the masses from their mediocrity; he saw his own transcendentalism as a faith to rouse others from mental and spiritual torpor, and to realize the divine potential within. This was, perhaps, the source of his buoyant optimism when confronting the social ills of his own country.

Emerson's political philosophy strove to reconcile respect for the freedom of the individual with the good of society as a whole, a view held by other transcendentalists such as William Ellery Channing, Henry David Thoreau, Walt Whitman, and

Theodore Parker. Emerson believed in a divine power he named the "Over-Soul," of which all humanity could partake with equality; all external distinctions between people were, therefore, artificial and should be discarded. Through the application of intuitive reason, all people would eventually free themselves from materialism and achieve a spiritual greatness.

This elevation of the individual and confidence in self-reliance, however, did not mask an underlying tendency toward anarchy. The best government, according to Emerson, is the one that is organized to promote the needs of its citizens and not obstruct them. His ideal state would be unobtrusive with three main responsibilities—to instruct the ignorant, to supply the poor with work, and to mediate between want and supply. This arrangement would be the most productive in facilitating the material quality of life and the spiritual development of its citizens. Emerson's "anarchy" would essentially require each individual to govern himself.

The transcendentalist movement provided Emerson with an outlet for his religious beliefs and political ideals. He became a leading figure in the "Transcendental Club" or the "Hedge Club," as it was known after its founder, Frederic Henry Hedge. He co-edited with Thoreau and Margaret Fuller a review of transcendentalist ideas, called the *Dial*. Through this forum and through his essential writings, he spoke out against the rationalism that was prevalent in the Unitarian Church, placing faith in intuitive reason, "a still, inner voice" that would call all men and women into communion with infinite truth, goodness, and beauty. He knew and was known by prominent men from among the most influential literary, philosophical, and political circles of his time, and he profoundly inspired many to affirm spiritual ideals. His image of the essential dignity of the individual remains significant.

Overview of Biographical Sources

A plethora of biographical material has been produced on Emerson, members of his family, and fellow transcendentalists. In 1885, Oliver Wendell Holmes, another literary luminary of nineteenth-century New England, published one of the first biographies of Emerson, and he acknowledges his debt to the Emerson family for supplying letters and other valuable information. In 1887, a two-volume biography, *A Memoir of Ralph Waldo Emerson*, was published by James Elliot Cabot, Emerson's last editor. His brother, Edward Waldo Emerson, contributed *Emerson in Concord* (1890). Another two-volume book by Daniel Conway Moncure, *Autobiography, Memories and Experiences* (1904), continues the sympathetic portrayal of Emerson provided by those who were closest to him.

In the last forty years, many new works have emerged. Ralph Rusk, *The Life of Ralph Waldo Emerson* (1949), has become a standard reference volume on the facts of his life. This very useful volume, however, tends to gloss over or ignore several facets of Emerson's life which have captured the attention of more recent biographers, namely the dynamics of his relationships with family and friends, and the significance of his writings in the context of American social and intellectual history. Gay Wilson Allen, *Waldo Emerson* (1981), interprets his subject's emotional disposition and literary character, discusses the intellectual climate of his time, and describes the personalities who influenced Emerson's psychology and his work. John McAleer, *Ralph Waldo Emerson: Days of Encounter* (1984), endeavors to capture the elusive essence of Emerson through exploring his personal and professional relationships.

Books about the family, in which Ralph Waldo Emerson is prominent, include Mary Miller Engel, *I Remember the Emersons* (1941); and *The Letters of Ellen Tucker Emerson* (1941), edited by Edith E. W. Gregg. Books which focus on Emerson's relationship with his wives are Henry F. Pommer, *Emerson's First Marriage* (1967); and *The Life of Lidian Jackson* (1980), edited by Delores Carpenter Bird.

Evaluation of Principal Biographical Sources

Allen, Gay Wilson. *Waldo Emerson: A Biography*. New York: Viking Press, 1981. (A) Written by a leading chronicler of Emerson's life and work, this book is an in-depth exploration of the emotional currents of the early years, and an insightful penetration into Emerson's relations with family and companions in the later years. Individual works are related closely with the events of his life; especially helpful is the analysis of his poetry. This biography provides the reader with factual information, as well as a vivid sense of the cultural context of Emerson's time. An extensive bibliography is included to aid further research.

Bode, Carl, ed. *Ralph Waldo Emerson: A Profile*. New York: Hill and Wang, 1968. (A) A collection of essays in the American Profiles Series from such authors as Whipple, Rusk, Brooks, Holmes, Norton, Perry, Hubble, Aaron, and Kleinfield. Representing various time periods and attitudes, these essays range from character studies to political analyses. The different pieces are balanced between blind admiration and more critical appraisals of his work and influence. The bibliography seems a bit outdated.

Holmes, Oliver Wendell. *Ralph Waldo Emerson*. Reprint. New York: Chelsea House, 1980. (A, G) A reproduction of Holmes's original 1885 work that provides a knowing commentary on Emerson's background from one who also emerged from among the New England Brahmins. Holmes's sometimes wittily acerbic comments reflect his own bias away from the mystical toward the scientific; nevertheless, his observations are as instructive for an understanding of Emerson as they are entertaining.

McAleer, John. *Ralph Waldo Emerson: Days of Encounter*. Boston: Little, Brown, 1984. (A, G) An eminently lucid and clearly written account that seeks to capture the essence of Emerson's unique personality through a series of encounters with significant persons in his life. Life events and his written words are woven together to present a living portrait. A very comprehensive bibliography is included.

Rusk, Ralph L. *The Life of Ralph Waldo Emerson*. New York: Columbia University Press, 1949. **(A, G)** The definitive biography for thirty years following its publication, this work is still useful on the facts of Emerson's life. Though rather colorless, Rusk's biography is meticulously researched and objective, avoiding any speculation about its subject's personal life.

Staebler, Warren. *Ralph Waldo Emerson*. New York: Twayne, 1973. **(A, G)** A volume in the Great American Thinkers Series that devotes too much time to familiar material. Generally admiring in tone, but a final chapter breaks new ground by relating Emerson's ideas and "influences" to current social and political events.

Yannella, Donald. *Ralph Waldo Emerson*. Boston: Twayne, 1982. **(G)** A compact volume in the United States Authors Series that is an invaluable resource to the general reader, who should start with this work rather than Rusk's or Allen's. This book serves as a concise, factual introduction to Emerson's life and works. Especially noteworthy is the author's informative treatment of the main ideas of the transcendentalist movement.

Overview and Evaluation of Primary Sources

Ralph Waldo Emerson has left a voluminous amount of written material in several different genres. His writings include sermons, essays, lectures and addresses, poetry, letters, and personal journals, and deal with the widest possible range of subjects—events of his personal life, philosophical thoughts, opinions on the political events and personalities of his era. Many different collections of his work are available. The best collection to consult for autobiographical information is the sixteen-volume *Journals and Miscellaneous Notebooks of Ralph Waldo Emerson* (Cambridge: Harvard University Press, 1960–1982; **A, G**).

Of his speeches, several have been singled out as especially noteworthy. On August 31, 1837, he delivered the "American Scholar Address" at Harvard, which was described by Oliver Wendell Holmes as "our intellectual Declaration of Independence." He decries the dependence of American scholars on European academia and urges students to strike out along creative, individual paths, rather than succumb to "worship" of traditions that have merely been handed down from others.

On July 15, 1838, several years after his resignation as a Unitarian minister, he delivered his controversial "Harvard Divinity School Address." This speech boldly outlines the evolution of his religious ideas and challenges the "outworn, formalized creed" of the Unitarian clergy.

Emerson's essays were no less provocative in his time than his speeches. Of special significance in the history of American letters was the publication of three volumes of essays: *Nature* (1836; **A, G**), *Essays: First Series* (1841; **A, G**), and *Essays: Second Series* (1844; **A, G**). Perhaps, the most popular of these collected essays was published in the 1841 volume as "Self-Reliance." This is an impassioned declaration of the dignity, sanctity, and authority of the individual; the self must be trusted over and above society; "who so would be a man, must be a nonconformist."

Readers may encounter Emerson's opinions on political, social, and economic questions in such works as "Politics" and "Power," also in *Essays: First Series*. In *Representative Men* (1850; **A, G**), Emerson analyzes the attributes and character flaws of six major figures of western civilization: Plato, Swedenborg, Montaigne, Shakespeare, Napoleon, and Goethe. For further exploration of his views on social and political life, see also *The Conduct of Life* (1866; **A, G**), a collection of lectures on success, wealth, and the economy.

Emerson's poetic theory emerges in "Poetry and the Imagination" (1875; **A, G**); this essay provides a useful introduction to his poetry. He published three volumes in his lifetime: *Poems* (1846; **A, G**), *May-Day and Other Pieces* (1866; **A, G**), and *Selected Poems* (1876; **A, G**). Much of his poetry is an evocation of some form of the transcendental experience.

Museums, Historical Landmarks, Societies

Emerson Home (Concord, MA). A national landmark, operated by the Ralph Waldo Emerson Association and open to the public in April and May. The Association sponsors an annual convention which traditionally is held sometime during these months.

Other Sources

Anderson, John Q. *The Liberating Gods: Emerson on Poets and Poetry*. Coral Gables: University of Miami Press, 1971. A useful study of Emerson's theory of the poet as orphic seer and visionary.

Bishop, Jonathan. *Emerson on the Soul*. Cambridge: Harvard University Press, 1964. A thorough examination of one of Emerson's basic philosophical concepts.

Carpenter, Frederic Ives. *Emerson and Asia*. Cambridge: Harvard University Press, 1930. Still the best study of Emerson's orientalism, particularly his interest in neoplatonism, Persian poetry, and Hindu thought.

Konvitz, Milton R. *The Recognition of Ralph Waldo Emerson: Selected Criticism Since 1837*. Ann Arbor: University of Michigan Press, 1972. A survey of Emerson's growing reputation, based on a selection of prominent writers and critics.

Konvitz, Milton R., and Stephen E. Whicher. *Emerson: A Collection of Critical Essays*. Englewood Cliffs: Prentice-Hall, 1962. A valuable collection of mid-century Emerson scholarship, with a number of important essays not collected elsewhere.

Packer, Barbara L. *Emerson's Fall: A New Interpretation of the Major Essays*. New York: Continuum, 1982. A penetrating new study of Emerson the writer and of the relationship between his journals and essays.

Lenore Gussin

Ralph Waldo Emerson, 1940

DAVID FARRAGUT
1801-1870

Chronology

Born James Glasgow Farragut on July 5, 1801, at Campbell's Station, Tennessee, the second son in a family of five children born to George Farragut, a naval and army officer, and Elizabeth Shine Farragut; *1807* moves to New Orleans with family; *1808* mother dies; is informally adopted by Commodore David Porter, who arranges for his midshipman's warrant in 1810; *1811-1814* cruises in Porter's *Essex* until their capture by the British; *1813* Farragut commands his first ship, the prize vessel *Alexander Barclay*, at the age of twelve; *1814* takes the name David Glasgow Farragut in honor of the Commodore; *1815-1820* on routine sea and land duty in the Mediterranean; *1822* serves aboard the *John Adams* carrying the American minister to Mexico; *1823-1824* returns to duty with Porter, combatting piracy in the West Indies; *1823* marries Susan Marchant, settling in Norfolk, his home until 1861; *1825* attains the rank of lieutenant; *1825-1838* serves regular tours of sea and land duty out of Norfolk; *1838* observes the French naval capture of the castle of San Juan de Ulloa off Vera Cruz; *1838-1843* serves several tours on the Brazil Station; *1840* wife dies after long illness; *1841* appointed commander; *1843* marries Virginia Loyall; *1847* on blockade duty in the Mexican War; *1848-1858* establishes the Mare Island Navy Yard, California; *1855* commissioned captain, highest rank then in navy; *1859-1860* commands the *Brooklyn* in the Gulf of Mexico; *1860-1861* awaits orders at Norfolk and New York while the Union navy department debates the trustworthiness of this southern-born officer; *1862* commands West Gulf Blockading Squadron and captures New Orleans on April 25, for which he receives the thanks of Congress and the first rear admiralcy in the navy on July 16; *1862-1863* blockades the gulf and assists the army forces in opening the Mississippi River; *1864* defeats the Confederate flotilla in Mobile Bay on August 5 and receives his appointment as vice admiral December 31; *1866* appointed the navy's first full admiral; *1867-1868* commands the European Squadron on a goodwill tour; *1870* dies on August 14 at Portsmouth, New Hampshire; buried at Woodlawn Cemetery, New York after public funeral on September 30.

Activities of Historical Significance

Had the Civil War never been fought, David Glasgow Farragut would still have been known within the navy as a steady and capable senior officer of long service. His two famous victories during the war, however, came at times of uncertain Union fortunes and endeared him as a hero to the nation as well as to the navy. His victory at New Orleans in early 1862 made him famous for his courage and daring. Farragut's orders required him to bombard Forts Saint Philip and Jackson below

493

the city, capture them, then threaten New Orleans for the army to capture. Quickly finding that the forts withstood his bombardment, Farragut steamed his fleet up the river in a running fight with Confederate land and river vessels, passed the batteries, and forced the surrender of the city to his naval forces, giving the Union a strategic southern base to operate on the Mississippi River. His August 1864 victory at Mobile Bay had a similarly electrifying effect on northern morale. The energy, innovation, leadership, courage and aggressive self-confidence Farragut displayed in leading his fleet through the minefields of the bay and defeating the Confederate naval forces there made him the model of an ideal naval officer for generations thereafter and materially assisted Abraham Lincoln's reelection in the presidential election of 1864. His promotion to admiral in July 1866 made him the navy's first admiral in every sense of the term. His famous "Damn the torpedoes" battle cry has become one of the symbols of naval daring and leadership in crisis.

Overview of Biographical Sources

Farragut has been a popular subject for writers since his 1862 victory at New Orleans. His first biographer, Phineas Camp Headley, wrote *Life and Naval Career of Vice-Admiral David Glasgoe Farragut* (1865) in the first wave of popular adulation at the war's end and is entirely uncritical of his subject. Other admiring works quickly followed, notably J. T. Headley's *Farragut and Our Naval Commanders* (1867), William Henry Davenport Adams's *Farragut and Other Great Commanders: A Series of Naval Biographies* (ca. 1871), and James Barnes's *David G. Farragut* (1899). After Farragut's death, Loyall Farragut acceded to his father's wishes and produced his *Life of David Glasgow Farragut, The First Admiral of the United States Navy, Embodying His Journal and Letters* (1879), which became the primary source material for later writers on Farragut. Alfred Thayer Mahan wrote his analytical *Admiral Farragut* in 1892, and set the tone for most later studies, including the more narrative *David Glasgow Farragut* (1941–1943) by Charles Lee Lewis. Although his biographers have exhaustively chronicled the official life of the navy's most popular historical figure, the paucity of primary source material on his personal life has made any assessment of Farragut as a man difficult. The most successful operational analyses are Mahan's work and Jim Dan Hill's balanced essay in his *Sea Dogs of the Sixties: Farragut and Seven Contemporaries* (1935). William N. Still, Jr.'s essay, "David Glasgow Farragut: The Union's Nelson" (1986), is a recent synthesis of the literature and a good introduction to Farragut's strategy and tactics.

Evaluation of Principal Biographical Sources

Adams, William Henry Davenport. *Farragut and Other Great Commanders: A Series of Naval Biographies*. New York: George Routledge and Sons, n.d. **(G)** A wooden recounting of facts and dates dependent on extensive quotation from other books and after-action reports.

Barnes, James. *David G. Farragut*. Boston: Small, Maynard, 1899. **(G)** An extended essay prepared with the assistance of Farragut's son which quotes some official and personal correspondence but adds little to the public's knowledge of the man.

Headley, J. T. *Farragut and Our Naval Commanders*. New York: E. B. Treat, 1867. **(G)** A popular, admiring character sketch with more emphasis on Farragut's personality than his actions.

Headley, Phineas Camp. *Life and Naval Career of Vice-Admiral David Glasgoe Farragut*. New York: William H. Appleton, 1865. **(G)** The earliest and most speculative of Farragut's popular biographies, it has been easily superseded despite the author's use of Farragut as a source.

Hill, Jim Dan. *Sea Dogs of the Sixties: Farragut and Seven Contemporaries*. Minneapolis: University of Minnesota Press, 1935. **(A, G)** An insightful, clever, and compelling analysis of Farragut's Civil War career.

Homans, James Edward. *Our Three Admirals: Farragut, Porter, Dewey*. New York: James T. White, 1899. **(G)** In his longest essay Homans presents a fairly standard biographical sketch notable for the use of some letters and memoirs of Farragut's junior officers.

Lewis, Charles Lee. *David Glasgow Farragut*. 2 vols. Annapolis: United States Naval Institute, 1941–1943. **(A)** A thorough, scholarly biography, utilizing most known manuscripts, which chronicles Farragut's life in exhaustive detail.

Macartney, Clarence Edward Noble. *Mr. Lincoln's Admirals*. New York: Funk & Wagnalls, 1956. **(G)** A standard biographical sketch with some insight into Farragut's relations with his subordinates.

Mahan, Alfred Thayer. *Admiral Farragut*. New York: D. Appleton, 1892. **(A, G)** More analytical than the narrative study by Lewis, Mahan places Farragut within the context of nineteenth-century naval life and remains probably his best biographer.

Martin, Christopher. *Damn the Torpedos! The Story of America's First Admiral: David Glasgow Farragut*. New York: Abelard-Schuman, 1970. **(G)** A popular, readable biography which suffers from some inaccuracies.

Spears, John Randolph. *David G. Farragut*. Philadelphia: G. W. Jacobs, 1905. **(G)** An unremarkable account dependent upon earlier publications.

Still, William N., Jr. "David Glasgow Farragut: The Union's Nelson." In *Captains of the Old Steam Navy*, edited by James C. Bradford. Annapolis, MD: Naval

Institute Press, 1986, pp. 166–193. **(A, G)** A good short synthesis of modern scholarship on Farragut.

Evaluation of Biographies for Young People

Barnes, James. *Midshipman Farragut*. New York: Appleton, 1896. A popular, readable children's book still in print after more than ninety years.

Beebe, Mabel Borton. *The Story of Admiral Farragut for Young Readers*. New York: Werner School Book Co., 1899. A book for young children, intended to entertain as well as to instruct with fair factual accuracy.

Chavanne, Rose Nelson. *David Farragut, Midshipman*. New York: Coward-McCann, 1941. The author uses Loyall Farragut's book as the basis for this work, which succeeds in capturing the flavor of Farragut's early life at sea but remains more fictional than historical.

Latham, Jean Lee. *Anchor's Aweigh: The Story of David Glasgow Farragut*. New York: Harper Jr. Books, 1968. A well-written book for young adults with some illustrated maps.

―――――. *David Glasgow Farragut: Our First Admiral*. Champaign, IL: Garrard, 1967. Intended for a younger audience, this book is good and colorfully illustrated.

Long, Laura. *David Farragut, Boy Midshipman*. Indianapolis: Bobbs-Merrill, 1950. A highly fictionalized but adequate grade school account of some incidents in Farragut's life.

Mudra, Maria. *David Farragut: Sea Fighter*. New York: Julian Messner, 1953. Although advertised as fiction, this lively youth biography includes helpful bibliographies and chronologies and is probably the best introduction to Farragut for junior high readers.

Overview and Evaluation of Primary Sources

Farragut wrote no more than he had to, and collections of his letters remain small. The best official correspondence has been printed in the U.S. Navy Department's *Official Records of the Union and Confederate Navies in the War of the Rebellion*, 31 vols. (Washington, DC: Government Printing Office, 1894–1927; **A, G**) and the War Department's *The War of the Rebellion: Official Records of the Union and Confederate Armies*, 70 vols. in 128 serials (Washington, DC: Government Printing Office, 1880–1901; **A, G**). Loyall Farragut's accurate, admiring work, *The Life of David Glasgow Farragut, The First Admiral of the United States Navy, Embodying His Journal and Letters* (New York: D. Appleton, 1879; **A, G**), is primarily a collection of quotations from his father's private journal and correspondence. The largest collections of Farragut documents are at the Henry E. Huntington Library, San Marino, California, and the Naval Historical Foundation, Washington, D.C., and are not large, while a tiny collection of Farragut items can be found at the Library of Congress, Manuscript Division.

The largest single repository of Farragut documents is undoubtedly the National Archives, which houses hundreds of Farragut letters in naval and army record groups. The Library of Congress also holds Farragut correspondence in various other collections. Manuscripts relating to Farragut can also be found among the holdings of the William L. Clements Library, Ann Arbor, Michigan; the United States Naval Academy Museum, Annapolis, Maryland; the Virginia Historical Society, Richmond; the University of Michigan Transportation Library, Ann Arbor; the Missouri Historical Society, St. Louis; the Earl Gregg Swem Library, College of William and Mary; the Tennessee State Library and Archives; Syracuse University Library; Burrow Library, Southwestern at Memphis, Tennessee; the Maryland Historical Society Library; and the University of Virginia Library. An 1864 diary of Farragut's private secretary, Alexander McKinley, can be found at the Eleutherian Mills Historical Library, Greenville, Delaware. Some of Farragut's ordnance reports have been compiled and published in the U.S. Navy Ordnance Bureau's *Experiments to Ascertain the Strength and Endurance of Navy Guns* (Washington, DC: A. O. P. Nicholson, 1854).

Fiction and Adaptations

Farragut is the subject of Noel Bertram Gerson's novel *Clear for Action!* (1970). Farragut has also appeared in a few popular movies. The silent version of Cyrus Townsend Brady's novel *The Southerners*, filmed in 1914, highlights Farragut's battle in Mobile Bay. Lew Ayres's 1936 film *Hearts in Bondage* included scenes depicting shipbuilder John Ericsson's attempts to convince Farragut and President Abraham Lincoln of the importance of ironclad vessels. Oliver Wendell Holmes and Henry Howard Brownwell are among the poets who have written verses commemorating Farragut's victories at sea.

Museums, Historical Landmarks, Societies

Farragut Square (Washington, DC). A popular bronze statue by Vinnie Ream stands at the intersection of two subway lines in the nation's capital.

Madison Square (New York, NY). An 1881 statue of Farragut by Augustus St. Gaudens, placed by the Farragut Monument Association, graces the square.

Marine Park (South Boston, MA). Another statue of Farragut stands here, completed by H. H. Kitson in 1893.

Navy Memorial Museum (Washington, DC). Portions of Farragut's most famous wartime flagship, the *Hartford*, are displayed here.

United States Naval Academy Chapel (Annapolis, MD). A striking memorial stained glass window and one of Farragut's prayer books commemorate his leadership and achievements.

Four U.S. Navy vessels (a torpedo boat, a torpedo boat destroyer, a destroyer, a guided missile frigate) and a World War II naval training center in Idaho were named for the admiral.

Other Sources

Montgomery, James Eglinton. *Our Admiral's Flag Abroad: The Cruise of Admiral D. G. Farragut, Commanding the European Squadron in 1867–68, in the Flag-Ship Franklin*. New York: G. P. Putnam & Son, 1869. A detailed, narrative account of Farragut's last voyage with good illustrations and a full chronology.

Paullin, Charles O. "David Glasgow Farragut." In *The Dictionary of American Biography*, edited by Allen Johnson and Dumas Malone, 6: 286–90. New York: Charles Scribner's Sons, 1931. A factual and interpretive narrative sketch by a distinguished naval writer.

Tamara Moser Melia
Naval Historical Center, Washington, D.C.

MILLARD FILLMORE
1800–1874

Chronology

Born Millard Fillmore on January 7, 1800, in a log cabin, in Locke Township, Cayuga County, in western New York State, the first son of transplanted New Englanders Nathaniel Fillmore, a farmer, and Phoebe Millard Fillmore; *1800–1819* grows up in rural, western New York, where family settles in East Aurora; spends early youth as farmer, apprentice cloth dresser, and textile mill worker; *1819–1823* develops an interest in law career, clerks while teaching and is admitted to the bar; *1826* marries his former teacher, Mary Powers of Moravia, New York, daughter of a Baptist minister; *1829–1831* emerges from a successful law practice to become a New York State assemblyman, supports Anti-Masonic Party and champions revision of the state's bankruptcy and imprisonment-for-debt laws; permanently moves to the City of Buffalo; *1833–1835* serves as U.S. congressman; *1837–1843* serves three more terms in Congress; supports Whig party and becomes leading member; elected chairman of the House Ways and Means Committee; *1844* is narrowly defeated as the Whig nominee for governor of New York; *1848–1849* is elected comptroller of New York State; *1849–1850* serves as U.S. vice president under Zachary Taylor, having been nominated on the second ballot of the Whig national nominating convention; *1850–1853* becomes president on the death of Taylor; completes term but is not renominated by his party; *1853* moves back to Buffalo grieved by the earlier death of his wife, who apparently contracted pneumonia at the inauguration of President-elect Pierce; *1854* his only daughter dies during an outbreak of cholera in Buffalo; *1856* as he tours Europe, is nominated as president of the American party, a nativist political organization; returns and campaigns, but the party is badly defeated by the Democrats; *1857–1874* retires from public life; becomes very active in civic affairs, serving as first chancellor of the University of Buffalo; is a founding and active member of the Buffalo Historical Society; *1874* dies on March 8 after suffering a paralytic stroke at his Buffalo home.

Activities of Historical Significance

Fillmore's political career mirrored the fortunes of the Whig party. He became an influential politician and helped form and guide the Whig party in western New York State, an area of increasing political and economic importance. As a Whig congressman and chairman of the House Ways and Means Committee, he helped draft and steer through Congress the protective tariff of 1842, an important piece of national legislation. Fillmore's role as a state and national leader was confirmed by his nomination as the Whig vice-presidential candidate in the 1848 election.

As president during one of the most difficult and argumentative periods in American history, Fillmore signed the Compromise of 1850, a measure that included enforcement of the Fugitive Slave Act. His support of the Compromise Act, though he personally opposed the institution of slavery, personified his commitment to the ideals of national union.

Fillmore's foreign policy initiatives during his short term were also significant. An expansionist but not a belligerent, he dispatched four warships under Matthew Perry to negotiate and open trade channels with Japan. He also resolved to maintain and expand American interests in the Hawaiian Islands.

Fillmore's support of the nativist American party was controversial. Fillmore was not blatantly anti-Catholic, but he did oppose state aid to Catholic schools. Fillmore also believed that unrestricted Irish immigration would disrupt the American election process. He hoped that the American party would stabilize the fragmentation of political parties in the 1850s.

Overview of Biographical Sources

Biographical material concerning Millard Fillmore is not extensive. A small number of late nineteenth- and early twentieth-century biographies were primarily uncritical and superficial chronicles about Fillmore's life and career. The first major study, Robert J. Rayback, *Millard Fillmore: Biography of a President*, was not published until 1959. Since Rayback's study, only one other significant biographical survey has appeared. The dearth of materials on Fillmore can be attributed to a number of reasons. Until Rayback's study, historians were satisfied that Fillmore was a weak politician and ineffectual president. This view was perpetuated by contemporary detractors as well as by Fillmore's political allies, including the shrewd and influential New Yorker, Thurlow Weed. Also, Fillmore was not a popular president. Unionist and compromising views were becoming more untenable in antebellum America. He was overshadowed by more popular and oratorical contemporaries, such as Henry Clay and Daniel Webster. Lastly, biographers had long assumed that a substantial portion of the president's personal correspondence had been destroyed after his death. This was a provision of the will of Millard Powers Fillmore, the president's only son. Despite the apparent recovery of these materials in the 1960s, Robert Rayback's study remains the most complete and concise biography.

Evaluation of Principal Biographical Sources

Barre, W. L. *The Life and Public Services of Millard Fillmore*. Buffalo, NY: Wanzer, McKim & Co., 1856. **(A, G)** A campaign biography written to support Fillmore's candidacy as presidential nominee of the American party. This book was addressed to the nation's "Young Men" as a primer of correct political and moral values.

[Chamberlain, Ivory]. *Biography of Millard Fillmore*. Buffalo, NY: Thomas and Lathrops, 1856. **(G)** Another highly laudatory and uncritical biography intended to support and justify Fillmore's role with the nativist American party.

Grayson, Benson L. *The Unknown President: The Administration of President Millard Fillmore*. Lanham, MD: University Press of America, 1981. **(A, G)** This most recent biographical study concentrates primarily on the president's political career. Grayson provides some rehabilitation of the president's past image by showing him as a principled and courageous individual. The book is thinly documented, however, and adds no new interpretation or revision of Fillmore since Rayback's 1957 study. Grayson stresses the president's often overlooked role in the field of American foreign policy.

Griffis, William E. *Millard Fillmore, Constructive Statesman, Defender of the Constitution, President of the United States*. Ithaca, NY: Andrus and Church, 1915. **(G)** A more interesting and detailed study of Fillmore's life and public career. This is a sympathetic work which praised Fillmore's commitment to national union.

Rayback, Robert. *Millard Fillmore: Biography of a President*. Buffalo, NY: Henry Stewart, 1959. **(A, G)** This remains the most complete and definitive biography of Millard Fillmore to date. Balanced and concise, the author relies heavily on existing primary source material. The study is particularly strong on state and national party politics and political maneuvering during the president's public career.

Overview and Evaluation of Primary Sources

A compilation of Fillmore's important presidential speeches is contained in James D. Richardson, comp., *A Compilation of the Messages and Papers of the Presidents*, 10 vols. (Washington, D.C.: Government Printing Office, 1903; **A, G**). The Buffalo Historical Society holds the major collection of Fillmore's papers, especially those related to his public career. This collection includes a small but important group of papers and writings that were collated and edited by Frank H. Severance in volumes 10 and 11 of *Publications* (Buffalo: Buffalo Historical Society, 1907; **A, G**). This collection also contains a substantial amount of Fillmore's political speeches, addresses, and an interesting autobiography of his early years that he completed a few years before his death. A second group of papers thought to have been destroyed was discovered in a Buffalo attic in 1911. Recognized as the bulk of Fillmore's Presidential Papers, this collection contains approximately 8500 pieces. Despite the size of this collection and its importance, much of the material represents inbound correspondence.

A second important group of Fillmore's papers is housed in the Library of the State University of New York at Oswego. Discovered in a house in New Haven, Connecticut, in the 1960s, this collection also includes numerous incoming correspondence to the president. Approximately 70 letters from Dorothea Dix revealed a close relationship between the president and this noted social reformer and activist. An important and interesting volume of this correspondence was edited by Charles Snyder, *The Lady and the President: The Letters of Dorothea Dix and Millard Fillmore* (Lexington: University Press of Kentucky, 1975; **A, G**). The Oswego collection also includes a draft of Fillmore's first public address, an index that the president maintained of his incoming correspondence, furnishings that the president took when he departed from the White House, and a list of books contained in the president's personal library.

Important but smaller collections of Fillmore's papers can be found in the Thurlow Weed, William Henry Seward, and Francis Granger Papers at the University of Rochester Library; the Millard Fillmore Papers at the Library of Congress; the Hamilton Fish Letterbook at the Library of Congress; and the Millard Fillmore Papers at Harvard University Library.

Considering the length and breadth of his public service, the number of extant speeches, addresses, and letters written by Fillmore is not considerable. For whatever reason, perhaps the reserved and diplomatic nature of the president's character, the scarcity of his outbound correspondence has made full discussion of Fillmore's views and personality more difficult.

Museums, Historical Landmarks, Societies

Buffalo Historical Society (Buffalo, NY). Besides containing Fillmore's papers, the society has a collection of Fillmore's photographs and a number of his personal effects.

Forest Lawn Cemetery (Buffalo, NY). The gravesite of Millard Fillmore is marked by a simple stone obelisk. There is no mention of the fact that he served as 13th president of the United States.

Millard Fillmore Museum and Homestead (East Aurora, NY). A national historic landmark and the only Fillmore residence still standing. This circa 1825 house was built by Fillmore for his first wife. He lived in this house until 1830. The main house contains Fillmore memorabilia and period furnishings.

Other Sources

DeGregorio, William A. *The Complete Book of U.S. Presidents*. New York: Dembner Books, 1984. An interesting and useful quick reference survey of the president's life and public career.

Gienapp, William. "Nativism and the Creation of a Republican Majority in the North before the Civil War." *Journal of American History* 72 (December 1985): 529–559. A recent examination of the motives and political maneuverings of the American Nativist party.

Graebner, Norman. "Zachary Taylor/Millard Fillmore." In *The Presidents: A Reference History*, edited by Henry Graff. New York: Charles Scribner's Sons, 1984. A brief though useful examination of the presidential administrations of Zachary Taylor and Millard Fillmore.

Martin, Fenton, and Goehlert Martin, eds. *American Presidents: A Bibliography*. Washington, DC: Congressional Quarterly, 1987. A valuable source listing of both recent and older bibliographical material.

Russel, Robert R. "What Was the Compromise of 1850." *Journal of Southern History* 22 (August 1956): 292–309. An important study of the Fillmore administration's most noteworthy domestic policy decision.

Vaughn, William P. *The Anti-Masonic Party in the United States 1826–1843*. Lexington: University Press of Kentucky, 1983. A helpful study of the first political party which attracted the attention of Millard Fillmore.

Donald Richards
Herbert Lehman College

GERALD R. FORD
1913

Chronology

Born Leslie Lynch King, Jr., on July 14, 1913, in Omaha, Nebraska, the son of Dorothy Gardner King and Leslie Lynch King; *1916* mother divorces King and remarries Gerald Rudolph Ford, the owner and operator of a small paint factory; is adopted and renamed Gerald R. Ford, Jr.; reared in Grand Rapids, Michigan, with three younger stepbrothers; gains prominence as prep athlete; *1931–1935* attends University of Michigan on a football scholarship; *1936* turns down a pro football contract with the Green Bay Packers to become assistant football coach at Yale University; *1938* enters Yale Law School as a part-time student while still coaching; *1941* receives his law degree and ranks among the top third of a distinguished class; *1942* interrupts a Grand Rapids law practice to enlist in the U.S. Navy; *1942–1945* serves aboard the aircraft carrier *U.S.S. Monterey* in the South Pacific and receives many citations for valor in battle; *1946* is discharged from service as lieutenant commander; *1947* heads Home Front, a Republican organization seeking municipal reform in Grand Rapids; *1948* enters the Republican primary for Congress; marries Elizabeth (Betty) Bloomer on October 15; is elected to the House of Representatives in the fall election as a Republican from Michigan's Fifth Congressional District; *1949–1973* serves thirteen consecutive terms in the House of Representatives, while aspiring to speakership; *1963* is elected Chairman of the House Republican Conference; is selected by President Lyndon Johnson to serve on the Warren Commission to investigate the assassination of John F. Kennedy; *1964* criticizes President Johnson's military conduct of the Vietnam War; *1965–1973* is repeatedly chosen as the GOP House Minority Leader; *1965–1969* teams with Senate Minority Leader Everett Dirksen on the "Ev and Jerry Show," using television to publicize the position of the loyal opposition; *1968* is chosen permanent chairman of the Republican National Convention; *1970* leads an unsuccessful attempt to impeach Supreme Court Justice William O. Douglas; *1973* is nominated by President Richard Nixon and confirmed by Congress on December 6 as vice president to fill the vacancy left by the resignation of Spiro Agnew; *1974* becomes the 38th president on August 9 after President Nixon resigns from office; nominates Governor Nelson A. Rockefeller of New York to be vice president; pardons Nixon on September 17 to heal the divisive effects of the Watergate affair; attends a summit meeting with Leonid Brezhnev at Vladivostok; *1975* initiates an air rescue of military personnel and Vietnamese civilians after the fall of South Vietnam to the communist forces of the North; orders military retaliation after the American vessel *S.S. Mayaguez* is seized by the Cambodian Khmer Rouge; signs Helsinki Accords on human rights; sends Secretary of State Henry Kissinger to mediate peace between Egypt and Israel; appoints John Paul Stevens to the Supreme Court; survives two assassination attempts in September, both in California; *1976* repeatedly uses the veto to curtail deficit spending and check inflation; issues an executive order to instigate reforms of intelligence gathering agencies; wins the GOP presidential nomination over Ronald Reagan on the first ballot at the Republican National Convention in Kansas City; loses the presidential election to Democratic nominee Jimmy Carter by a close electoral vote of 297 to 240; *1979* writes his memoir, *A Time to Heal; 1980* is seriously considered by presidential candidate Ronald Reagan as a running mate; remains active during post-presidency as a political campaigner, elder statesman of party, educator, and business entrepreneur.

Activities of Historical Significance

Ford was the nation's first nonelected vice president selected under the twenty-fifth amendment and also became the first nonelected president. His administration, which lasted only 835 days, was marked by political controversy stemming from the legacy of the Watergate scandal, his grant of a presidential pardon to Nixon, and the turmoil following the American withdrawal from Vietnam. He was only partially successful in resisting the national mood of neoisolationism and thwarting the intent of a strong Democratic Congress to prevent further overseas military involvement. Ford made formidable use of his veto power (using it over fifty times) to check excess government spending while pursuing a conservative fiscal policy to reduce the negative economic impact of high inflation. Nevertheless, Ford was never a rigid ideologue and sought compromise with Congress whenever possible.

In the realm of international affairs, where he was greatly influenced by the views of Henry Kissinger, Ford pursued a policy of détente with the Soviet Union; diplomatic rapprochement with the People's Republic of China; transfer of the Panama Canal to the Republic of Panama; peace through a balance of power between Egypt and Israel in the Middle East; and containment of communist expansion in Africa. Ford's foreign policy was challenged by liberal, "dovish" Democrats as being too belligerent and by conservative, "hawkish" Republicans for being ineffective in stopping the advance of communist imperialism.

After beating back a strong challenge from Ronald Reagan for the 1976 GOP presidential nomination, Ford waged a hard-fought campaign as the underdog to try to win the White House on his own. His chances were hurt by frequent media references to Watergate; by a persistent public image as a clumsy bungler; by his firing of Secretary of Agriculture Earl Butz for making a racial slur while telling an off-color joke; and by the poor showing of his running mate, Senator Robert Dole, in a public debate with Democratic nominee Walter Mondale. Ford's own misstatement in a televised debate with Jimmy Carter, in which he denied Poland was under the domination of the Soviet Union, severely hurt his chances for election. Although winning twenty-seven states to Carter's twenty-three (and the District of

Columbia), Ford lost the popular vote by 1,678,069 out of a total of 81.5 million votes cast nationally. Despite his relatively short tenure, he is remembered as a president who, with personal candor and decency, restored honor and integrity to the presidency while preserving basic executive prerogatives during a stormy period in American politics.

Overview of Biographical Sources

The early biographies of Ford are by journalists who wrote without the benefit of archival sources or the perspective of time. All were written while he was president and thus reflect the political passions of that era. Most noteworthy of these is Jerald F. terHorst, *Gerald R. Ford and the Future of the Presidency* (1974). Others of this genre include Bud Vestal, *Jerry Ford, Up Close* (1974); Richard Reeves, *A Ford, Not a Lincoln* (1975); Clark Mollenhoff, *The Man Who Pardoned Nixon* (1976); and John Osborne, *White House Watch: The Ford Years* (1977).

A second category of books about Ford are those written by associates who served him while President. Most were published within five years after Ford left the White House and reflect the point of view of insiders who were generally sympathetic to the president and his actions. These include Malcom MacDougall, *We Almost Made It* (1977); John J. Casserly, *The Ford White House: Diary of a Speechwriter* (1977); Ron Nessen, *It Sure Looks Different from the Inside* (1978); David Kennerly, *Shooter* (1979); Robert T. Hartmann, *Palace Politics: An Insider's Account of the Ford Years* (1980); and Henry Kissinger, *White House Years* (1979) and *Years of Upheaval* (1982). Also useful is Sheila Rabb Weidenfeld, *First Lady's Lady: With the Fords in the White House* (1979).

Evaluation of Principal Biographical Sources

Casserly, John J. *The Ford White House: Diary of a Speechwriter*. Boulder: Colorado Associated University Press, 1977. **(G)** Personal recollections based on the diary of a White House speechwriter. It is subjective but contains useful information, as well as judgmental comments on Ford's tenure.

Hartmann, Robert T. *Palace Politics: An Insider's Account of the Ford Years*. New York: McGraw-Hill, 1980. **(A, G)** Though highly critical of some White House staffers, this is one of the most informative accounts written by an insider who served as an aide to Ford while he was minority leader, vice president, and president. It reveals the author's own biases, but is frank and contains a critical evaluation.

Kissinger, Henry A. *White House Years*. Boston and Toronto: Little, Brown, 1979; *Years of Upheaval*. Boston and Toronto: Little, Brown, 1982. **(A)** A superbly written account of foreign policy decisions made during the Ford years as interpreted by the former Secretary of State. It concentrates more on Nixon's presidency than Ford's, but is nevertheless useful.

McDougall, Malcom D. *We Almost Made It*. New York: Crown Publishers, 1977. **(G, Y)** An inside version of the Ford presidential campaign by a media specialist who planned it.

Mollenhoff, Clark R. *The Man Who Pardoned Nixon*. New York: St. Martin's Press, 1976. **(G, Y)** A highly unflattering study written in the sensationalist style of an investigative reporter. It reflects the suspicious "Watergate" mentality of the press during an election year.

Nessen, Ron. *It Sure Looks Different from the Inside*. New York: Simon and Schuster, 1978. **(G, Y)** Recounts interesting episodes involving Ford as well as anecdotes and inside information as told by a former presidential press secretary.

Osborne, John. *White House Watch: The Ford Years*. Washington, D.C.: New Republic, 1977. **(G, Y)** A compilation of articles written by a liberal reporter for the *New Republic* magazine while Ford was president.

Reeves, Richard. *A Ford, Not a Lincoln*. New York: Harcourt Brace Jovanovich, 1975. **(G, Y)** A critical portrait presented by a journalist who approaches his subject in an unsympathetic manner.

terHorst, Jerald F. *Gerald Ford and the Future of the Presidency*. New York: Third Press, 1974. **(G, Y)** The coverage of Ford's early years is excellent, but, since this ex-press secretary to the president resigned over the Nixon pardon, the narrative stops at that point.

Vestal, Bud. *Jerry Ford, Up Close: An Investigative Biography*. New York: Coward, McCann and Geoghagen, 1974. **(G, Y)** Written in a reportorial style with a tendency toward faultfinding as befits an investigative journalist.

Weidenfeld, Sheila Rabb. *First Lady's Lady: With the Fords at the White House*. New York: Putnam, 1979. **(G, Y)** Although informal and gossipy in tone, it reveals the problems encountered by Betty Ford as First Lady.

Overview and Evaluation of Primary Sources

The starting point for studying Ford's life and career is to read his candid personal memoir, *A Time to Heal: The Autobiography of Gerald R. Ford* (New York: Harper and Row/Reader's Digest, 1979; **A, G**). In a straightforward manner he relates the details of his early life and the highlights of his political career. It is valuable for an understanding of why Ford took particular political stands and the circumstances under which he made certain crucial decisions as a congressman, vice president, and president. Also useful are the reminiscences of Betty Ford in her *The Times Of My Life* (New York: Harper and Row/Reader's Digest, 1979; **G, Y**) and to a lesser extent *Betty: A Glad Awakening* (Garden City: Doubleday, 1987; **G, Y**). The first of these books relates primarily her relations with Ford as his wife, but also comments on White House events during her years as First Lady. The second autobiography discusses her personal ordeal with alcoholism and drug dependency.

The largest collection of primary materials, which are indispensable in researching Ford's life and career, are located in the Gerald R. Ford Library at Ann Arbor, Michigan. All of Ford's papers and the papers of many who served in his administration are deposited here; it is the prime archival source for historical research dealing with all phases of Ford's long career as a public servant.

Significant materials dealing with Ford's role as a municipal reformer in Grand Rapids are found in the Bentley Historical Library at Ann Arbor, Michigan. Much useful material relating to Ford's tenure in Congress can be found in the following presidential libraries: Harry S Truman Library (Independence, Missouri); Dwight D. Eisenhower Library (Abilene, Kansas); John F. Kennedy Library (Cambridge, Massachusetts); and the Lyndon Baines Johnson Library (Austin, Texas). The Everett McKinley Dirksen Congressional Leadership Library at Pekin, Illinois, contains significant material relating to Ford as GOP House Minority Leader.

An invaluable collection of published documents is the multi-volume *Public Papers and Addresses of the Presidents, Gerald R. Ford, 1973–1977* (Washington: Government Printing Office, 1975–1979; **A, G**). Also helpful for preliminary research is George Lankevich, *Gerald R. Ford-Chronology-Documents-Bibliographical Aids* (Dobbs Ferry, NY: Oceana Publications, 1977; **A, G, Y**).

Museums, Historical Landmarks, Societies

Gerald R. Ford Birthplace Memorial Park (Omaha, NE). Located where the house in which Ford was born stood before an accidental fire destroyed it. An exhibit case within a gazebo displays photographs of the home as it looked at the time of Ford's birth. The park contains a rose garden dedicated to Betty Ford.

Gerald R. Ford Museum (Grand Rapids, MI). Houses memorabilia, exhibits, displays, photographs, and significant documents relating to Ford's life and political career. Films are shown daily and special programs are presented that deal with contemporary and historical events.

Other Sources

A Discussion With Gerald R. Ford, The American Presidency. Washington, D.C.: American Enterprise Institute for Public Policy Research, 1977. President Ford discusses the achievements and failures of his administration.

"How Good A President? An Appraisal of the Middle American in the White House." *Newsweek* 99 (October 18, 1976): 28–31. A pre-election evaluation of Ford's presidency in terms of his midwestern conservatism.

Huckshorn, Robert J. "Gerald R. Ford." In *The Encyclopedia Americana*. Danbury, CT: Grolier, 1948. A factual, straightforward account of Ford's life and political career.

Kraus, Sidney, ed. *The Great Debates: Carter vs. Ford, 1976*. Bloomington and London: Indiana University Press, 1979. The exact text and critical analysis of the 1976 presidential debate between Ford and Carter.

Natoli, Marie D. "The Vice Presidency: Gerald Ford as Healer?" *Presidential Studies Quarterly* 10 (Fall 1980): 662–664. A short but significant appraisal of Ford as vice president.

Reichley, A. James. *Conservatism in an Age of Change, The Nixon and Ford Administrations*. Washington, D.C.: The Brookings Institution, 1981. Focuses on the continuity between the Nixon and Ford presidencies as it relates to domestic and foreign policy.

Schapsmeier, Edward L., and Frederick H. Schapsmeier. "Gerald R. Ford's Roots in Omaha." *Nebraska History* 68 (Summer 1987): 56–62. Elaborates on Ford's relations with his biological father, his subsequent adoption by Gerald R. Ford, Sr., and the impact of the latter on his life.

Sloan, John W. "The Ford Presidency: A Conservative Approach to Economic Management." *Presidential Studies Quarterly* 14 (Fall 1984): 526–537. Presents a favorable assessment of Ford's economic policies from a conservative viewpoint.

terHorst, Jerald F. "Gerald R. Ford." In *The World Book Encyclopedia*. Chicago: World Book, 1986. A succinct and well written account of Ford's political career.

Turner, Michael. *The Vice President As Policy Maker: Rockefeller in the Ford White House*. Westport, CT: Greenwood Press, 1982. Discusses Rockefeller's relations with Ford and the former's role as vice president.

Edward L. Schapsmeier
Illinois State University

HENRY FORD
1863–1947

Chronology

Born Henry Ford on July 30, 1863, in Greenfield Township (now Dearborn), Michigan, the second of eight children of William Ford and Mary Litogot Ford; *1863–1879* grows up on family farm; attends local schools; acquires fascination with machinery; *1879–1899* moves to Detroit; learns machinist trade; marries Clara Bryant; experiments with engines; is employed as engineer by Edison Illuminating Company; builds operable gasoline-fueled car; *1899–1903* fails at first two automobile manufacturing ventures; turns to automobile racing as publicity device; gains sufficient financial backing to launch Ford Motor Company; *1903–1909* acquires majority of firm's stock; adopts policy of standardized design, interchangeable parts, and low price to reach mass market; introduces Model T; begins construction of massive plant at Highland Park, north of Detroit; *1909–1915* successfully challenges patent monopoly of Association of Licensed Automobile Manufacturers; expands dealership network; installs continuously moving assembly line; adopts eight-hour shift and $5-a-day basic wage for workers; consolidates industry leadership; *1915–1920* turns out millionth Model T; opposes military preparedness and United States involvement in World War I; finances "Peace Ship" project for ending war; supports President Woodrow Wilson's reelection and United States membership in the League of Nations; wins Democratic nomination for United States Senator but is narrowly defeated by Republican Truman H. Newberry; installs son Edsel as company president but retains personal control; becomes embroiled in legal battle with minority stockholders over dividend policy, and threatens to start a rival firm to buy out their holdings; the firm becomes completely family-owned; sues *Chicago Tribune* for libel; *1920–1927* conducts virulent anti-Semitic campaign in the *Dearborn Independent* until forced to backtrack by resulting defamation suit; raises money to pay off bank loans to finance buy-out of minority stockholders by pressuring dealers to take cars; weakens company by driving out independent-minded lieutenants; purchases Lincoln Motor Car Company; builds immense River Rouge industrial complex in Dearborn; extends holdings to include glass factory, rubber plantation, iron and coal mines, railroad, and aircraft manufacturing; makes bid to purchase government-built hydroelectric facilities at Muscle Shoals on the Tennessee River; is spoken of seriously as possible presidential candidate; loses automobile industry leadership to General Motors; *1927–1933* discontinues production of Model T; introduces Model A; replaces Model A with Ford V-8; begins to devote more and more attention to building museum for early American artifacts and miniature rural village at Dearborn; *1933–1941* is strongly hostile to New Deal; refuses to cooperate with National Recovery Administration; adamantly resists unionization; sees company slide to third place behind General Motors and Chrysler; opposes U.S. involvement in World War II; suffers from deteriorating physical and mental health; *1941* is forced to recognize United Auto Workers; *1943* resumes company presidency after death of son Edsel; *1945* is replaced by grandson, Henry Ford II; retires from active role in company; *1947* dies on April 7 of a massive cerebral hemorrhage at his Fair Lane estate in Dearborn.

Activities of Historical Significance

Ford's personal role in revolutionizing the motor car industry is difficult to assess. Much of the firm's success is attributable to James Couzens, who managed the business until resigning in 1915 to protest Ford's use of company advertising to promote his political views. Ford's achievements on the production side also owed much to key lieutenants such as C. Harold Wills, William S. Knudsen, and Charles E. Sorenson. Ford did not play a significant role in the development of the basic technology of the motor car, although he was responsible for such improvements as the Model T's four-cylinder, single-block, water-cooled engine and the eight-cylinder V-8 engine introduced in 1932. His major contribution lay in transforming the automobile from a luxury into a necessity. The key to that achievement was the adoption of a standardized design using interchangeable parts and cutting costs through mass production techniques. His introduction of the assembly line made the Ford name synonomous with the most advanced and efficient production methods. And he, more than anyone else, foresaw the development of a mass production-consumption economy based upon low prices, high wages, and volume output.

Ford's policy of putting the bulk of the profits back into the company was responsible for its rapid growth. But his tight-fisted limiting of stock dividends embroiled him in a bitter legal battle with the minority stockholders. Ford exploited his threat of starting a rival company to buy out their holdings in 1919, thereby making the firm totally family-owned. But his dictatorial style proved a long-run liability as one after another of his more able lieutenants left. Although Ford installed his son Edsel as company president in 1918, he never gave him enough authority to run the firm. Ford himself eventually became a figurehead, manipulated first by his personal secretary, Ernest G. Liebold, and then by his security chief, Harry H. Bennett. As a result, no one was in a position to halt the company's decline in the face of competition from General Motors and Chrysler.

By the mid-1920s, Ford's once magic touch appeared to desert him. His ambitious plans to make the River Rouge complex a model of vertical integration never fully succeeded. Most important, Ford himself grew increasingly rigid in his views and out of touch with changing public tastes. The Model T's sturdiness, lightness, cheapness, and low operating costs made the car the favorite of rural and small-town America. At the height of its popularity—1921—the Model T accounted for approximately 56 percent of all cars sold in the United States. Increasingly, however, Americans were coming to want more from a car than simply utilitarian transportation; they were looking rather for comfort, style, and status. General Motors took advantage of this new marketing environment. Ford stood adamantly by the Model T. Symbolic of this rigidity was his decision to produce only black cars from 1914 to 1926. The introduction of the Model A in 1927 and of the Ford V-8 five years later failed to halt the company's decline. By 1936, Ford had slipped to third place in the industry, behind General Motors and Chrysler.

Ford had become a folk hero to millions of Americans and had even been seriously considered as a possible presidential candidate in the early 1920s. His popularity had survived the exposure of the large wartime profits made by the company despite promises to the contrary. By the 1930s, however, Ford's reputation began to lose much of its former luster. A strong opponent of United States involvement in World War II and supporter of America First, he was accused of pro-Hitler sympathies because of his acceptance of a medal from the Nazi government. But the major focal point of controversy became his company's labor relations. Despite the much vaunted "Five Dollar Day" wage policy, a substantial number of Ford employees never received that much. In fact, by the 1930s, Ford was regarded as having the lowest wages and worst working conditions in the industry. Ford adamantly resisted unionization efforts by the United Auto Workers with a violent campaign masterminded by Harry Bennett. After repeated findings of unfair labor practices by the National Labor Relations Board, he finally had to recognize the union in 1941.

World War II probably saved the company from collapse. But its productive achievements—most notably, the gigantic facility at Willow Run, Michigan, for building B-24 bombers—were largely the work of Charles E. Sorenson. After his son Edsel died in May 1943, Ford resumed the company presidency despite his deteriorating physical and mental health. Effective power, however, fell into the hands of Bennett, who forced Sorenson out in 1944. In 1945, Ford's eldest grandson, Henry Ford II, took over the presidency during a countercoup. The old man faded into quiet retirement until his death from a massive cerebral hemorrhage at his Fair Lane estate in Dearborn. The bulk of his stock in the Ford Motor Company was left to the Ford Foundation, which then became the world's richest private foundation.

Ford's personality was strangely contradictory. He had an idealistic strain, evidenced by his pacifism in World War I, admiration for Woodrow Wilson, support of American membership in the League of Nations, and labor policies. But he could be ruthless, unscrupulous, and vindictive. The pressure Ford exerted upon his dealers in 1921 to raise the cash to pay off the bank loans he had secured to buy out his minority stockholders serves as an example of these traits.

Although he had an instinctive genius for things mechanical, outside that area he was ill-informed, provincial, and bigoted. As he grew older, the negative side of his personality dominated. Hurt by the abuse he suffered because of his antipreparedness stand and by the ridicule directed against his "Peace Ship" project, Ford was even further embittered by his defeat for the United States Senate in 1918. Ford's bitterly fought race against Truman H. Newberry was marked by allegations that Ford and his son were unpatriotic. Ford retaliated by financing an investigation of alleged malpractice in the Newberry campaign that eventually led to Newberry's forced resignation from the Senate. The final blow was dealt Ford during his million-dollar libel suit against the *Chicago Tribune* over an editorial that had called him an "anarchist" and "an ignorant idealist" for opposing "preparedness." During their cross-examination, the *Tribune's* lawyers publicly humiliated him by exposing his ignorance on matters of general knowledge. Consequently, the jury, while it found the *Tribune* guilty of libel, awarded Ford only an insulting six cents in damages.

Ford's conviction that he was the target of a conspiracy by his enemies was most strikingly revealed in the virulent anti-Semitic campaign he launched through his weekly *Dearborn Independent* in 1920. Ford's resulting feud with a Chicago lawyer led to a defamation suit that Ford was forced to settle out-of-court in 1927.

As a young man, Ford was no admirer of farm life. By the latter 1920s, however, he had succumbed to a romanticized nostalgia for the good old days before the machine age that he himself had done so much to advance. He devoted more and more of his time to building a museum of early American artifacts (first named the Edison Institute after his friend, inventor Thomas A. Edison; in 1952 renamed the Henry Ford Museum) and an adjoining miniature rural community known as Greenfield Village, which were opened to the public in 1933. The total cost was approximately $30 million.

Overview of Biographical Sources

Much of the immense body of writing on Ford published during his lifetime was highly uncritical. Typical of this genre were Charles Merz, *And Then Came Ford* (1929), and William A. Simonds, *Henry Ford: His Life, His Work, His Genius* (1943). At the other extreme were such hostile polemics as Jonathan N. Leonard's *The Tragedy of Henry Ford* (1932) and Upton Sinclair's *The Flivver King* (1937). Another large body of works consisted of recollections by former associates. The most insightful and valuable are Samuel S. Marquis, *Henry Ford, An Interpretation* (1923); Garet Garrett, *The Wild Wheel* (1952); and Charles E. Sorenson, *My Forty Years with Ford* (1956). By contrast, Harry Bennett's *We Never Called Him Henry* (1951) is a blatantly self-serving account that must be read with caution. The first attempt at a biography based upon solid research was Keith Sward's *The Legend of Henry Ford* (1958). Sward had to rely for the most part upon the public record—newspapers, court proceedings, government investigations and reports—and his aim, as his title suggests, was debunking. Still, the work remains a landmark contribution as the first scholarly treatment of Ford. Other works warranting attention are William C. Richards's anecdotal *The Last Billionaire* (1948); Roger Burlingame's brief and readable *Henry Ford: A Great Life in Brief* (1954); and Anne Jardim's exercise in psychobiography, *The First Henry Ford: A Study in Personality and Business Leadership* (1970). But the fullest and most thoroughly researched account of Ford and his company is the monumental three-volume work by Allan Nevins and Frank Ernest Hill, published between 1954 and 1963. The Nevins-Hill work, in turn, became the major source for such later popularized accounts as James Brough's *The Ford Dynasty: An American Story* (1977) and Robert Lacey's *Ford: The Men and the Machines* (1986).

Evaluation of Principal Biographical Sources

Bennett, Harry, as told to Paul Marcus. *We Never Called Him Henry*. New York: Gold Medal Books, 1951. **(G)** A self-serving account by Ford's security chief and right-hand man that glosses over or denies personal responsibility for the abuses suffered by the company's workers.

Brough, James. *The Ford Dynasty: An American Story*. Garden City, NY: Doubleday, 1977. **(G)** A pot-boiler written for the popular market.

Burlingame, Roger. *Henry Ford: A Great Life in Brief*. New York: Alfred A. Knopf, 1954. **(G)** A brief, readable, and reasonably balanced biographical sketch. Although Burlingame appears to have consulted some Ford Archives materials, the work is intended for a popular audience.

Garrett, Garet. *The Wild Wheel*. New York: Pantheon, 1952. **(G)** A perceptive character sketch by a journalist who had known Ford for more than thirty years.

Jardim, Anne. *The First Henry Ford: A Study in Personality and Business Leadership*. Cambridge, MA: MIT Press, 1970. **(A)** An exercise in psychobiography that blames the contradictions in Ford's personality on his love-hate relationship with his father. Although the work is factually accurate, most readers will be put off by its flights into the realm of psychoanalytical fantasy.

Lacey, Robert. *Ford: The Men and the Machines*. Boston: Little, Brown, 1986. **(G)** Includes new material on Henry Ford II's tenure, but consists largely of familiar information about Henry Ford, Sr.

Leonard, Jonathan N. *The Tragedy of Henry Ford*. New York: G. P. Putnam's Sons, 1932. **(G)** Pictures Ford as a Frankenstein-like monster driven by his own personal demons. Like most of the early writing on Ford, whether pro or con, the work is undocumented.

Marquis, Samuel S. *Henry Ford, An Interpretation*. Boston: Little, Brown, 1923. **(G)** The author was an Episcopalian minister whom, in 1915, Ford named head of the company's Sociological Department, an experiment in welfare capitalism for workers and their families. Because Marquis was extremely close to Ford until he left the firm in the winter of 1920–1921, this character sketch is illuminating even if turgidly written.

Merz, Charles. *And Then Came Ford*. Garden City, NY: Doubleday, Doran, 1929. **(G)** Written in a breathless prose style that reads like a company press release.

Nevins, Allan, and Frank Ernest Hill. *Ford: The Times, the Man, the Company*. New York: Charles Scribner's Sons, 1954. **(A)** The first volume—covering up to 1915—of what will remain, for the foreseeable future, the definitive account of Ford and his company. An exemplary piece of scholarship based on a thorough mastery of the available sources—including the vast body of materials in the Ford Archives.

―――. *Ford: Expansion and Challenge, 1915–1933*. New York: Charles Scribner's Sons, 1957. **(A)** The second volume of this monumental study.

―――. *Ford: Decline and Rebirth, 1933–1962*. New York: Charles Scribner's Sons, 1963. **(A)** The third, and final, volume covers the company's gradual decline under its founder to its rebuilding under Henry Ford II.

Olsen, Sidney. *Young Henry Ford: A Picture History of the First Forty Years*. Detroit: Wayne State University Press, 1963. **(A, G)** The title accurately describes the contents.

Richards, William C. *The Last Billionaire*. New York: Charles Scribner's Sons, 1948. **(G)** A collection of readable anecdotes and stories about Ford.

Simonds, William A. *Henry Ford: His Life, His Work, His Genius*. Indianapolis: Bobbs-Merrill, 1943. **(G)** The most detailed of the early works on Ford, it suffers, however, from an absence of documentation, and the author's uncritical approach to his subject.

Sorenson, Charles E., with Samuel T. Williamson. *My Forty Years with Ford*. New York: W. W. Norton, 1956. **(A, G)** An invaluable autobiography by a key figure in the revolution in mass production techniques associated with Ford. The book covers his years with the company, from 1904 to his forced departure in 1944.

Sward, Keith. *The Legend of Henry Ford*. New York: Rinehart, 1958. **(A, G)** A former public relations counsel for the Congress of Industrial Organizations, Sward explores the gap between Ford's professed beliefs and his business practices, especially his labor policies. Sward's account, the first attempt at an in-depth investigation of the Ford empire, is limited by its reliance on the public record. But the work remains the best study for those lacking the stamina or time to tackle the three-volume work by Nevins and Hill.

Overview and Evaluation of Primary Sources

Henry Ford's autobiography, *My Life and Work* (Garden City, NY: Doubleday, Page, 1922; **G**), apparently dictated by Ford to ghostwriter Samuel Crowther, is factually unreliable. The follow-up volumes appearing under his name but written by Crowther—*Today and Tomorrow* (Garden City, NY: Doubleday, Page, 1926; **G**) and *Moving Forward* (Garden City, NY: Doubleday, Doran, 1931; **G**)—are even more blatant examples of press agent puffery. More straightforward is F. L. Faurote, *My Philosophy of Industry [by] Henry Ford: An Authorized Interview* (New York: Coward-McCann, 1929; **G**).

Also of some value as primary sources are the aforementioned works by Ford's colleagues Samuel S. Marquis, Garet Garrett, Charles E. Sorenson, and Harry Bennett.

The most extensive collection of materials is found in the Ford Archives, located in the Henry Ford Museum at Dearborn, Michigan. Consisting of several million items, the archives include family records, personal correspondence, memoranda, and diaries. Also included are company minute books; production, sales, and legal records; photographs; transcripts of hundreds of tape-recorded reminiscences of relatives, friends, and associates; and a large collection of newspaper clippings, magazine articles, pamphlets, and books.

Museums, Historical Landmarks, Societies

Fair Lane National Historic Landmark (Dearborn, MI). Ford lived and died on this estate, now in use as a conference center by the University of Michigan.

Ford Birthplace (Dearborn, MI). The site of the farm where Ford was born is designated by an historical marker.

Henry Ford Museum (Dearborn, MI). Located at Greenfield Village, a sprawling complex of museums and historic structures, the Ford museum has a vast collection of artifacts, automobiles, documents, photographs, and other items related to Ford and the industry he founded.

Other Sources

Arnold Horace L., and Fay L. Faurote. *Ford Methods and the Ford Shops*. New York: Engineering Magazine Company, 1915. Despite the authors' Ford-can-do-no-wrong bias, this work remains the classic description of the new mass-production techniques.

Barnard, John. *Walter Reuther and the Rise of the Auto Workers*. Boston: Little, Brown, 1983. Excellent on the bitter struggle between Ford and the United Auto Workers union.

Fine, Sidney. *The Automobile Under the Blue Eagle*. Ann Arbor: University of Michigan Press, 1963. Includes a full treatment of Ford's refusal to cooperate with the National Recovery Administration.

Flink, James J. *The Car Culture*. Cambridge, MA: MIT Press, 1975. Contains an excellent brief account of Ford's contribution to and role in America's love affair with the automobile.

Greenleaf, William. *Monopoly on Wheels: Henry Ford and the Selden Automobile Patent*. Detroit: Wayne State University Press, 1961. The fullest account of Ford's successful challenge of the patent monopoly aspired to by the Association of Licensed Automobile Manufacturers.

————. *From These Beginnings: The Early Philanthropies of Henry Ford and Edsel Ford, 1911–1936*. Detroit: Wayne State University Press, 1964. A detailed account of Ford's philanthrophic involvements—the most important of which were the Henry Ford Museum and Greenfield Village.

Kuhn, Arthur J. *GM Passes Ford, 1918–1938: Designing the General Motors Performance-Control System*. University Park: Pennsylvania State University Press, 1986. Illuminating on how Ford's intellectual rigidity and dictatorial, one-man rule allowed Alfred P. Sloan, Jr., and his team at General Motors to take over industry leadership.

Lewis, David L. *The Public Image of Henry Ford: An American Folk Hero and His Company*. Detroit: Wayne State University Press, 1976. An encyclopedic review of Ford's image.

Rae, John B. *The American Automobile: A Brief History*. Chicago: University of Chicago Press, 1965. A succinct though informative history of the automobile industry that places Ford's role in its larger context.

Upward, Geoffrey, C. *A Home for Our Heritage: The Building and Growth of Greenfield Village and Henry Ford Museum, 1929–1979*. Dearborn, MI: Henry Ford Museum, 1979. The official history.

Wik, Reynold M. *Henry Ford and Grass-roots America*. Ann Arbor: University of Michigan Press, 1972. Illuminating on Ford as a cultural hero for rural and small-town America in the 1920s.

Wilkins, Mira, and Frank Ernest Hill. *American Business Abroad: Ford on Six Continents*. Detroit: Wayne State University Press, 1964. Traces the growth of the Ford Company's overseas operations.

John Braeman
University of Nebraska-Lincoln

NATHAN BEDFORD FORREST
1821-1877

Chronology

Born Nathan Bedford Forrest, on July 13, 1821, along with a twin sister, at the family homestead in what will become Chapel Hill, Tennessee, the oldest of nine children of William Forrest, a pioneer blacksmith from North Carolina, and Mariam Beck Forrest; *1821-1837* grows up on the frontier in Tennessee, and later, in Mississippi, where the family moves in 1834; receives about six months of formal schooling; his father dies in 1837, leaving young Nathan to provide for his mother and eight siblings; *1837-1851* works at farming, storekeeping, livestock trading, and in the livery stable business in Mississippi; *1841* leads a company of volunteers to Texas to fight in defense of the Republic against a threatened Mexican attack, but sees no action; *September 25, 1845* marries Mary Ann Montgomery, who comes from a socially prominent family in Hernando, Mississippi; *1851-1861* moves to Memphis and develops an extensive business trading in livestock, slaves, land, and cotton; acquires two large plantations in Mississippi; serves as alderman; *1861* in June, enlists in the Confederate Army as a private, along with his brother and fifteen-year-old son; in October, receives commission as a lieutenant colonel; raises, finances, and equips a cavalry battalion, taking along forty-five of his male slaves as teamsters (promising them manumission if they serve faithfully); shows enterprise in small actions and reconnaissance missions in Western Tennessee and Kentucky; his battalion joins the garrison at Fort Donelson on the Cumberland River; *1862* in February, the fort comes under siege by federal troops, but Forrest and his men escape before the surrender; in April, after joining the main Confederate Army of Tennessee, he plays a conspicuous role in the Battle of Shiloh, and in the withdrawal of the army in its aftermath, but is seriously wounded; in July, receives commission as brigadier general, and organizes a cavalry brigade; *September 1862-April 1863* conducts a series of brilliant raids deep behind federal lines in Kentucky and Tennessee; returns to Confederate territory with few losses, many recruits, and large quantities of captured horses, equipment, and supplies; *April-May 1863* Union Colonel Abel Streight leads a large expedition from Nashville to find and defeat Forrest; during an epic chase across three states, the pursuit is reversed, and Streight surrenders to Forrest's much smaller forces near Rome, Georgia; *May-November 1863* commands a division of cavalry, making major contributions to the victory at Chickamauga; refuses to continue serving under the command of General Braxton Bragg, accusing him of failing to follow up the Chickamauga victory adequately; *November-December 1863* promoted to Major General and takes command of the Department of North Mississippi and West Tennessee, most of which is under enemy occupation; raises and equips new forces, mainly from enemy resources; *December 1863-December 1864* outwits three major expeditions sent to hunt him down; conducts raids into Kentucky and Tennessee, creating havoc and slowing General Sherman's progress toward Atlanta; rejoins the main Confederate Army in November, commanding part of the cavalry during the disastrous offensive around Nashville and Franklin, Tennessee; *January–April 1864* with declining forces, opposes massive federal cavalry raids in Alabama; is promoted to Lieutenant General in February; is overwhelmed at Selma, Alabama, the next month, and surrenders to General James H. Wilson; is paroled; urges South to accept defeat and live peacefully; *1865–1877* takes up farming again in Mississippi; later moves to Memphis, where he engages in railroad and levee construction; *1867* is probably elected "Grand Wizard" of the recently formed Ku Klux Klan; *c.1868* orders the group dissolved; *1871* appears before a congressional committee to whom he gives lengthy, but inconclusive testimony on the KKK; *1877* dies on October 29 in Memphis.

Activities of Historical Significance

All of his biographers, and most students of military history, agree that Forrest was a natural military genius who would have been even greater had he been better prepared or given more opportunity to demonstrate his skills. The Confederacy had a number of daring cavalry leaders, but Forrest's bravado was complemented by an instinct for military effectiveness. Highly dedicated to his cause, courageous, and persevering, he displayed a great intelligence and aptitude for military leadership. His effectiveness with inferior resources rested upon an ability to synthesize information from many sources; to intuitively assess the opposition and grasp the essential points about movements, concentration, and terrain; and to pursue every opportunity for advantage with aggressive and unflagging determination. Perhaps most importantly, Forrest had the ability to inspire confidence and commitment in those he led. For a long period, his campaigns were required study for British army officers, and his leadership and wile are always likely to be of interest to students of military science.

Overview of Biographical Sources

Despite Forrest's controversial reputation, most biographers have been laudatory rather than critical in their approach to his life and career. During and after the Civil War, Forrest was something of a *bête noir* to Northerners, and was charged with many atrocities. But nearly all of these wartime legends have been discounted by later investigators. It is easy to understand why Forrest acquired this reputation; he personified the characteristics that outsiders disliked about the South, creating such fear and frustration in the North that he became a particular focus of hatred. Yet, during the war, Forrest deliberately promoted his reputation for ferocity, considering it a military asset because it spread confusion and hesitation among his adversaries.

The definitive biography, which also best tackles this facet of Forrest's life, is Robert Selph Henry's *"First with the Most" Forrest* (1944). Although historians have cleared Forrest of wrongdoing in most cases, Henry examines the episode that remains the most controversial: the alleged massacre of black Union soldiers that occurred during or after Forrest's capture of Fort Pillow, Tennessee, in April 1864. Yet the evidence remains inconclusive as to Forrest's involvement in the slaughter.

There has been little development or change in the biographical literature on Forrest. The facts of his life before and after the war are documented sufficiently to be fairly well established, but not extensively enough to allow much elaboration. His biographers tend to summarize these parts of his life, usually resorting to the same traditional legends to illustrate his prowess and courage. Popularized episodes of his life include those in which the young Forrest used a knife to kill a panther; wrestled the carriage containing his wife-to-be and her mother out of a mudhole: and single-handedly rescued the intended victim of a lynch mob in Memphis.

Likewise, biographical accounts of Forrest's military service tend to relate the same campaigns, albeit with differing detail and emphasis. His business activities after the war require little elaboration, and, by the nature of the case, his involvement with the Ku Klux Klan must rest upon conjecture and fragments of controversial information.

Evaluation of Principal Biographical Sources

Gentry, Claude. *General Nathan Bedford Forrest: The Boy and the Man.* Baldwyn, MS: Magnolia Publishers, 1972. (**Y**) An informal and colorful account of Forrest's early life and exploits, written for younger readers.

Henry, Robert Selph. *"First with the Most" Forrest.* Indianapolis and New York: Bobbs-Merrill, 1944. (**A, G**) A detailed, thoroughly researched, and well-illustrated work, this is the definitive life of Forrest.

Jordan, Thomas, and John P. Pryor. *The Campaigns of Gen. N. B. Forrest, and of Forrest's Cavalry.* 1868. Reprint. Dayton, OH: Morningside Bookshop Press, 1977. (**A, G**) Well written by a pair of Confederate staff officers who had access to Forrest, his subordinates, and his papers immediately after the war, this is the best and earliest source for much information on Forrest's military career.

Lytle, Andrew. *Bedford Forrest and His Critter Company.* 1931. Rev. ed. Seminole, FL: Green Key Press, 1984. (**G, Y**) Lytle, a Southern novelist, portrays Forrest as a mythic hero of the Old Southwest. Several revised editions have appeared since its original publication, the most recent being the 1984 Green Key Press volume.

Mathes, J. Harvey. *General Forrest*. New York: D. Appleton, 1902. **(G)** An early, detailed, and factual military study written for a series on "Great Commanders."

Sheppard, Eric Williams. *Bedford Forrest, the Confederacy's Greatest Cavalryman*. New York: Dial Press, 1930. **(G)** A British army officer's appreciation of Forrest's military exploits.

Wolseley, Garnet. "General Forrest." *United Service Magazine* 5 (April/May 1892). **(A, G)** An influential interpretation of Forrest as a great natural military genius, written by a British field marshall and viscount. Wolseley originated the popular point of reference that pegs Forrest as an untraditional cavalry officer who led an infantry into battle on horseback and then dismounted to fight.

Wyeth, John Allan. *Life of General Nathan Bedford Forrest*. 1899. Reprinted as *That Devil Forrest: Life of General Nathan Bedford Forrest*. New York: Harper and Brothers, 1959. **(A, G, Y)** Wyeth, a seasoned Confederate cavalryman who went on to become a noted surgeon and president of the American Medical Association, made a hobby of exhaustively authenticating the facts of Forrest's life and campaigns; here, he presents his findings in a reliable and colorful work. The original edition contains excellent illustrations.

Overview and Evaluation of Primary Sources

Although there is no one comprehensive collection of Forrest's papers, many small collections of Forrest's manuscripts and other primary sources are scattered throughout many libraries and private collections. The largest single collection, in the Duke University Library, contains less than 400 items. Many of the facts, especially of his earlier life, are known only through recollections of acquaintances, recorded in early works such as that of Jordan and Pryor, and many veterans' reminiscences. By far the greatest source of primary material relating to Forrest, his commands, his superiors, and his opponents, is found in the extensive and well indexed series, *War of the Rebellion: A Compilation of the Official Records of the Union and Confederate Armies*, 70 vols. (Washington: U.S. Government Printing Office, 1881–1901; **A, G**).

Fiction and Adaptations

Forrest's military campaigns were carried out over an area of the eastern Mississippi Valley consisting of Bluegrass and Western Kentucky, Middle and West Tennessee, and Northern Mississippi and Alabama. All of Forrest's men came from this Confederate region which, throughout the Civil War, was either occupied or regularly invaded by federal troops. It is not surprising that, in this region, Forrest became a folk hero of epic proportions, personifying the Lost Cause in the same way that General Lee did for the older Southern states.

This region has produced numerous writers, and thus Forrest has had a considerable presence in Southern literature. He looms in the background of many of William Faulkner's works, most explicitly in the short story "My Great Grandmother Millard and General Nathan Bedford Forrest and the Battle of Owl Creek." More recently, Forrest crops up several times in the reflections of modern Southerners in some of Walker Percy's novels. Donald Davidson has written a long epic poem, "The Running of Streight," to tell the story of Forrest's capture of Colonel Streight and his raiders, published in his *Lee in the Mountains and Other Poems* (1949). Forrest also emerges vividly in Shelby Foote's novel *Shiloh* (1952). Perhaps the most authentic and moving of the novels in which Forrest appears is Caroline Gordon's *None Shall Look Back* (1937), which tells the tragic story of some of the men who followed Forrest and who took "a one way ticket to the war."

Other Sources

Boatner, Mark Mayo. *The Civil War Dictionary*. New York: David McKay, 1959. This contains good concise summaries of Forrest's major battles and campaigns.

Foote, Shelby. *The Civil War: A Narrative*. 3 vols. New York: Random House, 1958–1974. A vivid and convincing portrait of Forrest emerges from this comprehensive account of the Civil War, although it is woven through a vast amount of other material.

Henry, Robert Selph, ed. *As They Saw Forrest: Some Recollections and Comments of Contemporaries*. Jackson, TN: McCowat-Mercer Press, 1956. Contains lengthy excerpts from memoirs of private soldiers who served under Forrest, and provides guidance for further study of such materials.

Ku Klux Conspiracy. Report of the Joint Select Committee to Inquire into the Condition of Affairs in the Late Insurrectionary States. Senate Report No. 41, 42nd Congress, 2nd Session, 1872. Contains extensive and often unevaluated material on the Ku Klux Klan in the early Reconstruction period.

Morton, John Watson. *The Artillery of Nathan Bedford Forrest's Cavalry: "The Wizard of the Saddle."* Nashville and Dallas: Methodist Episcopal Church South Publishing House, 1909. Morton, Forrest's artillery chief, provides a vivid account of the experiences of men who took part in the campaigns.

Young, John P. *The Seventh Tennessee Cavalry (Confederate): A History*. 1890. Reprint. Dayton, OH: Morningside Bookshop Press, 1976. Perhaps the best published reminiscence of private soldiers who served with Forrest.

Clyde N. Wilson
University of South Carolina

FELIX FRANKFURTER
1882–1965

Chronology

Born Felix Frankfurter on November 15, 1882, in Vienna, Austria, the son of Leopold Frankfurter, a rabbinical student turned businessman, and Emma Winter Frankfurter; *1882–1894* spends boyhood in Vienna where father struggles to make living; *1894–1903* comes with family to New York City; attends public elementary school where he learns English; completes combined high school-college course at the College of the City of New York and receives B.A.; works in the tenement house division of the city government; *1903–1906* compiles a distinguished academic record at Harvard Law School; *1906–1910* joins a leading New York law firm and then the staff of United States Attorney Henry L. Stimson; *1910–1913* serves as legal officer of the Bureau of Insular Affairs of the War Department; *1914–1917* appointed first Byrne Professor of Administrative Law at Harvard Law School; becomes active in the Zionist movement; *1917–1919* takes leave of absence to serve first as secretary and counsel to the President's Mediation Commission dealing with labor disputes in war industries, and then as secretary of the War Labor Policies Board; marries Marion Denman; *1919–1933* returns to Harvard Law School; active in defense of civil liberties in postwar red scare; champions Sacco and Vanzetti; coauthors *The Business of the Supreme Court* and *The Labor Injunction*; *1933–1938* acts as adviser to President Franklin D. Roosevelt; plays important role in staffing New Deal agencies with his protégés; *1939–1962* is appointed associate justice of the U.S. Supreme Court; continues to play influential behind-the-scenes role in mobilization and foreign policy matters before and after U.S. entry into World War II; becomes the focal point of a bitter split on the Court over civil liberties issues; *1962–1965* retires from the bench after a stroke; *1965* dies on November 15 from a coronary affliction in Washington, D.C.

Activities of Historical Significance

As a legal scholar, Frankfurter made his mark in three areas: the history and role of the Supreme Court; public utilities law; and, most important, administrative law. He was an apostle of the progressive faith that the disinterested application of intelligence by trained experts was the key to solving the complex problems of industrial society. He was, in broad terms, a legal realist hostile to a mechanical and immutable jurisprudence. His major target was the pre-1937 Court's dogmatic adherence to *laissez faire* in opposition to government economic regulation. Reflecting his pro-union sympathies, he attacked the abuse of judicially-issued injunctions in labor disputes. The reverse side of his commitment to social reform was his dedication to the protection of civil liberties. His most noteworthy involvement in

523

that area was his leadership of the campaign for a new trial for the Italian immigrant anarchists Sacco and Vanzetti after their conviction for murder in a trial tainted by ethnic and political prejudice. A third passion was Zionism. A protégé of Justice Louis D. Brandeis, Frankfurter acted as Brandeis's surrogate in a wide range of activities and, in return, received a financial subsidy to assist in the expenses involved.

Frankfurter became a major figure on the national scene during the New Deal. An influential adviser to President Franklin D. Roosevelt, he placed his former students in key positions within the New Deal and was the leader of the so-called Brandeisians, or trustbusters, within the administration, favoring a more vigorous attack upon big business. He personally disliked Roosevelt's Court-packing plan of 1937, but remained loyal. His reward was an appointment to the high court bench.

His performance on the Supreme Court disappointed many liberal admirers. In reaction against what he saw as the pre-1937 Court's abuse of power, he became the leading exponent of judicial self-restraint—that is, deference to the decisions of the politically responsible branches of government—although he himself did not always adhere to that position when values about which he felt deeply, such as separation of church and state and the Fourth Amendment, were at stake.

He retained a Brandeisian commitment to upholding a large area of autonomy for local and state governments. In the years after 1941, the justices divided sharply over how far the Court should go in striking down restrictions upon free expression and imposing upon the states uniform standards of criminal procedure. Frankfurter's major antagonist on the Court was Justice Hugo L. Black. Frankfurter favored a balancing approach to First Amendment issues in contrast with Black's absolutism. The two similarly clashed—Black for, Frankfurter opposed—over nationalization of the criminal law provisions of the Bill of Rights. From 1942 to 1946, Frankfurter was on the losing side more often than not; after 1946, his views generally prevailed until his retirement opened the door for the activism of the Warren Court. His crucial role in achieving unanimity in the 1954 *Brown* decision outlawing racial segregation in the public schools may have been Frankfurter's most significant contribution.

Overview of Biographical Sources

Frankfurter has been written about extensively, partly because of his own importance, partly because of the abundance of rich source materials. The first attempt at a comprehensive treatment, *Felix Frankfurter: Scholar on the Bench* by Helen S. Thomas (1960), was primarily an analysis of his judicial opinions. Although Liva Baker drew upon Frankfurter's personal papers, her 1969 biography, *Felix Frankfurter*, was a laudatory journalistic account aimed at the general reader. Though they provide personal sidelights, the reminiscences in Wallace Mendelson, ed., *Felix Frankfurter: A Tribute* (1964), are eulogistic. Later biographical treatments, such as Joseph Lash's introduction to *From the Diaries of Felix Frankfurter* (1975) and especially H. N. Hirsch's *The Enigma of Felix Frankfurter* (1981), reflect the disfavor Frankfurter had fallen into with many liberals enamored by Warren Court-style activism.

The fullest account of his pre-Supreme Court years is Michael E. Parrish, *Felix Frankfurter and His Times: The Reform Years* (1982). The Frankfurter-Brandeis relationship has attracted substantial attention, most notably by Norman Dawson (1980), Bruce Allen Murphy (1982), and Leonard Baker (1984). The voluminous commentary about Frankfurter on the Supreme Court tends to be highly polarized ideologically, but a recurring focal theme is the conflict between him and Justice Hugo L. Black.

Evaluation of Principal Biographical Sources

Baker, Leonard. *Brandeis and Frankfurter: A Dual Biography*. New York: Harper & Row, 1984. **(A, G)** A lively, sympathetic treatment of their personal relationship as well as their contribution to twentieth-century American Liberalism.

Baker, Liva. *Felix Frankfurter*. New York: Coward-McCann, 1969. **(G)** A laudatory, but journalistically superficial, account aimed at the lay reader.

Dawson, Nelson L. *Louis D. Brandeis, Felix Frankfurter and the New Deal*. Hamden, CT: Archon, 1980. **(A, G)** A pedestrian, though still useful, treatment of Frankfurter's leadership of the Brandeisian group within the New Deal.

Hirsch, H. N. *The Enigma of Felix Frankfurter*. New York: Basic Books, 1981. **(A, G)** An exercise in psychobiography that sees Frankfurter's judicial philosophy as shaped by his neurotic lack of inner self-confidence and accompanying compensatory drive to dominate others. Distorted by the author's all-too-evident dislike for his protagonist.

Jacobs, Clyde. *Justice Frankfurter and Civil Liberties*. Berkeley and Los Angeles: University of California Press, 1961. **(A, G)** A workmanlike survey of Frankfurter's position on the civil liberties issues before the Court.

Lash, Joseph, ed. *From the Diaries of Felix Frankfurter*. New York: W. W. Norton, 1975. **(A, G)** Lash's introduction is a substantial biographical essay that admires Frankfurter's pre-Court liberalism, but concludes that Black was more attuned to "what the future required."

Mendelson, Wallace, ed. *Felix Frankfurter: The Judge*. New York: Reynal, 1964. **(A, G)** Generally sympathetic appraisals of Frankfurter's judicial record.

Mendelson, Wallace. *Justices Black and Frankfurter: Conflict in the Court*. Chicago: University of Chicago Press, 1961. **(A, G)** A treatment of the Black/Frankfurter rivalry by a strongly pro-Frankfurter partisan.

Murphy, Bruce Allen. *The Brandeis/Frankfurter Connection: The Secret Political Activities of Two Supreme Court Justices*. New York: Oxford University Press, 1982. **(A, G)** Although deliberately oversensationalizing the financial aspects of the Brandeis-Frankfurter relationship, the author does raise provocative questions about the propriety of off-the-bench political involvement by Supreme Court Justices, a practice of which both men were guilty—Frankfurter more egregiously so than his mentor.

Parrish, Michael E. *Felix Frankfurter and His Times: The Reform Years*. New York: Free Press, 1982. **(A, G)** This work is the fullest available treatment of the pre-Court years, and will probably remain the definitive treatment. Thoroughly researched, lucidly written, and judiciously balanced, this is a model biography.

Silverstein, Mark. *Constitutional Faiths: Felix Frankfurter, Hugo Black, and the Process of Judicial Decision Making*. Ithaca: Cornell University Press, 1984. **(A, G)** A prize-winning study that avoids the polemical tone afflicting most treatments of the Black-Frankfurter rivalry. Rather than seeking to denigrate or exalt one or the other, the author illuminates the sources of their differences.

Thomas, Helen S. *Felix Frankfurter: Scholar on the Bench*. Baltimore: Johns Hopkins Press, 1960. **(A, G)** More a sympathetic analysis of his judicial performance and philosophy based upon his Supreme Court opinions than a full biography.

Overview and Evaluation of Primary Sources

Frankfurter was self-consciously interested in presenting a favorable historical image, even to the extent of carrying out a selective "weeding" of his papers before his death. The collection in the Library of Congress consists mostly of personal correspondence; the bulk of his Supreme Court case files are in the Harvard Law School Library. Guides are: Reference Department, Manuscript Division, *Felix Frankfurter: A Register of His Papers In the Library of Congress* (Washington, D.C.: Library of Congress, 1971; **A**), and Erika S. Chadbourn, ed., *Felix Frankfurter: An Inventory of His Papers in the Harvard Law School Library* (Cambridge: Manuscript Division, Harvard Law School Library, 1982; **A**). His correspondence with Franklin D. Roosevelt is in Max Freedman, ed., *Roosevelt and Frankfurter: Their Correspondence* (Boston: Little, Brown, 1967; **A**). Fragmentary diaries for 1911, 1928, 1933, 1943, and 1945–1948 are published in Joseph Lash, ed., *From the Diaries of Felix Frankfurter* (New York: W. W. Norton, 1975; **A, G**); his autobiographical reflections for the Columbia University Oral History Collection are contained in Harlan B. Phillips, ed., *Felix Frankfurter Reminisces* (New York: Reynal, 1960; **A**). His occasional writings have been collected in Archibald MacLeish and E. F. Prichard, Jr., eds., *Law and Politics: Occasional Papers of Felix Frankfurter, 1913–1938* (New York: Harcourt, Brace, 1939; **A**); Philip Elman, ed., *Of Law and Men: Papers and Addresses of Felix Frankfurter* (New York: Harcourt, Brace, 1956; **A**); Philip B. Kurland, ed., *Of Law and Life and Other Things That Matter: Papers and Addresses of Felix Frankfurter 1956–1963* (Cambridge: Belknap Press of Harvard University Press, 1967; **A**); and Kurland, ed., *Felix Frankfurter on the Supreme Court: Extrajudicial Essays on the Court and the Constitution* (Cambridge: Belknap Press of Harvard University Press, 1970; **A**). Kurland, *Mr. Justice Frankfurter and the Constitution* (Chicago: University of Chicago Press, 1971; **A**), is a handy collection of topically-arranged excerpts from his Supreme Court opinions.

Other Sources

Fine, Sidney. *Frank Murphy: The Washington Years*. Ann Arbor: University of Michigan Press, 1985. Although Fine is sympathetic to Murphy, who was at odds with Frankfurter during most of his time on the Court from 1940 through 1948, this work provides an unequalled look at the Court's inner workings.

Harrison, Robert. "The Breakup of the Roosevelt Supreme Court: The Contribution of History and Biography." *Law and History Review* 2 (Fall 1984): 165–221. Illuminates the factors responsible for the split among the Roosevelt appointees that developed after 1941.

Jacobsohn, Gary. *Pragmatism, Statesmanship, and the Supreme Court*. Ithaca: Cornell University Press, 1977. Critical of what the author regards as the shortcomings in Frankfurter's view of the judicial role.

Jaffe, Louis L. "The Judicial Universe of Mr. Justice Frankfurter." *Harvard Law Review* 62 (January 1949): 357–412. A thorough and sympathetic analysis of the philosophical bases of Frankfurter's jurisprudence.

Magee, James. *Justice Black: Absolutist on the Court*. Charlottesville: University Press of Virginia, 1980. An incisive and balanced analysis of Frankfurter's major antagonist on the Court.

Mason, Alpheus T. *Harlan Fiske Stone: Pillar of the Law*. New York: Viking Press, 1956. An illuminating account of the workings of the Court based upon the late Chief Justice's voluminous papers.

Pritchett, C. Herman. *The Roosevelt Court: A Study in Judicial Politics and Values, 1937–1947*. New York: Macmillan, 1948. A landmark quantitative, behaviorialistic analysis of the justices' voting patterns.

———. *Civil Liberties and the Vinson Court*. Chicago: University of Chicago Press, 1954. A similar analysis for 1946–1953.

Rauh, Joseph. "Felix Frankfurter: Civil Libertarian." *Harvard Civil Rights-Civil*

Liberties Law Reform 11 (Summer 1976): 496–520. An appreciation of Frankfurter's contribution to civil liberties before and after his elevation to the bench.

Schwartz, Bernard. "Felix Frankfurter and Earl Warren: A Study of a Deteriorating Relationship." In *Supreme Court Review 1980*, edited by Philip B. Kurland and Gerhard Casper. Chicago: University of Chicago Press, 1981. Traces the widening split between Frankfurter and Chief Justice Earl Warren over judicial activism versus restraint.

Spaeth, Harold. "The Judicial Restraint of Mr. Justice Frankfurter—Myth or Reality." *Midwest Journal of Political Science* 8 (February 1964): 22–38. Argues that Frankfurter's espousal of judicial restraint was simply a cloak for his own increasingly conservative personal views.

John Braeman
University of Nebraska-Lincoln

BENJAMIN FRANKLIN
1706–1790

Chronology

Born Benjamin Franklin on January 17, 1706, in Boston, Massachusetts, the fifteenth child and youngest son of Josiah Franklin, a soap boiler and tallow chandler, and Abiah Folger Franklin, Josiah's second wife; *1714–1716* studies first at Boston Grammar (now Boston Latin) School and then at George Brownell's English School; *1716–1717* works for his father; *1718–1723* serves as apprentice to his brother James, a printer, and writes ballads and essays; *1722* writes fourteen essays under the pseudonym "Silence Dogood," so that his brother will print them in the *New-England Courant*; *1723* becomes the titular editor of the *Courant* so that his brother can avoid censorship by the Massachusetts Assembly; *September 25, 1723* flees from his brother's shop to seek work in New York; *October 6, 1723* arrives in Philadelphia after failure in New York; *October 7, 1723* hired by Samuel Keimer as journeyman printer; *1724–1726* works as printer in London, writes and prints *A Dissertation on Liberty and Necessity, Pleasure and Pain* (1725); *1726–1727* works as a shopkeeper in Philadelphia; *1727–1728* works again in Keimer's print-shop; creates the Junto; *1728* opens his own printing establishment with Hugh Meredith, publishes his *Articles of Belief and Acts of Religion; 1729* writes "Busy-Body" essays and *A Modest Enquiry into the Nature and Necessity of a Paper Currency*; purchases *Pennsylvania Gazette; 1729 or 1730* sires William, his illegitimate son; *1730* named printer for the Pennsylvania Assembly; becomes sole owner of the *Pennsylvania Gazette* by buying out Meredith's share; enters into common-law union with Deborah Read Rogers, whose husband has abandoned her, and takes William into his home; *1731* initiated as a Freemason; founds Library Company of Philadelphia; *1732* publishes first *Poor Richard: An Almanack* (published annually until 1758); *1735* writes pamphlets defending Presbyterian minister Samuel Hemphill against charges of unorthodoxy; *1736* attains contract to print New Jersey currency; appointed clerk of Pennsylvania Assembly (serves until 1751); founds Philadelphia's first fire company; his son Francis dies of smallpox at the age of four; *1737* becomes postmaster of Philadelphia; *1740–1744* serves as official printer for New Jersey; *1741 or 1742* designs and advertises the "Pennsylvania fireplace" or Franklin stove; *1743* founds American Philosophical Society; daughter Sarah is born; *1745–1747* conducts electrical experiments; *1747* publishes *Plain Truth* to warn of the colony's need for defense against attacks; organizes Pennsylvania's first militia; *1748* serves as soldier in militia; retires from printing business; becomes slave-holder; elected to Philadelphia Common Council; *1749* named Philadelphia Justice of the Peace; named grand master of Pennsylvania Masons; writes *Proposals Relating to the Education of Youth in Pennsylvania; 1750* proposes construction of lightning rods to protect buildings; plans electrical experiments; *1751* devises plan for public and private support for Pennsylvania Hospital;

his *Experiments and Observations on Electricity* is edited and published in London; proposes first fire insurance company; elected as alderman of Philadelphia; *1751–1764* serves in Pennsylvania Assembly; *1752* proves lightning is electricity with his kite experiment; installs a lightning rod on his house; develops a flexible catheter for bladder stone sufferers; *1753* publishes *Supplemental Experiments and Observations* on electricity; receives honorary M.A. degrees from Harvard and Yale; wins Copley Medal of the Royal Society for his electrical experiments; gains appointment as deputy postmaster general of the colonies; negotiates a treaty with the Ohio Indians; *1754* publishes America's first political cartoon; attends Albany Congress and proposes a plan for colonial union (with the assent of Thomas Hutchinson) that is rejected by colonies and British government; publishes *New Experiments and Observations on Electricity* in London; protests taxation without representation and defends colonial self-government in letters to Governor Shirley of Massachusetts; *1755* assists General Braddock in defense of Pennsylvania from Indian attacks; named colonel of Philadelphia regiment; *1756* elected a Fellow of the Royal Society of London, and a corresponding member of the Royal Society of Arts; gets bills passed by Assembly to provide street lights and night watchmen in Philadelphia; receives honorary M.A. degree from the College of William and Mary; *1757–1762, 1764–1775* serves as agent in London for the Pennsylvania Assembly; *1757* writes "Father Abraham's Speech" or "The Way to Wealth"; *1758* invents stove damper; *1759* receives honorary LL.D. degree from University of St. Andrews; *1760* writes and publishes *The Interest of Great Britain Considered* on the importance of Canada; elected chairman of the Associates of Dr. Bray, which sponsors schools for blacks in America; gains Privy Council approval of the taxation of Pennsylvania's proprietary estates after the Assembly's act allowing such taxation had been overturned by the Board of Trade; *1762* receives honorary D.C.L. degree from Oxford University; invents the glass armonica, a musical instrument; sails to Philadelphia; helps his son William acquire post of royal governor of New Jersey; *1764* elected speaker of Pennsylvania Assembly in May; supports switch of colony to a royal charter; instructs the Assembly's agent in London to oppose the Stamp Act, modify the Sugar Act, and uphold the principle of "no taxation without representation"; loses seat in Assembly after an acrimonious campaign; returns to London as an agent of the Assembly; *1765* works with other agents to repeal the Stamp Act without success; succeeds in convincing British government to amend the Quartering Act; writes articles for English newspapers, some parodying English views of America and some seriously defending the colonies against the recent acts; *1766* defends American position against the Stamp Act before the Committee of the Whole of the House of Commons and contributes to the Act's repeal; elected to Royal Academy of Sciences at Göttingen; *1768* becomes an agent for the Georgia Assembly (continues until 1774); publishes *Causes of the American Discontents before 1768*; maps are printed using his theories on the course of the Gulf Stream; *1769* elected president of the American Philosophical Society (he is re-elected every year for the rest of his life); engages in scheme to secure royal land grants in the Ohio Valley; becomes agent for the New Jersey House of Representatives (serves until 1775); *1770* appointed agent of Massachusetts House of Representatives (serves until 1775); *1771* begins to write his *Autobiography* or *Memoirs*; *1772* writes "The Sommersett Case and the Slave Trade," an anti-slavery tract; elected to the French Academy of Sciences; obtains correspondence of Thomas Hutchinson, forwards it to Massachusetts House of Representatives; *1773* forwards Massachusetts House petition for Hutchinson's removal to Lord Dartmouth, colonial secretary; writes "Rules by Which a Great Empire May Be Reduced to a Small One"; *1774* denounced by Solicitor General Wedderburn before the Privy Council over the Hutchinson correspondence affair; loses deputy postmaster generalship for North America; forwards petitions from First Continental Congress to King George III, writes "Hints for a Durable Union Between England and America"; his wife Deborah, whom he has not seen in ten years, dies in Philadelphia; *1775* returns to Philadelphia after Parliament declares Massachusetts in rebellion; elected to the Second Continental Congress and the Pennsylvania Committee of Safety; designs Continental currency; suggests Articles of Confederation and Perpetual Union of the United Colonies, the latter is not accepted; serves on committee of secret correspondence; *1776* resigns from Pennsylvania Assembly; travels to Canada as Congressional commissioner; serves on committee to draft a Declaration of Independence and suggests a few changes in Jefferson's text; votes in favor of independence; elected president of Pennsylvania state convention; travels to France as Congressional commissioner (with Silas Deane and Arthur Lee); *1777* requests aid from France; becomes a great celebrity in Paris; writes and prints essays, pamphlets, and bagatelles; *1778* negotiates a grant of six million livres, and alliance, amity, and commerce treaties, with France; elected minister plenipotentiary to France in September; *1779* non-scientific writings are compiled in London; *1781* appointed commissioner (along with Adams, Jay, Jefferson, and Henry Laurens) to negotiate peace; *1782* negotiates and signs (with Adams and Jay) preliminary articles of peace treaty with Great Britain, while neglecting the French opinion; acquires another loan from France; *1783* with Adams, declares armistice after France and Spain accede to the preliminary treaty; co-signs definitive treaty of peace with Great Britain in September; *1784* writes the second section of the *Autobiography* and publishes *Information to Those Who Would Remove to America*; with Adams and Jefferson, negotiates treaties with various European nations and the Barbary States; *1785* describes his invention of bifocal lenses; co-signs treaty with Prussia; returns to Philadelphia; elected president of the Supreme Executive Council of Pennsylvania (serves until 1788); *1787* elected president of the Society for Political Enquiries and the Pennsylvania Society for Promoting the Abolition of Slavery; attends the national Constitutional Convention as a Pennsylvania delegate; ends the deadlock over the issue of representation by proposing equal representation for each state in the Senate and representation according to the size of a state's population in the House of Representatives; urges delegates to approve the Constitution; *1788–1789* writes third section of his *Autobiography*;

1789–1790 writes anti-slavery tracts; *1790* dies on April 17 of pleurisy at his home in Philadelphia.

Activities of Historical Significance

Few individuals have led lives full of the variety and accomplishment achieved by Benjamin Franklin. Only a few Americans have contributed as much to their country's history. His career as a printer and writer greatly influenced American journalism (he published what was probably the first American political cartoon and the first illustrated news story). His *Autobiography*, or *Memoirs* as he called it, was the precursor to Horatio Alger's tales of youths who rose from "rags to riches" through "luck and pluck," and provided a model for many other didactic memoir-writers. Franklin reorganized the American postal system as postmaster of Philadelphia and deputy postmaster general of North America, facilitating the intercolonial communication that was necessary for the development of incipient American nationalism and recognition of common purpose. His public enterprises included the formation of a fire company, a fire insurance company, a hospital, an academy (and later a university), the American Philosophical Society, a colonial militia, and street lights and patrolmen.

His inventions and experiments with electricity made him one of America's foremost practitioners of applied science, which he used to solve practical problems. His work on electricity also made him the first American to win international renown. His reputation as a thinker and scientist was in part responsible for his success as a diplomat.

As a public servant, Franklin proposed colonial union and self-government long before they were possible, and then played an important role in making them realities. As an agent for the representative bodies of four colonies, Franklin became an even more important national figure and saw first-hand how national governments rule. He lent authority to the Continental Congress, the committee to draft the Declaration of Independence, and the Constitutional Convention.

Franklin was the prototypical self-made American, the first "tinkering genius," a thinker who was still a doer. He provided Americans with a model of public-mindedness. Even though his private life and unorthodox religious views have been subjects of controversy, his virtues have kept him securely within the pantheon of American heroes.

Overview of Biographical Sources

It is hardly surprising that a man of such diverse accomplishments has inspired numerous biographies emphasizing various aspects of his life. In the first stage of Franklin biography-writing, the moralizers held sway: Mason Locke Weems, *The Life of Benjamin Franklin* (1817); John L. Jewett, *Franklin—His Genius, Life, and*

Character (1849); and *Benjamin Franklin: A Book for the Young and the Old: For All* (1852), an unsigned pamphlet attributed to Samuel Hutchins, all suggest that Americans emulate Franklin. James Parton's two-volume *Life and Times of Benjamin Franklin* (1864) was the first complete biography and, combined with the publication of the first complete American edition of Franklin's *Autobiography*, insured his standing as an American hero. Parton's Franklin (and the Franklin of the *Autobiography*) was a natural choice as patron saint of the emerging middle class. He stressed thrift and opportunism but, at the same time, assisted young competitors in other colonies. John Bach McMaster continued the trend of laudatory biographies with *Benjamin Franklin as a Man of Letters* (1887).

At the end of the nineteenth century the scene shifted, and Franklin was allowed his faults as well as his virtues and achievements. Several authors demonstrated a more cynical style as they attempted to come closer to the "real" Franklin. Sydney George Fisher, *The True Benjamin Franklin* (1898); Paul Leicester Ford, *The Many-Sided Franklin* (1898); Elbert Hubbard, *Little Journeys to the Homes of American Statesmen* (1898); and Paul Elmer More, *Benjamin Franklin* (1900), all depicted a Franklin who was more heroic precisely because he was so human and fallible. Debunking biography was popular again in the 1920s: Bernard Faÿ wrote *Franklin: The Apostle of Modern Times* (1929) and Paul Wilstach contributed *Patriots Off Their Pedestals* (1927). At the same time, others were content to use heroes pragmatically, as shown by the authors of *The Amazing Benjamin Franklin*, edited by J. Henry Smythe, Jr. (1929). Three interesting and professional accounts appeared during the 1930s. Carl L. Becker wrote a brief sketch of Franklin's career for the *Dictionary of American Biography* (1931) which ascribed Franklin's views to "the tang of the soil." Carl Van Doren's massive volume, *Benjamin Franklin* (1938), was the most complete biography since Parton's. Van Doren used all the major editions of Franklin's papers to document his life as Franklin might have done had he finished his *Autobiography*. Van Doren's is still a useful book on most aspects of Franklin's career. Verner W. Crane's scholarly *Benjamin Franklin, Englishman and American* (1936) and *Benjamin Franklin and a Rising People* (1954) are both illuminating studies. Paul W. Conner, *Poor Richard's Politicks: Benjamin Franklin and His New American Order* (1965), however, takes issue with Crane's assumption that Franklin never formulated a systematic or consistent philosophy of government. Gerald Stourzh also considers Franklin's ideas in *Benjamin Franklin and American Foreign Policy* (1954).

Many historians writing in the latter half of the twentieth century have concentrated on specific aspects of Franklin's life. For Franklin as a scientist, see I. Bernard Cohen's *Benjamin Franklin, Scientist and Statesman* (1972, 1975) and *Franklin and Newton* (1956). Another area of Franklin's life that has been recently rediscovered is his private life. Claude-Anne Lopez explains how Franklin used influential, interesting, and amusing people as a means of securing aid for the rebellious new states in *Mon Cher Papa: Franklin and the Ladies of Paris* (1966), and then, with Eugenia W. Herbert, explores other troubling aspects of Franklin's relations with his family and other people in *The Private Franklin: The Man and His Family* (1975). Willard Sterne Randall investigates Franklin's rejection of his son William further in *A Little Revenge: Benjamin Franklin and His Son* (1984). Finally, Esmond Wright lends a British perspective to Franklin's life and significance in *Franklin of Philadelphia* (1986). Wright's final chapter is particularly helpful in pointing out the numerous questions about the philosopher's career that can only yield informed conjecture and more biographies.

Evaluation of Principal Biographical Sources

Becker, Carl L. *Benjamin Franklin: A Biographical Sketch by Carl L. Becker, Late Professor of History in Cornell University*. 1931. Reprint. Ithaca: Cornell University, 1946. **(A, G)** Reprinted from the *Dictionary of American Biography* with a preface by Julian P. Boyd, this brief account by a master historian of the Enlightenment is filled with insights and a number of errors. Becker locates the origin of Franklin's spirit and outlook in America's agrarian ideals. Becker also pleads too strongly for Franklin's status as a pure scientist.

Cohen, I. Bernard. *Benjamin Franklin: Scientist and Statesman*. 1972. Reprint. New York: Scribner's, 1975. **(A, G)** Reprinted from the *Dictionary of Scientific Biography*, this essay summarizes and updates Cohen's arguments in *Franklin and Newton* (Philadelphia: American Philosophical Society, 1956; **A, G**). Cohen acknowledges that most of Franklin's experiments had practical applications, but maintains that Franklin was becoming more of a "pure" scientist before public service distracted him from his scientific work.

Conner, Paul W. *Poor Richard's Politicks: Benjamin Franklin and His New American Order*. New York: Oxford University Press, 1965. **(A, G)** In this insightful monograph, Conner rejects the notion that Franklin was an eternal pragmatist, shifting his political stance to reflect changing political and social exigencies. Conner's Franklin formulated a systematic model of society and politics. Unfortunately, Conner does not attempt to chart the changes of Franklin's ideas during his long, active life.

Crane, Verner W. *Benjamin Franklin and a Rising People*. Boston: Little, Brown, 1954. **(A, G, Y)** This is a solid narrative of Franklin's life which concludes that he lacked real commitment to any of his occupations, and never formed a consistent philosophy of life, yet managed to succeed at almost everything he did. Lacks footnotes.

Fisher, Sydney George. *The True Benjamin Franklin*. Philadelphia: J. B. Lippincott, 1898. **(G)** Pre-dating the debunkers of the 1920s, Fisher and several of his contemporaries tried to strip away some of the myths surrounding Franklin to rescue him from prudery. Fisher gives greater emphasis to Franklin's foibles, but finds him heroic nevertheless.

Ford, Paul Leicester. *The Many-Sided Franklin*. 1898. Reprint. Freeport, NY: Books for Libraries Press, 1972. **(A, G)** Ford was a prolific scholar and expert on Frankliniana. He captures much of what makes Franklin interesting, but he does not include footnotes or a bibliography. The volume is well-illustrated.

[Hutchins, Samuel]. *Benjamin Franklin: A Book for the Young and the Old: For All*. Cambridge: n.p., 1852. **(G, Y)** Continuing in the hagiographic and moralistic tradition of Mason Weems, Hutchins's Franklin was unanimously admired. Any negative aspect of Franklin's life "has been or should be forgotten."

Lopez, Claude-Anne. *Mon Cher Papa: Franklin and the Ladies of Paris*. New Haven: Yale University Press, 1966. **(A, G)** The author, one of the editors of the *Franklin Papers*, uses papers now being published that document Franklin's manipulation of influential friends and acquaintances while commissioner and minister to France. This is an intriguing peek at an important chapter of Franklin's life.

Lopez, Claude-Anne, and Eugenia W. Herbert. *The Private Franklin: The Man and His Family*. New York: W. W. Norton, 1975. **(A, G)** This contains the best analysis of Franklin's "home life." His relations with his family were often marked by insensitivity, but he could also be affectionate to his wife, children, and grandchildren. Franklin emerges as a fallible but understandable patriarch. His transformation from a slaveholder to a writer of antislavery tracts is also documented.

More, Paul Elmer. *Benjamin Franklin*. Riverside Biographical Series, no. 3. Cambridge: Houghton Mifflin, 1900. **(A, G, Y)** More, a literary critic and philosopher, slights Franklin for his "paganism" but is fascinated with Franklin's successes. This study lies between the more stylistic biographies of the nineteenth century and the more academic attempts of the twentieth.

Parton, James. *Life and Times of Benjamin Franklin*. 2 vols. Boston: Houghton Mifflin, 1864. **(A, G, Y)** Although for decades this was the best biography, its errors require comparisons with more recent books. Parton emphasizes Franklin's achievements but covers enough of his life to show some of his failings as well.

Randall, Willard Sterne. *A Little Revenge: Benjamin Franklin and His Son*. Boston: Little, Brown, 1984. **(A, G)** Randall re-emphasizes William Franklin's significance as a figure in his own right, and points out the extent to which Benjamin Franklin was preoccupied by his son's loyalism. The book is marred in a number of places by a misunderstanding of the trans-Atlantic world of the eighteenth century.

Stourzh, Gerald. *Benjamin Franklin and American Foreign Policy*. Chicago: University of Chicago Press, 1954. **(A, G)** Stourzh analyzes Franklin's ideas on foreign policy.

Van Doren, Carl. *Benjamin Franklin*. New York: Viking, 1938. **(A, G, Y)** Although a half-century of research has challenged some of Van Doren's assertions, this book is still one of the essential sources for any study of Franklin, and one of the best-written. Van Doren sees Franklin as a democratic hero and is so sympathetic that at times all of Franklin's rivals seem petty and short-sighted. Franklin appears almost omniscient in comparison. Van Doren's bibliography is the best to 1938.

Weems, Mason Locke. *The Life of Benjamin Franklin*. 1817. Reprint of 1822 ed. New York: AMS Press, 1988. (**A, G, Y**) "Parson" Weems is better known for his *Lives* of Washington and Francis Marion, but this volume is another good example of didactic biography.

Whipple, Wayne. *The Story of Young Benjamin Franklin*. Philadelphia: Henry Altemus, 1916. (**Y**) Whipple's book, aimed at pre-adolescents, proves that the moralizing spirit of Samuel Hutchins had not died by 1916.

Wright, Esmond. *Franklin of Philadelphia*. Cambridge: Belknap Press of Harvard University Press, 1986. (**A, G, Y**) Wright, a British historian, manages to portray Franklin again as the first "Yankee," the first middle-class American hero. From his foreign perspective, Wright's argument that Franklin was the progenitor of distinctively American traits seems more credible than those of earlier, American authors. Wright incorporates a fair amount of recent scholarship, and, like Lopez and Herbert, uses the recently edited *Franklin Papers* from Yale University Press (up through 1777). The notes and bibliography are adequate. This volume should be consulted to correct and supplement Van Doren's and Crane's general studies.

Overview and Evaluation of Primary Sources

Franklin wrote on so many topics, in so many genres—almanacs, articles, bagatelles, essays, letters, memoirs and documents—that scores of people from his time to the present have felt impelled to compile his writings into comprehensible anthologies. As early as 1751, John Fothergill and Peter Collinson edited Franklin's letters to Collinson as *Experiments and Observations on Electricity*. Franklin edited the fourth edition in London in 1769. Barbeu Dubourg included some previously unpublished pieces in *Oeuvres de M. Franklin . . .*, 2 vols. (Paris: n.p., 1773; **A, G**). Non-scientific writings were included in Benjamin Vaughan's edition of Franklin's *Political, Miscellaneous, and Philosophical Pieces* (London: J. Johnson, 1779; **A, G**). Some of the philosophical works omitted from the latter volumes were published by Charles Dilly as *Philosophical and Miscellaneous Papers. Lately Written by B. Franklin, L.L.D. . . .* (London: n.p., 1787; **A, G**). Some of Franklin's pamphlets had been published separately, such as *A Dissertation on Liberty and Necessity, Pleasure and Pain* (London: n.p., 1725; **A, G**) and *A Modest Enquiry into the Nature and Necessity of a Paper-Currency* (Philadelphia: n.p.,

1729; **A, G**). The *Poor Richard's Almanacks* (1733–1758) were also printed separately, of course. Individual pieces from *The New-England Courant, The Pennsylvania Gazette*, or other periodicals had often been unattributed and, therefore, needed to be evaluated and compiled in anthologies. During the early nineteenth century, both William Duane and Franklin's grandson, William Temple Franklin, had access to manuscripts and articles that had not been published, and both published several volumes. Each included material the other lacked. Duane's *The Works of Dr. Benjamin Franklin . . .* [title varies], 6 vols. (Philadelphia: William Duane, 1808–1818; **A, G, Y**) and William Temple Franklin's *Memoirs of the Life and Writings of Benjamin Franklin, L.L.D. . . .* [title varies], 3 vols. (London: H. Colburn, 1817–1818; **A, G, Y**) were both useful yet still incomplete. Jared Sparks then edited ten volumes of Franklin's writings and biography, *The Works of Benjamin Franklin* (Boston: Hillard, Gray, 1836–1840; **A, G, Y**), including hundreds of essays and letters missed by his predecessors. The first editor to use a chronological arrangement in his volumes, John Bigelow was also the editor of the first complete American version of Franklin's autobiography, *The Life of Franklin* (Philadelphia: Lippincott, 1868; **A, G, Y**). In *The Complete Works of Benjamin Franklin*, 10 vols. (New York: G. P. Putnam's, 1887–1889; **A, G, Y**), Bigelow added a few hundred articles to Spark's tally. The next major edition of Franklin's writings was Albert Henry Smyth, ed., *Writings of Benjamin Franklin*, 10 vols. (New York: Macmillan, 1905–1907; **A, G, Y**). Smyth used the collections of the University of Pennsylvania, and the American Philosophical Society, as well as many private collections. Smyth added, for instance, the "Silence Dogood" essays from the *New-England Courant* and omitted some of the most questionable items from earlier versions. He did not have space for everything he found, however, and he included few letters addressed to Franklin. Smyth's work served as the primary source for Franklin scholars for over fifty years. Other editors supplemented Smyth: Paul Leicester Ford, *Franklin Bibliography: A List of Books Written by or Relating to Benjamin Franklin* (Brooklyn: n.p., 1889; **A, G**); Worthington Chauncey Ford, *List of the Benjamin Franklin Papers in the Library of Congress* (Washington, DC: Government Printing Office, 1905; **A, G**); I. Minis Hays, *Calendar of the Papers of Benjamin Franklin in the American Philosophical Society*, 5 vols. (Philadelphia: n.p., 1908; **A, G**) and *Calendar of the Papers of Benjamin Franklin in the Library of the University of Pennsylvania* (Philadelphia: n.p., 1908; **A, G**); Carl Van Doren, *The Letters of Benjamin Franklin and Jane Mecom* (Princeton, NJ: Princeton University Press, 1950; **A, G**) and *Letters and Papers of Benjamin Franklin and Richard Jackson, 1753–1785* (Philadelphia: American Philosophical Society, 1947; **A, G**); William Greene Roelker, *Benjamin Franklin and Catharine Ray Greene: Their Correspondence, 1755–1790* (Philadelphia: American Philosophical Society, 1949; **A, G**); James Madison Stifler, *"My Dear Girl": The Correspondence of Benjamin Franklin with Polly Stevenson, Georgiana and Catherine Shipley* (New York: George H. Doran, 1927; **A, G, Y**); and Whitfield Bell, " 'All Clear Sunshine': New Letters of Franklin and Mary Stevenson Hewson,"

Papers of the American Philosophical Society 100 (December 1956; **A, G**). Verner W. Crane tackles Franklin's England years in *Benjamin Franklin's Letters to the Press, 1758–1775* (Chapel Hill: University of North Carolina Press, 1950; **A, G**).

Despite these additions to Smyth's anthology, there remained a need for a comprehensive, annotated edition of Franklin's writings and correspondence. In 1954 the American Philosophical Society and Yale University began to locate and duplicate the Frankliniana from hundreds of repositories, including their own vast holdings, the Library of Congress, the National Archives, the Historical Society of Pennsylvania, the University of Pennsylvania, the Massachusetts Historical Society, and the French Foreign Office, as well as the smaller but still significant collections elsewhere. The first volume alone boasted inclusions from approximately 110 individuals and 220 institutions. The editors, Leonard W. Labaree, Whitfield J. Bell, Jr., et al., intended to be comprehensive, including every document reasonably concluded to have been written by Franklin (alone or with others), all state papers in the drafting of which he played a significant role, and all letters to or from him. Only business records or the documents he clerked would be excluded. Over 27,000 manuscript pieces were collected by the editors (compared to 2,000 in Smyth's *Writings*). The first volume of *The Papers of Benjamin Franklin* (New Haven: Yale University Press; **A, G, Y**) appeared in 1959, and twenty-four additional volumes have been published to date, covering Franklin's writings to February 1778. The volumes contain excellent introductions and extensive annotation. The frustratingly slow pace of the project has led to some complaints that the editors have been too inclusive. Smyth's edition is still necessary for the materials from 1778–1790. Some amendments to the *Papers* have been made by J. A. Leo Lemay, *The Canon of Benjamin Franklin, 1722–1776: New Attributions and Reconsiderations* (Newark: University of Delaware Press, 1986; **A**). Lemay has also edited a useful single volume of Franklin's letters, bagatelles, articles, essays, *Poor Richard's Almanacks*, and the *Autobiography* for the Library of America series, *Benjamin Franklin: Writings* (New York: Library of America, 1987; **A, G, Y**). Lemay includes helpful notes and a detailed chronology of Franklin's life.

There are several other accessible editions of the *Autobiography*: Leonard W. Labaree, et al., eds., *The Autobiography of Benjamin Franklin* (New Haven: Yale University Press, 1964; **A, G, Y**); the Modern Library edition of *The Autobiography of Benjamin Franklin and Selections from His Other Writings* (New York: Random House, 1950; **A, G, Y**); and the parallel text edition of Max Farrand, ed., *Benjamin Franklin's Memoirs* (Berkeley: University of California Press, 1949; **A, G**). See also J. A. Leo Lemay and P. M. Zall, eds., *The Autobiography of Benjamin Franklin: A Genetic Text* (Knoxville: University of Tennessee Press, 1981; **A, G**), which uses the manuscript in the Huntington Library.

Fiction and Adaptations

Franklin's life has inspired novelists and film-makers. Franklin appears as a stifling father-figure in Herman Melville's *Israel Potter* (1854). Robert Lawson gives children a mouse-eye view of Franklin's Philadelphia in *Ben and Me: A New and Astonishing Life of Benjamin Franklin as Written by His Good Mouse, Amos* (1939). Lion Feuchtwanger's *Proud Destiny* (*Waffen für Amerika*) was translated into English in 1947. It depicts Franklin's attempts to forge an alliance between the emerging United States and Louis XVI's France, the squabbles between Franklin and his fellow commissioners, the machinations of Beaumarchais to provide the rebels with arms and funds, and the intrigues of Louis's court.

1776: A Musical Play (1970) features music and lyrics by Sherman Edwards. After a run on Broadway, Jack L. Warner produced a movie version of the musical in 1972, starring Howard Da Silva as Franklin, Bill Daniels as John Adams, and Ken Howard as Thomas Jefferson. The revolutionaries are caricatures; Da Silva's Franklin has an adage for all occasions. Da Silva performed a reprise of his role for the film *Benjamin Franklin: Portrait of a Family* (1976), shown at the Franklin Court of Independence National Historic Park. In this film, Franklin reflects on his life in Philadelphia, based on his letters to his family. Issues such as his son's and grandson's illegitimacy are avoided. The visitor center of Independence National Historic Park runs the film *Independence*, directed by John Huston, and starring Eli Wallach as Franklin, Patrick O'Neal as Washington, and Ken Howard once again as Jefferson. As in *Benjamin Franklin: Portrait of a Family*, the characters are supposed to be ghosts returning to Philadelphia. And, as in *1776*, the myth of a single signing of the Declaration of Independence is perpetuated.

Franklin has been treated in numerous television adaptations. Both J. Bronowski (*Ascent of Man*, BBC & PBS, February 25, 1972) and Alistair Cooke (*America*, NBC, November 28, 1972) discussed Franklin as a "scholar-citizen," an inventor, and an opportunist. Neither segment was particularly long or detailed. CBS aired a four-part series, *Franklin* (1974–1975), featuring four different actors—Eddie Albert, Lloyd Bridges, Richard Widmark, and Melvyn Douglas—as the title character. Directed by Glenn Jordan, the series explored the connection between Franklin's public and private lives. The final episode, "The Statesman" was particularly effective, as Melvyn Douglas portrayed Franklin at the end of his life. In 1985, WHA-TV in Madison, Wisconsin, aired a taped version of Alexis Lauren's one-man stage play, *Portrait of Ben Franklin: In His Own Words*. Produced by Lauren and Carl Battaglia, the teleplay covered a long span of Franklin's life and effectively gave a sample of Franklin's ideas and accomplishments.

Museums, Historical Landmarks, Societies

Franklin Institute (Philadelphia, PA). Houses archives and the Benjamin Franklin National Memorial, which includes a sculpture of Franklin by J. E. Fraser, and displays of objects and portraits relating to Franklin.

Historical Society of Pennsylvania (Philadelphia, PA). This society holds large numbers of Franklin's papers and other related items.

Independence National Historic Park (Philadelphia, PA). The park includes Franklin Court, which has a visitor center at the site where Franklin's house once stood. Portraits, documents, and a film are on display. The Visitor Center for the Park and Independence Hall offers additional interpretation. The Franklin printing shop features a costumed printer and a working press.

Library Company of Philadelphia (Philadelphia, PA). Founded by Franklin, the company is a repository for statuary and portraiture as well as written Frankliniana.

Other Sources

Ambler, Louise Todd. *Benjamin Franklin: A Perspective*. Cambridge: Fogg Art Museum, 1975. A catalogue written for a Franklin exhibition of the same title.

Bailyn, Bernard. *The Ordeal of Thomas Hutchinson*. Cambridge: Belknap Press of Harvard University Press, 1974. This study, by a preeminent scholar of the American Revolution, includes an excellent account of Franklin and the Hutchinson letters affair.

Kammen, Michael G. *A Rope of Sand: The Colonial Agents, British Politics, and the American Revolution*. Ithaca, NY: Cornell University Press, 1968. An incisive examination of the role of the colonial agents, including Franklin.

Metropolitan Museum of Art. *Benjamin Franklin and His Circle*. New York: Plantin Press, 1936. A book written to coincide with the museum's exhibition.

Sellers, Charles Coleman, ed. *Benjamin Franklin in Portraiture*. New Haven, CT: Yale University Press, 1962. A guide to the many, scattered paintings of Franklin. The plates are reproduced well.

————. *Exhibition of Portraits Marking the 250th Anniversary of the Birth of the Society's Founder, Benjamin Franklin*. Philadelphia: American Philosophical Society, 1956. A catalogue written for the American Philosophical Society's exhibit.

Michael D. Cook
The Strong Museum

JOHN C. FREMONT
1813–1890

Chronology

Born John Charles Frémont on January 21, 1813, in Savannah, Georgia, the first of four children of French emigré Charles Frémont, a wandering teacher, and Ann Beverley Whiting, who scandalized Richmond, Virginia, by leaving her elderly husband, John Pryor, to run away with her lover; *1818* the father dies, and the boy is reared by his mother in Charleston, South Carolina; *1829* enrolls in the Scientific Department of the College of Charleston, but is dismissed in 1831, three months short of graduation, for "incorrigible negligence"; five years later he applies for and is granted the B.A. degree; *1833–1838* as a civilian, successively teaches mathematics to midshipmen on board the U.S.S. *Natchez*, assists in surveying the Charleston, Louisville and Cincinnati Railroad and the Cherokee country, and helps the French scientist, Joseph Nicolas Nicollet, make a scientific reconnaissance of the Minnesota country; *1838* receives a commission as a lieutenant in the United States Corps of Topographical Engineers; *1839–1840* makes a second examination of the Minnesota country with Nicollet and works in Washington, D.C., on the maps from this expedition; *1841* surveys the lower course of the Des Moines River; elopes with Jessie Anne, the seventeen-year-old daughter of the influential Senator Thomas Hart Benton of Missouri; *1842* commands an expedition to South Pass and the Wind River Mountains; *1843–1844* leads another exploring party to Oregon and California; effects a controversial midwinter crossing of the Sierra Nevada mountains; *1845* interprets his survey orders as license to enter California again, and participates in the war between the United States and Mexico, hailed by some as the "Conqueror of California"; *1848* is court-martialled and convicted on charges of mutiny, disobedience, and conduct prejudicial to military discipline because of his defiance of the authority of Stephen Watts Kearny in California; President James K. Polk remits the penalty, but Frémont resigns from the army; *1848–1849* makes his fourth western expedition (privately financed) seeking passes for a Pacific railroad and loses eleven men in the bitter winter of the San Juan Mountains; *1849–1855* attempts to develop his gold-rich Mariposa estate in California; negotiates contracts to feed the Indians in California; serves briefly as a U. S. Senator from California; makes his fifth and final expedition into the West; *1856* the newly formed Republican Party nominates him for the presidency and thousands march to the slogan, "Free Soil, Free Men, Frémont and Victory," but he is defeated by James Buchanan; *1857–1861* Mariposa affairs again occupy his attention; journeys to Europe a second time to raise capital; with the coming of the Civil War, he is commissioned a major-general of the Union Army and given command of the Department of the West with headquarters at St. Louis; military defeat, politics, and his proclamation emancipating Missouri rebels' slaves lead

President Lincoln to remove him; *1862* holds briefly the command of the Department of Western Virginia; *1864* is again nominated for the presidency by the radical wing of the Republican party, but soon withdraws; establishes a home at Pocaho in New York and attempts to make a fortune in railroading, but questionable business practices and bankruptcy in 1870 blemish his reputation and leave him virtually penniless; *1878* seeks and receives an appointment as governor of the Arizona Territory, but long absences in the East, promoting various land and railroad schemes, lead to considerable criticism and a request for his resignation, which he submits in the Fall of 1881; *1886* works on his *Memoirs*; *1890* Congress authorizes the president to appoint him a major general in the army and to place him on the retired list for pension purposes; *1890* dies on July 13 of peritonitis in a New York City boarding house.

Activities of Historical Significance

Frémont's proudest legacy was exploring the West and then describing it through narratives and maps. His first expedition to South Pass and the rugged Wind River Mountains of Wyoming was pathbreaking, and his spectacular unfurling of the national flag on one of the highest peaks in the chain complemented by his remarkable report, written with the help of his wife, stirred the imaginations of Americans, doing more than any previous explorer to point the way west.

He became more famous when, two years later, Americans read the report of his 1843–1844 circuit of the West and pored over an accompanying map. This work was to become a classic in exploration literature and changed conceptions of the West. Both houses of Congress ordered printings of 10,000 copies and it was taken up by commercial publishers at home and abroad. Within a short time, Frémont had an international reputation and was awarded gold medals by the British Royal Geographical Society and the Prussian government.

At home, his description of the valleys along Bear River undoubtedly influenced the Mormons' decision to settle in Salt Lake Valley; the swelling tide of westward-moving emigrants found that his reports gave vital information about terrain, campsites, water, vegetation, wildlife and weather. Some of the names Frémont gave to land features did not possess much staying power, but others were permanently transmitted; among the most famous are the Golden Gate, the Humboldt River and Mountains, Carson River and Lake, Walker River and Lake, and the Kern River. Eventually, twelve towns east and west of the Mississippi and countless city streets would bear the name of Frémont. Appropriately, one of the nine stamps commemorating the Trans-Mississippi Exposition held in Omaha in 1898 is of Frémont raising the flag on a Rocky Mountain peak.

Overview of Biographical Sources

Given his prominence and controversial career, there are fewer biographies of Frémont than one might expect. In 1850, his father-in-law, Thomas Hart Benton, anonymously authored a twenty-one-page *Thrilling Sketch* of his life, which was published and circulated in England along with John Skirving's panoramic painting of the overland expeditions. The presidential campaign of 1856 brought a number of eulogistic compilation-style biographies; those by John Bigelow, Charles W. Upham, and S. M. Smucker are still on the shelves of major libraries. The seventeen-page *Life of Col. Fremont*, attributed to Horace Greeley, circulated widely and was translated into German.

In 1914, G. P. Putnam's Sons published Frederick S. Dellenbaugh's *Frémont and '49*, a scientific and critical account of Frémont's explorations. Sixteen years later, Cardinal L. Goodwin wrote a brief and hostile account of Frémont under the title *John Charles Frémont: An Explanation of His Career*. To date, the best and most complete biography of Frémont is by Allan Nevins.

Evaluation of Principal Biographical Sources

Brandon, William E. *The Men and the Mountain: Frémont's Fourth Expedition*. New York: William Morrow, 1955. **(A, G)** A gripping account of how the men of Frémont's fourth expedition fought the winter and the mountains for thirty-two days, were defeated, and for another thirty-two days fought to escape. Recent studies have corrected portions of Brandon's tracing of the route.

Egan, Fero. *Frémont: Explorer for a Restless Nation*. Garden City: Doubleday, 1977. **(A, G)** A well-written account of Frémont's life through the period of exploration. The final chapter is an inadequate summary of the last thirty-six years of the explorer's life, which were often filled with controversy.

Gienapp, William E. *The Origins of the Republican Party, 1852–1856*. New York: Oxford University Press, 1987. **(A)** A richly detailed study of the creation of the Republican Party. Several chapters deal with Frémont's nomination and campaign. Undoubtedly it will replace Ruhl J. Bartlett, *John C. Frémont and the Republican Party* (1930).

Hine, Robert V. *In the Shadow of Frémont: Edward Kern and the Art of Exploration, 1845–60*. Norman: University of Oklahoma Press, 1982. **(A, G)** Essentially a revision of Hine's *Edward Kern and American Expansion*, published in 1962 by Yale University Press. Edward Kern was an artist with Frémont's third and fourth expeditions. Hine devotes a large portion of the volume to the relationship between Ned Kern and Frémont and the rupture of that relationship. The account is interesting, factual, and interpretive.

Nevins, Allan. *Frémont: Pathmarker of the West.* New York: Longmans, Green, 1955. **(A, G)** This remains the best and most comprehensive biography of Frémont. The late Professor Nevins, a prolific scholar at Columbia University, was fascinated by Frémont. He published a two-volume laudatory biography in 1928 with the subtitle *The West's Greatest Adventurer*, rewrote it in 1939 with "Pathmarker" in the title, and made a final critical revision in 1955. Essentially, Nevins remains sympathetic to Frémont.

Parrish, William E. *Turbulent Partnership: Missouri and the Union, 1861-1865.* Columbia: University of Missouri Press, 1963. **(A, G)** Examines Frémont's Civil War command in Missouri, his relationship with the provisional government, his emancipation proclamation, and his removal by President Lincoln.

Overview and Evaluation of Primary Sources

The first three chapters of Frémont's *Memoirs of My Life* (Chicago: Belford, Clarke, 1886; **A, G**) contain a rapid account of his education, his early adventures, and his work with Joseph Nicollet. Chapters four through seven are based on the reports of his first and second expeditions and add little to them. The last chapters deal, often sketchily, with the events of the third expedition and the war in California up to the capitulation of the Mexicans at Cahuenga. This volume breaks off at that point, but after her husband's death, Jessie and her son, Frank, continued work on what she hoped would constitute the second volume of Frémont's *Memoirs*. The manuscript, now in the Bancroft Library at the University of California, Berkeley, was never published.

The United States Government published as Congressional documents the reports which Frémont wrote following his 1842 and 1843-1844 expeditions. It also published the *Geographical Memoir upon Upper California, in Illustration of His Map of Oregon and California.* These 1842-1844 reports, the *Geographical Memoir*, the record of his court-martial trial, Solomon Nunes Carvalho's account of the fifth expedition, the *Plantae Fremontainae*, maps relevant to the five expeditions and all of the known correspondence of the explorer to October 1854 may conveniently be found in Donald Jackson and Mary Lee Spence, eds., *The Expeditions of John Charles Frémont*, 3 vols. Supplement, and Map Portfolio (Urbana: University of Illinois Press, 1970-1984; **A**).

The collected diaries of the participants on the 1848-1849 expedition have been published by LeRoy R. Hafen and Ann W. Hafen in *Frémont's Fourth Expedition: A Documentary Account of the Disaster of 1848-49* (Glendale, CA: Arthur H. Clark, 1960; **A**).

The 1856 presidential campaign produced an abundance of pamphlet literature, pro-and anti-Frémont, much too vast to list here. Information about the Memphis, El Paso, and Pacific Railroad can be found in Senate Miscellaneous Documents 96 and 121, 41st Congress, 2nd Session.

Artists and photographers of his time found Frémont an attractive subject. Marcus A. Root, Mathew Brady, and George Rockwood all photographed him. Paintings by Thomas Hicks, Otis Bass, William Jewett, Solomon Nunes Carvalho, Charles Elliott, and Guiseppi Fagnani hang respectively in the Henry E. Huntington Museum, the University of Michigan Art Gallery, the National Gallery of Art, the Pennsylvania Academy of Fine Arts, the Brooklyn Museum, and the Olin Military Room of the Missouri Historical Society in St. Louis. All convey differing images of the man.

The Frémonts' daughter, Elizabeth, burned her parents' personal papers in 1907, but as they were both such public figures, many of their letters can be located in other people's collections scattered around the country. The largest quantity are in the Library of Congress, the National Archives (because of Frémont's official posts), and three California institutions: the Bancroft Library, the Henry E. Huntington Library, and the Southwest Museum.

Fiction and Adaptations

David Nevin wrote a very popular novel, *Dream West*, about the Frémonts which was published in 1984 by G. P. Putnam's Sons. Two years later, CBS televised a seven-hour mini-series based on the novel and used the same title. It was a Sunn Classic Pictures production, starring Richard Chamberlain as John C. Frémont, Alice Krige as Jessie Benton Frémont, Fritz Weaver as Thomas H. Benton, and Rip Torn as Kit Carson. The series was filled with many historical inaccuracies, failed to capture the spirit of the age, and was a disappointment to the casual viewer as well as the historian.

Museums, Historical Landmarks, Societies

Frémont House (Prescott, AZ). Now a part of the Sharlott Hall Museum Complex, Frémont rented this house during the first years of his tenure as territorial governor.

Frémont House Museum (Tucson, AZ). Frémont's home includes collections relating to his life and governance of Arizona.

Other Sources

Fireman, Bert M. "Frémont's Arizona Adventure." *American West* (Spring 1964): 8–19. Sheds light on a phase of Frémont's career that is often neglected.

Herr, Pamela. *Jessie Benton Frémont: A Biography*. New York: Franklin Watts, 1987. This book is a sensitive treatment of Frémont's wife, one of America's notable women. It is essential for understanding Frémont's private life. Herr's research is impeccable; she has read every letter to, from, and about Mrs. Frémont which she could locate. The biography will supersede Catherine Coffin Phillips's out-of-print *Jessie Benton Frémont: A Woman Who Made History* (1935).

Miner, H. Craig. *The St. Louis-San Francisco Transcontinental Railroad: The Thirty-fifth Parallel Project, 1853–1890*. Lawrence: University of Kansas Press, 1972. Biographers have not dealt in depth with Frémont's railroad promotions and speculations. One of the chapters in this book deals with his Atlantic and Pacific Railroad Company.

Rolle, Andrew. "Exploring an Explorer: Psychohistory and John Charles Frémont." *Pacific Historical Review* 51 (1982): 135–163. Suggests that many of Frémont's difficulties stem from his attempt "to wall himself off from powerful feelings of sorrow over the loss of his father [when he was five] and his own illegitimacy."

Royce, Josiah. "Frémont." *Atlantic Monthly* 66 (October 1890): 548–557. A philosopher of Frémont's day, who considered him an "enigma," and a "creature of shadow land," "who possessed all the qualities of genius except ability." Probably the inspiration for Rolle's article mentioned above.

Weber, David J. *Richard H. Kern: Expeditionary Artist in the Far Southwest, 1848–1853*. Albuquerque: University of New Mexico Press, 1985. Like his brother Edward Kern, mentioned above, Richard was also an artist and a member of Frémont's fourth expedition. This volume is beautifully illustrated with drawings and paintings from that expedition.

Mary Lee Spence
University of Illinois at Urbana-Champaign

Frémont on the Rocky Mountains, 1898

BETTY FRIEDAN
1921

Chronology

Born Betty Naomi Goldstein on February 4, 1921, in Peoria, Illinois, to Harry Goldstein, a jeweler, and Miriam Horowitz Goldstein, a newspaper columnist before her marriage; *1921-1939* grows up in Peoria as the eldest of three children, keenly feeling her marginality as a Jew in the midwest; founds a literary magazine in high school and graduates as valedictorian of her class; *1939-1942* attends Smith College, majors in psychology, and studies with Kurt Koffka, one of the leading Gestalt psychologists; works during summers as a clinical psychologist, doing early work in the field of group dynamics; serves as editor of Smith's student newspaper and cofounds the Smith literary magazine; *1942* graduates *summa cum laude* and receives a research fellowship to begin graduate work in psychology at the University of California, Berkeley; *1943* receives the offer of another research fellowship which would have obligated her to the doctoral program and a career as a professional psychologist; rejects the fellowship and moves to New York City to work in a series of editing jobs; *1947* marries Carl Friedan, a producer of summer stock theatre and later an advertising executive; *1947-1957* has three children, Daniel, Jonathan, and Emily, and lives in Parkway Village, an apartment complex in Queens that was somewhat communally organized; *1957* moves with family to an eleven-room Victorian home in suburban Rockland County; begins to experience and observe the phenomenon she is later to call "the Feminine Mystique"; sends a questionnaire to her Smith College classmates as well as to the graduates of Radcliffe and other Ivy League women's colleges in order to identify what she calls the "problem that has no name"; *1960* publishes an article based on survey results entitled "Women Are People Too!" in *Good Housekeeping* (September), and public response leads her to begin a book on the subject, based on extensive research in personal interviews, popular culture, sociology, and psychology; *1963* publishes *The Feminine Mystique* and it becomes a widely-excerpted, widely-translated, and extremely influential best seller that advocates the necessity for women to develop their full intellectual capacities through meaningful employment; *1966* founds the National Organization for Women (NOW), a group committed to the improvement of women's civil rights and becomes its first president; *1969* divorces her husband; *1970* proclaims and leads the first women's strike day on August 26, the fiftieth anniversary of women's suffrage; *1970-1976* travels throughout America, Europe, Mexico, South America, and India speaking on behalf of the women's issues she sees as crucial: abortion, day care centers, and equal job and educational opportunities; *1971-1973* cofounds and serves on the policy council of the National Women's Political Caucus; *1972-1974* serves as vice president of the National Association to Repeal Abortion Laws; *1975* receives the Humanist of the Year award; *1976* publishes *It Changed My Life: Writings on the Women's Movement*, a series of essays on how *The Feminine Mystique* affected the lives of women by changing their consciousness and actions; *1981* publishes *The Second Stage*, a book that grew out of her conviction that the contemporary feminist movement must enter a new phase of accommodation to the demands of women as both careerists and mothers; *1982–present* continues to travel, speak, and write on behalf of child care reform, maternity and paternity leave for working parents, shared housekeeping and a breakdown of rigid sex roles.

Activities of Historical Significance

The publication of *The Feminine Mystique* (1963) is considered to be the inauguration of the contemporary women's movement in America. This work is generally considered to be the first to attribute women's problems to a sex-biased society and not to the personal failures of individual women.

The founding of the National Organization of Women (NOW) in 1970 is considered to be a major contemporary step forward in politicizing women's demands for reform.

As a leader and organizer of the Women's Strike Day for Equality (August 26, 1970), Friedan tried to mobilize women to fight for passage of the Equal Rights Amendment (ERA) and for the right to abortion and subsidized child-care. She was confronted at the strike by more radical women who demanded much more in terms of political, social, and sexual rights. This infighting factionalized the women's movement and weakened its effectiveness.

As founder of the National Women's Political Caucus and a member of its policy board, Friedan worked to encourage and support women's bids for political offices in the 1972 election. She herself considered these efforts to have been "abortive" because of the increasing polarization that divided women into pro- and anti-ERA camps during this period.

Although Friedan's writings and positions have been criticized as conservative and traditionalist by more radical feminists, her practical suggestions and moderate voice in *The Second Stage* may prove more influential for the liberation of women and men from traditional sexual roles than extremists realize.

Overview of Biographical/Critical Sources

There are no better sources on Friedan's life than the autobiography that emerges throughout her own three books (*The Feminine Mystique, It Changed My Life*, and *The Second Stage*). Brief biographies appear in *American Women Writers*, vol. 2 (1980); *Current Biography* (1970); and *Contemporary Authors*, vol. 65–68. June Sochen's *Movers and Shakers: American Women Thinkers and Activists 1900–1970* (1973) is particularly important because it places Friedan and her contemporaries in a historical framework. No full biographies have yet appeared on Friedan, but several works contain critiques of her controversial ideas.

Evaluation of Principal Biographical/Critical Sources

"Betty Friedan." In *American Women Writers*, edited by Lina Mainiero. Vol. 2. New York: Ungar, 1980. **(A, G)** A brief but useful biographical and critical portrait.

Eisenstein, Hester. *Contemporary Feminist Thought*. Boston: G. K. Hall, 1983. **(A)** A valuable historical survey of the contemporary American feminist movement, which discusses Friedan's role in a chapter entitled "Uncovering the Patriarchal Power Structure."

Janeway, Elizabeth. *Man's World, Woman's Place*. New York: Morrow, 1971. **(A, G)** Using Friedan's findings about women and the family, Janeway concludes that women want autonomy: "control over their own lives and authority or influence commensurate with their abilities in the external world."

Sochen, June. *Movers and Shakers: American Women Thinkers and Activists 1900–1970*. New York: Quadrangle, 1973. **(A, G)** In the contemporary section of this study, Sochen places Friedan, Kate Millett, Robin Morgan and others into a lengthy historical framework of which they themselves have not always been aware.

Overview and Evaluation of Primary Sources

Friedan's reputation was established by her first book, *The Feminine Mystique* (New York: Norton, 1963; **G**), a huge publishing success and a force for social, political, and economic change for women. In hindsight, critics have accused the book of presenting only the problems of educated, white, middle and upper-middle class women, and of not advocating radical enough social and institutional changes.

It Changed My Life: Writings on the Women's Movement (New York: Random House, 1976; **G**), Friedan's second book, consists of a series of open letters and essays in which Friedan assesses the progress of the women's movement and the role she has played in it. The book contains both personal and political history and advocates human liberation, which will only be possible when all people transcend sexual polarization.

The Second Stage (New York: Summit, 1981; **G**), her most recent book, contains Friedan's current theories on women's successes and failures so far. She denounces the attempts by lesbians and extreme man-haters to factionalize the movement, while at the same time she battles against women who would block the ERA and abortion rights. The book solidifies her position as a moderate feminist.

The Schlesinger Library of Radcliffe College maintains a collection of Friedan's personal papers.

Other Sources

Bird, Caroline. *Born Female: The High Cost of Keeping Women Down*. New York: Pocket, 1972. Bird distinguishes herself from Friedan by claiming that Friedan puts the burden of change on individual women, whereas Bird asserts that social institutions themselves must be transformed.

Haber, Barbara. *Women in America: A Guide to Books, 1963–1975*. Urbana: University of Illinois Press, 1981. Contains several discussions of Friedan's major books. An extremely valuable annotated bibliography on hundreds of books written by and about women.

Lerner, Gerda. *The Female Experience: An American Documentary*. Indianapolis: Bobbs-Merril, 1977. This anthology excerpts primary sources from the women's movement, including Friedan's writings, and arranges them around the life cycle of women.

Mitchell, Juliet. *Psychoanalysis and Feminism*. New York: Pantheon, 1974. Mitchell attacks Friedan's condemnation of Freud and argues that Freud's theories are not recommendations for behavior, but instead are critiques of the patriarchy.

Ryan, Mary P. *Womanhood in America: From Colonial Times to the Present*. New York: New Viewpoints, 1975. Ryan looks at women's history by separating cultural attitudes from actual behavior, and concludes that an equitable society will only emerge when women form a strong socialist feminist movement.

Sochen, June. *Herstory: A Woman's View of American History*. New York: Alfred, 1974. A personal view of men's treatment of women, blacks, Native Americans, and the environment.

————. *The New Feminism in Twentieth-Century America*. Lexington, Mass. Heath, 1971. A collection of feminist writings from the nineteenth-century suffrage movement, the feminism of the 1910s, and the revival of the 1960s.

Diane Long Hoeveler
Marquette University

J. WILLIAM FULBRIGHT
1905

Chronology

Born James William Fulbright on April 9, 1905, in Sumner, Missouri, the third child of six to Jay Fulbright, a successful banker, entrepreneur, and Republican notable in the Missouri-Arkansas region, and Roberta Waugh Fulbright, a college-educated country school teacher; *1905-1920* grows up in Fayetteville, Arkansas; enjoys secure relationship with both father and mother; *1921-1922* studies at the University of Arkansas, president of his fraternity and school, and member of student senate; *1923* father dies and J. William leaves studies for year to run family businesses; *1924* returns to University; *1925* receives A.B.; *1925-1928* as Rhodes Scholar, begins process of intellectual awakening under tutelage of Oxford don R. B. McCallum; visits Paris; *1928* receives B.A. from Oxford University, moves to Vienna, travels through the Balkans and Greece with Hungarian journalist M. W. Fodor; *1929* returns to the U.S. due to illness; *1930-1933* attends and graduates George Washington University Law School; *1932* marries Philadelphia debutante Elizabeth Williams; *1934* serves as Special Attorney in Justice Department's antitrust division; *1935* becomes a legal instructor at George Washington University; *1936-1939* returns to Fayetteville where he runs family business and teaches at the University of Arkansas; *1939-1941* serves as President of the University of Arkansas, the youngest university president in the U.S.; *1940* criticizes U.S. isolationism; *1942* elected to House of Representatives from the 3rd District of Arkansas; *1943-1944* House Foreign Affairs Committee member, he authors the Fulbright Resolution, committing the United States to planning for entry into a post-World War II United Nations organization; *1944* elected Senator from Arkansas; *1945* sponsors legislation providing for proceeds from the sale of U.S. military equipment to finance a student exchange program dubbed Fulbright Scholarships; *1949* becomes member of Senate Foreign Relations Committee; *1950* is reelected to Senate from Arkansas; *1951* establishes himself as the leading Democratic critic of Truman's domestic policy following investigation of unethical conduct by Truman appointees to the Reconstruction Finance Corporation; is also leading Senate critic of Senator Joseph McCarthy; *1956* is elected to Senate from Arkansas for third time; *1957* signs the Southern Manifesto opposing Supreme Court rulings on racial issues; *1959* assumes Chairmanship of the Senate Foreign Relations Committee; *1962* opposes Bay of Pigs invasion; is elected Senator from Arkansas for the fourth time; *1963* publishes *Prospects for the West* and leads fight for passage of the Limited Test Ban Treaty; *1964* publishes *Old Myths and New Realities and Other Commentaries* and manages passage of the Gulf of Tonkin Resolution in Congress; *1966* publishes *The Arrogance of Power* and holds hearings on U.S. involvement in Vietnam; *1968* holds second Foreign Relations Committee hearings on Vietnam; is reelected to fifth term as Senator from Arkansas; *1970* publishes *The Pentagon Propaganda Machine*; *1974* publishes *The Crippled Giant*; is defeated in Democratic Party primary; *1975–1987* acts counsel for firm of Hogan and Hartson in Washington, D.C.; occasionally participates in national forums on foreign policy issues.

Activities of Historical Significance

Fulbright's powerful dissent from American intervention in Vietnam while chairman of the Senate Foreign Relations Committee in the 1960s stands as one of the most courageous and principled oppositions to executive action in American history. The fact that Johnson had been a close personal friend made the task all the more difficult. Fulbright's telling criticism of the hubris of the Johnson regime's misadventure made him a hero to those elements of the American electorate that had come to doubt the White House's ability to dictate events in Southeast Asia. His actions helped promote a reexamination of the relationship of means and ends in American foreign policy. As a result of his leadership, a new era was born in executive-legislative relations in the area of foreign policy. Fulbright's dissent gave powerful stimulus to Congressional attempts to check the drift of power into the hands of the president.

Prior to his famous dissent from cold war orthodoxy, Fulbright had distinguished himself by standing virtually alone in voicing public criticism of the formidable Joseph McCarthy in the early 1950s.

During his thirty-two years in Congress, J. William Fulbright pondered how American power could best be used in world affairs. For the most part he remained an advocate of liberal internationalism; albeit he often justified his plea for American magnanimity with arguments based on hard-headed self-interest. Symptomatic of his outlook was his promotion of a new approach to U.S. relations with the world through sponsorship of the international scholarship program that bears his name. In addition to education, Fulbright sponsored economic aid and cultural exchange programs, activities befitting the Senate's first Rhodes Scholar.

In his later years in the Senate, Fulbright emerged as a critic of the military-industrial complex, arguing that the American military is a principal obstacle to arms control agreements and asserting that the American people have more to fear from domestic hawks than Russian bears.

Overview of Biographical Sources

The biographical literature on Fulbright has told a great deal about a narrow, albeit important, part of his life. To date, two major biographical studies of the Senator have appeared, along with a fair number of more scholarly assessments of different aspects of his life and thought. The biographies, both written at the height of Fulbright's Vietnam dissent, are limited to telling the story of his life up to that moment. Moreover, because they devote far more attention to Fulbright's personality and foreign policy concepts, the subjects of greatest popular and scholarly interest, they remain sketchy on a number of important aspects of his life and career. Prior to the mid-1960s, Fulbright was mainly the subject of short journalistic pieces. Though nearly all major works about him have been written with the cooperation of the Senator, who has made himself and his public papers available to chroniclers and researchers alike, Fulbright has yet to receive a treatment that painstakingly examines his entire life's work.

The serious treatments of Fulbright's life that are currently available are informed by his Senate speeches and the four major books that he authored during his public career. His Vietnam dissent has received the greatest detailed analysis, while fairly detailed treatments address the roots of his dissent in the 1950s and earlier as well. Relatively little has been written covering his chairmanship during the Nixon administration, his abysmal civil rights record, or his power base in Arkansas.

Evaluation of Principal Biographical Sources

Brown, Eugene. *J. William Fulbright: Advice and Dissent.* Iowa City: University of Iowa Press, 1982. **(A, G)** Perhaps the most penetrating study of the Senator's foreign policy concepts available. Brown stresses the astute but limited nature of Fulbright's dissent from the U.S. global mission, which he defines as a disagreement about means, not ends. The Fulbright that emerges from this portrait is less a philosopher than an advisor trying to reconcile power and rational planning.

Coffin, Tristram. *Senator Fulbright; Portrait of a Public Philosopher.* New York: E. P. Dutton, 1966. **(G)** This work is the first biography of the Senator. It provides a sketchy account of his early years. Moreover, the author tends to exaggerate the philosophical nature of Fulbright's opposition to Lyndon Johnson's escalation. He presents the Senator's dissent as a sort of culmination of a scholastic pacifist philosophy developed throughout his life.

Daughan, George C. *From Lodge to Fulbright: The Chairman of the Senate Foreign Relations Committee.* Doctoral Dissertation, Harvard University, 1970. **(A)** The author places the Senator within a larger and uneven tradition of Chairman of the Senate Foreign Relations Committee.

Davenport, Walter. "Just a Boy From the Ozarks." *Colliers* (February 10, 1945). **(G, Y)** This is the first published portrait.

Grundy, Kenneth W. "The Apprenticeship of J. William Fulbright." *Virginia Quarterly* (1967): 382–399. **(A, G)** A scholarly assessment of the roots of Fulbright's 1960s dissent, which the author locates in the Senator's break with John Foster Dulles in 1956 over the Eisenhower Administration's handling of the Middle East.

Johnson, Haynes, and Bernard M. Gwertzman. *Fulbright The Dissenter*. New York: Doubleday, 1968. **(G)** A brief but critical biography of Fulbright's life and political career up to 1967. Emphasizes his role as a dissenter from the cardinal assumptions of U.S. globalism, but also makes note of the Senator's retrogressive civil rights stand.

Kemler, Edgar. "The Fulbright Fellow." *The Nation* (February 20, 1954). **(G)** This is a short treatment of Fulbright's courageous opposition to Joseph McCarthy.

Kenworthy, E. W. "Fulbright Becomes a National Issue." *New York Times Magazine* (October 1, 1961). **(G, Y)** A left-liberal assessment of Fulbright's career in the early 1960s.

Lynn, Naomi B. *Senator J. William Fulbright's Views on Presidential Power in Foreign Policy*. Lawrence, KS: University Press of Kansas, 1970. **(A, G)** The author convincingly demonstrates how Fulbright changed some of his ideas later in his career as reflected in his critical assessment of the role of the president and his call for Congressional restraint of executive actions based on Fulbright's experience with the Gulf of Tonkin and Dominican Republic crises.

Lynn, Naomi, and Arthur McClure. *The Fulbright Premise*. Lewisburg, PA: Bucknell University Press, 1973. **(A, G)** The authors trace the Senator's change of mind about the trend toward increasing executive power.

Perry, Bruce. *Senator J. William Fulbright on European and Atlantic Unity*. Doctoral Dissertation, University of Pennsylvania, 1969. **(A)** This work discusses Fulbright's belief in European and Atlantic cooperation and integration.

Smith, Beverly, Jr. "Egghead from the Ozarks." *Saturday Evening Post* (May 2, 1959). **(G, Y)** This is an important sympathetic sketch.

Trask, David F. "The Congress as Classroom: J. William Fulbright and the Crisis of American Power." In *Makers of American Diplomacy: From Benjamin Franklin to Henry Kissinger*, edited by Frank J. Merli and Theodore A. Wilson. New York: Charles Scribner's Sons, 1974. **(A, G)** A penetrating study which provides an incisive summary of Fulbright's career and focuses mainly on the themes of his published works. Viewing Fulbright as educator rather than philosopher, Trask maintains that Fulbright sought to teach successive administrations to doubt foreign policy catchwords and clichés, to face new realities, and to learn from history. Trask was the first to note the phases through which Fulbright's thought proceeded, although he is not always correct about which aspects of the Senator's thought changed.

Twersar, Kurt W. *Changing Patterns of Political Beliefs: The Foreign Policy Operational Codes of J. William Fulbright, 1943– 1967*. Beverly Hills: Sage Publications, 1974. **(A)** This work discusses how Fulbright's early internationalism gave way during the onset of the cold war to a preference for executive action, only to be transformed again during Vietnam into a new view of the universe.

Overview and Evaluation of Primary Sources

Fulbright's published writings and speeches offer a detailed guide to the development of his political philosophy and policy preferences. They contain many excellent examples of his polished style and ample erudition. Samples of his speeches and writings from the period before 1960 have been collected under the title *Fulbright of Arkansas: Public Positions of a Private Philosopher*, edited by Karl Meyer (Washington: R. B. Luce, 1963; **A, G**). These provide ample evidence of the limited character of Fulbright's dissent from foreign policy orthodoxy before Vietnam and also some measure of his doubts about democratic control of government.

Upon reaching the chairmanship of the Senate Foreign Relations Committee, Fulbright was often asked to present lectures at universities on American foreign policy. These occasions became the basis for his best known books. In 1963 he delivered the Clayton lectures at Harvard University, which he subsequently published as *Prospects for the West* (Cambridge, MA: Harvard University Press, 1963; **A, G**), a work which details his case for strengthening the role of the executive in foreign policy. *Old Myths and New Realities* (New York: Random House, 1964; **A, G**) in turn sought to warn the executive of what Fulbright perceived to be the growing divergence between policy preconceptions and political developments in the communist and third world. Lectures at Johns Hopkins University formed the basis for his most important and influential statement, *The Arrogance of Power* (New York: Random House, 1966; **A, G**), a work which marked his pivotal turn against the war in Vietnam. Fulbright's increasing skepticism about the role of the military in policy formation and manipulation of public opinion is presented in a muckraking vein in *The Pentagon Propaganda Machine* (New York: Liveright, 1970; **A, G**). The Senator's ambivalent reaction to the Nixon-Kissinger foreign policy can be followed in *The Crippled Giant* (New York: Random House, 1974; **A, G**).

Since leaving the Senate, Fulbright has continued to offer observations on contemporary policy, such as *SALT II: An Obligation or an Option?* (Washington: American Enterprise Institute Defense Review, 1978; **A, G**). The Senator can be heard debating Charles Frankel on an audio-cassette entitled "The Elite and the Electorate: The Limits to Government by the People" (Center for Cassette Studies, Center for the Study of Democratic Institutions, 1975, 52 minutes). The debate originally took place in 1962. More recently, Fulbright restated his internationalism in "The Future of the United Nations," a roundtable held on November 16, 1976 (Washington: American Enterprise Institute, 1977).

Beyond his own published writings, the Senator retains a sizable collection of primary material pertaining to his life and career, to which he has occasionally allowed researchers access, although he has yet to turn them over to a principal repository.

Other Sources

Johnson, Walter, and Francis J. Colligan. *The Fulbright Program: A History.* Chicago: University of Chicago Press, 1965. Offers a useful assessment of the achievements of the Fulbright scholarship grant program over its first two decades.

Julian J. DelGaudio
California State University, Long Beach

MARGARET FULLER
1810–1850

Chronology

Born Sarah Margaret Fuller on May 23, 1810, in Cambridgeport, Massachusetts, the first of nine children of Timothy Fuller, a lawyer and politician, and Margaret Crane Fuller, a former schoolteacher; *1810–1824* is rigorously tutored by her father, learning Latin at age six, and reading the classics in her father's library; *1821* briefly attends Dr. Park's School in Boston; *1824* attends Miss Prescott's School in Groton, Massachusetts; *1826–1833* returns to Cambridge, where she studies French, Italian, and philosophy at home, and learns Greek at Cambridgeport Private Grammar School; acquires a wide reputation as a prodigy and conversationalist among her peers; *1833–1836* returns with family to a farm at Groton; tutors her younger brothers and sisters while reading Goethe, Schiller, and philosophy; *1835* father dies of cholera; *1836–1837* spends two weeks with the Emersons; takes private students and a teaching position at Bronson Alcott's experimental Temple School in Providence, Rhode Island; publishes translation of Eckermann's *Conversations with Goethe*; begins writing life of Goethe; moves with mother and younger siblings to Jamaica Plain; earns a living by holding intellectual "Conversations" with eminent women in Boston; *1840–1842* moves to Cambridge; joins Emerson and others in producing and editing the *Dial*; *1842* publishes translation of some *Correspondence of Fraulein Gunderode with Bettina von Arnim*; *1843* travels to the West; *1844* publishes *Summer on the Lakes, in 1843*; becomes literary critic for Horace Greeley's *New York Tribune*; *1845* publishes *Woman in the Nineteenth Century*; *1846* publishes a collection of critical essays, *Papers on Literature and Art*; becomes the *Tribune*'s foreign correspondent in Europe, where she meets William Wordsworth, George Sand, Frédéric Chopin, Giuseppe Mazzini, Pierre Jean de Béranger, Thomas Carlyle, and Robert and Elizabeth Barrett Browning; *1847–1848* meets Giovanni Angelo, Marchese d'Ossoli in Rome; marries Ossoli; gives birth to his child, Angelo Eugenio; *1849* directs hospital for the wounded during the French siege of Rome; begins a history of the short-lived Roman Revolution; *1850* sails to America with Ossoli and their child, and dies on July 19 when their ship sinks near Fire Island, New York; only the child's body is recovered.

Activities of Historical Significance

During the four years of her popular Conversations, Margaret Fuller helped women to think systematically and express themselves boldly on subjects outside their "sphere"; she gathered a circle of devoted friends and established a lasting reputation as a conversationalist and a crystallizer of ideas. Though she agreed with some of the ideas of the Transcendentalists, she was much more accepting of the religious and philosophical ideas of Goethe, whom she revered as a "father."

As a translator, she introduced the works of Goethe and other German authors to English-speaking readers. She created some of her best literary work in her critical essays on Goethe, and in her translation of the letters of Bettina Brentano and Caroline von Gunderode.

As the editor of the *Dial*, she was an organizer and force behind what T. W. Higginson called "the first thoroughly American literary enterprise." Her methods of literary criticism shifted the standards from the "tomahawk theory" of revenge, fault-finding, and didacticism to absolute truthfulness, determined balance, and impartiality. A romantic critic, she judged each writer a law unto himself, insisting the critic must enter each work from within, forgetting rules and preconceived formulas. In spite of the "Carlyleisms" of her idiosyncratic, even ungrammatical style, she is considered (with Poe) the best literary critic America had yet seen. Her critical writing collected in *Papers on Literature and Art* (1846) set standards of practical literary criticism in the United States.

Her book *Woman in the Nineteenth Century* (1845), widely read in America and Europe for its daring feminism, philosophically influenced the Seneca Falls Convention on woman's rights in 1848 and remains an important document in the history of feminism. As the first professional American newspaperwoman and the first female foreign correspondent and war correspondent, Margaret Fuller was sometimes lampooned or satirized for her precocity and intellectualism. In her own time, her tendency to sarcastic wit and rebuttal may have strained even her closest friends; yet "her natural element" of serious conversation gained her many distinctive friends and wide influence. For later generations, interest in her remarkable personality and active life seems to have overshadowed her literary legacy.

Overview of Biographical/Critical Sources

Historians may never recover the "real" Margaret Fuller from the mythical woman shaped by her biographers, whose works began appearing two years after her death. Ralph Waldo Emerson, James Freeman Clarke, and especially William H. Channing, expurgated her papers irreparably in their *Memoirs of Margaret Fuller Ossoli* (1852), although Thomas Wentworth Higginson corrected this earlier work in his study *Margaret Fuller Ossoli* (1884). Other biographies appeared at regular intervals, including Katherine Anthony, *Margaret Fuller: A Psychological Biography* (1921), a Freudian psychoanalysis of Fuller's personality.

Fuller's love letters to James Nathan were edited by Julia Ward Howe and published in 1903, spawning new biographies and helping to sustain public interest in her love affair, marriage and participation in the Roman Revolution, as well as her tragic early death.

In 1940, Mason Wade produced *Margaret Fuller: Whetstone of Genius*, surpassing all other biographies in balance and critical insight, but lacking footnotes. Most recently, feminists have reassessed Fuller's writings and life, notably in Bell Gale Chevigny's *The Woman and the Myth* (1976), and in Paula Blanchard's scholarly biography, *Margaret Fuller: From Transcendentalism to Revolution* (1978).

Evaluation of Principal Biographical/Critical Sources

Anthony, Katherine. *Margaret Fuller: A Psychological Biography*. New York: Harcourt, Brace, 1921. (**A, G**) Relates Fuller's feminist views, revolutionary activity, and reactions to European crises, analyzing her as a perfect model for Freud's theories on female hysteria and the Electra complex. Includes brief biographical, psychological, and general sources.

Bell, Margaret. *Margaret Fuller*. New York: Charles Boni, 1930. (**A, G, Y**) A fictionalized, dramatic biography, this study provides psychological insights into Margaret Fuller's infatuation with Samuel Ward and James Nathan, revealed in letters published in 1903.

Blanchard, Paula. *Margaret Fuller: From Transcendentalism to Revolution*. New York: Delacorte Press, 1978. (**A, G**) This feminist, scholarly study demonstrates how Fuller fought against the societal forces that stymied her feminist ideas. Lively prose describes the social, political, and religious context of Fuller's life, and probes her sexuality, mysticism, parental influences, and her work as a housekeeper. Extensive bibliography and footnotes.

Braun, Frederick Augustus. *Margaret Fuller and Goethe*. New York: Henry Holt, 1910. (**A, G**) A professor of German gives the only existing scholarly estimate of Fuller's readings, translations, and devotions to Goethe and other German writers. Footnotes and bibliography.

Brown, Arthur. *Margaret Fuller*. New York: Twayne, 1964. (**A, G**) "An essentially revolutionary" Fuller appears in this brief, readable, dramatic biography in which Brown gives his critical estimate of Fuller's "non-distinctive" literary style. Annotated, selected bibliography and footnotes.

Deiss, Joseph Jay. *The Roman Years of Margaret Fuller*. New York: Thomas Y. Crowell, 1969. (**A, G**) Based on his presumption that Ossoli and Margaret Fuller were lovers before they were married, Deiss builds a dramatic biography of a romance between a middle-aged puritan intellectual American woman and a youthful Italian nobleman. Brief chapter notes and bibliography.

Higginson, Thomas Wentworth. *Margaret Fuller Ossoli*. Boston: Houghton Mifflin, 1884. (**A, G, Y**) A friend of Fuller's younger brothers, Higginson brings her out of the intellectual and spiritual clouds shaped by the editors of her *Memoirs* and Howe's biography, finding she desired a career combining thought and action. His restricted use of family manuscripts enlarges the picture of her daily practical labors for her family and friends, and defends her against charges of vanity and self-absorption. Extensive bibliography.

Howe, Julia Ward. *Margaret Fuller*. Boston: Roberts Brothers, 1883. **(A, G, Y)** In very flowery prose, Howe depicts a woman intent on self-culture, oblivious to the limitations of the brain or the body, and a critic whose sincerity is arbitrary and whose standards unrealistic.

Stern, Madeleine B. *The Life of Margaret Fuller*. New York: E. P. Dutton, 1942. **(A, G, Y)** To bring Fuller to life for the reader, Stern invents dramatic conversations drawn from historical materials; she proposes motivations for which there is not evidence. Chapter by chapter bibliography of sources.

Wade, Mason. *Margaret Fuller: Whetstone of Genius*. 1940. Reprint. Fairfield, NJ: Augustus M. Kelley, 1973. **(A, G)** Wade's critical balance, careful psychological insights, and ability to find new information in old material has gained his biography deserved and lasting attention. Includes bibliography, but regrettably lacks footnotes.

Overview and Evaluation of Primary Sources

Four anthologies of Fuller's writings have been issued in this century: *The Writings of Margaret Fuller*, edited by Mason Wade (New York: Viking Press, 1941; **A, G**); an edition selected and edited by Perry Miller (New York: Doubleday, 1963; **A, G**); *The Woman and the Myth: Margaret Fuller's Life and Writings*, edited by Bell Gale Chevigny (New York: The Feminist Press, 1976; **A, G**); and *Margaret Fuller: Essays on American Life and Letters*, edited by Joel Myerson (New Haven, CT: College and University Press, 1977; **A, G**). In these collections, and in the *Memoirs of Margaret Fuller Ossoli*, edited by Ralph Waldo Emerson, W. H. Channing, and J. F. Freeman (Boston: Phillips, Simpson, 1852; **A, G**), one can find many of Fuller's letters, and critical essays for the *Dial* and *New York Tribune*, as well as her *Woman in the Nineteenth Century* (1845), parts of her translation of *Eckermann's Conversations with Goethe* (1839), *Summer on the Lakes, in 1843* (1844) and her poetry. Her style is difficult to read, but her intelligence, wit, and learning make the effort enriching and even delightful.

The translation of *Eckermann's Conversations with Goethe in the Last Years of His Life* (Boston: Hilliard, Gray, 1839; **A, G**) was Fuller's first book, and the only completed work on her proposed life of Goethe. T. W. Higginson considers *Gunderode: A Translation from the German* (Boston: Elizabeth Peabody, 1842; **A, G**) to be Fuller's finest literary work, because she captures the "airy style" of the young girls' letters. This small pamphlet was completed by another translator in 1860.

Fuller's first original book was *Summer on the Lakes, in 1843* (Boston: Charles C. Little and James Brown, 1844; **A, G, Y**). Her descriptions of people are the most valuable aspect of this travelogue, which sold poorly but brought her to the attention of Horace Greeley. *Woman in the Nineteenth Century* (1845. Reprint. New York: W. W. Norton, 1971; **A, G**) expands her essay for the *Dial*, "The Great Lawsuit. Man versus Men. Woman versus Women." Considered her most important work and a major document in the history of American feminism, the book attacks stereotyped roles for men and women. Fuller's book sold well in America and in a pirated edition in England, gaining her a literary reputation and entrée abroad.

Papers on Literature and Art (1846. Reprint. New York: AMS Press, 1972; **A, G**) contains critical reviews on English, American, and European literature and art. Fuller's critiques were candid and accurate, especially in assessing American poets. Printed posthumously, *At Home and Abroad*, edited by A. B. Fuller (1856. Reprint. Port Washington, NY: Kennikat Press, 1971; **A, G**) includes portions of *Summer on the Lakes, in 1843*, *Tribune* letters from Europe, and memorials to deceased members of Fuller's family. A. B. Fuller also edited *Life Without and Life Within* (1860. Reprint. Westport, CT: Greenwood Press, 1970; **A, G, Y**), which includes Fuller's reviews of Goethe, Beethoven, Poe, and several French novelists; poems; essays on Christmas, Thanksgiving, and New Years Day; an exceptionally lovely, romantic description of the magnolia flower of Lake Pontchartrain; and an essay entitled "Thoughts on Sunday Morning When Prevented by a Snowstorm from Going to Church," all of which were first printed in the *New York Tribune*. These short works reveal a better humored writer than Fuller's biographers have indicated.

Fuller's correspondence to James Nathan, published as *Love Letters of Margaret Fuller 1845–1846* (1903. Reprint. Westport, CT: Greenwood Press, 1969; **A, G**), reveal the faithful, longing heart of a busy, professional newspaperwoman writing to a man who eventually jilted her.

The Houghton Library at Harvard University holds the Fuller Family Papers. The Boston Public Library's Department of Rare Books and Manuscripts has a collection of Fuller's journals and papers.

Museums, Historical Landmarks, Societies

Memorial Stone (Fire Island, NY). Located at the shore near Fire Island, in the area where Fuller drowned in a shipwreck off the coast.

Viale Margaret Ossoli Fuller (Rome, Italy). A tree-shaded walkway inside Janiculum walls.

Other Sources

Kearns, Francis E. "Margaret Fuller and the Abolition Movement." *Journal of the History of Ideas* (January 1964): 120–127. A chapter from Kearns's doctoral dissertation, "Margaret Fuller's Social Criticism," University of North Carolina, 1960. Kearns argues that Fuller was more radical than the abolitionists in her fight to liberate women and blacks.

McMaster, Helen Neill. "Margaret Fuller as a Literary Critic." *University of Buffalo Studies* (December 1928). Master's thesis.

Myerson, Joel. "Sarah Margaret Fuller, Marchesa D'Ossoli." In *American Renaissance in New England*, Vol. 1 of the *Dictionary of Literary Biography*. Detroit: Gale Research, 1978. Descriptive, critical essay by Fuller's biographer and the editor of the volume.

Gretchen R. Sutherland
Cornell College

ROBERT FULTON
1765–1815

Chronology

Born Robert Fulton on November 14, 1765, on the family farm near Quarryville, Lancaster County, Pennsylvania, the only son of Robert Fulton, Sr., and Mary Smith Fulton; *1772* the family is forced to sell the farm and return to Lancaster, where Robert Fulton, Sr., resumes his trade as a tailor; *1774* Robert Fulton, Sr., dies; *early 1780s* the young Fulton advertises in the Philadelphia papers as a miniature painter and "worker in hair"; *1786* goes to London to study painting with Benjamin West; *1793* invents a machine for cutting and polishing marble during a visit to Torquay, Devonshire; *June 1794* gets a British patent for mechanized slopes and other canal-related transportation equipment; *March 1, 1796* publishes *A Treatise on the Improvement of Canal Navigation*, containing his ideas on the nature of inventive genius; *Fall 1797* goes to France; *1798* begins designing a submarine; *October 10, 1802* signs an agreement with Robert R. Livingston, American minister plenipotentiary to France, to construct a steamboat to provide passenger service between New York City and Albany on the Hudson River; *August 9, 1803* successful trial run of his first steamboat on the Seine; *August 18, 1807* Fulton's and Livingston's steamboat, the *Clermont*, begins her maiden voyage from New York City, returning on August 21; *January 7, 1808* Fulton marries Livingston's second cousin, Harriet Livingston; *January 1, 1809* applies for a United States patent for his steamboat design; *1810* publishes *Torpedo War and Submarine Explosions*; *1812* a Fulton steamboat offers passenger service on the Mississippi River; *1815* Fulton dies on February 23 of pneumonia in his New York City home.

Activities of Historical Significance

To many Americans, Robert Fulton's name is synonymous with steamboats. But while Fulton did indeed play a crucial role in the successful application of steam technology to transportation, he also made significant contributions to the fields of canal and naval engineering.

His first invention, a machine for cutting and polishing marble, won a silver medal from the British Society for the Encouragement of Arts, Commerce, and Manufacture. Fulton then focused his energies on the problems of canal design and construction. He summed up many of his ideas in *A Treatise on the Improvement of Canal Navigation* (1796), including a rather radical assertion that inventive genius did not lie in creating a completely new mechanism, but rather in using previously discovered concepts to improve or transcend existing technology. This philosophy, which he followed in his own work, would later entangle him in patent disputes and litigation.

While Fulton was in France looking for financial backing for his canal schemes, he became interested in the idea of submarine warfare. He built a working submarine, the *Nautilus*, under contract to the French government. He later tried unsuccessfully to sell the plans to the British and American governments. Much of his work in this field proved useful to later engineers.

His involvement with steamboats began in 1802, when he met Robert R. Livingston. The New York state legislature had granted Livingston a monopoly on steam navigation of the Hudson River, but he had not yet found someone to build an acceptable steamboat. He liked Fulton's ideas on the subject and offered him a partnership in the venture in return for designing a boat. Fulton's boat, the *Clermont*, began service in 1807, and Fulton applied for and received a United States patent for it in 1809. Much of the *Clermont*'s success lay in Fulton's fusion of previously known principles into a design more practical than earlier ones. But other inventors resented his use of their ideas and disputed the validity of his patent. Fulton, in turn, felt misunderstood and unappreciated. He died an embittered and embattled man.

Overview of Biographical Sources

There is very little satisfying literature on Fulton. The first biography of Fulton was a eulogistic celebration of his virtue and genius, *The Life of Robert Fulton* (1817), written by his associate and legal adviser Cadwallader D. Colden. J. Franklin Reigart, *The Life of Robert Fulton* (1856), and Alice Crary Sutcliffe (Fulton's great-granddaughter), *Robert Fulton* (1915), continued in this vein. In contrast, Henry W. Dickinson, *Robert Fulton, Engineer and Artist, His Life and Works* (1913), was reasonably objective and exhaustively researched. Cynthia Owen Philip, *Robert Fulton: A Biography* (1985), covered much of the same ground but also analyzed his personality and motivation. James Thomas Flexner, *Steamboats Come True* (1978), and Alice Crary Sutcliffe, *Robert Fulton and the Clermont* (1908), discuss Fulton's place in steam technology, while Parsons evaluates his submarine work. The Naval Institute has published other monographs on the subject, but they are highly technical and jargon-riddled. Biographies of friends and associates, such as George Dangerfield, *Chancellor Robert R. Livingston of New York, 1746–1813* (1960); Talbot Hamlin, *Benjamin Henry Latrobe* (1955); and Archibald D. Turnbull, *John Stevens: An American Record* (1928), provide insight into Fulton's professional relationships and the environment of American inventiveness.

Evaluation of Principal Biographical Sources

Dickinson, Henry W. *Robert Fulton, Engineer and Artist, His Life and Works.*

London: John Lane, 1913. **(A, G)** The most thorough biography of Fulton, making excellent use of primary sources and reproductions of his drawings and plans.

Evans, Dorinda. *Benjamin West and His American Students*. Washington: Smithsonian Institution Press, 1980. **(A, G)** Evans includes a good short account of Fulton's association, both private and professional, with West.

Flexner, James Thomas. *Steamboats Come True: American Inventors in Action*. Boston: Little, Brown, 1978. **(A, G)** Flexner's discussion of the pioneers of American steam technology is engaging and instructive.

Henry, Joanne Landers. *Robert Fulton, Steamboat Builder*. Scarsdale: Garrard Publishing, 1975. **(Y)** A good short account of Fulton's achievements, this book is aimed specifically at a younger audience.

Morgan, John S. *Robert Fulton*. New York: Mason/Charter, 1977. **(A, G)** This pedestrian but adequate biography sheds no new light on Fulton.

Parsons, William Barclay. *Robert Fulton and the Submarine*. New York: Columbia University Press, 1922. **(A, G)** The best monograph to focus on this important aspect of Fulton's life.

Philip, Cynthia Owen. *Robert Fulton: A Biography*. New York: Franklin Watts, 1985. **(A, G)** Philip's biography is the most recent, and offers a coherent interpretation of Fulton's thought and actions.

Sutcliffe, Alice Crary. *Robert Fulton*. New York: Macmillan, 1915. **(A, G)** Sutcliffe's biography is not as good as Dickinson's or Philip's, but it does include some interesting family stories.

―――――. *Robert Fulton and the Clermont*. New York: Century, 1908. **(A, G)** Sutcliffe drew on private family papers and stories to construct this account of Fulton's steamboat operations on the Hudson River.

Virginskii, V. S. *Robert Fulton 1765–1815*. Translated by Vijay Pandit. New Delhi, India: Smithsonian Institution and National Science Foundation, 1976. **(A, G)** This Marxist interpretation of Fulton as a proto-communist who wanted to harness the power of steam for the good of the proletariat is inaccurate and trivial.

Overview and Evaluation of Primary Sources

Anyone seriously interested in Fulton should consult the six major collections of his papers at the New-York Historical Society, the Clermont State Historic Park, the New York Public Library, the Library of Congress, the Archives Nationales de France, and in the Stanhope Manuscripts at the Kent County Archives in England. Some early Fulton family papers are in the Historical Society of Pennsylvania. A disastrous fire in 1836 destroyed the early records of the Patent Office, but some of the correspondence between Fulton and the superintendent of patents, William Thornton, has been collected in a new National Archives microfilm project, *The Papers of the Patent Office, 1802–1836*. Some of his patent drawings are in the Records of the Patent Office, Patent Drawings, in the National Archives.

The papers of Fulton's friends, associates, and adversaries are also useful. Those especially worth consulting are the Livingston Family Papers at the New-York Historical Society; the Joel Barlow collections at the Houghton Library at Harvard and the Beinecke at Yale; the Stevens Family Papers at the New Jersey Historical Society; the Benjamin Henry Latrobe Papers at the Maryland Historical Society; the John Fitch Papers in the Peter Force Collection; and the William Thornton Papers at the Library of Congress. Selected letterpress editions of the correspondence of Latrobe and Thornton are in preparation.

Museums, Historical Landmarks, Societies

Clermont State Historic Park (Germantown, NY). The state runs and maintains the estate and house of Chancellor Robert R. Livingston, where Fulton spent much time. The *Clermont* used to call at the estate's landing on the Hudson.

Robert Fulton Birthplace (Quarryville, PA). A late-nineteenth-century stone farmhouse stands on the site of Fulton's birth.

Jean V. Berlin
Wofford College

ALBERT GALLATIN
1761–1849

Chronology

Born Abraham Alfonse Albert Gallatin on January 29, 1761, in Geneva, Switzerland, second child of Jean Gallatin, a merchant, and Sophie Albertine Rolaz du Rosey Gallatin; *1775–1779* attends the famous Academy of Geneva and studies with such renowned scholars as the historian Johannes von Muller, the physicist George-Louis Le Sage, and the naturalist Horace-Benedict de Saussure, who impart a lasting respect for empirical precision and thoroughness; *1780* runs away without warning to America; *1780–1783* arrives in Boston, embarks on an unsuccessful trading expedition to Machias, Maine, then returns to Boston to eke out a living as a French tutor; *1783* moves to western Pennsylvania to pursue land speculation and founds the town of New Geneva, near the Monongahela River; *1788* makes his political debut as a delegate from Fayette County to the Antifederalist Harrisburg convention; *1789* marries Sophie Allegre, who dies only months later, and serves as delegate to the state constitutional convention in Philadelphia; *1790* is elected to the first of three one-year terms in the Pennsylvania state legislature, gains recognition as a financial expert and a forceful opponent of Hamilton's financial program; *1793* is elected to the U.S. Senate but has not been a citizen for the required nine years and is denied a seat by Federalists; marries Hannah Nicholson, daughter of Commodore James Nicholson of New York, an influential politician; *1794* plays a moderating role in western Pennsylvania's Whiskey Rebellion; wins the first of three elections to the House of Representatives; *1795–1801* rallies opposition in the House against Federalist domestic and foreign policies, becoming, with Jefferson and Madison, a founder of the Democratic-Republican party; *1801–1814* serves as Secretary of Treasury under Presidents Jefferson and Madison; *1814* leaves the Treasury to participate in negotiations that result in the Treaty of Ghent with Great Britain, ending the War of 1812; *1816–1823* serves as minister to France; *1826–1827* serves as minister to England; *1830* retires from public life; helps establish New York University; *1831* is named president of the National Bank of New York; *1842* is elected president of the New-York Historical Society and the American Ethnological Society; *1849* dies on August 13 in Astoria, Long Island.

Activities of Historical Significance

During his first twenty-five years in public life, from the time he entered the Pennsylvania legislature until he stepped down from the Treasury, Gallatin was best known for his dogged opposition to public indebtedness. The debt became a subject of national controversy when Alexander Hamilton persuaded Congress to consolidate the unpaid bills of the Revolution, state as well as federal, and to reduce them gradually through a device known as a sinking fund.

567

To Gallatin, and many other Americans, this was an invitation to political and social disaster. History (especially British history) persuaded them that prolonged national indebtedness led to corruption, legislative impotence, executive tyranny, inequality, speculation, and even personal indolence. The only proper course for a republic, they said, was to pay what it owed immediately and borrow more only when absolutely necessary.

During the 1790s, armed with masses of statistics, Gallatin emerged as the shrewdest, best-informed exponent of these principles in Congress. Almost single-handedly, he identified the new Democratic-Republican party with the cause of balanced budgets, fiscal integrity, and legislative vigilance over appropriations. He was chiefly responsible for the creation in 1795 of a standing Ways and Means Committee in the House to watch over the government's finances.

His views reached a national audience with the publication of numerous speeches, reports, and pamphlets, among them *A Sketch of the Finances of the United States* (1796) and *Views of the Public Debt, Receipts, and Expenditures of the United States* (1800).

Gallatin was the obvious choice for Treasury Secretary for both Presidents Jefferson and Madison, but his twelve years in that office (no one has ever served longer) were less than successful. His attempts to eliminate the national debt were repeatedly frustrated by events such as war with the Barbary Pirates, the purchase of Louisiana, and the long crisis with Great Britain that culminated in the War of 1812. To make matters worse, Gallatin's relations with the more dogmatic members of his party deteriorated when he came out in favor of rechartering the Bank of the United States, one of Hamilton's pet projects, and pressed Congress to support an extensive program of federally-financed internal improvements.

With considerable relief Gallatin left the Treasury to take part in the peace conference at Ghent, the successful outcome of which historians have credited to his exceptional diligence, shrewdness, and cosmopolitanism. Diplomacy henceforth appealed to him far more than domestic politics, and he happily accepted subsequent appointments as minister to France and to Great Britain. Gallatin's years abroad were, for the most part, uneventful, although his negotiations with the British in 1818 over the Canadian-American boundary did pave the way for subsequent American occupation of the Pacific Northwest.

Retirement from public life in 1830 enabled Gallatin to pursue a long-standing interest in Native American languages, culture, and history. The results of Gallatin's research into Native American culture include *A Synopsis of the Indian Tribes Within the United States East of the Rocky Mountains, and in the British and Russian Possessions of North America* (1836), which remained for many years the standard work on that subject.

Gallatin managed to churn out an astonishing number of books and pamphlets defending such controversial causes as hard money, free banking, and free trade. Among his better-known titles were *Considerations on the Currency and Banking System of the United States* (1831) and *Suggestions on the Banks and Currency of the Several United States, in Reference Principally to the Suspension of Specie Payments* (1841). His opposition to the annexation of Texas and Oregon led him to write *The Oregon Question* (1846), and when war broke out with Mexico he took up his pen to denounce it in *Peace with Mexico* (1847).

Overview of Biographical Sources

Despite his importance in the early national period, Gallatin has been the subject of only two authoritative biographies: Henry Adams, *Life of Albert Gallatin* (1879) and, eighty years later, Raymond Walters, Jr., *Albert Gallatin: Jeffersonian Financier and Diplomat* (1957). For most purposes, Walters is the more accessible and useful of the two, although Adams's remains the superior work, magisterial in style and interpretation. John Austin Stevens, *Albert Gallatin* (1884), is essentially a tribute by a family relation that adds only anecdotal odds and ends to the Adams study.

Edwin G. Burrows, *Albert Gallatin and the Political Economy of Republicanism, 1761–1800* (1986), presents much new material on Gallatin's early life and attempts to set it in the context of international republicanism at the end of the eighteenth century. Chien Tseng Mai, *The Fiscal Policies of Albert Gallatin* (1930), and Alexander Balinky, *Albert Gallatin: Fiscal Theories and Policies* (1958), are, as their titles suggest, specialized studies with limited biographical value.

Evaluation of Principal Biographical Sources

Adams, Henry. *Life of Albert Gallatin*. Philadelphia: Lippincott, 1879. **(A, G)** Adams remains one of the great American historians, and in this early work he argues that Gallatin's pragmatism and fair-mindedness drew him away from Jeffersonian radicalism toward policies advocated by his Federalist forebears, Presidents John Adams and John Quincy Adams. The book's scholarship is now quite antiquated, but its interpretation of Gallatin met with no serious challenges for more than a century.

Burrows, Edwin G. *Albert Gallatin and the Political Economy of Republicanism, 1761–1800*. New York: Garland, 1986. **(A)** This study offers a full account of Gallatin's years in Geneva and argues, contrary to Adams and Walters, that his identification with Jeffersonianism did not occur until well after his arrival in the United States.

Walters, Raymond, Jr. *Albert Gallatin: Jeffersonian Financier and Diplomat*. New York: Macmillan, 1957. **(A, G)** The first modern biography of Gallatin since Henry Adams. Readers will find the style less forbidding than that of Adams. Walters adds personal and family material that Adams did not have access to (or chose to ignore), and he is less determined to advance a particular interpretation of Gallatin's life and career.

Overview and Evaluation of Primary Sources

The bulk of Gallatin's voluminous private papers are held by the New-York Historical Society in New York City. For a useful sampling of his letters, pamphlets, and other writings, consult Henry Adams, ed., *Writings of Albert Gallatin*, 3 vols. (Philadelphia: Lippincott, 1879; **A, G**), which may be considered a kind of elaborate appendix to the same author's biography. E. James Ferguson, ed., *Selected Writings of Albert Gallatin* (Indianapolis: Bobbs-Merrill, 1967; **A, G**), while covering much the same ground as the Adams collection, does have Gallatin's own brief autobiographical recollections.

Museums, Historical Landmarks, Societies

Friendship Hill National Historic Site (New Geneva, PA). Gallatin's western Pennsylvania homestead, built in stages from the 1790s to the 1820s and currently under restoration.

Other Sources.

Burrows, Edwin G., ed. "'Notes on Settling America': Albert Gallatin, New England, and the American Revolution [1780]" *New England Quarterly* 58 (September 1985): 442–453. The first published version, with an introduction and notes, of Gallatin's earliest impressions of the United States. It reveals how little enthusiasm he had at first for Americans or for their Revolution and raises the question of when, and why, his ideas began to change.

Edwin G. Burrows
Brooklyn College, City University of New York

JAMES A. GARFIELD
1831-1881

Chronology

Born James Abram Garfield on November 19, 1831, in a rude hut near Orange, Ohio, to Abram Garfield, a pioneer farmer, and Eliza Ballou Garfield; *1831–1851* raised by his widowed mother; *1851–1854* attends Western Reserve Eclectic Institute (later Hiram College); *1854–1856* attends and graduates from Williams College; *1856–1861* serves as a teacher and president of Hiram College; *1858* marries Lucretia Rudolph; *1859–1861* is a Republican member of the Ohio Senate; *1861–1863* helps organize the Forty-Second Ohio Infantry and rises from lieutenant colonel to major general; fights at Middle Creek, Shiloh, Chickamauga; *1863–1880* serves as a Republican member, House of Representatives, from Ohio; gains reputation for oratory, knowledge of finance; ultimately heads Appropriations Committee; *1876* serves on electoral commission deciding Hayes-Tilden election; *1880* heads Ohio delegation to Republican national convention and nominated as dark horse candidate for president; elected to Senate but never takes seat; is elected president; *1881* is shot by Charles J. Guiteau and dies September 19 in Elberon, New Jersey.

Activities of Historical Significance

Moving from the battlefield to Congress before the Civil War ended, Garfield rose steadily through party ranks. At first his pedantic demeanor made him extremely unpopular with his House colleagues, but by 1871 he was part of the group that ruled the chamber. Something of a paradox, he was a pacifist turned soldier, a clergyman turned economist, and a man of letters thrust into the role of party chieftain. As a man, he was intelligent, sensitive, and alert, and his knowledge of government was unmatched. He possessed more than a streak of self-righteousness, and though not really guilty in the Crédit Mobilier scandal of 1873, his testimony could have been much franker.

Because he was assassinated so soon after taking office, his presidency remains something of a question mark. He saw his office primarily in administrative terms and, by winning a crucial patronage victory over the Stalwart wing of the Republican party, he kept the power of appointment in his own hands. He had, however, yet to be tested on matters of public policy. Moreover, he often lacked judgment at crucial points, and he was so strongly dependent upon his Secretary of State and leader of his party's Half-Breed faction, James G. Blaine, that one wonders if he would have been his own man. Because of his Civil War service, personal pietism, and apparent martyrdom to civil service reform, Garfield's death met with a tremendous outpouring of grief, and many monuments were erected. However, the causes which he found sacred—hard currency, laissez-faire economics, and am-

571

nesty for the South—soon appeared irrelevant to a nation in the throes of industrialization, and by the turn of the century adulation had given way to indifference. In retrospect, he is best seen as a transitional figure, a way station on the road leading from the weak leadership of Andrew Johnson to the forceful direction of Theodore Roosevelt.

Overview of Biographical Sources

For many years, there was no serious biographical work on Garfield. Although his impoverished boyhood and subsequent "rise" made him a campaign manager's dream, the biographies surrounding the 1880 race and subsequent assassination offer little of substance to the serious researcher. The tone of many earlier works was set by Horatio Alger's *From Canal Boy to President, or the Boyhood and Manhood of J. A. Garfield* (1880) and William N. Thayer's *From Log-Cabin to the White House: Life of James A. Garfield* (1881). Even in the late nineteenth century, however, there were some notable exceptions: Jonas Mills Bundy's *The Life of James Abram Garfield* (1880), in which the editor of the *New York Evening Mail* draws upon interviews with Garfield's mother; Corydon E. Fuller, *Reminiscences of James A. Garfield with Notes Preliminary and Collateral* (1887), written by one of Garfield's personal friends; Burke Aaron Hinsdale, ed., *The Works of James Abram Garfield*, 2 vols. (1883), and Burke Aaron Hinsdale, *Garfield and Education* (1882), both contributed by the president of Hiram College and the man closest to Garfield; and Jacob Dolson Cox, *Military Reminiscences of the Civil War*, 2 vols. (1900), written by the Ohio governor and secretary of the interior under Grant who knew Garfield in the Ohio Senate, the Union army, and the House of Representatives. Scholarly biography began with Theodore Clarke Smith's *The Life and Letters of James Abram Garfield* (1925); Robert Granville Caldwell's *James A. Garfield: Party Chieftain* (1931). Garfield's entire era is treated with hostility and superficiality in Matthew Josephson's *The Politicos, 1865–1896* (1938), a work that helped create the general picture of the Gilded Age as a "great barbecue" and "saturnalia of plunder." However, two works now interpret Garfield and his age on their own terms. Allan Peskin's definitive biography *Garfield* (1978) shows Garfield's role in such crucial matters as Reconstruction, industrialization, and party politics, and also gives a sensitive, detailed picture of Garfield the man. Justus D. Doenecke, *The Presidencies of James A. Garfield and Chester A. Arthur* (1981), the first single volume to focus on Garfield's administration, offers a revisionist tone. Challenging such portraits as Josephson's, Doenecke gives a renewed appreciation of Garfield the man and puts the presidency into a wide political, economical, and social context.

Evaluation of Principal Biographical Sources

Caldwell, Robert Granville. *James A. Garfield: Party Chieftain*. New York:

Dodd, Mead, 1931. **(A, G)** Once a leading scholarly source, it has long been superseded.

Doenecke, Justus D. *The Presidencies of James A. Garfield and Chester A. Arthur.* Lawrence: University Press of Kansas, 1981. **(A, G)** Doenecke offers a general picture of American economic and intellectual trends in 1880, then moves to the party system, state and local government, and the weakness of the presidency. He examines Garfield's background, views on the presidency, and personal strengths and drawbacks. The author claims that the question as to whether Garfield would have made a successful president remains open. Much background is given on foreign policy, the civil service, Indians, blacks, and the spoils system.

Leech, Margaret, and Harry J. Brown. *The Garfield Orbit.* New York: Harper and Row, 1978. **(G)** Up to the Civil War, the account is Leech's product, but material on Garfield's congressional career and short period as chief executive is written by Brown. The book does much with the women in Garfield's life (his mother, wife, and two others who were in love with him), and has helpful data on his education, theological transition, and military experience. However, it is marred by a gushing style and, as far as reliability goes, the first half should be used with care.

Peskin, Allan. *Garfield.* Kent, OH: Kent State University Press, 1978. **(A, G)** In this thorough yet readable account, based heavily upon the Garfield papers, Peskin illuminates the era as well as the man. His treatment of Crédit Mobilier and of Stalwart boss Roscoe Conkling might be too revisionist for some tastes, but new material is offered on Civil War engagements as well as Garfield's views of blacks, Indians, the South, and women's rights. He shows that, contrary to myth, Garfield worked on canals for only six weeks, was not an outstanding college student, and never fully sided with civil service reformers.

Pletcher, David M. *The Awkward Years: American Foreign Relations under Garfield and Arthur.* Columbia: University of Missouri Press, 1961. **(A)** A leading diplomatic historian shows that Garfield left behind no monuments to diplomatic achievement. He left foreign policy in the hands of James G. Blaine, a blundering diplomat who betrayed his amatuerism from Chile to Great Britain.

Smith, Theodore Clark, ed. *The Life and Letters of James Abram Garfield.* 2 vols. New Haven, CT: Yale University Press, 1925. **(A, G)** This work, once definitive, is still helpful on all aspects of Garfield's life, though one must use his quotations with care.

Taylor, John M. *Garfield of Ohio: The Available Man.* New York: W. W. Norton, 1970. **(G)** A State Department hand offers a journalistic account, superficial in the extreme.

Overview and Evaluation of Primary Sources

The most important primary source is Harry James Brown and Frederick D. Williams, *The Diary of James A. Garfield* (East Lansing: Michigan State University Press, 1967–1973; **A**). A superb source on Garfield's thought, it begins in 1848 and stops at 1877; hence, it does not cover his presidency. Mary L. Hinsdale edited the *Garfield-Hinsdale Letters: Correspondence between James Abram Garfield and Burke Aaron Hinsdale* (Ann Arbor: University of Michigan Press, 1949; **A**). In this well-edited collection of some three hundred letters, Garfield reveals much about himself. His friendship with Hinsdale dated back to Hiram, and the two men remained close until Garfield's assassination. Most helpful on Garfield's military experience is Frederick D. Williams, ed., *The Wild Life of the Army: Civil War Letters of James A. Garfield* (East Lansing: Michigan State University Press, 1964; **A**). Also revealing is James D. Norris and Arthur H. Shaffer, eds., *Politics and Patronage in the Gilded Age: The Correspondence of James A. Garfield and Charles E. Henry* (Madison: State Historical Society of Wisconsin, 1970; **A**). This correspondence, covering the years 1869 to 1880, is between Congressman Garfield and his chief political lieutenant in Ohio's 19th congressional district. It shows how Garfield maintained his base of power at home, used patronage to build local political organizations, and skillfully gauged the effects of national issues on his constituents. Particularly revealing is Garfield's and Henry's genuine belief that the Democratic party was unsuited to governing the nation. Theodore Clarke Smith's biography (see above) has many letters.

The Papers of James A. Garfield are at the Library of Congress. This is a rich collection, for the president was one of the most assiduous hoarders in American history. Preserved as well on 177 reels of microfilm, the papers are remarkably candid, enough to be a boon to any biographer. The Western Reserve Historical Society also has several Garfield manuscripts. Volume 8 of James D. Richardson, ed., *A Compilation of the Messages and Papers of the Presidents, 1789–1902*, 10 vols. (Washington, DC: Government Printing Office, 1896–1907) contains Garfield's few state papers.

Museums, Historical Landmarks, Societies

Abram Garfield Farm Site Park (Moreland Hills, OH). Although the farm where Garfield was born is no longer in existence, the site is preserved as a park.

Garfield Home National Historic Landmark (Mentor, OH). Lawnfield, Garfield's mansion, whence he conducted his presidential campaign (the building that served as the headquarters is adjacent to the house), contains original furnishings, and personal and political artifacts. A replica of his rustic birthplace is also located here.

Lakeview Cemetery (Cleveland, OH). Garfield's burial place is marked by a 180-foot Romanesque turret, lavishly decorated with mosaics and bas-relief, illustrating every phase of his career. Inside is a memorial shrine, dominated by a heroic statue of the president, carved from a solid block of Italian marble. A winding staircase leads to a gloomy basement crypt which houses his bronze casket. His wife Lucretia is also buried here.

Other Sources

Rosenberg, Charles E. *The Trial of the Assassin Guiteau: Psychiatry and Law in the Gilded Age*. Chicago: University of Chicago Press, 1968. Though this work focuses on the question of Guiteau's sanity, it is the best general work on the background of the assassination.

Justus D. Doenecke
New College of the University of South Florida

WILLIAM LLOYD GARRISON
1805–1879

Chronology

Born William Lloyd Garrison on December 10, 1805, in Newburyport, Massachusetts, the son of Abijah Garrison, a seaman with a drinking problem, and Frances Lloyd Garrison; *1808* suffers the desertion of his father; *1814–1818* serves unhappy apprenticeships as a shoemaker and a cabinetmaker; *1818–1826* learns the newspaper business while serving as an apprentice printer at the Newburyport *Herald*; *1826–1828* edits several small newspapers in Boston and in Vermont; meets Benjamin Lundy and acquires an interest in the antislavery movement; *1829* delivers his first antislavery oration on July 4 in Boston's Park Street Church; moves to Baltimore and edits with Lundy a weekly journal, *Genius of Universal Emancipation*; *1830* serves jail term after conviction for libel against Francis Todd, a ship captain engaged in the coastal slave trade; *January 1, 1831* back in Boston produces first issue of the *Liberator* and calls for uncompensated, immediate abolition of slavery; *1832* organizes the New England Antislavery Society; publishes *Thoughts on African Colonization*, a bitter attack upon those who favored gradual abolition and the deportation of blacks; *1833* takes first trip to England and receives encouragement from British antislavery leaders; attends first convention of American Antislavery Society in Philadelphia and writes the Declaration of Sentiments; *October 21, 1835* withstands attack by mob in the streets of Boston; *1835–1838* criticizes New England clergy who do not share his views about immediate emancipation; espouses equal rights for women and nonresistance to human authority; *May 1840* captures control of American Antislavery Society from New York faction whose members denounce nonresistance and call for political action; *1841* boycotts World Antislavery Convention in London after that body excluded women delegates; *1844* prods American Antislavery Society to call for disunion with southern slaveholders; *1847* takes lecture tour of the West with Frederick Douglass; *1850* opposes Missouri Compromise legislation and the new fugitive slave law; *1854* burns copy of Constitution at Framingham, Massachusetts; *1859* reluctantly defends John Brown's actions at Harpers Ferry; *1861* endorses northern participation in the Civil War; *1862–1863* defends Abraham Lincoln but urges more aggressive emancipation policy; *1864–1865* provokes rift with longtime friend and supporter Wendell Phillips over his support for Lincoln and his opinions about the future of freed slaves; withdraws from American Antislavery Society at the conclusion of the war; *December 29, 1865* gives valedictory editorial in the *Liberator* and shuts down the journal; *1868* accepts national testimonial of $31,000 which relieves his financial distress; *1869–1879* spends his final decade writing occasional articles and calling for justice to the freedmen; *1879* dies on May 24 in New York of complications from kidney disease.

Activities of Historical Significance

The appearance of the *Liberator* on January 1, 1831, marked both a new departure in the antislavery movement and the beginning of William Lloyd Garrison's impact upon the nation. Garrison's call for immediate emancipation and for equal rights for blacks launched a war against those who favored a gradual end to slavery and the deportation of the freedmen. In 1832, his *Thoughts on African Colonization* accelerated that war, and soon Garrison had pushed colonization to the periphery of the antislavery movement.

Slaveholders quickly recognized the danger posed by Garrison and his *Liberator*. Reacting to Garrison's harsh, provocative language and overestimating his influence, southern statesman blamed the New England reformer for Nat Turner's Rebellion (August 1831) and for disrupting sectional harmony. Garrison would remain the most despised figure in the plantation South until the Civil War.

Garrison helped to forge the American Antislavery Society in 1833, but he did not dominate the movement. His self-righteous attitude disturbed colleagues. His espousal of women's rights, anticlericalism, and Christian pacifism troubled moderates. Above all, his hostility toward the government and the Constitution and his rejection of political tactics alienated practical reformers. By the 1840s, political abolitionists and Garrisonians had nestled into competing and at times hostile camps.

Although politics furnished the battleground over slavery during the late 1840s and the 1850s, Garrison's influence had not disappeared. To millions throughout the North disturbing events, including the Fugitive Slave Act, the Kansas-Nebraska Act and the Dred Scott decision, seemed to confirm the existence of the "Slave Power" that Garrison had warned against over twenty years before. By the start of the Civil War millions of northern citizens shared Garrison's opinions about slaveholders and the South.

When the fighting started Garrison abandoned his pacifism and pronounced the conflict God's just punishment upon slaveholders. He buttressed the northern war effort with his support for Abraham Lincoln, especially after the Emancipation Proclamation. Finally exhibiting insight into the nature of politics, Garrison accepted Lincoln's cautious plans for the rehabilitation of the slaves. Nonetheless, after Lincoln's assassination he joined with the more radical Republicans in their assault upon Andrew Johnson, and he demanded a more vigorous program for the freedmen.

Deeply loved by his small band of followers and despised by his enemies, William Lloyd Garrison touched the American consciousness for four decades. His religious zeal and his unremitting verbal attacks substantially contributed to a great war and to the eradication of a great social evil.

Overview of Biographical Sources

Numerous scholars have chronicled the stormy career of William Lloyd Garrison, and interpretations about his motives, character, and accomplishments have fluctuated over the decades. Family members and close associates produced the first accounts of his life. These renditions are glowing testimonials that affirm Garrison's central position in the antislavery movement. Works in this category include Francis Jackson Garrison and Wendell Phillips Garrison, *William Lloyd Garrison, 1805–1879: The Story of His Life Told By His Children* (1885–1889); Oliver Johnson, *William Lloyd Garrison and His Times* (1881); and Fanny Garrison Villard, *William Lloyd Garrison on Non-Resistance* (1924). Early twentieth-century scholars continued to describe Garrison in laudatory terms. Lindsay Swift, *William Lloyd Garrison* (1911), and John Jay Chapman, *William Lloyd Garrison* (1913), are sympathetic, uncritical appraisals. These early biographies created the legend of the heroic Garrison who stood in the forefront of the abolitionist crusade.

By the 1930s, revisionist historians who considered the Civil War a needless conflict brought about by the blunders of antebellum leaders seriously tarnished Garrison's reputation. Throughout their works, scholars such as Avery Craven and James G. Randall portrayed all abolitionists as fanatics who led the nation into war. Partially sympathetic to the revisionists, Gilbert H. Barnes in his influential treatise, *The Antislavery Impulse, 1830–1844* (1933), sees Garrison as a misguided extremist who hindered the productive and enlightened efforts of Theodore D. Weld and other western reformers. Barnes also insists that Garrison and his New England followers who shunned political action played no substantial role in the campaign against slavery. The "Barnes Thesis" and the harsh criticism of the revisionists produced a most unsympathetic image of Garrison that lingered in textbooks until the 1960s.

The resurgence of the civil rights movement after World War II prompted scholars to reexamine Garrison. Ralph Korngold, *Two Friends of Man: The Story of William Lloyd Garrison and Wendell Phillips and Their Relationship with Abraham Lincoln* (1950), defends Garrison from the revisionist denunciations. Russell B. Nye, *William Lloyd Garrison and the Humanitarian Reformers* (1955), suggests that his career was shaped not by blind fanaticism but rather by militant Protestant evangelism. Louis Filler, *The Crusade Against Slavery, 1830–1860* (1960), the first modern survey of abolitionism, places Garrison and the New England reformers once again at the center of the movement. Two lengthy biographies of Garrison appeared in 1963. Both John L. Thomas, *The Liberator: William Lloyd Garrison, A Biography*, and Walter M. Merrill, *Against Wind and Tide: A Biography of William Lloyd Garrison*, portray their subject as a sincere, flawed reformer. Finally, Aileen Kraditor, *Means and Ends in American Abolitionism: Garrison and His Critics on Strategy and Tactics, 1834–1850* (1967), completely refurbishes Garrison's image. She dismisses the notion that Garrison and the abolitionists were fanatical or unreasonable and argues that these reformers pursued a logical, consistent strategy in the face of an implacable enemy.

Evaluation of Principal Biographical Sources

Archer, Jules. *Angry Abolitionist: William Lloyd Garrison*. New York: Julian Messner, 1969. **(Y)** Written by a prolific author of children's books, this account offers younger readers a factual, sympathetic story about Garrison's campaign to free the slaves. The text is written for the junior high school level.

Chapman, John Jay. *William Lloyd Garrison*. New York: Moffat, Yard, 1913. **(G)** Lacking documentation, this work is merely a tribute to a figure that the author considers the greatest man of the nineteenth century.

Fredrickson, George, ed. *William Lloyd Garrison*. Englewood Cliffs, NJ: Prentice-Hall, 1968. **(A, G)** This valuable book contains excerpts from Garrison's speeches and *Liberator* editorials, commentary about Garrison from his contemporaries, and a summary of Garrison historiography over the last century. Fredrickson's introduction contains the best evaluation of Garrison's significance to antebellum America.

Garrison, Francis Jackson, and Wendell Phillips Garrison. *William Lloyd Garrison, 1805–1879: The Story of His Life Told By His Children*. New York: Century, 1885–1889. **(A, G)** This highly laudatory summary of Garrison's career stood as the definitive biography until the 1960s. The study is valuable for its chronology and for the copious amount of letters woven into the narrative. The biased interpretations found in this work formed the foundations for the positive legend of Garrison that persisted into the twentieth century.

Johnson, Oliver. *William Lloyd Garrison and His Times*. Boston: Houghton Mifflin, 1881. **(G)** Written by a Garrison co-worker and close friend, this account supplements well the adulatory rendition of Garrison's sons.

Korngold, Ralph. *Two Friends of Man: The Story of William Lloyd Garrison and Wendell Phillips and Their Relationship With Abraham Lincoln*. Boston: Little, Brown, 1950. **(A, G)** This book contains a regrettably short account of Garrison's pre-war career as an abolitionist, yet that summary does comprise the first complimentary treatment of Garrison since the work of the revisionists. The absence of footnotes and a reliance upon older published sources detract from Korngold's interpretations.

Kraditor, Aileen. *Means and Ends in American Abolitionism: Garrison and His Critics on Strategy and Tactics, 1834–1850*. New York: Pantheon Books, 1967. **(A)** This brilliant study examines the factions within the antislavery movement and assesses the tactics that each camp utilized. Garrison is the central figure in this work, and Kraditor argues effectively that he offered a reasonable program and developed logical tactics. In her view, Garrison's fiery verbal assaults upon southerners were proper weapons to employ against slaveholders, the real extremists of nineteenth-century America.

Merrill, Walter M. *Against Wind and Tide: A Biography of William Lloyd Garrison*. Cambridge: Harvard University Press, 1963. **(A, G)** Based on manuscript collections that had not been available to earlier scholars, this full-scale biography portrays Garrison as a flawed, self-seeking man who became the master publicist of the antislavery movement. Merrill does argue that Garrison's concern for the slaves was genuine and that he supported the freedman long after his departure from the American Antislavery Society.

Nye, Russell B. *William Lloyd Garrison and the Humanitarian Reformers*. Boston: Little, Brown, 1955. **(A, G)** This concise, analytical account portrays Garrison as a man driven by deep religious impulses. Nye maintains that Garrison was a powerful symbol to Americans from both sections, but he reinforces the "Barnes Thesis" by insisting that western political abolitionists wielded far more influence upon the course of events than did his visionary subject.

Swift, Lindsay. *William Lloyd Garrison*. Philadelphia: George W. Jacobs, 1911. **(G)** Based exclusively upon the correspondence in the Garrison brothers' biography of their father and secondary sources, this work is another laudatory account that faithfully preserves the Garrison legend.

Thomas, John L. *The Liberator: William Lloyd Garrison, A Biography*. Boston: Little, Brown, 1963. **(A, G)** This well-written, highly critical account is the best full-scale biography of Garrison. Thomas interprets Garrison's zeal for reform as an obsession to acquire power and respect. In sharp contrast to the views of Merrill, Thomas denounces Garrison for abandoning the freedmen and for failing to exert his considerable influence towards the creation of a democratic society in the aftermath of the Civil War.

Villard, Fanny Garrison. *William Lloyd Garrison on Non-Resistance*. New York: Nation Press Printing, 1924 **(A, G)** This work contains Fanny Garrison's reminiscences about her father, William Lloyd Garrison's explanations about his concept of Non-resistance, and a tribute to the abolitionist from Russian literary figure Leo Tolstoy.

Overview and Evaluation of Primary Sources

Although he chose not to write an autobiography, William Lloyd Garrison left behind an abundance of source material. The *Liberator* offers a continuous thirty-five-year record of Garrison's views about the issues and personalities of his age. Scholars who seek only a sampling of Garrison's editorials should turn to Truman Nelson, ed., *Documents of Upheaval: Selections From William Lloyd Garrison's "Liberator," 1831–1865* (New York: Hill and Wang, 1966; **A, G**). Garrison also published numerous tracts and speeches. His *Thoughts On African Colonization* (1832; Reprint. New York: Arno Press, 1968; **A, G**) comprises a harsh attack against his first set of public enemies. His *Selections From the Writings and*

Speeches of William Lloyd Garrison (Boston: R. F. Wallcut, 1852; **A, G**) is a twenty-year summary of his public opinions. Garrison considered himself a literary figure of some importance. His *Sonnets and Other Poems* (1843; Reprint. Upper Saddle River, NJ: Literature House, 1970; **A, G**) consists of forty-eight poems that contribute little to the legacy of nineteenth-century American literature but provide insight into the author's feelings and values.

Garrison's letters comprise the most important source of primary material. Walter M. Merrill and Louis Ruchames, eds., *The Letters of William Lloyd Garrison*, 6 vols. (Cambridge: Harvard University Press, 1971–1981; **A, G**), faithfully reproduce all of the Garrison letters that have been located. These volumes do not contain the correspondence that Garrison received, and scholars must turn for that valuable material to the archives that house significant William Lloyd Garrison collections: the Boston Public Library, Harvard University, and Smith College.

Fiction and Adaptations
A character representing William Lloyd Garrison appears briefly during the opening scenes of D. W. Griffith's silent film classic, *The Birth of a Nation* (1915). Garrison has not reappeared as a specific subject in motion pictures or historical novels, yet fictional abolitionists in such works often display his zeal and religious intensity.

Museums, Historical Landmarks, Societies
Garrison Family Home (Roxbury, MA). This house is a National Historical Landmark, but it is privately owned and closed to the public.

Garrison Statue (Boston, MA). Constructed by Olin L. Warner in 1885, this statue occupies a prominent place on the Commonwealth Avenue Mall.

Museum of Afro American History (Boston, MA). Formerly the Old African Meeting House, this facility houses artifacts and archival material relevant to the history of black residents of New England. On these premises in 1832, Garrison held the first meeting of the New England Antislavery Society.

Park Street Church (Boston, MA). This was the site of Garrison's first antislavery oration on July 4, 1829.

Other Sources
Friedman, Lawrence J. "Insurgents of the Boston Clique." In *Gregarious Saints: Self and Community in American Abolitionism, 1830–1870*. Cambridge: Cambridge University Press, 1982. Utilizing the tools of psychohistory, the author

examines the close, family-like relationship between Garrison and his loyal cadre of supporters.

Ruchames, Louis. "William Lloyd Garrison and the Negro Franchise." *Journal of Negro History* 50 (January 1965): 37–49. This article rebukes the contention by John L. Thomas that Garrison abandoned American blacks after the Civil War.

Stewart, James B. "The Aims and Impact of Garrisonian Abolitionism, 1840–1860." *Civil War History* 15 (June 1969): 197–209. This study maintains that Garrisonians contributed significantly to the ultimate success of northern Republican politicians by weakening popular respect for the Constitution, the Union, and compacts with slaveholders.

Wyatt-Brown, Bertram. "William Lloyd Garrison and Antislavery Unity: A Reappraisal." *Civil War History* 13 (March 1967): 5–24. This important article suggests that Garrison was a unifying force within the antislavery movement during the late 1850s and argues that his pacifism prevented many frustrated reformers from resorting to violent projects similar to Harpers Ferry.

Jack Patrick
Youngstown State University

APPENDIX I
HISTORICAL FIGURES GROUPED BY ERA

AGE OF EXPLORATION/COLONIAL (pre–1776)

Samuel Adams
John Adams
Daniel Boone
Joseph Brant
William Byrd II
Christopher Columbus
Coronado
John Dickinson
Mary Dyer
Jonathan Edwards
Benjamin Franklin
Patrick Henry
Anne Hutchinson

Thomas Hutchinson
Cotton Mather
William Penn
Pocahontas
Chief Pontiac
Sir Walter Raleigh
Junípero Serra
John Smith
Hernando de Soto
George Washington
Roger Williams
John Winthrop

REVOLUTIONARY/EARLY NATIONAL (1776–1827)

Abigail Adams
John Adams
John Quincy Adams
Samuel Adams
Benedict Arnold
John Jacob Astor
Daniel Boone
Joseph Brant
Aaron Burr
John C. Calhoun
George Rogers Clark
Henry Clay
James Fenimore Cooper
John Dickinson
Benjamin Franklin
Robert Fulton
Albert Gallatin
Nathanael Greene
Alexander Hamilton
William Henry Harrison
Patrick Henry
John Jay

Thomas Jefferson
John Paul Jones
Marquis de Lafayette
Benjamin Henry Latrobe
Meriwether Lewis & William Clark
Dolley Madison
James Madison
Francis Marion
John Marshall
James Monroe
Gouverneur Morris
Robert Morris
Thomas Paine
Oliver Hazard Perry
Benjamin Rush
Winfield Scott
Zachary Taylor
Tecumseh
George Washington
Daniel Webster
Eli Whitney

JACKSONIAN/ANTEBELLUM (1828–1860)

George Bancroft
Henry Ward Beecher
Thomas Hart Benton
John Brown
James Buchanan
John C. Calhoun
Kit Carson
Henry Clay
James Fenimore Cooper
Davy Crockett
Jefferson Davis
Dorothea Dix
Stephen A. Douglas
Frederick Douglass
Ralph Waldo Emerson
Millard Fillmore
John C. Frémont
Margaret Fuller
William Lloyd Garrison
Horace Greeley
Angelina & Sarah Grimké
William Henry Harrison
Joseph Henry
Sam Houston
Andrew Jackson

Abraham Lincoln
Horace Mann
Samuel F. B. Morse
Theodore Parker
Francis Parkman
Matthew Calbraith Perry
Wendell Phillips
Franklin Pierce
James K. Polk
William Hickling Prescott
Winfield Scott
William Gilmore Simms
Joseph Smith
Harriet Beecher Stowe
Charles Sumner
Roger Brooke Taney
Zachary Taylor
Henry David Thoreau
Harriet Tubman
Nat Turner
John Tyler
Martin Van Buren
Daniel Webster
Walt Whitman
Brigham Young

CIVIL WAR AND RECONSTRUCTION (1861–1877)

Charles Francis Adams
Louis Agassiz
Susan B. Anthony
George Bancroft
Clara Barton
P. G. T. Beauregard
Henry Ward Beecher
Judah P. Benjamin
James G. Blaine
Benjamin F. Butler
Salmon P. Chase
Crazy Horse

Jefferson Davis
Dorothea Dix
David Farragut
Nathan Bedford Forrest
William Lloyd Garrison
Ulysses S. Grant
Horace Greeley
Joseph Henry
Stonewall Jackson
Jesse James
Andrew Johnson
Robert E. Lee

Abraham Lincoln
George B. McClellan
Thomas Nast
Francis Parkman
Wendell Phillips
Carl Schurz
William Seward
William T. Sherman
Edwin M. Stanton

Alexander H. Stephens
Thaddeus Stevens
Charles Sumner
Roger Brooke Taney
Harriet Tubman
William M. Tweed
Gideon Welles
Walt Whitman
Brigham Young

LATE NINETEENTH CENTURY (1878–1899)

Henry Adams
Jane Addams
Horatio Alger, Jr.
Susan B. Anthony
Chester A. Arthur
Clara Barton
Henry Ward Beecher
Alexander Graham Bell
Edward Bellamy
Billy the Kid
James G. Blaine
Andrew Carnegie
Grover Cleveland
George A. Custer
Eugene V. Debs
George Dewey
John Dewey
Mary Baker Eddy
Thomas Edison
Charles W. Eliot
Richard T. Ely
James A. Garfield
Washington Gladden
Emma Goldman
Samuel Gompers
Marcus Alonzo Hanna

Benjamin Harrison
John Hay
Rutherford B. Hayes
William Randolph Hearst
Oliver Wendell Holmes, Jr.
Jesse James
William James
Chief Joseph
Florence Kelley
Alfred Thayer Mahan
William McKinley
J. Pierpont Morgan
John Muir
Thomas Nast
Terence V. Powderly
Jacob Riis
John D. Rockefeller
Elizabeth Cady Stanton
William Graham Sumner
Frederick W. Taylor
Frederick Jackson Turner
Lester Frank Ward
Booker T. Washington
Thomas Watson
Frances Willard

PROGRESSIVE ERA (1900–1916)

Jane Addams

Charles A. Beard

Mary McLeod Bethune

Louis D. Brandeis

William Jennings Bryan

George Washington Carver

Clarence Darrow

Eugene V. Debs

John Dewey

W. E. B. Du Bois

Henry Ford

Charlotte Perkins Gilman

Washington Gladden

Emma Goldman

Samuel Gompers

D. W. Griffith

William D. Haywood

William Randolph Hearst

Oliver Wendell Holmes, Jr.

Charles Evans Hughes

Florence Kelley

Robert M. La Follette

Walter Lippmann

Henry Cabot Lodge

H. L. Mencken

J. Pierpont Morgan

Carry Nation

George W. Norris

John J. Pershing

Gifford Pinchot

John Reed

Jacob Riis

John D. Rockefeller

Theodore Roosevelt

Elihu Root

Margaret Sanger

Alfred E. Smith

Lincoln Steffens

William Graham Sumner

William H. Taft

Thorstein Veblen

Lester Frank Ward

Booker T. Washington

Thomas Watson

William Allen White

Woodrow Wilson

Wilbur & Orville Wright

WORLD WAR I THROUGH WORLD WAR II (1917–1945)

Irving Babbitt

Bernard M. Baruch

Charles A. Beard

Mary McLeod Bethune

William E. Borah

Louis D. Brandeis

William Jennings Bryan

Al Capone

George Washington Carver

Calvin Coolidge

Charles E. Coughlin

Clarence Darrow

John Dewey

Thomas E. Dewey

W. E. B. Du Bois

Amelia Earhart

Albert Einstein

Dwight D. Eisenhower

Henry Ford

Felix Frankfurter

Marcus M. Garvey

Emma Goldman

D. W. Griffith

Warren G. Harding

William D. Haywood

William Randolph Hearst

Oliver Wendell Holmes, Jr.

Herbert Hoover

J. Edgar Hoover
Charles Evans Hughes
Cordell Hull
Fiorello La Guardia
John L. Lewis
Charles A. Lindbergh, Jr.
Walter Lippmann
Henry Cabot Lodge
Huey Long
Clare Boothe Luce
Henry R. Luce
Douglas MacArthur
George C. Marshall
Aimee Semple McPherson
H. L. Mencken
Billy Mitchell
Albert Jay Nock
George W. Norris
J. Robert Oppenheimer
George S. Patton, Jr.
Frances Perkins
John J. Pershing
Ulrich B. Phillips
Gifford Pinchot
A. Philip Randolph
John Reed
Eleanor Roosevelt
Franklin D. Roosevelt
Nicola Sacco & Bartolomeo Vanzetti
Margaret Sanger
Alfred E. Smith
Henry L. Stimson
Robert A. Taft
William H. Taft
Norman Thomas
Harry S Truman
Thorstein Veblen
William Allen White
Wendell L. Willkie
Woodrow Wilson

POST-WORLD WAR II (1946–present)

Dean Acheson
William F. Buckley, Jr.
Rachel Carson
Jimmy Carter
Whittaker Chambers
Richard J. Daley
Thomas E. Dewey
John Foster Dulles
Dwight D. Eisenhower
Gerald R. Ford
Felix Frankfurter
Betty Friedan
J. William Fulbright
Billy Graham
Alger Hiss
J. Edgar Hoover
Hubert H. Humphrey
Lyndon B. Johnson
John F. Kennedy
Robert F. Kennedy
Martin Luther King, Jr.
Henry A. Kissinger
John L. Lewis
Clare Boothe Luce
Henry R. Luce
Douglas MacArthur
Malcolm X
George C. Marshall
Joseph R. McCarthy
Margaret Mead
Thomas Merton
Ralph Nader
Richard M. Nixon
J. Robert Oppenheimer
A. Philip Randolph
Ronald Reagan
Jackie Robinson
Nelson A. Rockefeller

Eleanor Roosevelt
Julius & Ethel Rosenberg
Margaret Sanger
Adlai E. Stevenson
Robert A. Taft

Norman Thomas
Harry S Truman
George C. Wallace
Henry A. Wallace
Earl Warren

APPENDIX II
SELECTED MUSEUMS AND HISTORICAL LANDMARKS

ALABAMA
Montgomery
Dexter Avenue Baptist Church (Martin Luther King, Jr.)
First White House of the Confederacy (Jefferson Davis)

Tuskegee
George Washington Carver Museum

Tuskegee Institute
Tuskegee Institute National Historic Site (Booker T. Washington)

ALASKA
Glacier Bay National Park
Muir Glacier

ARIZONA
Hereford
Coronado National Memorial

Prescott
Frémont House

Tucson
Frémont House Museum

ARKANSAS
Eureka Springs
Hatchet Hall Museum and Art Studio (Carry Nation)

CALIFORNIA
Alcatraz
Alcatraz Prison (Al Capone)

Cambria
San Simeon Castle (William Randolph Hearst)

Carmel
Carmel Mission (Junípero Serra)

Los Angeles
Temple Museum (Aimee Semple McPherson)

Marin County
Muir Woods National Monument

Martinez
John Muir National Historic Site

Sacramento
Governors' Mansion State Historical Monument (Ronald Reagan, Lincoln
    Steffens, and Earl Warren)

San Diego
Junípero Serra Museum
Mission San Diego de Alcala (Junípero Serra)

Sierra Nevada Mountains
John Muir Trail

COLORADO
La Junta
Bent's Old Fort National Historic Site (Kit Carson)

Las Animas
Kit Carson Museum and Historical Society

CONNECTICUT
Hamden
Eli Whitney Museum

Hartford
Nook Farm (Harriet Beecher Stowe)

New Haven
New Haven Colony Historical Society (Benedict Arnold)

DISTRICT OF COLUMBIA
Washington
American Red Cross (Clara Barton)
Charles Sumner School
Decatur House (Benjamin Henry Latrobe)
Dumbarton Oaks (John C. Calhoun)
Ford's Theatre (Abraham Lincoln)
Frederick Douglass Home
J. Edgar Hoover FBI Building
Jefferson Memorial
Lincoln Memorial
Mary McLeod Bethune Landmark
Navy Memorial Museum (David Farragut)
Octagon Museum (James and Dolley Madison)
St. John's Church (Benjamin Henry Latrobe)

Amelia Earhart
Amelia Earhart, 1963

Smithsonian Institution
United States Capitol
Washington Monument
Woodrow Wilson House

DELAWARE
Dover
Dickinson Mansion National Historic Landmark

FLORIDA
Bradenton
De Soto National Memorial

Daytona Beach
Mary McLeod Bethune Home

Ellenton
Judah P. Benjamin Confederate Memorial

Fort Myers
Edison Winter Home and Museum

GEORGIA
Atlanta
Jimmy Carter Library Museum
Martin Luther King, Jr., Center for Nonviolent Social Change
Martin Luther King, Jr., National Historic Site and Preservation District

Cobb County
Kennesaw Mountain National Battlefield Park

Crawfordville
Liberty Hall (Alexander H. Stephens)

Plains
Carter Museum

Savannah
Nathanael Greene Monument

Warm Springs
Little White House (Franklin D. Roosevelt)

ILLINOIS
Carthage
Carthage Jail (Joseph Smith)

Martin Luther King, Jr.
Martin Luther King, 1979

Cedarville
Cedarville Area Museum (Jane Addams)

Chicago
Jane Addams' Hull-House
Lexington Hotel (Al Capone)
Stephen A. Douglas State Memorial

Evanston
Willard Museum

Freeport
Stephenson County Historical Society (Jane Addams)

Galena
Grant Home

Menard County
New Salem State Park (Abraham Lincoln)

Nauvoo
Smith Family Properties (Joseph Smith)

Salem
Bryan Birthplace

Springfield
Lincoln's Home
Lincoln's Tomb
Old State Capitol National Historic Landmark (Stephen A. Douglas and Abraham
    Lincoln)

George Rogers Clark
George Rogers Clark, 1929

Vincennes
George Rogers Clark National Historical Park

INDIANA
Battle Ground
Tippecanoe Battlefield

Fort Wayne
Louis A. Warren Lincoln Library and Museum (Abraham Lincoln)

Indianapolis
Benjamin Harrison Home

Lafayette
Tippecanoe County Historical Museum (William Henry Harrison and Tecumseh)

Vincennes
Grouseland National Historic Landmark (William Henry Harrison)
Indiana Territory State Memorial (William Henry Harrison)

IOWA
Boone
Mamie Doud Eisenhower Birthplace (Dwight D. Eisenhower)

Tabor
Todd House (John Brown)

West Branch
Herbert Hoover National Historic Site

KANSAS
Abilene
Dwight D. Eisenhower Library

Emporia
William Allen White Memorial Library

Medicine Lodge
Carry Nation Home

Osawatamie
John Brown Memorial Museum

Wabaunsee
Beecher Bible and Rifle Church

KENTUCKY
Fort Knox
Patton Museum

Hodgenville
Abraham Lincoln Birthplace

Lexington
Ashland (Henry Clay)

Louisville
Locust Grove National Historic Site (George Rogers Clark)
Springfield National Historic Landmark (Zachary Taylor)
Thomas Edison House
University of Louisville Law School (Louis D. Brandeis)

George S. Patton, Jr.
VFW 75th Anniversary, 1974

Madison County
Fort Boonesborough State Park (Daniel Boone)

Maysville
Mason County Museum (Daniel Boone)

Trappist
Abbey of Our Lady of Gethsemani (Thomas Merton)

LOUISIANA
New Orleans
Beauregard House
Confederate Memorial Hall
Jackson Square National Historic Landmark (Andrew Jackson)
Jean Lafitte National Historic Park and Preserve (Andrew Jackson)

MAINE
Augusta
Blaine House

Coastal Marshes
Rachel Carson National Wildlife Refuge

Fort Kent
Fort Kent National Historic Landmark (Winfield Scott)

Hampden
Dorothea Dix Park

Lubec
Roosevelt Cottage National Historic Landmark (Franklin D. and Eleanor
    Roosevelt)

MARYLAND
Annapolis
U.S. Naval Academy

Baltimore
H. L. Mencken House
Roman Catholic Cathedral (Benjamin Henry Latrobe)

Glen Echo
Clara Barton National Historic Site

Sharpsburg
Antietam National Battlefield Site

MASSACHUSETTS

Boston
Dorchester Heights National Historic Site (George Washington)
Faneuil Hall (Wendell Phillips)
First Church of Boston (Anne Hutchinson)
John F. Kennedy Presidential Library and Museum
Museum of Afro American History
Park Street Church (William Lloyd Garrison)

Brookline
John F. Kennedy National Historic Site (John F. and Robert F. Kennedy)
Mary Baker Eddy Museum

Cambridge
Museum of Comparative Zoology (Louis Agassiz)

Chatham
Brandeis Summer Home

Chestnut Hill
Mary Baker Eddy Home

Concord
Concord Free Public Library (Henry David Thoreau)
Emerson Home
Walden Pond Restoration (Henry David Thoreau)

Great Barrington
Du Bois Boyhood Homesite National Historic Landmark

Lynn
Mary Baker Eddy Home

Northampton
Calvin Coolidge Memorial Room, Forbes Library

North Oxford
Clara Barton Birthplace

Plymouth
Plymouth Plantation Restoration (John Winthrop)

Quincy
John Adams and John Quincy Adams Birthplaces

Waltham
Brandeis University

West Roxbury
Theodore Parker Unitarian Church

Harriet Tubman
Harriet Tubman, 1978

MICHIGAN
Ann Arbor
Gerald R. Ford Library

Dearborn
Fair Lane National Historic Landmark (Henry Ford)
Henry Ford Birthplace
Henry Ford Museum and Greenfield Village (Thomas Edison, Henry Ford,
    Wilbur & Orville Wright)

Detroit
Great Lakes Indian Museum (Pontiac)

Grand Rapids
Gerald R. Ford Museum

Mackinac Island
Astor House

West Lake Erie
Put-in-Bay (Oliver Hazard Perry)

MINNESOTA
Little Falls
Lindbergh House

Twin Cities
Hubert H. Humphrey Institute for Public Affairs

MISSISSIPPI
Biloxi
Beauvoir (Jefferson Davis)

Greenville
Winterville Mounds State Historic Site (Hernando de Soto)

Vicksburg
Old Court House Museum (Jefferson Davis)
Vicksburg National Military Park

Woodville
Rosemont (Jefferson Davis)

MISSOURI
Booneville
Boone's Lick State Historical Site

Coffeyville
Coffeyville Historical Museum (Wendell L. Willkie)

Defiance
Daniel Boone Home

Diamond
George Washington Carver National Monument

Independence
Harry S Truman Library and Museum
Harry S Truman National Historic Site
Independence Temple (Joseph Smith)

Kearney
Jesse James Farm

Laclede
General John J. Pershing Boyhood Home State Historic Site

Lamar
Harry S Truman Birthplace State Historic Site

Liberty
Jesse James Bank Museum

Nevada
Bushwhacker Museum (Jesse James)

St. Joseph
Jesse James House Museum
St. Joseph Museum (Jesse James)

St. Louis
Lindbergh Museum

St. Louis County
White Haven (Ulysses S. Grant)

George Washington Carver
Dr. George Washington Carver, 1948

MONTANA
Billings
Pompey's Pillar (Lewis & Clark)

Chinook
Chief Joseph Battleground of the Bear's Paw

Crow Agency
Custer Battlefield National Monument (Crazy Horse and George Custer)

Cut Bank
Camp Disappointment (Lewis & Clark)

Wisdom
Big Hole National Battlefield

NEBRASKA
Lincoln
Fairview (William Jennings Bryan)

McCook
George W. Norris Home

NEVADA
Radium Springs
Fort Selden State Monument (Douglas MacArthur)

NEW HAMPSHIRE
Concord
New Hampshire Historical Society (Daniel Webster)

Franklin
Daniel Webster Birthplace

Hanover
Dartmouth College (Daniel Webster)

Hillsborough
Hillsborough Historical Society (Franklin Pierce)

NEW JERSEY
Bordentown
Free Public School (Clara Barton)

Caldwell
Cleveland Birthplace

Camden
Harleigh Cemetery (Walt Whitman)
Walt Whitman Association

Freehold
Monmouth Battlefield

Haledon
American Labor Museum

Morristown
Morristown National Historic Park (George Washington)
Villa Fortuna (Thomas Nast)

Princeton
Cleveland Memorial Tower .
Princeton Battlefield
Princeton University Physics Department (Joseph Henry)

West Orange
Edison Laboratory
Edison National Historic Site

NEW MEXICO
Bernalillo
Coronado State Monument

Ft. Sumner
Billy the Kid Museum

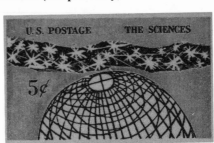

J. Robert Oppenheimer
Science, 1963

Las Vegas
Rough Riders Memorial and City Museum (Theodore Roosevelt)

Los Alamos
Bathtub Row House (J. Robert Oppenheimer)

Taos
Kit Carson Memorial Foundation

NEW YORK
Albany
Schuyler Mansion National Historic Landmark (Alexander Hamilton)

Auburn
Seward House
Tubman House National Historic Landmark

Brooklyn
Plymouth Church of the Pilgrims (Henry Ward Beecher)

Buffalo
Buffalo Historical Society (Millard Fillmore)
Theodore Roosevelt Inaugural Historic Site

Cooperstown
Fenimore House (James Fenimore Cooper)
National Baseball Museum and Hall of Fame (Jackie Robinson)

East Aurora
Millard Fillmore Museum and Homestead

Fayette
Peter Whitmer Farm (Joseph Smith)

Germantown
Clermont State Historic Park (Robert Fulton)

Huntington
Walt Whitman Birthplace

Hyde Park
Franklin D. Roosevelt Library and Museum (Franklin D. and Eleanor Roosevelt)

Katonah
John Jay Homestead State Historic Site

Kinderhook
Martin Van Buren National Historic Site

Lake Placid
John Brown's Farm

Long Island
Sagamore Hill (Theodore Roosevelt)

Mount McGregor
Grant Cottage

New Rochelle
Huguenot-Thomas Paine Historical Society

New York City
A. Philip Randolph Institute
American Museum of Natural History (Margaret Mead)
Astor Library
Brooklyn Museum (John D. Rockefeller)
Carnegie Mansion National Historic Landmark
General Grant National Memorial
Hamilton Grange National Memorial
Morris-Jumel Mansion (Aaron Burr)
National Academy of Design (Samuel F. B. Morse)
Pierpont Morgan Library
Pierpont Morgan Wing, Metropolitan Museum of Art
Theodore Roosevelt Birthplace National Historic Site

Newburgh
Hasbrouck House (George Washington)

Palmyra
Smith Family Farm, the Hill Cumorah, and the Sacred Grove (Joseph Smith)

Pocantico Hills
Rockefeller Archive Center (John D. Rockefeller)

Poughkeepsie
Locust Grove (Samuel F. B. Morse)

Rochester
Susan B. Anthony House

Sands Point
Falaise (Charles A. Lindbergh, Jr.)

Saratoga Springs
Saratoga National Battlefield Park

Elizabeth Cady Stanton
Woman Suffrage, 1970

Seneca Falls
National Women's Hall of Fame
Seneca Falls Historical Society (Elizabeth Cady Stanton)
Women's Rights National Historical Park (Elizabeth Cady Stanton)

Tarrytown
Historical Society of Tarrytown (John D. Rockefeller)

West Point
United States Military Academy

NORTH CAROLINA
Boone
Boone Memorial Gardens

Durham
Bennett Place State Historical Site (William T. Sherman)

Greensboro
Greensboro Historical Museum (Dolley Madison)

Johnston County
Bentonville Battleground

Kill Devil Hill
Wright Memorial

Mocksville
Daniel Boone State Park

Pineville
James K. Polk Memorial State Historic Site

Raleigh
Andrew Johnson Birthplace

Roanoke Island
Fort Raleigh National Historic Site (Sir Walter Raleigh)

NORTH DAKOTA
Mandan
Fort Abraham Lincoln State Historical Park (George A. Custer)

Medora
Theodore Roosevelt National Park-Visitor Center

Williston
Fort Union Trading Post National Historical Site (John Jacob Astor)

OHIO
Akron
John Brown Home Museum

Canton
McKinley's Tomb

Cincinnati
Ohio Historical and Philosophical Society (William Henry Harrison)
Stowe House Community Center (Harriet Beecher Stowe and Henry Ward
    Beecher)
William Howard Taft National Historic Site (William H. and Robert A. Taft)

Columbus
First Congregational Church (Washington Gladden)

Dayton
United States Air Force Museum (Billy Mitchell)

Fremont
Rutherford B. Hayes Presidential Center

Lancaster
Sherman Birthplace

Marion
Harding Home

Mentor
Garfield Home National Historic Landmark

Milan
Thomas Edison Birthplace

Niles
McKinley National Birthplace

Point Pleasant
Grant Birthplace

OKLAHOMA
Tonkawa
Nez Perce Reservation (Chief Joseph)

OREGON
Fort Astoria
Fort Astoria (John Jacob Astor)

John Jacob Astor
Commerce, 1975

Newberg
Minthorn House (Herbert Hoover)

Portland
Oregon Lewis and Clark Heritage Foundation

PENNSYLVANIA
Birdsboro
Daniel Boone Homestead

Boalsburg
Christopher Columbus Family Chapel

Bucks County
Washington Crossing State Park

Carlisle
Dickinson College

Chadds Ford
Brandywine Battlefield Park

Easton
American Friends of Lafayette

Gettysburg
Eisenhower National Historic Site
Gettysburg National Military Park

Harrisburg
William Penn Memorial Museum

Marquis de Lafayette
Marquis de Lafayette, 1977

Milford
Grey Towers (Gifford Pinchot)

Morrisville
Summerseat (Robert Morris)

New Geneva
Friendship Hill National Historic Site (Albert Gallatin)

Philadelphia
Bank of North America (Robert Morris)
Franklin Institute (Amelia Earhart and Benjamin Franklin)
Independence National Historical Park
Library Company of Philadelphia (Benjamin Franklin)
Olympia (George Dewey)
Pennsbury Manor (William Penn)

Pittsburgh
Carnegie Institute

Springdale
Rachel Carson Childhood Home

Swarthmore
Swarthmore College Peace Collection (Jane Addams)

Uniontown
Fort Necessity National Battlefield

Valley Forge
J. Edgar Hoover Library of the Freedoms Foundation
Valley Forge State Park

York County
Gifford Pinchot State Park

RHODE ISLAND
Coventry
Nathanael Greene Homestead

SOUTH CAROLINA
Charleston
Fort Sumter National Monument

Clemson
Fort Hill (John C. Calhoun)

Columbia
South Caroliniana Library (William Gilmore Simms)

Fort Jackson
Fort Jackson Museum (Andrew Jackson)

Andrew Carnegie
Andrew Carnegie, 1960

Nathanael Greene
George Washington and Nathanael Greene, 1936

Lancaster
Andrew Jackson State Park

Marion
Marion County Museum (Francis Marion)

Moncks Corner
Mepkin Plantation (Henry and Clare Boothe Luce)

SOUTH DAKOTA
Crazy Horse
Crazy Horse Memorial

Custer
Way Park Museum (George A. Custer)

Game Lodge
State Game Lodge (Calvin Coolidge)

TENNESSEE
Byrdston
Cordell Hull Birthplace

Chattanooga
Chickamauga and Chattanooga National Military Park

Columbia
Ancestral Home of James Knox Polk

Dayton
Rhea County Courthouse (Clarence Darrow and William Jennings Bryan)

Greene County
Davy Crockett Birthplace State Historic Area

Greeneville
Andrew Johnson Memorial Association
Andrew Johnson National Historic Site

Hardin County
Shiloh National Military Park

Hohenwald
Meriwether Lewis Monument

Maryville
Sam Houston Schoolhouse

Lewis and Clark
Lewis and Clark Expedition, 1954

Memphis
Chucalissa Indian Town (Hernando de Soto)
Lorraine Motel Exhibit (Martin Luther King, Jr.)

Morristown
David Crockett Tavern and Museum

Nashville
The Hermitage (Andrew Johnson)
Tennessee State Museum (Andrew Johnson and Davy Crockett)

Rutherford
David Crockett Cabin

Shiloh
Shiloh National Military Park

TEXAS
Austin
Lyndon B. Johnson Museum
Lyndon B. Johnson Presidential Library

Brownwood
Douglas MacArthur Academy of Freedom

Denison
Eisenhower Birthplace State Historic Site

Fort Davis
Fort Davis National Historic Site (Jefferson Davis)

Huntsville
Sam Houston House

Johnson City
Lyndon B. Johnson National Historical Park

San Antonio
The Alamo (Sam Houston and Davy Crockett)

San Jacinto
Battlefield of San Jacinto (Sam Houston)

UTAH
St. George
Brigham Young Winter Home and Office

Douglas MacArthur
Corregidor, 1944

Salt Lake City
Beehive House (Brigham Young)
Brigham Young Cemetery
Brigham Young Farm Home
Brigham Young's Office
Museum of Church History and Art of the Church (Joseph Smith and Brigham
 Young)

VERMONT
Brandon
Stephen A. Douglas Birthplace

Fairfield
President Chester A. Arthur Birthplace

Plymouth Notch
Coolidge Homestead National Historic Landmark

Sharon
Joseph Smith's Birthplace

VIRGINIA
Alexandria
Alexandria Historic District (George Washington)
Gadsby's Tavern (George Washington)
George Washington Masonic Temple
Mount Vernon (George Washington)

Appomattox
Appomattox Court House National Historical Park

Arlington
Arlington House (George Washington)
Arlington National Cemetery
Custis-Lee Mansion National Memorial (Robert E. Lee)

Beaver Dam
Scotchtown (Dolley Madison)

Brookneal
Patrick Henry Museum—Red Hill Shrine

Charles City
Berkeley National Historic Landmark (William Henry Harrison)
Sherwood Forest (John Tyler)
Westover (William Byrd II)

Charlottesville
Ash Lawn (James Monroe)
Monticello (Thomas Jefferson)
University of Virginia Historic District (Thomas Jefferson)

Falmouth
James Monroe Museum and Memorial Library

Fredericksburg
Fredericksburg-Spotsylvania National Military Park
George Washington Birthplace National Monument
Rising Sun Tavern (Thomas Jefferson)

Hardy
Booker T. Washington National Monument

Jamestown
Jamestown National Historic Site (John Smith and Pocahontas)

Lexington
George C. Marshall Research Foundation
Lee Chapel, Washington and Lee University
Stonewall Jackson House
Virginia Military Institute (Stonewall Jackson)

Manassas
Manassas National Battlefield Park

Norfolk
MacArthur Memorial

Orange
James Madison Museum
Montpelier (James and Dolley Madison)

Petersburg
Petersburg National Battlefield

Richmond
Hollywood Cemetery (Jefferson Davis)
John Marshall House
Museum of the Confederacy
Richmond National Battlefield Park
Valentine Museum (Dolley Madison)
Virginia Historical Society Collections (William Henry Harrison)
Virginia State Capitol (Thomas Jefferson)

Staunton
Woodrow Wilson Birthplace

Westmoreland County
Stratford Hall (Robert E. Lee)

Williamsburg
Colonial National Historical Park

WASHINGTON
Iwaco
Lewis and Clark Interpretive Center

Spalding
Nez Perce National Historical Park (Chief Joseph)

Vancouver
Gifford Pinchot National Forest
Grant House Museum

WEST VIRGINIA
Harpers Ferry
Harpers Ferry National Monument (Robert E. Lee and John Brown)

WISCONSIN
Couderay
The Hideout (Al Capone)

Madison
Richard T. Ely House

Marquette
Fountain Lake (John Muir)

Patrick Henry
Patrick Henry, 1961

RESEARCH GUIDE
TO AMERICAN
HISTORICAL BIOGRAPHY

Volume I
A-Garr
Appendices I, II

Robert Muccigrosso
Editor

Suzanne Niemeyer
Editorial Director

Beacham Publishing

Library of Congress
  Cataloging in Publication Data

Research Guide to American Historical Biography / edited by Robert
    Muccigrosso—Washington, D.C.: Beacham Publishing.
        3 v.; 24 cm.

        Bibliography: p.
        Includes index

        1. United States—Biography—Handbooks, manuals, etc. 2. United
    States—Bio-bibliography. I. Muccigrosso, Robert.

CT214.R47   1988   920'.073—dc19   88-19316

        Description and evaluation of the most important secondary and
primary sources for 278 American historical figures.

Library of Congress Card Number: 88-19316

ISBN: 0-933833-09-1 (set)

Printed in the United States of America
First printing, September 1988